# ROCKETO ™

## JOURNEY TO THE HIDDEN SEA

### VOLUME 1

*Frank Espinosa*

D1397882

I love Rocketo. Rocketo is one of those books that is a culmination of the best skills and vision that comics have to offer. The creation of a new world map filled with amazing wonders is a staple of fantasy lore, and the pulp magazine hero who takes us there is standard stuff that we all know, but it demands our attention when it's done this well. Frank Espinosa is one of the brightest new talents to grace comics, and by that I mean that I fully appreciate his time and efforts gracing this medium. Frank could have just as easily kept his skills in the animation field alone, where he's just come from. Frank spent many years guiding other talented artists with work he both illustrated and animated for Warner Bros. Consumer Products. This is where I got to know Frank and had the privilege to see Rocketo in development some time ago. What I've seen of Frank's vision for the series, the number of epic stories he has planned and the volume of artwork generated that he's yet to show, is nothing short of stunning.

Artistically, Frank has accomplished a wonderful hybrid style, combining the best figure modeling of animated feature films and the more liberated expressionist line of European comics. With resemblance to the classic comic strips of Chester Gould and Alex Raymond to the kinetic energy of Jack Kirby's work, Frank's style transcends the ages of the comic book. His look is inspired by the past and pushing us forward graphically into the future. His line only indicates the purity of his subject's gesture and position without always holding in the form to a rigid contour. Color is employed at an amazing level of accent only, restrained to a limited palate of mostly only two colors used at a single time. These innovations are put to an exceptional effect, creating a mood and graphic experience not likely to be found elsewhere. At his core there is Frank's strength of drawing keeping these bold steps together, making the images hold up for closer scrutiny. Coupled with his boundless creativity, Rocketo's artwork is married with a story of impressive tone, execution, and class. The panoramic format of this work is well-suited to the epic nature of events it documents, and it makes this new retro-future Earth seem all the more inviting.

It's a rare thing to find that craftsman who tells a passionate tale with such quality as both writer and artist and who has the commitment to make the journey. I know I'll be there to follow him on that journey, absorbing the inspirations that his labors bring.

**Alex Ross**
2005

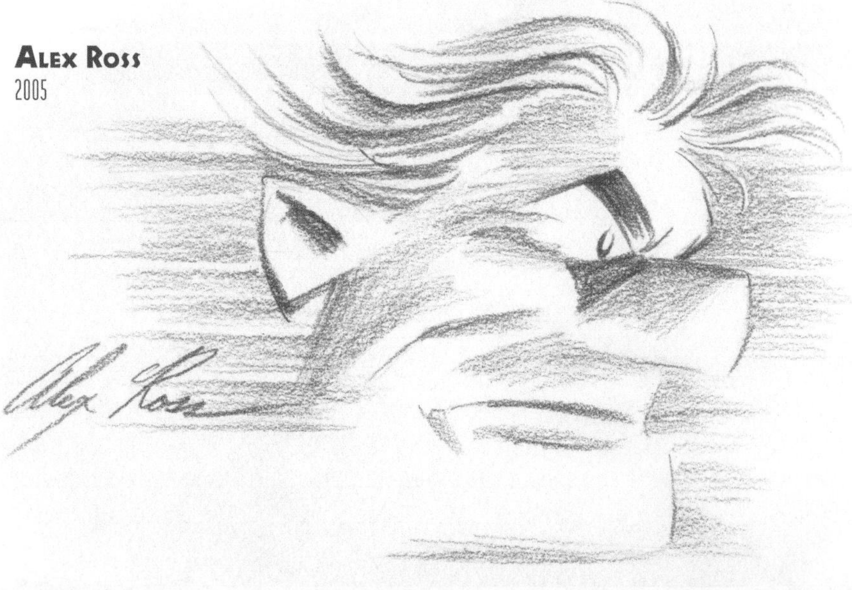
Alex Ross

IT HAS BEEN 2000 YEARS SINCE THE GREAT SHATTERING OF THE PLANET EARTH.
NEW MEN HAVE BEEN CREATED FOR THIS NEW WORLD.
AMONG THEM ARE THE MAPPERS WHO EXPLORE THE UNKNOWN CONTINENTS,
CHART THE DEPTHS OF OCEANS, NAVIGATING NEW JUNGLES AND DESERTS,
GUIDING OTHERS IN THE DISCOVERY OF THEIR WORLD.

THESE ARE THE JOURNEYS OF ROCKETO GARRISON.

# 0

# THE SIREN'S CALL

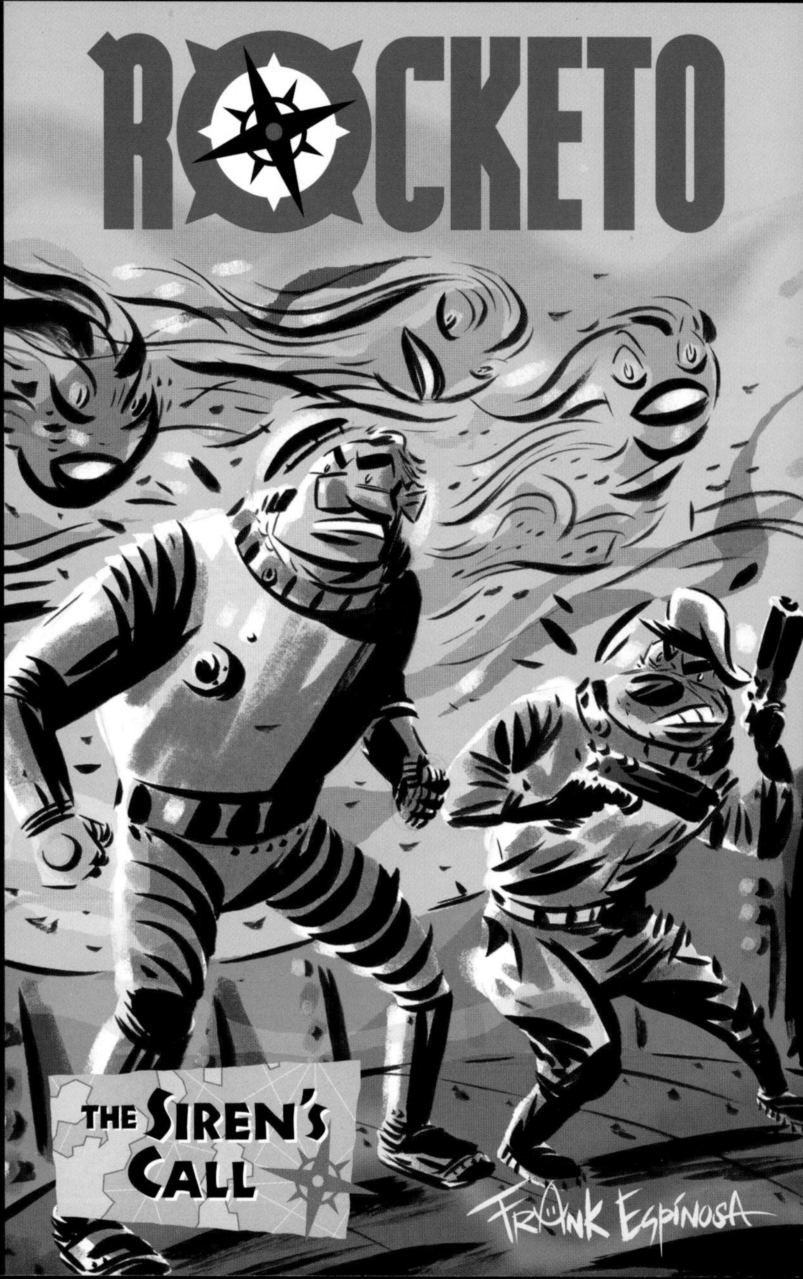
ROCKETO
THE SIREN'S CALL
FRANK ESPINOSA

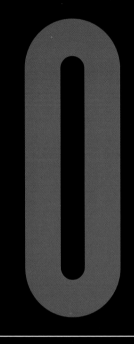

IT'S BEEN **TEN** SILENT YEARS SINCE
THE **LAST** GREAT **ADVENTURE.**

THE WORLD HAS **CHANGED** AGAIN, AND YET AGAIN.
MY OLD FRIEND HAS LONG BEEN GONE FROM **PORTO LOGAS.**
BUT HIS MAPS REMAIN ... AND FROM THE MAPS
THE **REMARKABLE** STORY OF HIS LIFE IS SEEN AND HEARD.

THE STORIES AND **EXPLORATION** OF A MAN'S LIFE..
ROCKETO GARRISON ONE OF THE GREATEST
**MAPPERS** OF THE **NEW WORLD..**

THE LAST TIME I **SAW** HIM, HE SAID, **"SPIRO**, HOLD ONTO THESE **MAPS.**
THEY ARE THE JOURNALS OF MY LIFE. THEY MIGHT BE A BEACON
ONE DAY TO THOSE WHOSE SPIRITS ARE DRAWN, AS MINE WAS,
TO GREAT **JOURNEYS."**

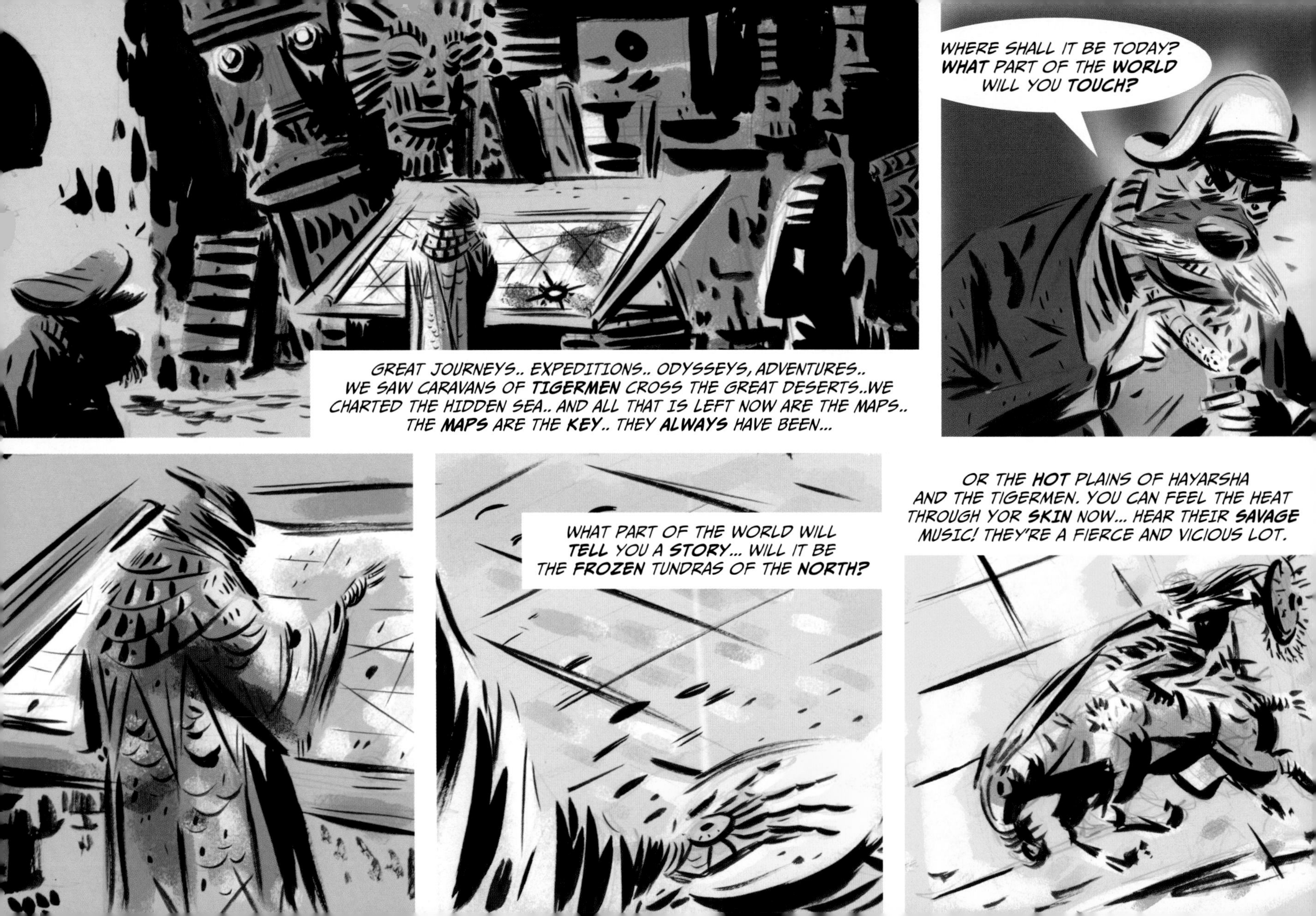
GREAT JOURNEYS.. EXPEDITIONS.. ODYSSEYS, ADVENTURES.. WE SAW CARAVANS OF TIGERMEN CROSS THE GREAT DESERTS..WE CHARTED THE HIDDEN SEA.. AND ALL THAT IS LEFT NOW ARE THE MAPS.. THE MAPS ARE THE KEY.. THEY ALWAYS HAVE BEEN...
WHERE SHALL IT BE TODAY? WHAT PART OF THE WORLD WILL YOU TOUCH?
WHAT PART OF THE WORLD WILL TELL YOU A STORY... WILL IT BE THE FROZEN TUNDRAS OF THE NORTH?
OR THE HOT PLAINS OF HAYARSHA AND THE TIGERMEN. YOU CAN FEEL THE HEAT THROUGH YOR SKIN NOW... HEAR THEIR SAVAGE MUSIC! THEY'RE A FIERCE AND VICIOUS LOT.

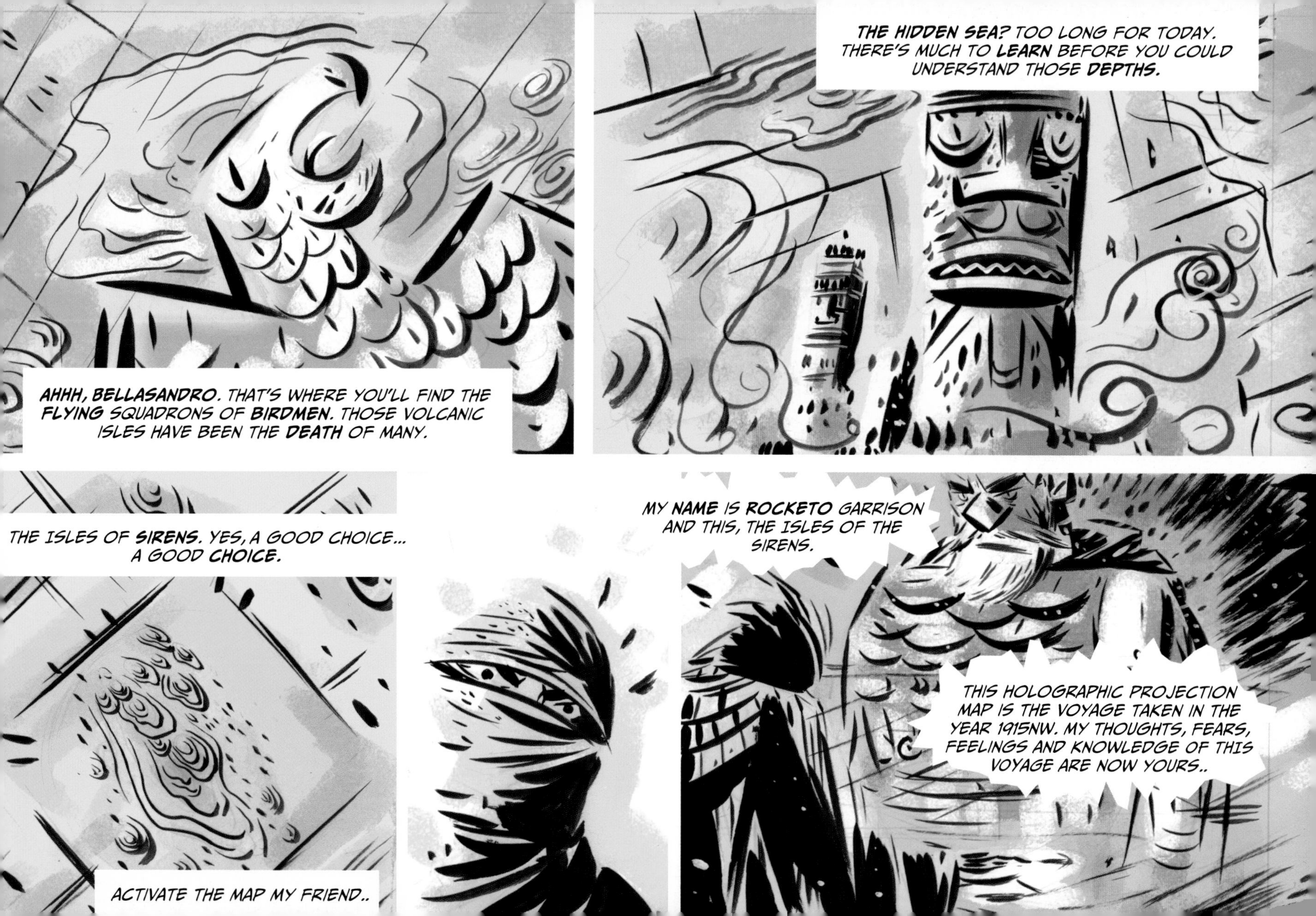

AHHH, BELLASANDRO. THAT'S WHERE YOU'LL FIND THE FLYING SQUADRONS OF BIRDMEN. THOSE VOLCANIC ISLES HAVE BEEN THE DEATH OF MANY.
THE HIDDEN SEA? TOO LONG FOR TODAY. THERE'S MUCH TO LEARN BEFORE YOU COULD UNDERSTAND THOSE DEPTHS.
THE ISLES OF SIRENS. YES, A GOOD CHOICE... A GOOD CHOICE.
ACTIVATE THE MAP MY FRIEND..
MY NAME IS ROCKETO GARRISON AND THIS, THE ISLES OF THE SIRENS.
THIS HOLOGRAPHIC PROJECTION MAP IS THE VOYAGE TAKEN IN THE YEAR 1915NW. MY THOUGHTS, FEARS, FEELINGS AND KNOWLEDGE OF THIS VOYAGE ARE NOW YOURS..

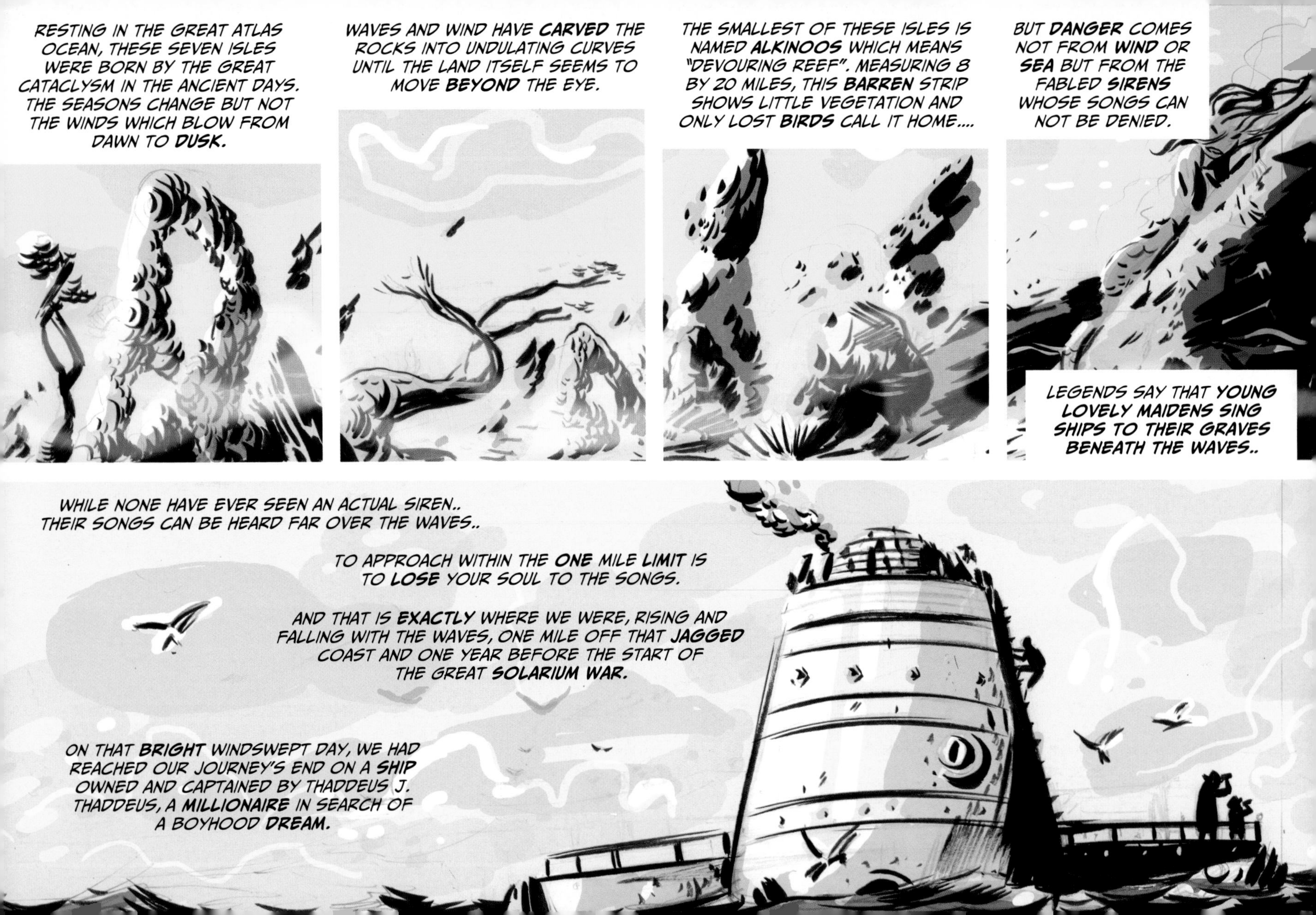
RESTING IN THE GREAT ATLAS OCEAN, THESE SEVEN ISLES WERE BORN BY THE GREAT CATACLYSM IN THE ANCIENT DAYS. THE SEASONS CHANGE BUT NOT THE WINDS WHICH BLOW FROM DAWN TO DUSK.
WAVES AND WIND HAVE CARVED THE ROCKS INTO UNDULATING CURVES UNTIL THE LAND ITSELF SEEMS TO MOVE BEYOND THE EYE.
THE SMALLEST OF THESE ISLES IS NAMED ALKINOOS WHICH MEANS "DEVOURING REEF". MEASURING 8 BY 20 MILES, THIS BARREN STRIP SHOWS LITTLE VEGETATION AND ONLY LOST BIRDS CALL IT HOME....
BUT DANGER COMES NOT FROM WIND OR SEA BUT FROM THE FABLED SIRENS WHOSE SONGS CAN NOT BE DENIED.
LEGENDS SAY THAT YOUNG LOVELY MAIDENS SING SHIPS TO THEIR GRAVES BENEATH THE WAVES..
WHILE NONE HAVE EVER SEEN AN ACTUAL SIREN.. THEIR SONGS CAN BE HEARD FAR OVER THE WAVES..
TO APPROACH WITHIN THE ONE MILE LIMIT IS TO LOSE YOUR SOUL TO THE SONGS.
AND THAT IS EXACTLY WHERE WE WERE, RISING AND FALLING WITH THE WAVES, ONE MILE OFF THAT JAGGED COAST AND ONE YEAR BEFORE THE START OF THE GREAT SOLARIUM WAR.
ON THAT BRIGHT WINDSWEPT DAY, WE HAD REACHED OUR JOURNEY'S END ON A SHIP OWNED AND CAPTAINED BY THADDEUS J. THADDEUS, A MILLIONAIRE IN SEARCH OF A BOYHOOD DREAM.

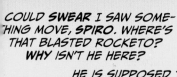

COULD **SWEAR** I SAW SOME-THING MOVE, **SPIRO.** WHERE'S THAT BLASTED ROCKETO? WHY ISN'T HE HERE?

HE IS SUPPOSED TO BE THE **BEST** MAPPER IN THIS WORLD.. **CHARTS** LOST ISLAND AND ALL THAT BOYHOOD STUFF!!

AND NOW HE HAS **GONE** AND DISAPPEARED! LEFT US **STRANDED!!**

**THERE!** WHAT DID I TELL YOU? THEY'RE ALL THERE! BLONDS, REDHEADS, **BRUNETTES.** THE MOST BEAUTIFUL WOMEN IN THE **WORLD.**

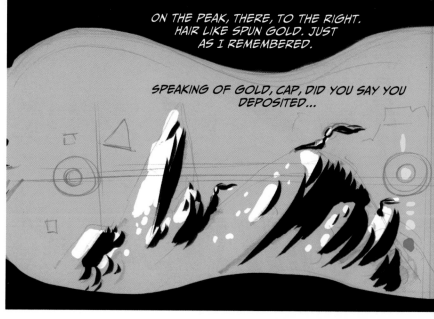

ON THE PEAK, THERE, TO THE RIGHT. HAIR LIKE SPUN GOLD. JUST AS I REMEMBERED.

SPEAKING OF GOLD, CAP, DID YOU SAY YOU DEPOSITED...

HE'LL BE HERE, **CAPTAIN.** BY THE WAY, DID YOU **DEPOSIT** THE **SWAG** TO OUR ACCOUNT IN **SANSEBO?**

YOU'LL GET YOUR BLASTED MONEY, YOU **PIRATE!**

JUST AS SOON AS I HAVE ONE OF THOSE **SIRENS.** NOW **WHERE'S** ROCKETO? WE CAN'T WASTE A MOMENT.

ROCKETO! COME IN, ROCKETO. THIS IS SPIRO.

I'VE WAITED **FORTY YEARS** FOR THIS MOMENT! I WANT HIM HERE **NOW!**

ON MY WAY, **SPIRO.** I GOT SOME GREAT **SAMPLES** FROM THE SEABED. IT LOOKS PRETTY **SOLID** UP TO THE **SHORE.**

ROCKETO! HE'S GONNA' **BLOW** A **GASKET.** GET UP HERE!

WHERE IS HE, SPIRO?! WHAT IS HE DOING AT THE BOTTOM OF THIS COLD OCEAN?!! DOESN'T HE KNOW HOW LONG I HAVE WAITED FOR THIS MOMENT

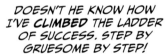

DOESN'T HE KNOW HOW I'VE **CLIMBED** THE LADDER OF SUCCESS. STEP BY GRUESOME BY STEP!

NO ONE TO **HELP** ME.

BUT WHEN I GOT THE **MONEY,** SUDDENLY I HAD FRIENDS. I BOUGHT THE BEST EQUIPMENT! SHIP! CREW THAT MONEY CAN BUY! I CAN BUY ANYTHING!

FORTY YEARS FOR THIS ONE **MOMENT...**

WHAT'S THE **WORD,** ROCKETO?

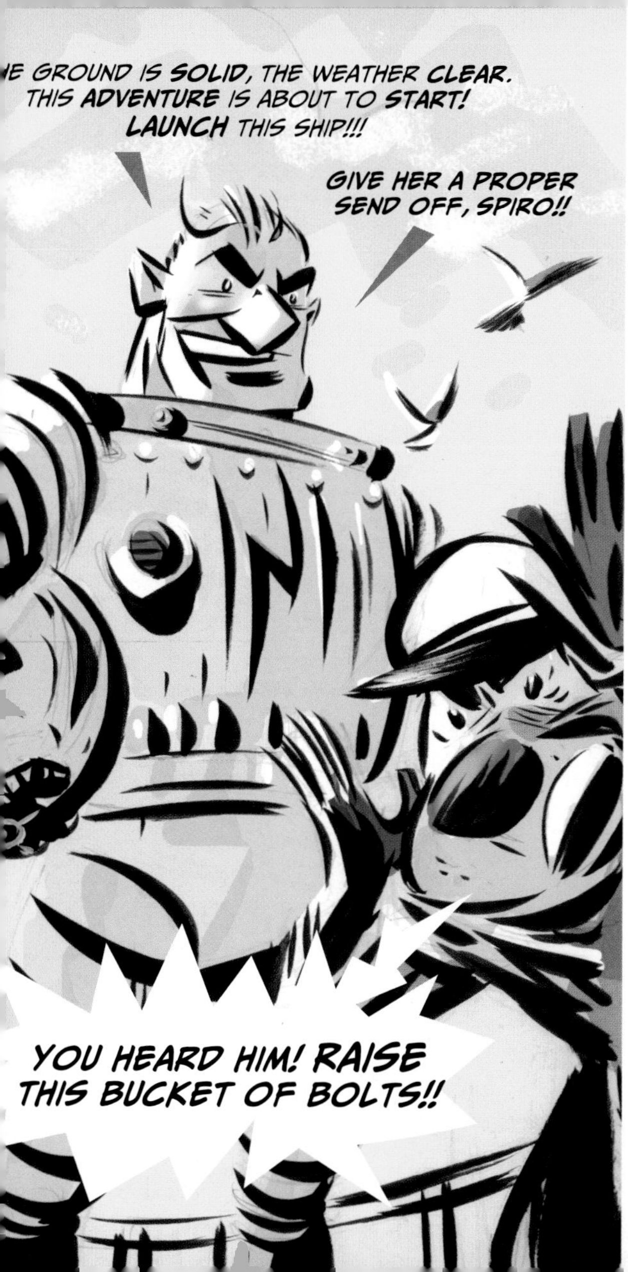
E GROUND IS SOLID, THE WEATHER CLEAR. THIS ADVENTURE IS ABOUT TO START! LAUNCH THIS SHIP!!!
GIVE HER A PROPER SEND OFF, SPIRO!!
YOU HEARD HIM! RAISE THIS BUCKET OF BOLTS!!

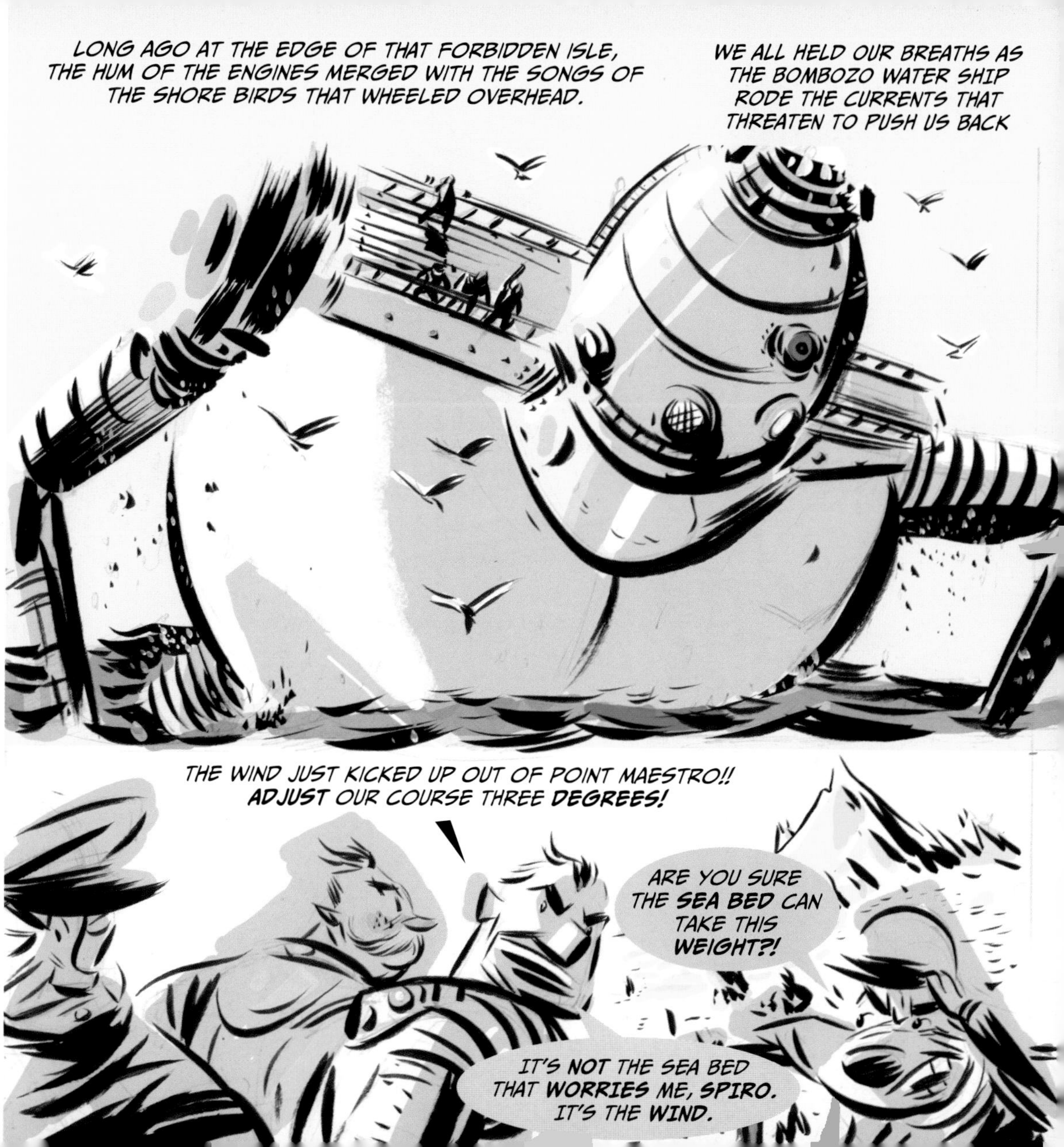
LONG AGO AT THE EDGE OF THAT FORBIDDEN ISLE, THE HUM OF THE ENGINES MERGED WITH THE SONGS OF THE SHORE BIRDS THAT WHEELED OVERHEAD.
WE ALL HELD OUR BREATHS AS THE BOMBOZO WATER SHIP RODE THE CURRENTS THAT THREATEN TO PUSH US BACK
THE WIND JUST KICKED UP OUT OF POINT MAESTRO!! ADJUST OUR COURSE THREE DEGREES!
ARE YOU SURE THE SEA BED CAN TAKE THIS WEIGHT?!
IT'S NOT THE SEA BED THAT WORRIES ME, SPIRO. IT'S THE WIND.

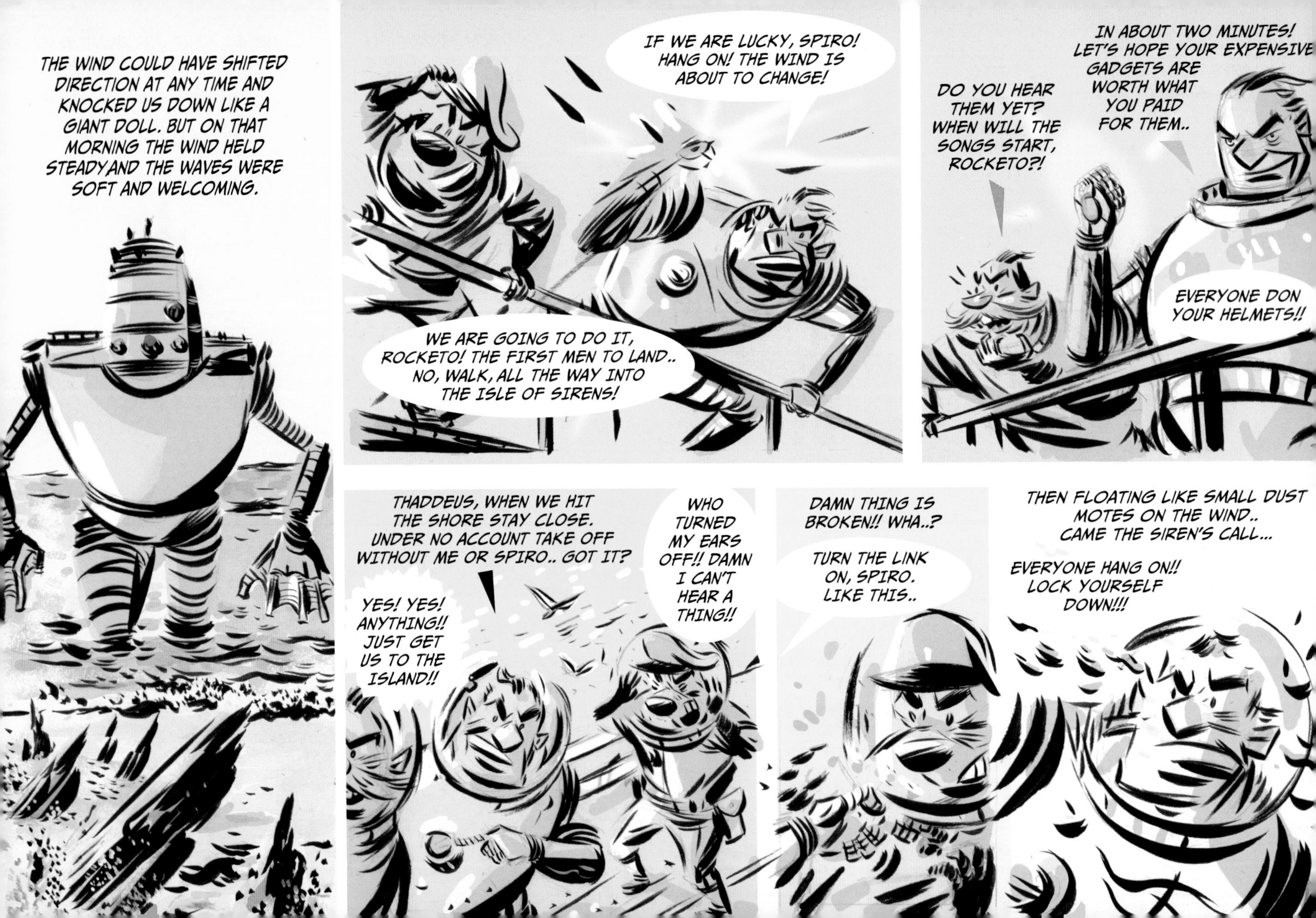
THE WIND COULD HAVE SHIFTED DIRECTION AT ANY TIME AND KNOCKED US DOWN LIKE A GIANT DOLL. BUT ON THAT MORNING THE WIND HELD STEADY,AND THE WAVES WERE SOFT AND WELCOMING.
IF WE ARE LUCKY, SPIRO! HANG ON! THE WIND IS ABOUT TO CHANGE!
WE ARE GOING TO DO IT, ROCKETO! THE FIRST MEN TO LAND.. NO, WALK, ALL THE WAY INTO THE ISLE OF SIRENS!
DO YOU HEAR THEM YET? WHEN WILL THE SONGS START, ROCKETO?!
IN ABOUT TWO MINUTES! LET'S HOPE YOUR EXPENSIVE GADGETS ARE WORTH WHAT YOU PAID FOR THEM..
EVERYONE DON YOUR HELMETS!!
THADDEUS, WHEN WE HIT THE SHORE STAY CLOSE. UNDER NO ACCOUNT TAKE OFF WITHOUT ME OR SPIRO.. GOT IT?
YES! YES! ANYTHING!! JUST GET US TO THE ISLAND!!
WHO TURNED MY EARS OFF!! DAMN I CAN'T HEAR A THING!!
DAMN THING IS BROKEN!! WHA..?
TURN THE LINK ON, SPIRO. LIKE THIS..
THEN FLOATING LIKE SMALL DUST MOTES ON THE WIND.. CAME THE SIREN'S CALL...
EVERYONE HANG ON!! LOCK YOURSELF DOWN!!!

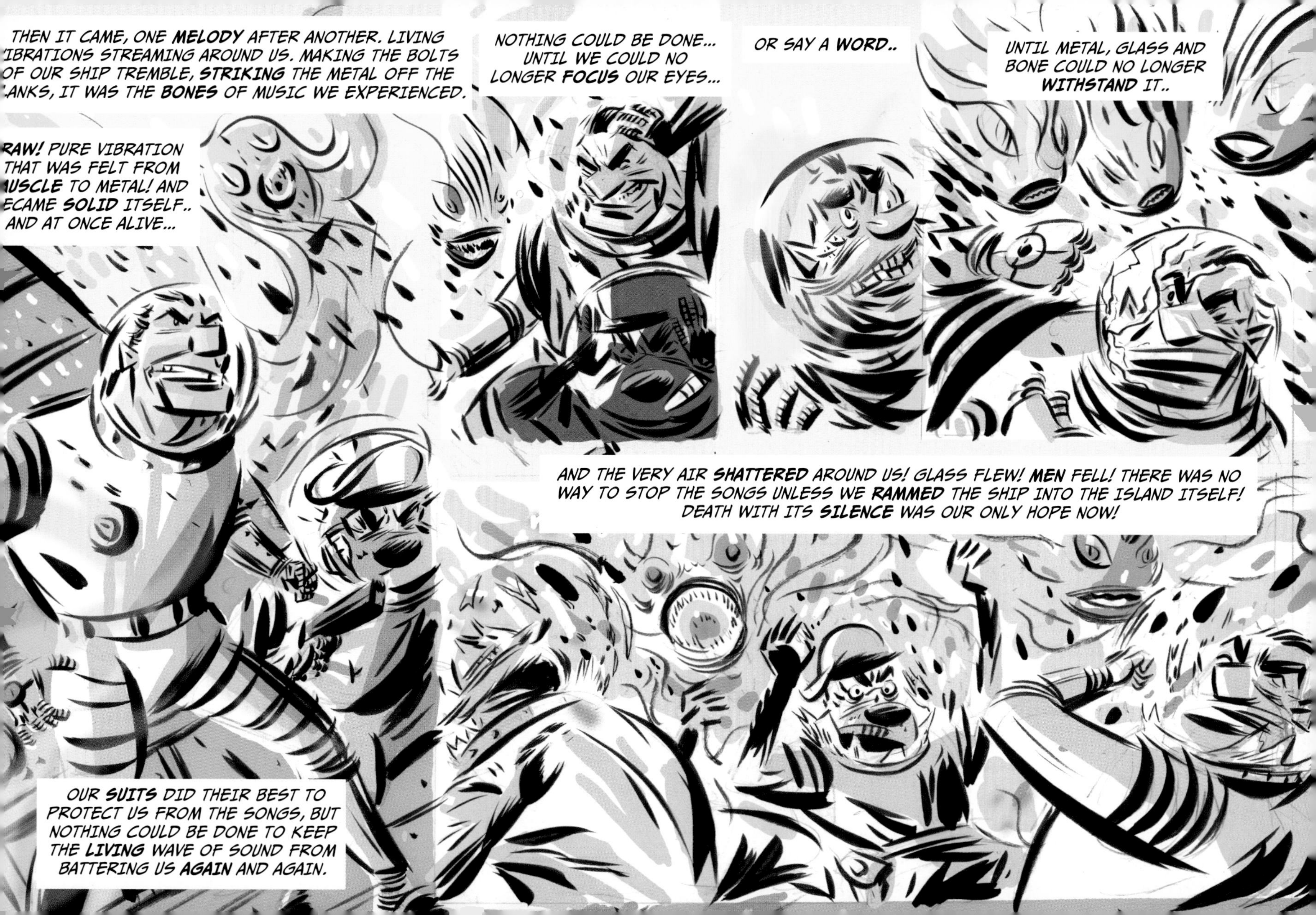
THEN IT CAME, ONE MELODY AFTER ANOTHER. LIVING
IBRATIONS STREAMING AROUND US. MAKING THE BOLTS
OF OUR SHIP TREMBLE, STRIKING THE METAL OFF THE
ANKS, IT WAS THE BONES OF MUSIC WE EXPERIENCED.
RAW! PURE VIBRATION THAT WAS FELT FROM USCLE TO METAL! AND ECAME SOLID ITSELF.. AND AT ONCE ALIVE...
NOTHING COULD BE DONE... UNTIL WE COULD NO LONGER FOCUS OUR EYES...
OR SAY A WORD..
UNTIL METAL, GLASS AND BONE COULD NO LONGER WITHSTAND IT..
AND THE VERY AIR SHATTERED AROUND US! GLASS FLEW! MEN FELL! THERE WAS NO WAY TO STOP THE SONGS UNLESS WE RAMMED THE SHIP INTO THE ISLAND ITSELF! DEATH WITH ITS SILENCE WAS OUR ONLY HOPE NOW!
OUR SUITS DID THEIR BEST TO PROTECT US FROM THE SONGS, BUT NOTHING COULD BE DONE TO KEEP THE LIVING WAVE OF SOUND FROM BATTERING US AGAIN AND AGAIN.

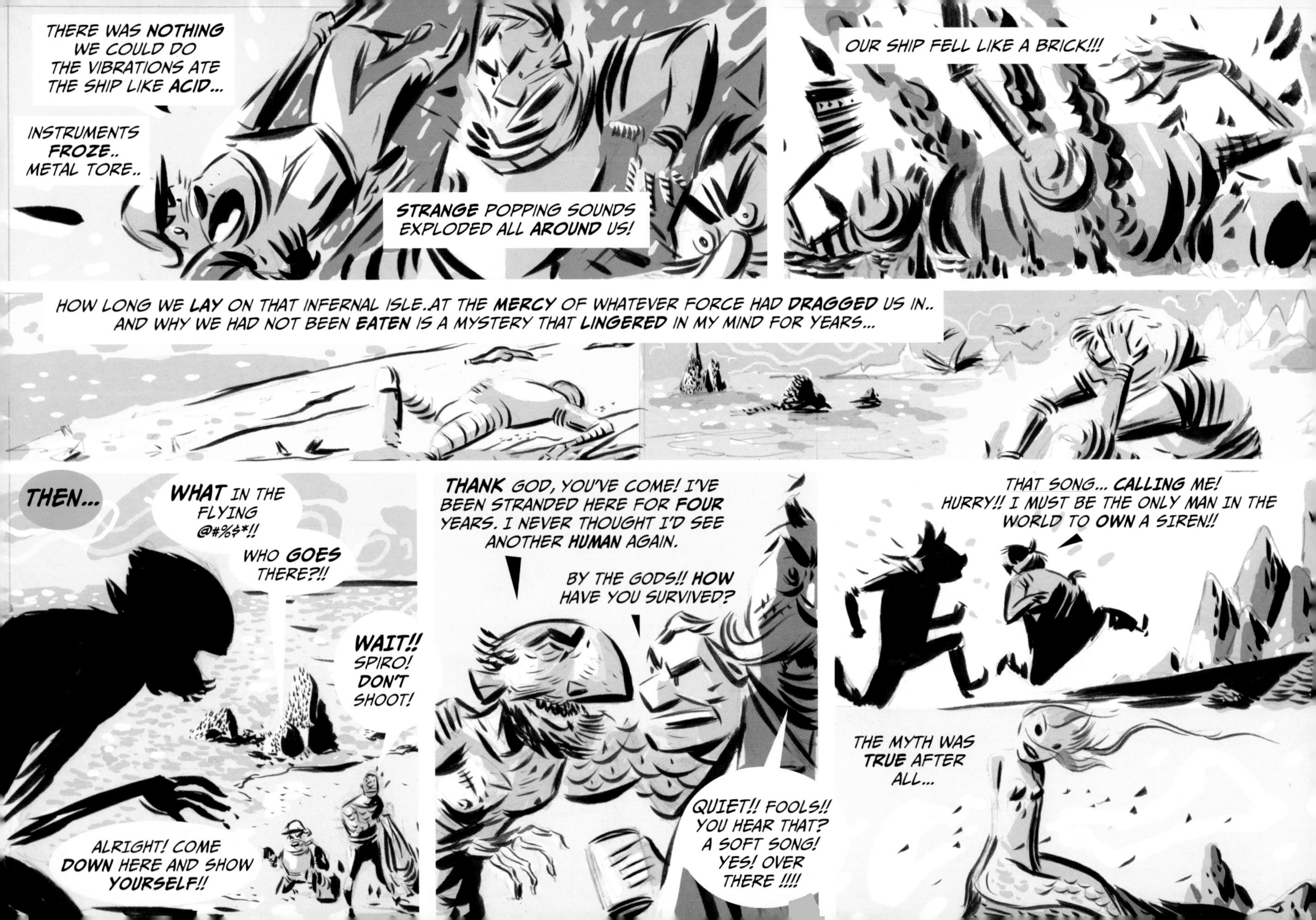
THERE WAS NOTHING WE COULD DO THE VIBRATIONS ATE THE SHIP LIKE ACID...
INSTRUMENTS FROZE.. METAL TORE..
STRANGE POPPING SOUNDS EXPLODED ALL AROUND US!
OUR SHIP FELL LIKE A BRICK!!!
HOW LONG WE LAY ON THAT INFERNAL ISLE..AT THE MERCY OF WHATEVER FORCE HAD DRAGGED US IN.. AND WHY WE HAD NOT BEEN EATEN IS A MYSTERY THAT LINGERED IN MY MIND FOR YEARS...
THEN...
WHAT IN THE FLYING @#%$*!!
WHO GOES THERE?!!
WAIT!! SPIRO! DON'T SHOOT!
ALRIGHT! COME DOWN HERE AND SHOW YOURSELF!!
THANK GOD, YOU'VE COME! I'VE BEEN STRANDED HERE FOR FOUR YEARS. I NEVER THOUGHT I'D SEE ANOTHER HUMAN AGAIN.
BY THE GODS!! HOW HAVE YOU SURVIVED?
QUIET!! FOOLS!! YOU HEAR THAT? A SOFT SONG! YES! OVER THERE !!!!
THAT SONG... CALLING ME! HURRY!! I MUST BE THE ONLY MAN IN THE WORLD TO OWN A SIREN!!
THE MYTH WAS TRUE AFTER ALL...

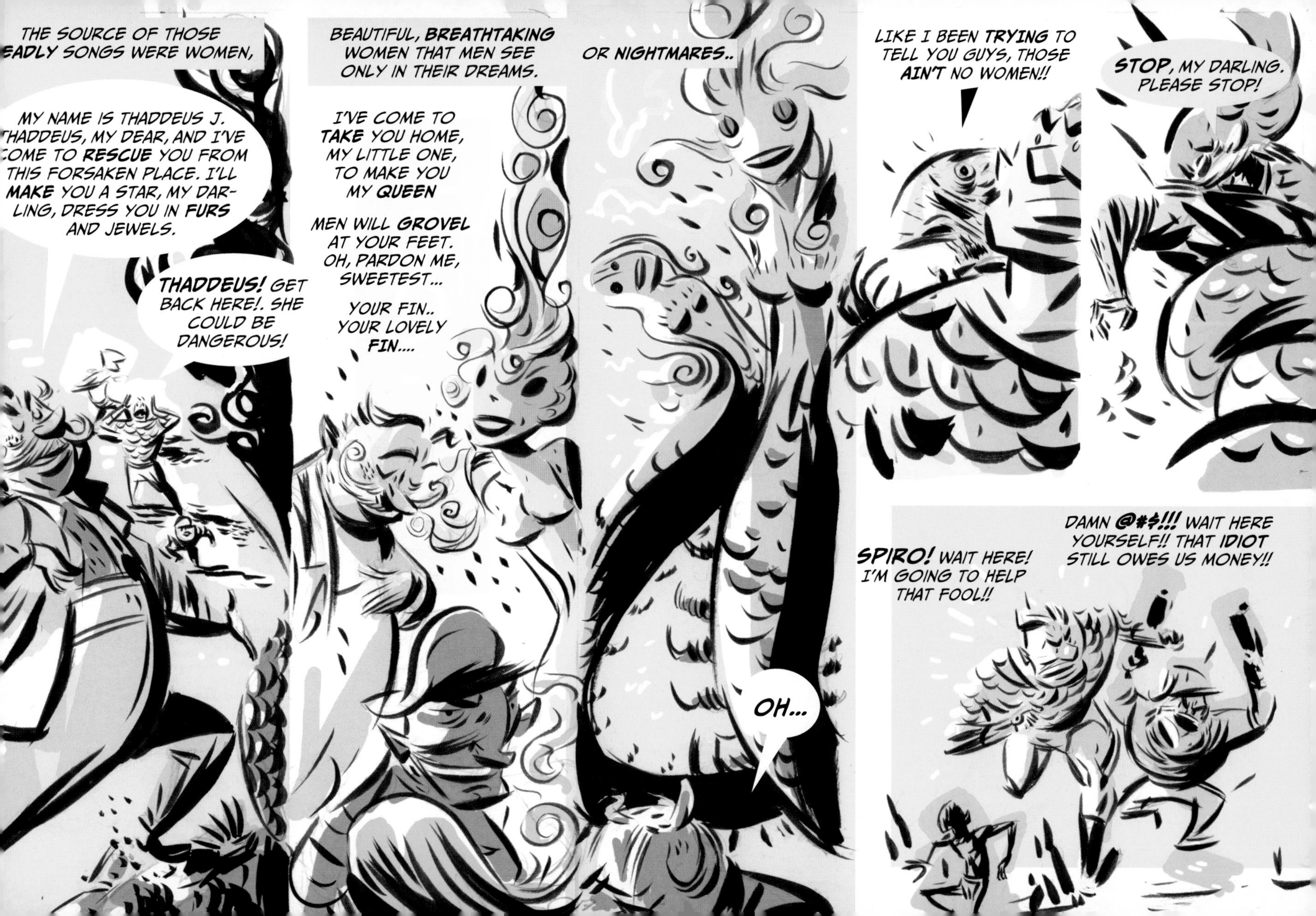

THE SOURCE OF THOSE DEADLY SONGS WERE WOMEN,
MY NAME IS THADDEUS J. THADDEUS, MY DEAR, AND I'VE COME TO RESCUE YOU FROM THIS FORSAKEN PLACE. I'LL MAKE YOU A STAR, MY DARLING, DRESS YOU IN FURS AND JEWELS.
THADDEUS! GET BACK HERE!. SHE COULD BE DANGEROUS!
BEAUTIFUL, BREATHTAKING WOMEN THAT MEN SEE ONLY IN THEIR DREAMS.
I'VE COME TO TAKE YOU HOME, MY LITTLE ONE, TO MAKE YOU MY QUEEN
MEN WILL GROVEL AT YOUR FEET. OH, PARDON ME, SWEETEST...
YOUR FIN.. YOUR LOVELY FIN....
OR NIGHTMARES..
OH...
LIKE I BEEN TRYING TO TELL YOU GUYS, THOSE AIN'T NO WOMEN!!
STOP, MY DARLING. PLEASE STOP!
SPIRO! WAIT HERE! I'M GOING TO HELP THAT FOOL!!
DAMN @#$!!! WAIT HERE YOURSELF!! THAT IDIOT STILL OWES US MONEY!!

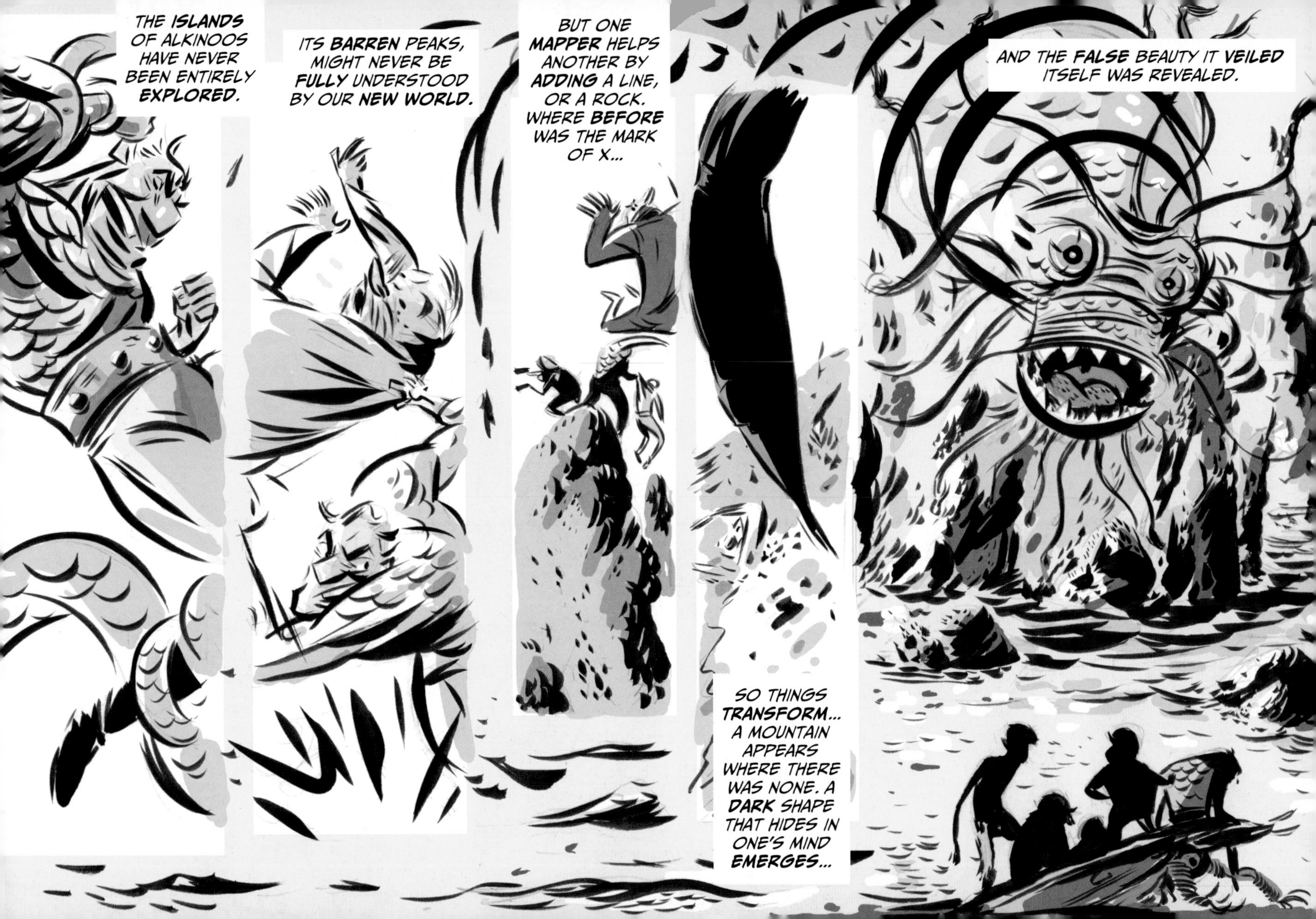
THE ISLANDS OF ALKINOOS HAVE NEVER BEEN ENTIRELY EXPLORED.
ITS BARREN PEAKS, MIGHT NEVER BE FULLY UNDERSTOOD BY OUR NEW WORLD.
BUT ONE MAPPER HELPS ANOTHER BY ADDING A LINE, OR A ROCK. WHERE BEFORE WAS THE MARK OF X...
SO THINGS TRANSFORM... A MOUNTAIN APPEARS WHERE THERE WAS NONE. A DARK SHAPE THAT HIDES IN ONE'S MIND EMERGES...
AND THE FALSE BEAUTY IT VEILED ITSELF WAS REVEALED.

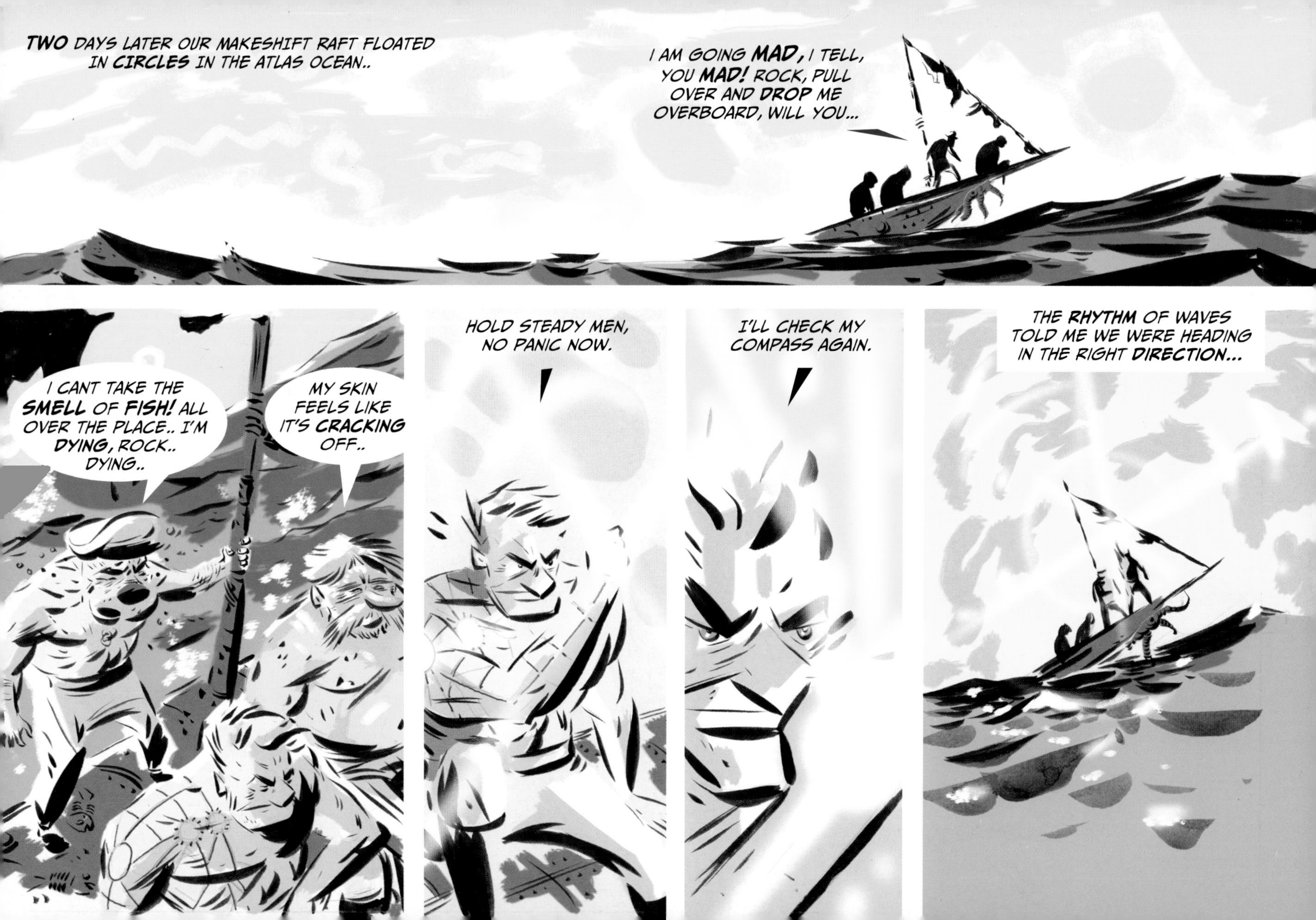
TWO DAYS LATER OUR MAKESHIFT RAFT FLOATED IN CIRCLES IN THE ATLAS OCEAN..
I AM GOING MAD, I TELL, YOU MAD! ROCK, PULL OVER AND DROP ME OVERBOARD, WILL YOU...
I CANT TAKE THE SMELL OF FISH! ALL OVER THE PLACE.. I'M DYING, ROCK.. DYING..
MY SKIN FEELS LIKE IT'S CRACKING OFF..
HOLD STEADY MEN, NO PANIC NOW.
I'LL CHECK MY COMPASS AGAIN.
THE RHYTHM OF WAVES TOLD ME WE WERE HEADING IN THE RIGHT DIRECTION...

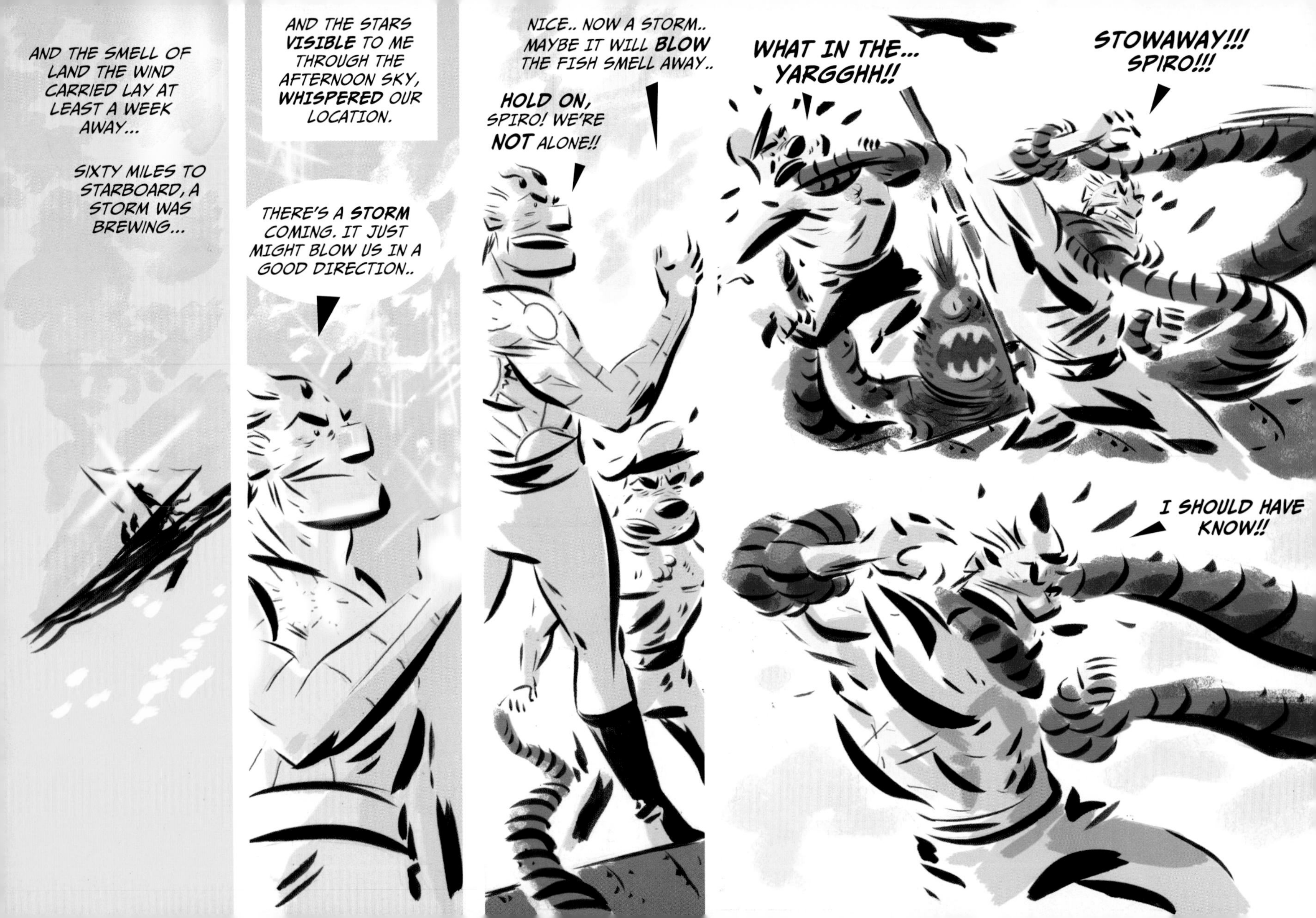
AND THE SMELL OF LAND THE WIND CARRIED LAY AT LEAST A WEEK AWAY...
SIXTY MILES TO STARBOARD, A STORM WAS BREWING...
AND THE STARS VISIBLE TO ME THROUGH THE AFTERNOON SKY, WHISPERED OUR LOCATION.
THERE'S A STORM COMING. IT JUST MIGHT BLOW US IN A GOOD DIRECTION..
NICE.. NOW A STORM.. MAYBE IT WILL BLOW THE FISH SMELL AWAY..
HOLD ON, SPIRO! WE'RE NOT ALONE!!
WHAT IN THE... YARGGHH!!
STOWAWAY!!! SPIRO!!!
I SHOULD HAVE KNOW!!

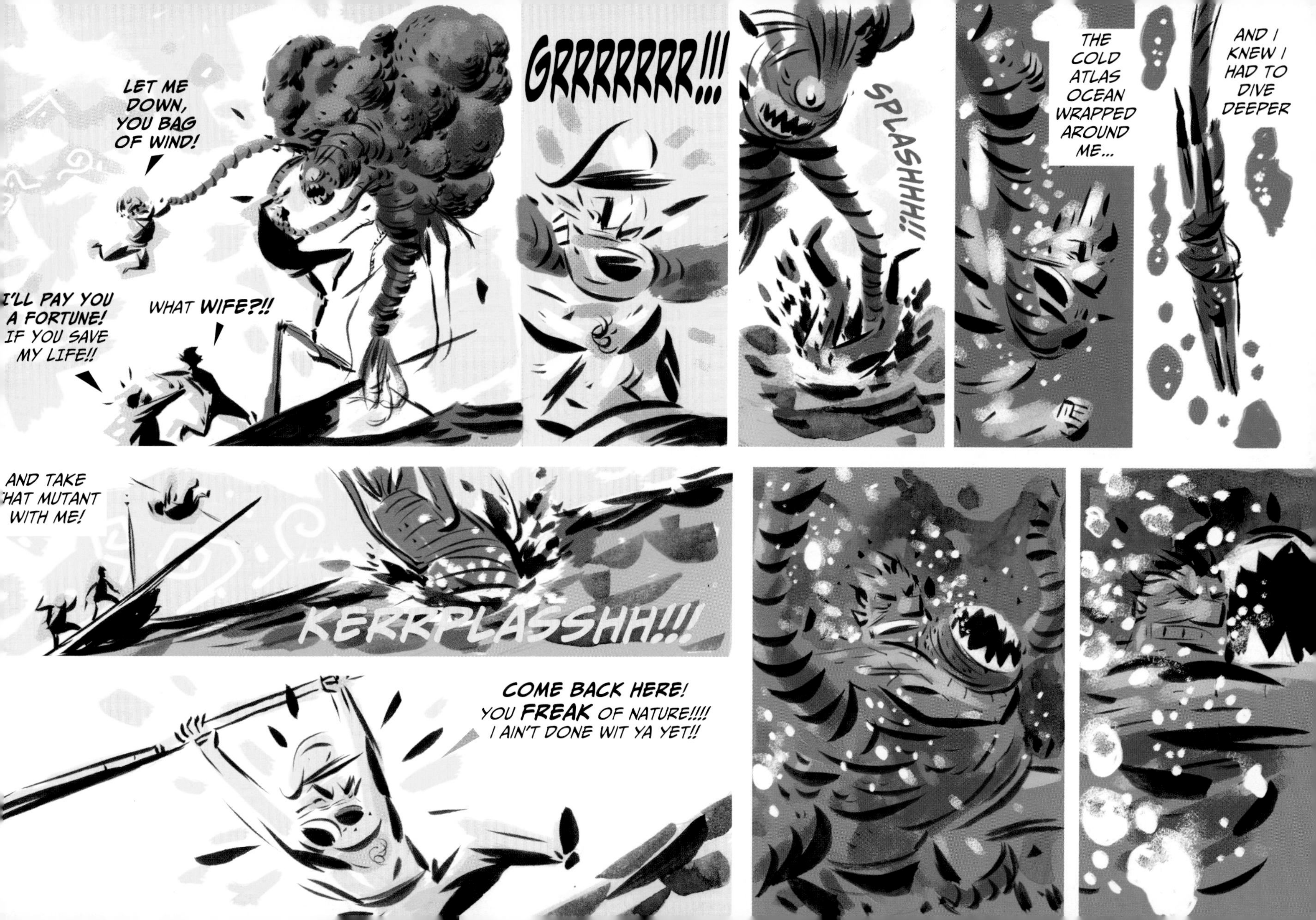
LET ME DOWN, YOU BAG OF WIND!
I'LL PAY YOU A FORTUNE! IF YOU SAVE MY LIFE!!
WHAT WIFE?!!
GRRRRRRR!!!
SPLASHHH!!
THE COLD ATLAS OCEAN WRAPPED AROUND ME...
AND I KNEW I HAD TO DIVE DEEPER
AND TAKE THAT MUTANT WITH ME!
KERRPLASSHH!!!
COME BACK HERE! YOU FREAK OF NATURE!!!! I AIN'T DONE WIT YA YET!!

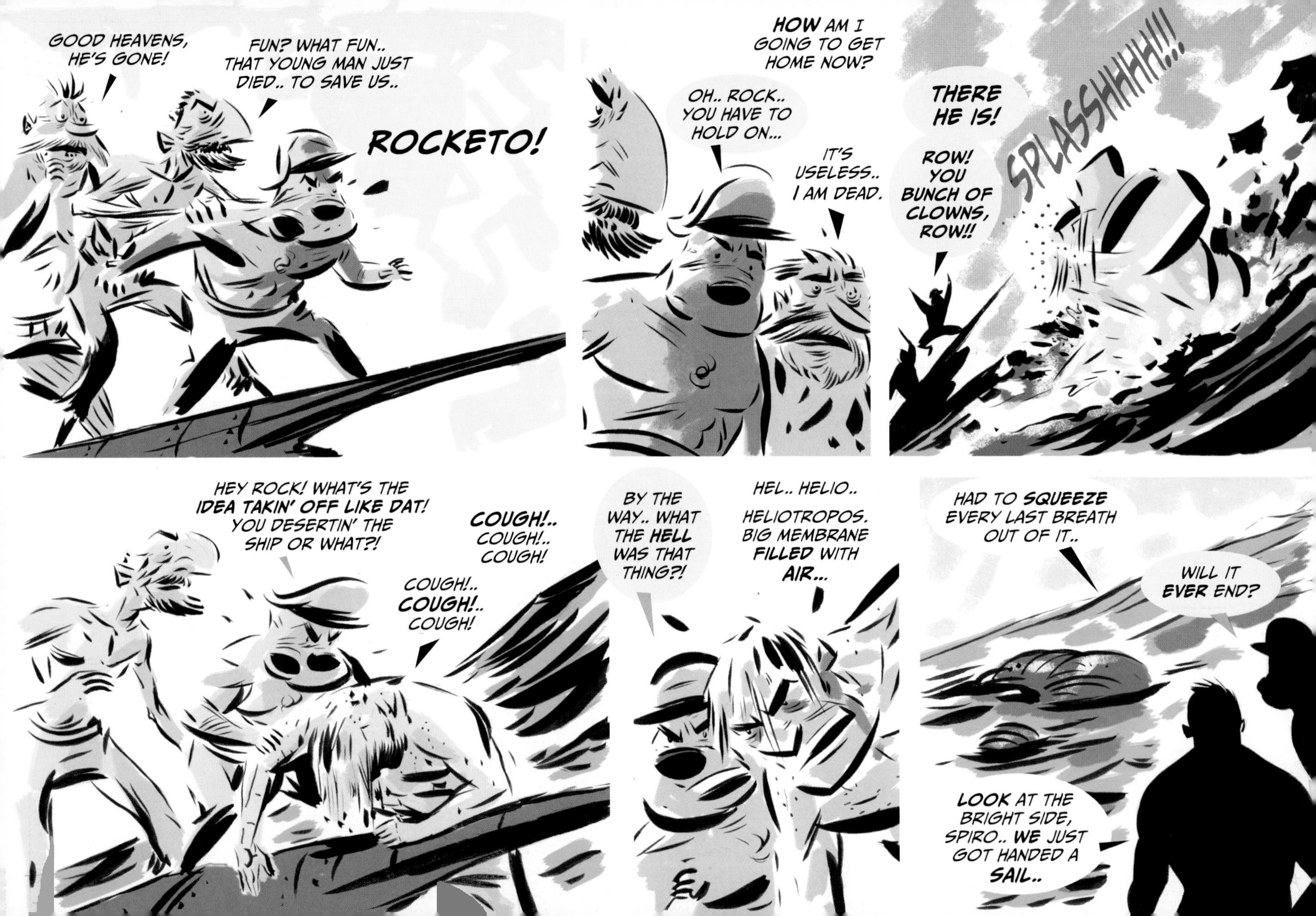

GOOD HEAVENS, HE'S GONE!
FUN? WHAT FUN.. THAT YOUNG MAN JUST DIED.. TO SAVE US..
ROCKETO!
HOW AM I GOING TO GET HOME NOW?
OH.. ROCK.. YOU HAVE TO HOLD ON...
IT'S USELESS.. I AM DEAD.
THERE HE IS!
ROW! YOU BUNCH OF CLOWNS, ROW!!
SPLASSHHHH!!!
HEY ROCK! WHAT'S THE IDEA TAKIN' OFF LIKE DAT! YOU DESERTIN' THE SHIP OR WHAT?!
COUGH!.. COUGH!.. COUGH!
COUGH!.. COUGH!.. COUGH!
BY THE WAY.. WHAT THE HELL WAS THAT THING?!
HEL.. HELIO..
HELIOTROPOS. BIG MEMBRANE FILLED WITH AIR...
HAD TO SQUEEZE EVERY LAST BREATH OUT OF IT..
WILL IT EVER END?
LOOK AT THE BRIGHT SIDE, SPIRO.. WE JUST GOT HANDED A SAIL..

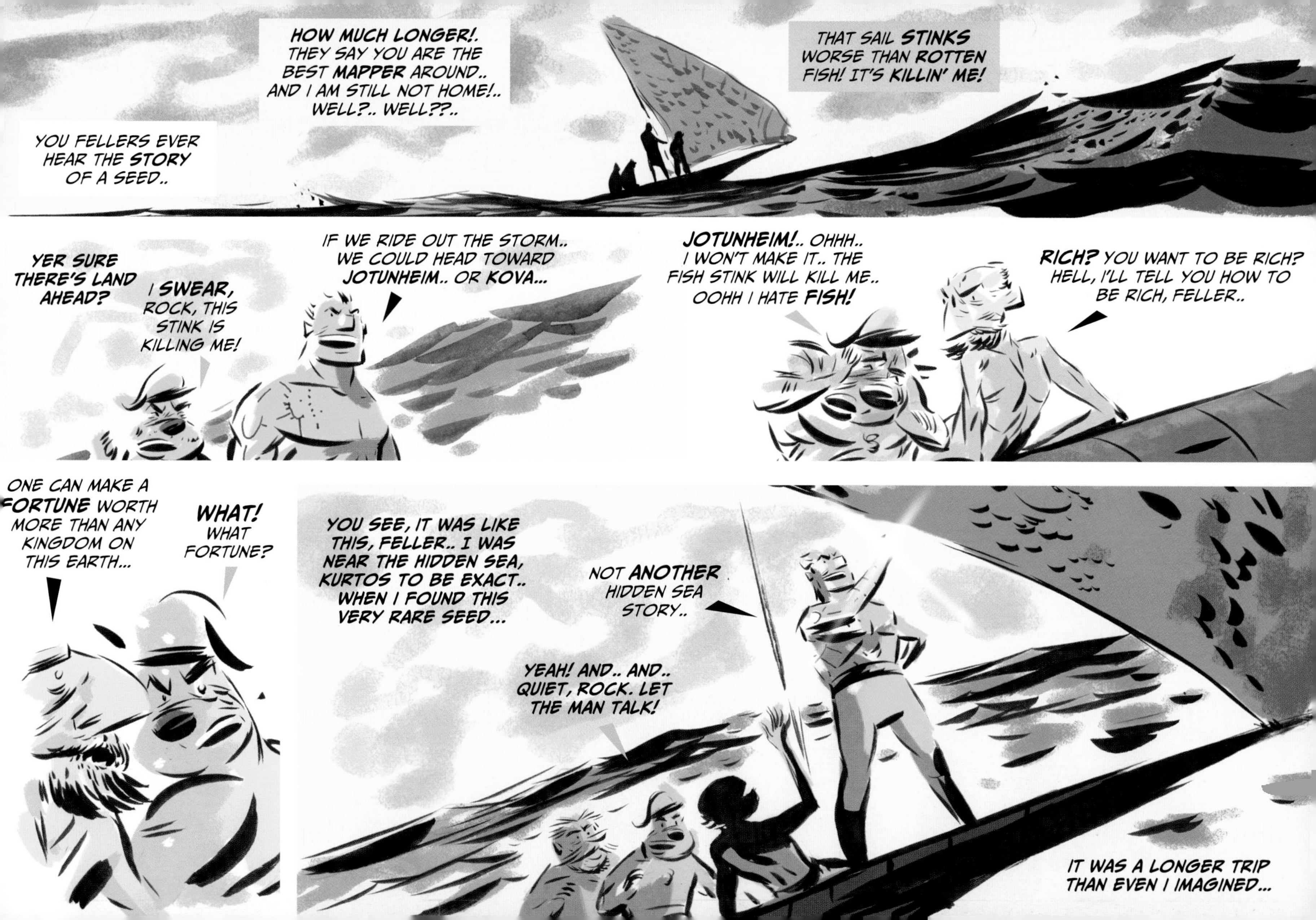

YOU FELLERS EVER HEAR THE STORY OF A SEED..
HOW MUCH LONGER!. THEY SAY YOU ARE THE BEST MAPPER AROUND.. AND I AM STILL NOT HOME!.. WELL?.. WELL??..
THAT SAIL STINKS WORSE THAN ROTTEN FISH! IT'S KILLIN' ME!
YER SURE THERE'S LAND AHEAD?
I SWEAR, ROCK, THIS STINK IS KILLING ME!
IF WE RIDE OUT THE STORM.. WE COULD HEAD TOWARD JOTUNHEIM.. OR KOVA...
JOTUNHEIM!.. OHHH.. I WON'T MAKE IT.. THE FISH STINK WILL KILL ME.. OOHH I HATE FISH!
RICH? YOU WANT TO BE RICH? HELL, I'LL TELL YOU HOW TO BE RICH, FELLER..
ONE CAN MAKE A FORTUNE WORTH MORE THAN ANY KINGDOM ON THIS EARTH...
WHAT! WHAT FORTUNE?
YOU SEE, IT WAS LIKE THIS, FELLER.. I WAS NEAR THE HIDDEN SEA, KURTOS TO BE EXACT.. WHEN I FOUND THIS VERY RARE SEED...
NOT ANOTHER HIDDEN SEA STORY..
YEAH! AND.. AND.. QUIET, ROCK. LET THE MAN TALK!
IT WAS A LONGER TRIP THAN EVEN I IMAGINED...

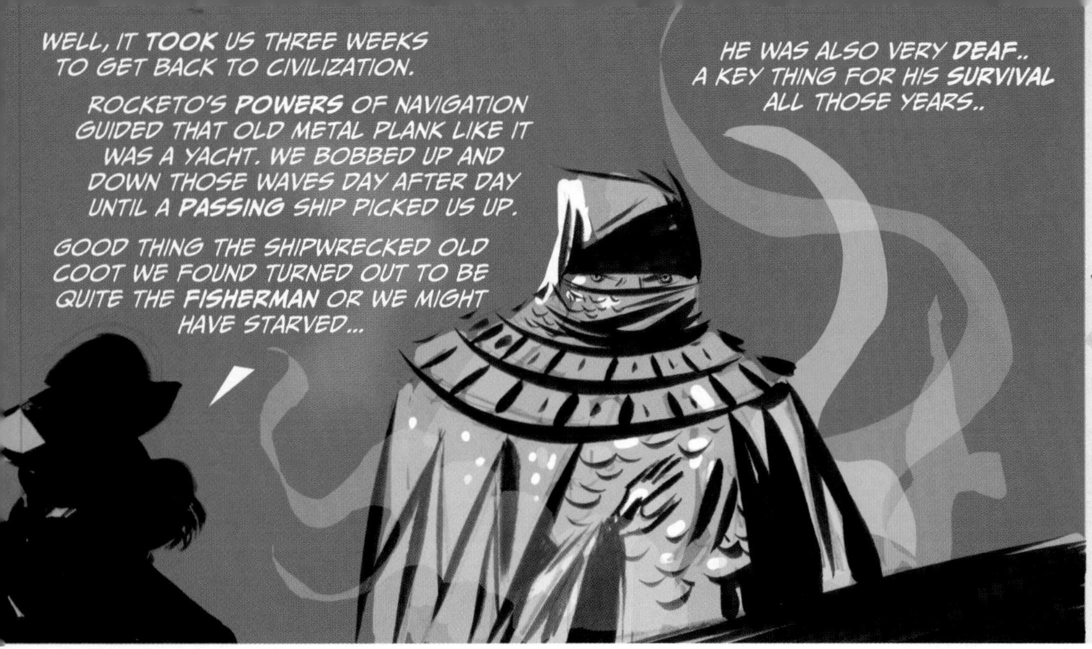
WELL, IT TOOK US THREE WEEKS TO GET BACK TO CIVILIZATION.
ROCKETO'S POWERS OF NAVIGATION GUIDED THAT OLD METAL PLANK LIKE IT WAS A YACHT. WE BOBBED UP AND DOWN THOSE WAVES DAY AFTER DAY UNTIL A PASSING SHIP PICKED US UP.
GOOD THING THE SHIPWRECKED OLD COOT WE FOUND TURNED OUT TO BE QUITE THE FISHERMAN OR WE MIGHT HAVE STARVED...
HE WAS ALSO VERY DEAF.. A KEY THING FOR HIS SURVIVAL ALL THOSE YEARS..

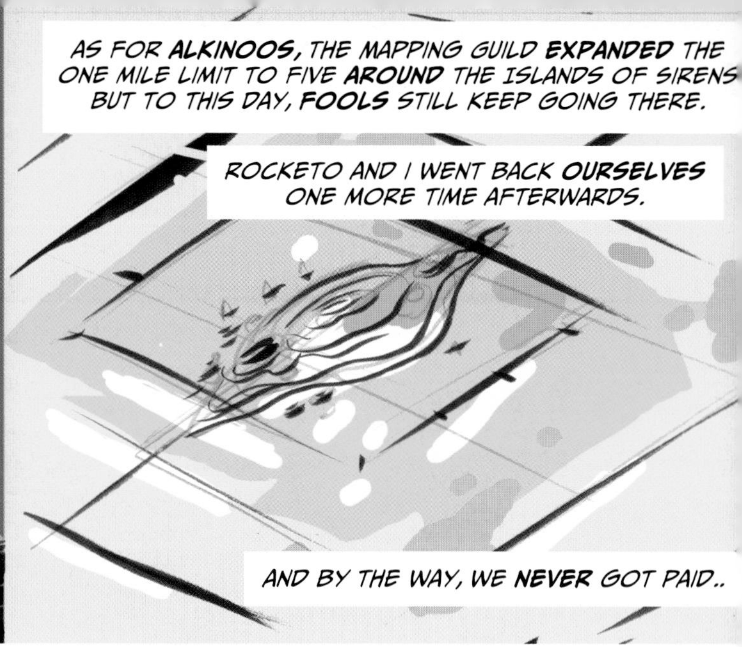
AS FOR ALKINOOS, THE MAPPING GUILD EXPANDED THE ONE MILE LIMIT TO FIVE AROUND THE ISLANDS OF SIRENS BUT TO THIS DAY, FOOLS STILL KEEP GOING THERE.
ROCKETO AND I WENT BACK OURSELVES ONE MORE TIME AFTERWARDS.
AND BY THE WAY, WE NEVER GOT PAID..

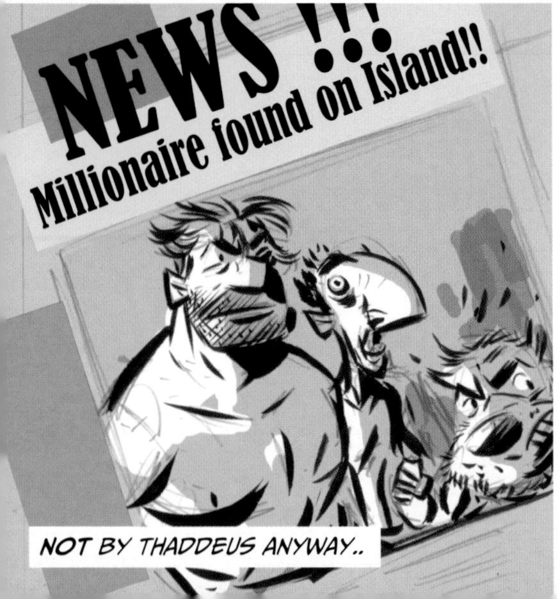
NEWS !!!
Millionaire found on Island!!
NOT BY THADDEUS ANYWAY..

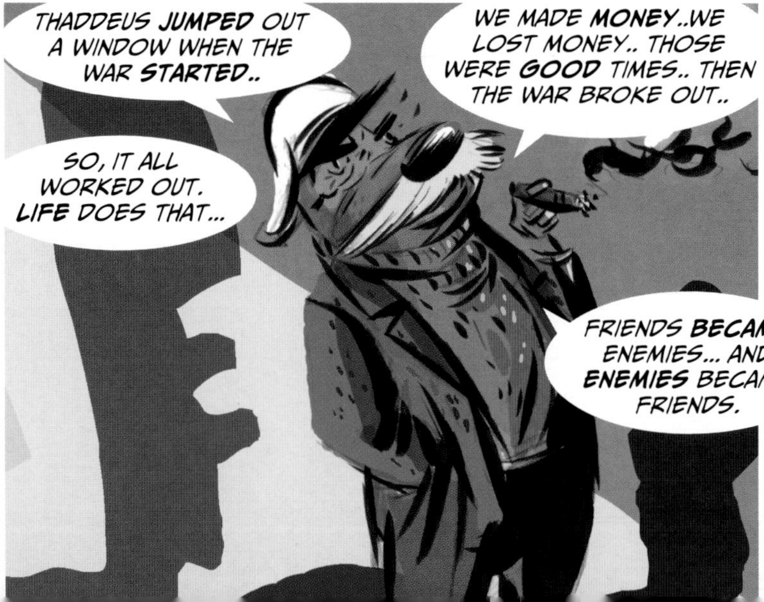
THADDEUS JUMPED OUT A WINDOW WHEN THE WAR STARTED..
SO, IT ALL WORKED OUT. LIFE DOES THAT...
WE MADE MONEY..WE LOST MONEY.. THOSE WERE GOOD TIMES.. THEN THE WAR BROKE OUT..
FRIENDS BECAME ENEMIES... AND ENEMIES BECAME FRIENDS.

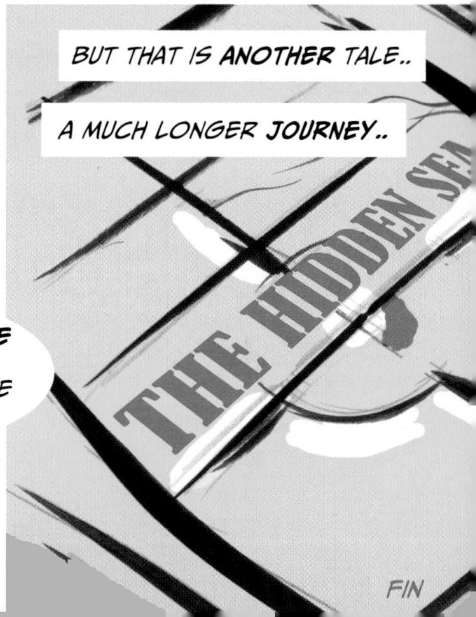
BUT THAT IS ANOTHER TALE..
A MUCH LONGER JOURNEY..
THE HIDDEN SEA
FIN

Included with this collection is the short story **The Siren's Call**.

Book 0 as it is sometimes called, was never meant to be a link with **Journey to the Hidden Sea**, only a preview for the 2005 San Diego Comic Con. The Siren's Call, always felt out of place added to this collection, without some revision. Now, with five new pages added, The Siren's Call can become part of the Hidden Sea story, in a more organic way than originally intended. It was so much fun to do, that it would be good to explore, what those other weeks at sea on the Atlas Ocean were like, in the next Rocketo trade.

# ROCKETO

# 1

## PROSPERITY

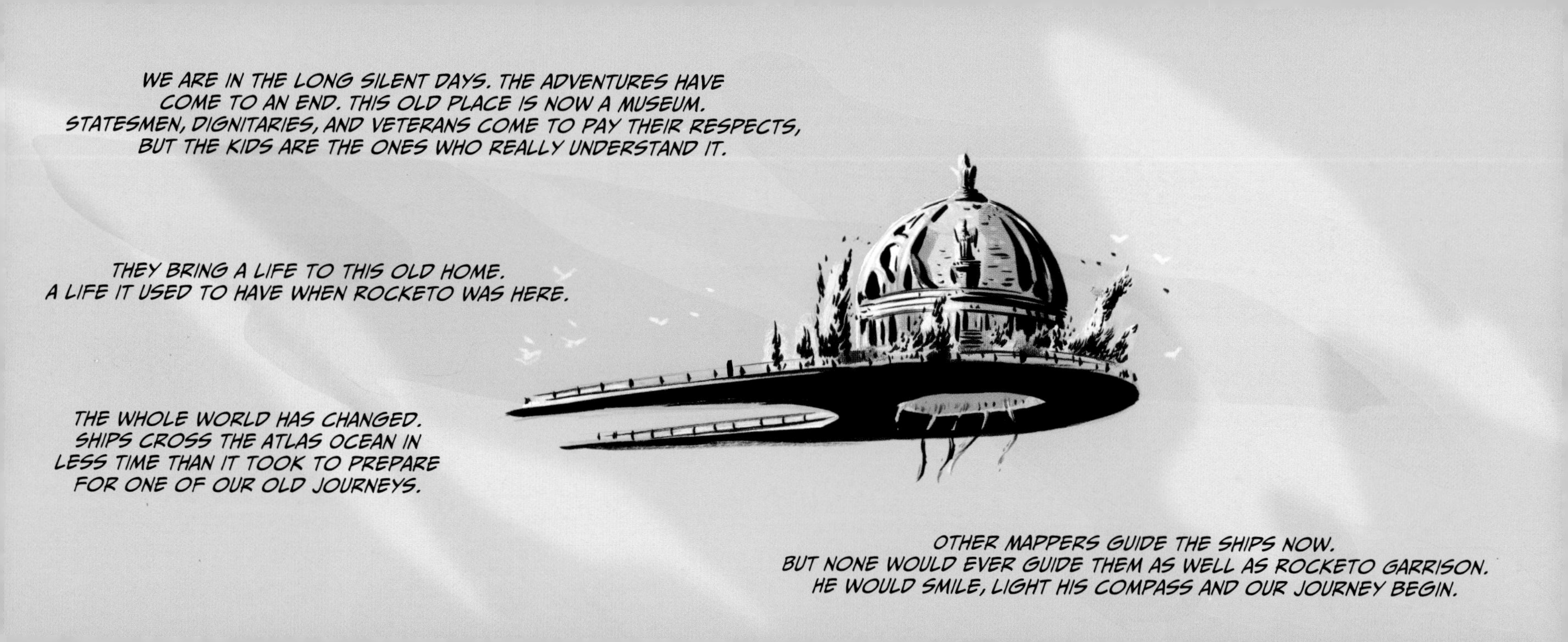
WE ARE IN THE LONG SILENT DAYS. THE ADVENTURES HAVE COME TO AN END. THIS OLD PLACE IS NOW A MUSEUM. STATESMEN, DIGNITARIES, AND VETERANS COME TO PAY THEIR RESPECTS, BUT THE KIDS ARE THE ONES WHO REALLY UNDERSTAND IT.
THEY BRING A LIFE TO THIS OLD HOME. A LIFE IT USED TO HAVE WHEN ROCKETO WAS HERE.
THE WHOLE WORLD HAS CHANGED. SHIPS CROSS THE ATLAS OCEAN IN LESS TIME THAN IT TOOK TO PREPARE FOR ONE OF OUR OLD JOURNEYS.
OTHER MAPPERS GUIDE THE SHIPS NOW. BUT NONE WOULD EVER GUIDE THEM AS WELL AS ROCKETO GARRISON. HE WOULD SMILE, LIGHT HIS COMPASS AND OUR JOURNEY BEGIN.

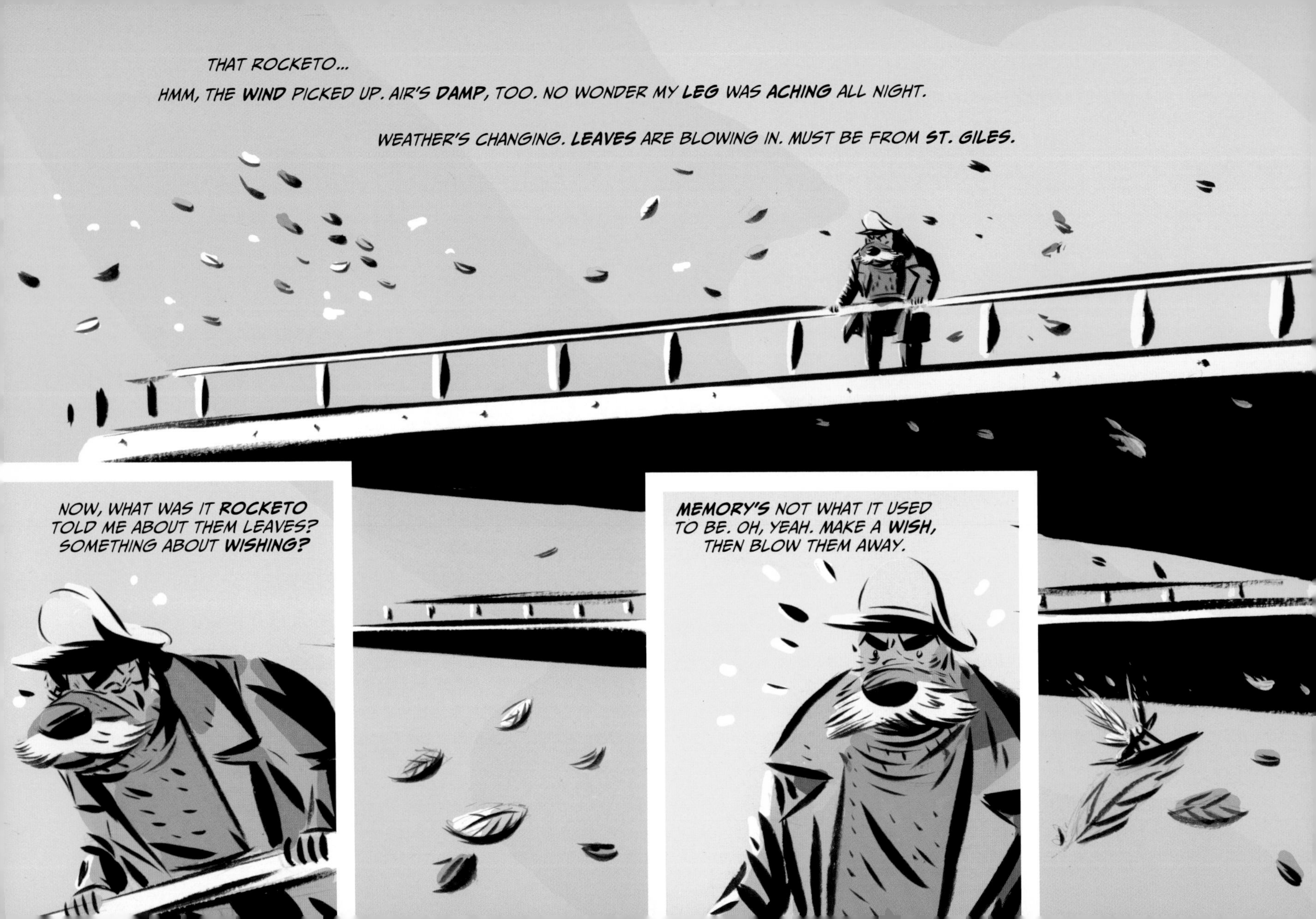
THAT ROCKETO...
HMM, THE WIND PICKED UP. AIR'S DAMP, TOO. NO WONDER MY LEG WAS ACHING ALL NIGHT.
WEATHER'S CHANGING. LEAVES ARE BLOWING IN. MUST BE FROM ST. GILES.
NOW, WHAT WAS IT ROCKETO TOLD ME ABOUT THEM LEAVES? SOMETHING ABOUT WISHING?
MEMORY'S NOT WHAT IT USED TO BE. OH, YEAH. MAKE A WISH, THEN BLOW THEM AWAY.

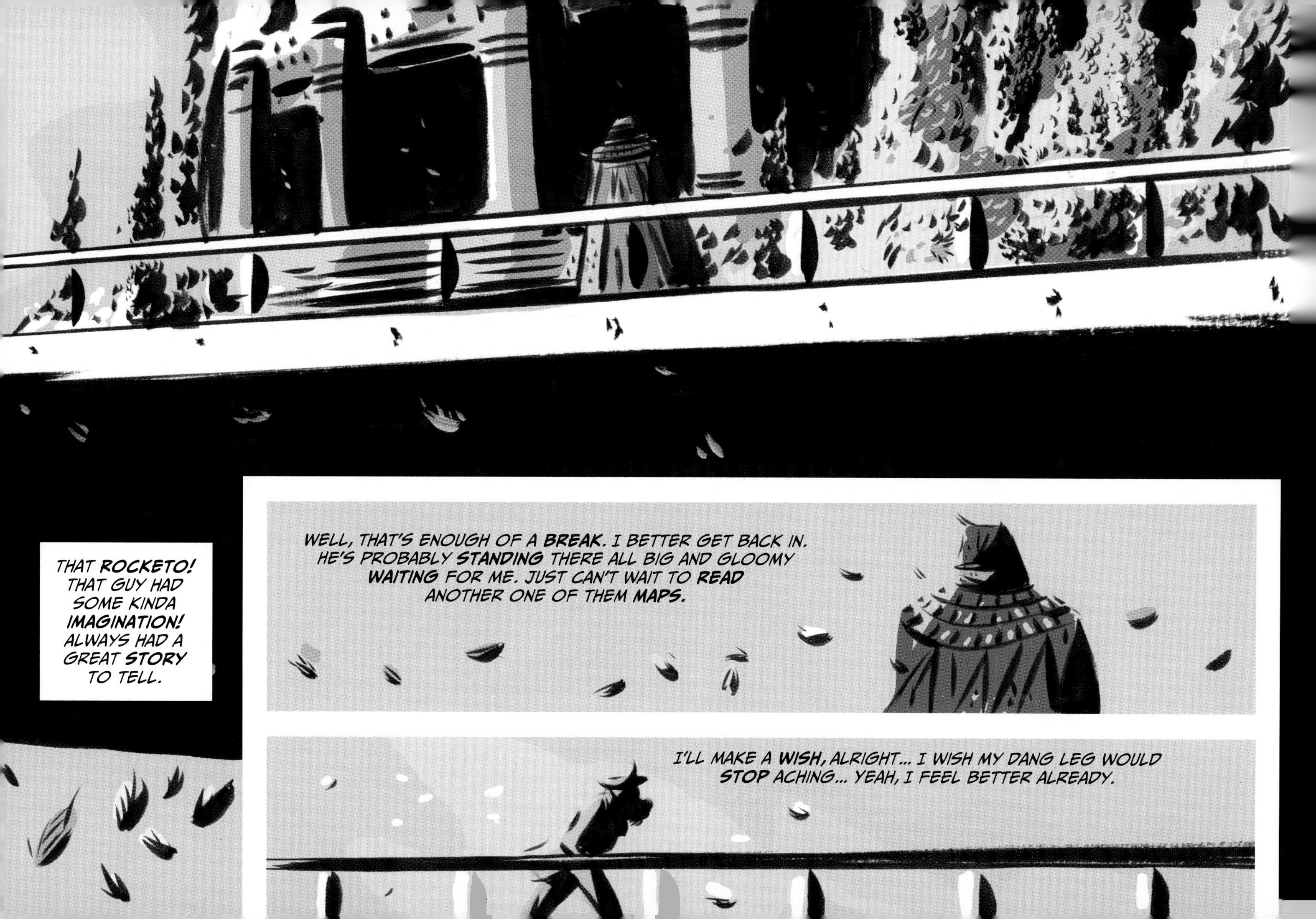
THAT ROCKETO! THAT GUY HAD SOME KINDA IMAGINATION! ALWAYS HAD A GREAT STORY TO TELL.
WELL, THAT'S ENOUGH OF A BREAK. I BETTER GET BACK IN. HE'S PROBABLY STANDING THERE ALL BIG AND GLOOMY WAITING FOR ME. JUST CAN'T WAIT TO READ ANOTHER ONE OF THEM MAPS.
I'LL MAKE A WISH, ALRIGHT... I WISH MY DANG LEG WOULD STOP ACHING... YEAH, I FEEL BETTER ALREADY.

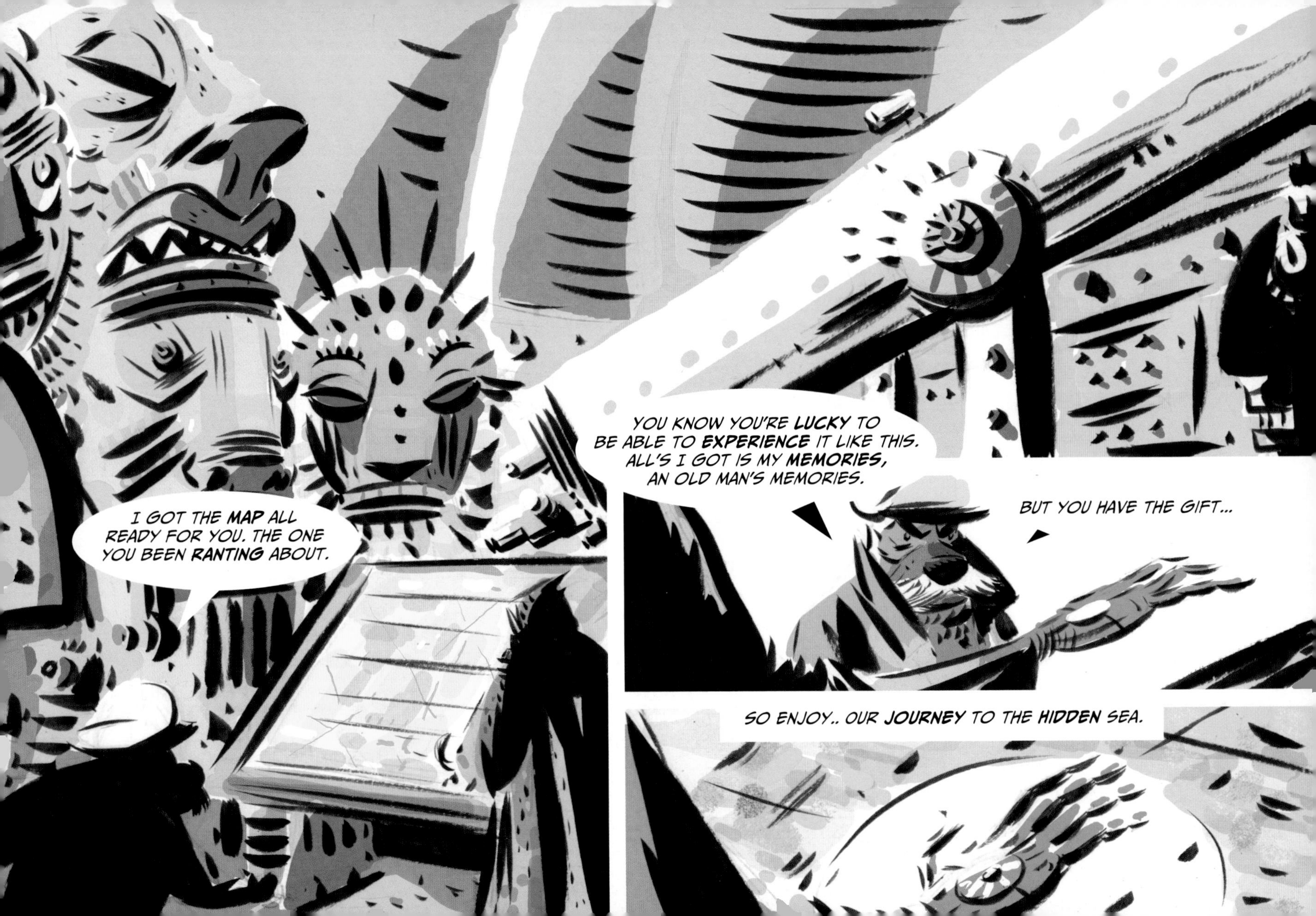
I GOT THE MAP ALL READY FOR YOU. THE ONE YOU BEEN RANTING ABOUT.
YOU KNOW YOU'RE LUCKY TO BE ABLE TO EXPERIENCE IT LIKE THIS. ALL'S I GOT IS MY MEMORIES, AN OLD MAN'S MEMORIES.
BUT YOU HAVE THE GIFT...
SO ENJOY.. OUR JOURNEY TO THE HIDDEN SEA.

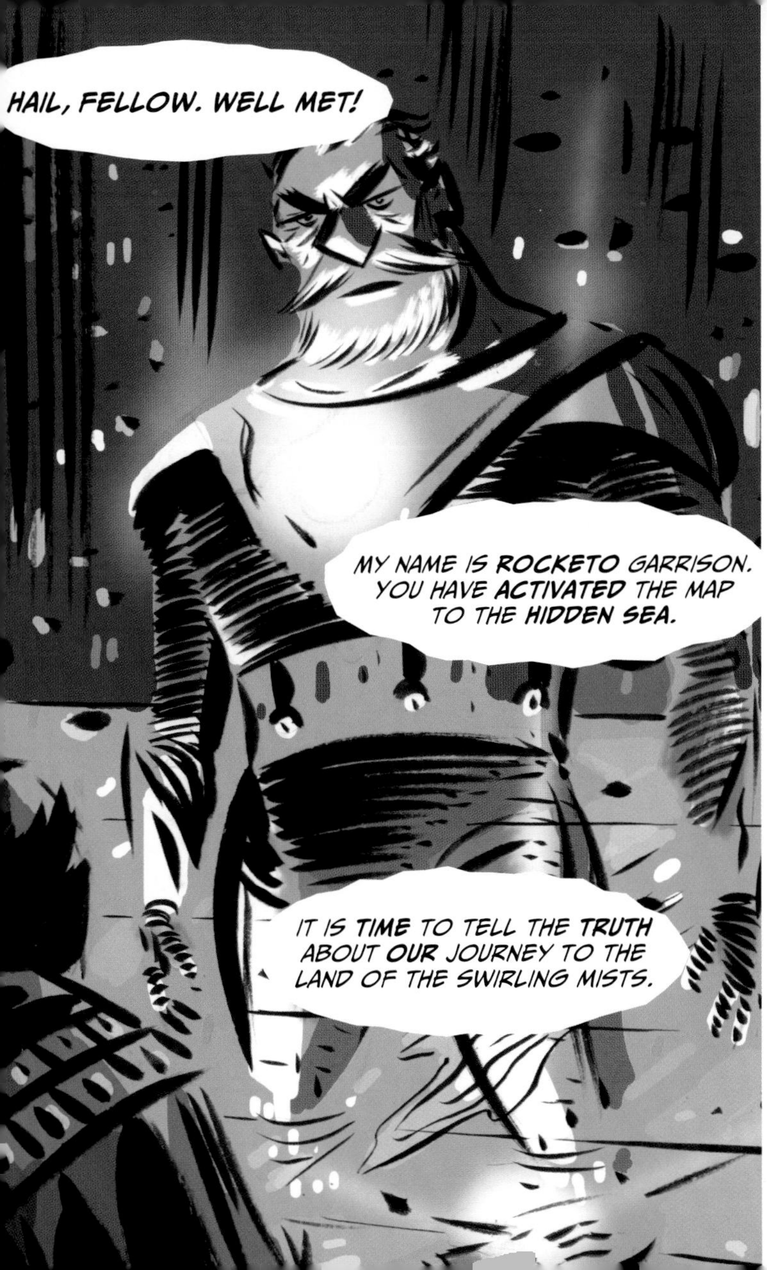
HAIL, FELLOW. WELL MET!
MY NAME IS ROCKETO GARRISON. YOU HAVE ACTIVATED THE MAP TO THE HIDDEN SEA.
IT IS TIME TO TELL THE TRUTH ABOUT OUR JOURNEY TO THE LAND OF THE SWIRLING MISTS.

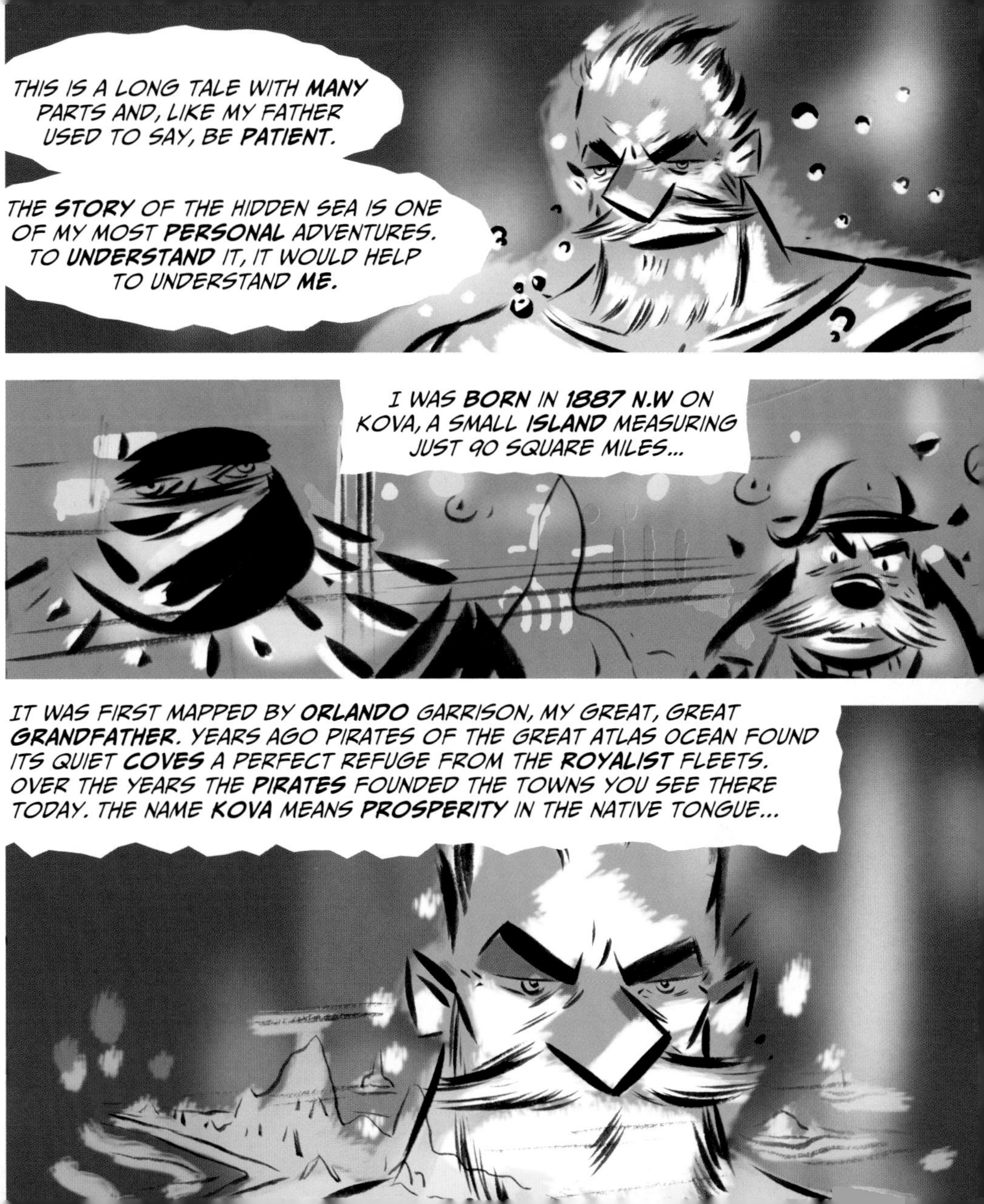
THIS IS A LONG TALE WITH MANY PARTS AND, LIKE MY FATHER USED TO SAY, BE PATIENT.
THE STORY OF THE HIDDEN SEA IS ONE OF MY MOST PERSONAL ADVENTURES. TO UNDERSTAND IT, IT WOULD HELP TO UNDERSTAND ME.
I WAS BORN IN 1887 N.W ON KOVA, A SMALL ISLAND MEASURING JUST 90 SQUARE MILES...
IT WAS FIRST MAPPED BY ORLANDO GARRISON, MY GREAT, GREAT GRANDFATHER. YEARS AGO PIRATES OF THE GREAT ATLAS OCEAN FOUND ITS QUIET COVES A PERFECT REFUGE FROM THE ROYALIST FLEETS. OVER THE YEARS THE PIRATES FOUNDED THE TOWNS YOU SEE THERE TODAY. THE NAME KOVA MEANS PROSPERITY IN THE NATIVE TONGUE...

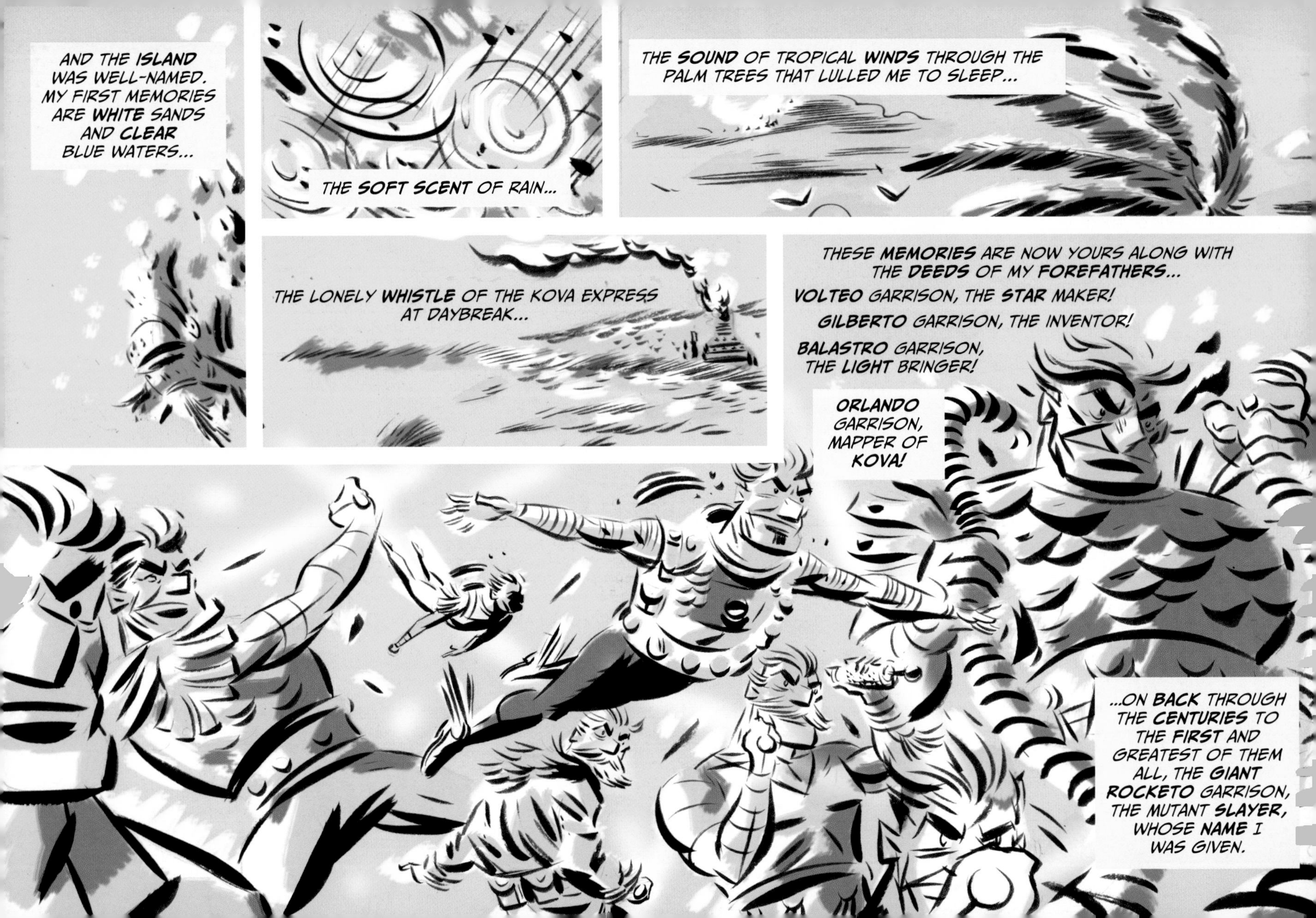
AND THE ISLAND WAS WELL-NAMED. MY FIRST MEMORIES ARE WHITE SANDS AND CLEAR BLUE WATERS...
THE SOFT SCENT OF RAIN...
THE SOUND OF TROPICAL WINDS THROUGH THE PALM TREES THAT LULLED ME TO SLEEP...
THE LONELY WHISTLE OF THE KOVA EXPRESS AT DAYBREAK...
THESE MEMORIES ARE NOW YOURS ALONG WITH THE DEEDS OF MY FOREFATHERS...
VOLTEO GARRISON, THE STAR MAKER!
GILBERTO GARRISON, THE INVENTOR!
BALASTRO GARRISON, THE LIGHT BRINGER!
ORLANDO GARRISON, MAPPER OF KOVA!
...ON BACK THROUGH THE CENTURIES TO THE FIRST AND GREATEST OF THEM ALL, THE GIANT ROCKETO GARRISON, THE MUTANT SLAYER, WHOSE NAME I WAS GIVEN.

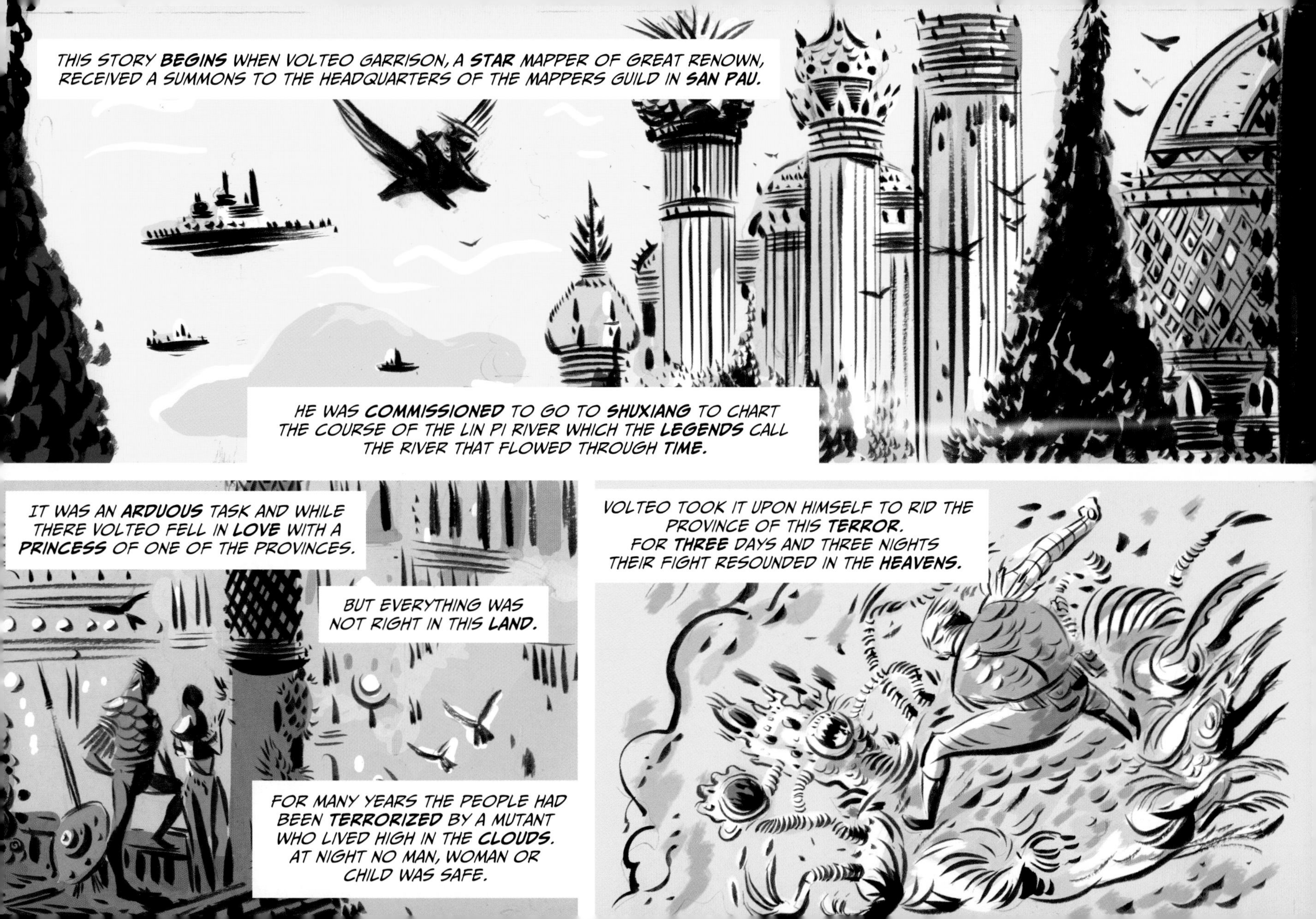
THIS STORY BEGINS WHEN VOLTEO GARRISON, A STAR MAPPER OF GREAT RENOWN, RECEIVED A SUMMONS TO THE HEADQUARTERS OF THE MAPPERS GUILD IN SAN PAU.
HE WAS COMMISSIONED TO GO TO SHUXIANG TO CHART THE COURSE OF THE LIN PI RIVER WHICH THE LEGENDS CALL THE RIVER THAT FLOWED THROUGH TIME.
IT WAS AN ARDUOUS TASK AND WHILE THERE VOLTEO FELL IN LOVE WITH A PRINCESS OF ONE OF THE PROVINCES.
BUT EVERYTHING WAS NOT RIGHT IN THIS LAND.
FOR MANY YEARS THE PEOPLE HAD BEEN TERRORIZED BY A MUTANT WHO LIVED HIGH IN THE CLOUDS. AT NIGHT NO MAN, WOMAN OR CHILD WAS SAFE.
VOLTEO TOOK IT UPON HIMSELF TO RID THE PROVINCE OF THIS TERROR. FOR THREE DAYS AND THREE NIGHTS THEIR FIGHT RESOUNDED IN THE HEAVENS.

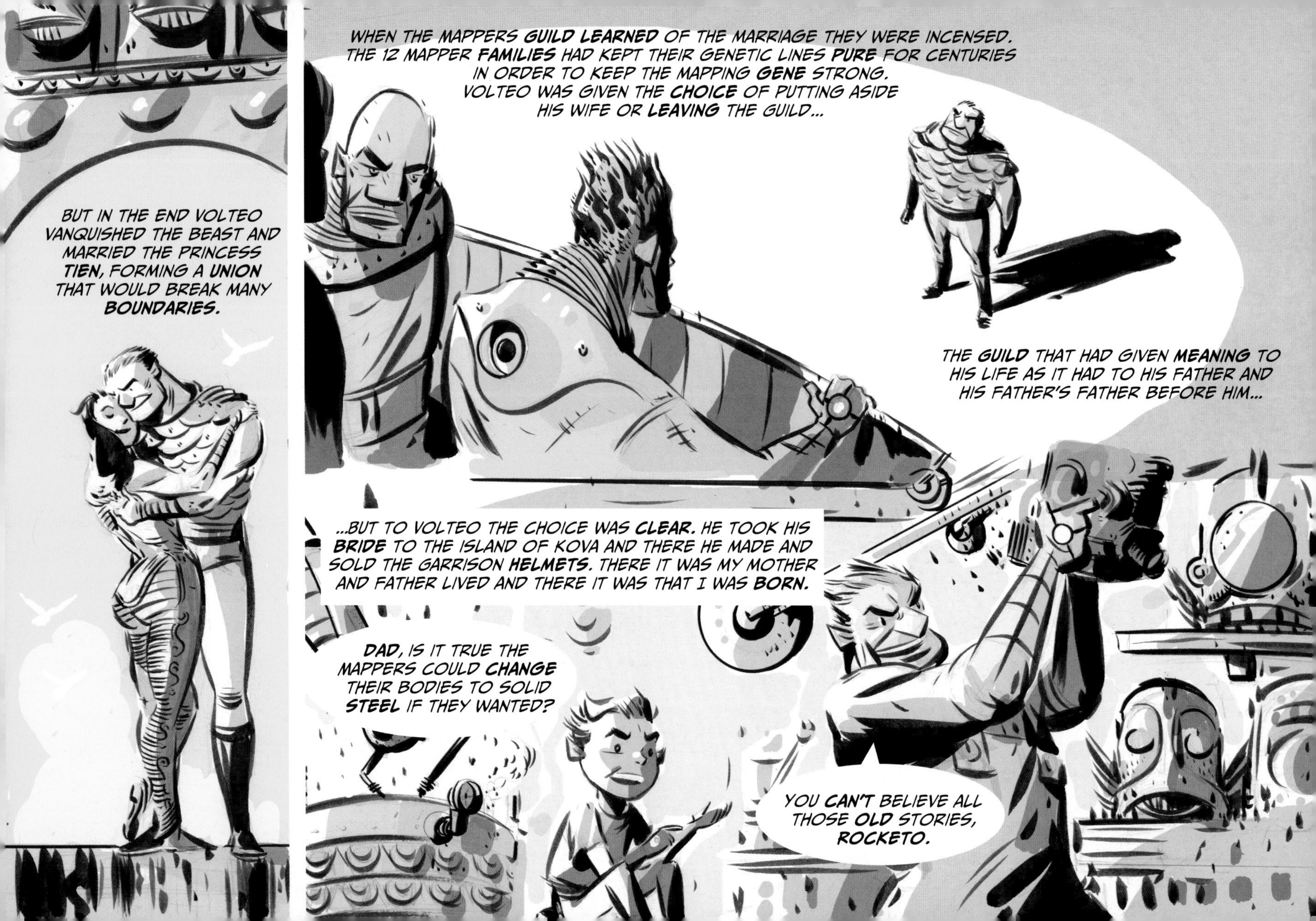
BUT IN THE END VOLTEO VANQUISHED THE BEAST AND MARRIED THE PRINCESS TIEN, FORMING A UNION THAT WOULD BREAK MANY BOUNDARIES.
WHEN THE MAPPERS GUILD LEARNED OF THE MARRIAGE THEY WERE INCENSED. THE 12 MAPPER FAMILIES HAD KEPT THEIR GENETIC LINES PURE FOR CENTURIES IN ORDER TO KEEP THE MAPPING GENE STRONG. VOLTEO WAS GIVEN THE CHOICE OF PUTTING ASIDE HIS WIFE OR LEAVING THE GUILD...
THE GUILD THAT HAD GIVEN MEANING TO HIS LIFE AS IT HAD TO HIS FATHER AND HIS FATHER'S FATHER BEFORE HIM...
...BUT TO VOLTEO THE CHOICE WAS CLEAR. HE TOOK HIS BRIDE TO THE ISLAND OF KOVA AND THERE HE MADE AND SOLD THE GARRISON HELMETS. THERE IT WAS MY MOTHER AND FATHER LIVED AND THERE IT WAS THAT I WAS BORN.
DAD, IS IT TRUE THE MAPPERS COULD CHANGE THEIR BODIES TO SOLID STEEL IF THEY WANTED?
YOU CAN'T BELIEVE ALL THOSE OLD STORIES, ROCKETO.

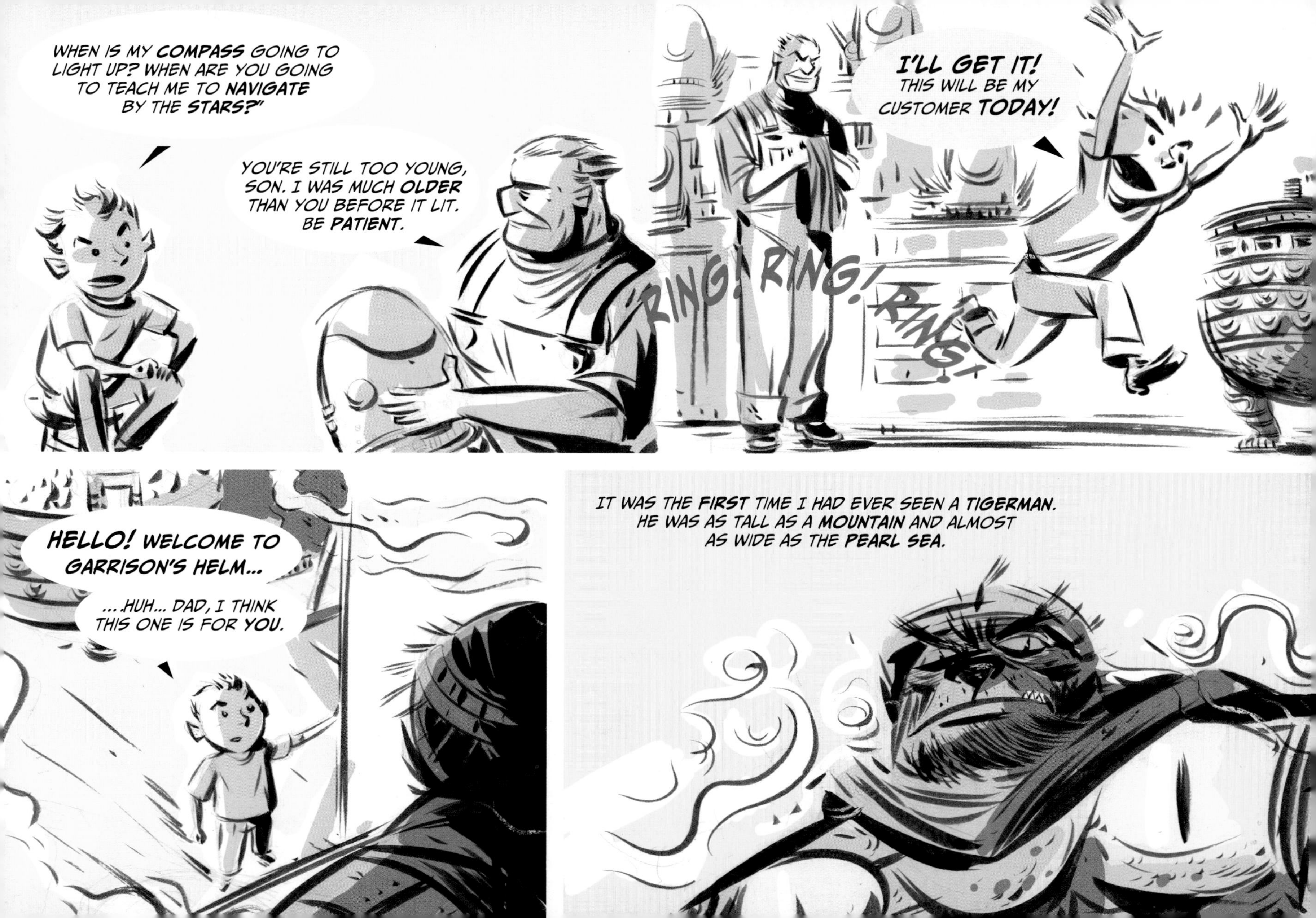
WHEN IS MY COMPASS GOING TO LIGHT UP? WHEN ARE YOU GOING TO TEACH ME TO NAVIGATE BY THE STARS?"
YOU'RE STILL TOO YOUNG, SON. I WAS MUCH OLDER THAN YOU BEFORE IT LIT. BE PATIENT.
RING! RING! RING!
I'LL GET IT! THIS WILL BE MY CUSTOMER TODAY!
HELLO! WELCOME TO GARRISON'S HELM...
...HUH... DAD, I THINK THIS ONE IS FOR YOU.
IT WAS THE FIRST TIME I HAD EVER SEEN A TIGERMAN. HE WAS AS TALL AS A MOUNTAIN AND ALMOST AS WIDE AS THE PEARL SEA.

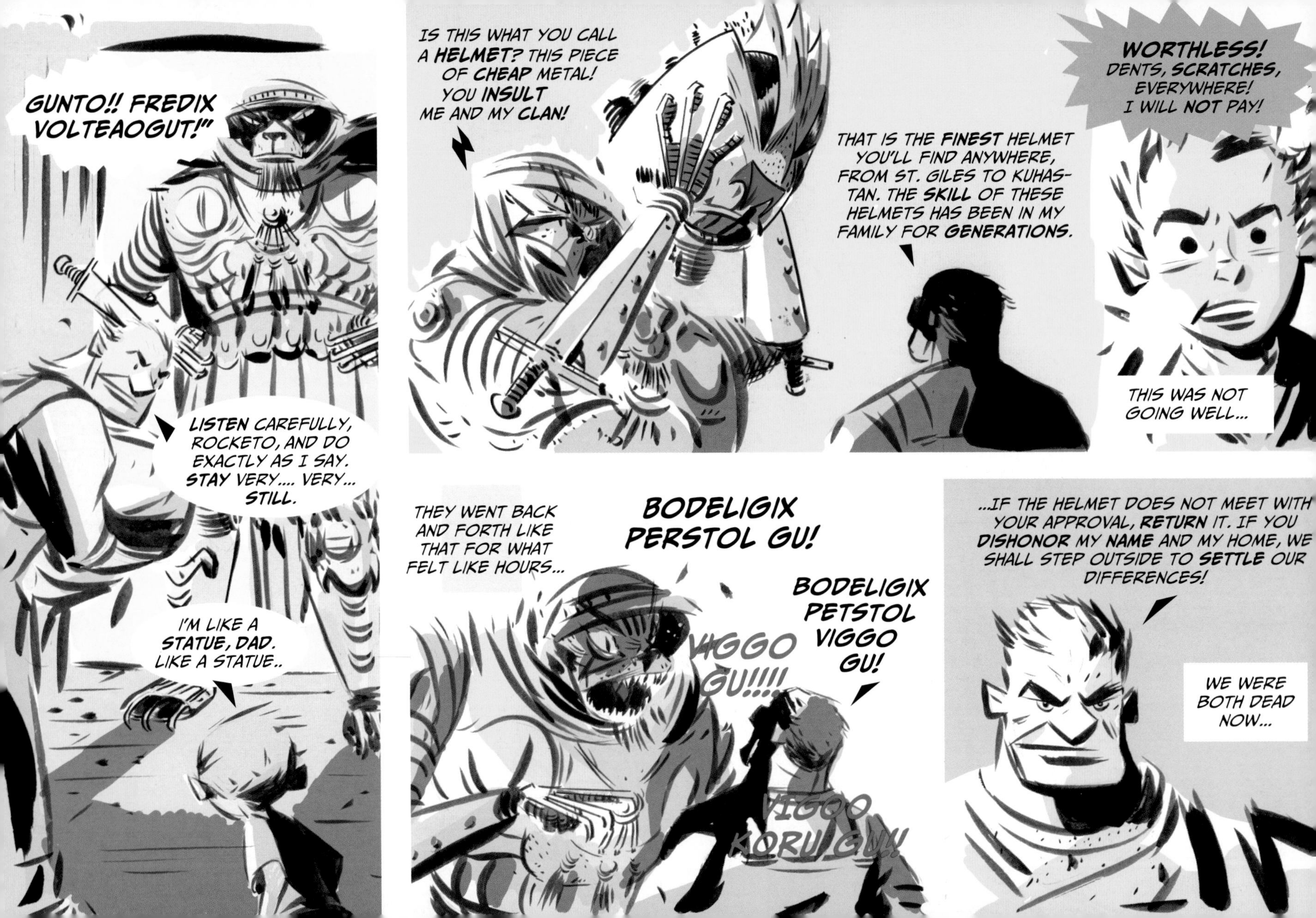

GUNTO!! FREDIX VOLTEAOGUT!"
LISTEN CAREFULLY, ROCKETO, AND DO EXACTLY AS I SAY. STAY VERY.... VERY... STILL.
I'M LIKE A STATUE, DAD. LIKE A STATUE..
IS THIS WHAT YOU CALL A HELMET? THIS PIECE OF CHEAP METAL! YOU INSULT ME AND MY CLAN!
THAT IS THE FINEST HELMET YOU'LL FIND ANYWHERE, FROM ST. GILES TO KUHAS-TAN. THE SKILL OF THESE HELMETS HAS BEEN IN MY FAMILY FOR GENERATIONS.
WORTHLESS! DENTS, SCRATCHES, EVERYWHERE! I WILL NOT PAY!
THIS WAS NOT GOING WELL...
THEY WENT BACK AND FORTH LIKE THAT FOR WHAT FELT LIKE HOURS...
BODELIGIX PERSTOL GU!
VIGGO GU!!!!
BODELIGIX PETSTOL VIGGO GU!
VIGGO KORU GU!!
...IF THE HELMET DOES NOT MEET WITH YOUR APPROVAL, RETURN IT. IF YOU DISHONOR MY NAME AND MY HOME, WE SHALL STEP OUTSIDE TO SETTLE OUR DIFFERENCES!
WE WERE BOTH DEAD NOW...

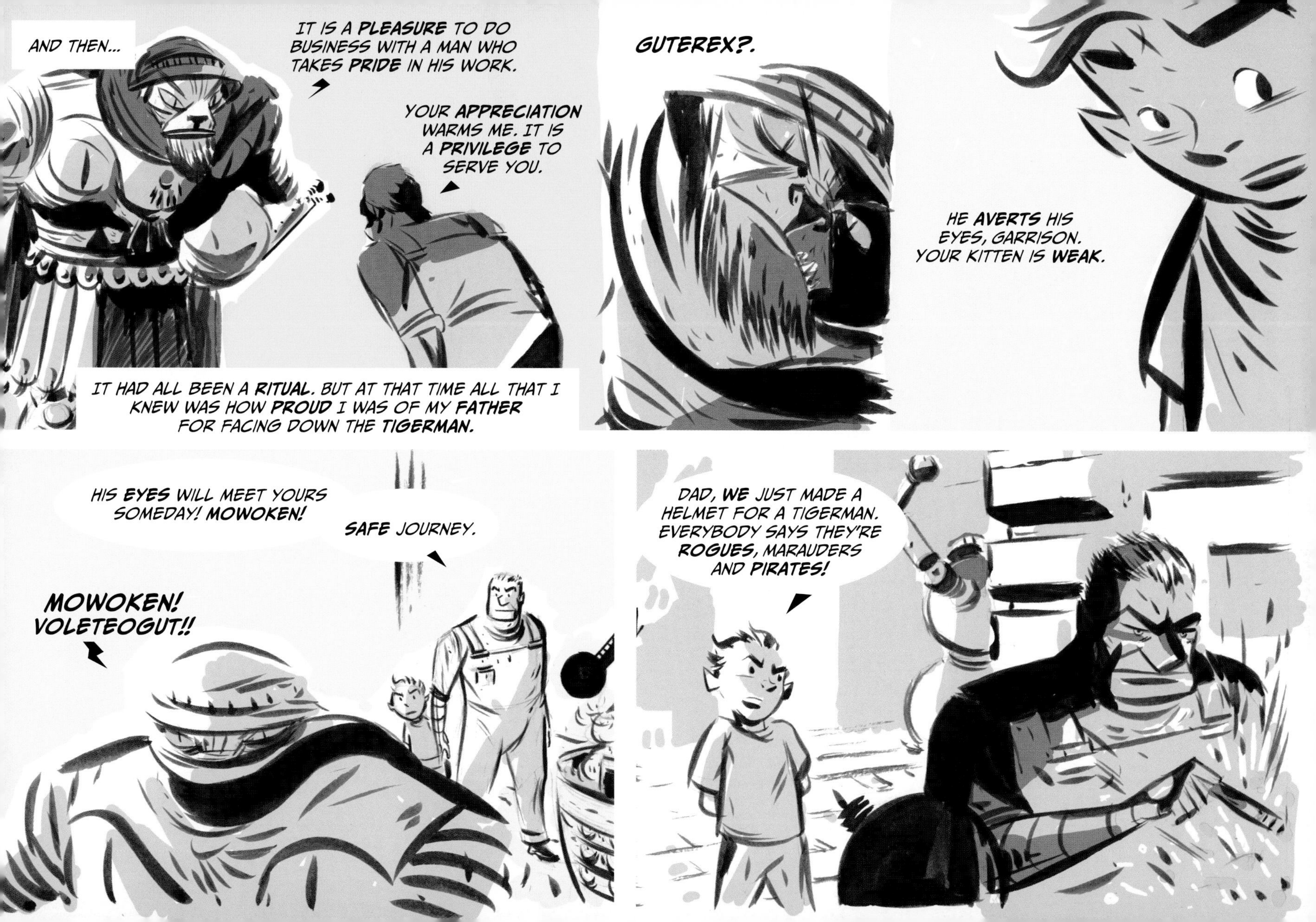
AND THEN...
IT IS A PLEASURE TO DO BUSINESS WITH A MAN WHO TAKES PRIDE IN HIS WORK.
YOUR APPRECIATION WARMS ME. IT IS A PRIVILEGE TO SERVE YOU.
IT HAD ALL BEEN A RITUAL. BUT AT THAT TIME ALL THAT I KNEW WAS HOW PROUD I WAS OF MY FATHER FOR FACING DOWN THE TIGERMAN.
GUTEREX?.
HE AVERTS HIS EYES, GARRISON. YOUR KITTEN IS WEAK.
HIS EYES WILL MEET YOURS SOMEDAY! MOWOKEN!
SAFE JOURNEY.
MOWOKEN! VOLETEOGUT!!
DAD, WE JUST MADE A HELMET FOR A TIGERMAN. EVERYBODY SAYS THEY'RE ROGUES, MARAUDERS AND PIRATES!

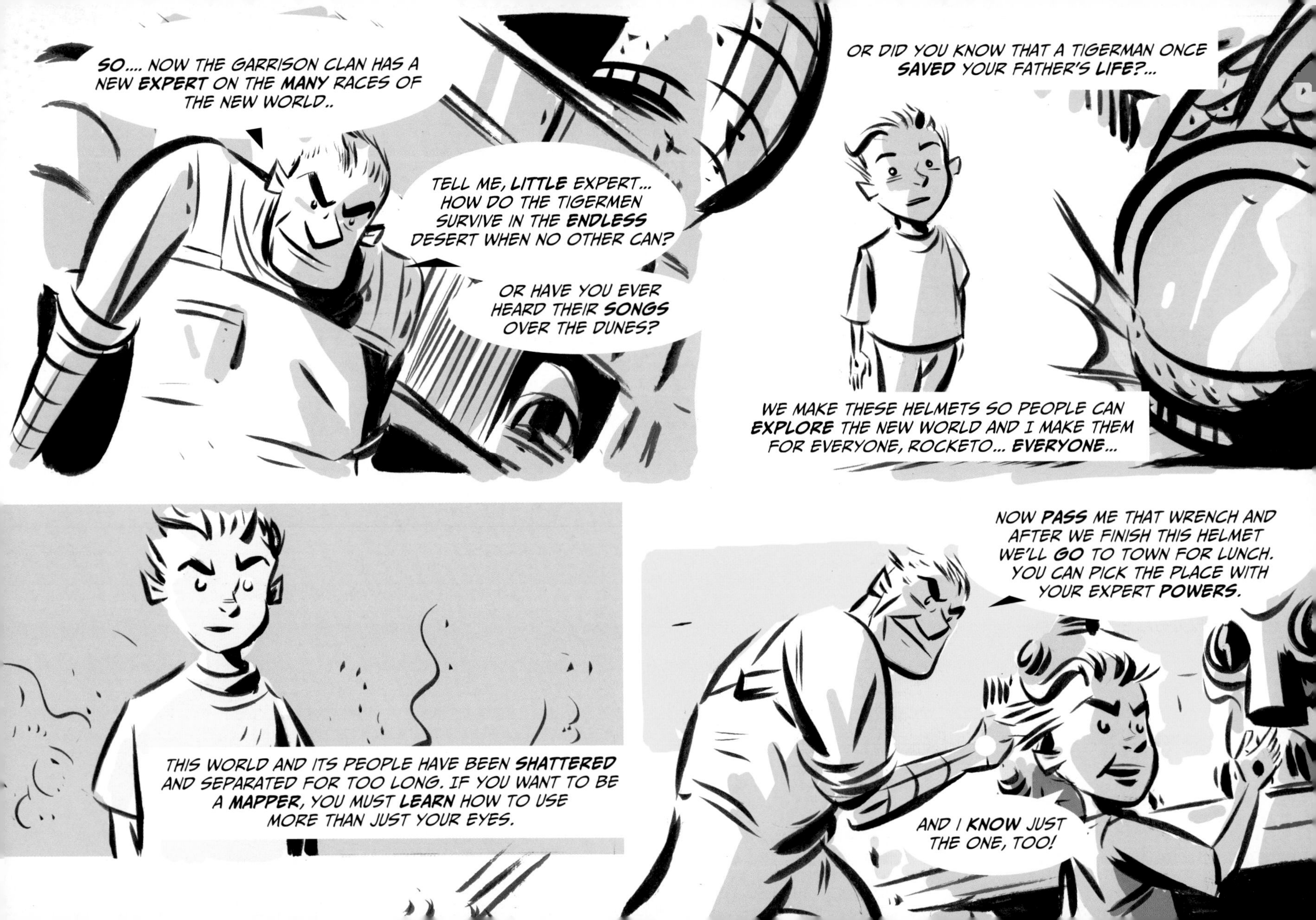
SO.... NOW THE GARRISON CLAN HAS A NEW EXPERT ON THE MANY RACES OF THE NEW WORLD..
TELL ME, LITTLE EXPERT... HOW DO THE TIGERMEN SURVIVE IN THE ENDLESS DESERT WHEN NO OTHER CAN?
OR HAVE YOU EVER HEARD THEIR SONGS OVER THE DUNES?
OR DID YOU KNOW THAT A TIGERMAN ONCE SAVED YOUR FATHER'S LIFE?...
WE MAKE THESE HELMETS SO PEOPLE CAN EXPLORE THE NEW WORLD AND I MAKE THEM FOR EVERYONE, ROCKETO... EVERYONE...
THIS WORLD AND ITS PEOPLE HAVE BEEN SHATTERED AND SEPARATED FOR TOO LONG. IF YOU WANT TO BE A MAPPER, YOU MUST LEARN HOW TO USE MORE THAN JUST YOUR EYES.
NOW PASS ME THAT WRENCH AND AFTER WE FINISH THIS HELMET WE'LL GO TO TOWN FOR LUNCH. YOU CAN PICK THE PLACE WITH YOUR EXPERT POWERS.
AND I KNOW JUST THE ONE, TOO!

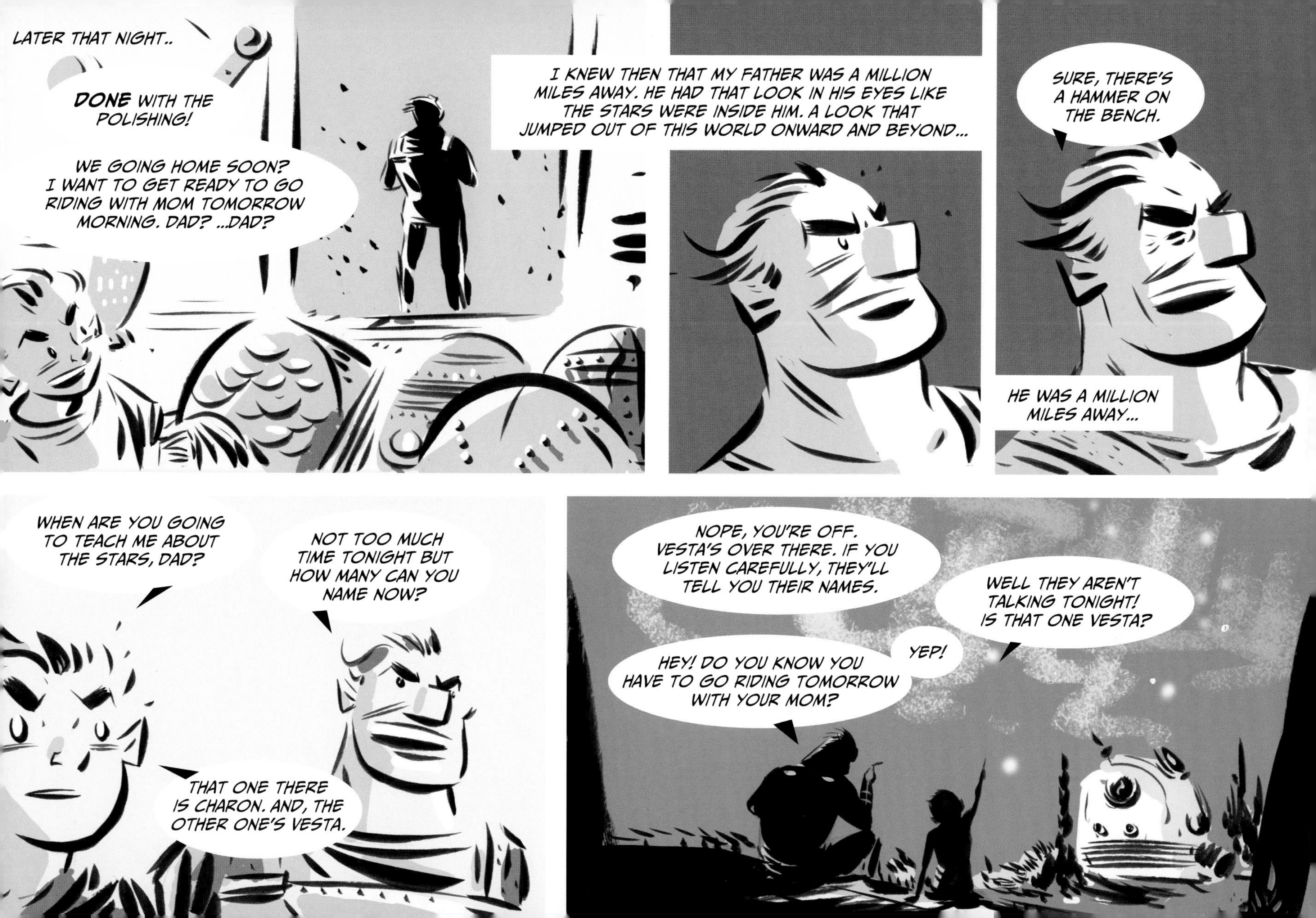
LATER THAT NIGHT..
**DONE** WITH THE POLISHING!
WE GOING HOME SOON? I WANT TO GET READY TO GO RIDING WITH MOM TOMORROW MORNING. DAD? ...DAD?
I KNEW THEN THAT MY FATHER WAS A MILLION MILES AWAY. HE HAD THAT LOOK IN HIS EYES LIKE THE STARS WERE INSIDE HIM. A LOOK THAT JUMPED OUT OF THIS WORLD ONWARD AND BEYOND...
SURE, THERE'S A HAMMER ON THE BENCH.
HE WAS A MILLION MILES AWAY...
WHEN ARE YOU GOING TO TEACH ME ABOUT THE STARS, DAD?
NOT TOO MUCH TIME TONIGHT BUT HOW MANY CAN YOU NAME NOW?
THAT ONE THERE IS CHARON. AND, THE OTHER ONE'S VESTA.
NOPE, YOU'RE OFF. VESTA'S OVER THERE. IF YOU LISTEN CAREFULLY, THEY'LL TELL YOU THEIR NAMES.
WELL THEY AREN'T TALKING TONIGHT! IS THAT ONE VESTA?
YEP!
HEY! DO YOU KNOW YOU HAVE TO GO RIDING TOMORROW WITH YOUR MOM?

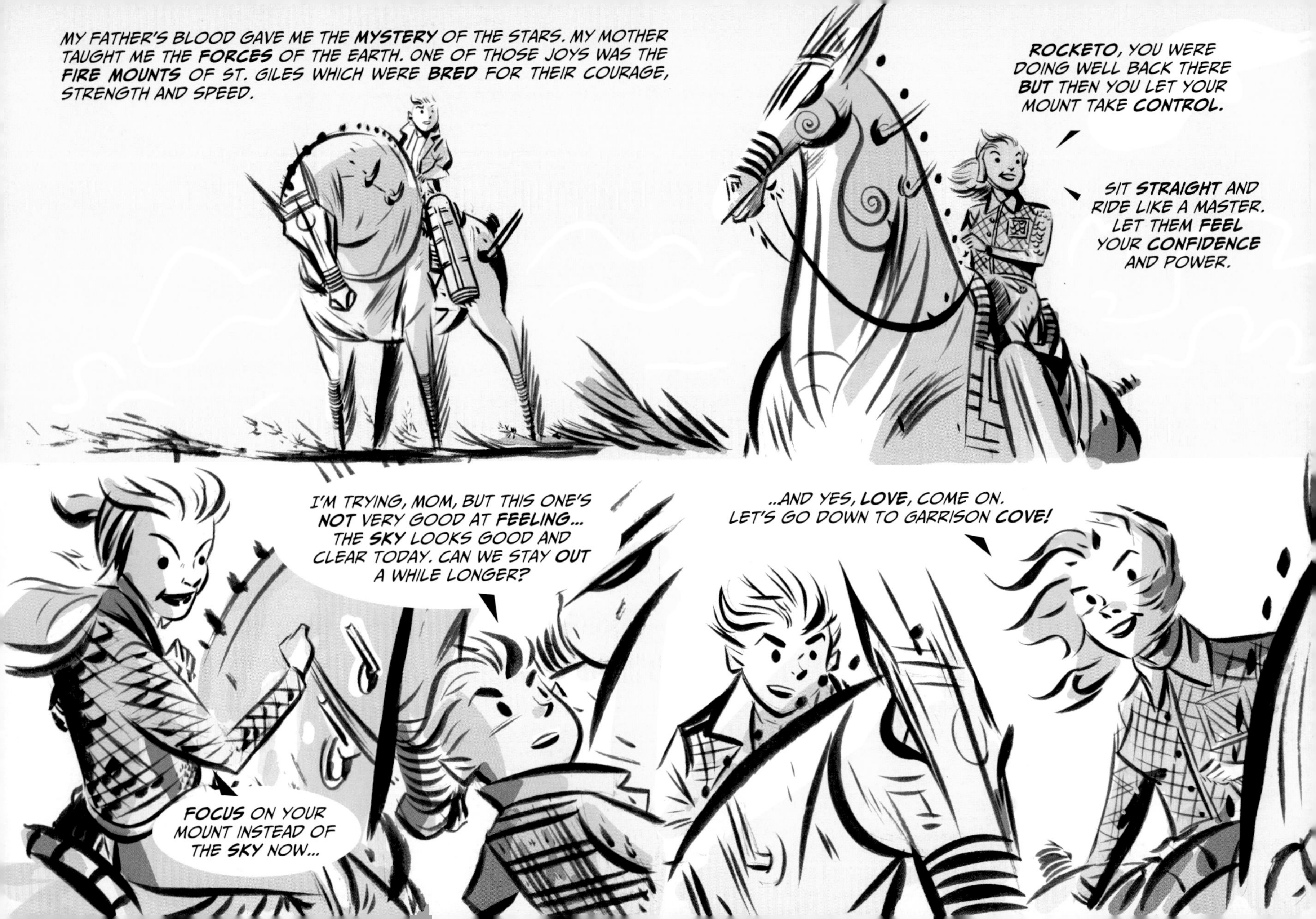

MY FATHER'S BLOOD GAVE ME THE MYSTERY OF THE STARS. MY MOTHER TAUGHT ME THE FORCES OF THE EARTH. ONE OF THOSE JOYS WAS THE FIRE MOUNTS OF ST. GILES WHICH WERE BRED FOR THEIR COURAGE, STRENGTH AND SPEED.
ROCKETO, YOU WERE DOING WELL BACK THERE BUT THEN YOU LET YOUR MOUNT TAKE CONTROL.
SIT STRAIGHT AND RIDE LIKE A MASTER. LET THEM FEEL YOUR CONFIDENCE AND POWER.
FOCUS ON YOUR MOUNT INSTEAD OF THE SKY NOW...
I'M TRYING, MOM, BUT THIS ONE'S NOT VERY GOOD AT FEELING... THE SKY LOOKS GOOD AND CLEAR TODAY. CAN WE STAY OUT A WHILE LONGER?
...AND YES, LOVE, COME ON. LET'S GO DOWN TO GARRISON COVE!

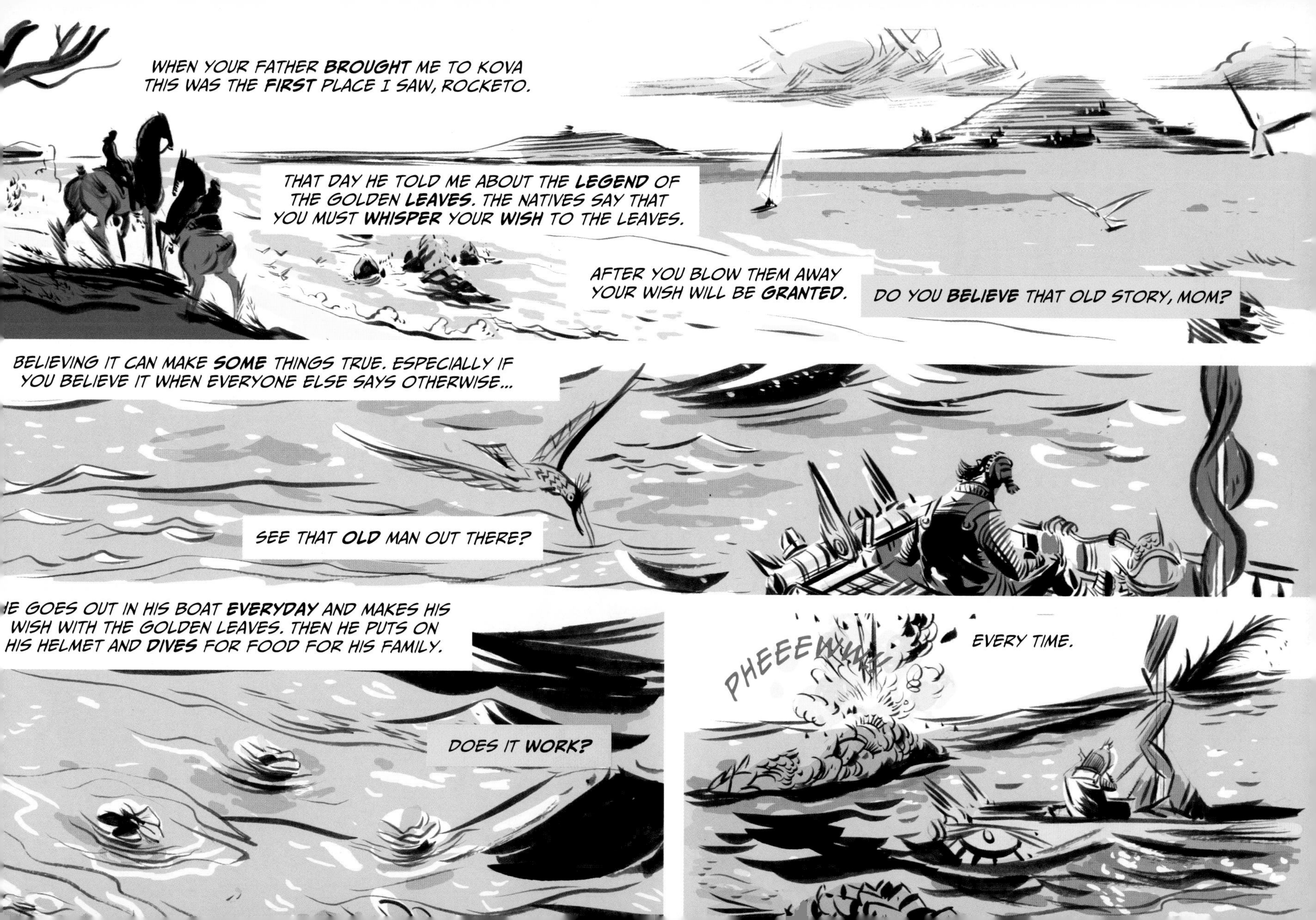
WHEN YOUR FATHER BROUGHT ME TO KOVA THIS WAS THE FIRST PLACE I SAW, ROCKETO.
THAT DAY HE TOLD ME ABOUT THE LEGEND OF THE GOLDEN LEAVES. THE NATIVES SAY THAT YOU MUST WHISPER YOUR WISH TO THE LEAVES.
AFTER YOU BLOW THEM AWAY YOUR WISH WILL BE GRANTED.
DO YOU BELIEVE THAT OLD STORY, MOM?
BELIEVING IT CAN MAKE SOME THINGS TRUE. ESPECIALLY IF YOU BELIEVE IT WHEN EVERYONE ELSE SAYS OTHERWISE...
SEE THAT OLD MAN OUT THERE?
HE GOES OUT IN HIS BOAT EVERYDAY AND MAKES HIS WISH WITH THE GOLDEN LEAVES. THEN HE PUTS ON HIS HELMET AND DIVES FOR FOOD FOR HIS FAMILY.
DOES IT WORK?
PHEEEWW
EVERY TIME.

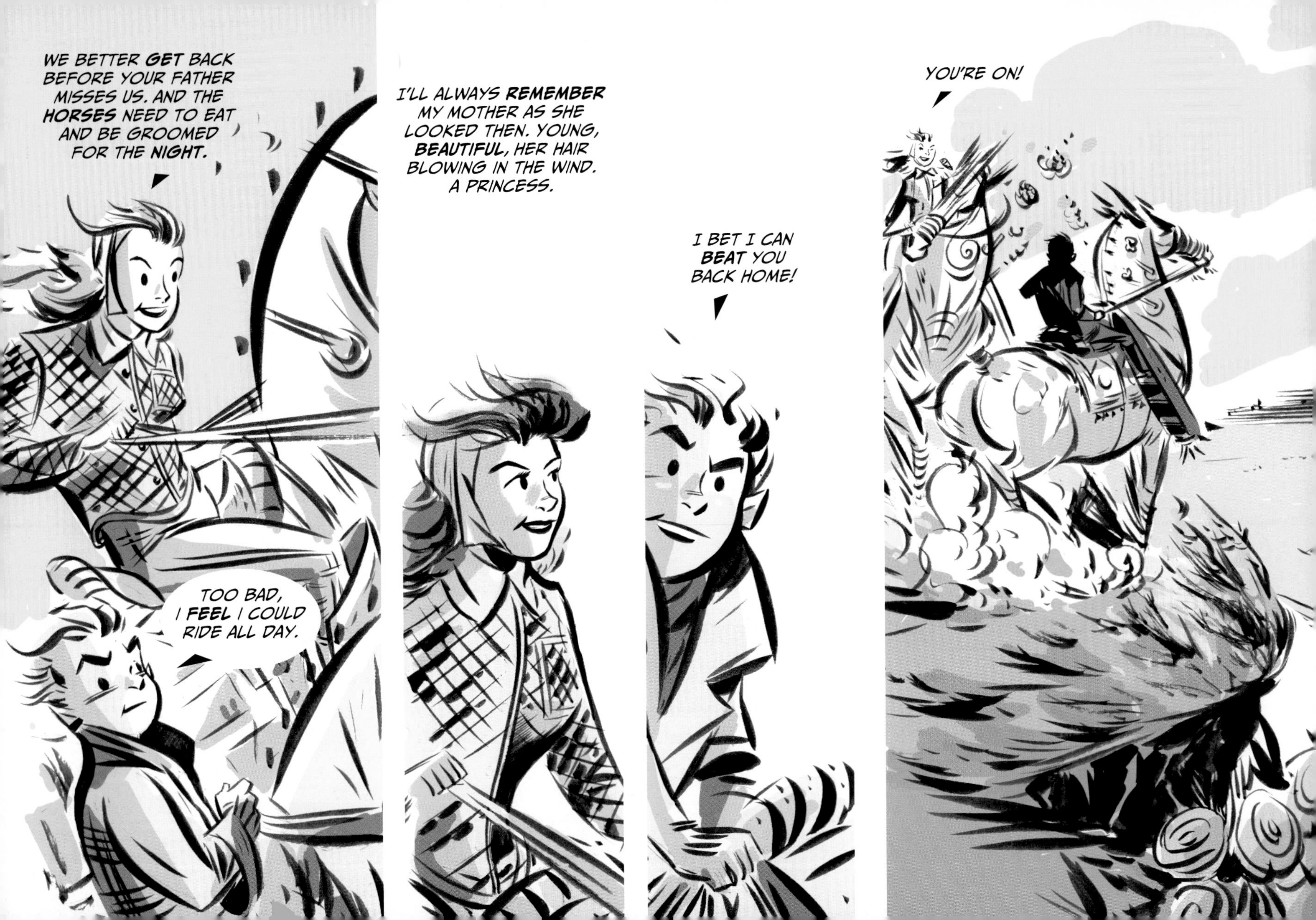
WE BETTER **GET** BACK BEFORE YOUR FATHER MISSES US. AND THE **HORSES** NEED TO EAT AND BE GROOMED FOR THE **NIGHT.**
TOO BAD, I **FEEL** I COULD RIDE ALL DAY.
I'LL ALWAYS **REMEMBER** MY MOTHER AS SHE LOOKED THEN. YOUNG, **BEAUTIFUL,** HER HAIR BLOWING IN THE WIND. A PRINCESS.
I BET I CAN **BEAT** YOU BACK HOME!
YOU'RE ON!

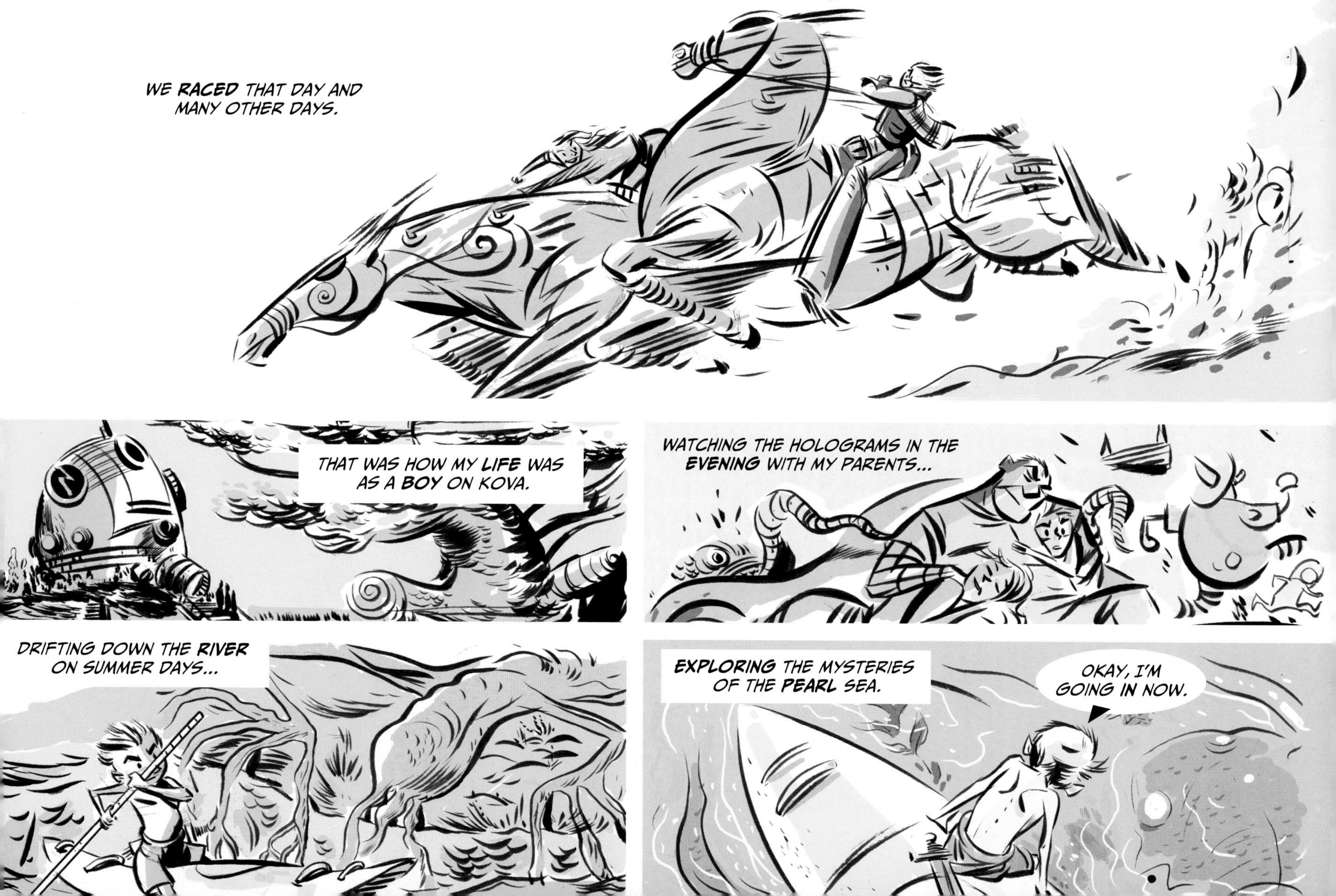
WE RACED THAT DAY AND MANY OTHER DAYS.
THAT WAS HOW MY LIFE WAS AS A BOY ON KOVA.
WATCHING THE HOLOGRAMS IN THE EVENING WITH MY PARENTS...
DRIFTING DOWN THE RIVER ON SUMMER DAYS...
EXPLORING THE MYSTERIES OF THE PEARL SEA.
OKAY, I'M GOING IN NOW.

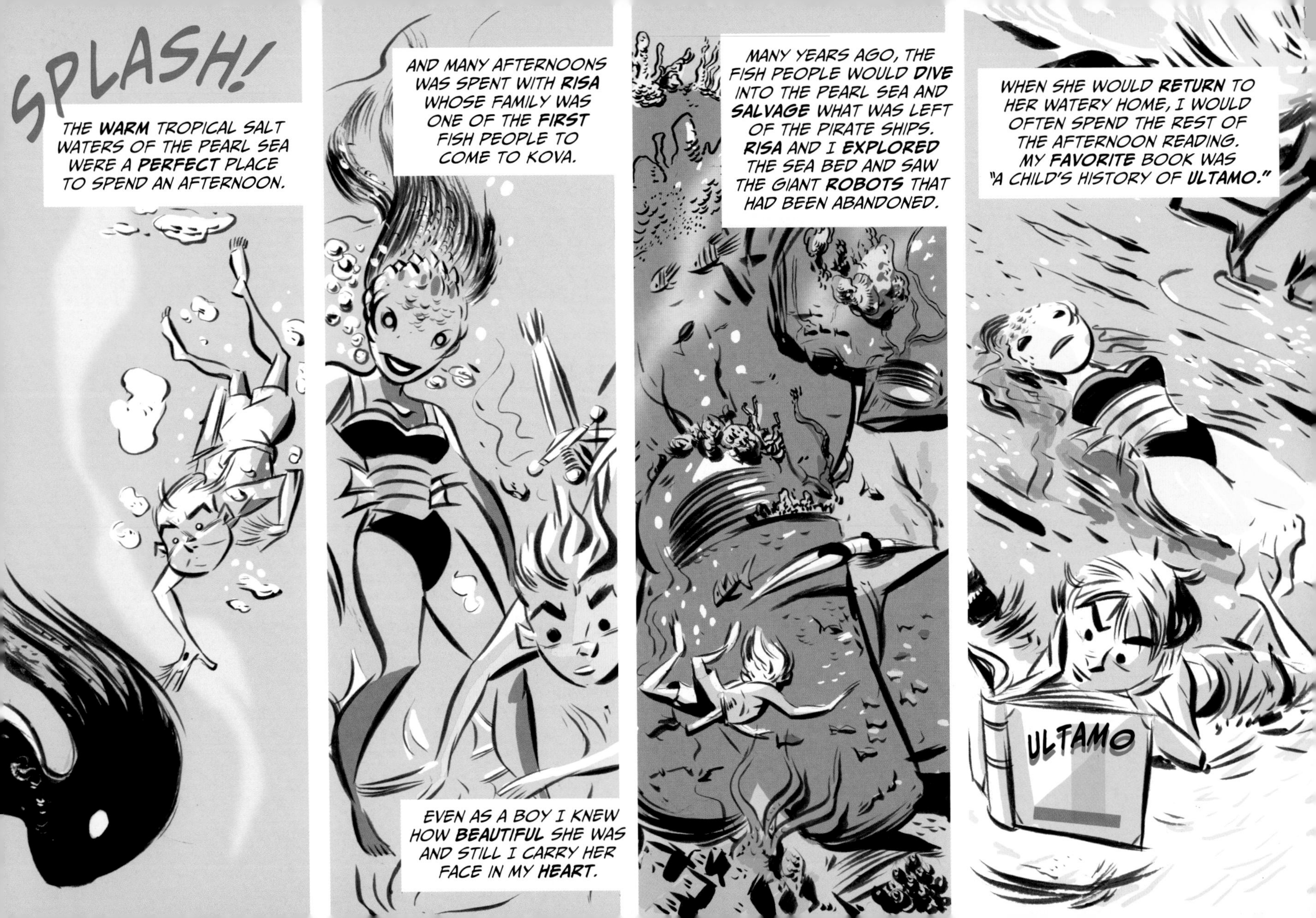
SPLASH!
THE WARM TROPICAL SALT WATERS OF THE PEARL SEA WERE A PERFECT PLACE TO SPEND AN AFTERNOON.
AND MANY AFTERNOONS WAS SPENT WITH RISA WHOSE FAMILY WAS ONE OF THE FIRST FISH PEOPLE TO COME TO KOVA.
EVEN AS A BOY I KNEW HOW BEAUTIFUL SHE WAS AND STILL I CARRY HER FACE IN MY HEART.
MANY YEARS AGO, THE FISH PEOPLE WOULD DIVE INTO THE PEARL SEA AND SALVAGE WHAT WAS LEFT OF THE PIRATE SHIPS. RISA AND I EXPLORED THE SEA BED AND SAW THE GIANT ROBOTS THAT HAD BEEN ABANDONED.
WHEN SHE WOULD RETURN TO HER WATERY HOME, I WOULD OFTEN SPEND THE REST OF THE AFTERNOON READING. MY FAVORITE BOOK WAS "A CHILD'S HISTORY OF ULTAMO."
ULTAMO

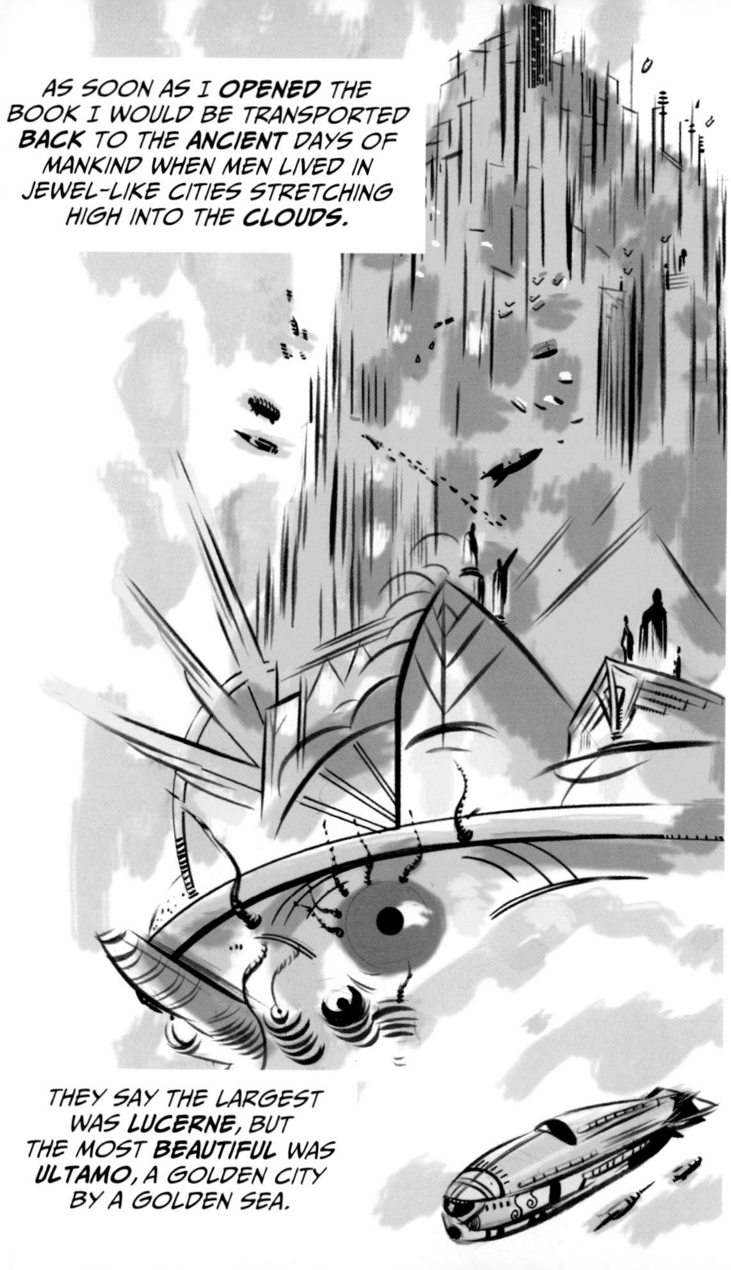
AS SOON AS I OPENED THE BOOK I WOULD BE TRANSPORTED BACK TO THE ANCIENT DAYS OF MANKIND WHEN MEN LIVED IN JEWEL-LIKE CITIES STRETCHING HIGH INTO THE CLOUDS.
THEY SAY THE LARGEST WAS LUCERNE, BUT THE MOST BEAUTIFUL WAS ULTAMO, A GOLDEN CITY BY A GOLDEN SEA.

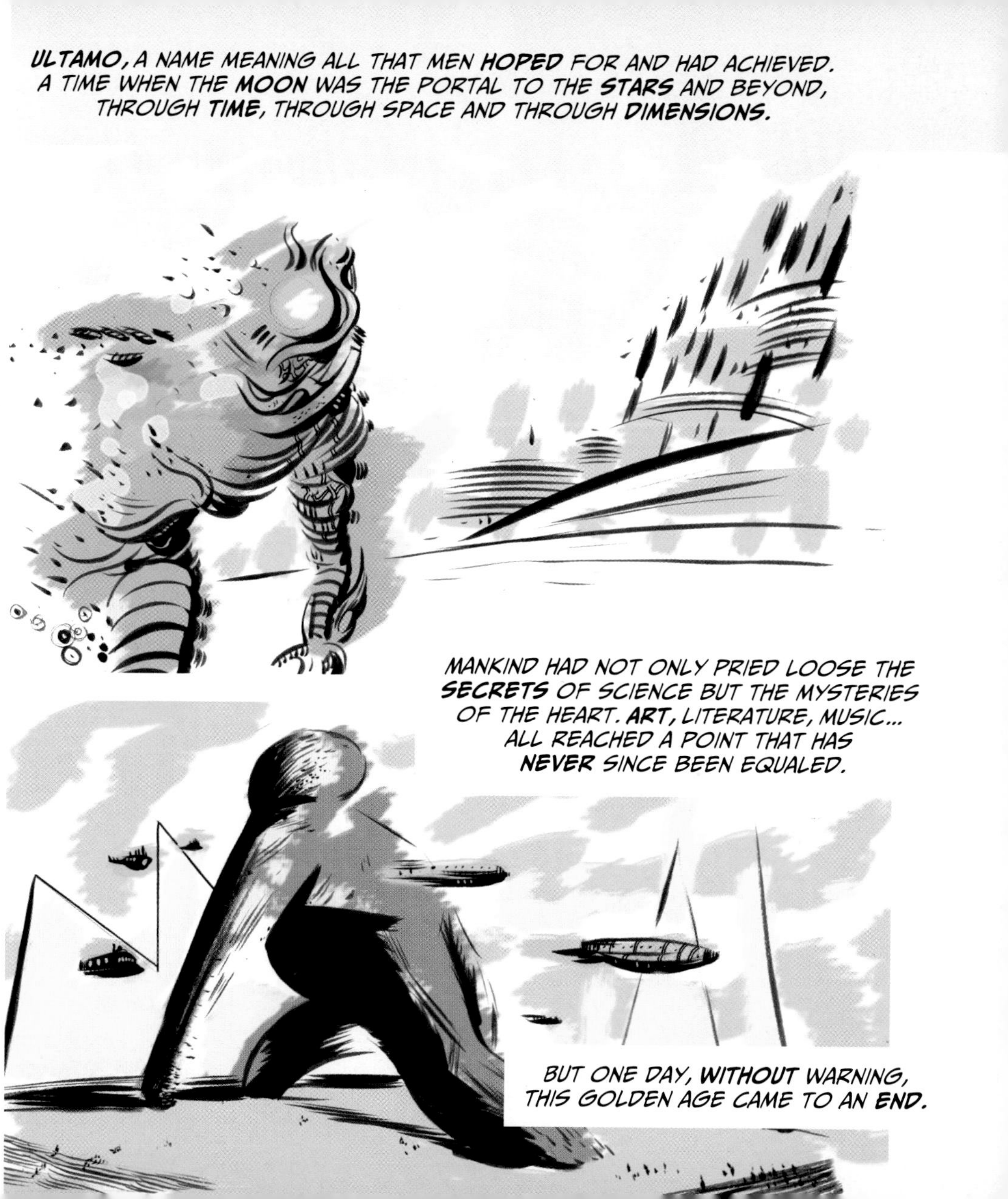
ULTAMO, A NAME MEANING ALL THAT MEN HOPED FOR AND HAD ACHIEVED. A TIME WHEN THE MOON WAS THE PORTAL TO THE STARS AND BEYOND, THROUGH TIME, THROUGH SPACE AND THROUGH DIMENSIONS.
MANKIND HAD NOT ONLY PRIED LOOSE THE SECRETS OF SCIENCE BUT THE MYSTERIES OF THE HEART. ART, LITERATURE, MUSIC... ALL REACHED A POINT THAT HAS NEVER SINCE BEEN EQUALED.
BUT ONE DAY, WITHOUT WARNING, THIS GOLDEN AGE CAME TO AN END.

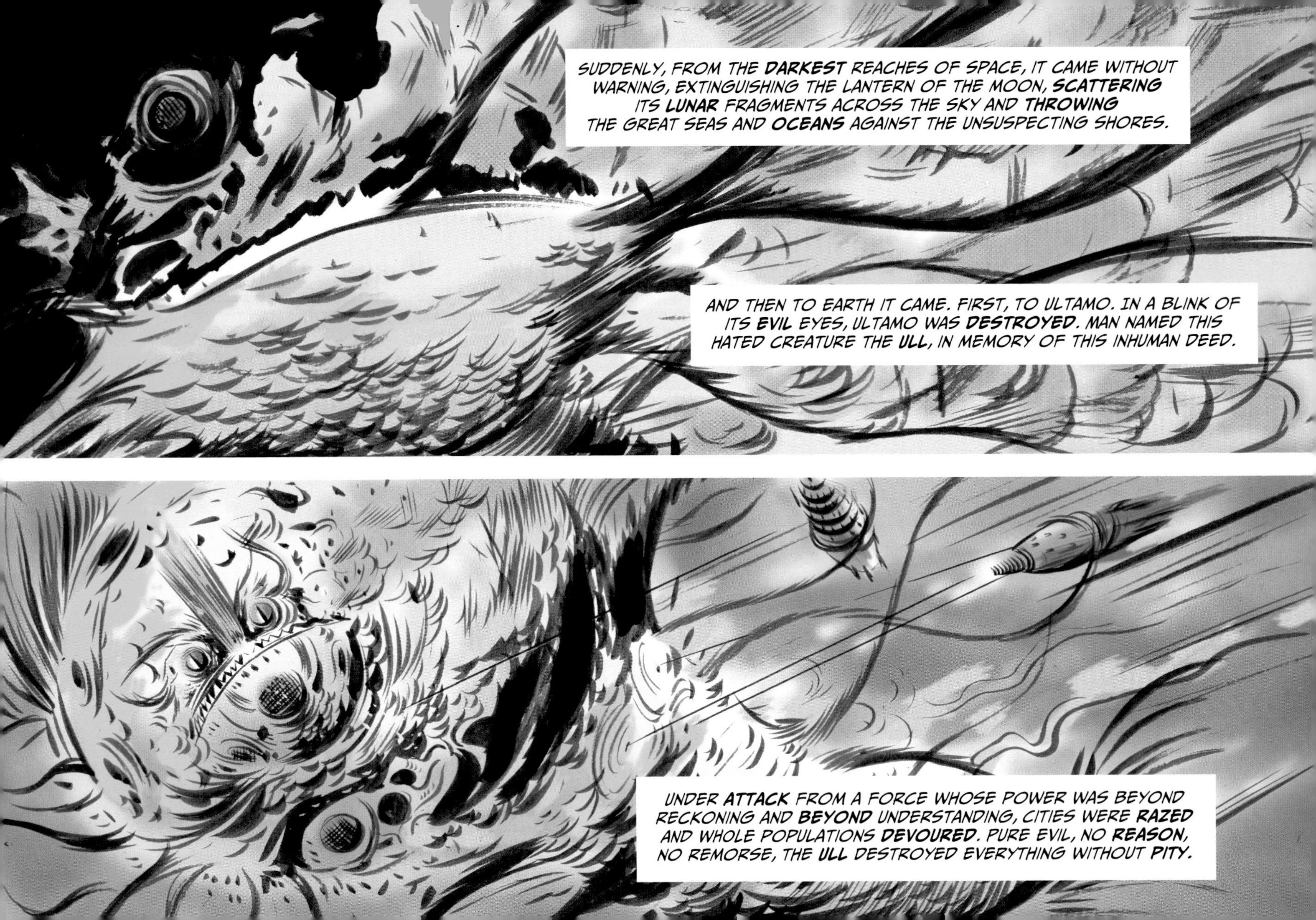
SUDDENLY, FROM THE DARKEST REACHES OF SPACE, IT CAME WITHOUT WARNING, EXTINGUISHING THE LANTERN OF THE MOON, SCATTERING ITS LUNAR FRAGMENTS ACROSS THE SKY AND THROWING THE GREAT SEAS AND OCEANS AGAINST THE UNSUSPECTING SHORES.
AND THEN TO EARTH IT CAME. FIRST, TO ULTAMO. IN A BLINK OF ITS EVIL EYES, ULTAMO WAS DESTROYED. MAN NAMED THIS HATED CREATURE THE ULL, IN MEMORY OF THIS INHUMAN DEED.
UNDER ATTACK FROM A FORCE WHOSE POWER WAS BEYOND RECKONING AND BEYOND UNDERSTANDING, CITIES WERE RAZED AND WHOLE POPULATIONS DEVOURED. PURE EVIL, NO REASON, NO REMORSE, THE ULL DESTROYED EVERYTHING WITHOUT PITY.

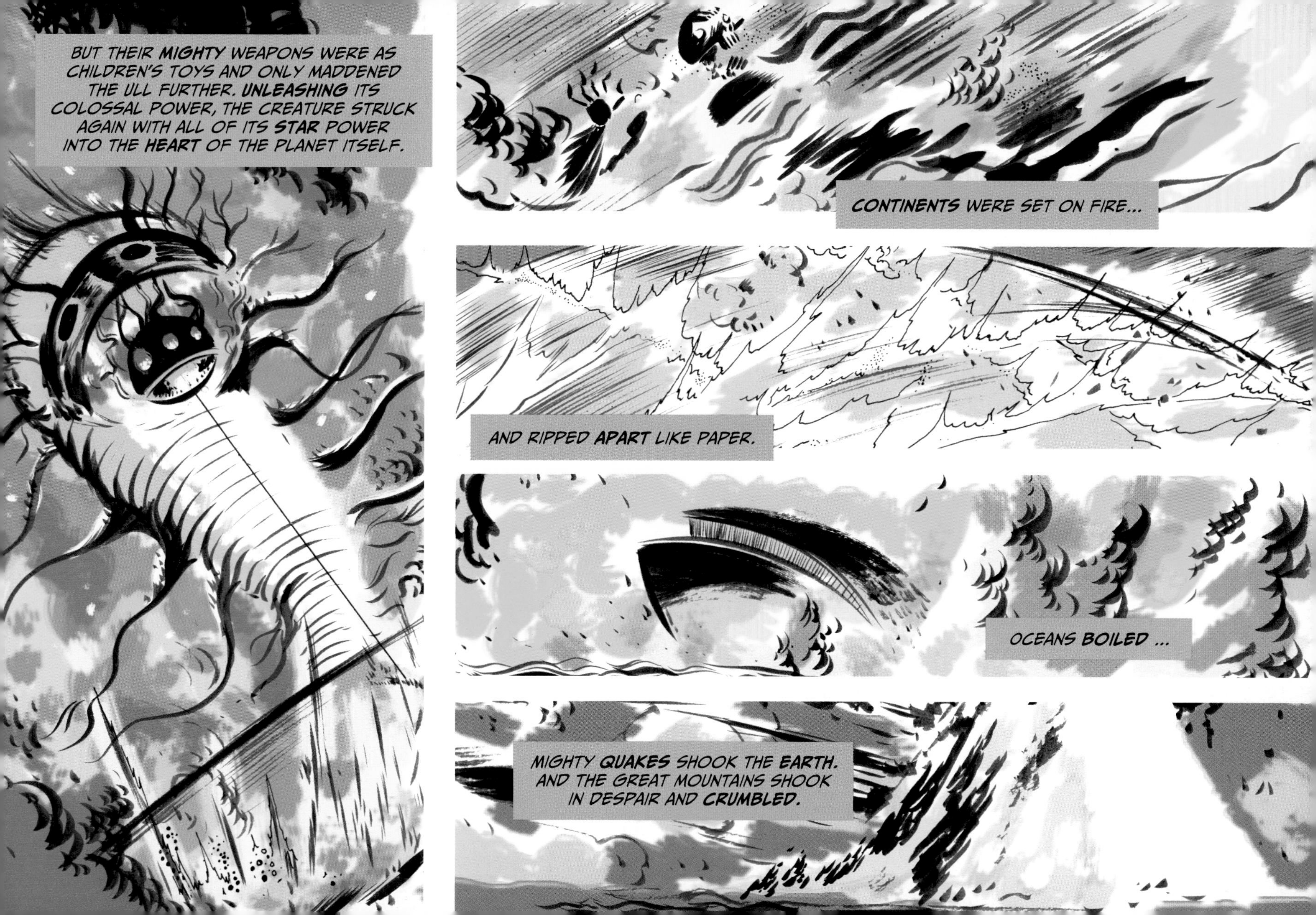
BUT THEIR MIGHTY WEAPONS WERE AS CHILDREN'S TOYS AND ONLY MADDENED THE ULL FURTHER. UNLEASHING ITS COLOSSAL POWER, THE CREATURE STRUCK AGAIN WITH ALL OF ITS STAR POWER INTO THE HEART OF THE PLANET ITSELF.
CONTINENTS WERE SET ON FIRE...
AND RIPPED APART LIKE PAPER.
OCEANS BOILED ...
MIGHTY QUAKES SHOOK THE EARTH. AND THE GREAT MOUNTAINS SHOOK IN DESPAIR AND CRUMBLED.

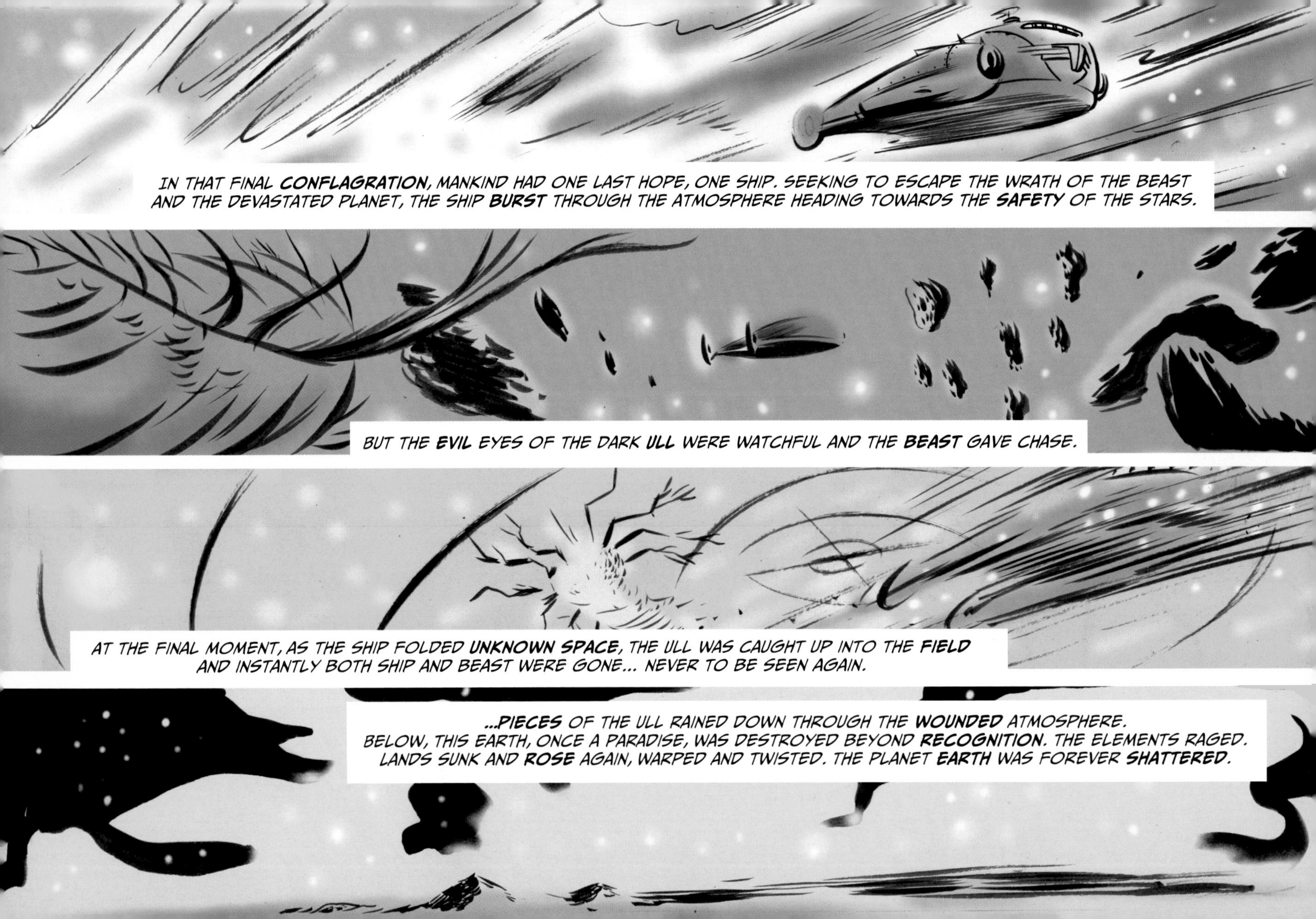
IN THAT FINAL **CONFLAGRATION**, MANKIND HAD ONE LAST HOPE, ONE SHIP. SEEKING TO ESCAPE THE WRATH OF THE BEAST AND THE DEVASTATED PLANET, THE SHIP **BURST** THROUGH THE ATMOSPHERE HEADING TOWARDS THE **SAFETY** OF THE STARS.
BUT THE **EVIL** EYES OF THE DARK **ULL** WERE WATCHFUL AND THE **BEAST** GAVE CHASE.
AT THE FINAL MOMENT, AS THE SHIP FOLDED **UNKNOWN SPACE**, THE ULL WAS CAUGHT UP INTO THE **FIELD** AND INSTANTLY BOTH SHIP AND BEAST WERE GONE... NEVER TO BE SEEN AGAIN.
...**PIECES** OF THE ULL RAINED DOWN THROUGH THE **WOUNDED** ATMOSPHERE. BELOW, THIS EARTH, ONCE A PARADISE, WAS DESTROYED BEYOND **RECOGNITION**. THE ELEMENTS RAGED. LANDS SUNK AND **ROSE** AGAIN, WARPED AND TWISTED. THE PLANET **EARTH** WAS FOREVER **SHATTERED**.

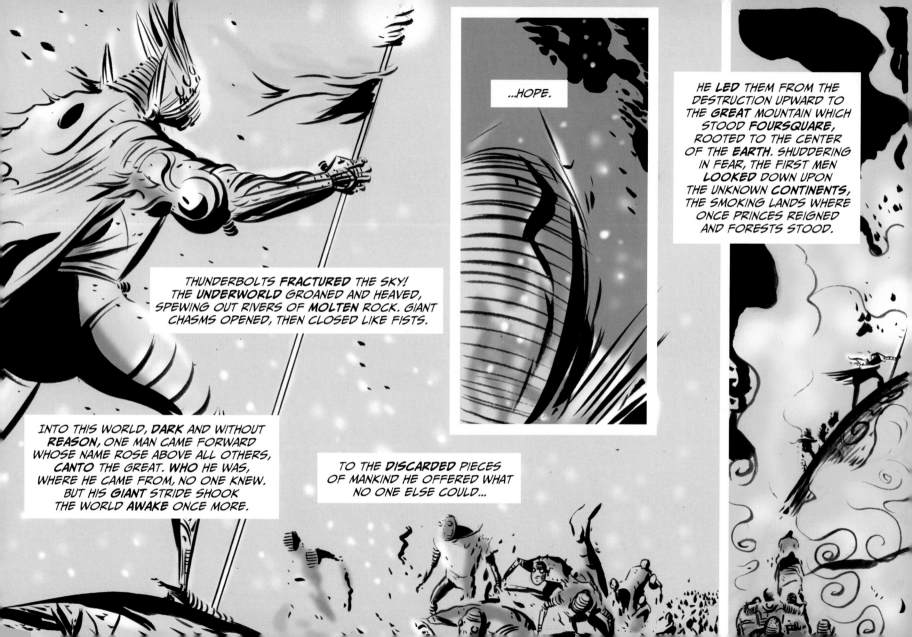

...HOPE.

HE **LED** THEM FROM THE DESTRUCTION UPWARD TO THE **GREAT** MOUNTAIN WHICH STOOD **FOURSQUARE**, ROOTED TO THE CENTER OF THE **EARTH**. SHUDDERING IN FEAR, THE FIRST MEN **LOOKED** DOWN UPON THE UNKNOWN **CONTINENTS**, THE SMOKING LANDS WHERE ONCE PRINCES REIGNED AND FORESTS STOOD.

THUNDERBOLTS **FRACTURED** THE SKY! THE **UNDERWORLD** GROANED AND HEAVED, SPEWING OUT RIVERS OF **MOLTEN** ROCK. GIANT CHASMS OPENED, THEN CLOSED LIKE FISTS.

INTO THIS WORLD, **DARK** AND WITHOUT **REASON**, ONE MAN CAME FORWARD WHOSE NAME ROSE ABOVE ALL OTHERS, **CANTO** THE GREAT. **WHO** HE WAS, WHERE HE CAME FROM, NO ONE KNEW. BUT HIS **GIANT** STRIDE SHOOK THE WORLD **AWAKE** ONCE MORE.

TO THE **DISCARDED** PIECES OF MANKIND HE OFFERED WHAT NO ONE ELSE COULD...

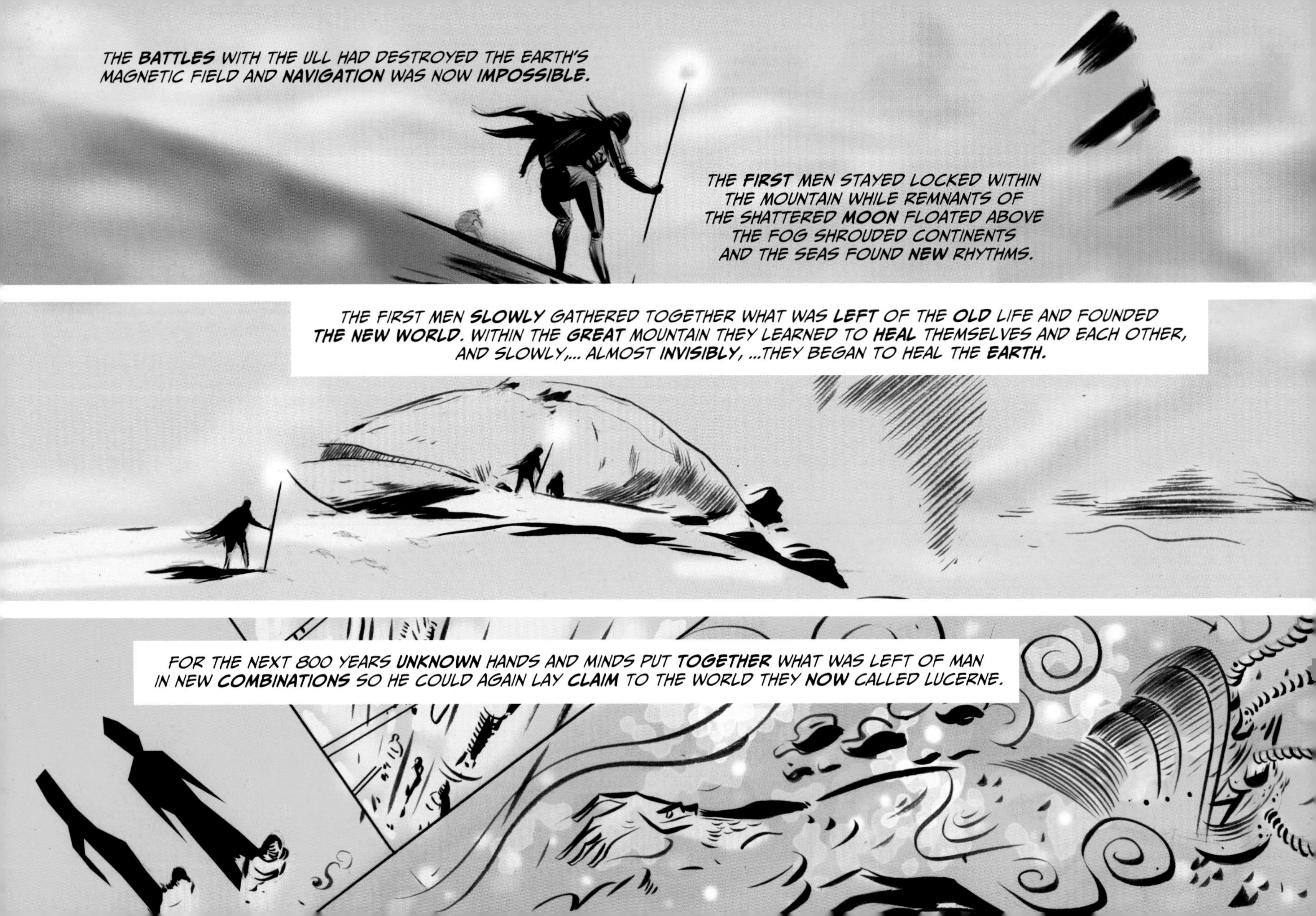
THE BATTLES WITH THE ULL HAD DESTROYED THE EARTH'S MAGNETIC FIELD AND NAVIGATION WAS NOW IMPOSSIBLE.
THE FIRST MEN STAYED LOCKED WITHIN THE MOUNTAIN WHILE REMNANTS OF THE SHATTERED MOON FLOATED ABOVE THE FOG SHROUDED CONTINENTS AND THE SEAS FOUND NEW RHYTHMS.
THE FIRST MEN SLOWLY GATHERED TOGETHER WHAT WAS LEFT OF THE OLD LIFE AND FOUNDED THE NEW WORLD. WITHIN THE GREAT MOUNTAIN THEY LEARNED TO HEAL THEMSELVES AND EACH OTHER, AND SLOWLY,... ALMOST INVISIBLY, ...THEY BEGAN TO HEAL THE EARTH.
FOR THE NEXT 800 YEARS UNKNOWN HANDS AND MINDS PUT TOGETHER WHAT WAS LEFT OF MAN IN NEW COMBINATIONS SO HE COULD AGAIN LAY CLAIM TO THE WORLD THEY NOW CALLED LUCERNE.

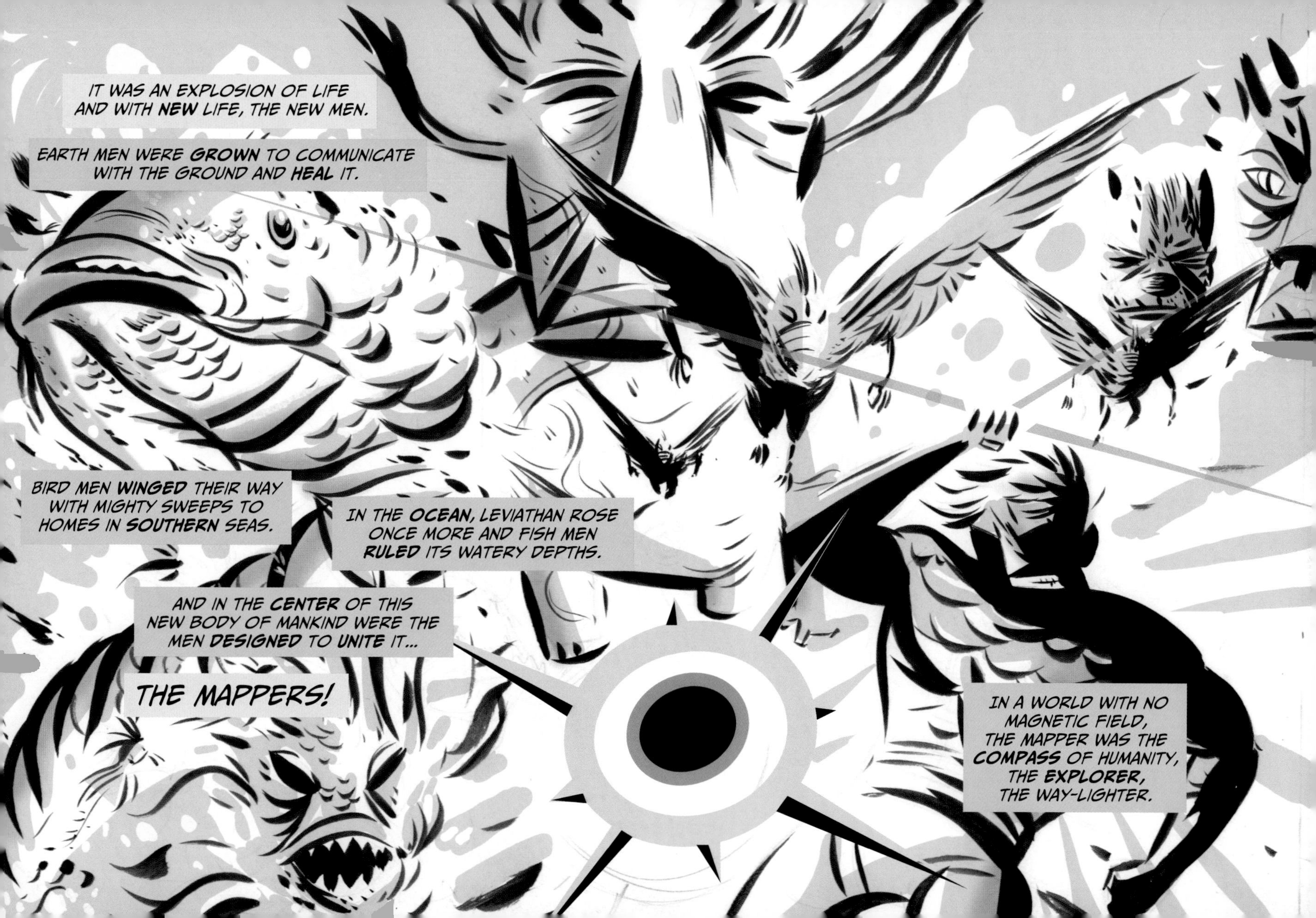
IT WAS AN EXPLOSION OF LIFE AND WITH **NEW** LIFE, THE NEW MEN.
EARTH MEN WERE **GROWN** TO COMMUNICATE WITH THE GROUND AND **HEAL** IT.
BIRD MEN **WINGED** THEIR WAY WITH MIGHTY SWEEPS TO HOMES IN **SOUTHERN** SEAS.
IN THE **OCEAN,** LEVIATHAN ROSE ONCE MORE AND FISH MEN **RULED** ITS WATERY DEPTHS.
AND IN THE **CENTER** OF THIS NEW BODY OF MANKIND WERE THE MEN **DESIGNED** TO **UNITE** IT...
THE MAPPERS!
IN A WORLD WITH NO MAGNETIC FIELD, THE MAPPER WAS THE **COMPASS** OF HUMANITY, THE **EXPLORER,** THE WAY-LIGHTER.

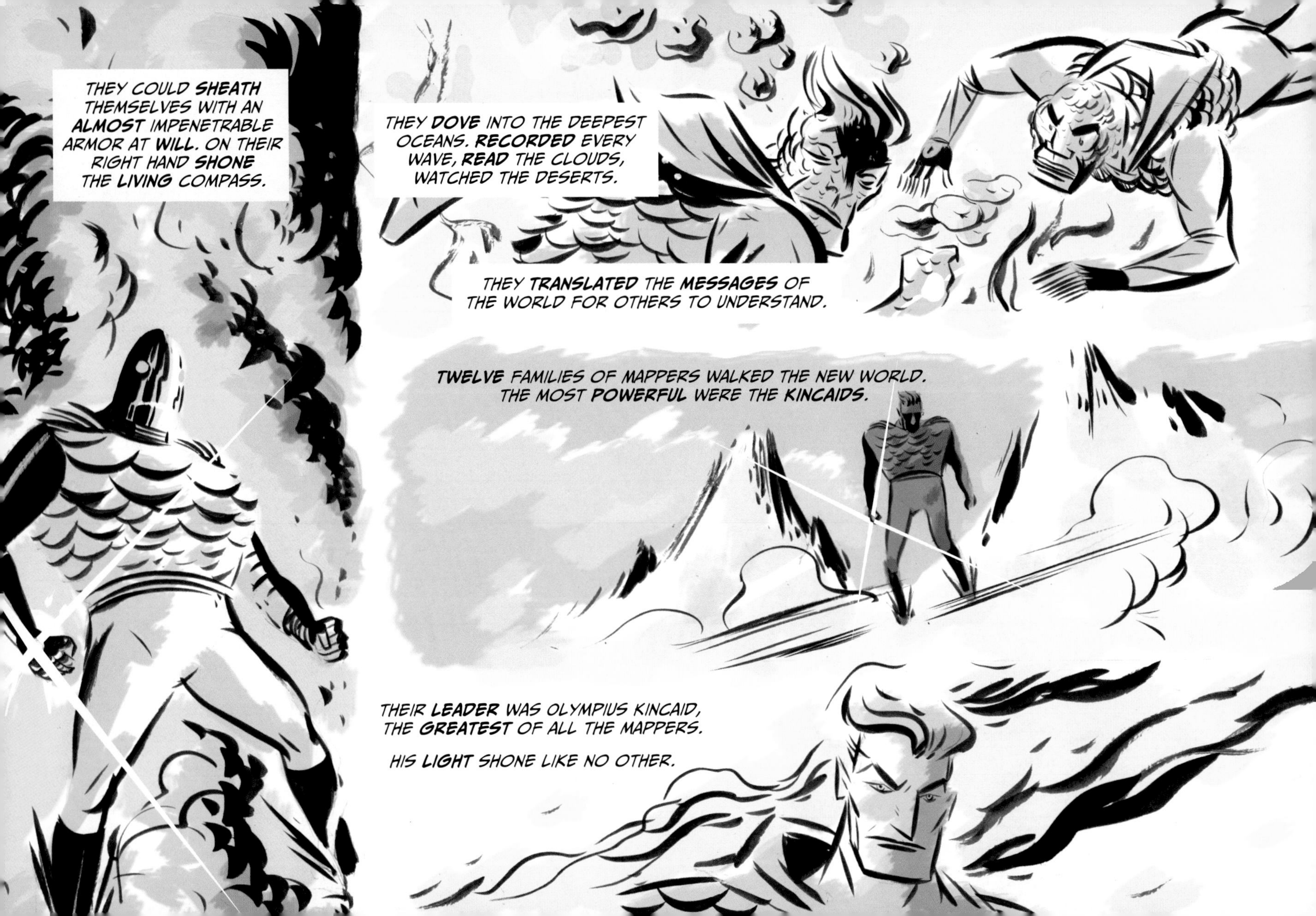
THEY COULD SHEATH THEMSELVES WITH AN ALMOST IMPENETRABLE ARMOR AT WILL. ON THEIR RIGHT HAND SHONE THE LIVING COMPASS.
THEY DOVE INTO THE DEEPEST OCEANS. RECORDED EVERY WAVE, READ THE CLOUDS, WATCHED THE DESERTS.
THEY TRANSLATED THE MESSAGES OF THE WORLD FOR OTHERS TO UNDERSTAND.
TWELVE FAMILIES OF MAPPERS WALKED THE NEW WORLD. THE MOST POWERFUL WERE THE KINCAIDS.
THEIR LEADER WAS OLYMPIUS KINCAID, THE GREATEST OF ALL THE MAPPERS.
HIS LIGHT SHONE LIKE NO OTHER.

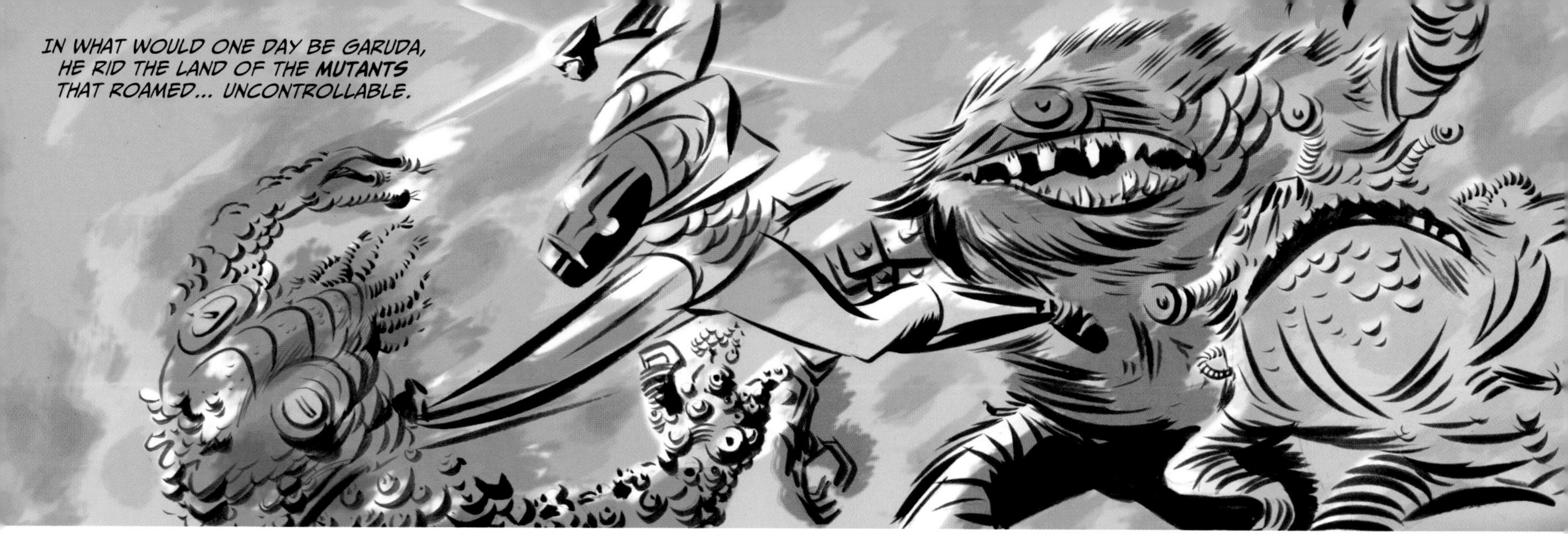
IN WHAT WOULD ONE DAY BE GARUDA, HE RID THE LAND OF THE MUTANTS THAT ROAMED... UNCONTROLLABLE.

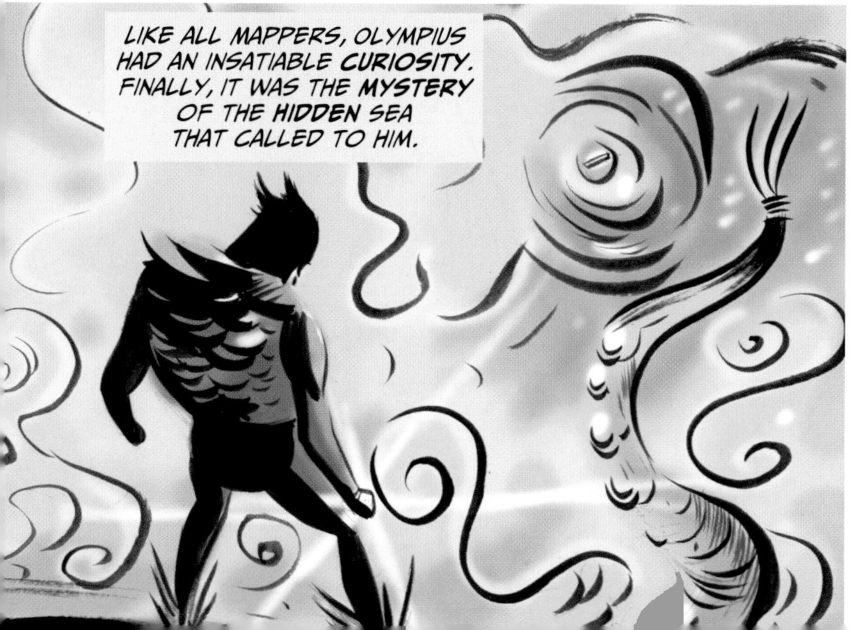
LIKE ALL MAPPERS, OLYMPIUS HAD AN INSATIABLE CURIOSITY. FINALLY, IT WAS THE MYSTERY OF THE HIDDEN SEA THAT CALLED TO HIM.

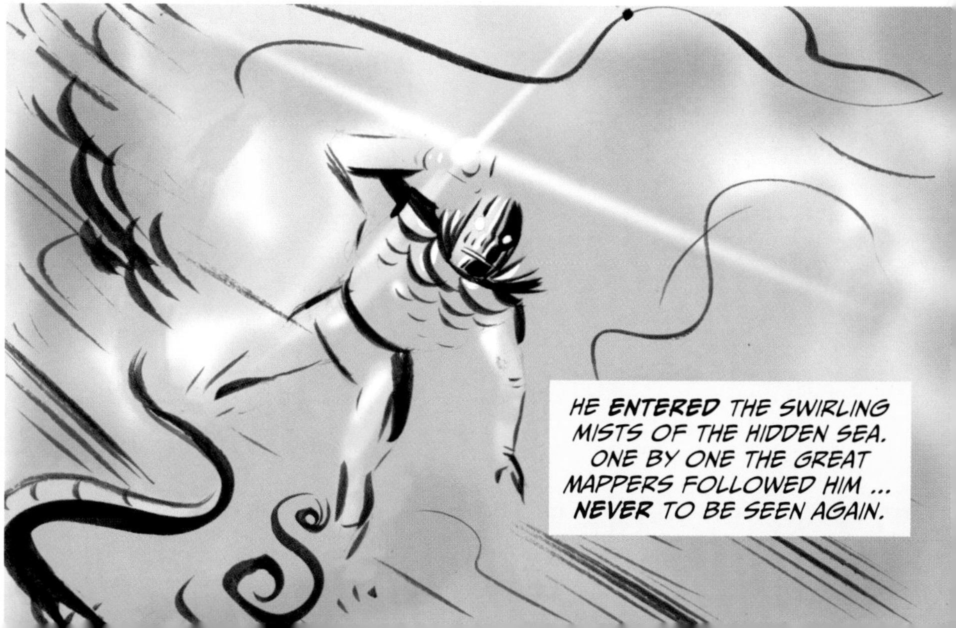
HE ENTERED THE SWIRLING MISTS OF THE HIDDEN SEA. ONE BY ONE THE GREAT MAPPERS FOLLOWED HIM ... NEVER TO BE SEEN AGAIN.

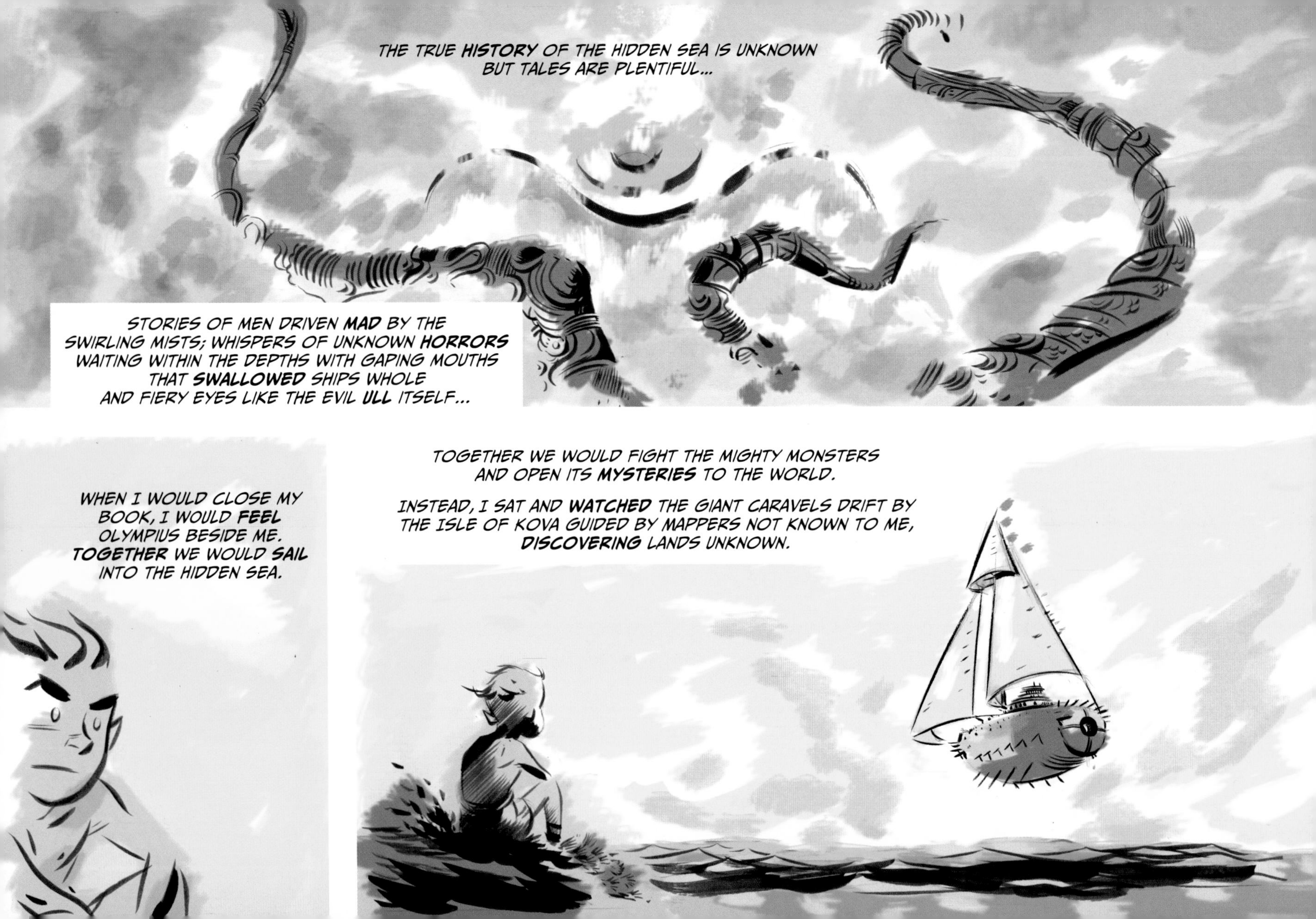
THE TRUE HISTORY OF THE HIDDEN SEA IS UNKNOWN BUT TALES ARE PLENTIFUL...
STORIES OF MEN DRIVEN MAD BY THE SWIRLING MISTS; WHISPERS OF UNKNOWN HORRORS WAITING WITHIN THE DEPTHS WITH GAPING MOUTHS THAT SWALLOWED SHIPS WHOLE AND FIERY EYES LIKE THE EVIL ULL ITSELF...
WHEN I WOULD CLOSE MY BOOK, I WOULD FEEL OLYMPIUS BESIDE ME. TOGETHER WE WOULD SAIL INTO THE HIDDEN SEA.
TOGETHER WE WOULD FIGHT THE MIGHTY MONSTERS AND OPEN ITS MYSTERIES TO THE WORLD.
INSTEAD, I SAT AND WATCHED THE GIANT CARAVELS DRIFT BY THE ISLE OF KOVA GUIDED BY MAPPERS NOT KNOWN TO ME, DISCOVERING LANDS UNKNOWN.

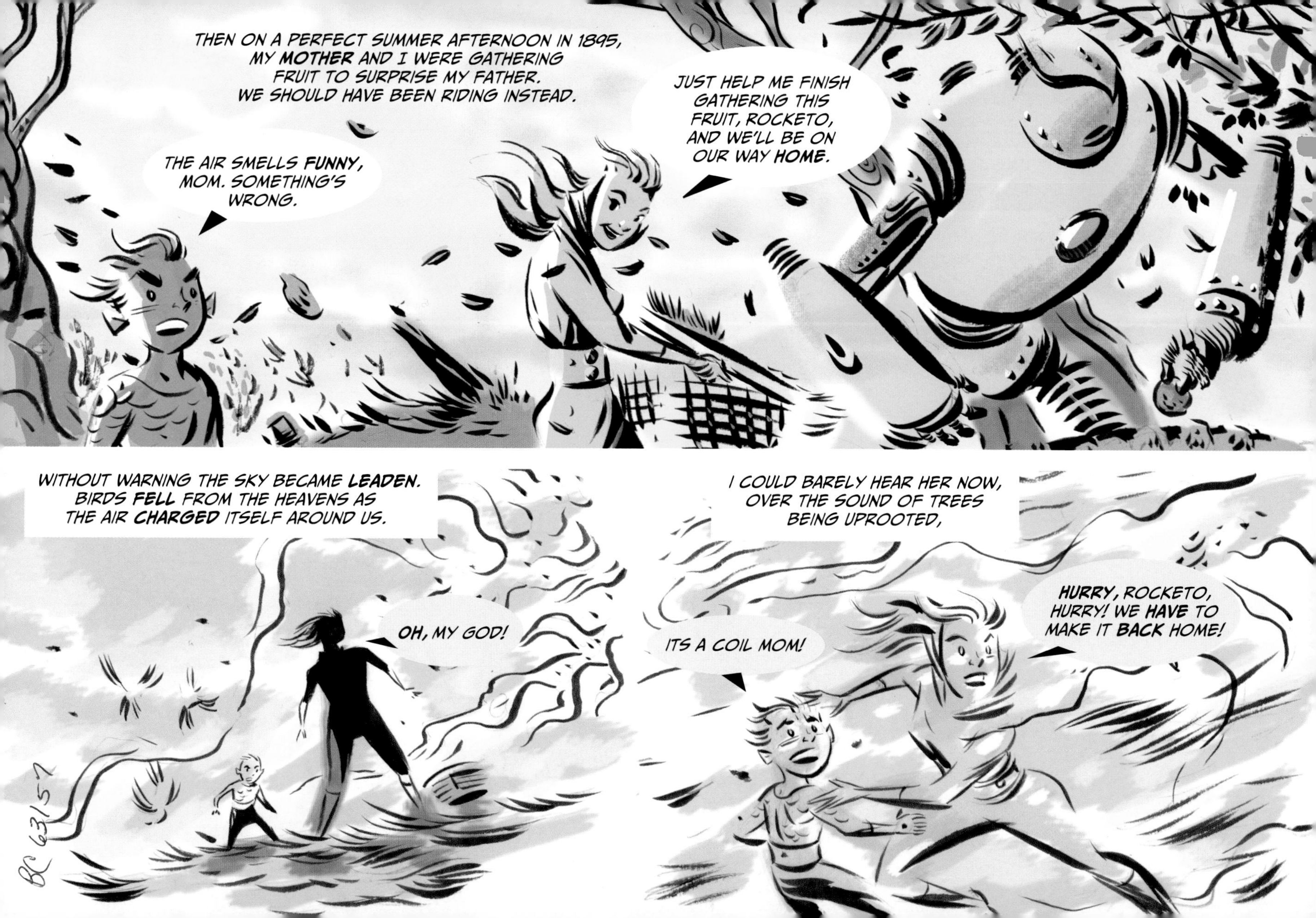
THEN ON A PERFECT SUMMER AFTERNOON IN 1895, MY MOTHER AND I WERE GATHERING FRUIT TO SURPRISE MY FATHER. WE SHOULD HAVE BEEN RIDING INSTEAD.
THE AIR SMELLS FUNNY, MOM. SOMETHING'S WRONG.
JUST HELP ME FINISH GATHERING THIS FRUIT, ROCKETO, AND WE'LL BE ON OUR WAY HOME.
WITHOUT WARNING THE SKY BECAME LEADEN. BIRDS FELL FROM THE HEAVENS AS THE AIR CHARGED ITSELF AROUND US.
OH, MY GOD!
I COULD BARELY HEAR HER NOW, OVER THE SOUND OF TREES BEING UPROOTED,
HURRY, ROCKETO, HURRY! WE HAVE TO MAKE IT BACK HOME!
ITS A COIL MOM!

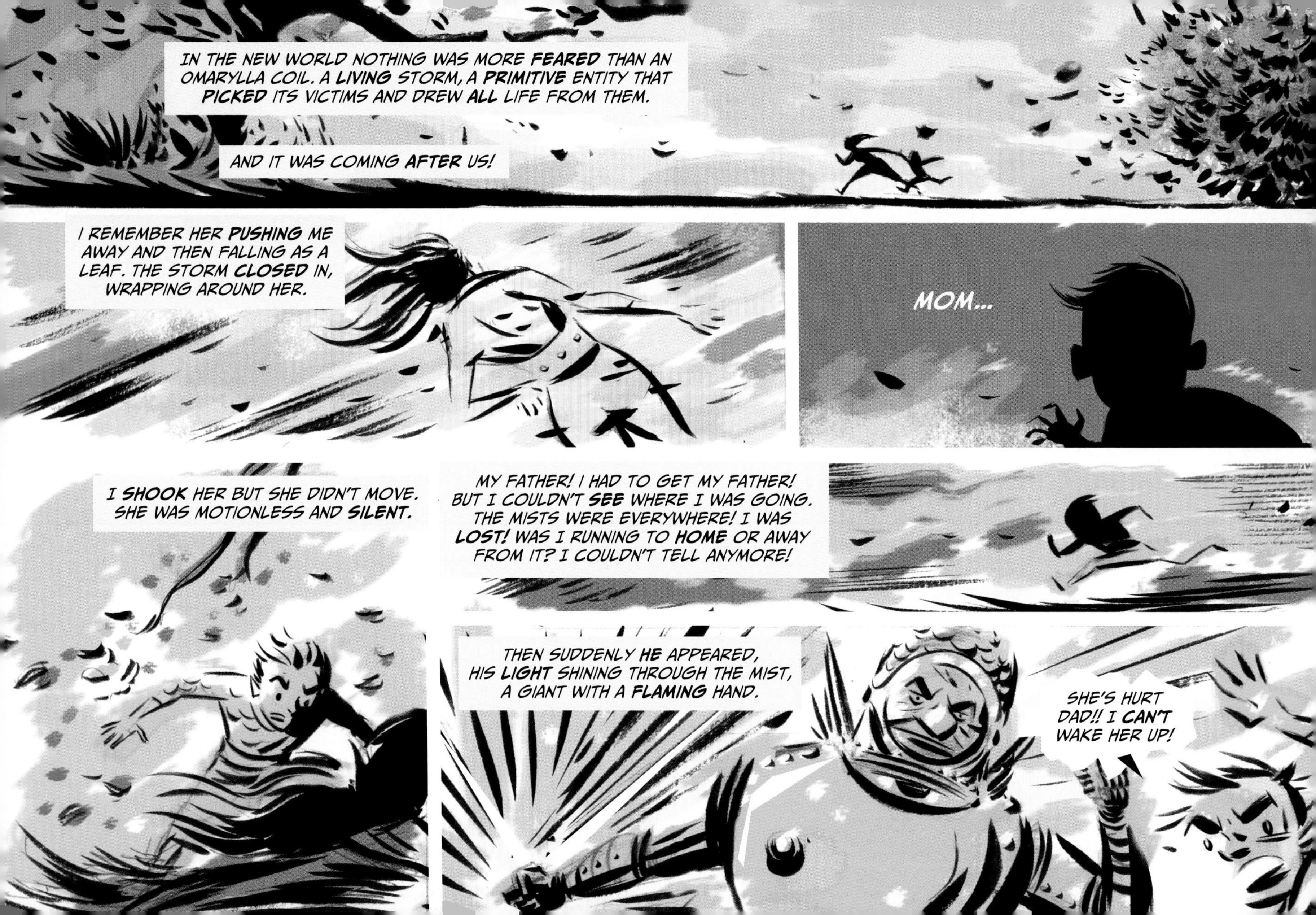

IN THE NEW WORLD NOTHING WAS MORE **FEARED** THAN AN OMARYLLA COIL. A **LIVING** STORM, A **PRIMITIVE** ENTITY THAT **PICKED** ITS VICTIMS AND DREW **ALL** LIFE FROM THEM.
AND IT WAS COMING **AFTER** US!
I REMEMBER HER **PUSHING** ME AWAY AND THEN FALLING AS A LEAF. THE STORM **CLOSED** IN, WRAPPING AROUND HER.
MOM...
I **SHOOK** HER BUT SHE DIDN'T MOVE. SHE WAS MOTIONLESS AND **SILENT.**
MY FATHER! I HAD TO GET MY FATHER! BUT I COULDN'T **SEE** WHERE I WAS GOING. THE MISTS WERE EVERYWHERE! I WAS **LOST!** WAS I RUNNING TO **HOME** OR AWAY FROM IT? I COULDN'T TELL ANYMORE!
THEN SUDDENLY **HE** APPEARED, HIS **LIGHT** SHINING THROUGH THE MIST, A GIANT WITH A **FLAMING** HAND.
SHE'S HURT DAD!! I **CAN'T** WAKE HER UP!

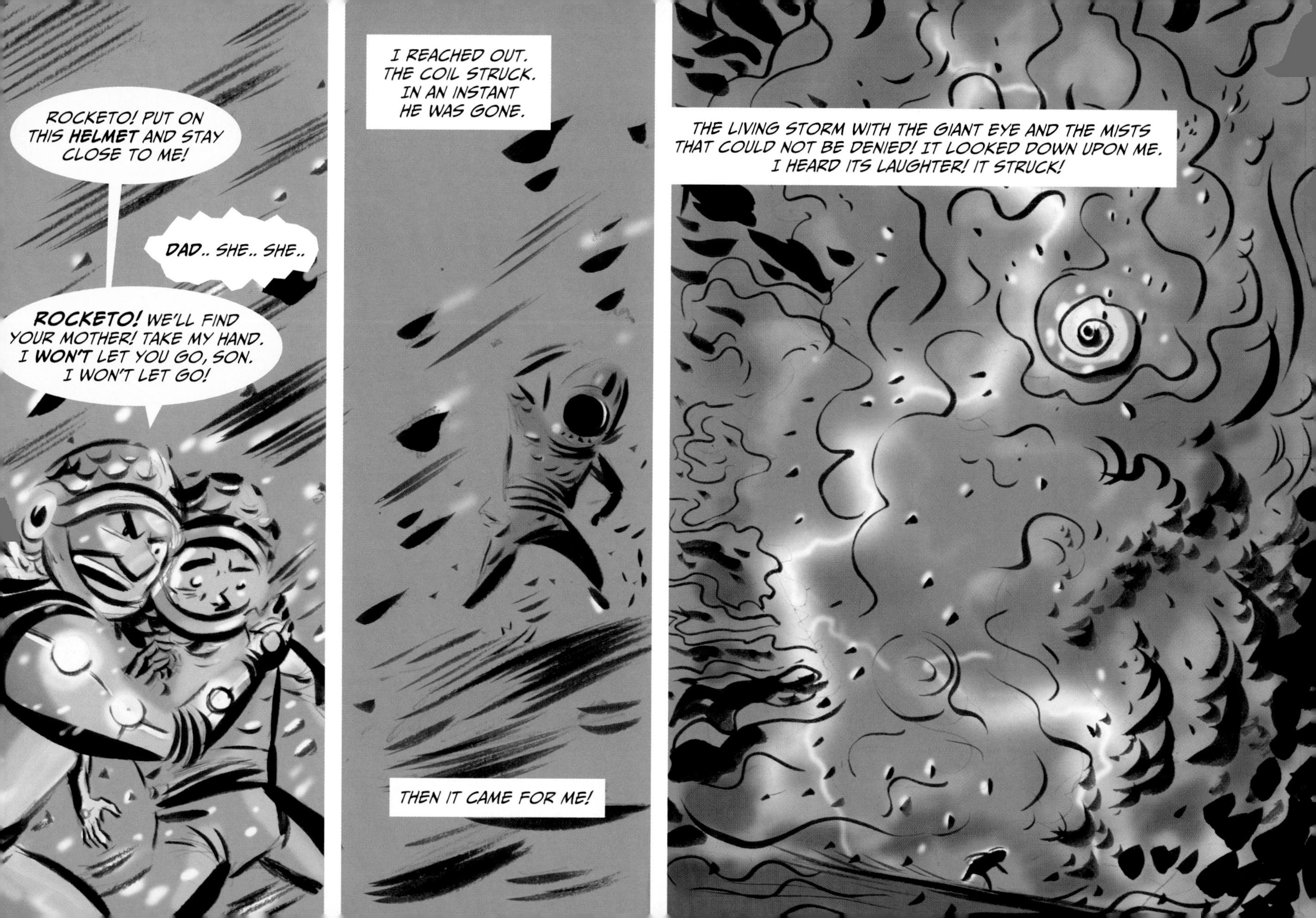
ROCKETO! PUT ON THIS HELMET AND STAY CLOSE TO ME!
DAD.. SHE.. SHE..
ROCKETO! WE'LL FIND YOUR MOTHER! TAKE MY HAND. I WON'T LET YOU GO, SON. I WON'T LET GO!
I REACHED OUT. THE COIL STRUCK. IN AN INSTANT HE WAS GONE.
THEN IT CAME FOR ME!
THE LIVING STORM WITH THE GIANT EYE AND THE MISTS THAT COULD NOT BE DENIED! IT LOOKED DOWN UPON ME. I HEARD ITS LAUGHTER! IT STRUCK!

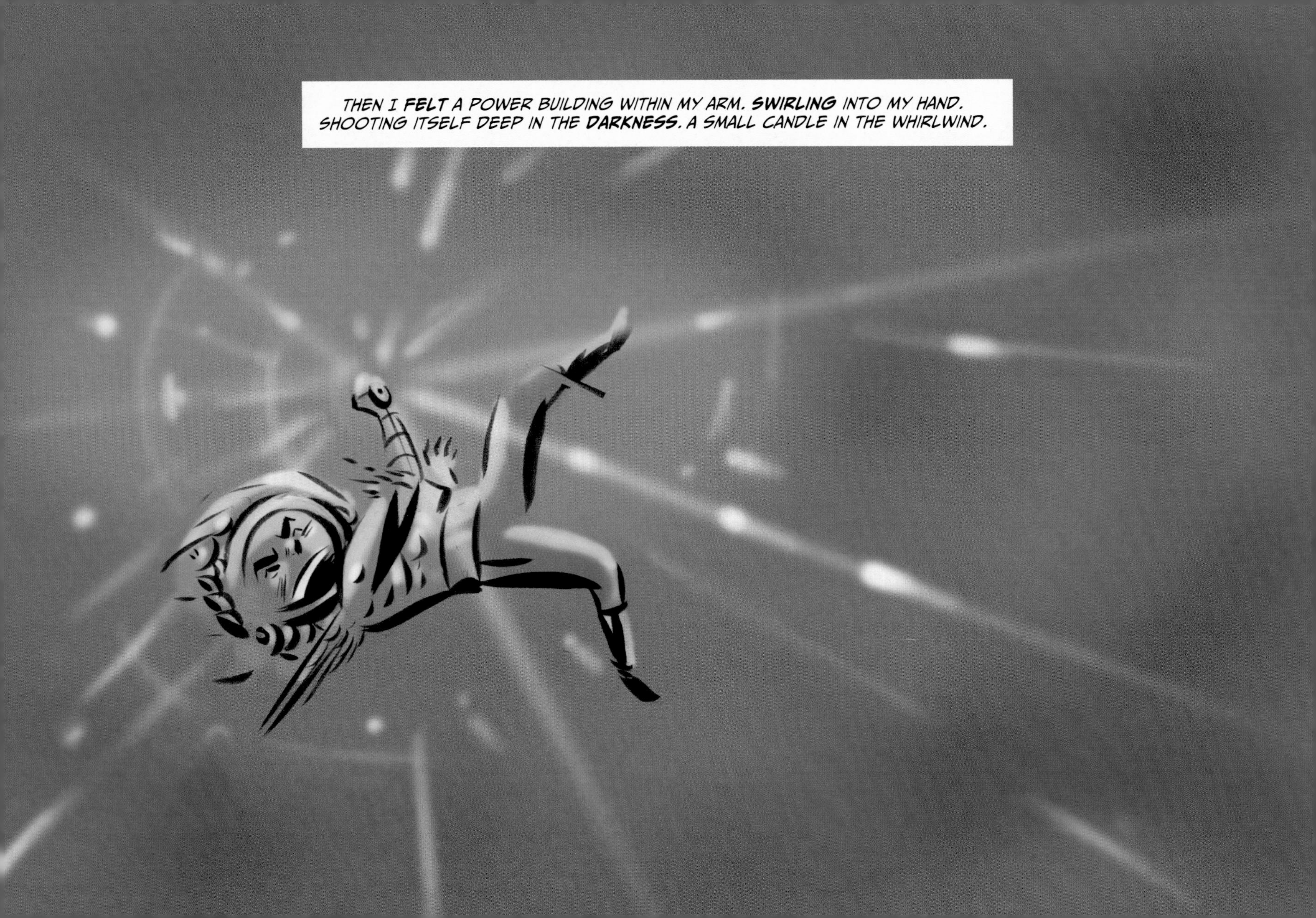
THEN I FELT A POWER BUILDING WITHIN MY ARM. SWIRLING INTO MY HAND. SHOOTING ITSELF DEEP IN THE DARKNESS. A SMALL CANDLE IN THE WHIRLWIND.

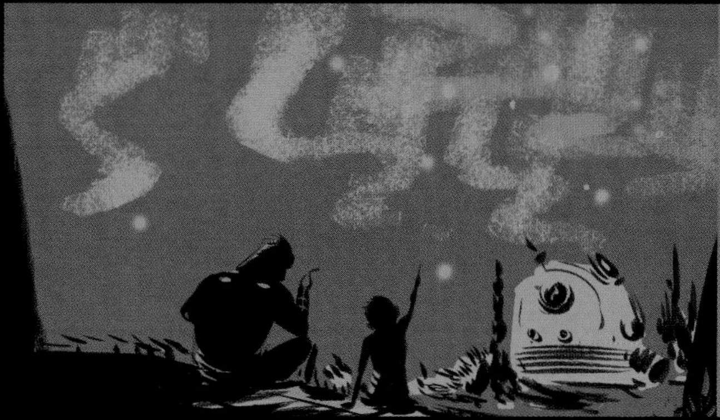

ROCKETO

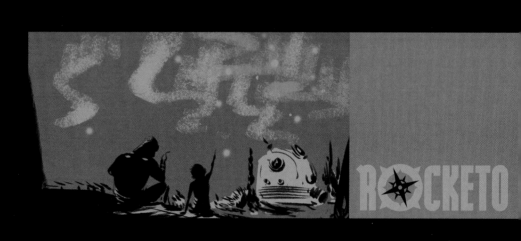

# 2

# CONFLICTS

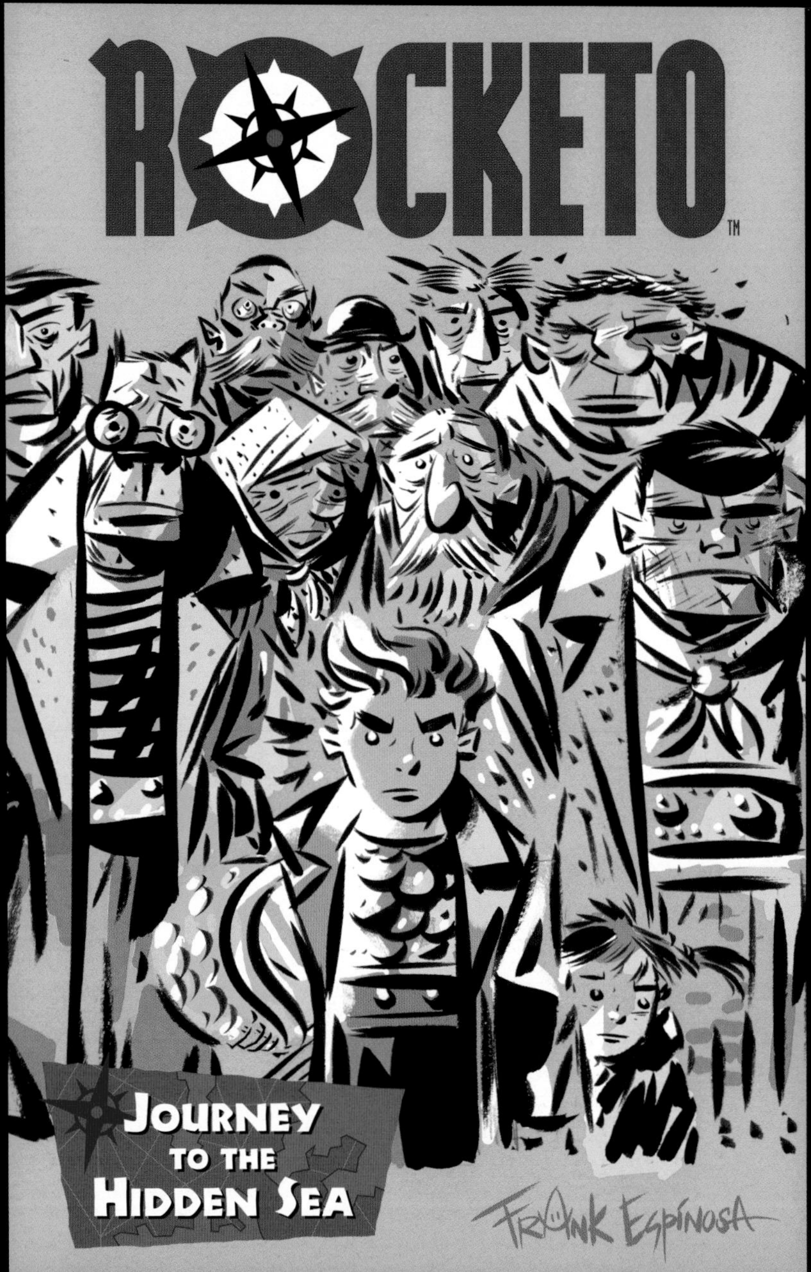
ROCKETO™
JOURNEY TO THE HIDDEN SEA
FRANK ESPINOSA

THE YEAR IS 1845, NEW WORLD TIME, THE ISLAND OF KOVA HAS BEEN RAVAGED BY A LIVING STORM KNOWN AS THE OMARYLLA COIL.

THE BIGGEST RESCUE MISSION IN THE HISTORY OF THE NEW WORLD WAS IMMEDIATELY LAUNCHED TO RESCUE SURVIVORS OF THE CATASTROPHE.

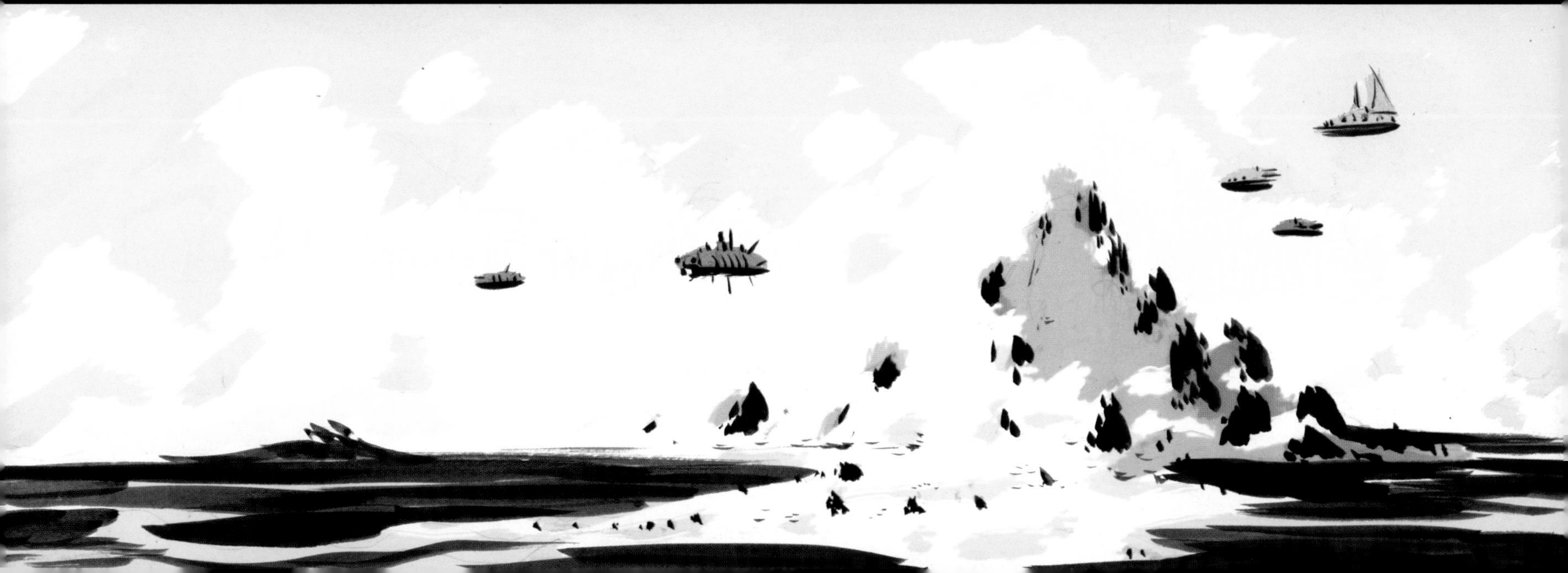

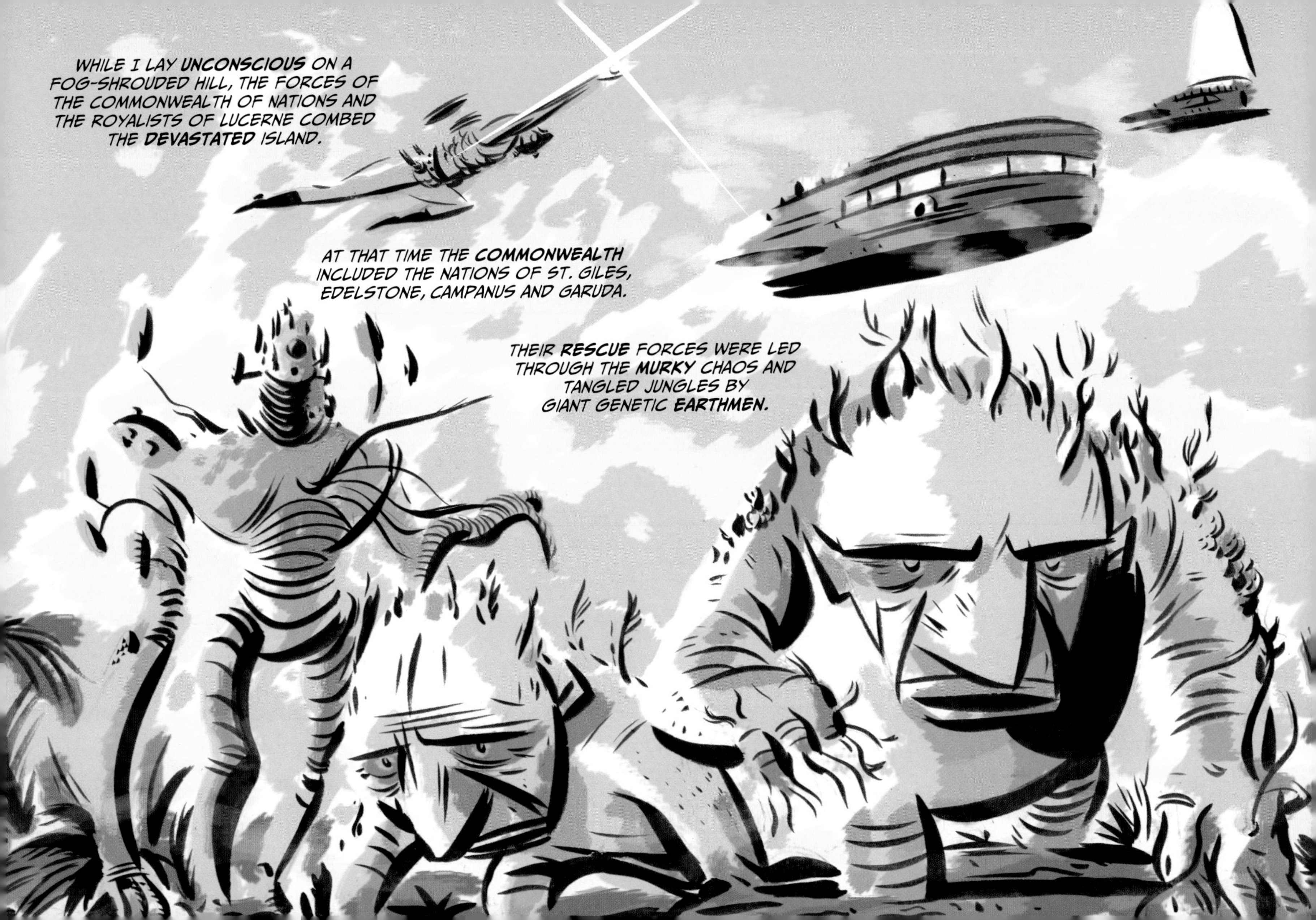
WHILE I LAY UNCONSCIOUS ON A FOG-SHROUDED HILL, THE FORCES OF THE COMMONWEALTH OF NATIONS AND THE ROYALISTS OF LUCERNE COMBED THE DEVASTATED ISLAND.
AT THAT TIME THE COMMONWEALTH INCLUDED THE NATIONS OF ST. GILES, EDELSTONE, CAMPANUS AND GARUDA.
THEIR RESCUE FORCES WERE LED THROUGH THE MURKY CHAOS AND TANGLED JUNGLES BY GIANT GENETIC EARTHMEN.

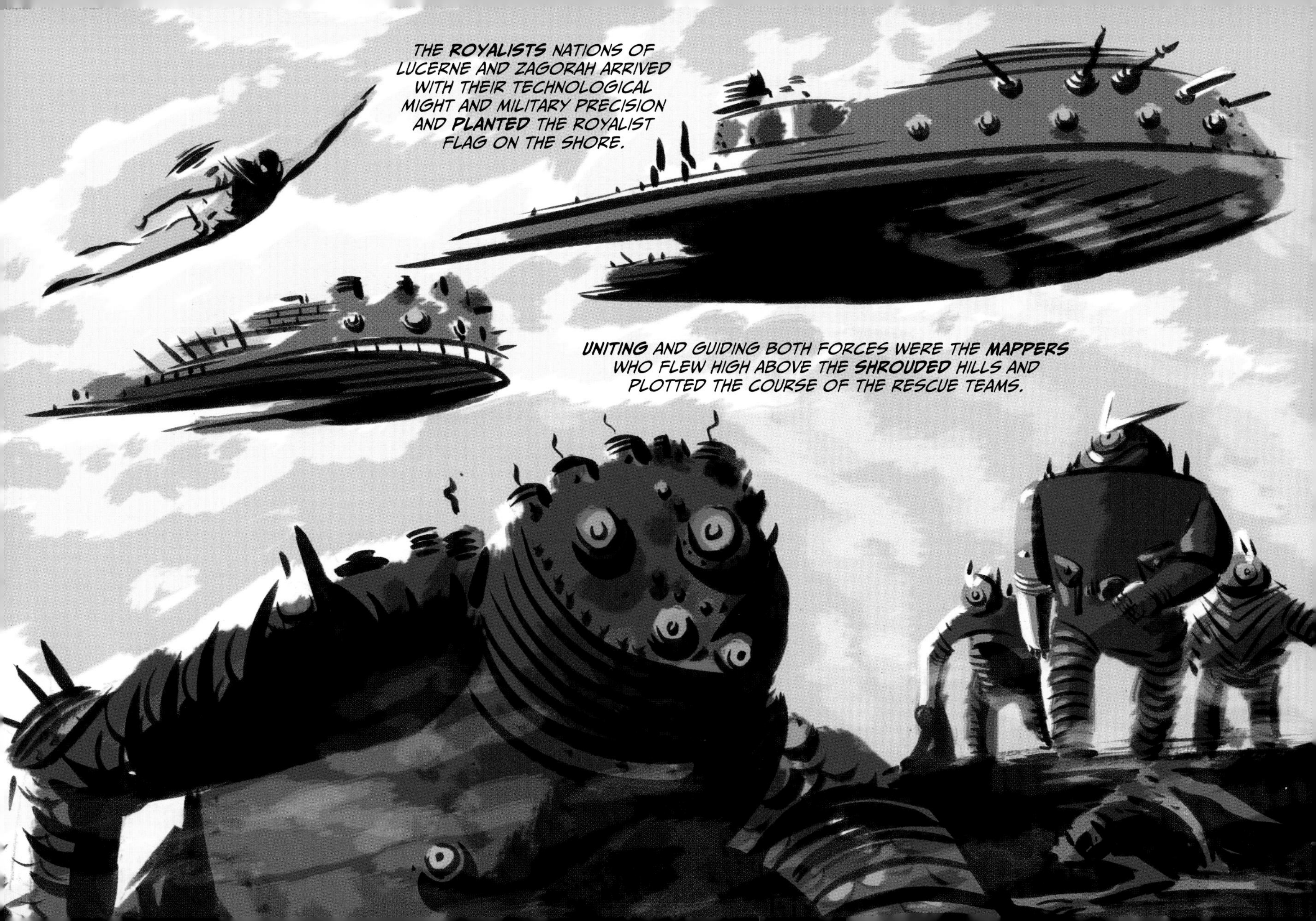
THE ROYALISTS NATIONS OF LUCERNE AND ZAGORAH ARRIVED WITH THEIR TECHNOLOGICAL MIGHT AND MILITARY PRECISION AND PLANTED THE ROYALIST FLAG ON THE SHORE.
UNITING AND GUIDING BOTH FORCES WERE THE MAPPERS WHO FLEW HIGH ABOVE THE SHROUDED HILLS AND PLOTTED THE COURSE OF THE RESCUE TEAMS.

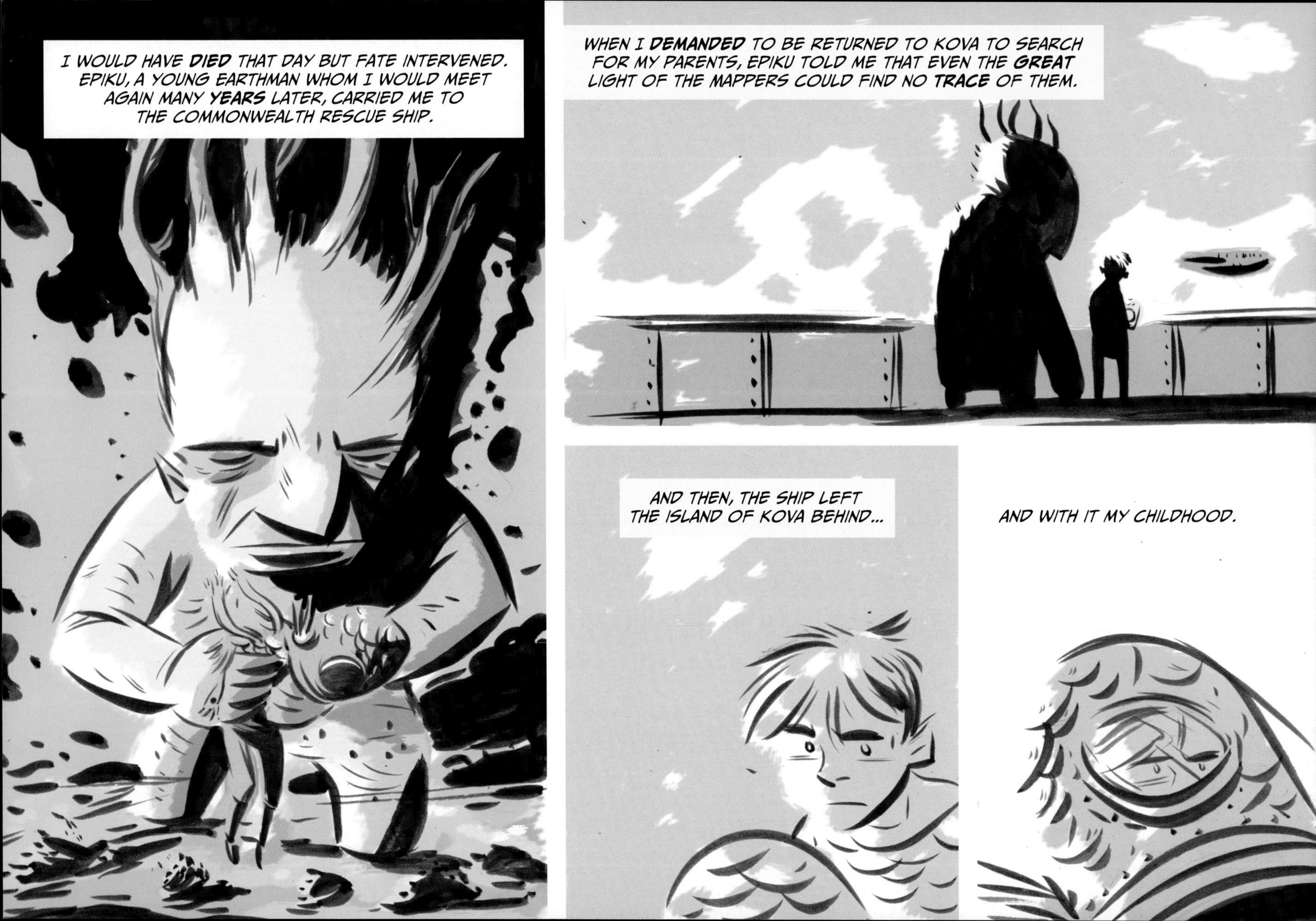
I WOULD HAVE DIED THAT DAY BUT FATE INTERVENED. EPIKU, A YOUNG EARTHMAN WHOM I WOULD MEET AGAIN MANY YEARS LATER, CARRIED ME TO THE COMMONWEALTH RESCUE SHIP.
WHEN I DEMANDED TO BE RETURNED TO KOVA TO SEARCH FOR MY PARENTS, EPIKU TOLD ME THAT EVEN THE GREAT LIGHT OF THE MAPPERS COULD FIND NO TRACE OF THEM.
AND THEN, THE SHIP LEFT THE ISLAND OF KOVA BEHIND...
AND WITH IT MY CHILDHOOD.

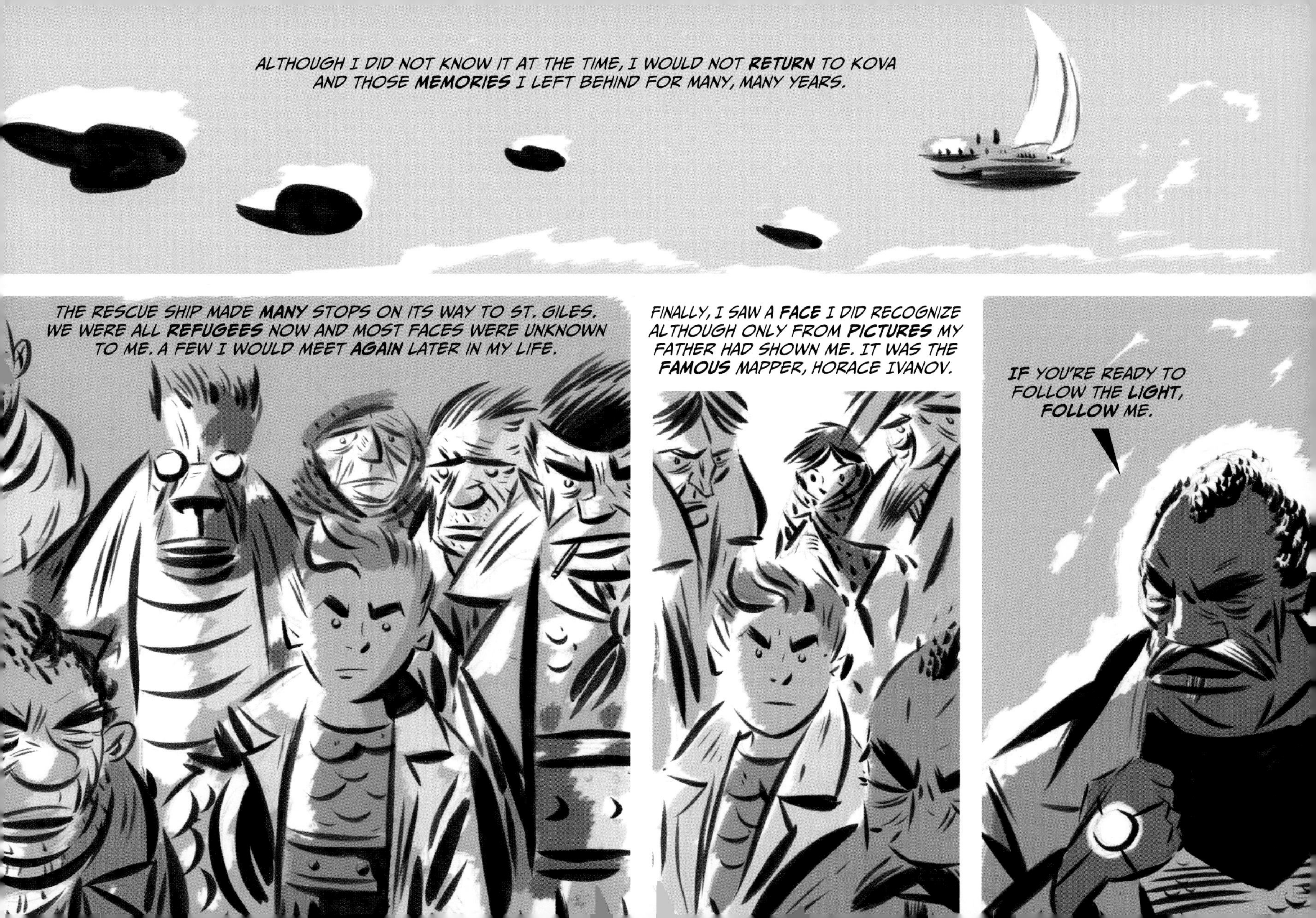
ALTHOUGH I DID NOT KNOW IT AT THE TIME, I WOULD NOT **RETURN** TO KOVA AND THOSE **MEMORIES** I LEFT BEHIND FOR MANY, MANY YEARS.
THE RESCUE SHIP MADE **MANY** STOPS ON ITS WAY TO ST. GILES. WE WERE ALL **REFUGEES** NOW AND MOST FACES WERE UNKNOWN TO ME. A FEW I WOULD MEET **AGAIN** LATER IN MY LIFE.
FINALLY, I SAW A **FACE** I DID RECOGNIZE ALTHOUGH ONLY FROM **PICTURES** MY FATHER HAD SHOWN ME. IT WAS THE **FAMOUS** MAPPER, HORACE IVANOV.
**IF** YOU'RE READY TO FOLLOW THE **LIGHT**, **FOLLOW** ME.

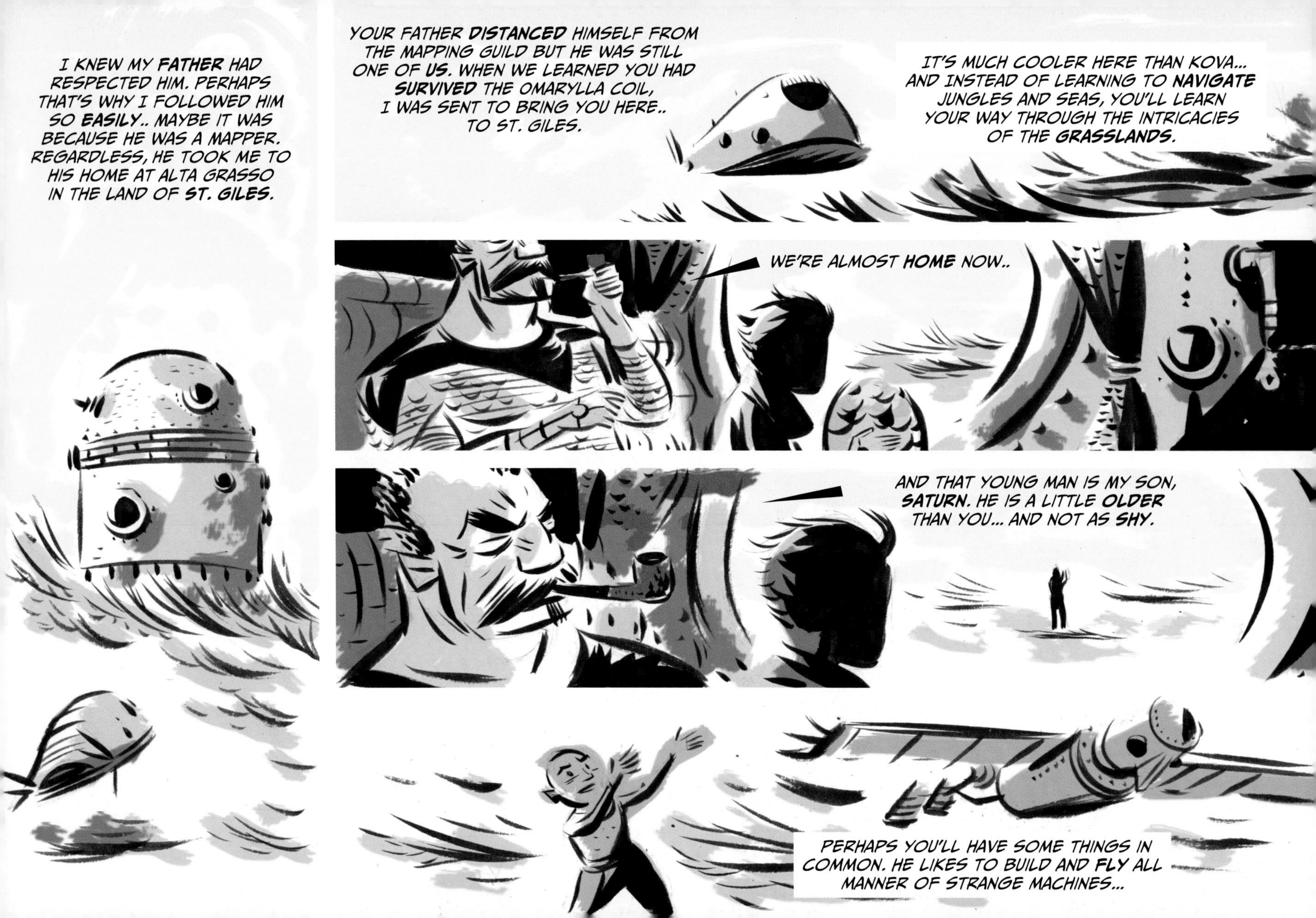
I KNEW MY **FATHER** HAD RESPECTED HIM. PERHAPS THAT'S WHY I FOLLOWED HIM SO **EASILY**.. MAYBE IT WAS BECAUSE HE WAS A MAPPER. REGARDLESS, HE TOOK ME TO HIS HOME AT ALTA GRASSO IN THE LAND OF **ST. GILES**.
YOUR FATHER **DISTANCED** HIMSELF FROM THE MAPPING GUILD BUT HE WAS STILL ONE OF **US**. WHEN WE LEARNED YOU HAD **SURVIVED** THE OMARYLLA COIL, I WAS SENT TO BRING YOU HERE.. TO ST. GILES.
IT'S MUCH COOLER HERE THAN KOVA... AND INSTEAD OF LEARNING TO **NAVIGATE** JUNGLES AND SEAS, YOU'LL LEARN YOUR WAY THROUGH THE INTRICACIES OF THE **GRASSLANDS**.
WE'RE ALMOST **HOME** NOW..
AND THAT YOUNG MAN IS MY SON, **SATURN**. HE IS A LITTLE **OLDER** THAN YOU... AND NOT AS **SHY**.
PERHAPS YOU'LL HAVE SOME THINGS IN COMMON. HE LIKES TO BUILD AND **FLY** ALL MANNER OF STRANGE MACHINES...

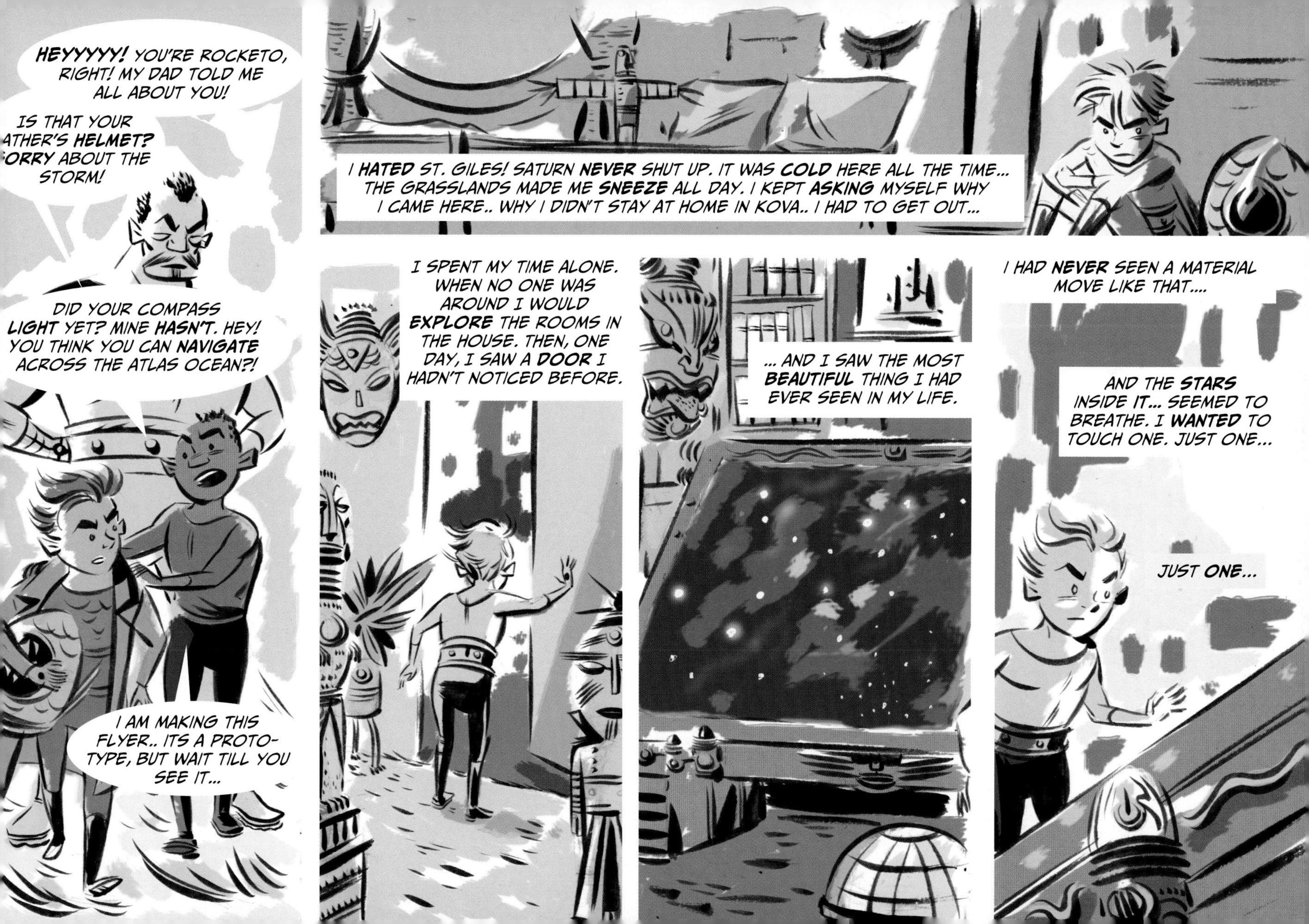
HEYYYYY! YOU'RE ROCKETO, RIGHT! MY DAD TOLD ME ALL ABOUT YOU!
IS THAT YOUR ATHER'S HELMET? ORRY ABOUT THE STORM!
DID YOUR COMPASS LIGHT YET? MINE HASN'T. HEY! YOU THINK YOU CAN NAVIGATE ACROSS THE ATLAS OCEAN?!
I AM MAKING THIS FLYER.. ITS A PROTO-TYPE, BUT WAIT TILL YOU SEE IT...
I HATED ST. GILES! SATURN NEVER SHUT UP. IT WAS COLD HERE ALL THE TIME... THE GRASSLANDS MADE ME SNEEZE ALL DAY. I KEPT ASKING MYSELF WHY I CAME HERE.. WHY I DIDN'T STAY AT HOME IN KOVA.. I HAD TO GET OUT...
I SPENT MY TIME ALONE. WHEN NO ONE WAS AROUND I WOULD EXPLORE THE ROOMS IN THE HOUSE. THEN, ONE DAY, I SAW A DOOR I HADN'T NOTICED BEFORE.
... AND I SAW THE MOST BEAUTIFUL THING I HAD EVER SEEN IN MY LIFE.
I HAD NEVER SEEN A MATERIAL MOVE LIKE THAT....
AND THE STARS INSIDE IT... SEEMED TO BREATHE. I WANTED TO TOUCH ONE. JUST ONE...
JUST ONE...

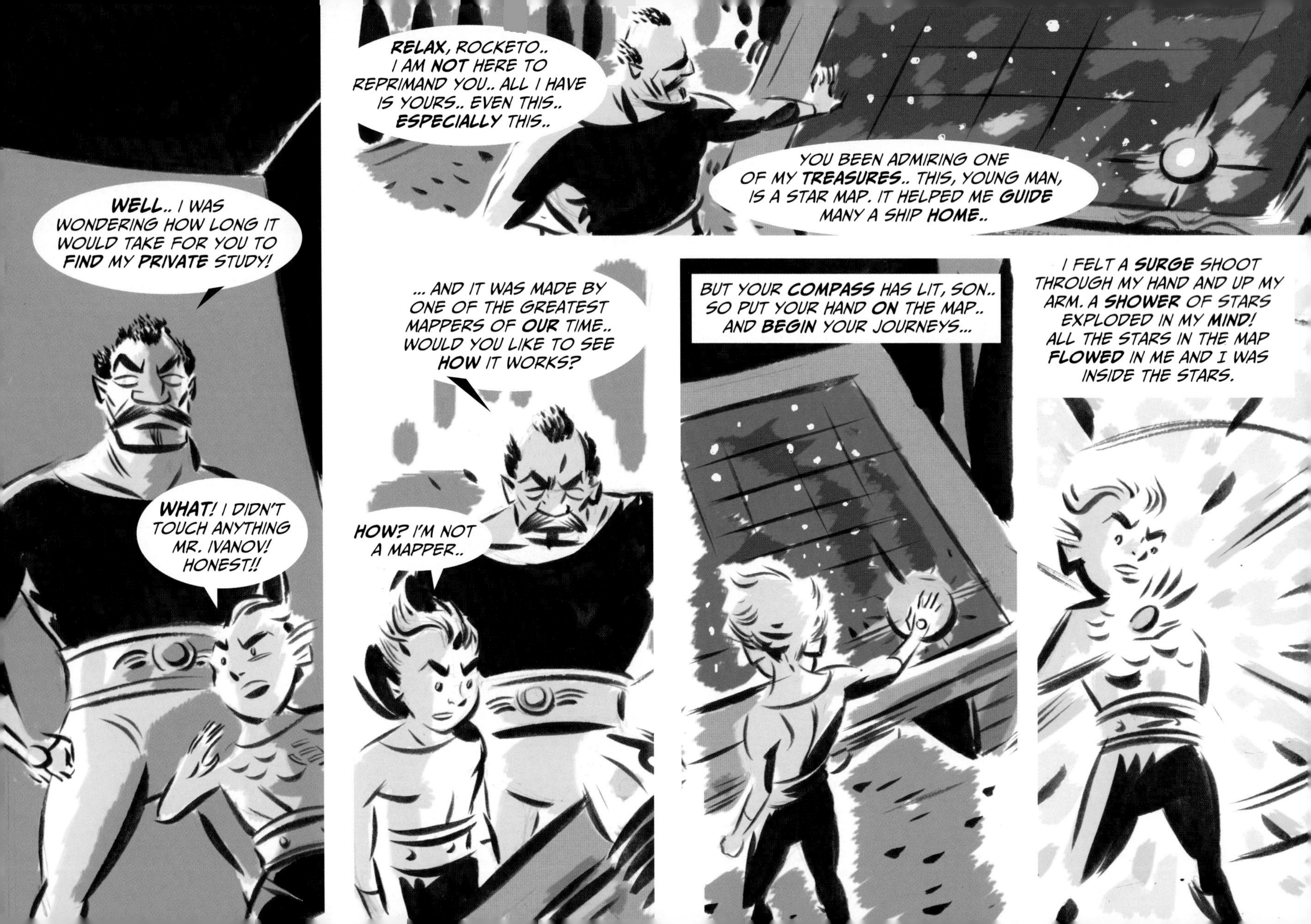
WELL.. I WAS WONDERING HOW LONG IT WOULD TAKE FOR YOU TO FIND MY PRIVATE STUDY!
WHAT! I DIDN'T TOUCH ANYTHING MR. IVANOV! HONEST!!
RELAX, ROCKETO.. I AM NOT HERE TO REPRIMAND YOU.. ALL I HAVE IS YOURS.. EVEN THIS.. ESPECIALLY THIS..
YOU BEEN ADMIRING ONE OF MY TREASURES.. THIS, YOUNG MAN, IS A STAR MAP. IT HELPED ME GUIDE MANY A SHIP HOME..
... AND IT WAS MADE BY ONE OF THE GREATEST MAPPERS OF OUR TIME.. WOULD YOU LIKE TO SEE HOW IT WORKS?
HOW? I'M NOT A MAPPER..
BUT YOUR COMPASS HAS LIT, SON.. SO PUT YOUR HAND ON THE MAP.. AND BEGIN YOUR JOURNEYS...
I FELT A SURGE SHOOT THROUGH MY HAND AND UP MY ARM. A SHOWER OF STARS EXPLODED IN MY MIND! ALL THE STARS IN THE MAP FLOWED IN ME AND I WAS INSIDE THE STARS.

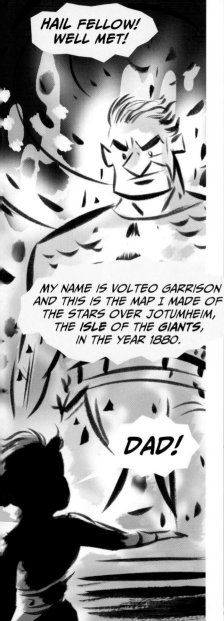

HAIL FELLOW! WELL MET!

MY NAME IS VOLTEO GARRISON AND THIS IS THE MAP I MADE OF THE STARS OVER JOTUMHEIM, THE **ISLE** OF THE **GIANTS**, IN THE YEAR 1880.

**DAD!**

DAD! IT'S **ME**! ROCKETO! CAN YOU SEE ME?

YOUR **COMPASS** TELLS ME YOU ARE OF THE GARRISON FAMILY. IT PLEASES ME THAT OUR **LINE** LIVES ON.

YOU **MUST** BE STRONG..

NOW, ROCKETO, **LEARN** THE STARS THAT WILL **GUIDE** YOUR **WAY** TO JOTUMHEIM.

THE **TAIL** OF CHARON **POINTS** INTO THE SNAKE THAT **ENCIRCLES** THE CONSTELLATION BELLOPHRON... THE GREAT HORSE.. THEN ON A CLEAR NIGHT YOU WILL SEE...

MORBITOS THE SLAIN..

GILGAMESH THE **GIANT** KING...

LAVINIA.. EMPRESS OF THE BLUE..

ABU.. THE WANDERER..

THE **FATHER** WHOM I NEVER THOUGHT TO SEE AGAIN, WHOSE **VOICE** I THOUGHT NEVER AGAIN TO HEAR, **TAUGHT** ME THE STAR WAY TO JOTUMHEIM.

VESTA.. **OUR** LIGHT.

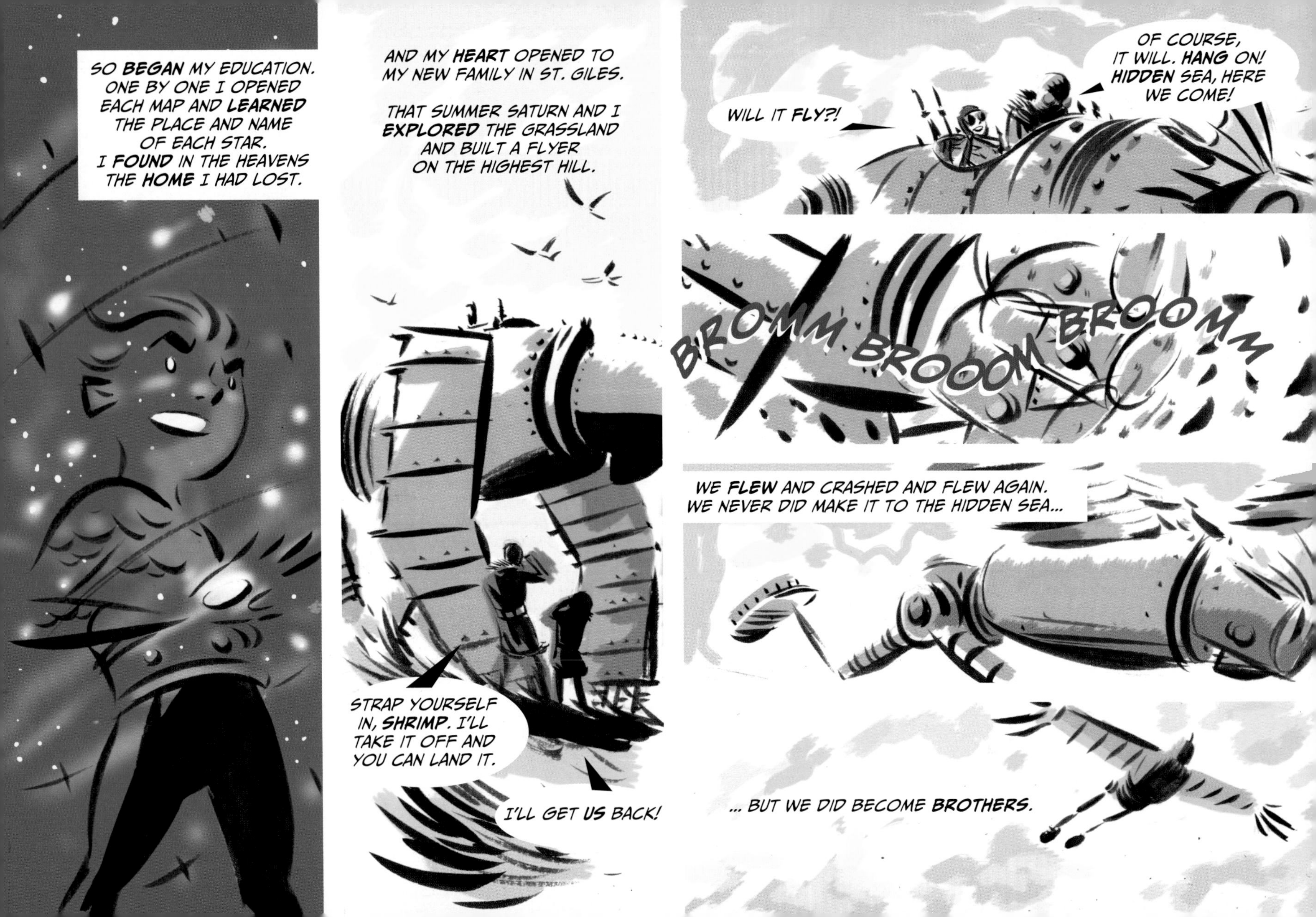
SO BEGAN MY EDUCATION. ONE BY ONE I OPENED EACH MAP AND LEARNED THE PLACE AND NAME OF EACH STAR. I FOUND IN THE HEAVENS THE HOME I HAD LOST.
AND MY HEART OPENED TO MY NEW FAMILY IN ST. GILES.
THAT SUMMER SATURN AND I EXPLORED THE GRASSLAND AND BUILT A FLYER ON THE HIGHEST HILL.
STRAP YOURSELF IN, SHRIMP. I'LL TAKE IT OFF AND YOU CAN LAND IT.
I'LL GET US BACK!
WILL IT FLY?!
OF COURSE, IT WILL. HANG ON! HIDDEN SEA, HERE WE COME!
BROMM BROOOM BROOMM
WE FLEW AND CRASHED AND FLEW AGAIN. WE NEVER DID MAKE IT TO THE HIDDEN SEA...
... BUT WE DID BECOME BROTHERS.

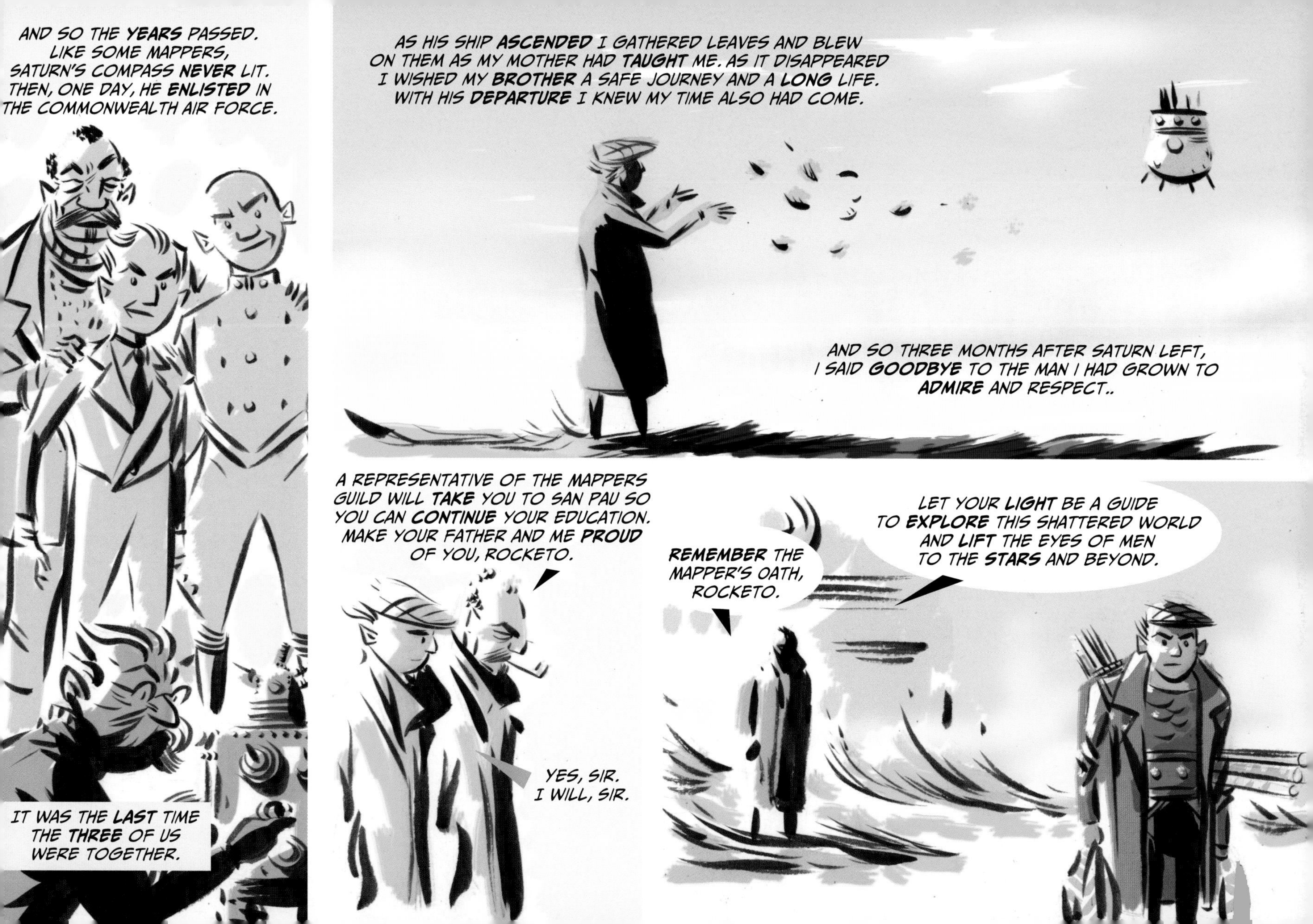
AND SO THE YEARS PASSED. LIKE SOME MAPPERS, SATURN'S COMPASS NEVER LIT. THEN, ONE DAY, HE ENLISTED IN THE COMMONWEALTH AIR FORCE.
IT WAS THE LAST TIME THE THREE OF US WERE TOGETHER.
AS HIS SHIP ASCENDED I GATHERED LEAVES AND BLEW ON THEM AS MY MOTHER HAD TAUGHT ME. AS IT DISAPPEARED I WISHED MY BROTHER A SAFE JOURNEY AND A LONG LIFE. WITH HIS DEPARTURE I KNEW MY TIME ALSO HAD COME.
AND SO THREE MONTHS AFTER SATURN LEFT, I SAID GOODBYE TO THE MAN I HAD GROWN TO ADMIRE AND RESPECT..
A REPRESENTATIVE OF THE MAPPERS GUILD WILL TAKE YOU TO SAN PAU SO YOU CAN CONTINUE YOUR EDUCATION. MAKE YOUR FATHER AND ME PROUD OF YOU, ROCKETO.
YES, SIR. I WILL, SIR.
REMEMBER THE MAPPER'S OATH, ROCKETO.
LET YOUR LIGHT BE A GUIDE TO EXPLORE THIS SHATTERED WORLD AND LIFT THE EYES OF MEN TO THE STARS AND BEYOND.

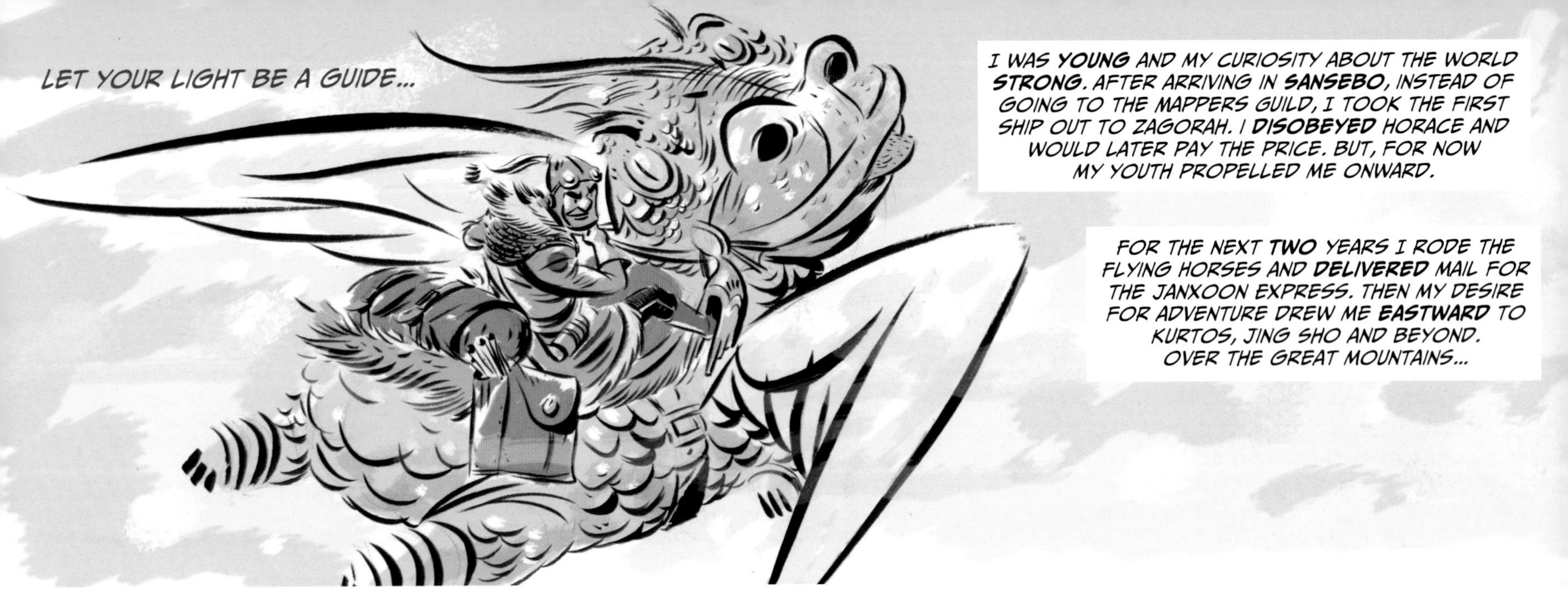
LET YOUR LIGHT BE A GUIDE...
I WAS YOUNG AND MY CURIOSITY ABOUT THE WORLD STRONG. AFTER ARRIVING IN SANSEBO, INSTEAD OF GOING TO THE MAPPERS GUILD, I TOOK THE FIRST SHIP OUT TO ZAGORAH. I DISOBEYED HORACE AND WOULD LATER PAY THE PRICE. BUT, FOR NOW MY YOUTH PROPELLED ME ONWARD.
FOR THE NEXT TWO YEARS I RODE THE FLYING HORSES AND DELIVERED MAIL FOR THE JANXOON EXPRESS. THEN MY DESIRE FOR ADVENTURE DREW ME EASTWARD TO KURTOS, JING SHO AND BEYOND. OVER THE GREAT MOUNTAINS...

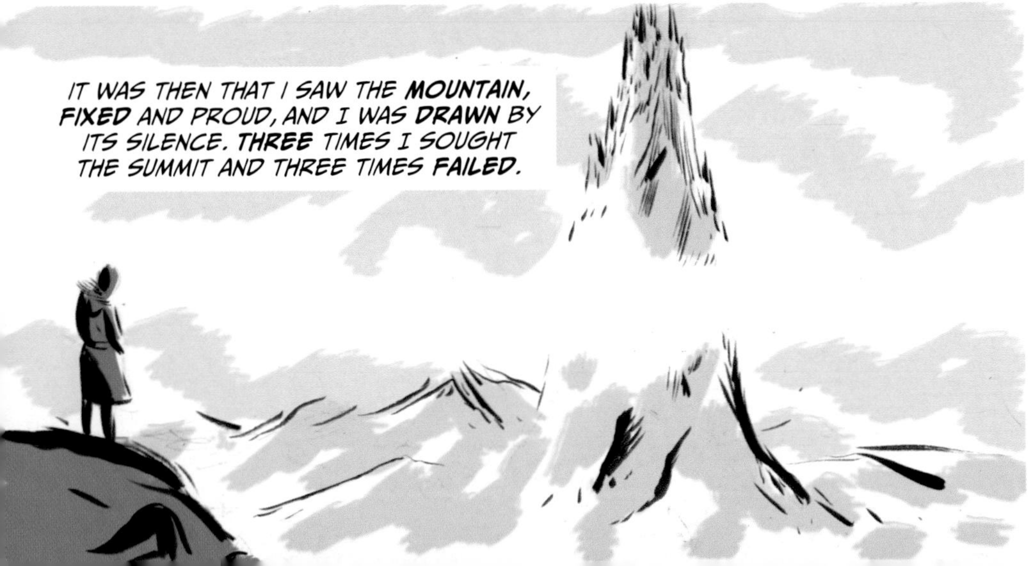
IT WAS THEN THAT I SAW THE MOUNTAIN, FIXED AND PROUD, AND I WAS DRAWN BY ITS SILENCE. THREE TIMES I SOUGHT THE SUMMIT AND THREE TIMES FAILED.

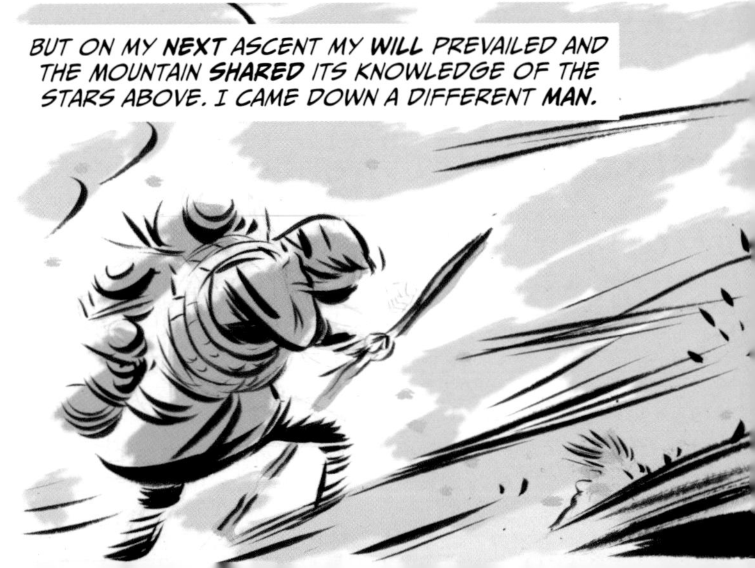
BUT ON MY NEXT ASCENT MY WILL PREVAILED AND THE MOUNTAIN SHARED ITS KNOWLEDGE OF THE STARS ABOVE. I CAME DOWN A DIFFERENT MAN.

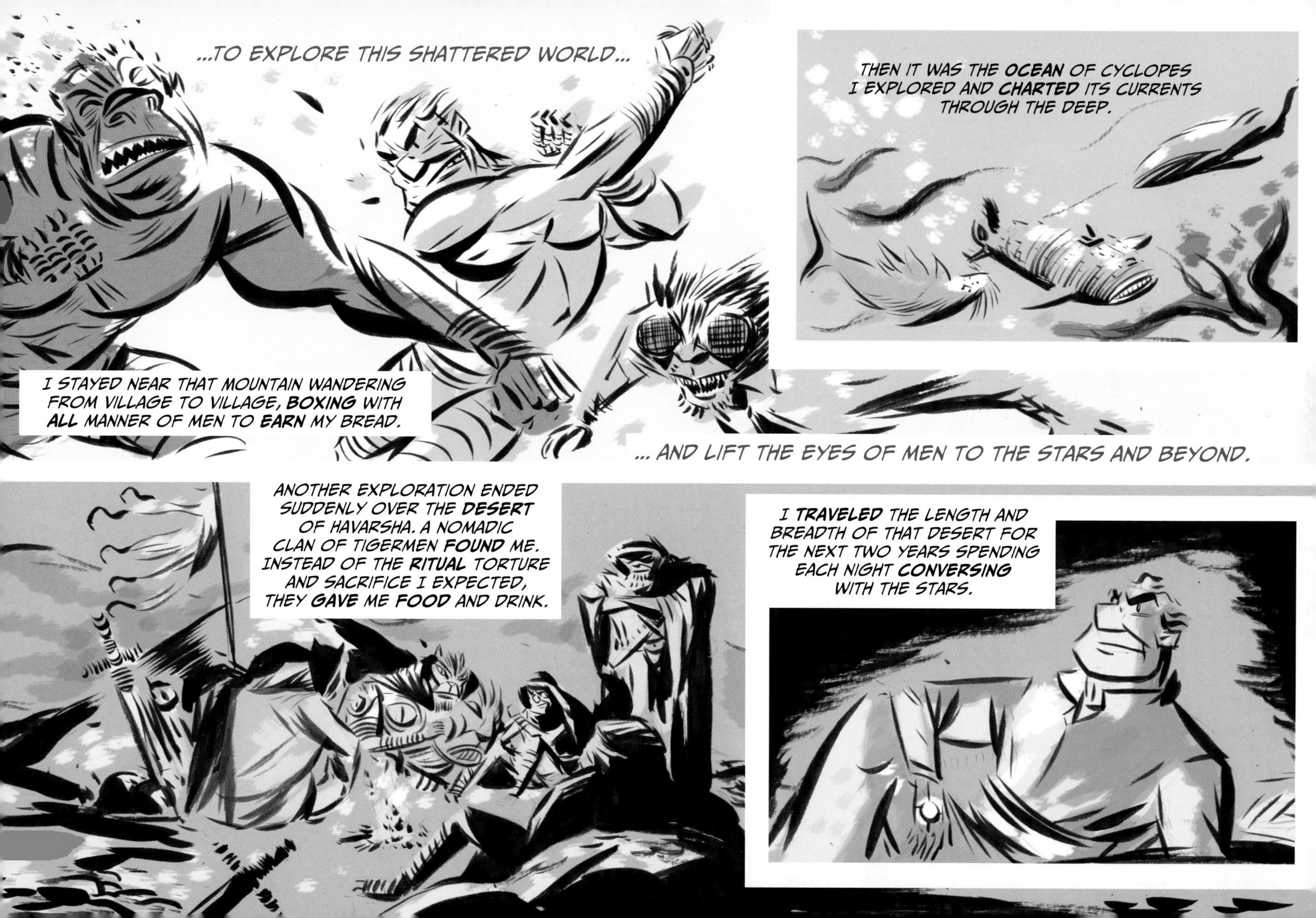
...TO EXPLORE THIS SHATTERED WORLD...
I STAYED NEAR THAT MOUNTAIN WANDERING FROM VILLAGE TO VILLAGE, BOXING WITH ALL MANNER OF MEN TO EARN MY BREAD.
THEN IT WAS THE OCEAN OF CYCLOPES I EXPLORED AND CHARTED ITS CURRENTS THROUGH THE DEEP.
... AND LIFT THE EYES OF MEN TO THE STARS AND BEYOND.
ANOTHER EXPLORATION ENDED SUDDENLY OVER THE DESERT OF HAVARSHA. A NOMADIC CLAN OF TIGERMEN FOUND ME. INSTEAD OF THE RITUAL TORTURE AND SACRIFICE I EXPECTED, THEY GAVE ME FOOD AND DRINK.
I TRAVELED THE LENGTH AND BREADTH OF THAT DESERT FOR THE NEXT TWO YEARS SPENDING EACH NIGHT CONVERSING WITH THE STARS.

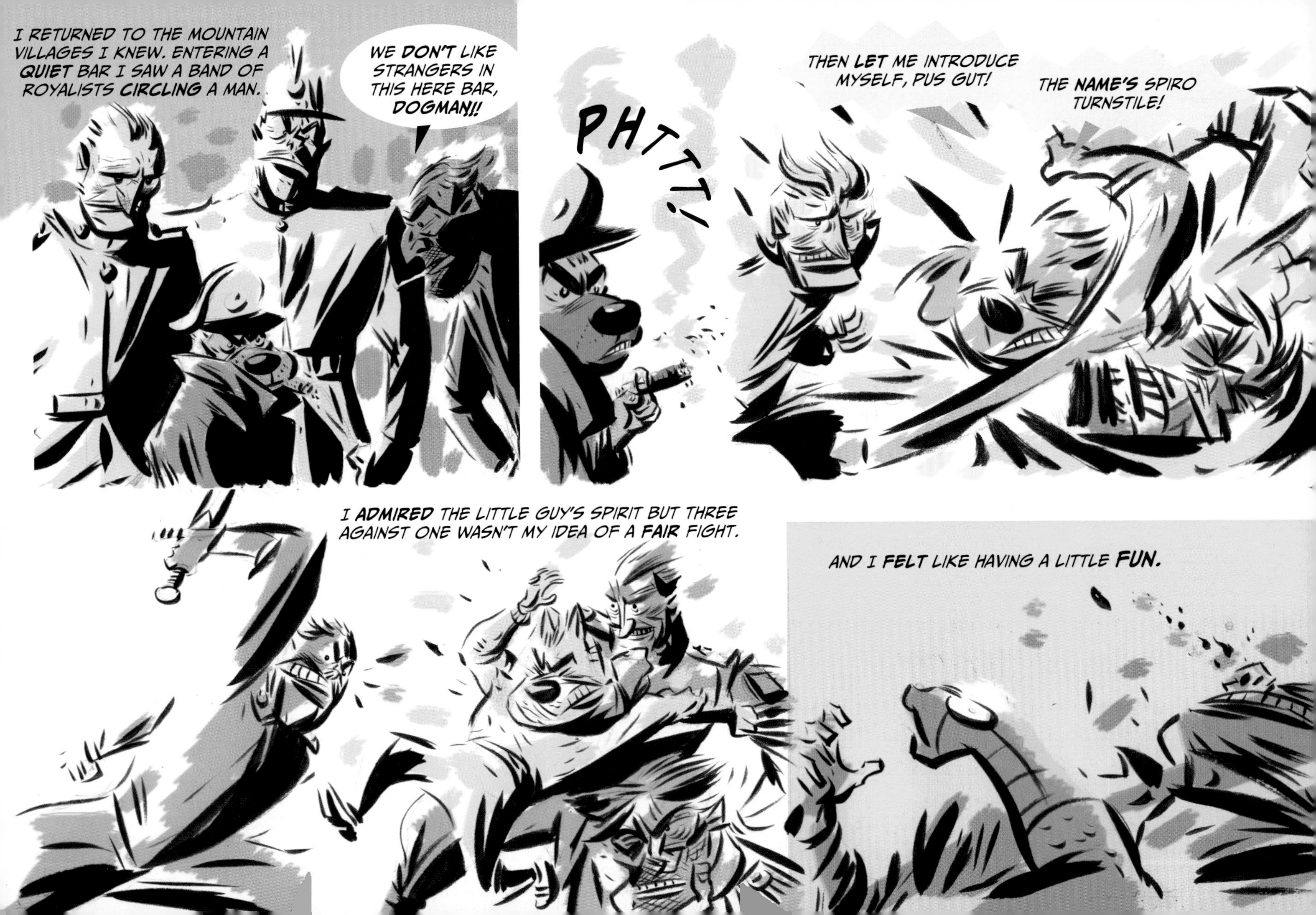
I RETURNED TO THE MOUNTAIN VILLAGES I KNEW. ENTERING A QUIET BAR I SAW A BAND OF ROYALISTS CIRCLING A MAN.
WE DON'T LIKE STRANGERS IN THIS HERE BAR, DOGMAN!!
PHTTT!
THEN LET ME INTRODUCE MYSELF, PUS GUT!
THE NAME'S SPIRO TURNSTILE!
I ADMIRED THE LITTLE GUY'S SPIRIT BUT THREE AGAINST ONE WASN'T MY IDEA OF A FAIR FIGHT.
AND I FELT LIKE HAVING A LITTLE FUN.

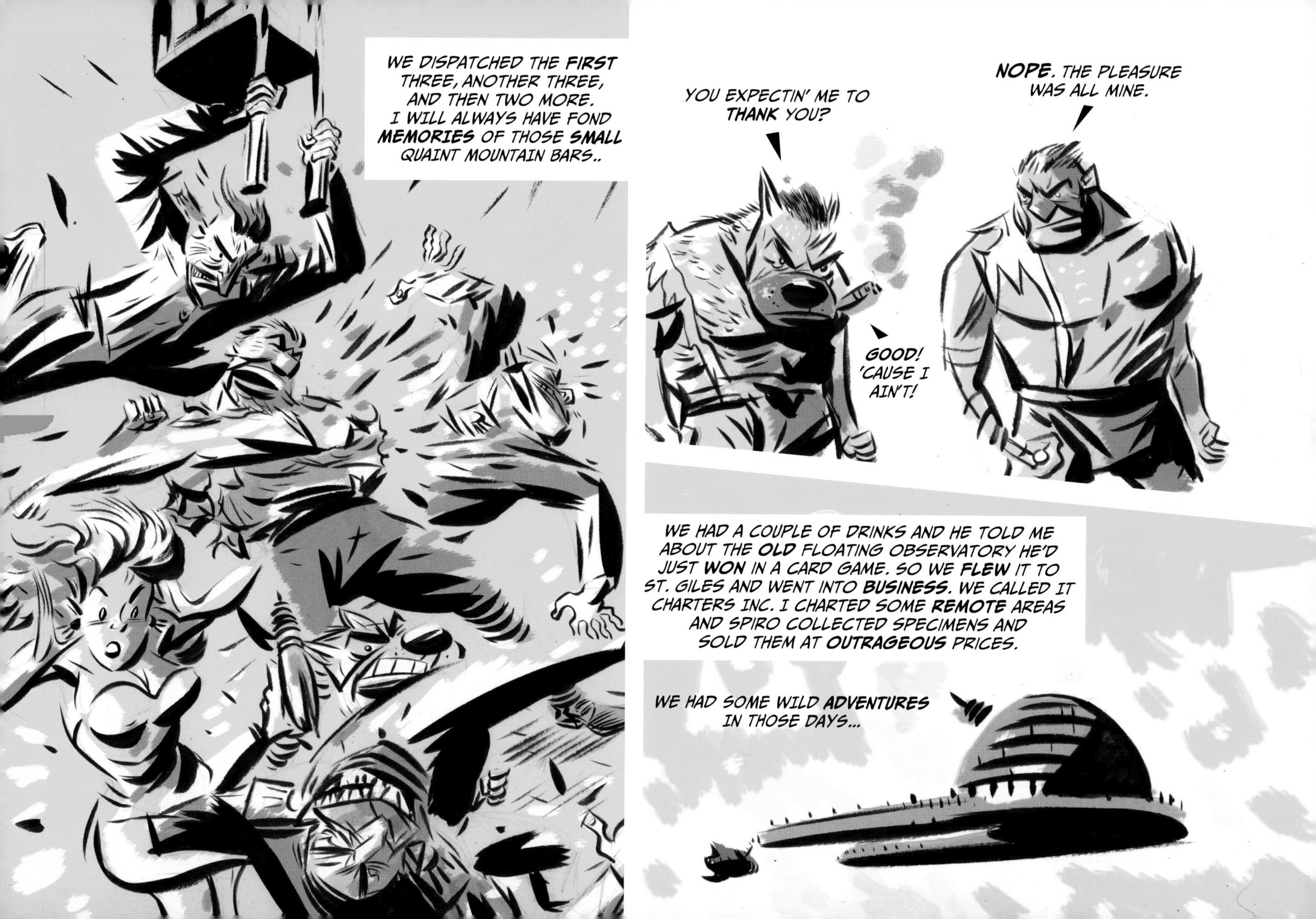
WE DISPATCHED THE FIRST THREE, ANOTHER THREE, AND THEN TWO MORE. I WILL ALWAYS HAVE FOND MEMORIES OF THOSE SMALL QUAINT MOUNTAIN BARS..
YOU EXPECTIN' ME TO THANK YOU?
NOPE. THE PLEASURE WAS ALL MINE.
GOOD! 'CAUSE I AIN'T!
WE HAD A COUPLE OF DRINKS AND HE TOLD ME ABOUT THE OLD FLOATING OBSERVATORY HE'D JUST WON IN A CARD GAME. SO WE FLEW IT TO ST. GILES AND WENT INTO BUSINESS. WE CALLED IT CHARTERS INC. I CHARTED SOME REMOTE AREAS AND SPIRO COLLECTED SPECIMENS AND SOLD THEM AT OUTRAGEOUS PRICES.
WE HAD SOME WILD ADVENTURES IN THOSE DAYS...

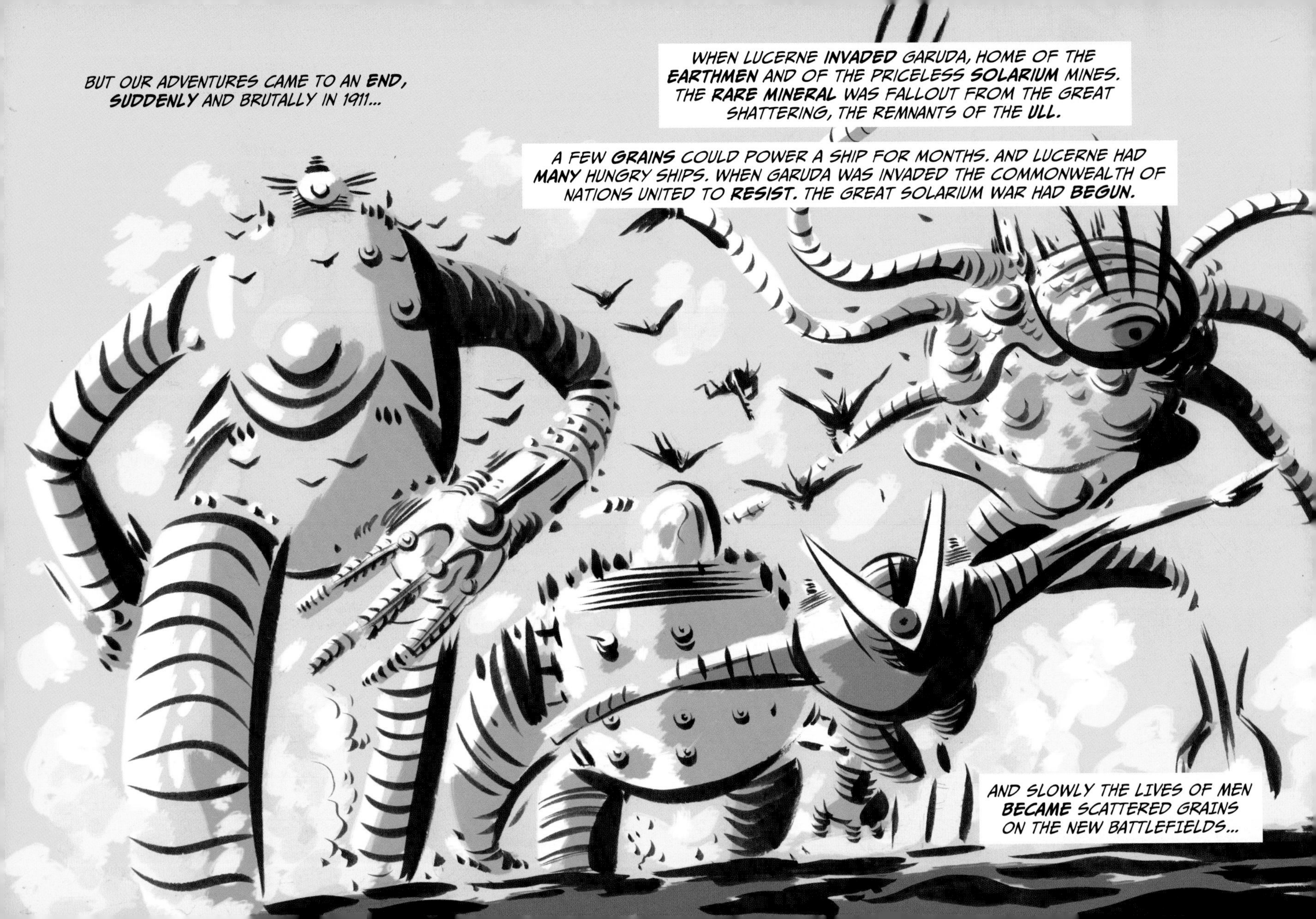
BUT OUR ADVENTURES CAME TO AN END, SUDDENLY AND BRUTALLY IN 1911...
WHEN LUCERNE INVADED GARUDA, HOME OF THE EARTHMEN AND OF THE PRICELESS SOLARIUM MINES. THE RARE MINERAL WAS FALLOUT FROM THE GREAT SHATTERING, THE REMNANTS OF THE ULL.
A FEW GRAINS COULD POWER A SHIP FOR MONTHS. AND LUCERNE HAD MANY HUNGRY SHIPS. WHEN GARUDA WAS INVADED THE COMMONWEALTH OF NATIONS UNITED TO RESIST. THE GREAT SOLARIUM WAR HAD BEGUN.
AND SLOWLY THE LIVES OF MEN BECAME SCATTERED GRAINS ON THE NEW BATTLEFIELDS...

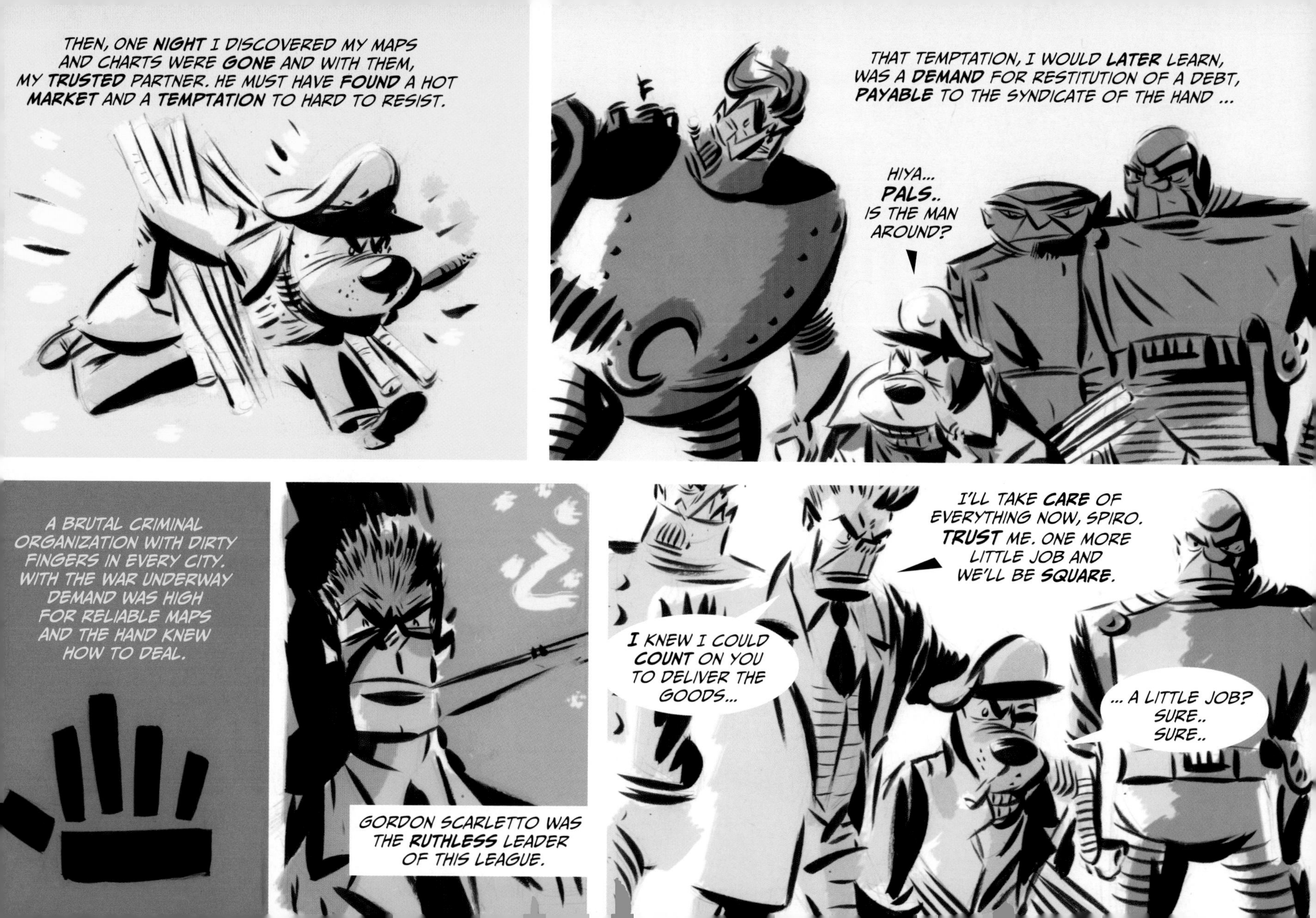
THEN, ONE NIGHT I DISCOVERED MY MAPS AND CHARTS WERE GONE AND WITH THEM, MY TRUSTED PARTNER. HE MUST HAVE FOUND A HOT MARKET AND A TEMPTATION TO HARD TO RESIST.
THAT TEMPTATION, I WOULD LATER LEARN, WAS A DEMAND FOR RESTITUTION OF A DEBT, PAYABLE TO THE SYNDICATE OF THE HAND ...
HIYA... PALS.. IS THE MAN AROUND?
A BRUTAL CRIMINAL ORGANIZATION WITH DIRTY FINGERS IN EVERY CITY. WITH THE WAR UNDERWAY DEMAND WAS HIGH FOR RELIABLE MAPS AND THE HAND KNEW HOW TO DEAL.
GORDON SCARLETTO WAS THE RUTHLESS LEADER OF THIS LEAGUE.
I'LL TAKE CARE OF EVERYTHING NOW, SPIRO. TRUST ME. ONE MORE LITTLE JOB AND WE'LL BE SQUARE.
I KNEW I COULD COUNT ON YOU TO DELIVER THE GOODS...
... A LITTLE JOB? SURE.. SURE..

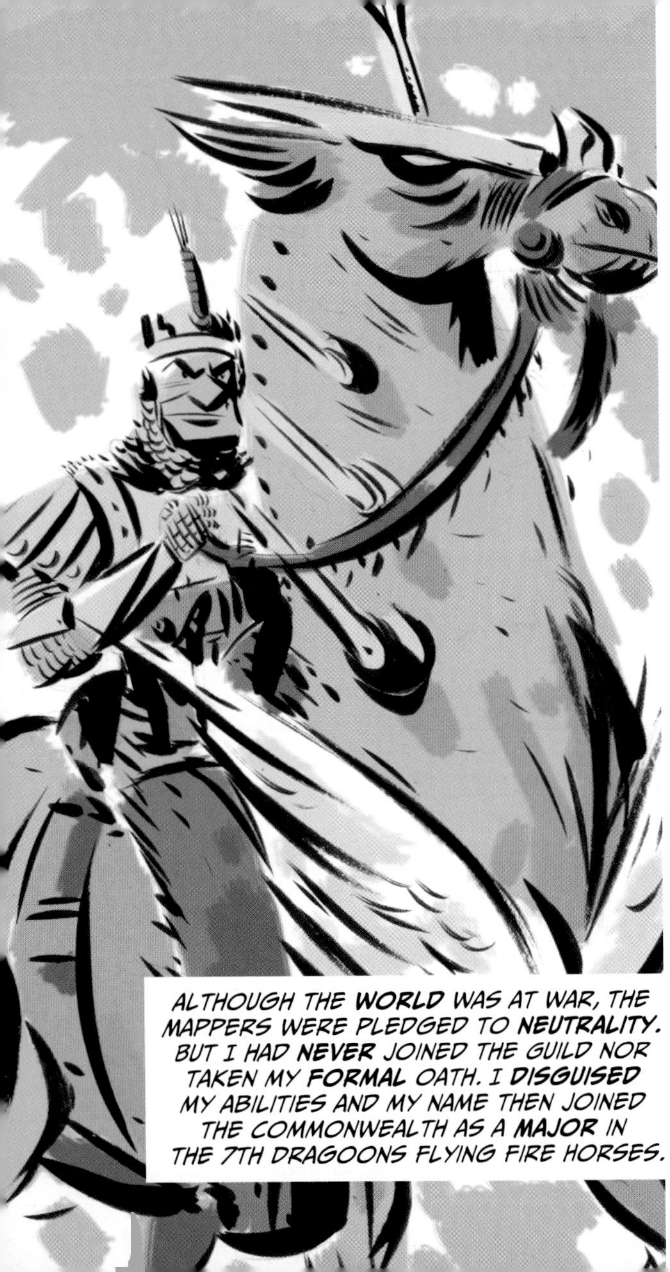
ALTHOUGH THE **WORLD** WAS AT WAR, THE MAPPERS WERE PLEDGED TO **NEUTRALITY.** BUT I HAD **NEVER** JOINED THE GUILD NOR TAKEN MY **FORMAL** OATH. I **DISGUISED** MY ABILITIES AND MY NAME THEN JOINED THE COMMONWEALTH AS A **MAJOR** IN THE 7TH DRAGOONS FLYING FIRE HORSES.

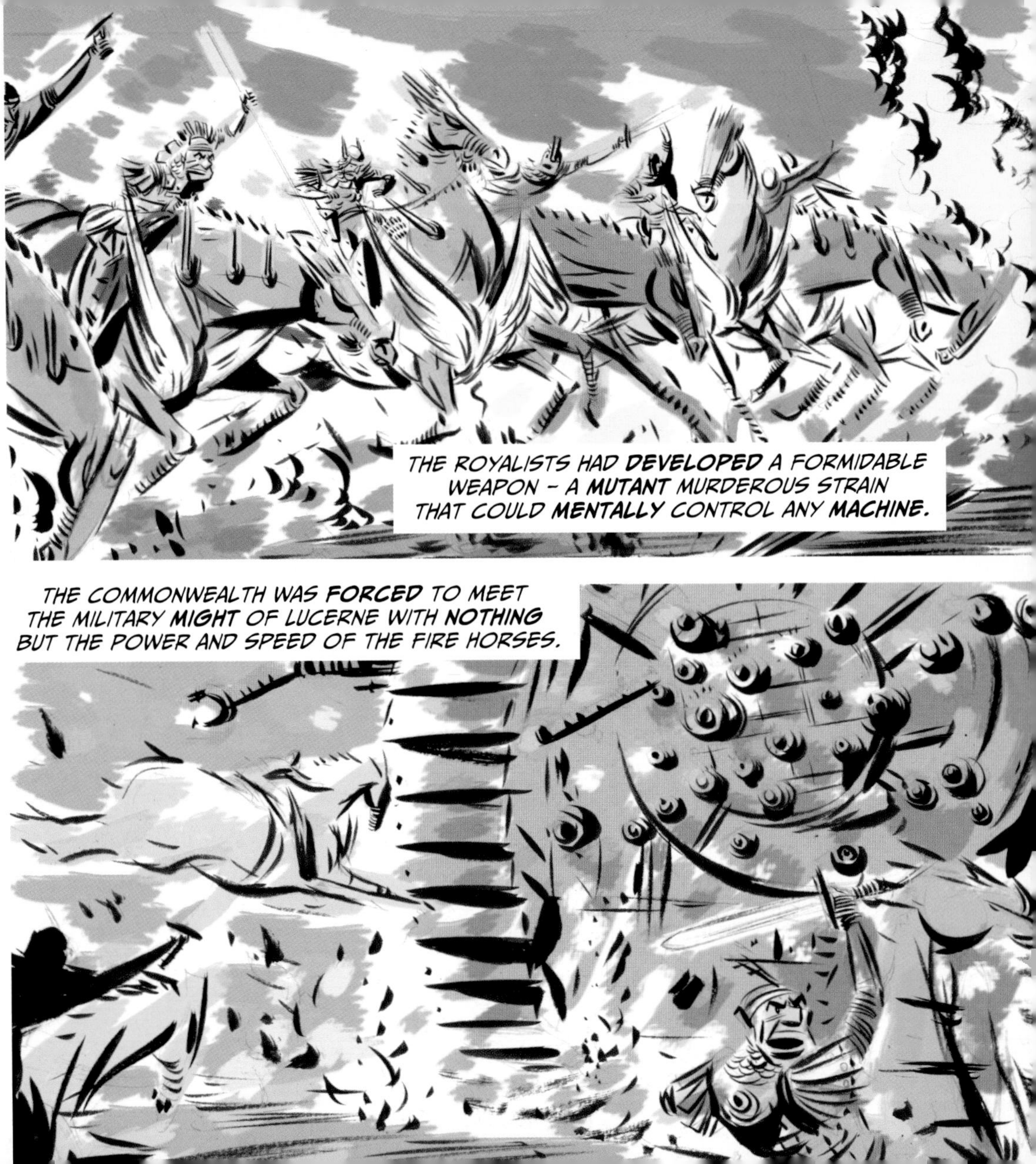
THE ROYALISTS HAD **DEVELOPED** A FORMIDABLE WEAPON – A **MUTANT** MURDEROUS STRAIN THAT COULD **MENTALLY** CONTROL ANY **MACHINE.**
THE COMMONWEALTH WAS **FORCED** TO MEET THE MILITARY **MIGHT** OF LUCERNE WITH **NOTHING** BUT THE POWER AND SPEED OF THE FIRE HORSES.

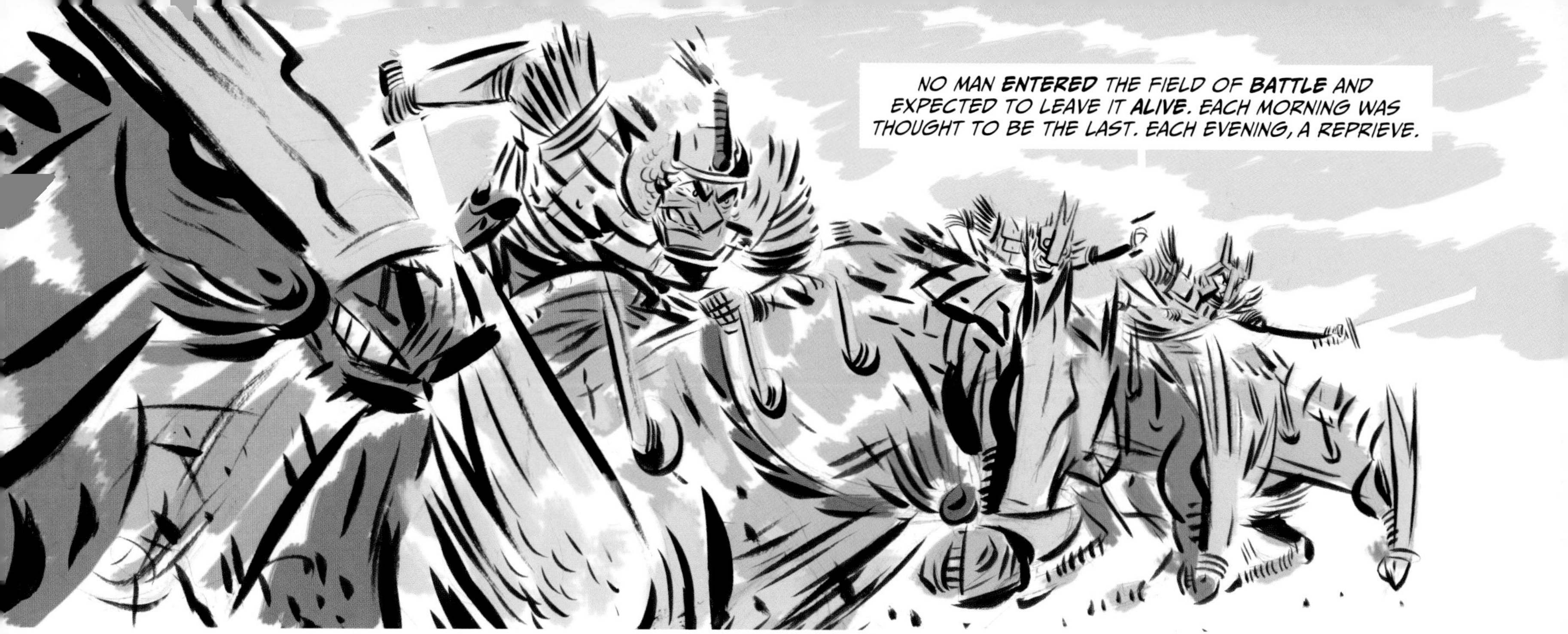
NO MAN ENTERED THE FIELD OF BATTLE AND EXPECTED TO LEAVE IT ALIVE. EACH MORNING WAS THOUGHT TO BE THE LAST. EACH EVENING, A REPRIEVE.

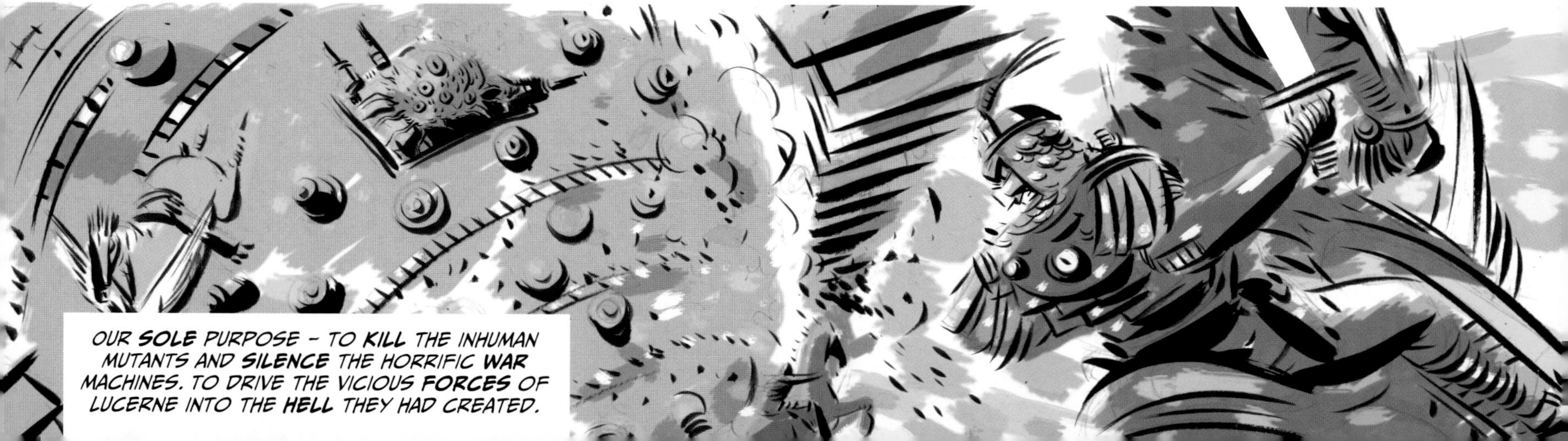
OUR SOLE PURPOSE – TO KILL THE INHUMAN MUTANTS AND SILENCE THE HORRIFIC WAR MACHINES. TO DRIVE THE VICIOUS FORCES OF LUCERNE INTO THE HELL THEY HAD CREATED.

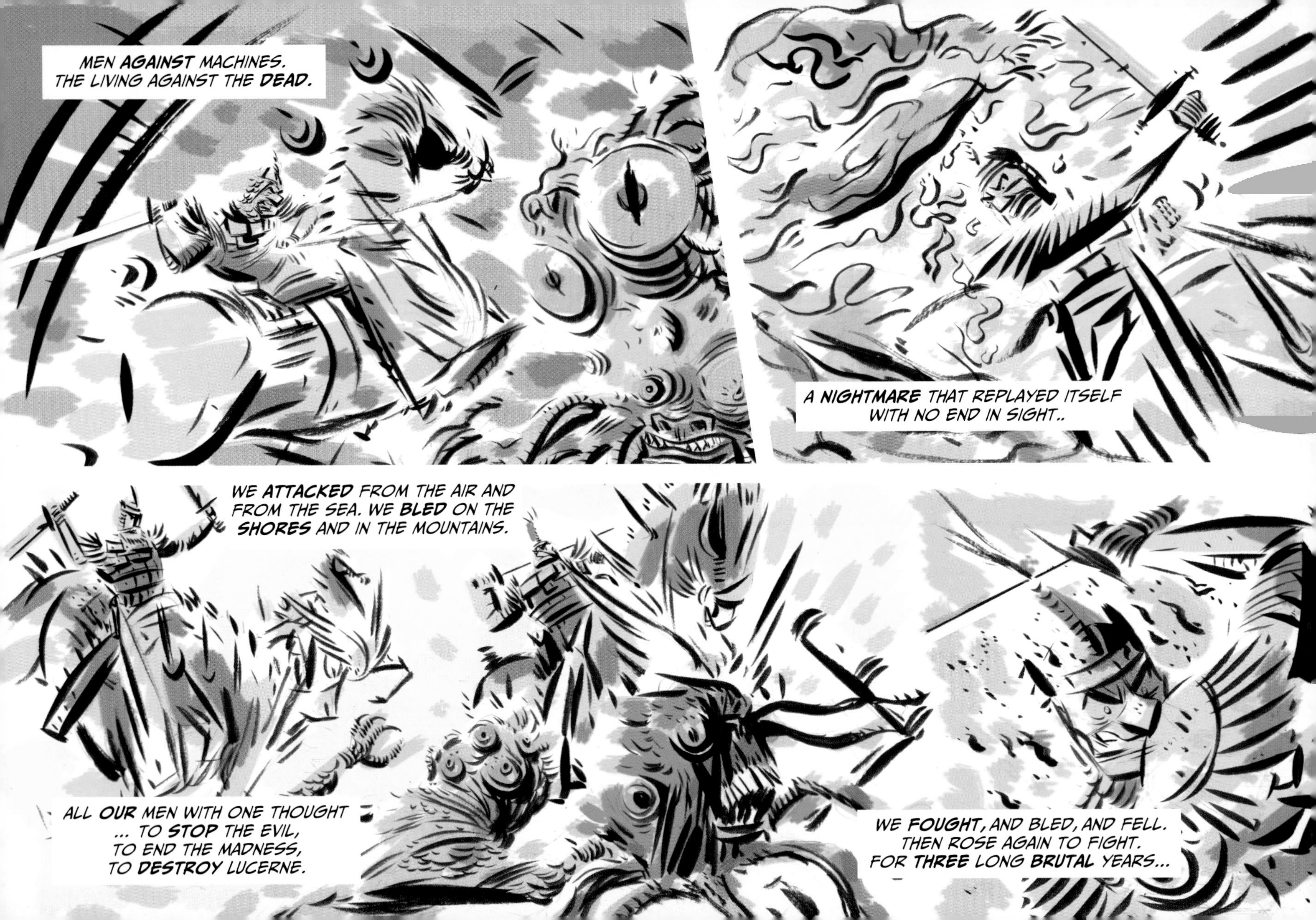
MEN AGAINST MACHINES.
THE LIVING AGAINST THE DEAD.
A NIGHTMARE THAT REPLAYED ITSELF WITH NO END IN SIGHT..
WE ATTACKED FROM THE AIR AND FROM THE SEA. WE BLED ON THE SHORES AND IN THE MOUNTAINS.
ALL OUR MEN WITH ONE THOUGHT ... TO STOP THE EVIL, TO END THE MADNESS, TO DESTROY LUCERNE.
WE FOUGHT, AND BLED, AND FELL. THEN ROSE AGAIN TO FIGHT. FOR THREE LONG BRUTAL YEARS...

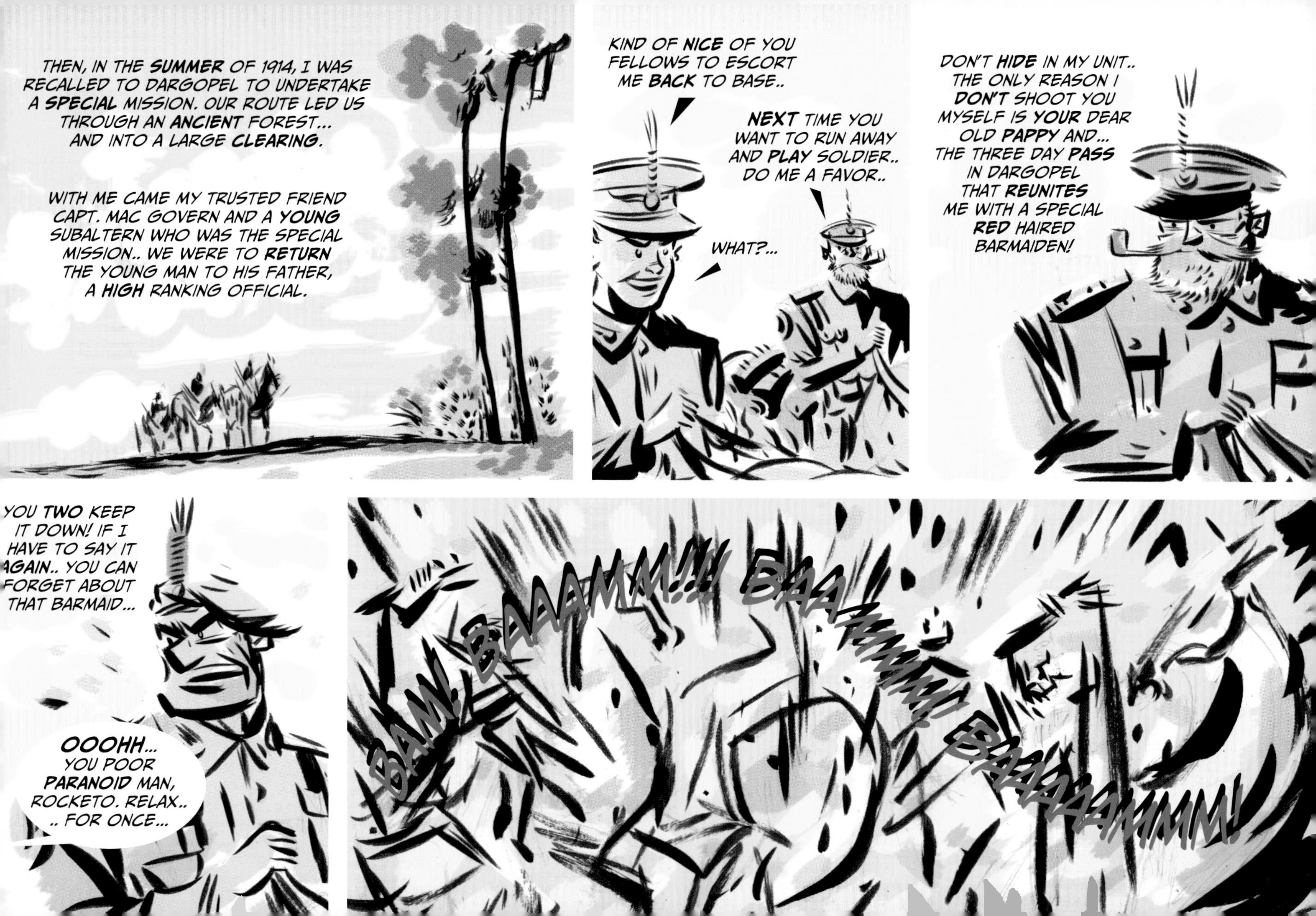
THEN, IN THE SUMMER OF 1914, I WAS RECALLED TO DARGOPEL TO UNDERTAKE A SPECIAL MISSION. OUR ROUTE LED US THROUGH AN ANCIENT FOREST... AND INTO A LARGE CLEARING.
WITH ME CAME MY TRUSTED FRIEND CAPT. MAC GOVERN AND A YOUNG SUBALTERN WHO WAS THE SPECIAL MISSION.. WE WERE TO RETURN THE YOUNG MAN TO HIS FATHER, A HIGH RANKING OFFICIAL.
KIND OF NICE OF YOU FELLOWS TO ESCORT ME BACK TO BASE..
NEXT TIME YOU WANT TO RUN AWAY AND PLAY SOLDIER.. DO ME A FAVOR..
WHAT?...
DON'T HIDE IN MY UNIT.. THE ONLY REASON I DON'T SHOOT YOU MYSELF IS YOUR DEAR OLD PAPPY AND... THE THREE DAY PASS IN DARGOPEL THAT REUNITES ME WITH A SPECIAL RED HAIRED BARMAIDEN!
YOU TWO KEEP IT DOWN! IF I HAVE TO SAY IT AGAIN.. YOU CAN FORGET ABOUT THAT BARMAID...
OOOHH... YOU POOR PARANOID MAN, ROCKETO. RELAX.. .. FOR ONCE...
BAM! BAAAAMM!!! BAAAMMMMM! BAAAAAAAMMMM!

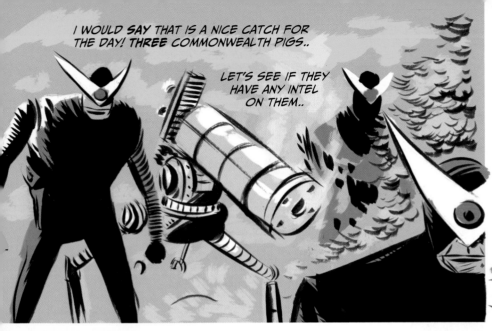

I WOULD **SAY** THAT IS A NICE CATCH FOR THE DAY! **THREE** COMMONWEALTH PIGS..

LET'S SEE IF THEY HAVE ANY INTEL ON THEM..

**HEEEY!! THIS** ONE STILL BREATHING. **FINISH** HIM OFF.

CLICK.. CLICK CLICK..

WHAT DO YOU KNOW.. GUN'S JAMMED..

NOT HIS **LUCKY** DAY TODAY...

HAAH!! HA HAAH HAA!!

I'LL HAVE TO FINISH HIM OFF THE **OLD** FASHION WAY THEN!

WHAT A **PLEASURE.**

I WANT YOU GUYS TO SEE THIS NEW BLADE IN ACTION!

**DON'T** TOUCH THAT ONE!

YOU **IDIOTS** MAY HAVE DONE ENOUGH **DAMAGE** ALREADY.. BRING HIM TO ME

**THIS** IS AN UNEXPECTED PRIZE.. VERY UNEXPECTED.. WE ARE **TAKING** HIM BACK WITH US.. FINISH THE **OTHERS.** LEAVE NOT A **SINGLE**... TRACE.. BEHIND..

AND **REMEMBER** THIS DAY FOR IT **MARKS** THE BEGINNING OF THE END. THE COMMONWEALTH HAS JUST **LOST** THE WAR..

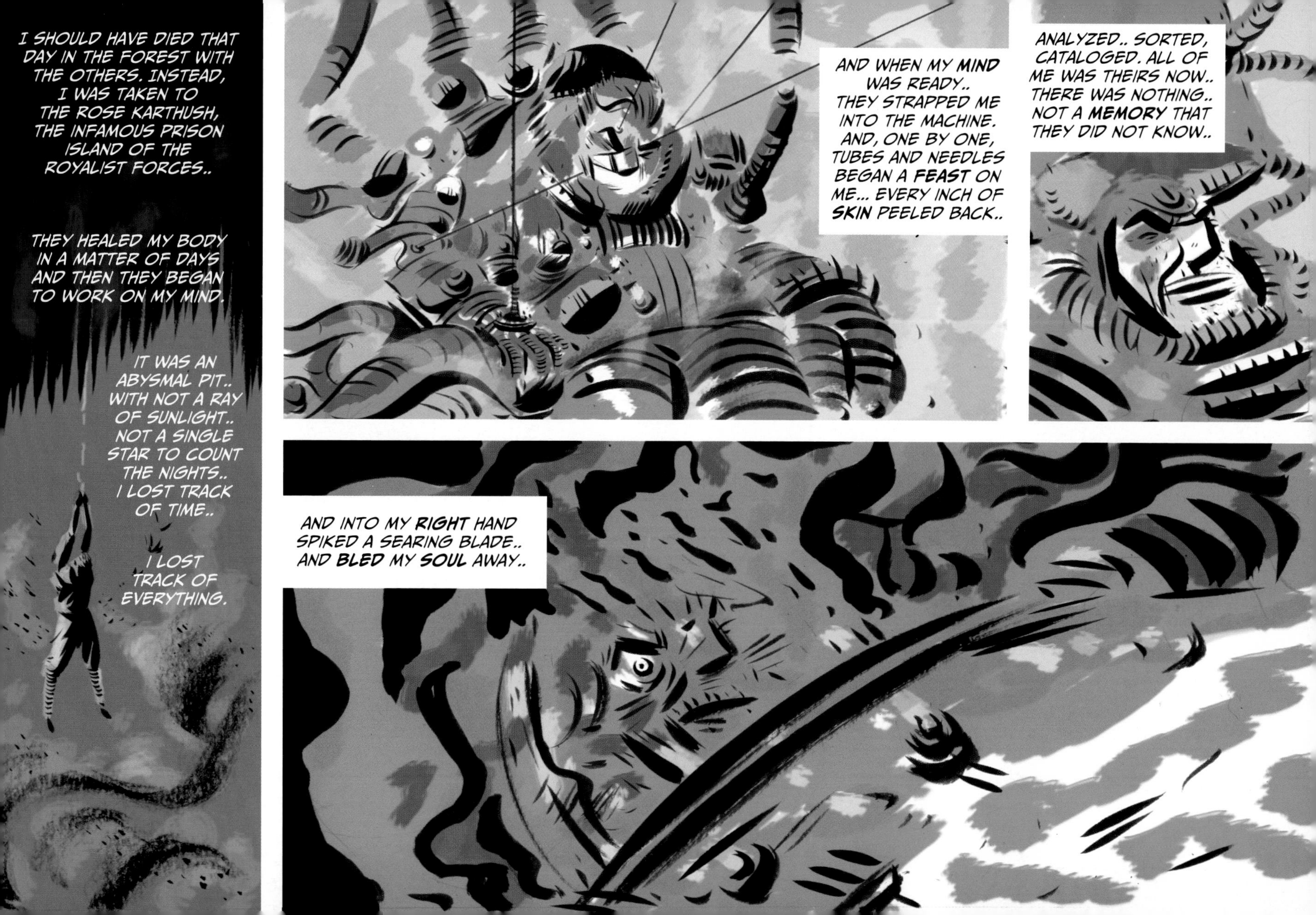
I SHOULD HAVE DIED THAT DAY IN THE FOREST WITH THE OTHERS. INSTEAD, I WAS TAKEN TO THE ROSE KARTHUSH, THE INFAMOUS PRISON ISLAND OF THE ROYALIST FORCES..
THEY HEALED MY BODY IN A MATTER OF DAYS AND THEN THEY BEGAN TO WORK ON MY MIND.
IT WAS AN ABYSMAL PIT.. WITH NOT A RAY OF SUNLIGHT.. NOT A SINGLE STAR TO COUNT THE NIGHTS.. I LOST TRACK OF TIME..
I LOST TRACK OF EVERYTHING.
AND WHEN MY MIND WAS READY.. THEY STRAPPED ME INTO THE MACHINE. AND, ONE BY ONE, TUBES AND NEEDLES BEGAN A FEAST ON ME... EVERY INCH OF SKIN PEELED BACK..
ANALYZED.. SORTED, CATALOGED. ALL OF ME WAS THEIRS NOW.. THERE WAS NOTHING.. NOT A MEMORY THAT THEY DID NOT KNOW..
AND INTO MY RIGHT HAND SPIKED A SEARING BLADE.. AND BLED MY SOUL AWAY..

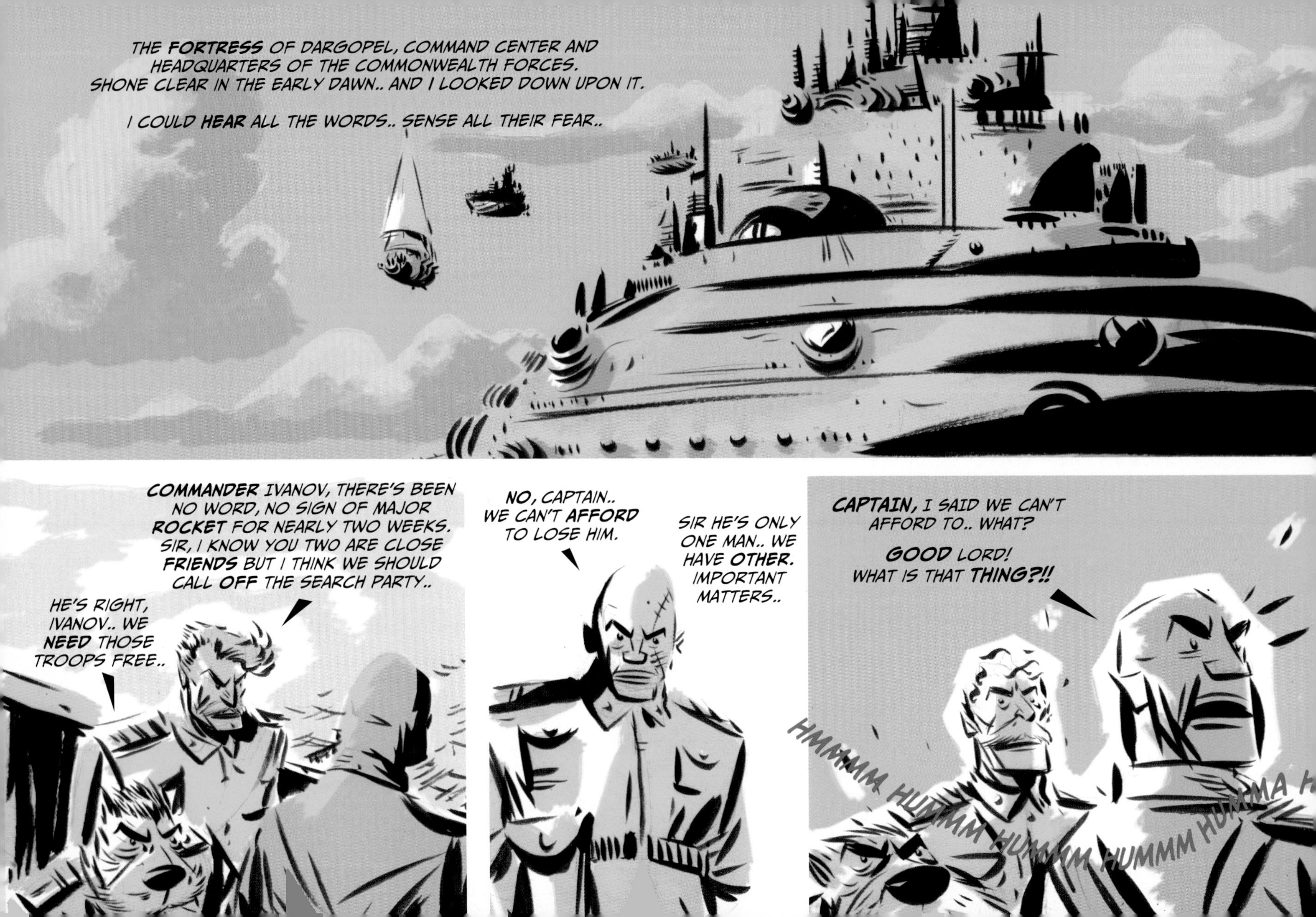
THE **FORTRESS** OF DARGOPEL, COMMAND CENTER AND HEADQUARTERS OF THE COMMONWEALTH FORCES. SHONE CLEAR IN THE EARLY DAWN.. AND I LOOKED DOWN UPON IT.
I COULD **HEAR** ALL THE WORDS.. SENSE ALL THEIR FEAR..
**COMMANDER** IVANOV, THERE'S BEEN NO WORD, NO SIGN OF MAJOR **ROCKET** FOR NEARLY TWO WEEKS. SIR, I KNOW YOU TWO ARE CLOSE **FRIENDS** BUT I THINK WE SHOULD CALL **OFF** THE SEARCH PARTY..
HE'S RIGHT, IVANOV.. WE **NEED** THOSE TROOPS FREE..
**NO,** CAPTAIN.. WE CAN'T **AFFORD** TO LOSE HIM.
SIR HE'S ONLY ONE MAN.. WE HAVE **OTHER.** IMPORTANT MATTERS..
**CAPTAIN,** I SAID WE CAN'T AFFORD TO.. WHAT?
**GOOD** LORD! WHAT IS THAT **THING?!!**
HUMMM HUMMM HUMMM HUMMA

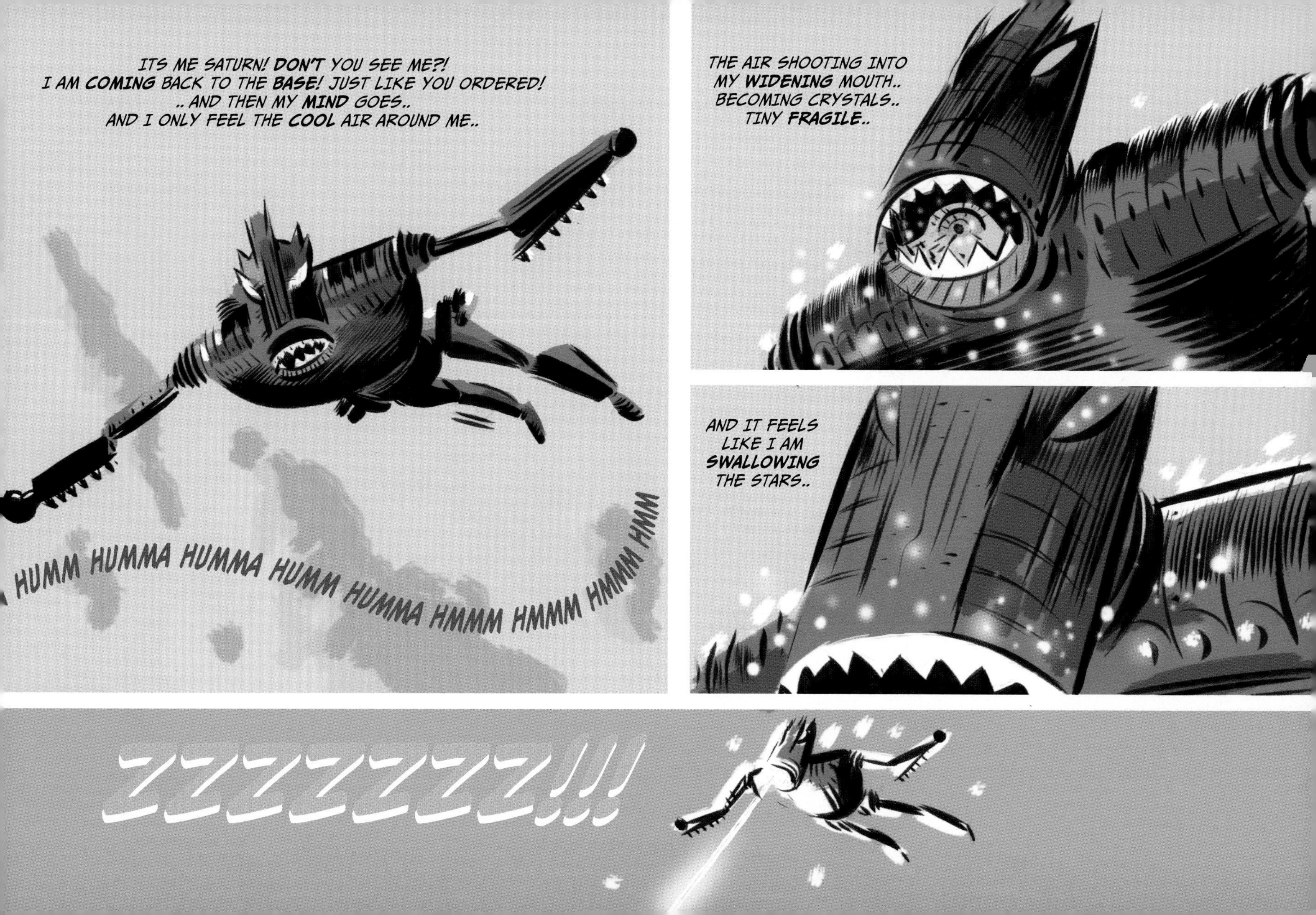
ITS ME SATURN! DON'T YOU SEE ME?! I AM COMING BACK TO THE BASE! JUST LIKE YOU ORDERED! .. AND THEN MY MIND GOES.. AND I ONLY FEEL THE COOL AIR AROUND ME..
HUMM HUMMA HUMMA HUMM HUMMA HMMM HMMM HMMM HMM
THE AIR SHOOTING INTO MY WIDENING MOUTH.. BECOMING CRYSTALS.. TINY FRAGILE..
AND IT FEELS LIKE I AM SWALLOWING THE STARS..
ZZZZZZZZ!!!

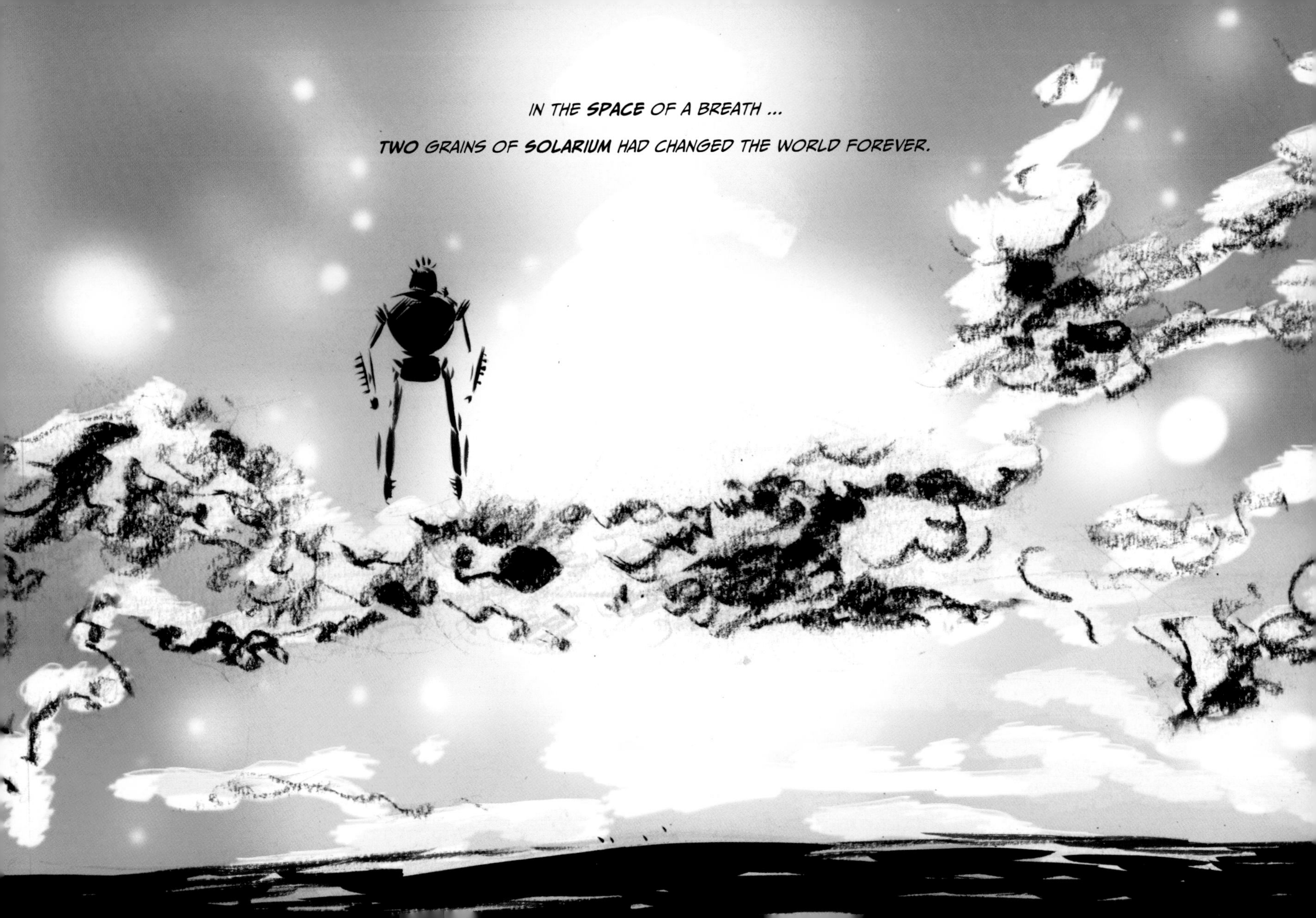
IN THE SPACE OF A BREATH ...
TWO GRAINS OF SOLARIUM HAD CHANGED THE WORLD FOREVER.

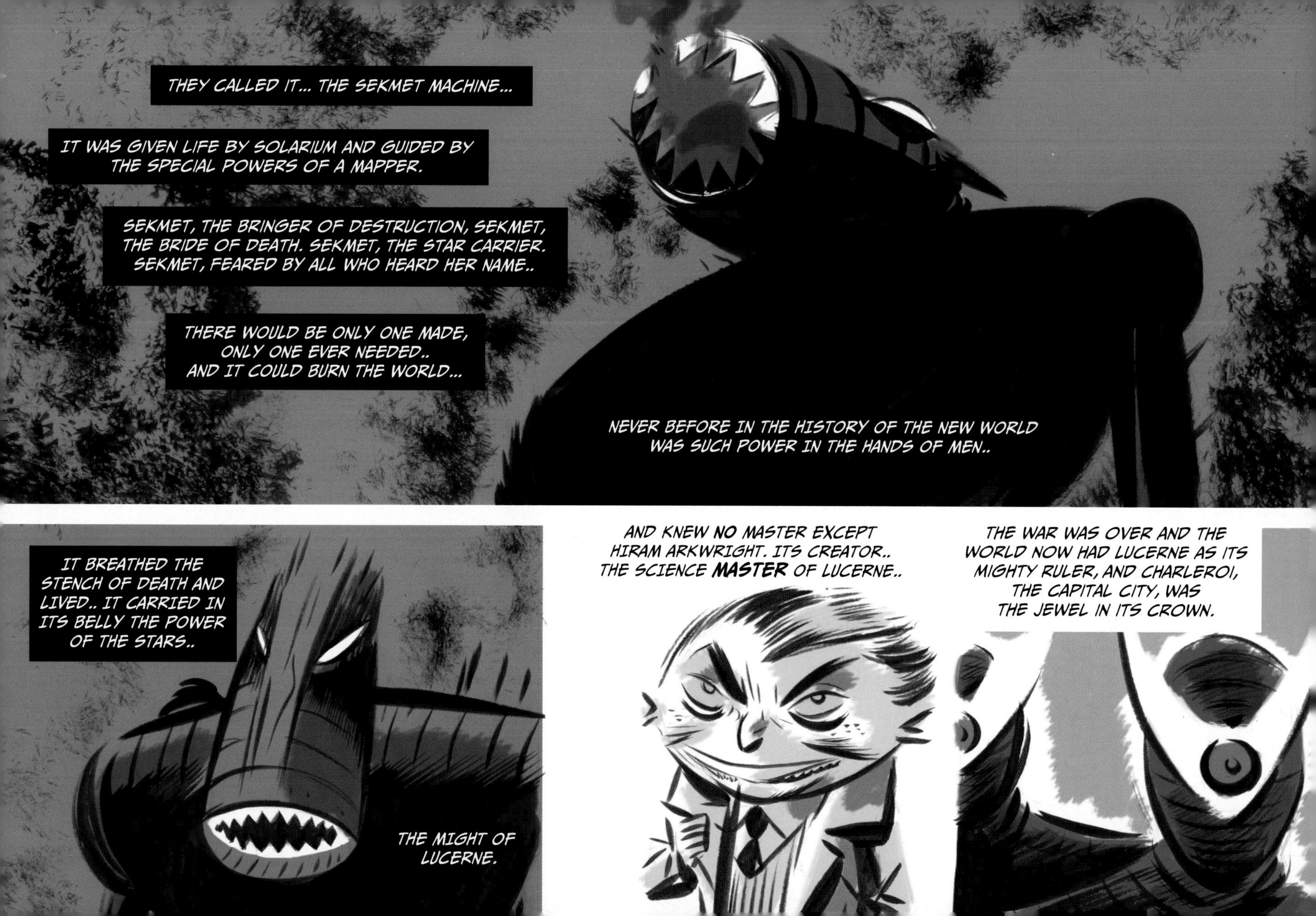
THEY CALLED IT... THE SEKMET MACHINE...
IT WAS GIVEN LIFE BY SOLARIUM AND GUIDED BY THE SPECIAL POWERS OF A MAPPER.
SEKMET, THE BRINGER OF DESTRUCTION, SEKMET, THE BRIDE OF DEATH. SEKMET, THE STAR CARRIER. SEKMET, FEARED BY ALL WHO HEARD HER NAME..
THERE WOULD BE ONLY ONE MADE, ONLY ONE EVER NEEDED.. AND IT COULD BURN THE WORLD...
NEVER BEFORE IN THE HISTORY OF THE NEW WORLD WAS SUCH POWER IN THE HANDS OF MEN..
IT BREATHED THE STENCH OF DEATH AND LIVED.. IT CARRIED IN ITS BELLY THE POWER OF THE STARS..
THE MIGHT OF LUCERNE.
AND KNEW **NO** MASTER EXCEPT HIRAM ARKWRIGHT. ITS CREATOR.. THE SCIENCE **MASTER** OF LUCERNE..
THE WAR WAS OVER AND THE WORLD NOW HAD LUCERNE AS ITS MIGHTY RULER, AND CHARLEROI, THE CAPITAL CITY, WAS THE JEWEL IN ITS CROWN.

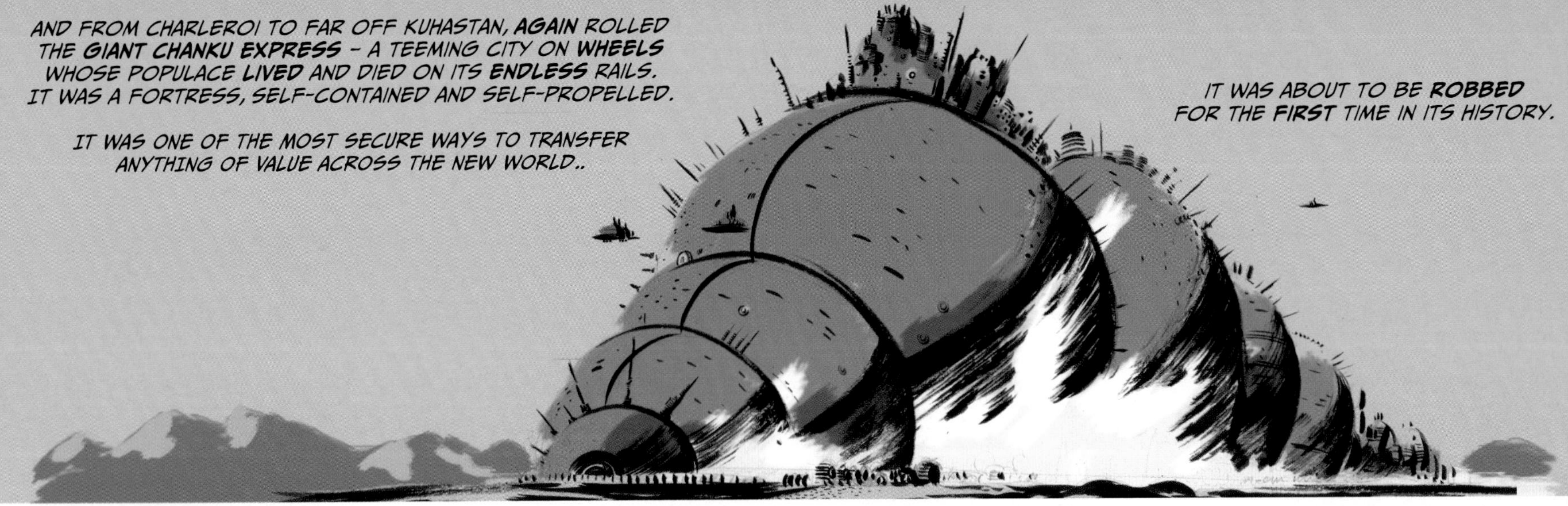
AND FROM CHARLEROI TO FAR OFF KUHASTAN, AGAIN ROLLED THE GIANT CHANKU EXPRESS - A TEEMING CITY ON WHEELS WHOSE POPULACE LIVED AND DIED ON ITS ENDLESS RAILS. IT WAS A FORTRESS, SELF-CONTAINED AND SELF-PROPELLED.
IT WAS ONE OF THE MOST SECURE WAYS TO TRANSFER ANYTHING OF VALUE ACROSS THE NEW WORLD..
IT WAS ABOUT TO BE ROBBED FOR THE FIRST TIME IN ITS HISTORY.

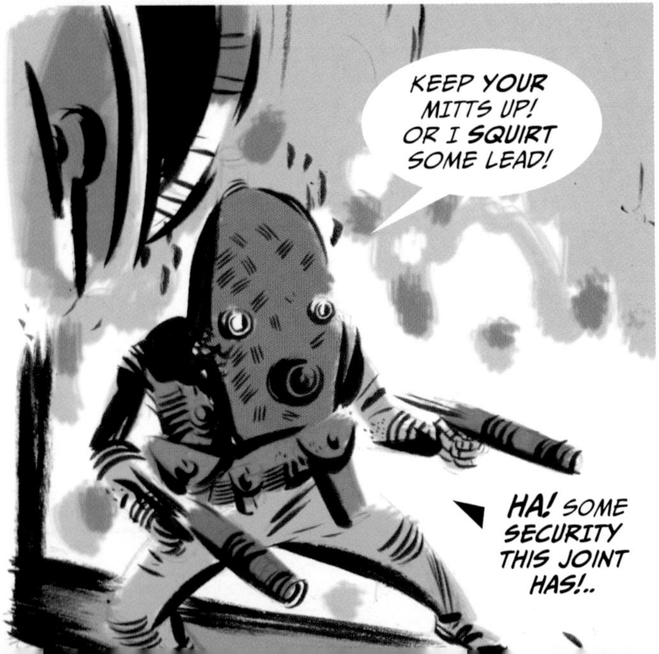
KEEP YOUR MITTS UP! OR I SQUIRT SOME LEAD!
HA! SOME SECURITY THIS JOINT HAS!..

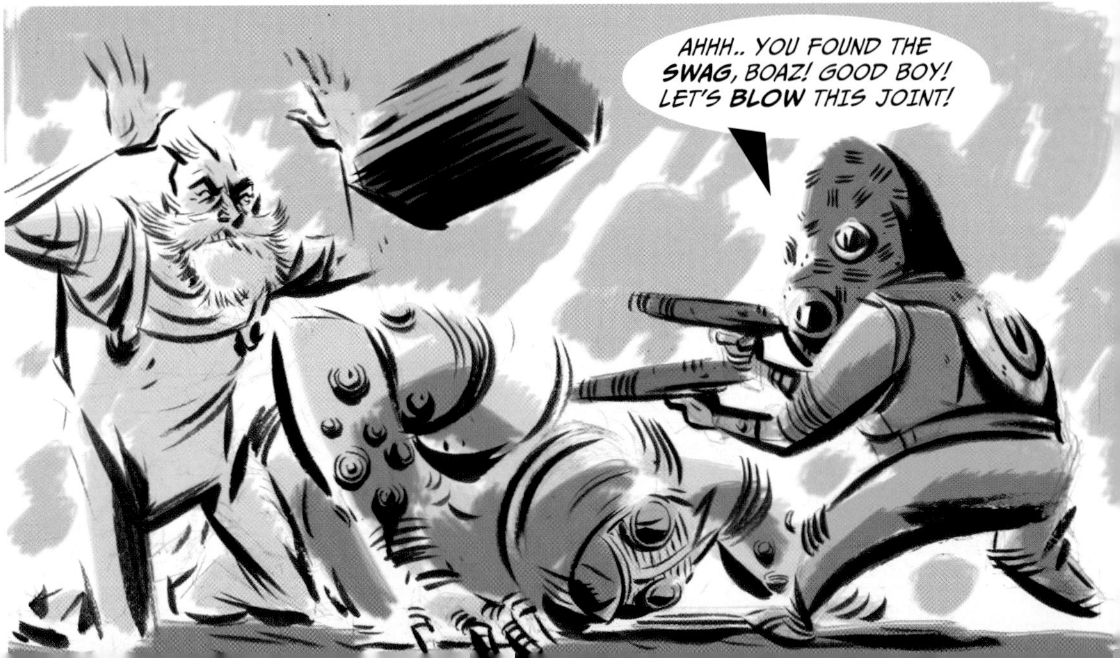
AHHH.. YOU FOUND THE SWAG, BOAZ! GOOD BOY! LET'S BLOW THIS JOINT!

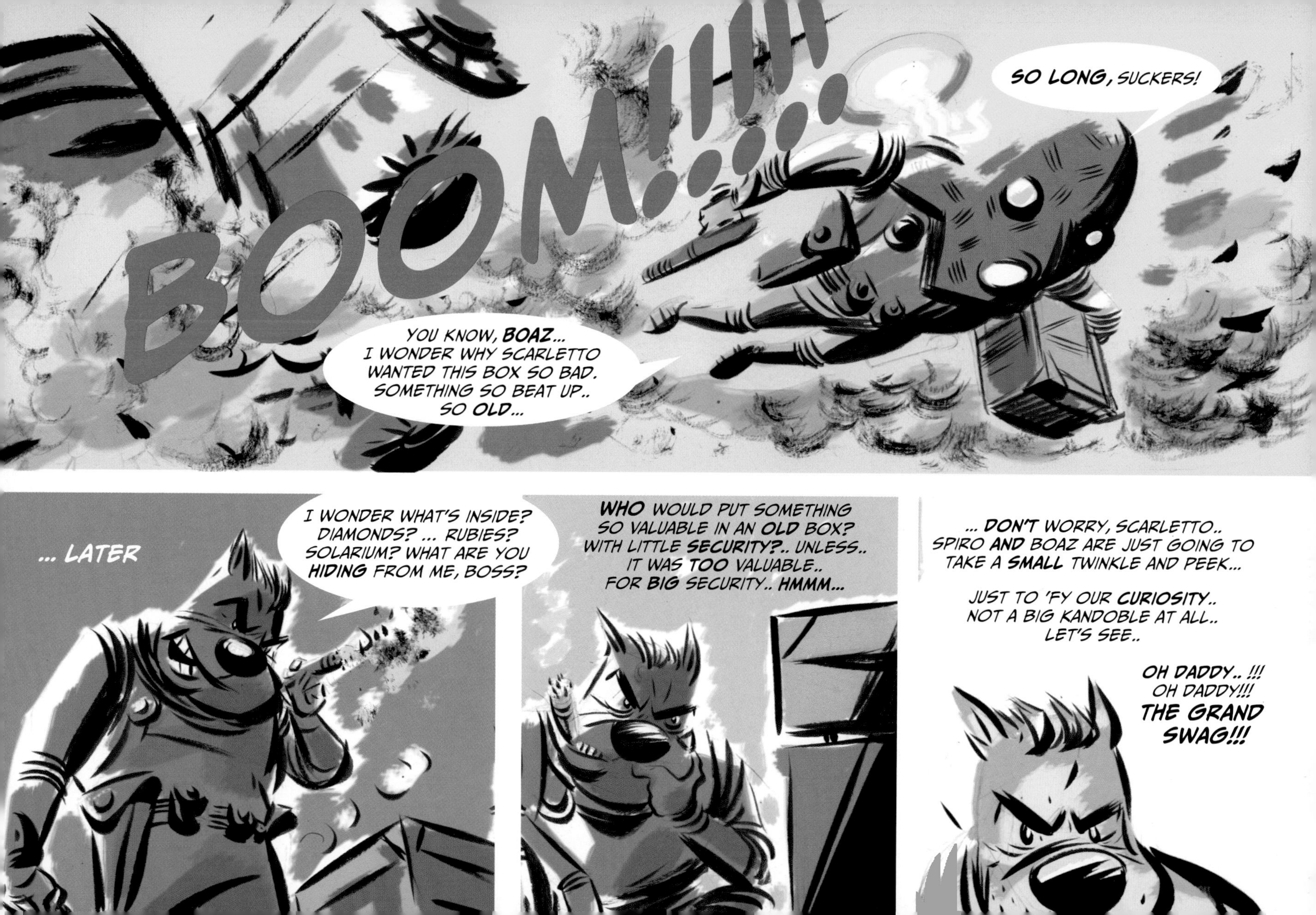
BOOM!!!!!
SO LONG, SUCKERS!
YOU KNOW, BOAZ... I WONDER WHY SCARLETTO WANTED THIS BOX SO BAD. SOMETHING SO BEAT UP.. SO OLD...
... LATER
I WONDER WHAT'S INSIDE? DIAMONDS? ... RUBIES? SOLARIUM? WHAT ARE YOU HIDING FROM ME, BOSS?
WHO WOULD PUT SOMETHING SO VALUABLE IN AN OLD BOX? WITH LITTLE SECURITY?.. UNLESS.. IT WAS TOO VALUABLE.. FOR BIG SECURITY.. HMMM...
... DON'T WORRY, SCARLETTO.. SPIRO AND BOAZ ARE JUST GOING TO TAKE A SMALL TWINKLE AND PEEK...
JUST TO 'FY OUR CURIOSITY.. NOT A BIG KANDOBLE AT ALL.. LET'S SEE..
OH DADDY.. !!! OH DADDY!!! THE GRAND SWAG!!!

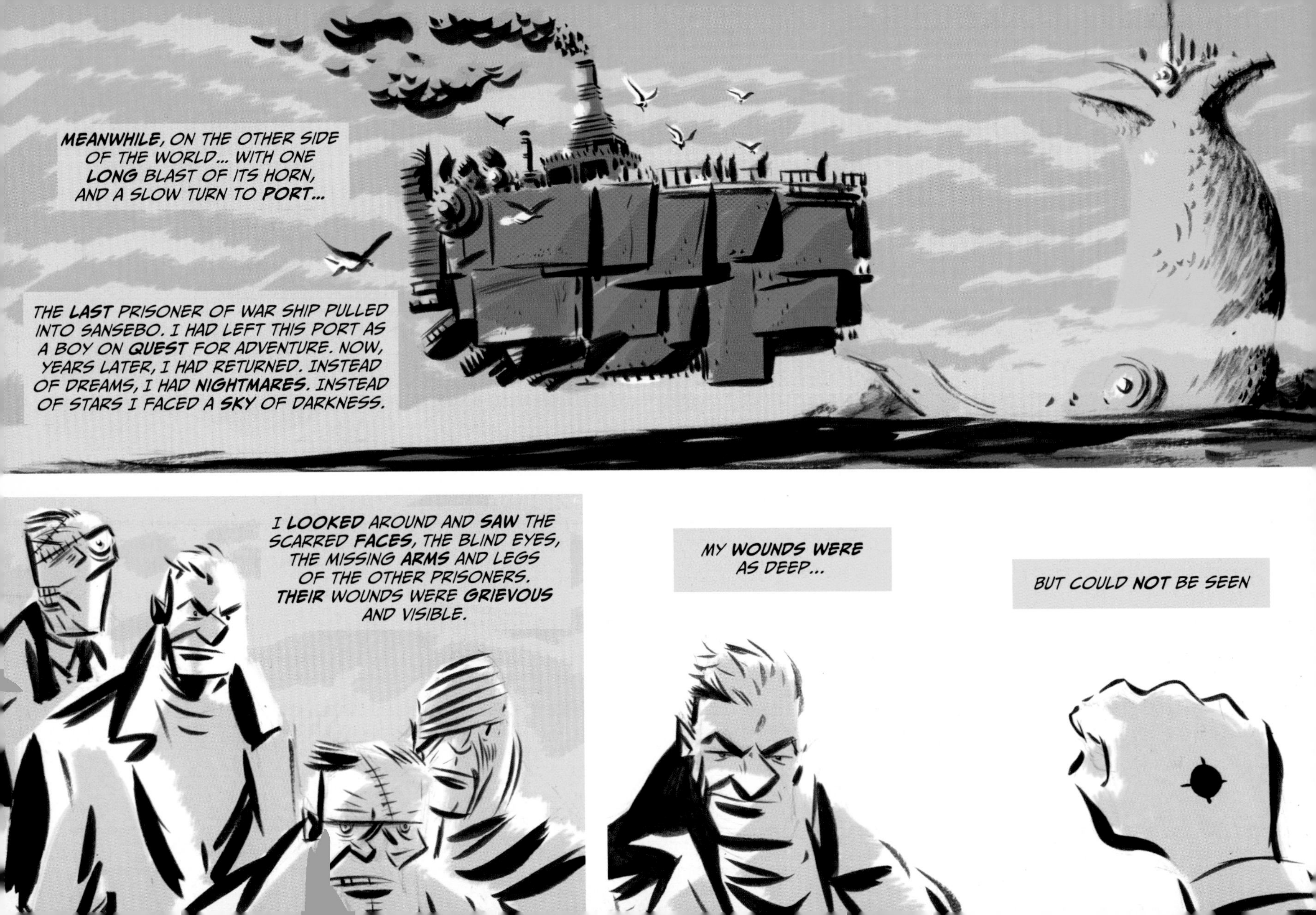
MEANWHILE, ON THE OTHER SIDE OF THE WORLD... WITH ONE LONG BLAST OF ITS HORN, AND A SLOW TURN TO PORT...
THE LAST PRISONER OF WAR SHIP PULLED INTO SANSEBO. I HAD LEFT THIS PORT AS A BOY ON QUEST FOR ADVENTURE. NOW, YEARS LATER, I HAD RETURNED. INSTEAD OF DREAMS, I HAD NIGHTMARES. INSTEAD OF STARS I FACED A SKY OF DARKNESS.
I LOOKED AROUND AND SAW THE SCARRED FACES, THE BLIND EYES, THE MISSING ARMS AND LEGS OF THE OTHER PRISONERS. THEIR WOUNDS WERE GRIEVOUS AND VISIBLE.
MY WOUNDS WERE AS DEEP...
BUT COULD NOT BE SEEN

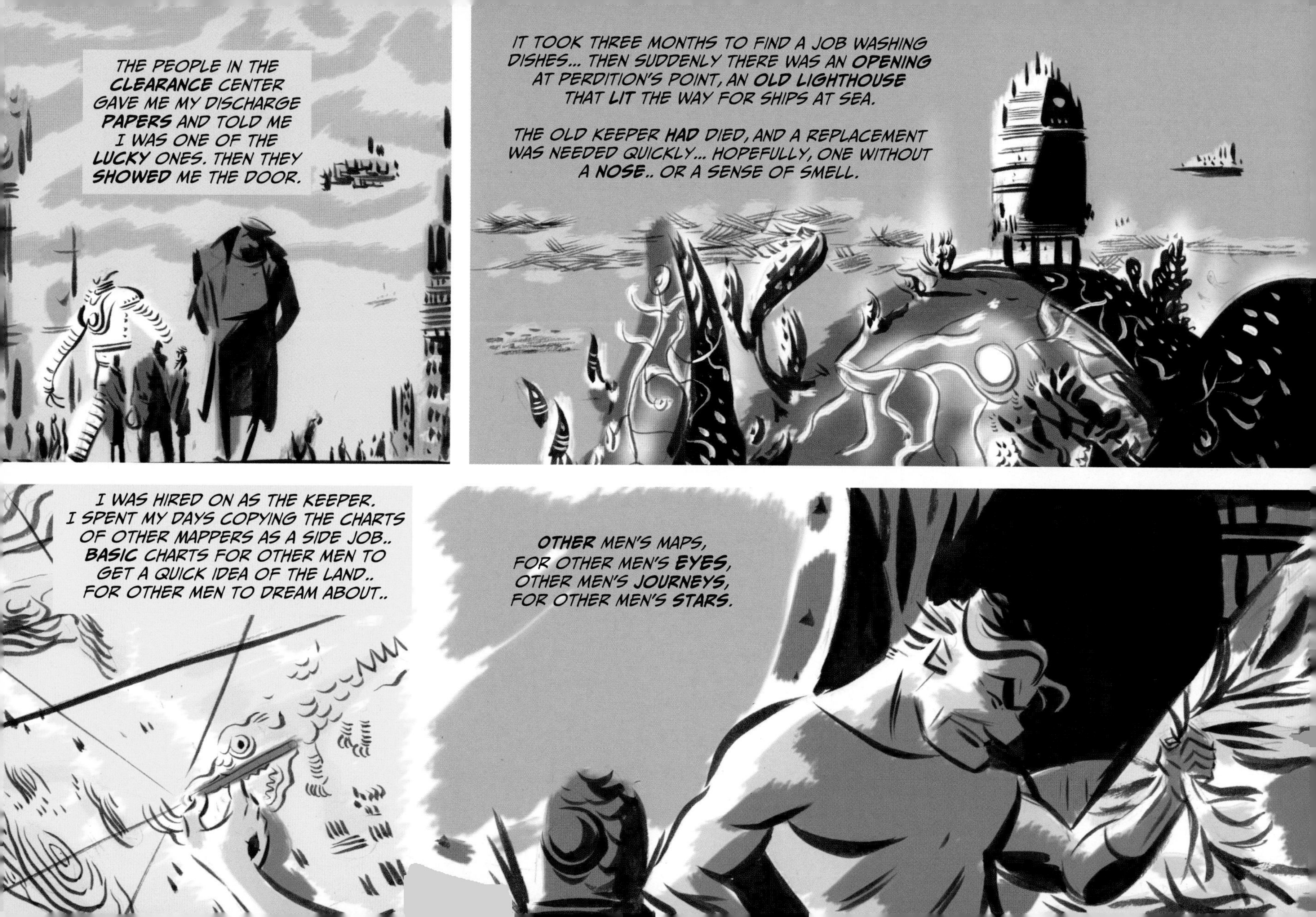
THE PEOPLE IN THE CLEARANCE CENTER GAVE ME MY DISCHARGE PAPERS AND TOLD ME I WAS ONE OF THE LUCKY ONES. THEN THEY SHOWED ME THE DOOR.
IT TOOK THREE MONTHS TO FIND A JOB WASHING DISHES... THEN SUDDENLY THERE WAS AN OPENING AT PERDITION'S POINT, AN OLD LIGHTHOUSE THAT LIT THE WAY FOR SHIPS AT SEA.
THE OLD KEEPER HAD DIED, AND A REPLACEMENT WAS NEEDED QUICKLY... HOPEFULLY, ONE WITHOUT A NOSE.. OR A SENSE OF SMELL.
I WAS HIRED ON AS THE KEEPER. I SPENT MY DAYS COPYING THE CHARTS OF OTHER MAPPERS AS A SIDE JOB.. BASIC CHARTS FOR OTHER MEN TO GET A QUICK IDEA OF THE LAND.. FOR OTHER MEN TO DREAM ABOUT..
OTHER MEN'S MAPS, FOR OTHER MEN'S EYES, OTHER MEN'S JOURNEYS, FOR OTHER MEN'S STARS.

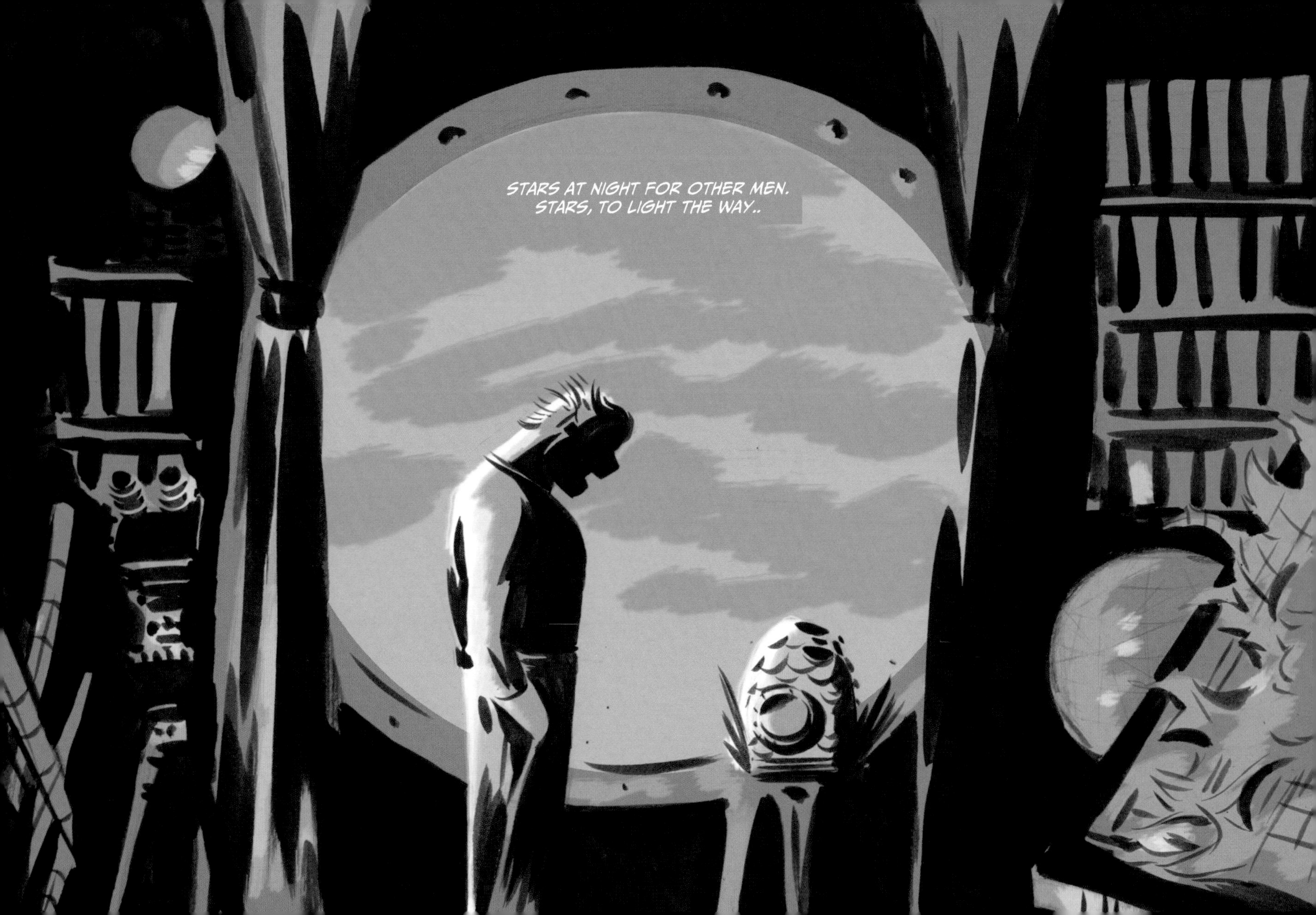
STARS AT NIGHT FOR OTHER MEN.
STARS, TO LIGHT THE WAY..

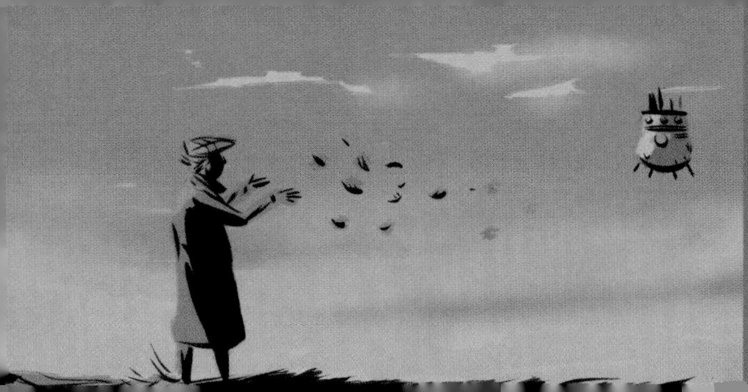

# ROCKETO

# 3

# DEPARTURES

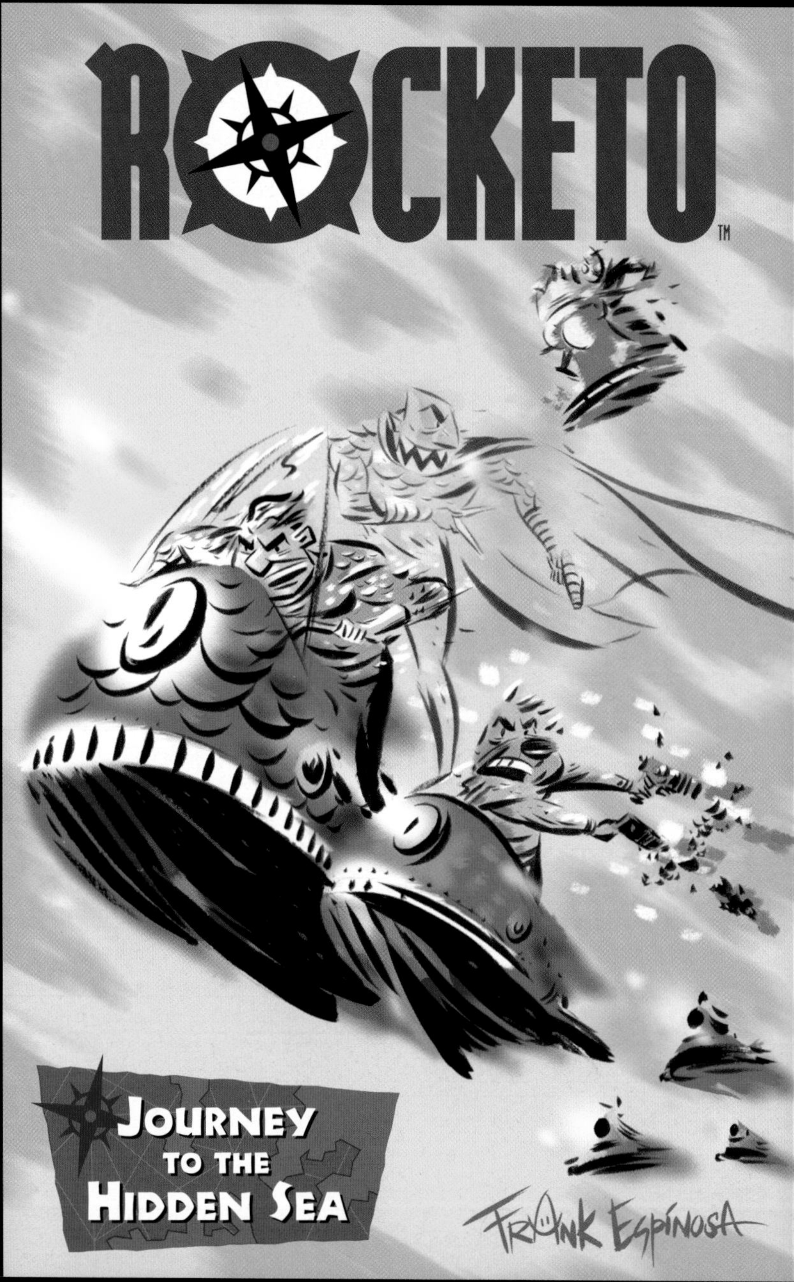
ROCKETO
TM
JOURNEY TO THE HIDDEN SEA
FRANK ESPINOSA

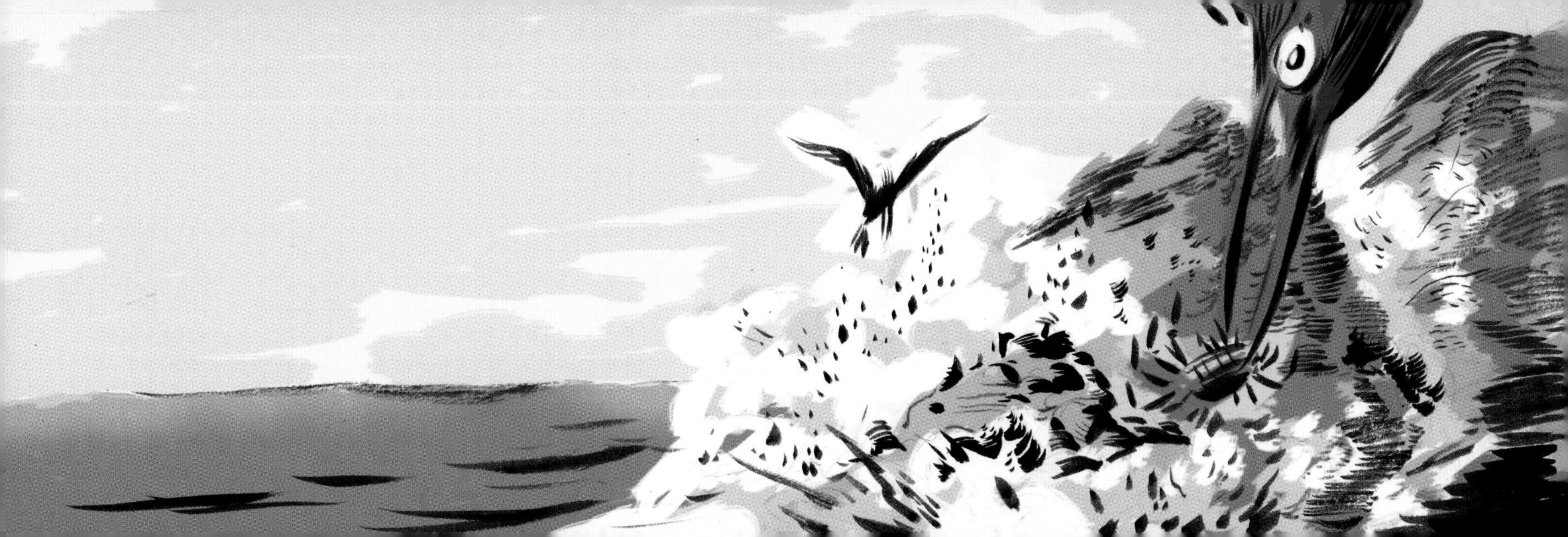

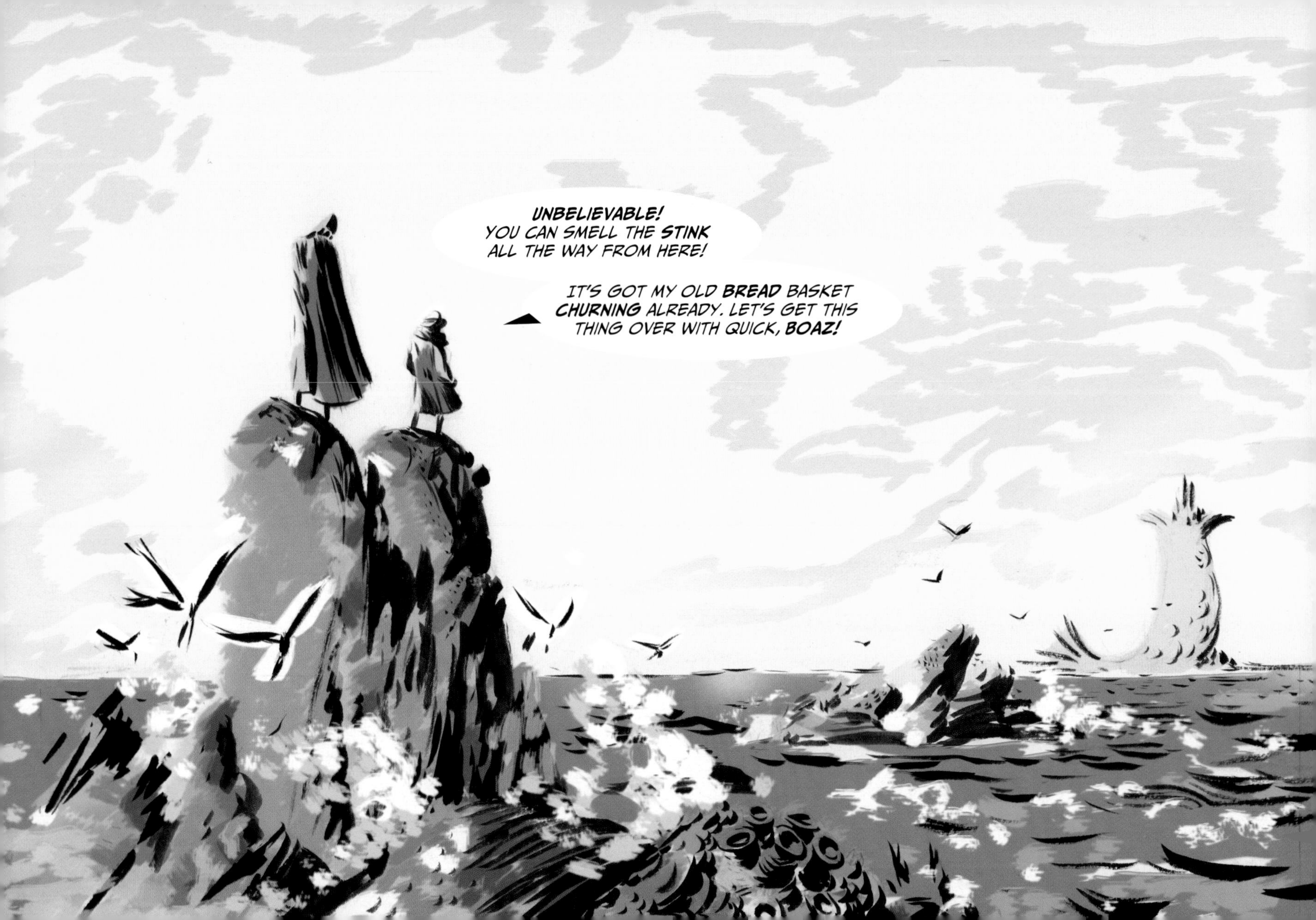
UNBELIEVABLE! YOU CAN SMELL THE STINK ALL THE WAY FROM HERE!
IT'S GOT MY OLD BREAD BASKET CHURNING ALREADY. LET'S GET THIS THING OVER WITH QUICK, BOAZ!

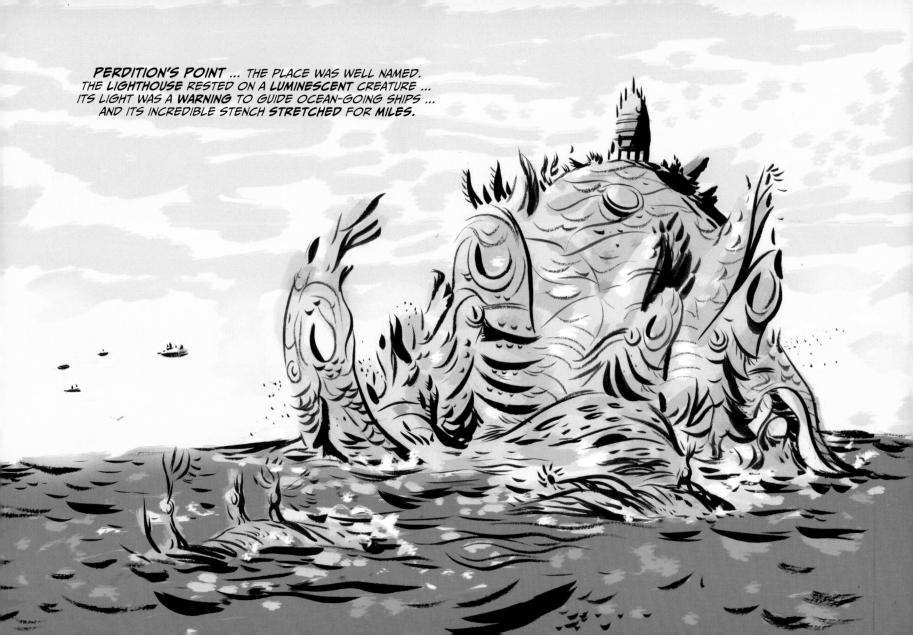

PERDITION'S POINT ... THE PLACE WAS WELL NAMED.
THE **LIGHTHOUSE** RESTED ON A **LUMINESCENT** CREATURE ...
ITS LIGHT WAS A **WARNING** TO GUIDE OCEAN-GOING SHIPS ...
AND ITS INCREDIBLE STENCH **STRETCHED** FOR MILES.

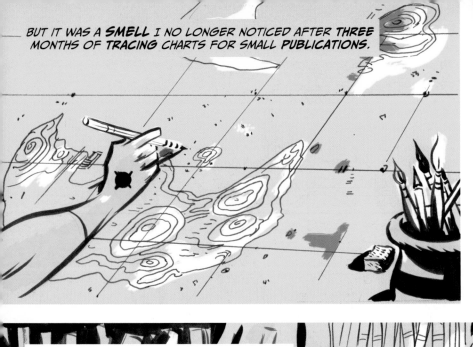

BUT IT WAS A **SMELL** I NO LONGER NOTICED AFTER **THREE** MONTHS OF **TRACING** CHARTS FOR SMALL **PUBLICATIONS**.

THREE **MONTHS** THINKING OF **VOYAGES** I WOULD NEVER TAKE...

DRAWING MAPS I WOULD **NEVER** FOLLOW...

DAY AFTER DAY, **LOOKING** AT A **HORIZON** I WOULD NEVER **CROSS**.

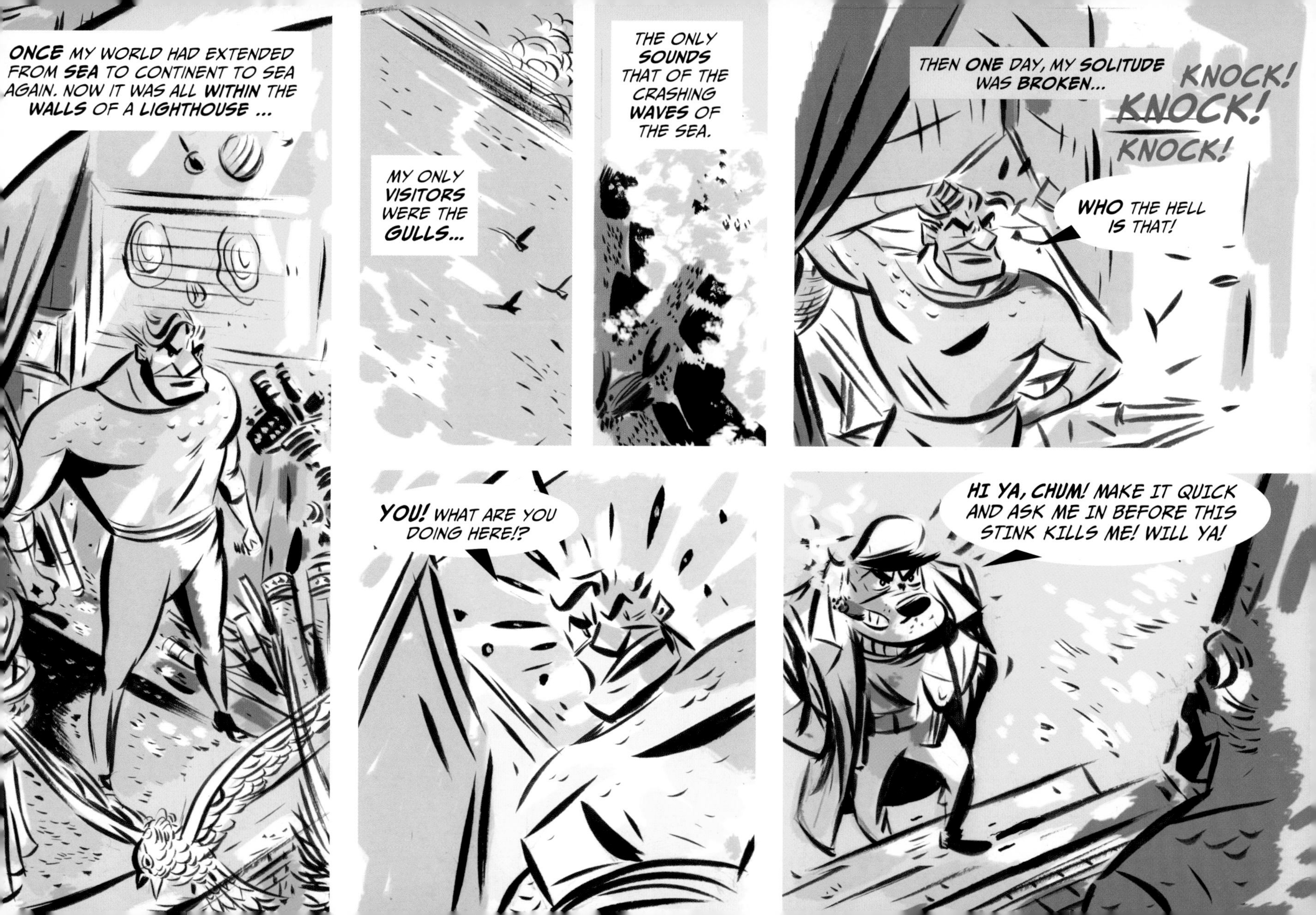
ONCE MY WORLD HAD EXTENDED FROM SEA TO CONTINENT TO SEA AGAIN. NOW IT WAS ALL WITHIN THE WALLS OF A LIGHTHOUSE ...
MY ONLY VISITORS WERE THE GULLS...
THE ONLY SOUNDS THAT OF THE CRASHING WAVES OF THE SEA.
THEN ONE DAY, MY SOLITUDE WAS BROKEN...
KNOCK! KNOCK! KNOCK!
WHO THE HELL IS THAT!
YOU! WHAT ARE YOU DOING HERE!?
HI YA, CHUM! MAKE IT QUICK AND ASK ME IN BEFORE THIS STINK KILLS ME! WILL YA!

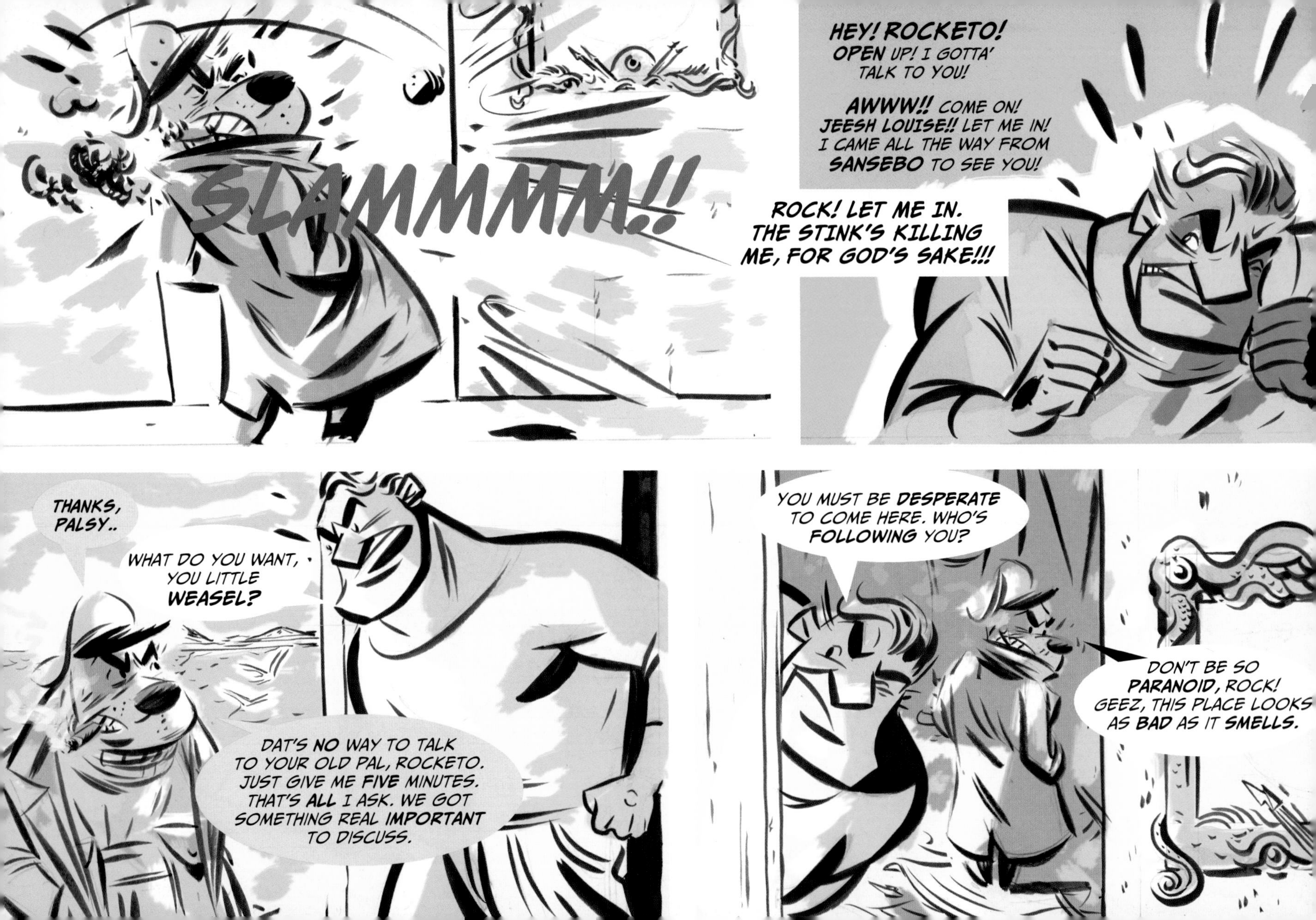
SLAMMMM!!
HEY! ROCKETO! OPEN UP! I GOTTA' TALK TO YOU!
AWWW!! COME ON! JEESH LOUISE!! LET ME IN! I CAME ALL THE WAY FROM SANSEBO TO SEE YOU!
ROCK! LET ME IN. THE STINK'S KILLING ME, FOR GOD'S SAKE!!!
THANKS, PALSY..
WHAT DO YOU WANT, YOU LITTLE WEASEL?
DAT'S NO WAY TO TALK TO YOUR OLD PAL, ROCKETO. JUST GIVE ME FIVE MINUTES. THAT'S ALL I ASK. WE GOT SOMETHING REAL IMPORTANT TO DISCUSS.
YOU MUST BE DESPERATE TO COME HERE. WHO'S FOLLOWING YOU?
DON'T BE SO PARANOID, ROCK! GEEZ, THIS PLACE LOOKS AS BAD AS IT SMELLS.

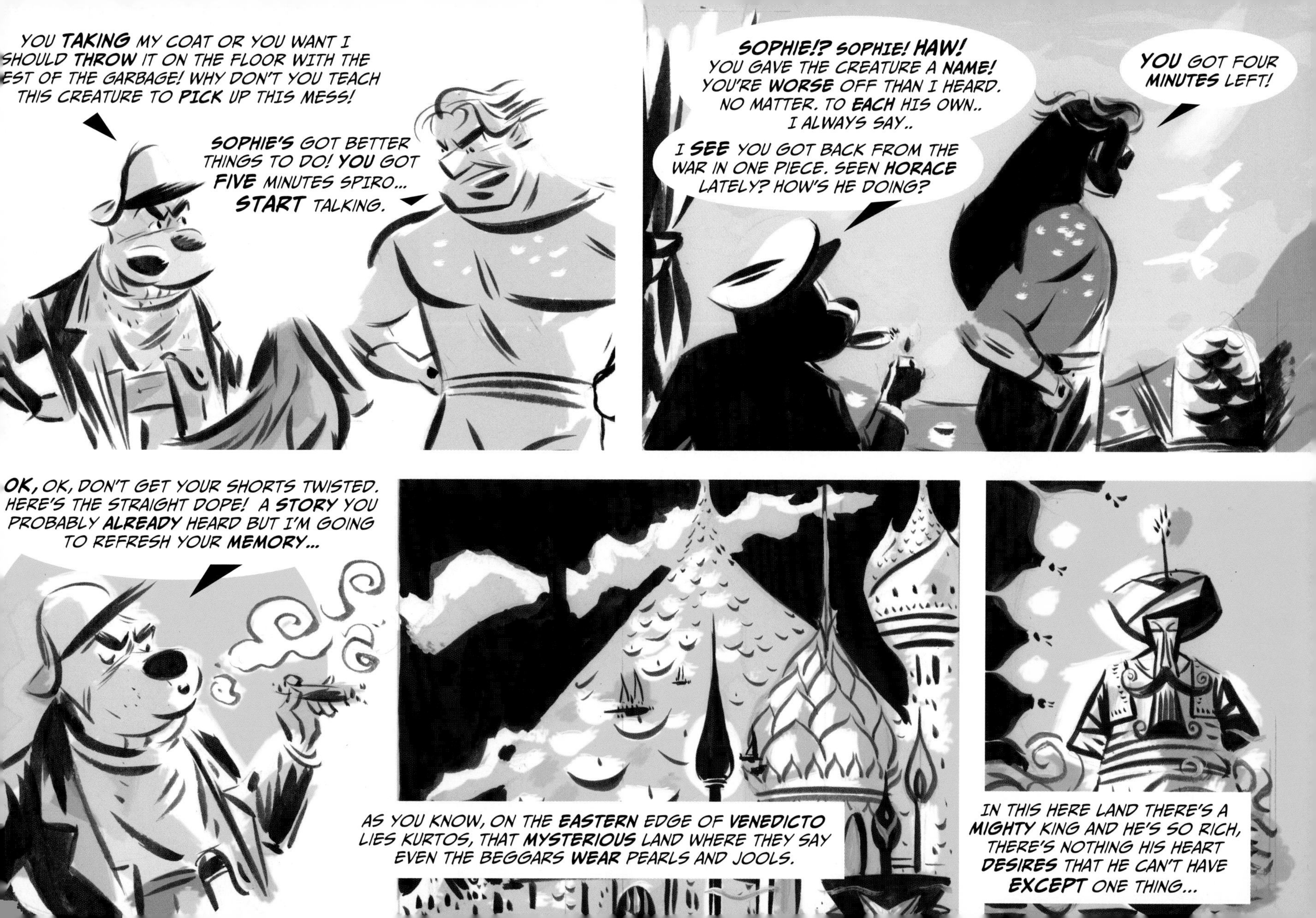
YOU TAKING MY COAT OR YOU WANT I SHOULD THROW IT ON THE FLOOR WITH THE EST OF THE GARBAGE! WHY DON'T YOU TEACH THIS CREATURE TO PICK UP THIS MESS!
SOPHIE'S GOT BETTER THINGS TO DO! YOU GOT FIVE MINUTES SPIRO... START TALKING.
SOPHIE!? SOPHIE! HAW! YOU GAVE THE CREATURE A NAME! YOU'RE WORSE OFF THAN I HEARD. NO MATTER. TO EACH HIS OWN.. I ALWAYS SAY..
I SEE YOU GOT BACK FROM THE WAR IN ONE PIECE. SEEN HORACE LATELY? HOW'S HE DOING?
YOU GOT FOUR MINUTES LEFT!
OK, OK, DON'T GET YOUR SHORTS TWISTED. HERE'S THE STRAIGHT DOPE! A STORY YOU PROBABLY ALREADY HEARD BUT I'M GOING TO REFRESH YOUR MEMORY...
AS YOU KNOW, ON THE EASTERN EDGE OF VENEDICTO LIES KURTOS, THAT MYSTERIOUS LAND WHERE THEY SAY EVEN THE BEGGARS WEAR PEARLS AND JOOLS.
IN THIS HERE LAND THERE'S A MIGHTY KING AND HE'S SO RICH, THERE'S NOTHING HIS HEART DESIRES THAT HE CAN'T HAVE EXCEPT ONE THING...

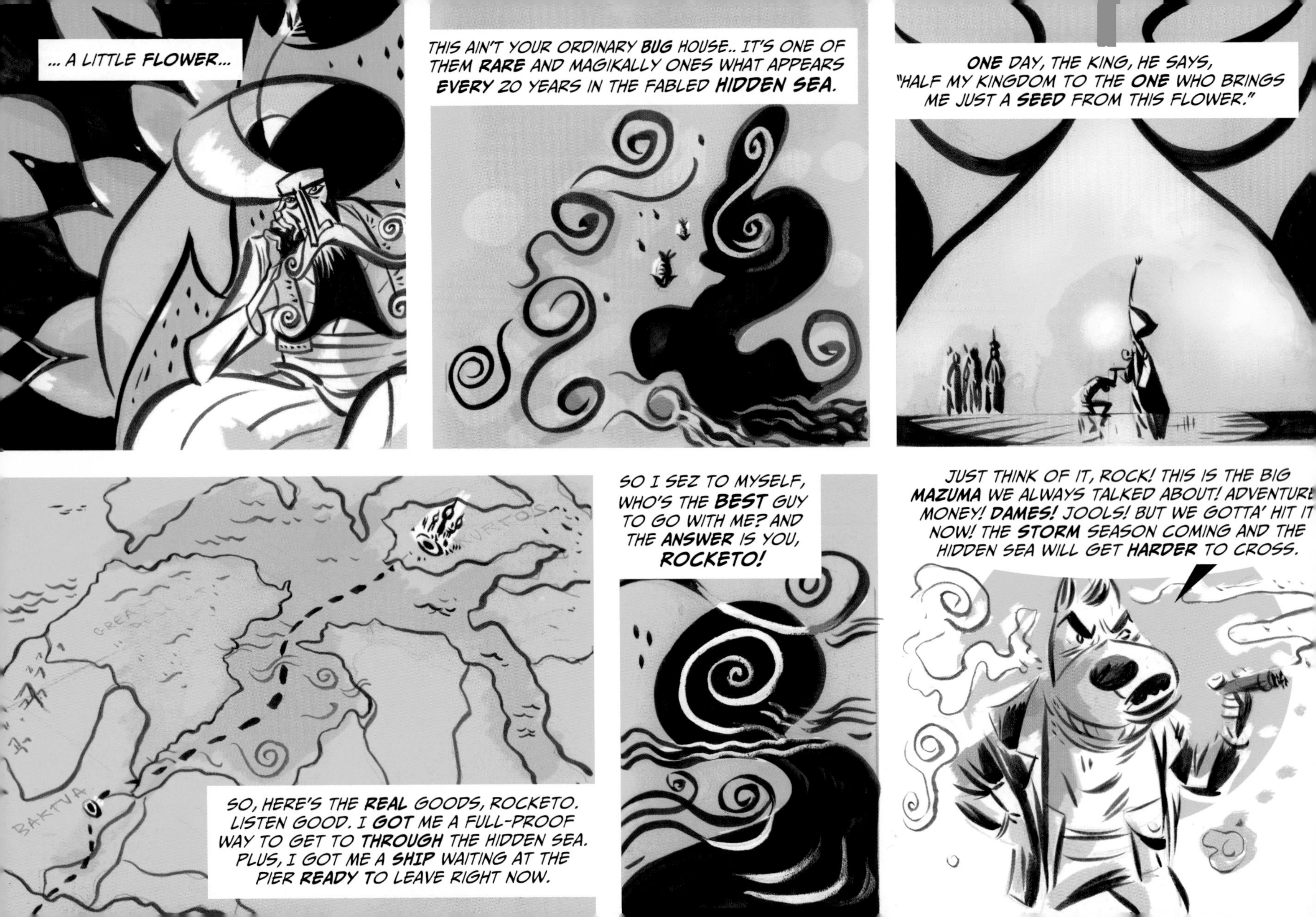

... A LITTLE FLOWER...
THIS AIN'T YOUR ORDINARY BUG HOUSE.. IT'S ONE OF THEM RARE AND MAGIKALLY ONES WHAT APPEARS EVERY 20 YEARS IN THE FABLED HIDDEN SEA.
ONE DAY, THE KING, HE SAYS, "HALF MY KINGDOM TO THE ONE WHO BRINGS ME JUST A SEED FROM THIS FLOWER."
SO, HERE'S THE REAL GOODS, ROCKETO. LISTEN GOOD. I GOT ME A FULL-PROOF WAY TO GET TO THROUGH THE HIDDEN SEA. PLUS, I GOT ME A SHIP WAITING AT THE PIER READY TO LEAVE RIGHT NOW.
SO I SEZ TO MYSELF, WHO'S THE BEST GUY TO GO WITH ME? AND THE ANSWER IS YOU, ROCKETO!
JUST THINK OF IT, ROCK! THIS IS THE BIG MAZUMA WE ALWAYS TALKED ABOUT! ADVENTURE MONEY! DAMES! JOOLS! BUT WE GOTTA' HIT IT NOW! THE STORM SEASON COMING AND THE HIDDEN SEA WILL GET HARDER TO CROSS.

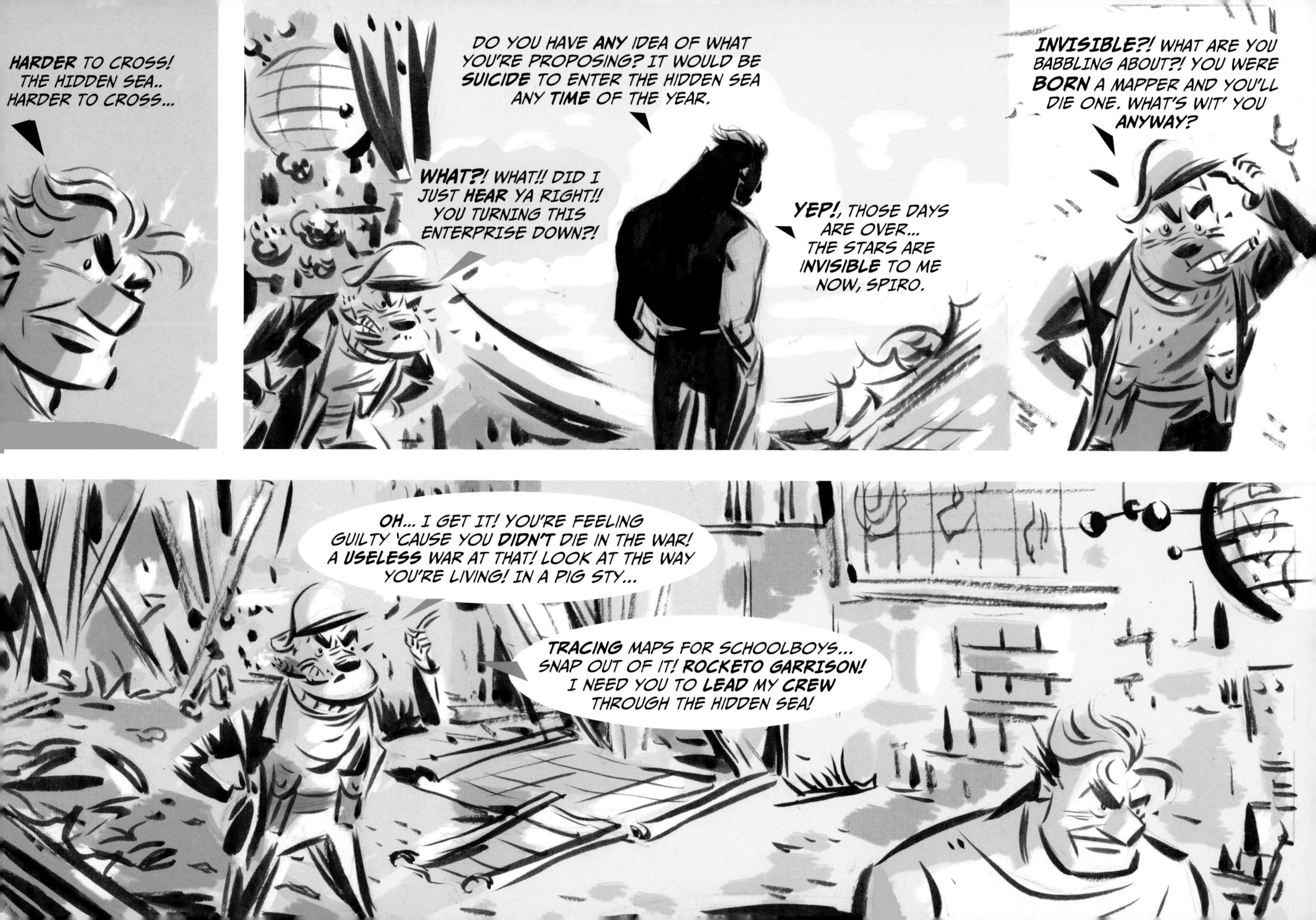

HARDER TO CROSS! THE HIDDEN SEA.. HARDER TO CROSS...
DO YOU HAVE ANY IDEA OF WHAT YOU'RE PROPOSING? IT WOULD BE SUICIDE TO ENTER THE HIDDEN SEA ANY TIME OF THE YEAR.
WHAT?! WHAT!! DID I JUST HEAR YA RIGHT!! YOU TURNING THIS ENTERPRISE DOWN?!
YEP!, THOSE DAYS ARE OVER... THE STARS ARE INVISIBLE TO ME NOW, SPIRO.
INVISIBLE?! WHAT ARE YOU BABBLING ABOUT?! YOU WERE BORN A MAPPER AND YOU'LL DIE ONE. WHAT'S WIT' YOU ANYWAY?
OH... I GET IT! YOU'RE FEELING GUILTY 'CAUSE YOU DIDN'T DIE IN THE WAR! A USELESS WAR AT THAT! LOOK AT THE WAY YOU'RE LIVING! IN A PIG STY...
TRACING MAPS FOR SCHOOLBOYS... SNAP OUT OF IT! ROCKETO GARRISON! I NEED YOU TO LEAD MY CREW THROUGH THE HIDDEN SEA!

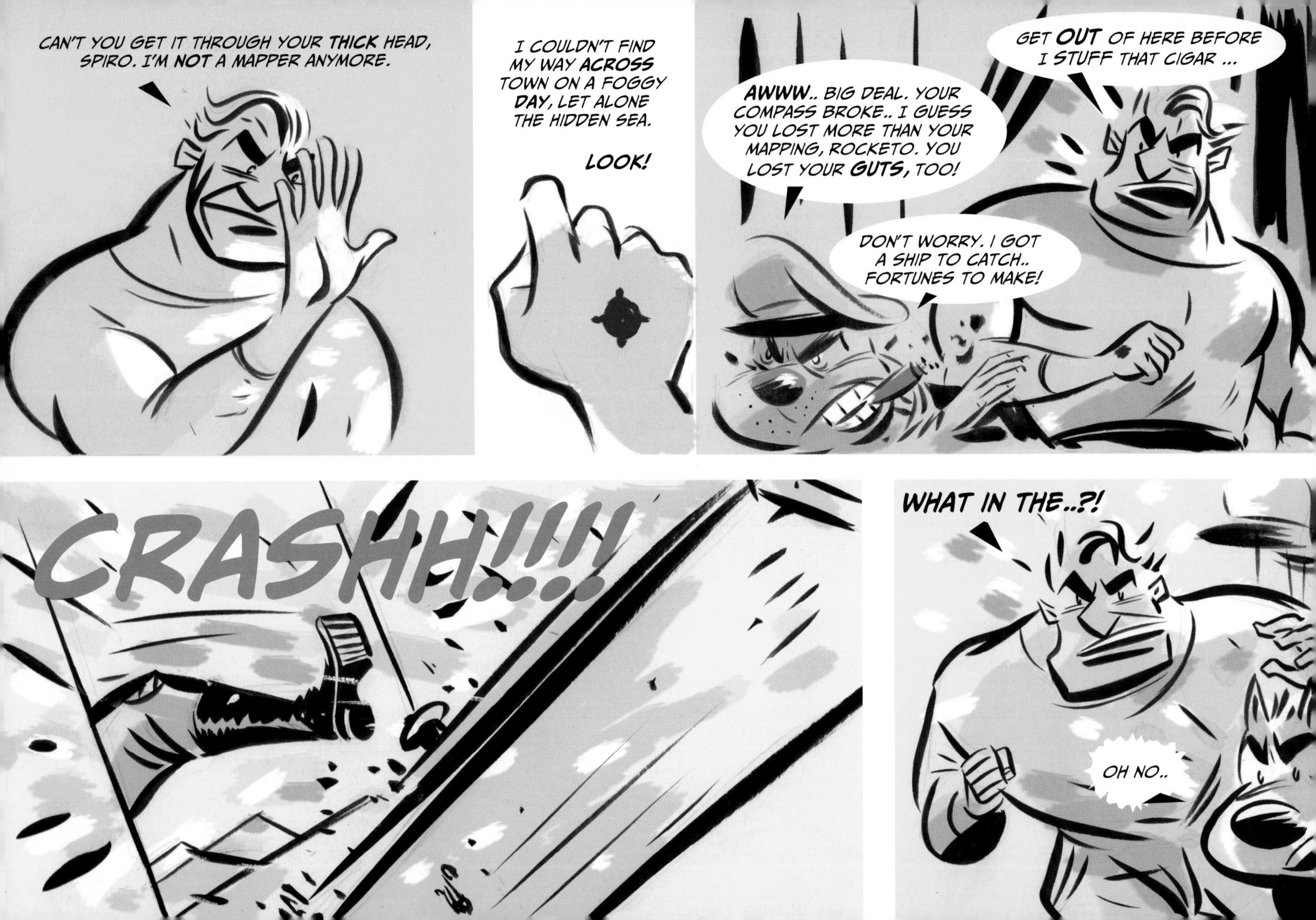
CAN'T YOU GET IT THROUGH YOUR THICK HEAD, SPIRO. I'M NOT A MAPPER ANYMORE.
I COULDN'T FIND MY WAY ACROSS TOWN ON A FOGGY DAY, LET ALONE THE HIDDEN SEA.
LOOK!
AWWW.. BIG DEAL. YOUR COMPASS BROKE.. I GUESS YOU LOST MORE THAN YOUR MAPPING, ROCKETO. YOU LOST YOUR GUTS, TOO!
GET OUT OF HERE BEFORE I STUFF THAT CIGAR ...
DON'T WORRY. I GOT A SHIP TO CATCH.. FORTUNES TO MAKE!
CRASHH!!!!
WHAT IN THE..?!
OH NO..

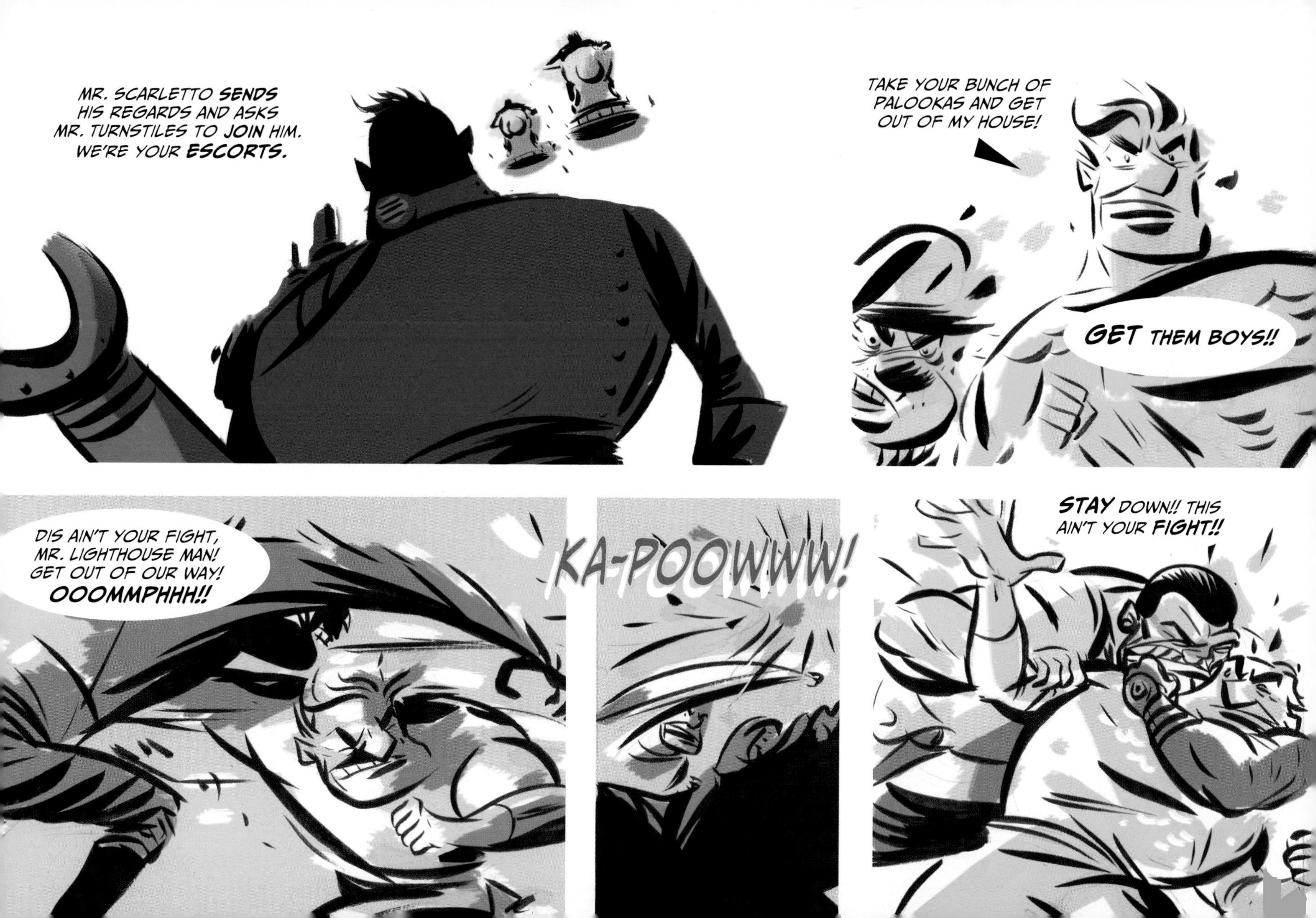
MR. SCARLETTO SENDS HIS REGARDS AND ASKS MR. TURNSTILES TO JOIN HIM. WE'RE YOUR ESCORTS.
TAKE YOUR BUNCH OF PALOOKAS AND GET OUT OF MY HOUSE!
GET THEM BOYS!!
DIS AIN'T YOUR FIGHT, MR. LIGHTHOUSE MAN! GET OUT OF OUR WAY! OOOMMPHHH!!
KA-POOWWW!
STAY DOWN!! THIS AIN'T YOUR FIGHT!!

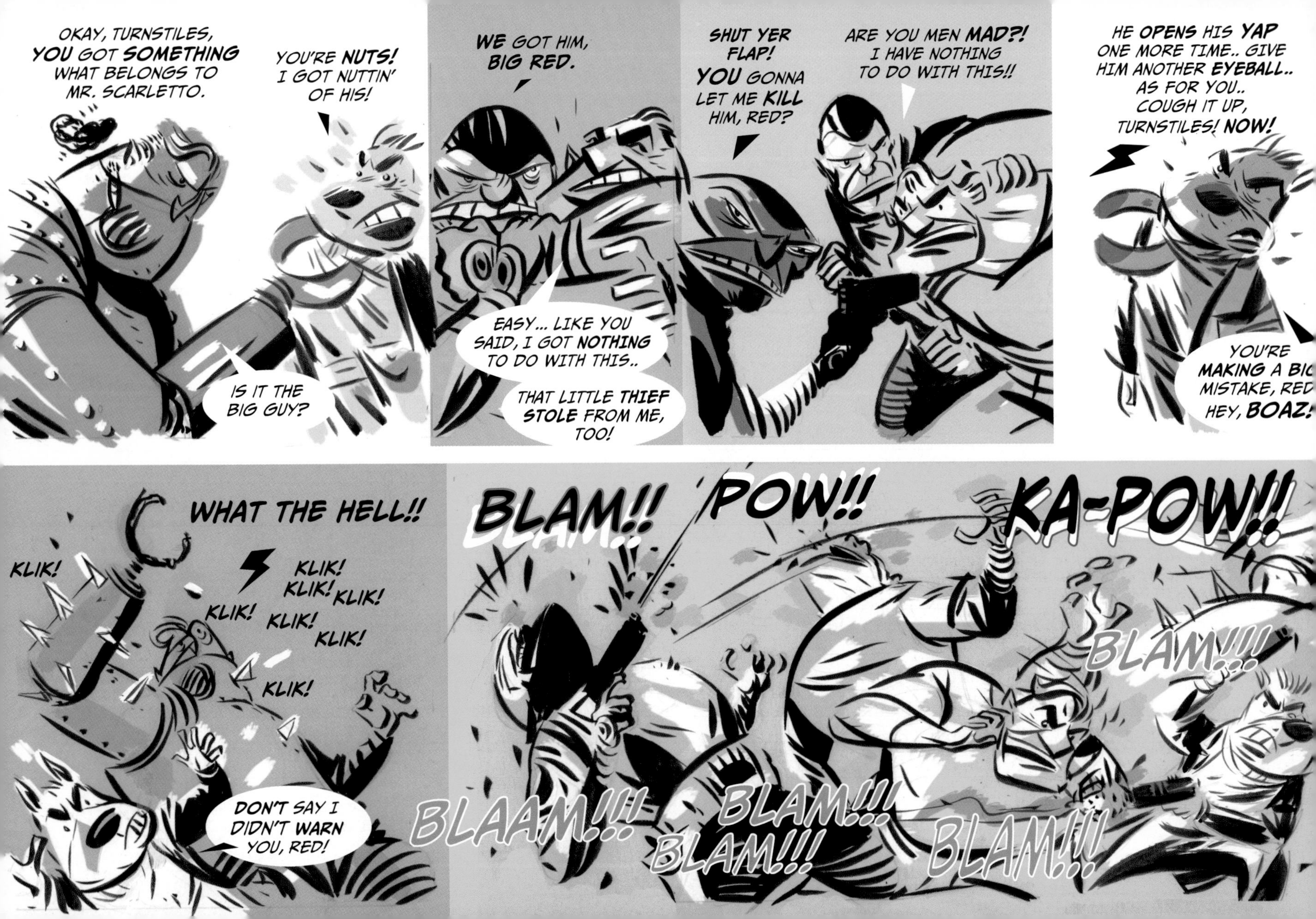

OKAY, TURNSTILES, YOU GOT SOMETHING WHAT BELONGS TO MR. SCARLETTO.
YOU'RE NUTS! I GOT NUTTIN' OF HIS!
IS IT THE BIG GUY?
WE GOT HIM, BIG RED.
EASY... LIKE YOU SAID, I GOT NOTHING TO DO WITH THIS..
THAT LITTLE THIEF STOLE FROM ME, TOO!
SHUT YER FLAP! YOU GONNA LET ME KILL HIM, RED?
ARE YOU MEN MAD?! I HAVE NOTHING TO DO WITH THIS!!
HE OPENS HIS YAP ONE MORE TIME.. GIVE HIM ANOTHER EYEBALL.. AS FOR YOU.. COUGH IT UP, TURNSTILES! NOW!
YOU'RE MAKING A BIG MISTAKE, RED HEY, BOAZ!
WHAT THE HELL!!
KLIK!
KLIK! KLIK! KLIK!
KLIK!
KLIK!
KLIK!
KLIK!
DON'T SAY I DIDN'T WARN YOU, RED!
BLAM!!
POW!!
KA-POW!!
BLAM!!!
BLAAM!!!
BLAM!!!
BLAM!!!
BLAM!!!

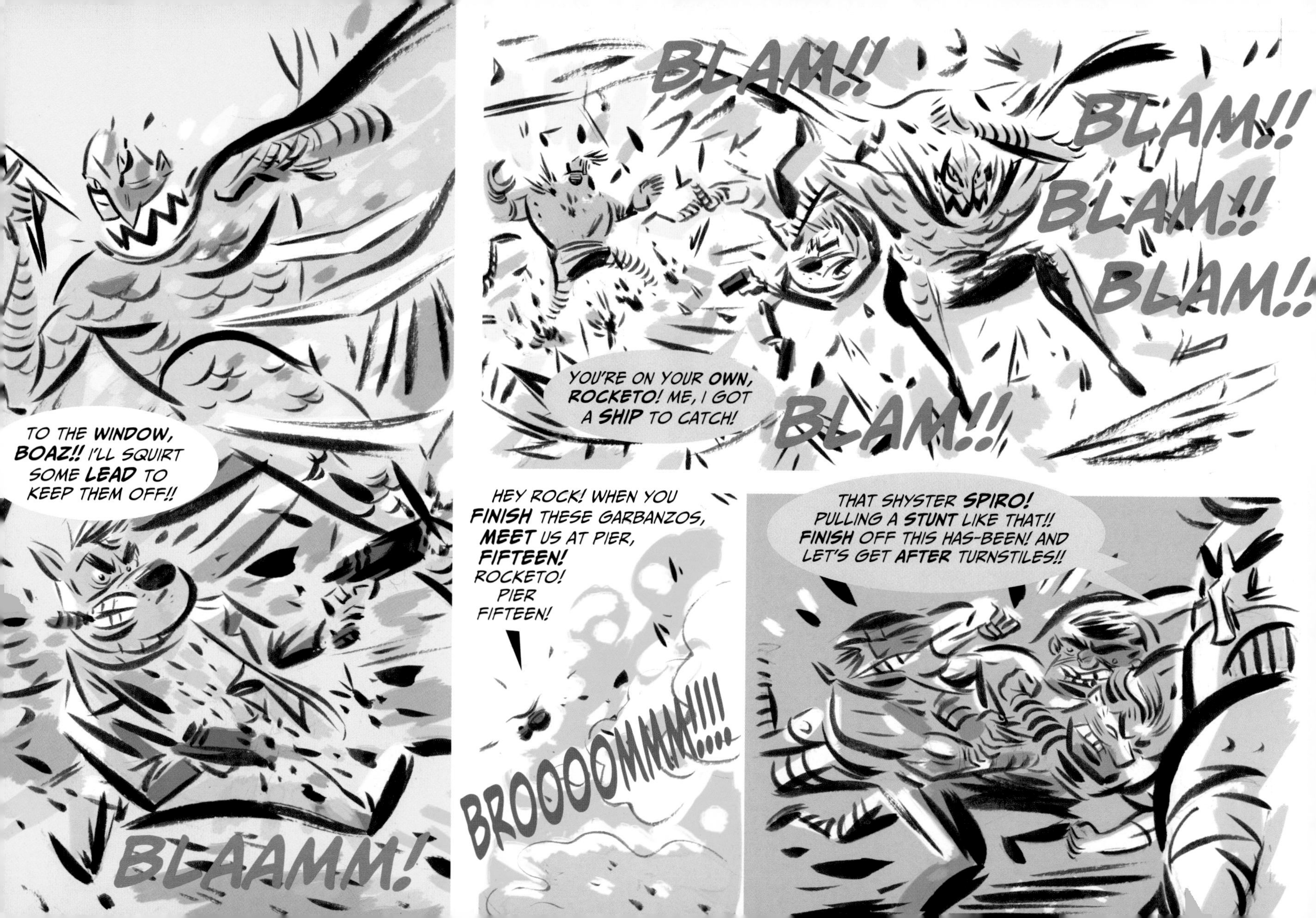
TO THE WINDOW, BOAZ!! I'LL SQUIRT SOME LEAD TO KEEP THEM OFF!!
BLAAMM!
BLAM!!
BLAM!!
BLAM!!
BLAM!!
YOU'RE ON YOUR OWN, ROCKETO! ME, I GOT A SHIP TO CATCH!
BLAM!!
HEY ROCK! WHEN YOU FINISH THESE GARBANZOS, MEET US AT PIER, FIFTEEN! ROCKETO! PIER FIFTEEN!
BROOOOMMM!!!...
THAT SHYSTER SPIRO! PULLING A STUNT LIKE THAT!! FINISH OFF THIS HAS-BEEN! AND LET'S GET AFTER TURNSTILES!!

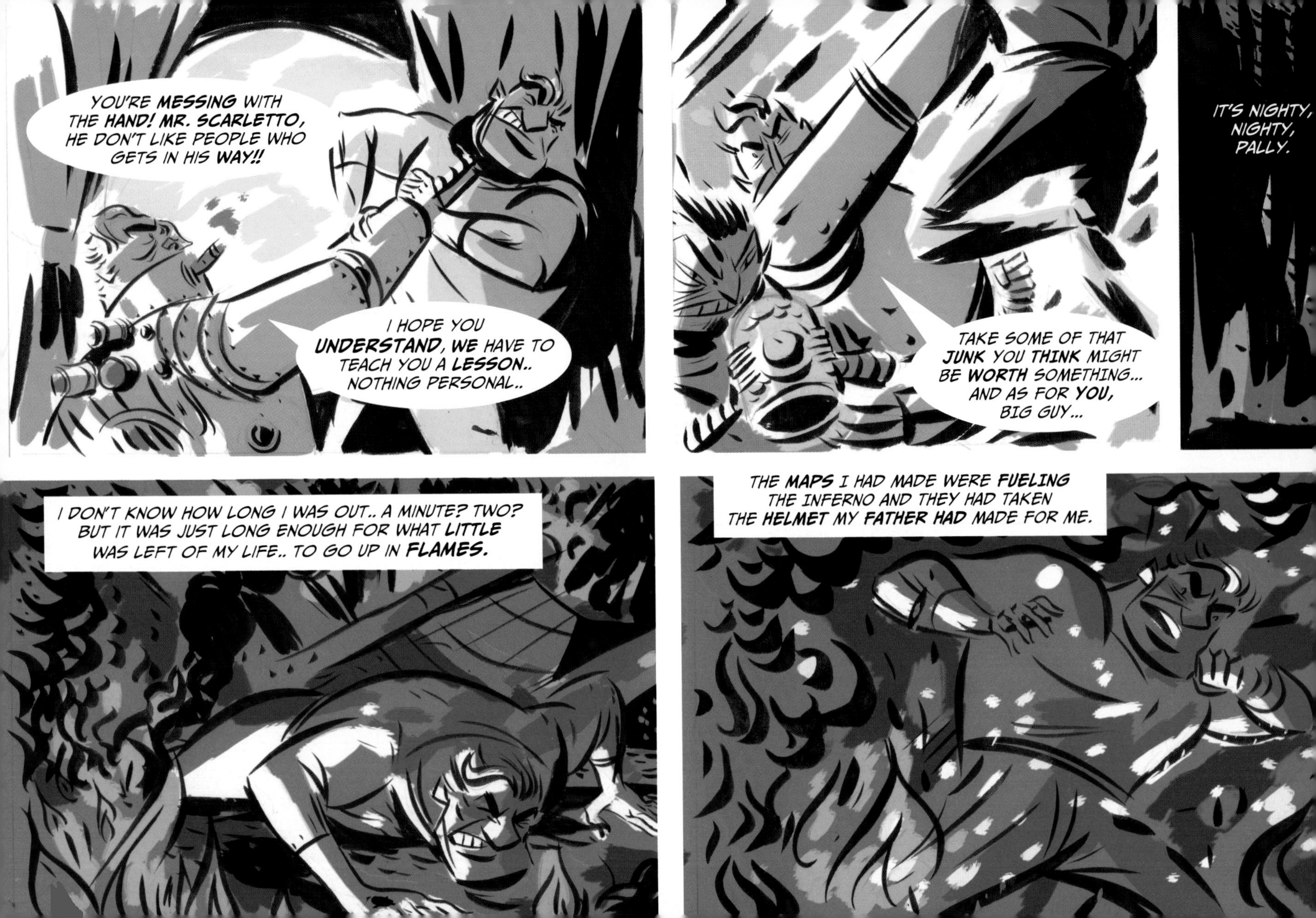
YOU'RE MESSING WITH THE HAND! MR. SCARLETTO, HE DON'T LIKE PEOPLE WHO GETS IN HIS WAY!!
I HOPE YOU UNDERSTAND, WE HAVE TO TEACH YOU A LESSON.. NOTHING PERSONAL..
TAKE SOME OF THAT JUNK YOU THINK MIGHT BE WORTH SOMETHING... AND AS FOR YOU, BIG GUY...
IT'S NIGHTY, NIGHTY, PALLY.
I DON'T KNOW HOW LONG I WAS OUT.. A MINUTE? TWO? BUT IT WAS JUST LONG ENOUGH FOR WHAT LITTLE WAS LEFT OF MY LIFE.. TO GO UP IN FLAMES.
THE MAPS I HAD MADE WERE FUELING THE INFERNO AND THEY HAD TAKEN THE HELMET MY FATHER HAD MADE FOR ME.

MY ONLY **HOPE** WAS SOPHIE.
I **PRAYED** THAT THE FIRE HAD
**AWAKENED** HER...

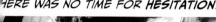

HERE WAS NO TIME FOR **HESITATION**..

JUST A QUICK PRAYER..

NO MORE TIME
FOR THINKING...

SOPHIE!!!

UMPHHH!

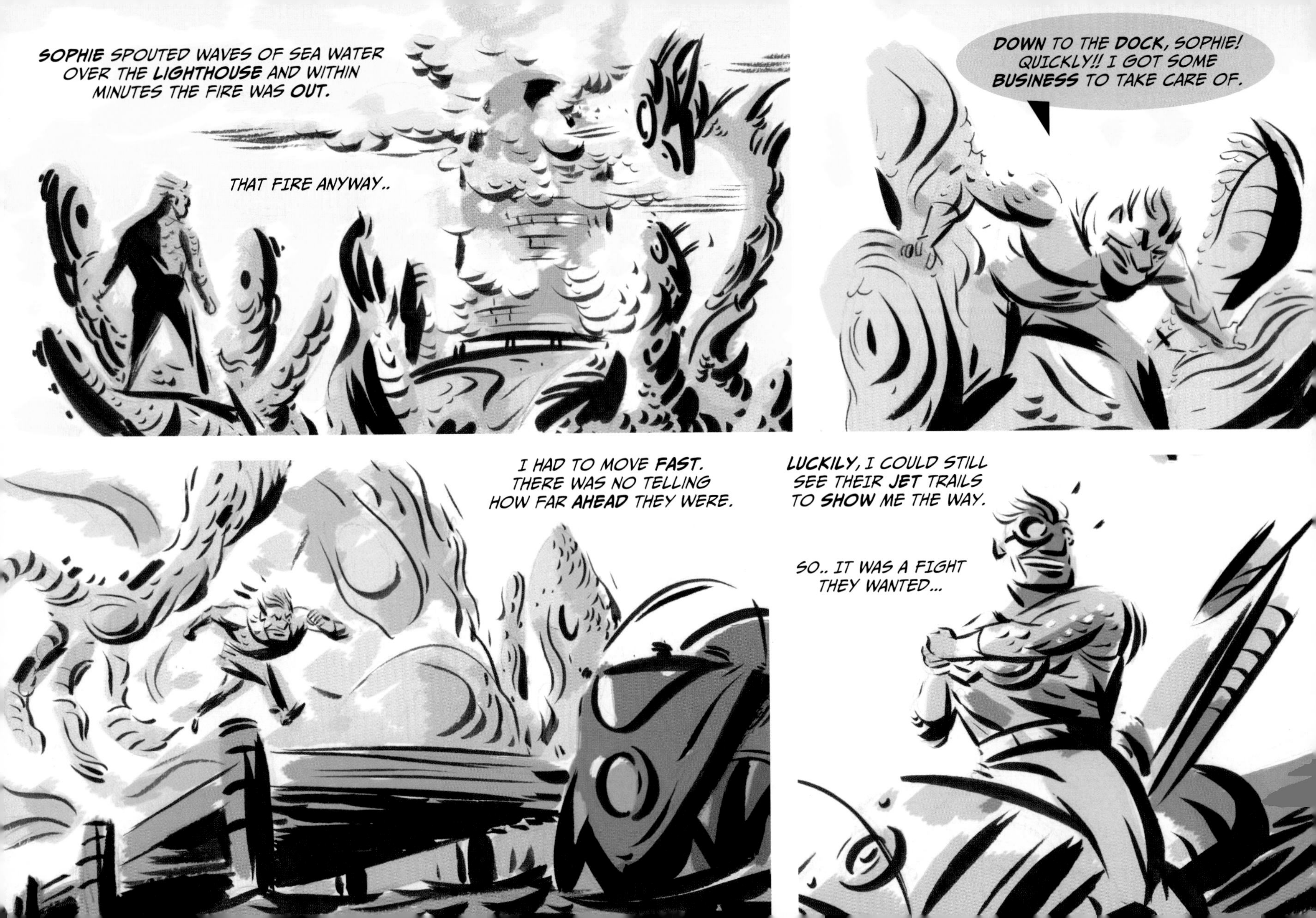
SOPHIE SPOUTED WAVES OF SEA WATER OVER THE LIGHTHOUSE AND WITHIN MINUTES THE FIRE WAS OUT.
THAT FIRE ANYWAY..
DOWN TO THE DOCK, SOPHIE! QUICKLY!! I GOT SOME BUSINESS TO TAKE CARE OF.
I HAD TO MOVE FAST. THERE WAS NO TELLING HOW FAR AHEAD THEY WERE.
LUCKILY, I COULD STILL SEE THEIR JET TRAILS TO SHOW ME THE WAY.
SO.. IT WAS A FIGHT THEY WANTED...

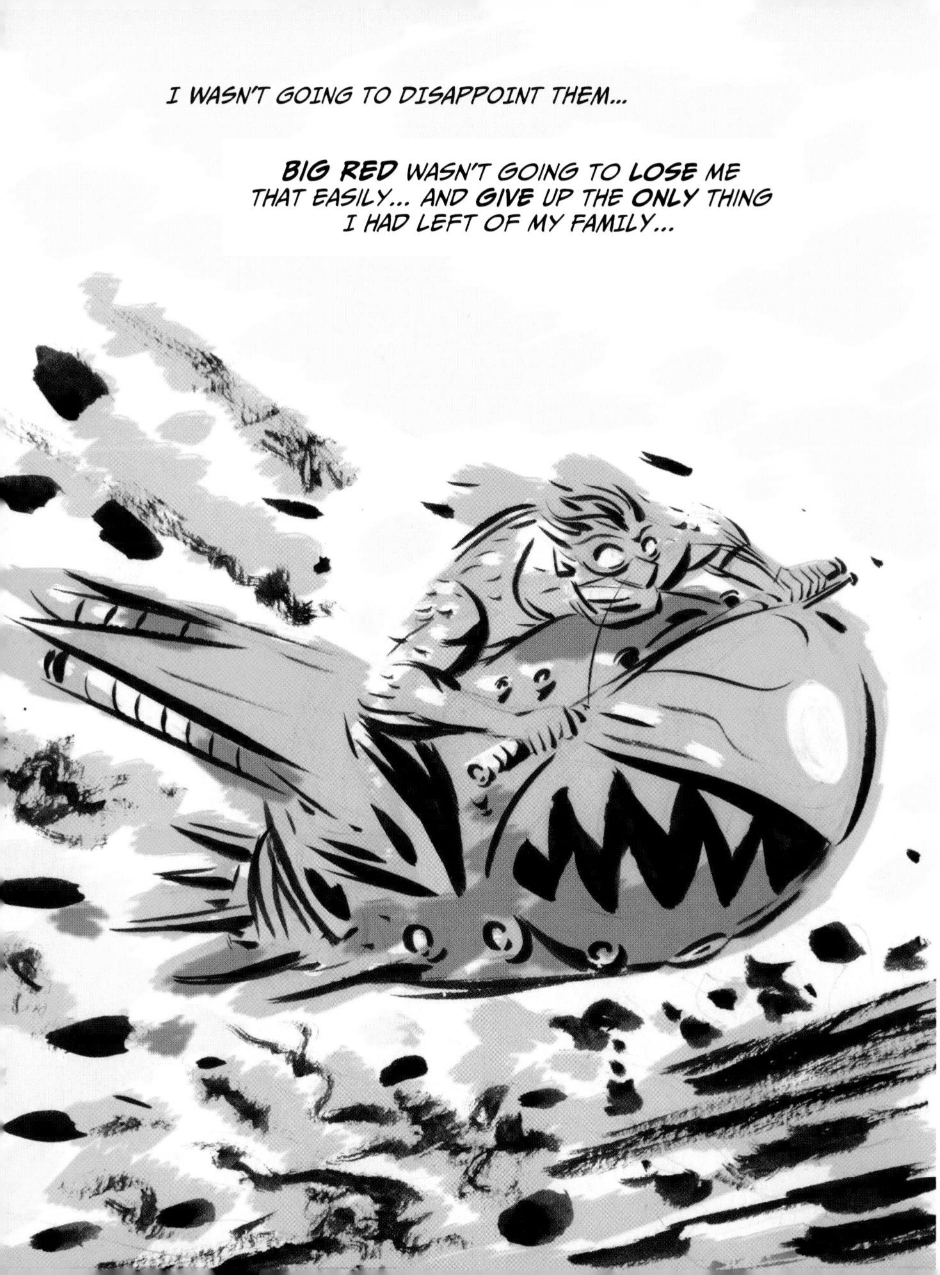
I WASN'T GOING TO DISAPPOINT THEM...
BIG RED WASN'T GOING TO LOSE ME THAT EASILY... AND GIVE UP THE ONLY THING I HAD LEFT OF MY FAMILY...

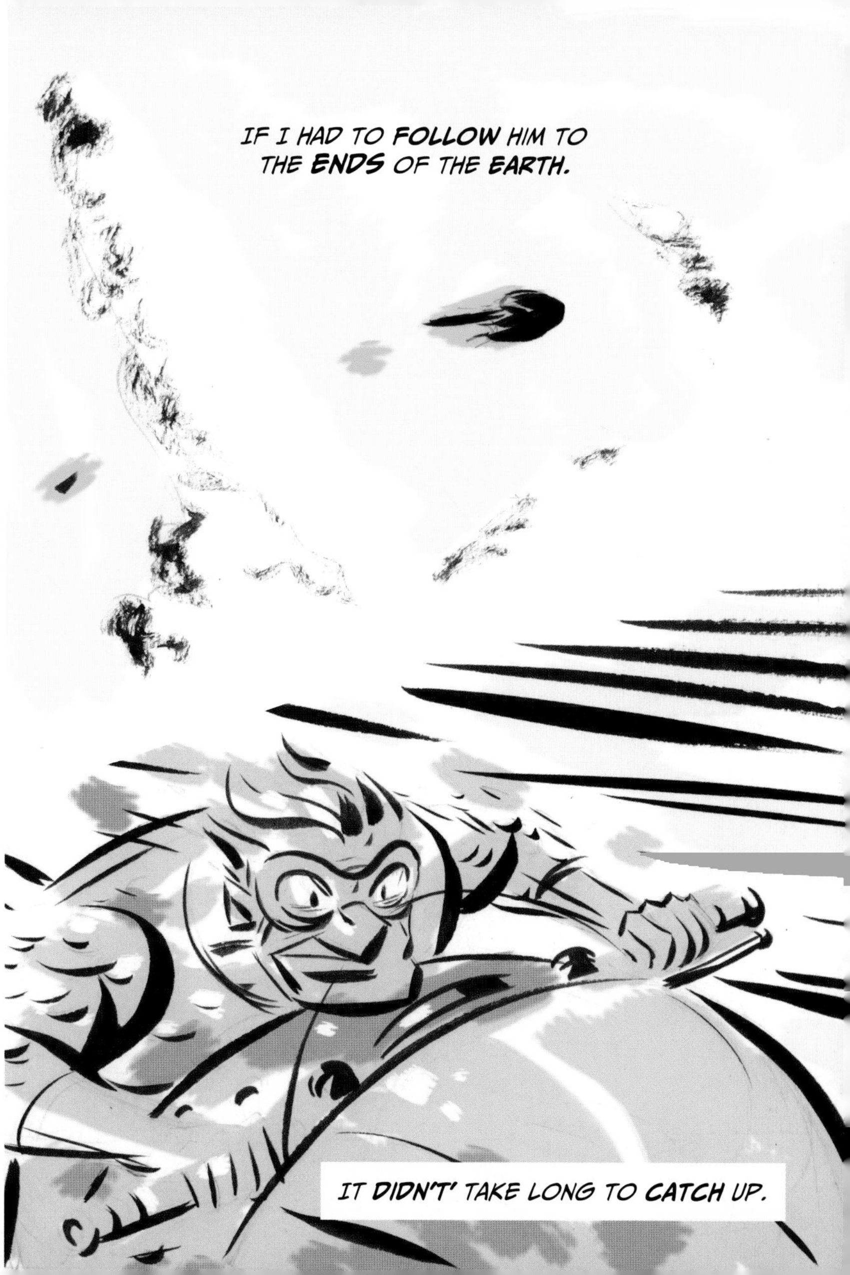
IF I HAD TO FOLLOW HIM TO THE ENDS OF THE EARTH.
IT DIDN'T' TAKE LONG TO CATCH UP.

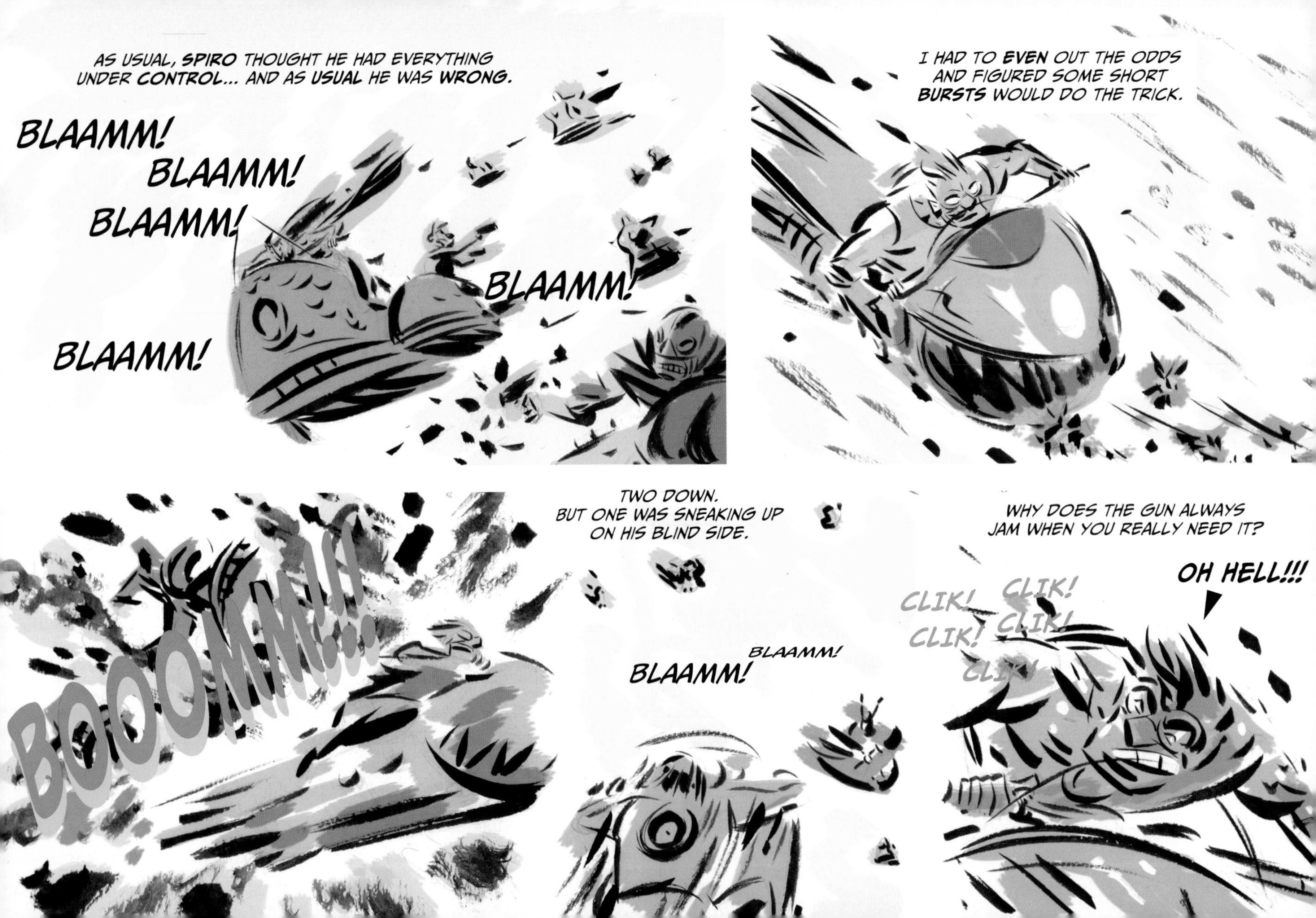
AS USUAL, SPIRO THOUGHT HE HAD EVERYTHING UNDER CONTROL... AND AS USUAL HE WAS WRONG.
BLAAMM!
BLAAMM!
BLAAMM!
BLAAMM!
BLAAMM!
I HAD TO EVEN OUT THE ODDS AND FIGURED SOME SHORT BURSTS WOULD DO THE TRICK.
BOOOMM!!!
TWO DOWN. BUT ONE WAS SNEAKING UP ON HIS BLIND SIDE.
BLAAMM!
BLAAMM!
WHY DOES THE GUN ALWAYS JAM WHEN YOU REALLY NEED IT?
CLIK!
CLIK!
CLIK!
CLIK!
OH HELL!!!

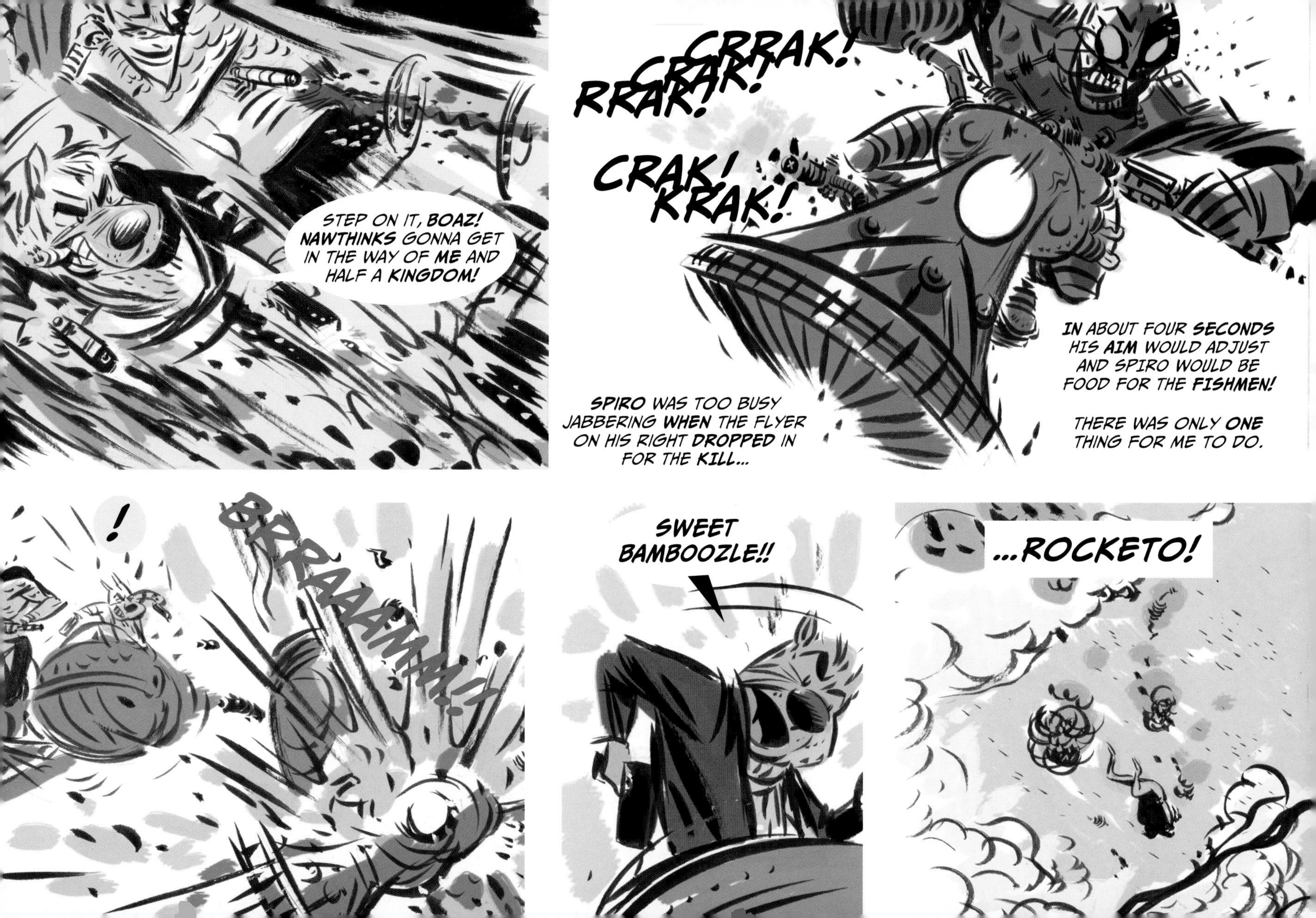
STEP ON IT, **BOAZ!** **NAWTHINKS** GONNA GET IN THE WAY OF **ME** AND HALF A **KINGDOM!**
CRRRAK!
CRAK!
RRAK!
CRAK!
KRAK!
**SPIRO** WAS TOO BUSY JABBERING **WHEN** THE FLYER ON HIS RIGHT **DROPPED** IN FOR THE **KILL...**
**IN** ABOUT FOUR **SECONDS** HIS **AIM** WOULD ADJUST AND SPIRO WOULD BE FOOD FOR THE **FISHMEN!**
THERE WAS ONLY **ONE** THING FOR ME TO DO.
!
BRRAAAMM!!
SWEET BAMBOOZLE!!
...ROCKETO!

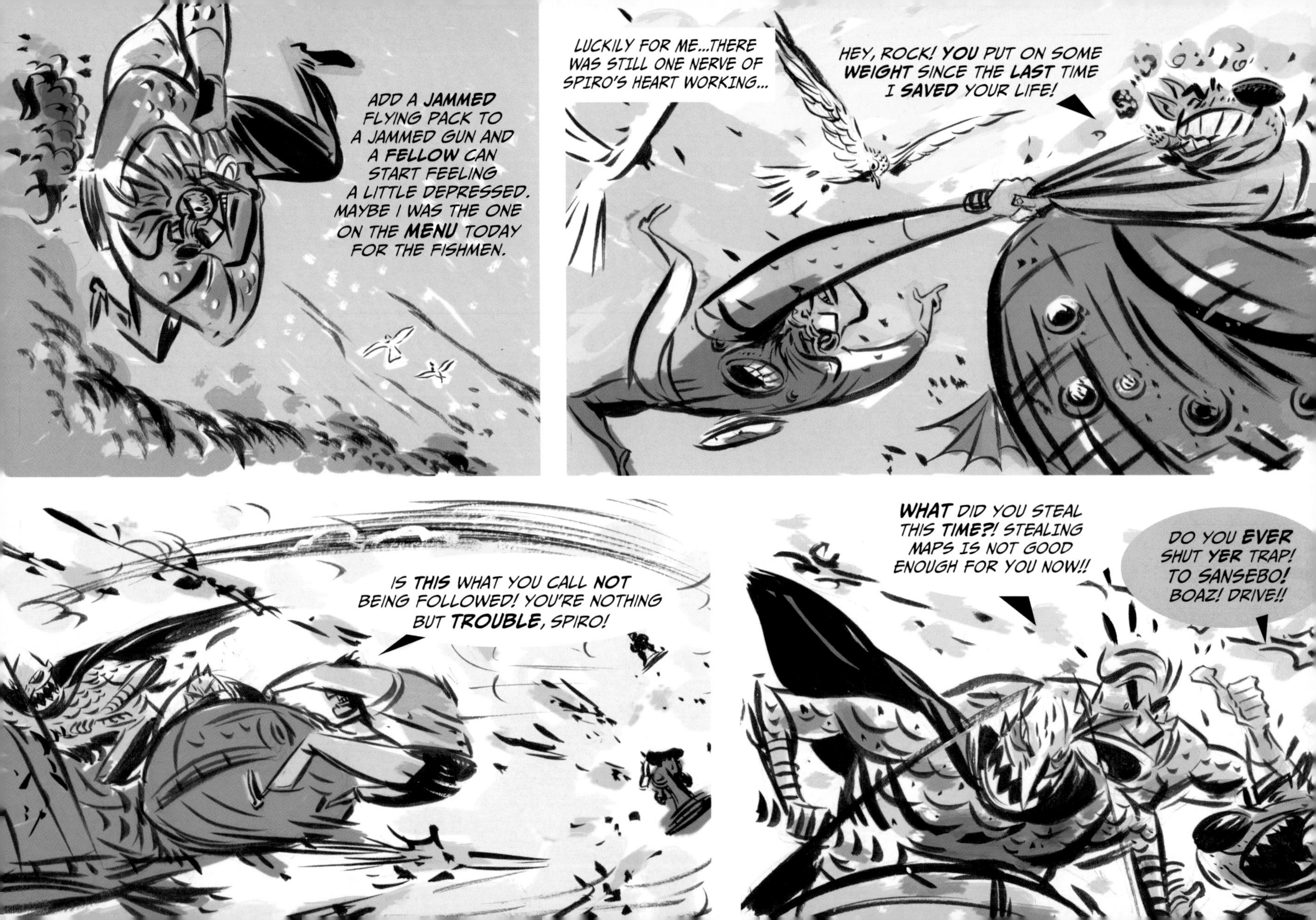
ADD A JAMMED FLYING PACK TO A JAMMED GUN AND A FELLOW CAN START FEELING A LITTLE DEPRESSED. MAYBE I WAS THE ONE ON THE MENU TODAY FOR THE FISHMEN.
LUCKILY FOR ME...THERE WAS STILL ONE NERVE OF SPIRO'S HEART WORKING...
HEY, ROCK! YOU PUT ON SOME WEIGHT SINCE THE LAST TIME I SAVED YOUR LIFE!
IS THIS WHAT YOU CALL NOT BEING FOLLOWED! YOU'RE NOTHING BUT TROUBLE, SPIRO!
WHAT DID YOU STEAL THIS TIME?! STEALING MAPS IS NOT GOOD ENOUGH FOR YOU NOW!!
DO YOU EVER SHUT YER TRAP! TO SANSEBO! BOAZ! DRIVE!!

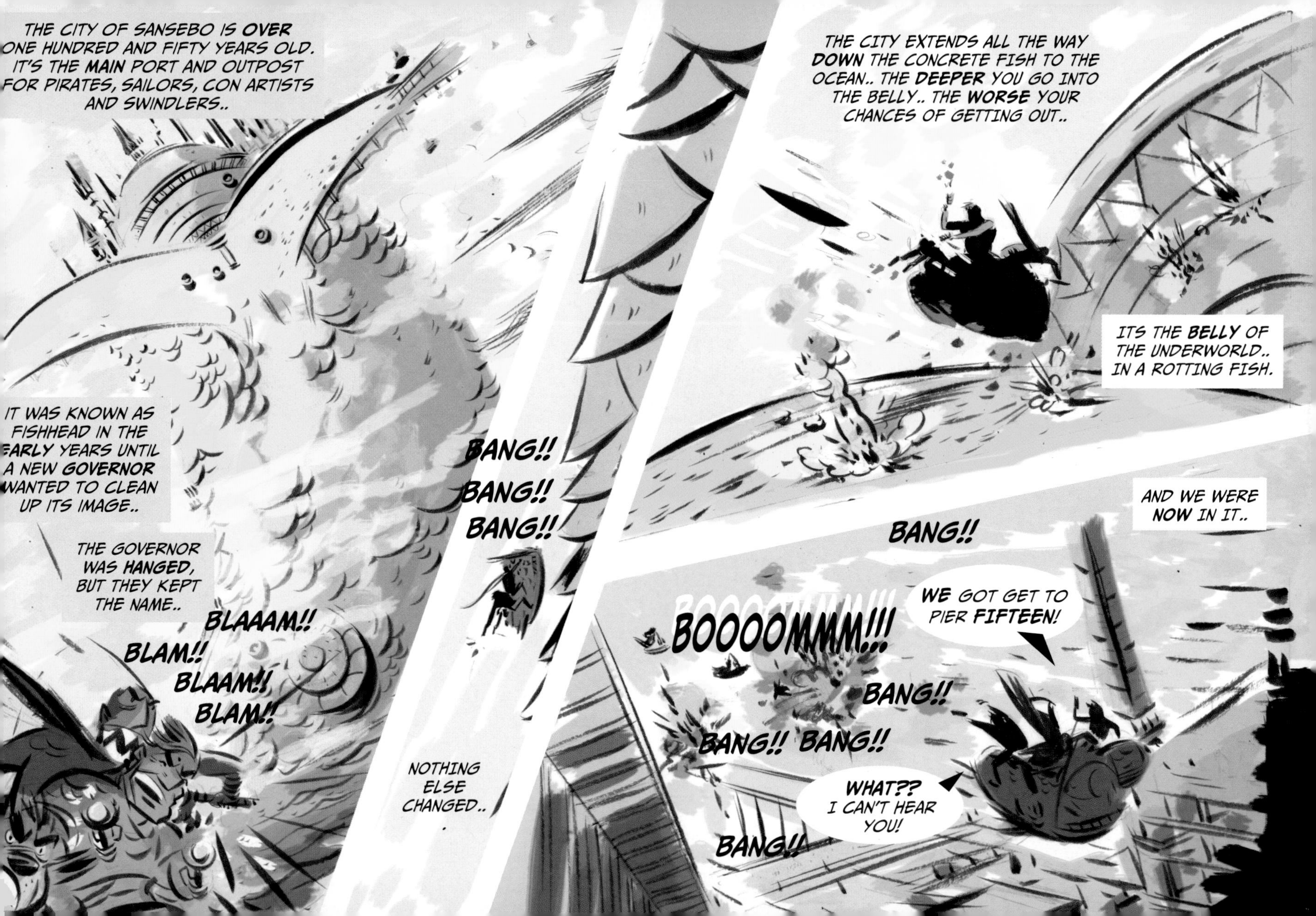
THE CITY OF SANSEBO IS OVER ONE HUNDRED AND FIFTY YEARS OLD. IT'S THE MAIN PORT AND OUTPOST FOR PIRATES, SAILORS, CON ARTISTS AND SWINDLERS..
IT WAS KNOWN AS FISHHEAD IN THE EARLY YEARS UNTIL A NEW GOVERNOR WANTED TO CLEAN UP ITS IMAGE..
THE GOVERNOR WAS HANGED, BUT THEY KEPT THE NAME..
BLAAAM!!
BLAM!!
BLAAM!!
BLAM!!
BANG!!
BANG!!
BANG!!
NOTHING ELSE CHANGED..
THE CITY EXTENDS ALL THE WAY DOWN THE CONCRETE FISH TO THE OCEAN.. THE DEEPER YOU GO INTO THE BELLY.. THE WORSE YOUR CHANCES OF GETTING OUT..
ITS THE BELLY OF THE UNDERWORLD.. IN A ROTTING FISH.
AND WE WERE NOW IN IT..
BANG!!
BOOOOMMM!!!
WE GOT GET TO PIER FIFTEEN!
BANG!!
BANG!! BANG!!
WHAT?? I CAN'T HEAR YOU!
BANG!!

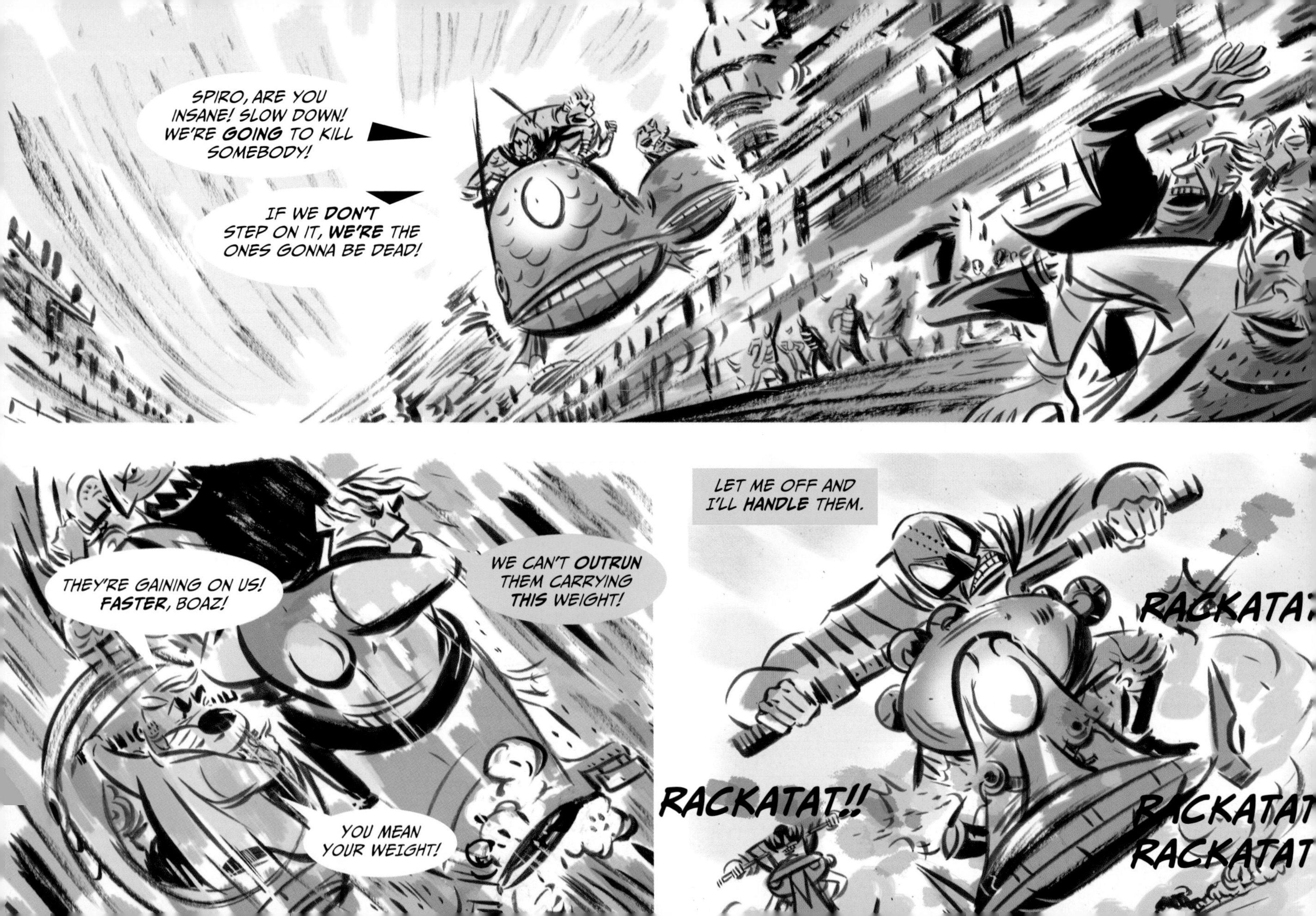
SPIRO, ARE YOU INSANE! SLOW DOWN! WE'RE **GOING** TO KILL SOMEBODY!
IF WE **DON'T** STEP ON IT, **WE'RE** THE ONES GONNA BE DEAD!
THEY'RE GAINING ON US! **FASTER**, BOAZ!
WE CAN'T **OUTRUN** THEM CARRYING **THIS** WEIGHT!
YOU MEAN YOUR WEIGHT!
LET ME OFF AND I'LL **HANDLE** THEM.
RACKATAT!!

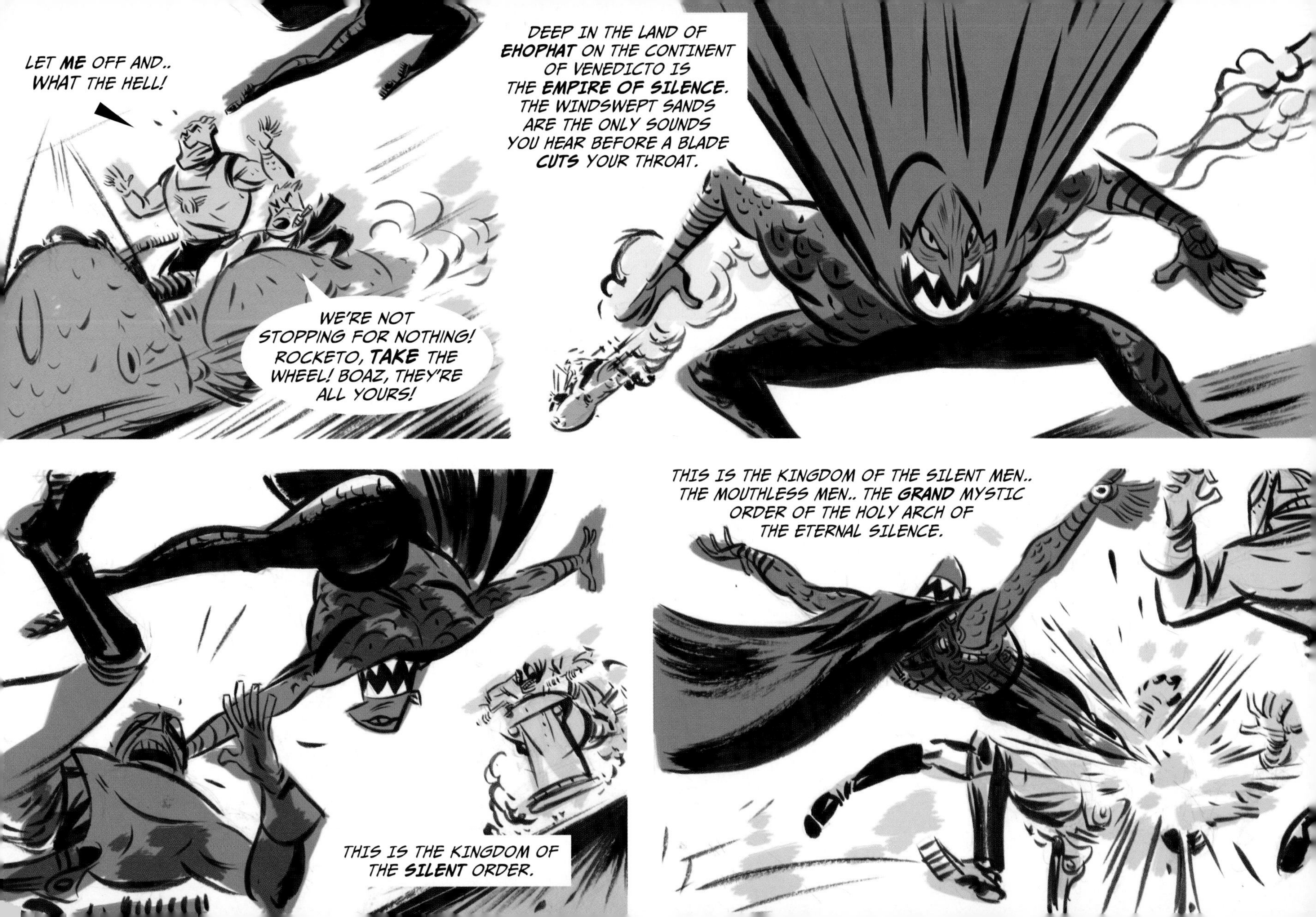
LET ME OFF AND.. WHAT THE HELL!
WE'RE NOT STOPPING FOR NOTHING! ROCKETO, TAKE THE WHEEL! BOAZ, THEY'RE ALL YOURS!
DEEP IN THE LAND OF EHOPHAT ON THE CONTINENT OF VENEDICTO IS THE EMPIRE OF SILENCE. THE WINDSWEPT SANDS ARE THE ONLY SOUNDS YOU HEAR BEFORE A BLADE CUTS YOUR THROAT.
THIS IS THE KINGDOM OF THE SILENT ORDER.
THIS IS THE KINGDOM OF THE SILENT MEN.. THE MOUTHLESS MEN.. THE GRAND MYSTIC ORDER OF THE HOLY ARCH OF THE ETERNAL SILENCE.

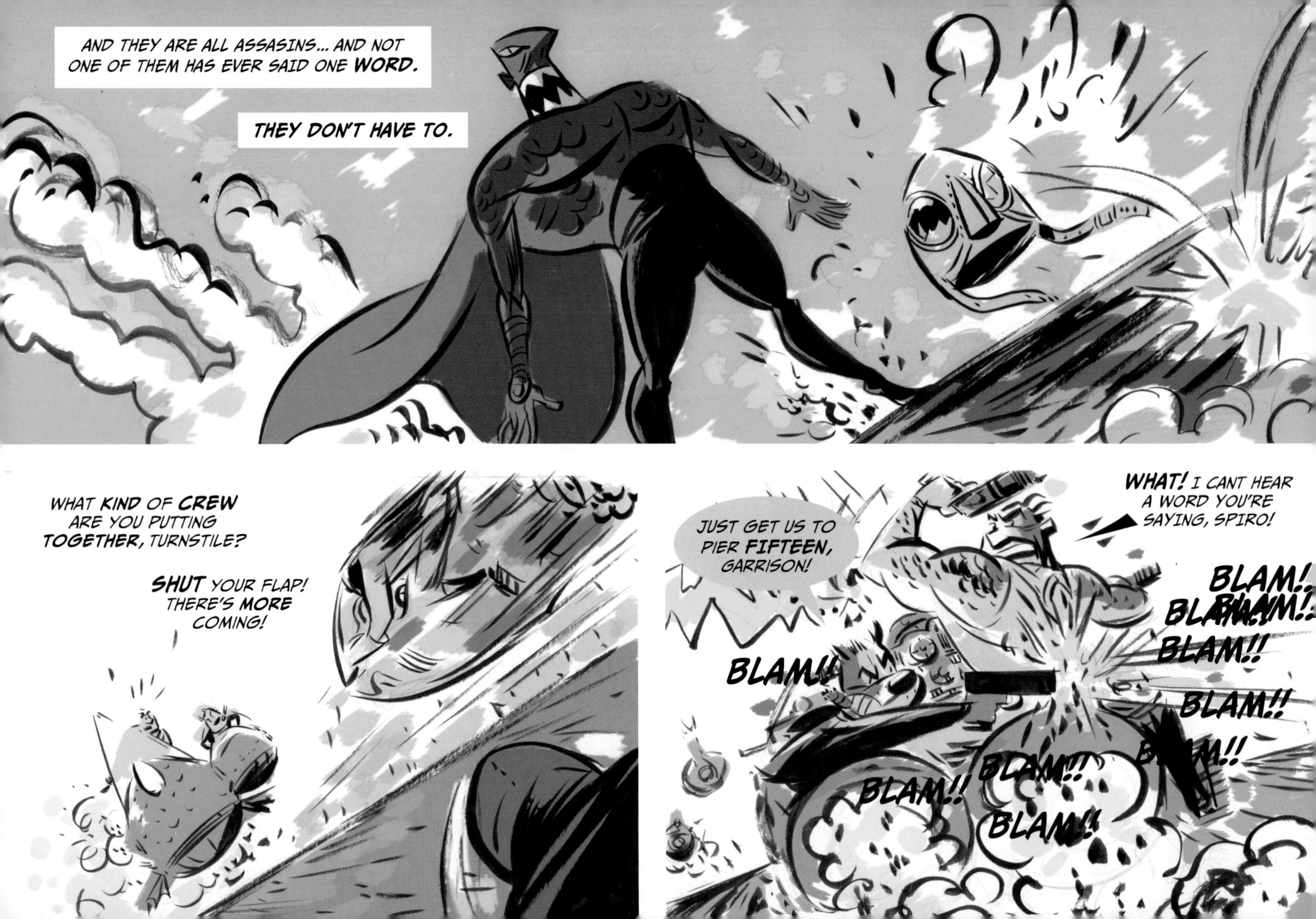
AND THEY ARE ALL ASSASINS... AND NOT ONE OF THEM HAS EVER SAID ONE WORD.
THEY DON'T HAVE TO.
WHAT KIND OF CREW ARE YOU PUTTING TOGETHER, TURNSTILE?
SHUT YOUR FLAP! THERE'S MORE COMING!
JUST GET US TO PIER FIFTEEN, GARRISON!
WHAT! I CANT HEAR A WORD YOU'RE SAYING, SPIRO!
BLAM!!
BLAM!!
BLAM!!
BLAM!!
BLAM!!
BLAM!!
BLAM!!
BLAM!!
BLAM!!
BLAM!!

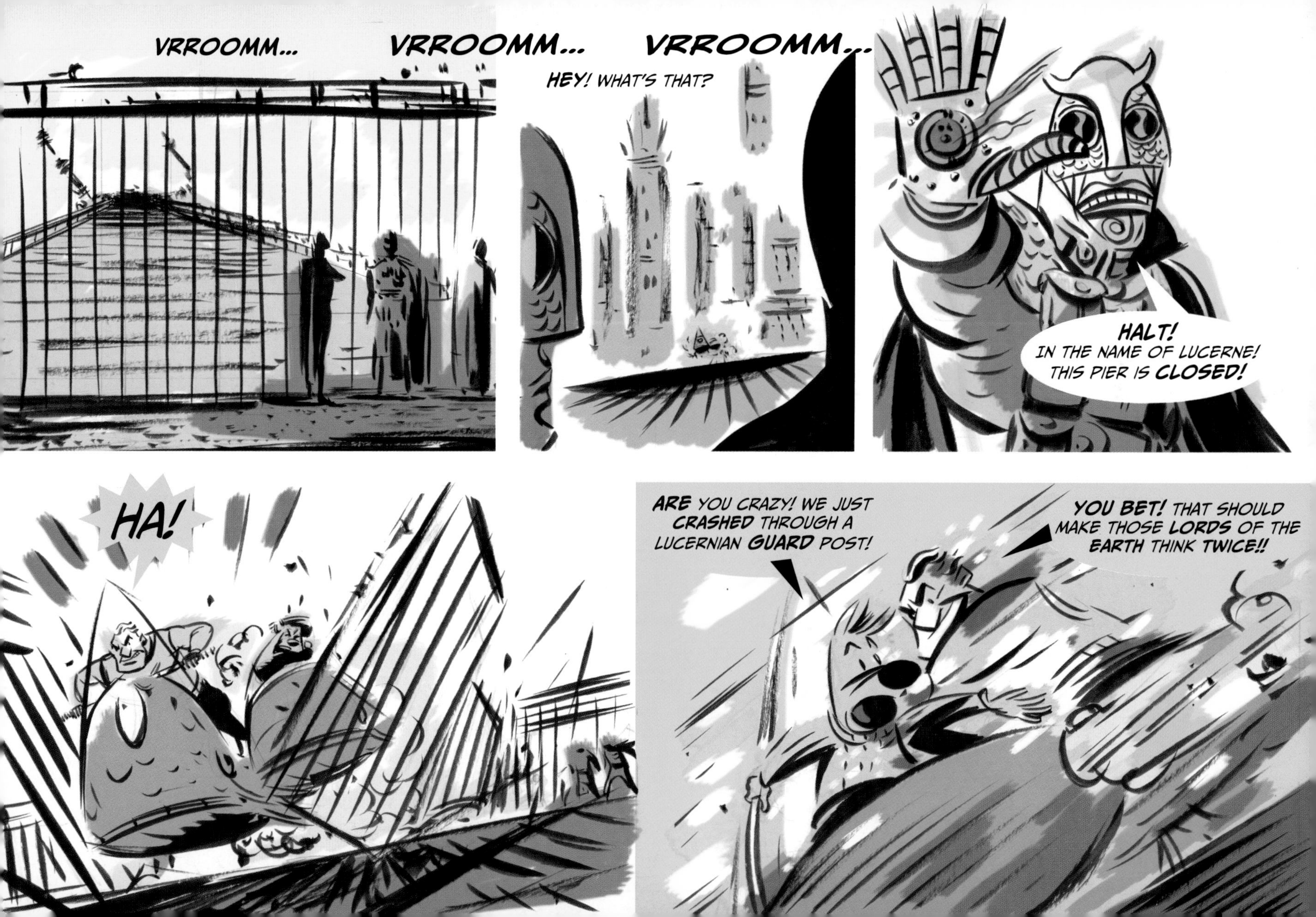
VRROOMM... VRROOMM... VRROOMM...
HEY! WHAT'S THAT?
HALT! IN THE NAME OF LUCERNE! THIS PIER IS CLOSED!
HA!
ARE YOU CRAZY! WE JUST CRASHED THROUGH A LUCERNIAN GUARD POST!
YOU BET! THAT SHOULD MAKE THOSE LORDS OF THE EARTH THINK TWICE!!

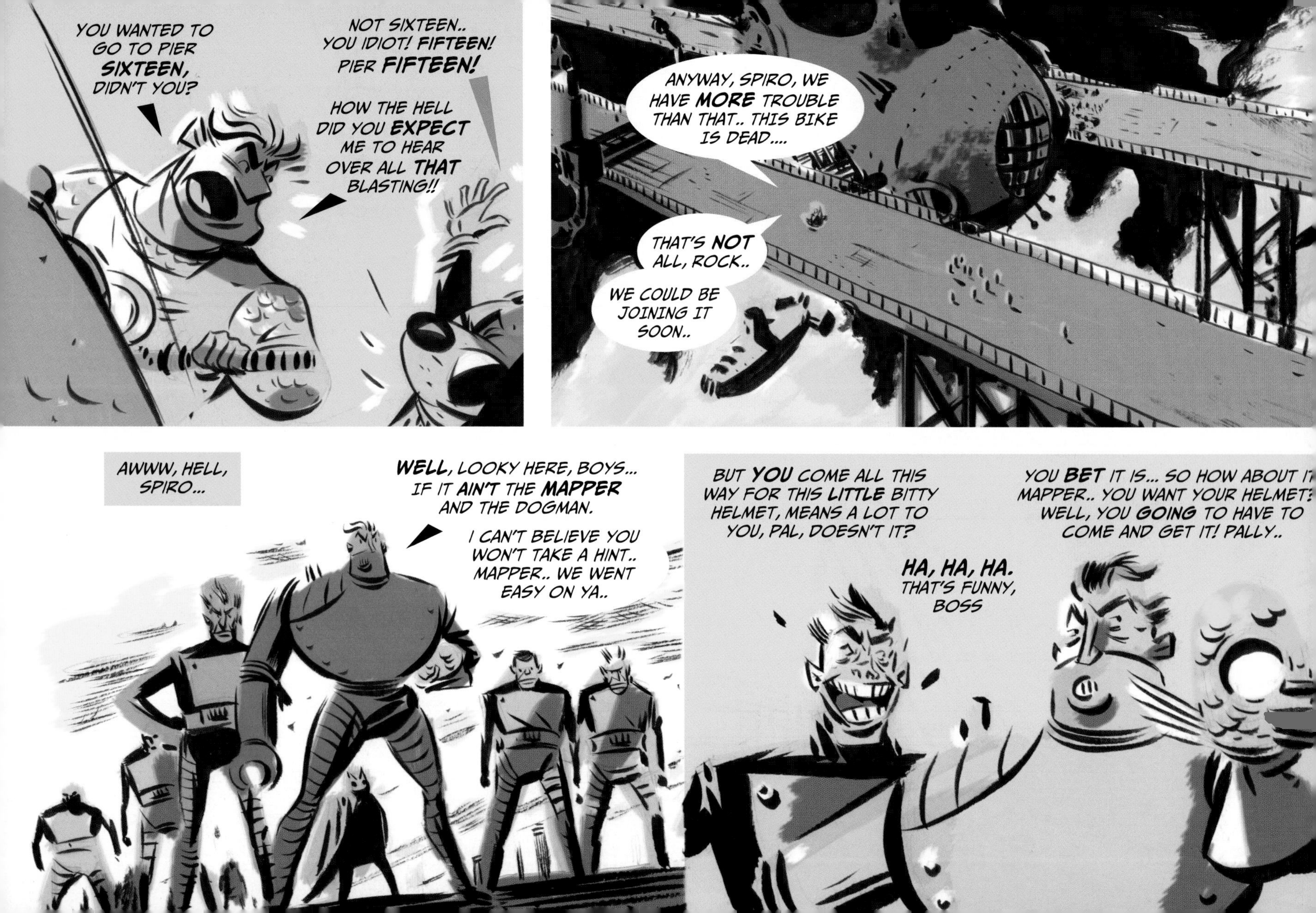

YOU WANTED TO GO TO PIER SIXTEEN, DIDN'T YOU?
NOT SIXTEEN.. YOU IDIOT! FIFTEEN! PIER FIFTEEN!
HOW THE HELL DID YOU EXPECT ME TO HEAR OVER ALL THAT BLASTING!!
ANYWAY, SPIRO, WE HAVE MORE TROUBLE THAN THAT.. THIS BIKE IS DEAD....
THAT'S NOT ALL, ROCK..
WE COULD BE JOINING IT SOON..
AWWW, HELL, SPIRO...
WELL, LOOKY HERE, BOYS... IF IT AIN'T THE MAPPER AND THE DOGMAN.
I CAN'T BELIEVE YOU WON'T TAKE A HINT.. MAPPER.. WE WENT EASY ON YA..
BUT YOU COME ALL THIS WAY FOR THIS LITTLE BITTY HELMET, MEANS A LOT TO YOU, PAL, DOESN'T IT?
YOU BET IT IS... SO HOW ABOUT IT MAPPER.. YOU WANT YOUR HELMET? WELL, YOU GOING TO HAVE TO COME AND GET IT! PALLY..
HA, HA, HA. THAT'S FUNNY, BOSS

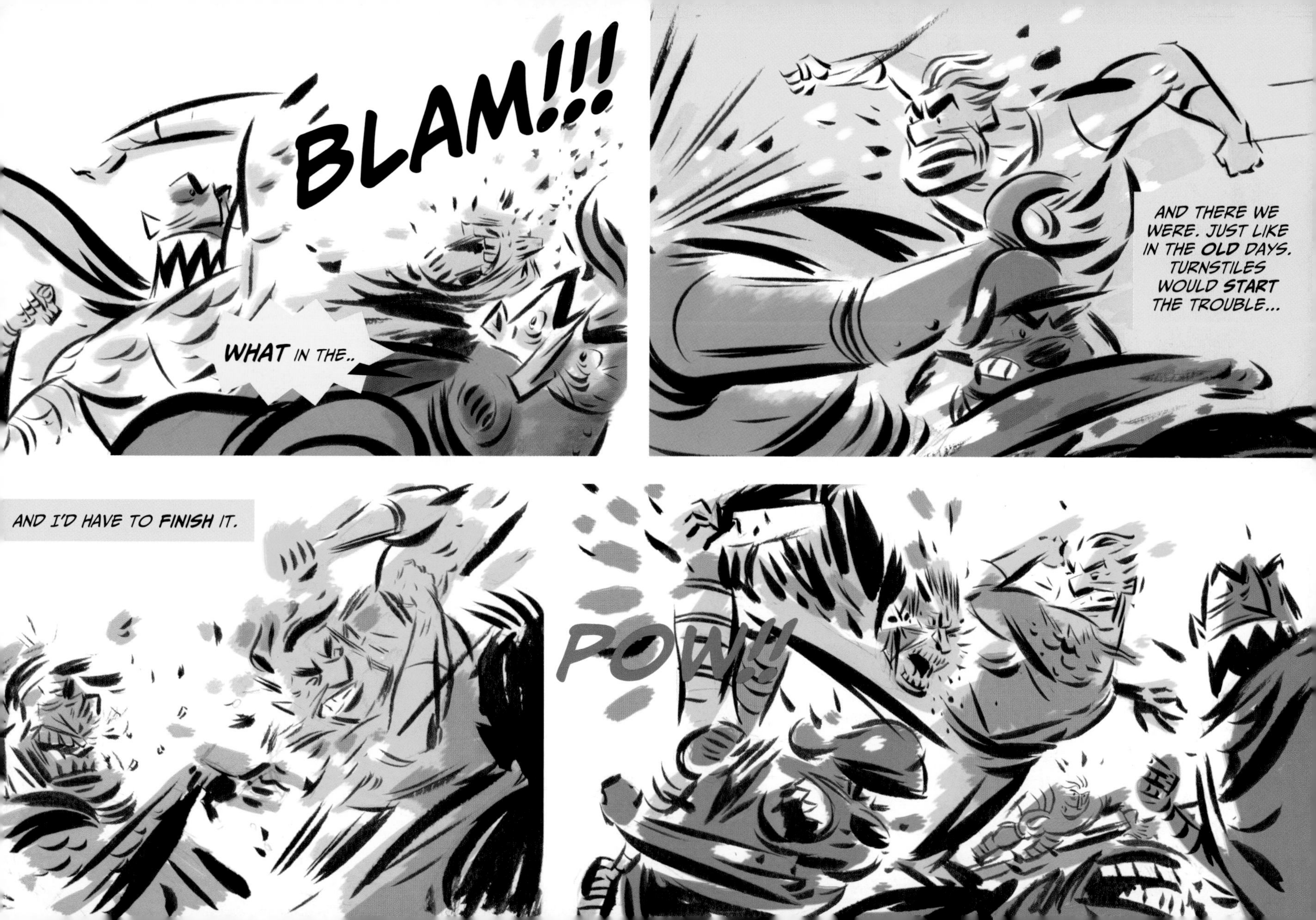
BLAM!!!
WHAT IN THE..
AND THERE WE WERE. JUST LIKE IN THE OLD DAYS. TURNSTILES WOULD START THE TROUBLE...
AND I'D HAVE TO FINISH IT.
POW!!

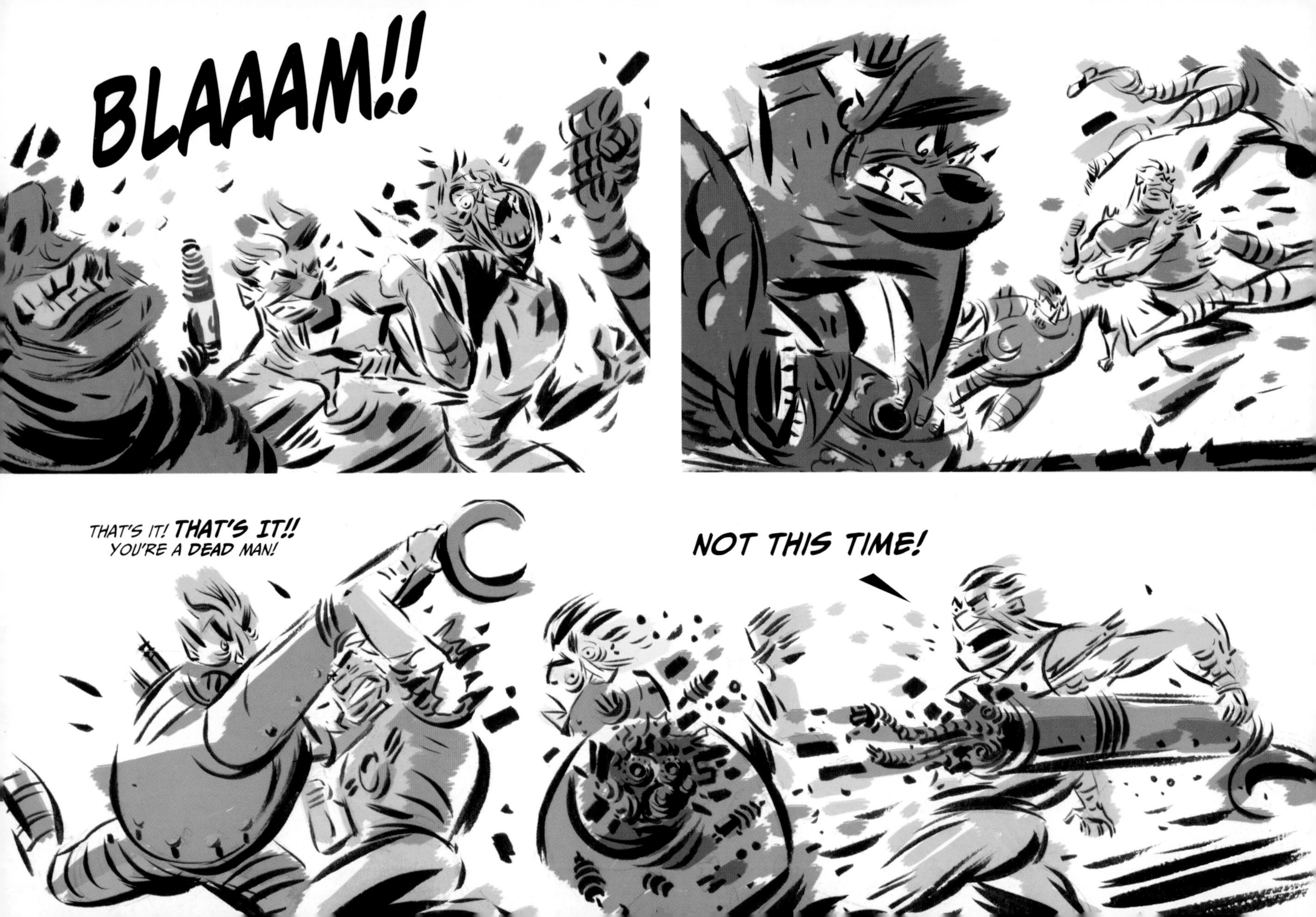
BLAAAM!!
THAT'S IT! THAT'S IT!! YOU'RE A DEAD MAN!
NOT THIS TIME!

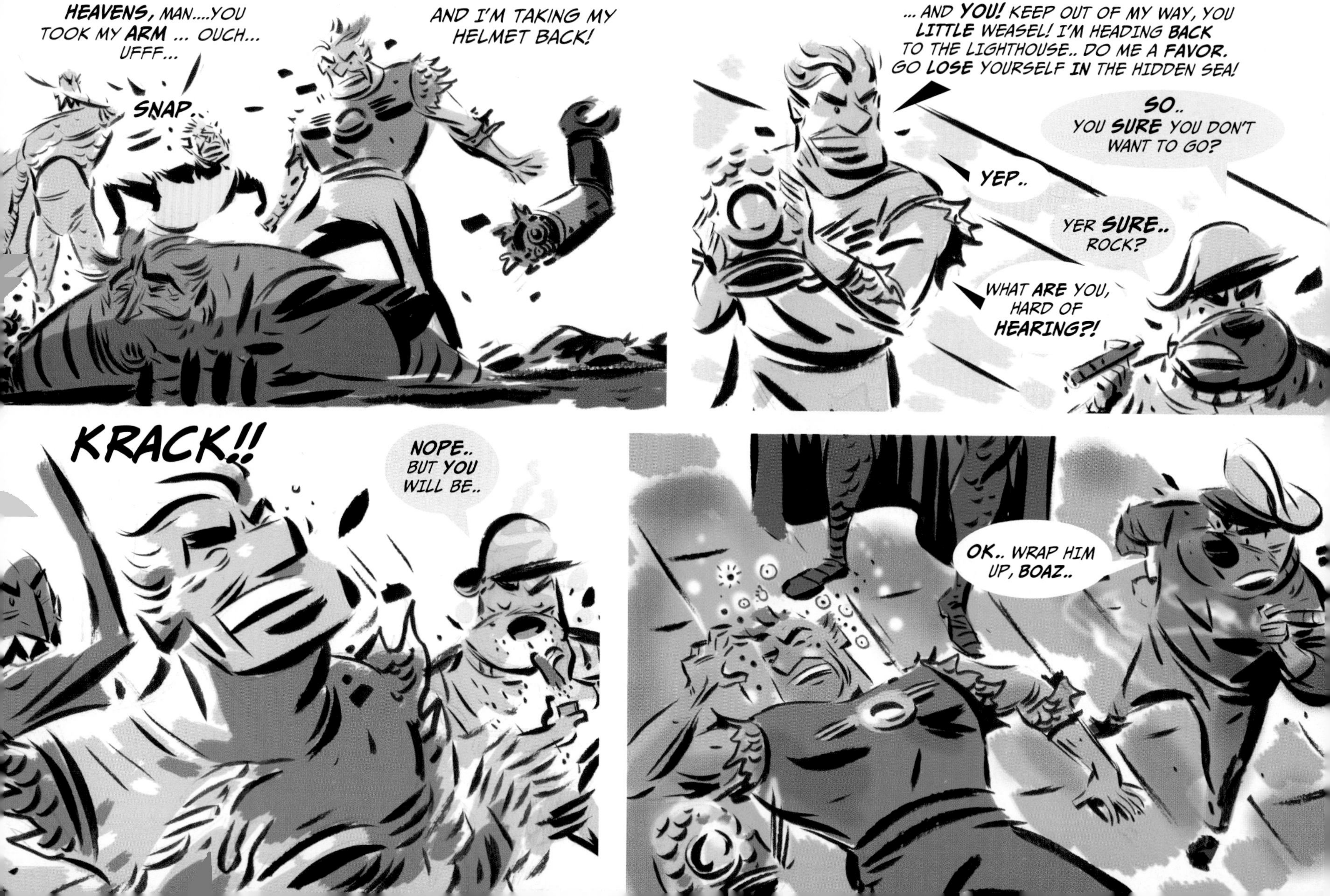
HEAVENS, MAN....YOU TOOK MY ARM ... OUCH... UFFF...
SNAP..
AND I'M TAKING MY HELMET BACK!
... AND YOU! KEEP OUT OF MY WAY, YOU LITTLE WEASEL! I'M HEADING BACK TO THE LIGHTHOUSE.. DO ME A FAVOR. GO LOSE YOURSELF IN THE HIDDEN SEA!
SO.. YOU SURE YOU DON'T WANT TO GO?
YEP..
YER SURE.. ROCK?
WHAT ARE YOU, HARD OF HEARING?!
KRACK!!
NOPE.. BUT YOU WILL BE..
OK.. WRAP HIM UP, BOAZ..

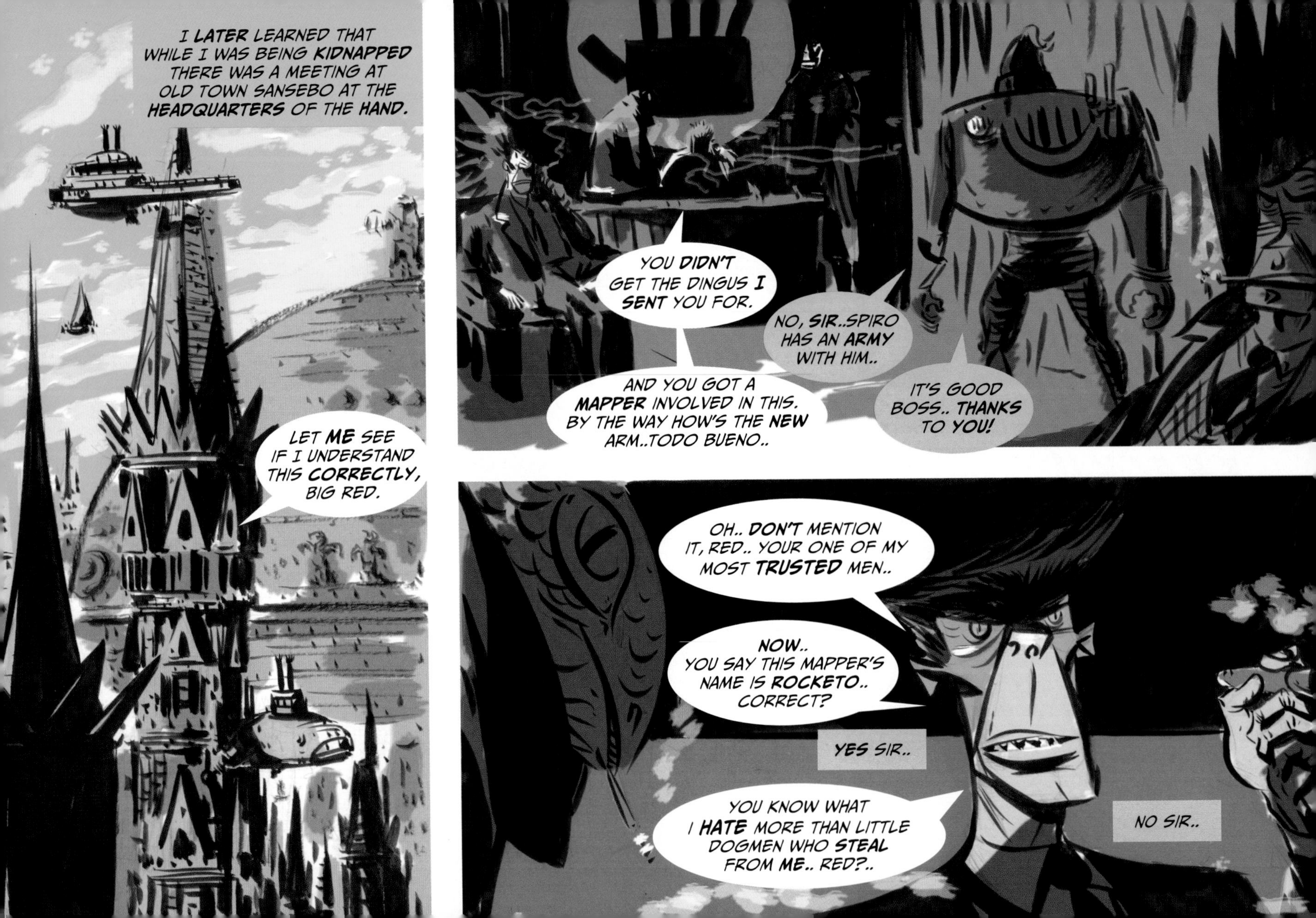
I LATER LEARNED THAT WHILE I WAS BEING KIDNAPPED THERE WAS A MEETING AT OLD TOWN SANSEBO AT THE HEADQUARTERS OF THE HAND.
LET ME SEE IF I UNDERSTAND THIS CORRECTLY, BIG RED.
YOU DIDN'T GET THE DINGUS I SENT YOU FOR.
AND YOU GOT A MAPPER INVOLVED IN THIS. BY THE WAY HOW'S THE NEW ARM..TODO BUENO..
NO, SIR..SPIRO HAS AN ARMY WITH HIM..
IT'S GOOD BOSS.. THANKS TO YOU!
OH.. DON'T MENTION IT, RED.. YOUR ONE OF MY MOST TRUSTED MEN..
NOW.. YOU SAY THIS MAPPER'S NAME IS ROCKETO.. CORRECT?
YES SIR..
YOU KNOW WHAT I HATE MORE THAN LITTLE DOGMEN WHO STEAL FROM ME.. RED?..
NO SIR..

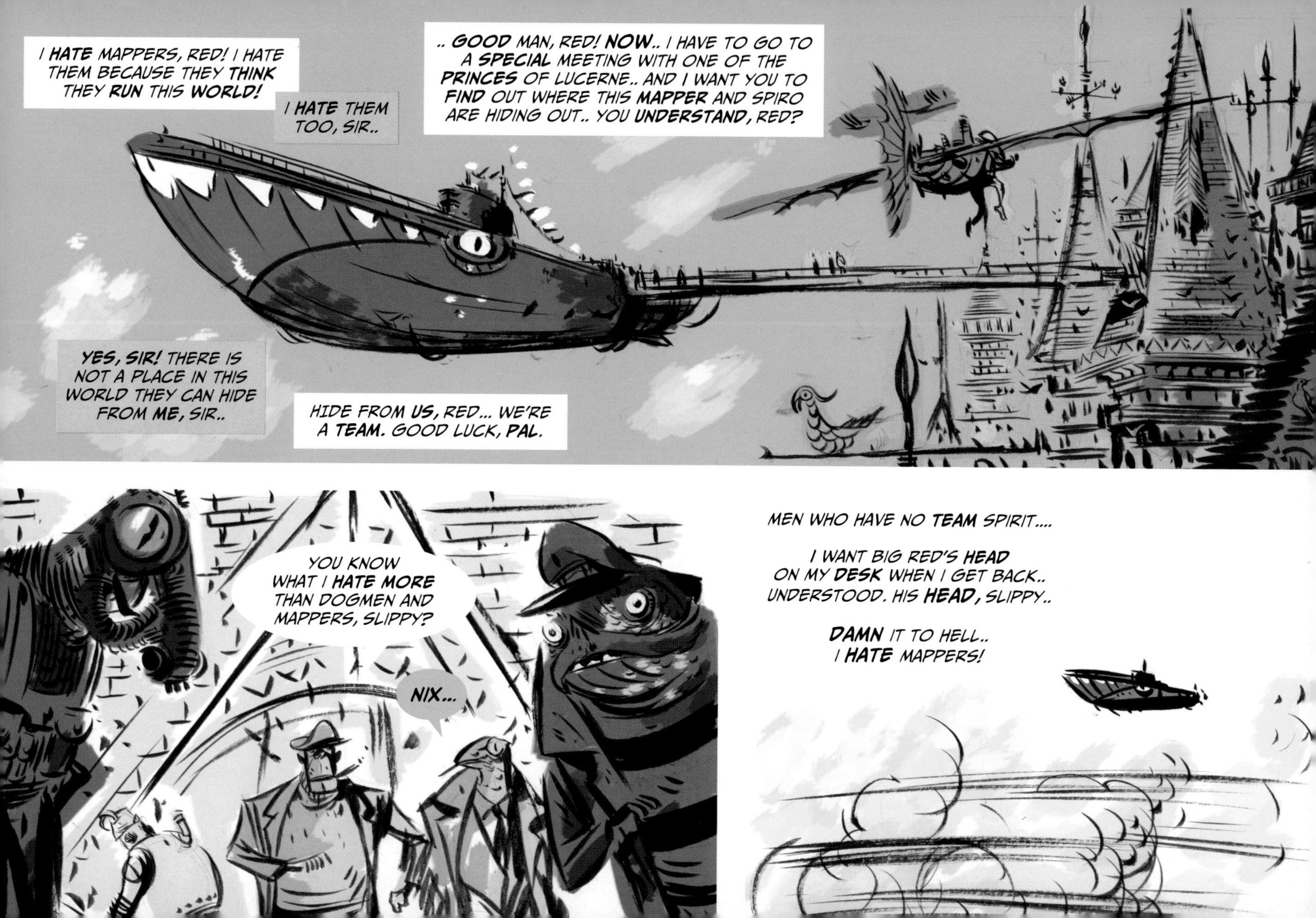
I HATE MAPPERS, RED! I HATE THEM BECAUSE THEY THINK THEY RUN THIS WORLD!
I HATE THEM TOO, SIR..
.. GOOD MAN, RED! NOW.. I HAVE TO GO TO A SPECIAL MEETING WITH ONE OF THE PRINCES OF LUCERNE.. AND I WANT YOU TO FIND OUT WHERE THIS MAPPER AND SPIRO ARE HIDING OUT.. YOU UNDERSTAND, RED?
YES, SIR! THERE IS NOT A PLACE IN THIS WORLD THEY CAN HIDE FROM ME, SIR..
HIDE FROM US, RED... WE'RE A TEAM. GOOD LUCK, PAL.
YOU KNOW WHAT I HATE MORE THAN DOGMEN AND MAPPERS, SLIPPY?
NIX...
MEN WHO HAVE NO TEAM SPIRIT....
I WANT BIG RED'S HEAD ON MY DESK WHEN I GET BACK.. UNDERSTOOD. HIS HEAD, SLIPPY..
DAMN IT TO HELL.. I HATE MAPPERS!

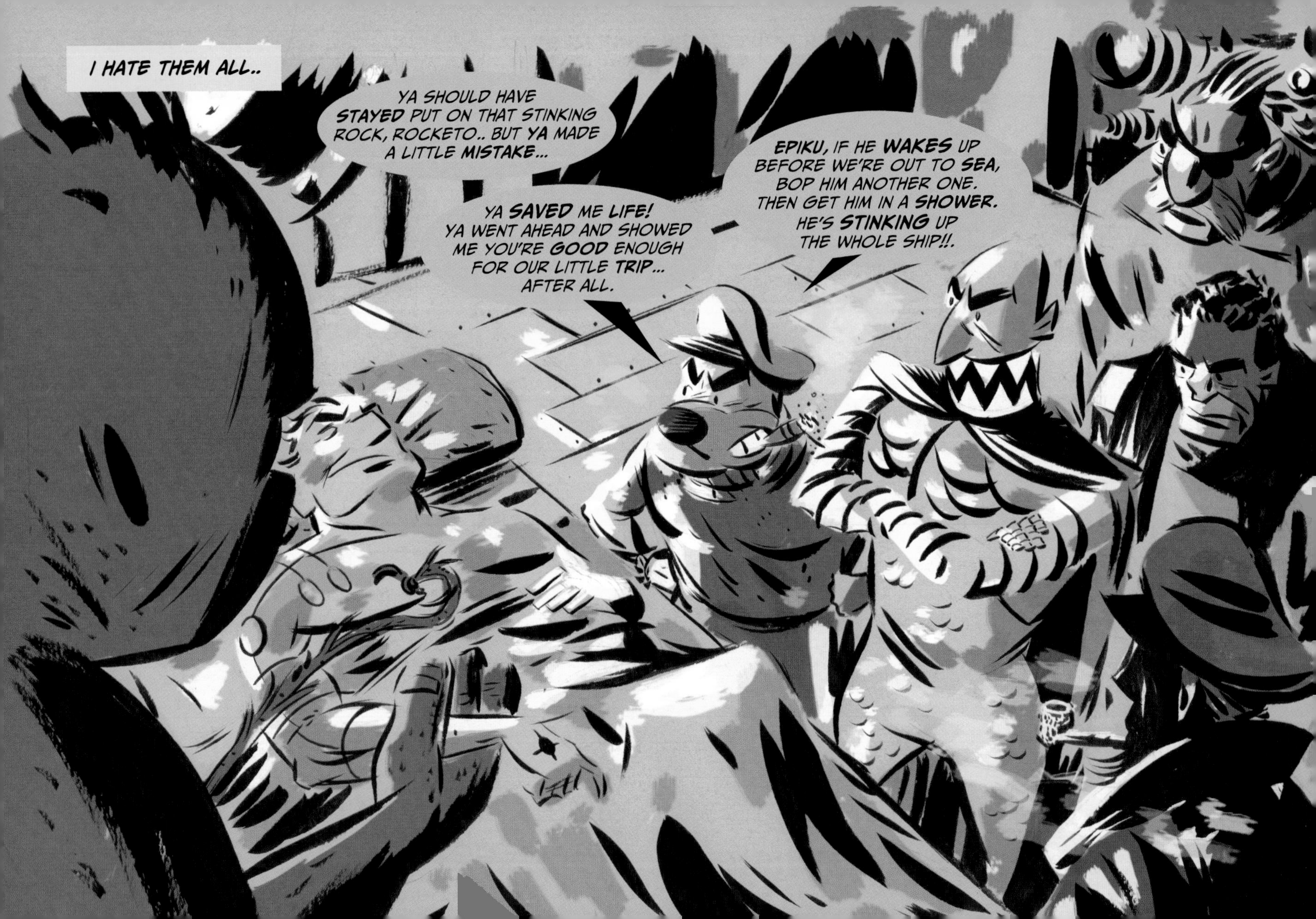
I HATE THEM ALL..
YA SHOULD HAVE STAYED PUT ON THAT STINKING ROCK, ROCKETO.. BUT YA MADE A LITTLE MISTAKE...
YA SAVED ME LIFE! YA WENT AHEAD AND SHOWED ME YOU'RE GOOD ENOUGH FOR OUR LITTLE TRIP... AFTER ALL.
EPIKU, IF HE WAKES UP BEFORE WE'RE OUT TO SEA, BOP HIM ANOTHER ONE. THEN GET HIM IN A SHOWER. HE'S STINKING UP THE WHOLE SHIP!!.

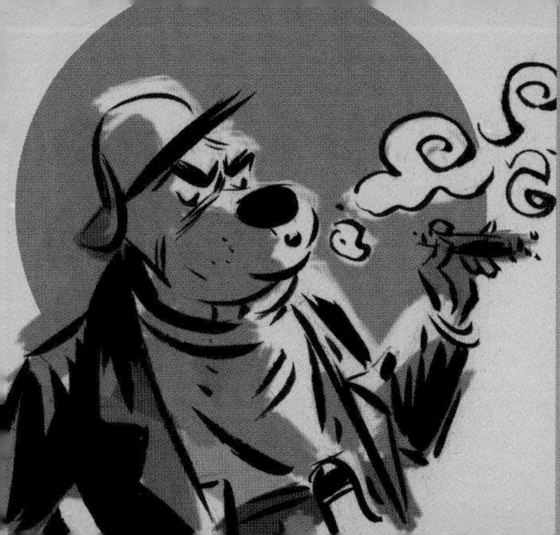

ROCKETO

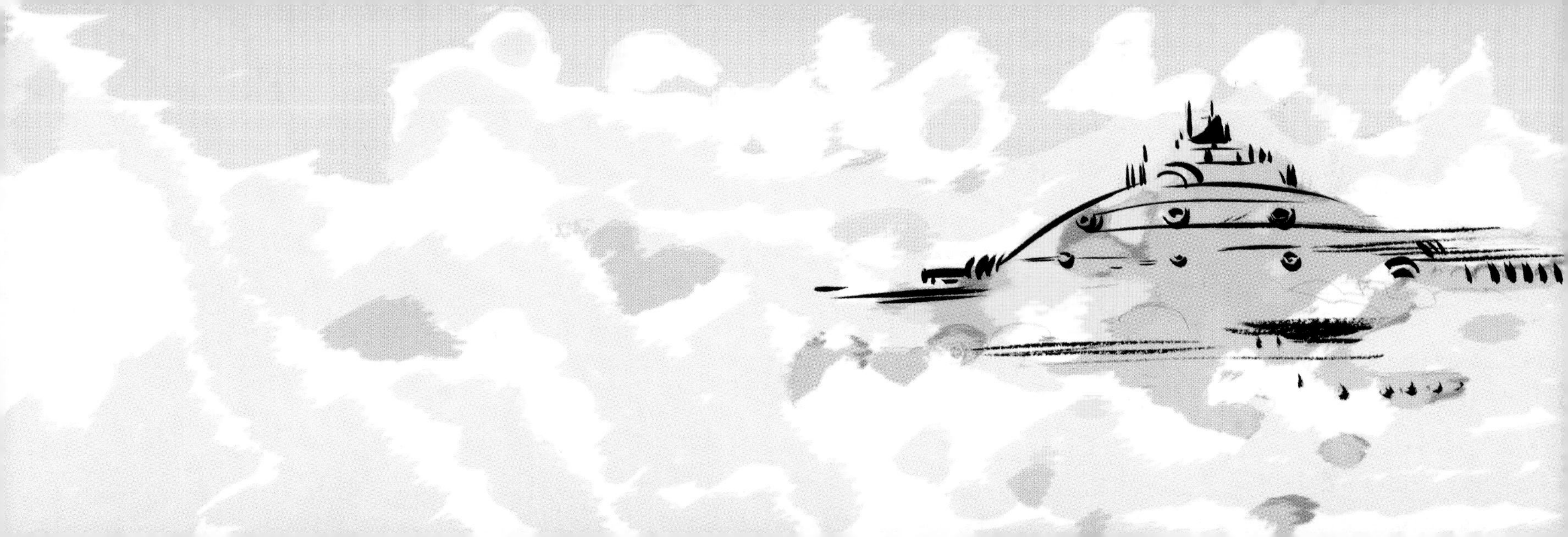

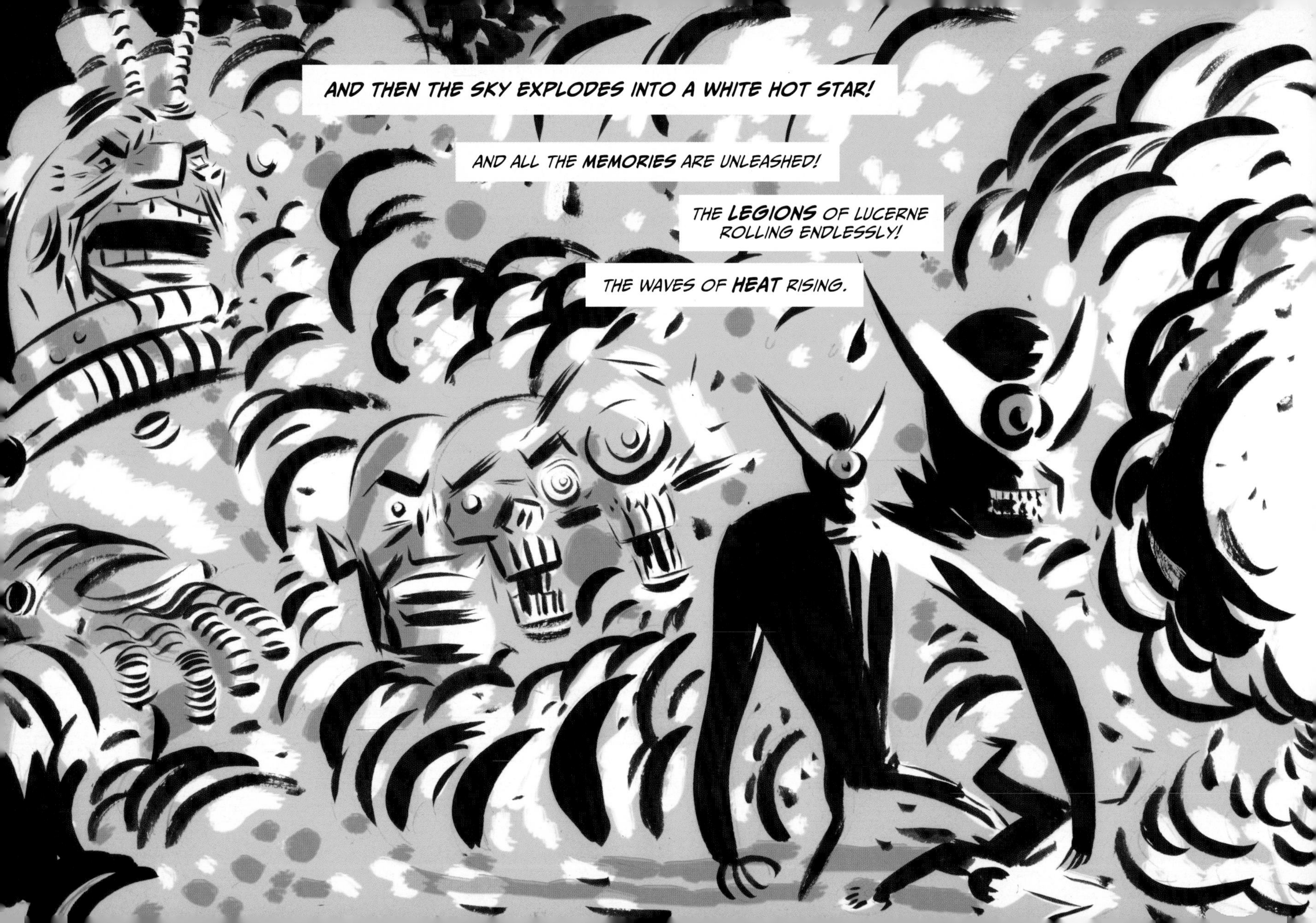
AND THEN THE SKY EXPLODES INTO A WHITE HOT STAR!
AND ALL THE **MEMORIES** ARE UNLEASHED!
THE **LEGIONS** OF LUCERNE ROLLING ENDLESSLY!
THE WAVES OF **HEAT** RISING.

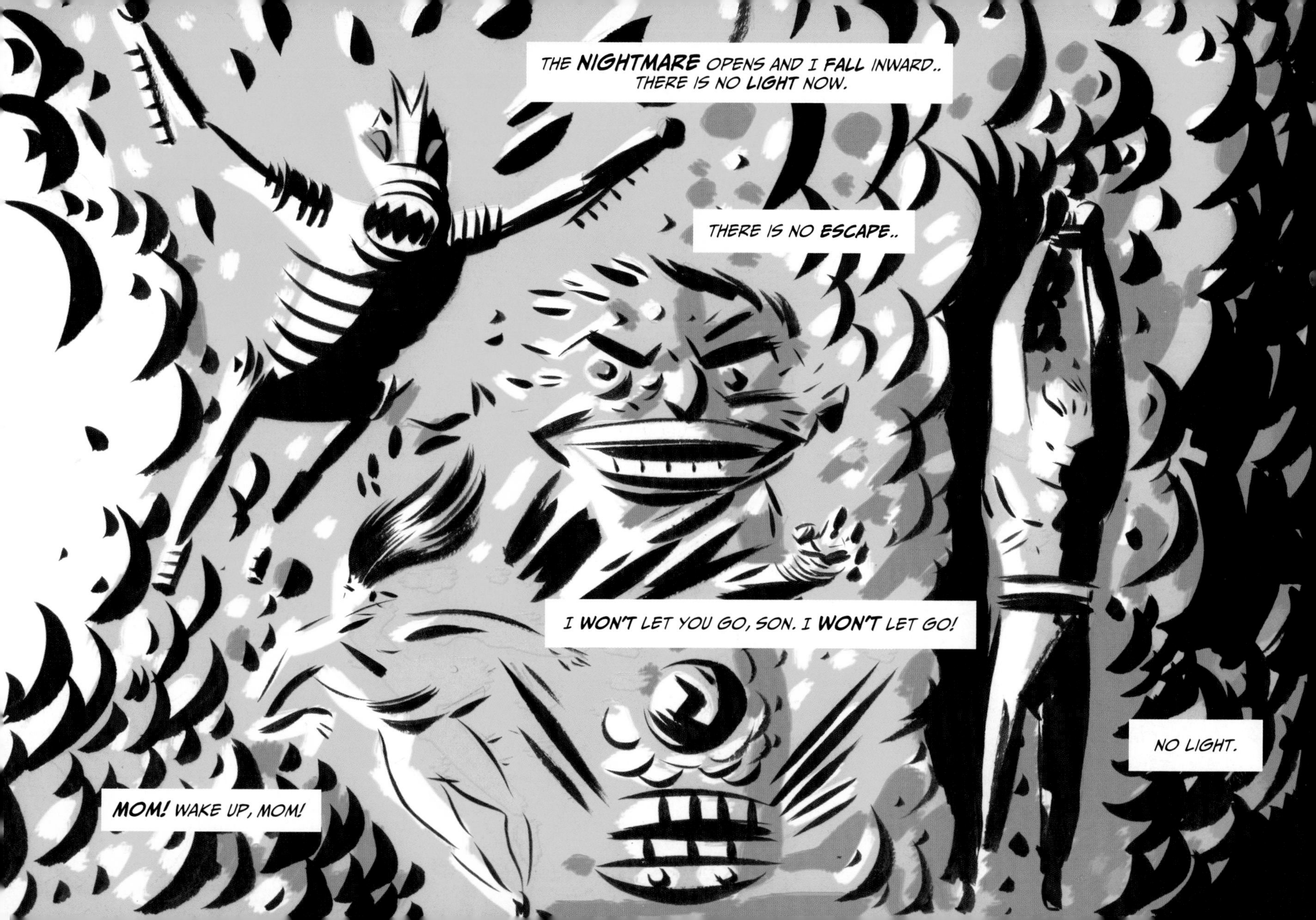
THE NIGHTMARE OPENS AND I FALL INWARD.. THERE IS NO LIGHT NOW.
THERE IS NO ESCAPE..
I WON'T LET YOU GO, SON. I WON'T LET GO!
NO LIGHT.
MOM! WAKE UP, MOM!

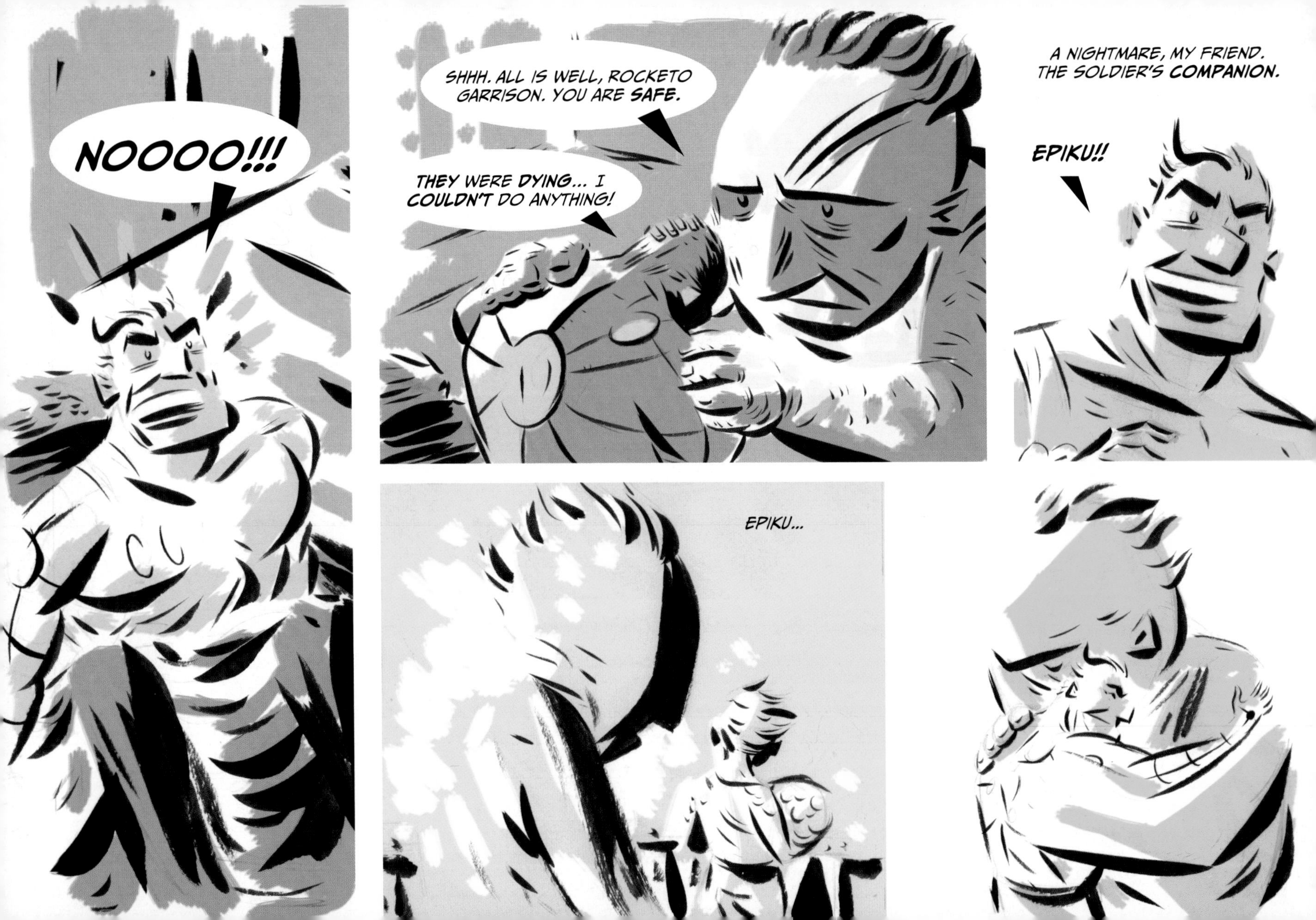
NOOOO!!!
SHHH. ALL IS WELL, ROCKETO GARRISON. YOU ARE **SAFE**.
THEY WERE **DYING**... I **COULDN'T** DO ANYTHING!
A NIGHTMARE, MY FRIEND. THE SOLDIER'S **COMPANION**.
EPIKU!!
EPIKU...

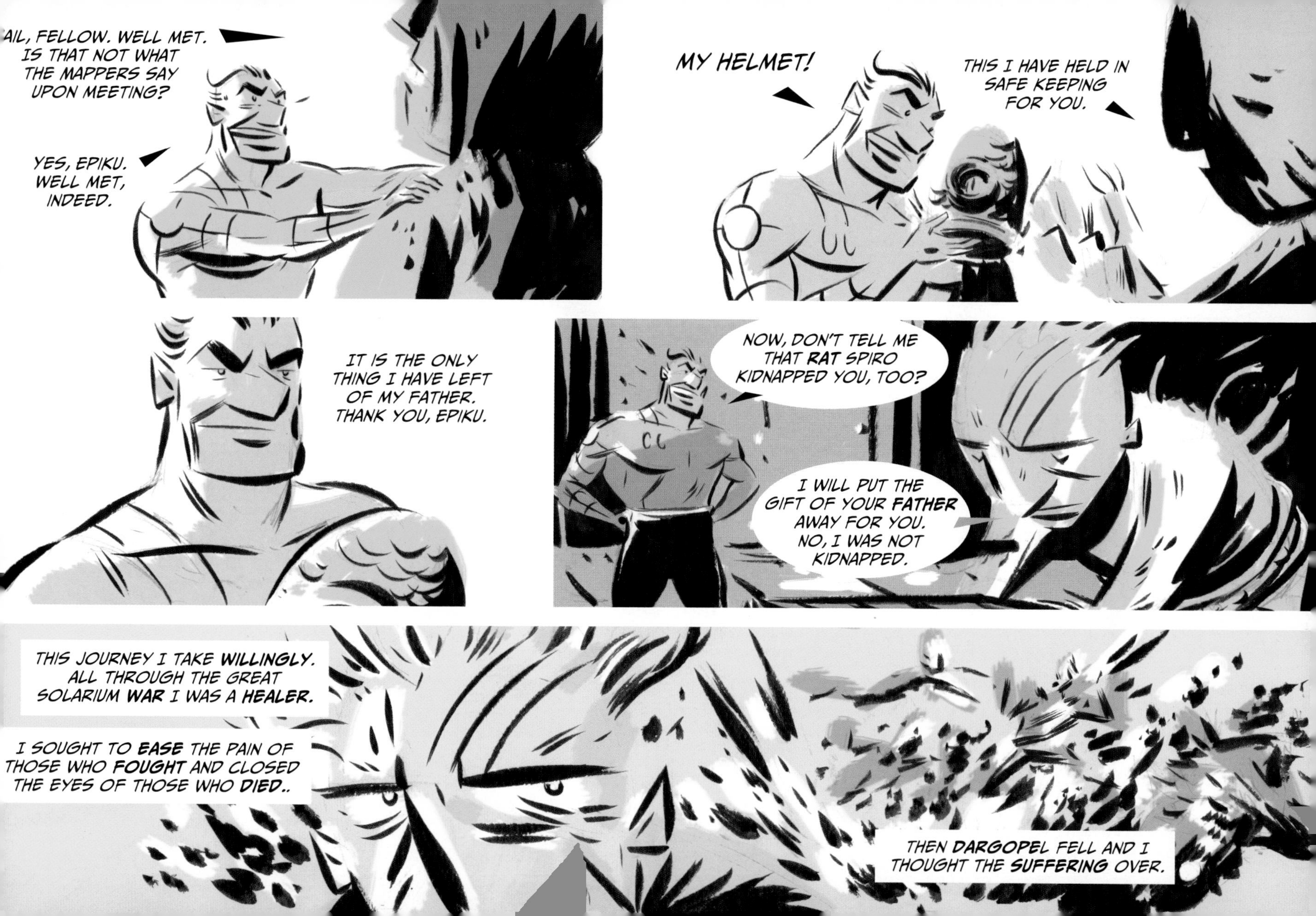
AIL, FELLOW. WELL MET. IS THAT NOT WHAT THE MAPPERS SAY UPON MEETING?
YES, EPIKU. WELL MET, INDEED.
MY HELMET!
THIS I HAVE HELD IN SAFE KEEPING FOR YOU.
IT IS THE ONLY THING I HAVE LEFT OF MY FATHER. THANK YOU, EPIKU.
NOW, DON'T TELL ME THAT RAT SPIRO KIDNAPPED YOU, TOO?
I WILL PUT THE GIFT OF YOUR FATHER AWAY FOR YOU. NO, I WAS NOT KIDNAPPED.
THIS JOURNEY I TAKE WILLINGLY. ALL THROUGH THE GREAT SOLARIUM WAR I WAS A HEALER.
I SOUGHT TO EASE THE PAIN OF THOSE WHO FOUGHT AND CLOSED THE EYES OF THOSE WHO DIED..
THEN DARGOPEL FELL AND I THOUGHT THE SUFFERING OVER.

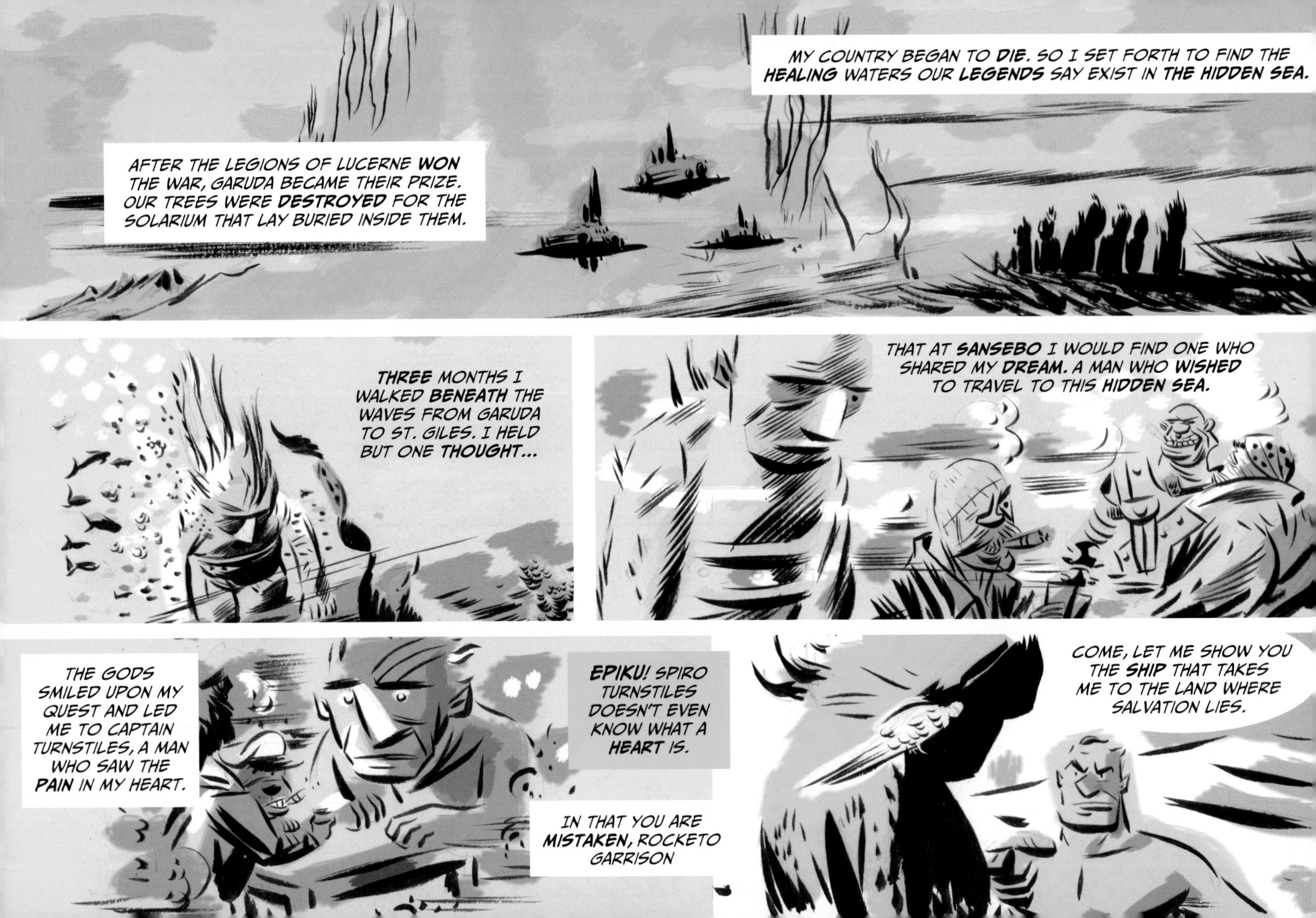
AFTER THE LEGIONS OF LUCERNE WON THE WAR, GARUDA BECAME THEIR PRIZE. OUR TREES WERE DESTROYED FOR THE SOLARIUM THAT LAY BURIED INSIDE THEM.
MY COUNTRY BEGAN TO DIE. SO I SET FORTH TO FIND THE HEALING WATERS OUR LEGENDS SAY EXIST IN THE HIDDEN SEA.
THREE MONTHS I WALKED BENEATH THE WAVES FROM GARUDA TO ST. GILES. I HELD BUT ONE THOUGHT...
THAT AT SANSEBO I WOULD FIND ONE WHO SHARED MY DREAM. A MAN WHO WISHED TO TRAVEL TO THIS HIDDEN SEA.
THE GODS SMILED UPON MY QUEST AND LED ME TO CAPTAIN TURNSTILES, A MAN WHO SAW THE PAIN IN MY HEART.
EPIKU! SPIRO TURNSTILES DOESN'T EVEN KNOW WHAT A HEART IS.
IN THAT YOU ARE MISTAKEN, ROCKETO GARRISON
COME, LET ME SHOW YOU THE SHIP THAT TAKES ME TO THE LAND WHERE SALVATION LIES.

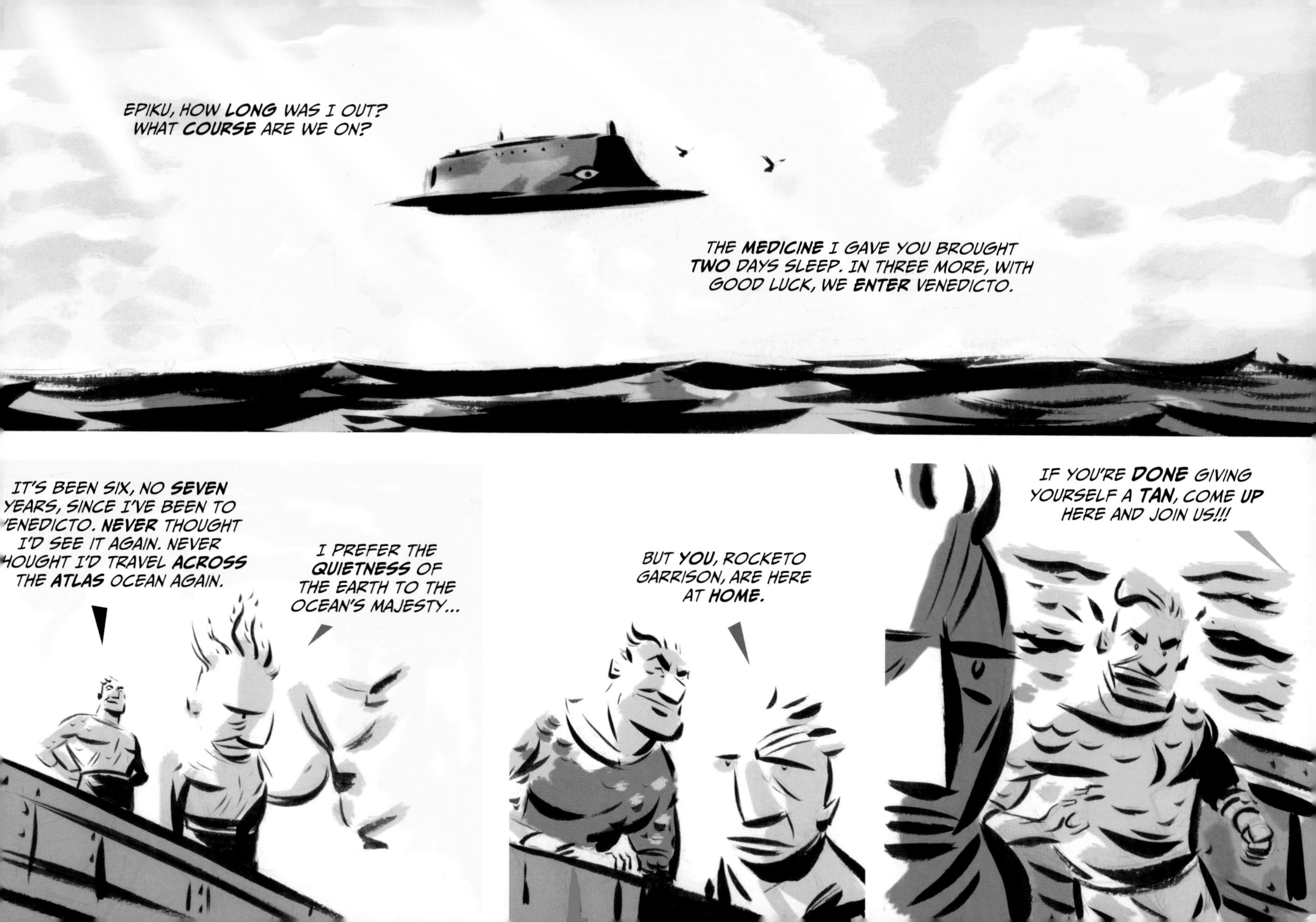

EPIKU, HOW LONG WAS I OUT? WHAT COURSE ARE WE ON?
THE MEDICINE I GAVE YOU BROUGHT TWO DAYS SLEEP. IN THREE MORE, WITH GOOD LUCK, WE ENTER VENEDICTO.
IT'S BEEN SIX, NO SEVEN YEARS, SINCE I'VE BEEN TO 'ENEDICTO. NEVER THOUGHT I'D SEE IT AGAIN. NEVER HOUGHT I'D TRAVEL ACROSS THE ATLAS OCEAN AGAIN.
I PREFER THE QUIETNESS OF THE EARTH TO THE OCEAN'S MAJESTY...
BUT YOU, ROCKETO GARRISON, ARE HERE AT HOME.
IF YOU'RE DONE GIVING YOURSELF A TAN, COME UP HERE AND JOIN US!!!

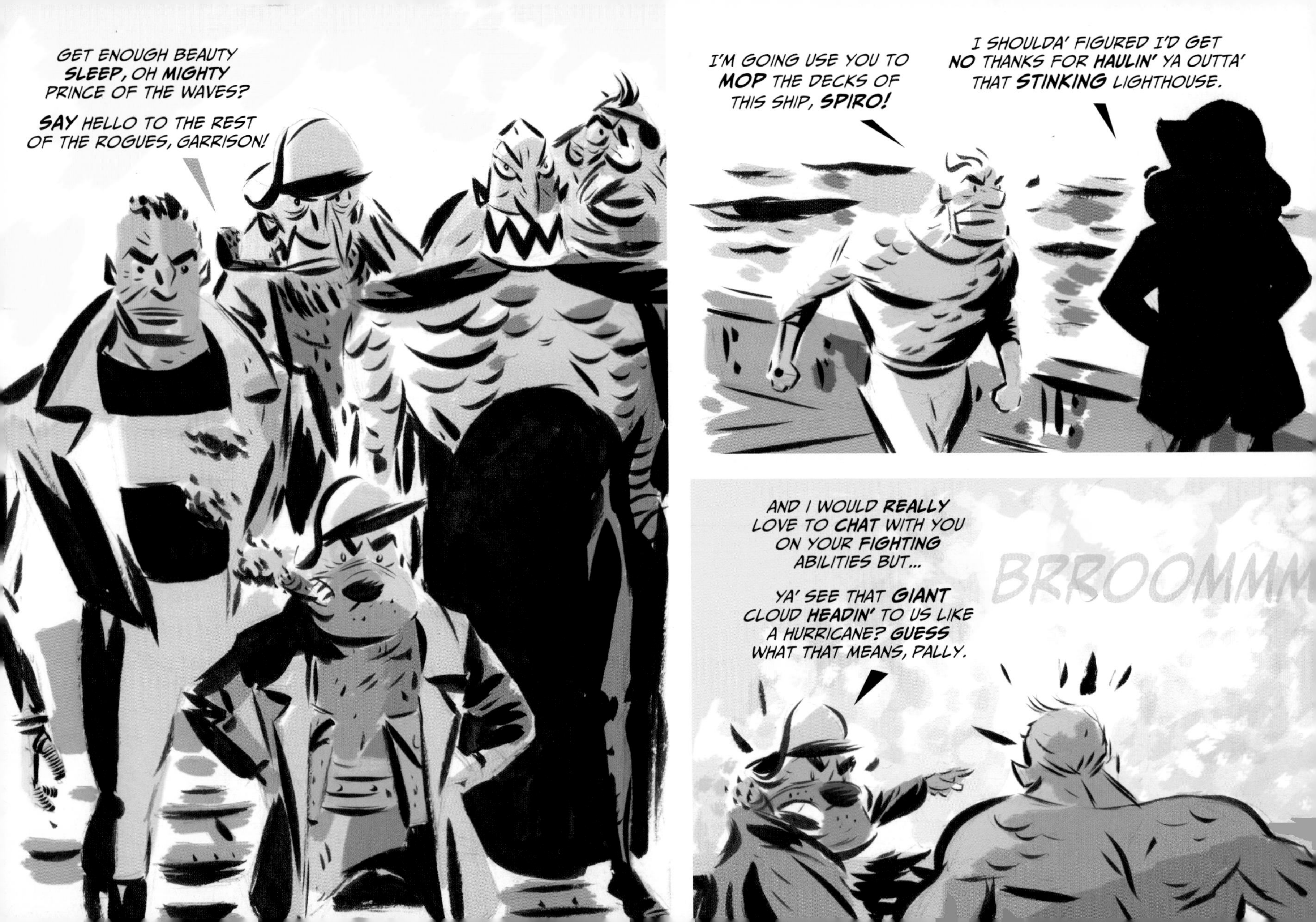
GET ENOUGH BEAUTY SLEEP, OH MIGHTY PRINCE OF THE WAVES?
SAY HELLO TO THE REST OF THE ROGUES, GARRISON!
I'M GOING USE YOU TO MOP THE DECKS OF THIS SHIP, SPIRO!
I SHOULDA' FIGURED I'D GET NO THANKS FOR HAULIN' YA OUTTA' THAT STINKING LIGHTHOUSE.
AND I WOULD REALLY LOVE TO CHAT WITH YOU ON YOUR FIGHTING ABILITIES BUT...
YA' SEE THAT GIANT CLOUD HEADIN' TO US LIKE A HURRICANE? GUESS WHAT THAT MEANS, PALLY.
BRROOMMM

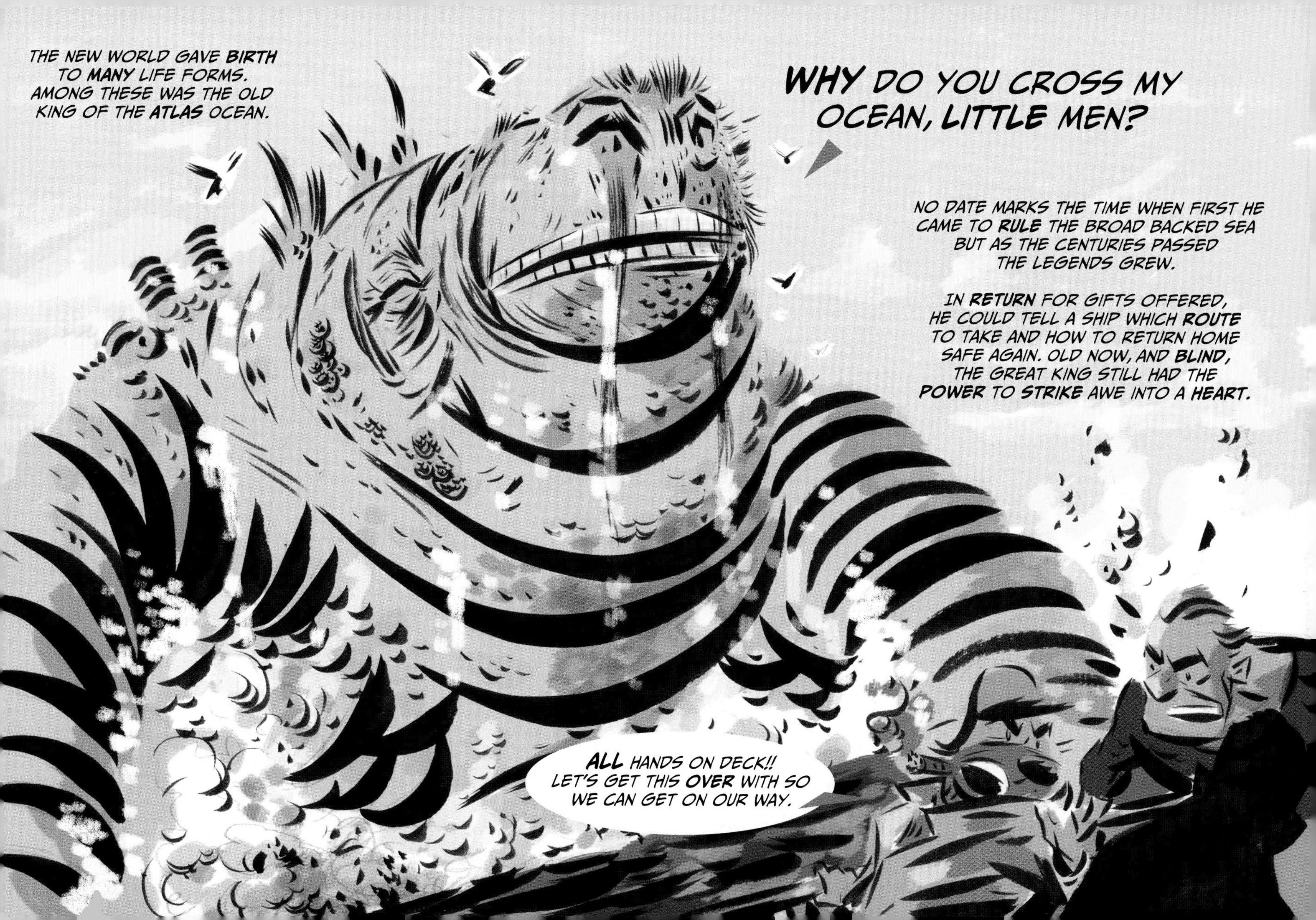
THE NEW WORLD GAVE BIRTH TO MANY LIFE FORMS. AMONG THESE WAS THE OLD KING OF THE ATLAS OCEAN.
WHY DO YOU CROSS MY OCEAN, LITTLE MEN?
NO DATE MARKS THE TIME WHEN FIRST HE CAME TO RULE THE BROAD BACKED SEA BUT AS THE CENTURIES PASSED THE LEGENDS GREW.
IN RETURN FOR GIFTS OFFERED, HE COULD TELL A SHIP WHICH ROUTE TO TAKE AND HOW TO RETURN HOME SAFE AGAIN. OLD NOW, AND BLIND, THE GREAT KING STILL HAD THE POWER TO STRIKE AWE INTO A HEART.
ALL HANDS ON DECK!! LET'S GET THIS OVER WITH SO WE CAN GET ON OUR WAY.

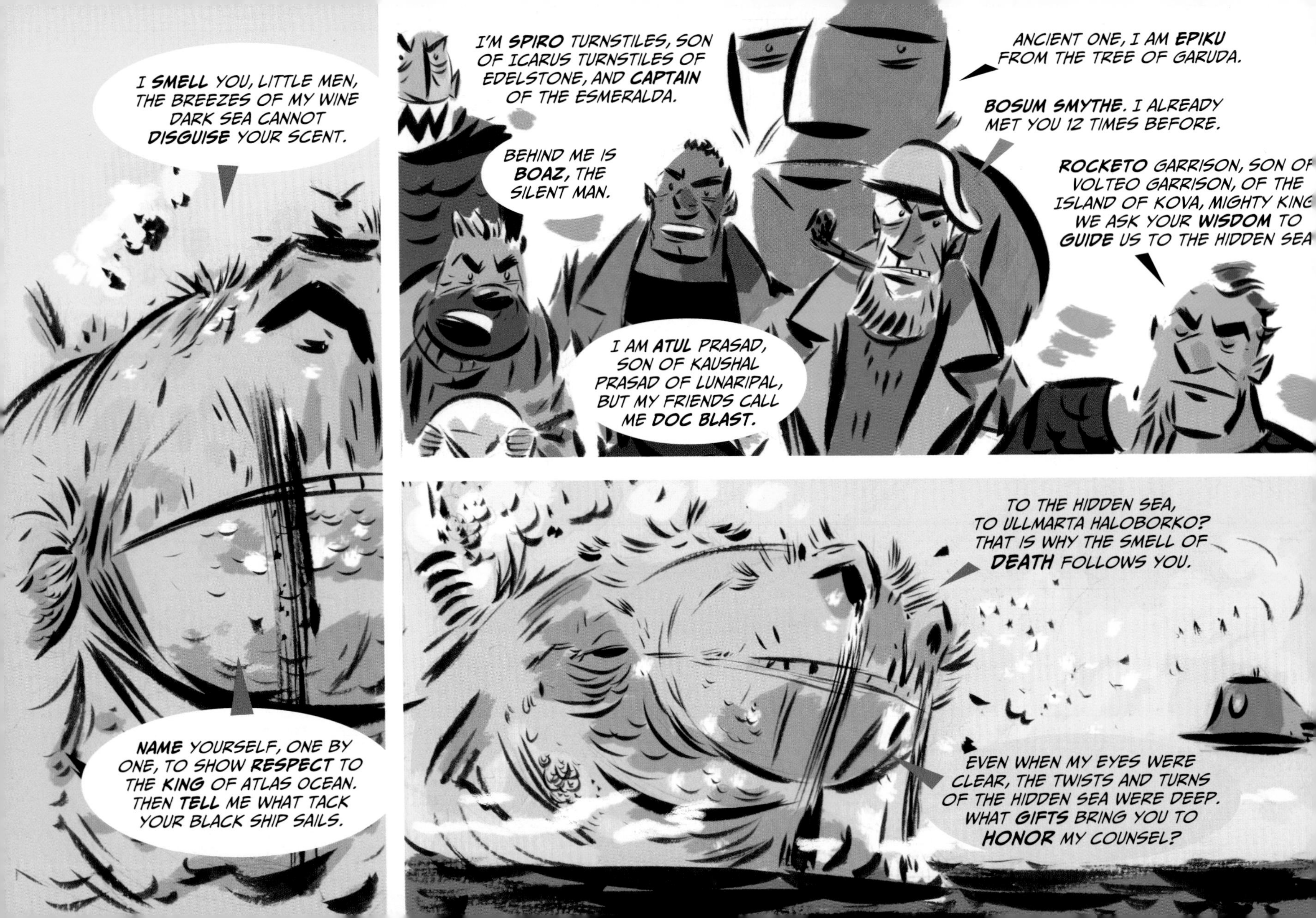
I SMELL YOU, LITTLE MEN, THE BREEZES OF MY WINE DARK SEA CANNOT DISGUISE YOUR SCENT.
NAME YOURSELF, ONE BY ONE, TO SHOW RESPECT TO THE KING OF ATLAS OCEAN. THEN TELL ME WHAT TACK YOUR BLACK SHIP SAILS.
I'M SPIRO TURNSTILES, SON OF ICARUS TURNSTILES OF EDELSTONE, AND CAPTAIN OF THE ESMERALDA.
BEHIND ME IS BOAZ, THE SILENT MAN.
I AM ATUL PRASAD, SON OF KAUSHAL PRASAD OF LUNARIPAL, BUT MY FRIENDS CALL ME DOC BLAST.
ANCIENT ONE, I AM EPIKU FROM THE TREE OF GARUDA.
BOSUM SMYTHE. I ALREADY MET YOU 12 TIMES BEFORE.
ROCKETO GARRISON, SON OF VOLTEO GARRISON, OF THE ISLAND OF KOVA, MIGHTY KING WE ASK YOUR WISDOM TO GUIDE US TO THE HIDDEN SEA
TO THE HIDDEN SEA, TO ULLMARTA HALOBORKO? THAT IS WHY THE SMELL OF DEATH FOLLOWS YOU.
EVEN WHEN MY EYES WERE CLEAR, THE TWISTS AND TURNS OF THE HIDDEN SEA WERE DEEP. WHAT GIFTS BRING YOU TO HONOR MY COUNSEL?

THIS HERE'S THE **LAST** OF THE MONEY MY **POOR GRANDMA** GAVE ME BEFORE SHE DIED. AND **BOAZ** HERE...

HE GIVES YOU A **SWORD** WHAT HE TOOK FROM A TIGERMAN.

PRASAD, O KING, BRINGS YOU THE **DESIGNS** OF THIS SHIP THAT TRAVELS YOUR MIGHTY OCEAN.

I, EPIKU, OFFER MY **HEALING ARTS.**

ROCKETO GARRISON OFFERS THE **RESPECT** DUE THE MIGHTY KING,

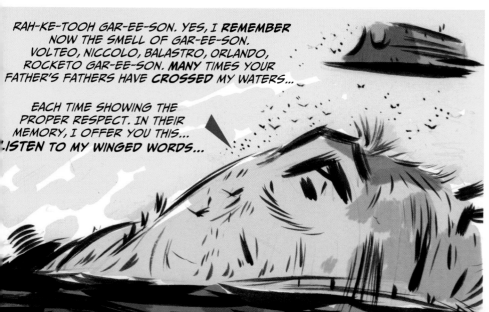

RAH-KE-TOOH GAR-EE-SON. YES, I **REMEMBER** NOW THE SMELL OF GAR-EE-SON. VOLTEO, NICCOLO, BALASTRO, ORLANDO, ROCKETO GAR-EE-SON. **MANY** TIMES YOUR FATHER'S FATHERS HAVE **CROSSED** MY WATERS...

EACH TIME SHOWING THE PROPER RESPECT. IN THEIR MEMORY, I OFFER YOU THIS... LISTEN TO MY WINGED WORDS...

LISTEN WELL AND LEARN, SON OF GAR-EE-SON, MASTER OF EXPLOITS. **LEARN** HOW TO CROSS THE HIDDEN SEA AND REACH HOME AT LAST.

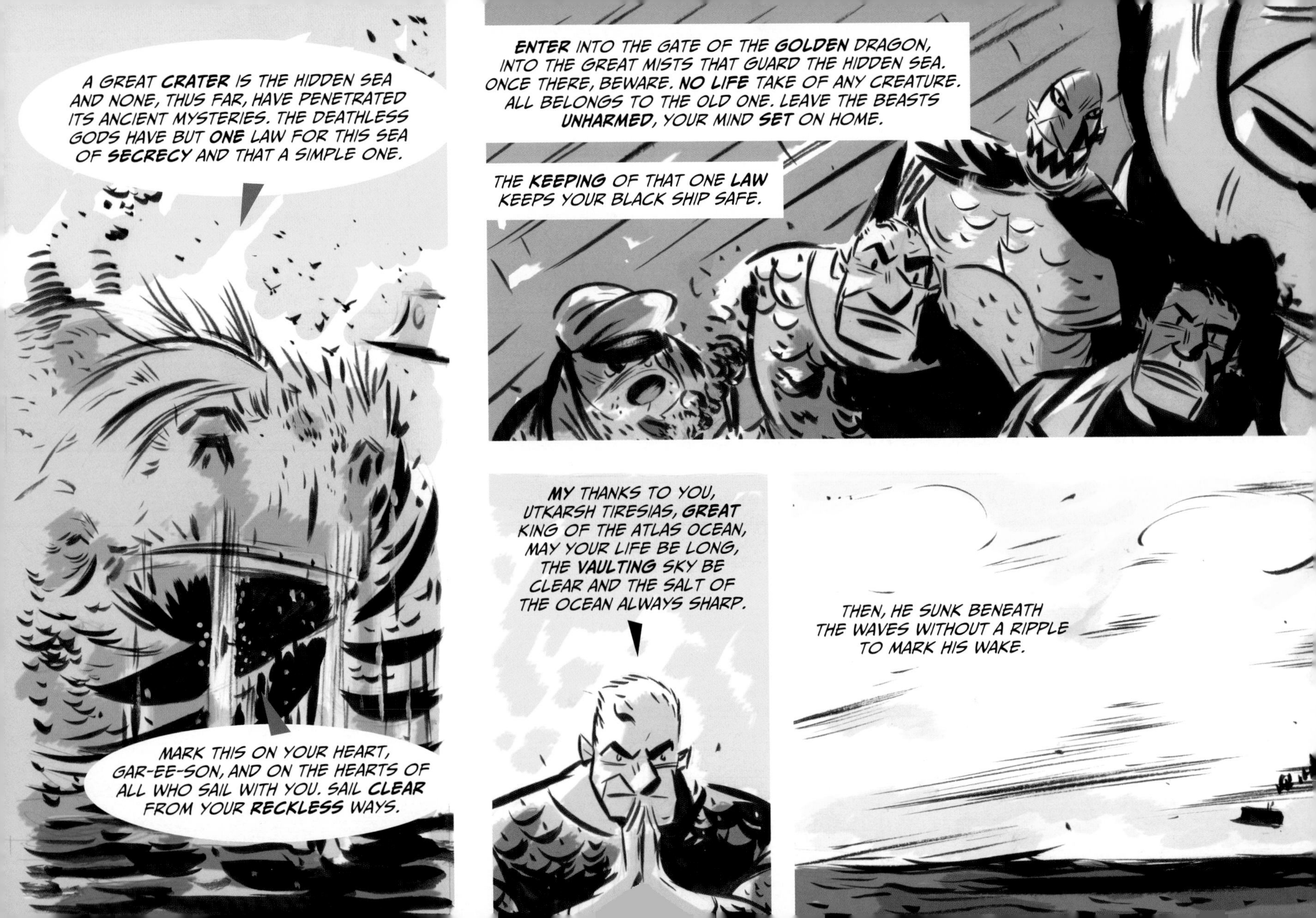

A GREAT **CRATER** IS THE HIDDEN SEA AND NONE, THUS FAR, HAVE PENETRATED ITS ANCIENT MYSTERIES. THE DEATHLESS GODS HAVE BUT **ONE** LAW FOR THIS SEA OF **SECRECY** AND THAT A SIMPLE ONE.
MARK THIS ON YOUR HEART, GAR-EE-SON, AND ON THE HEARTS OF ALL WHO SAIL WITH YOU. SAIL **CLEAR** FROM YOUR **RECKLESS** WAYS.
**ENTER** INTO THE GATE OF THE **GOLDEN** DRAGON, INTO THE GREAT MISTS THAT GUARD THE HIDDEN SEA. ONCE THERE, BEWARE. **NO LIFE** TAKE OF ANY CREATURE. ALL BELONGS TO THE OLD ONE. LEAVE THE BEASTS **UNHARMED**, YOUR MIND **SET** ON HOME.
THE **KEEPING** OF THAT ONE **LAW** KEEPS YOUR BLACK SHIP SAFE.
**MY** THANKS TO YOU, UTKARSH TIRESIAS, **GREAT** KING OF THE ATLAS OCEAN, MAY YOUR LIFE BE LONG, THE **VAULTING** SKY BE CLEAR AND THE SALT OF THE OCEAN ALWAYS SHARP.
THEN, HE SUNK BENEATH THE WAVES WITHOUT A RIPPLE TO MARK HIS WAKE.

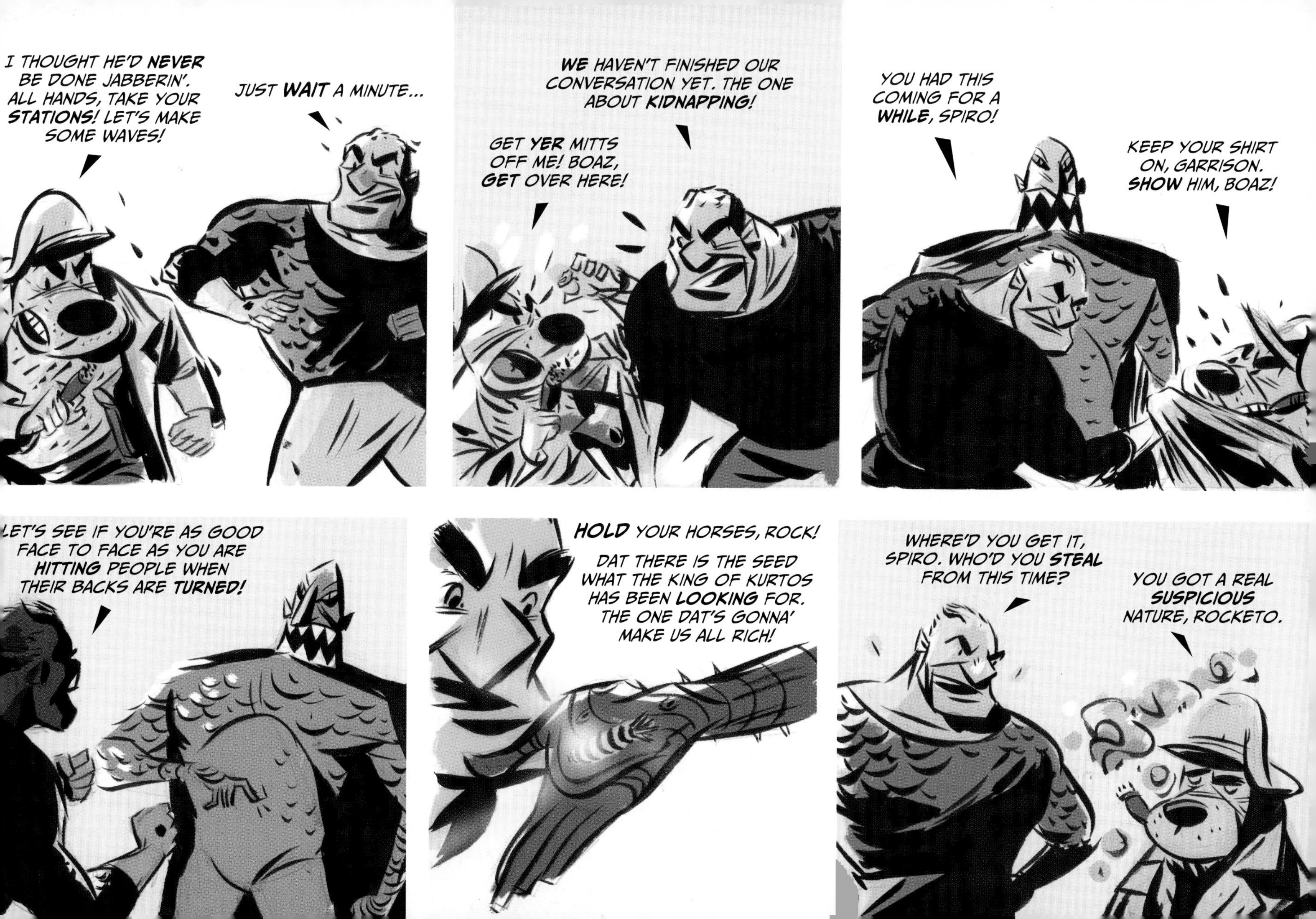
I THOUGHT HE'D NEVER BE DONE JABBERIN'. ALL HANDS, TAKE YOUR STATIONS! LET'S MAKE SOME WAVES!
JUST WAIT A MINUTE...
WE HAVEN'T FINISHED OUR CONVERSATION YET. THE ONE ABOUT KIDNAPPING!
GET YER MITTS OFF ME! BOAZ, GET OVER HERE!
YOU HAD THIS COMING FOR A WHILE, SPIRO!
KEEP YOUR SHIRT ON, GARRISON. SHOW HIM, BOAZ!
LET'S SEE IF YOU'RE AS GOOD FACE TO FACE AS YOU ARE HITTING PEOPLE WHEN THEIR BACKS ARE TURNED!
HOLD YOUR HORSES, ROCK!
DAT THERE IS THE SEED WHAT THE KING OF KURTOS HAS BEEN LOOKING FOR. THE ONE DAT'S GONNA' MAKE US ALL RICH!
WHERE'D YOU GET IT, SPIRO. WHO'D YOU STEAL FROM THIS TIME?
YOU GOT A REAL SUSPICIOUS NATURE, ROCKETO.

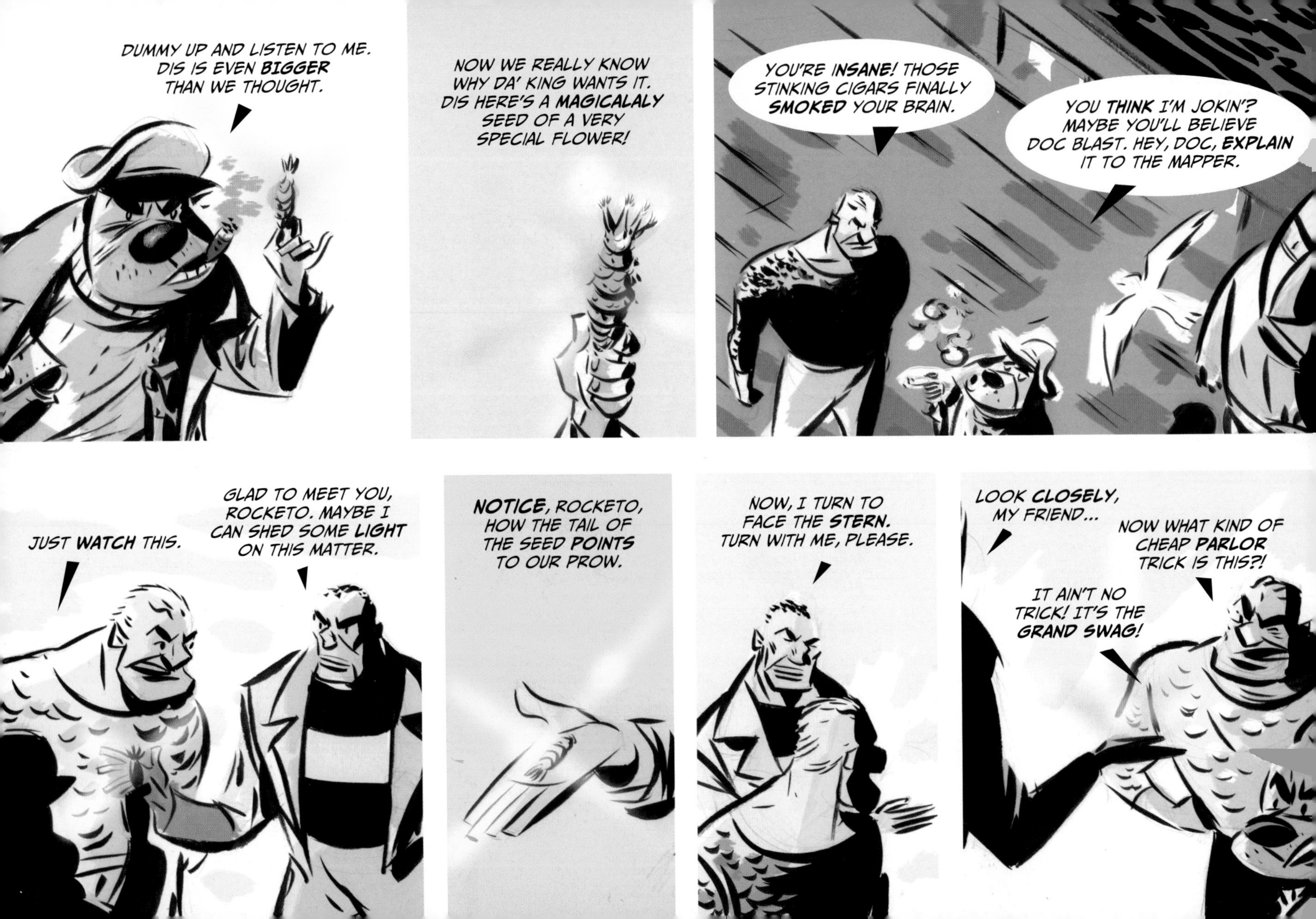
DUMMY UP AND LISTEN TO ME. DIS IS EVEN BIGGER THAN WE THOUGHT.
NOW WE REALLY KNOW WHY DA' KING WANTS IT. DIS HERE'S A MAGICALALY SEED OF A VERY SPECIAL FLOWER!
YOU'RE INSANE! THOSE STINKING CIGARS FINALLY SMOKED YOUR BRAIN.
YOU THINK I'M JOKIN'? MAYBE YOU'LL BELIEVE DOC BLAST. HEY, DOC, EXPLAIN IT TO THE MAPPER.
JUST WATCH THIS.
GLAD TO MEET YOU, ROCKETO. MAYBE I CAN SHED SOME LIGHT ON THIS MATTER.
NOTICE, ROCKETO, HOW THE TAIL OF THE SEED POINTS TO OUR PROW.
NOW, I TURN TO FACE THE STERN. TURN WITH ME, PLEASE.
LOOK CLOSELY, MY FRIEND...
NOW WHAT KIND OF CHEAP PARLOR TRICK IS THIS?!
IT AIN'T NO TRICK! IT'S THE GRAND SWAG!

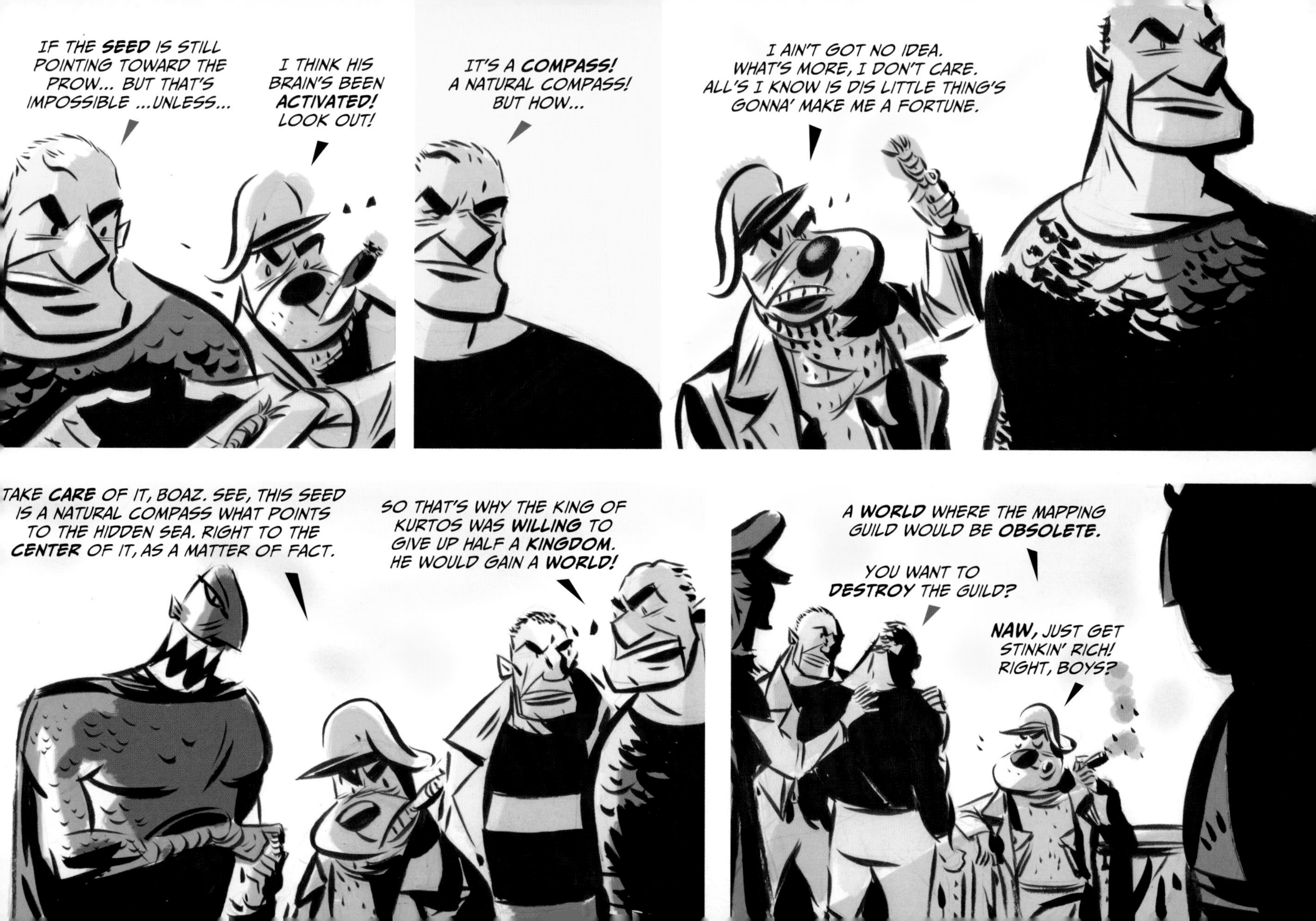
IF THE SEED IS STILL POINTING TOWARD THE PROW... BUT THAT'S IMPOSSIBLE ...UNLESS...
I THINK HIS BRAIN'S BEEN ACTIVATED! LOOK OUT!
IT'S A COMPASS! A NATURAL COMPASS! BUT HOW...
I AIN'T GOT NO IDEA. WHAT'S MORE, I DON'T CARE. ALL'S I KNOW IS DIS LITTLE THING'S GONNA' MAKE ME A FORTUNE.
TAKE CARE OF IT, BOAZ. SEE, THIS SEED IS A NATURAL COMPASS WHAT POINTS TO THE HIDDEN SEA. RIGHT TO THE CENTER OF IT, AS A MATTER OF FACT.
SO THAT'S WHY THE KING OF KURTOS WAS WILLING TO GIVE UP HALF A KINGDOM. HE WOULD GAIN A WORLD!
A WORLD WHERE THE MAPPING GUILD WOULD BE OBSOLETE.
YOU WANT TO DESTROY THE GUILD?
NAW, JUST GET STINKIN' RICH! RIGHT, BOYS?

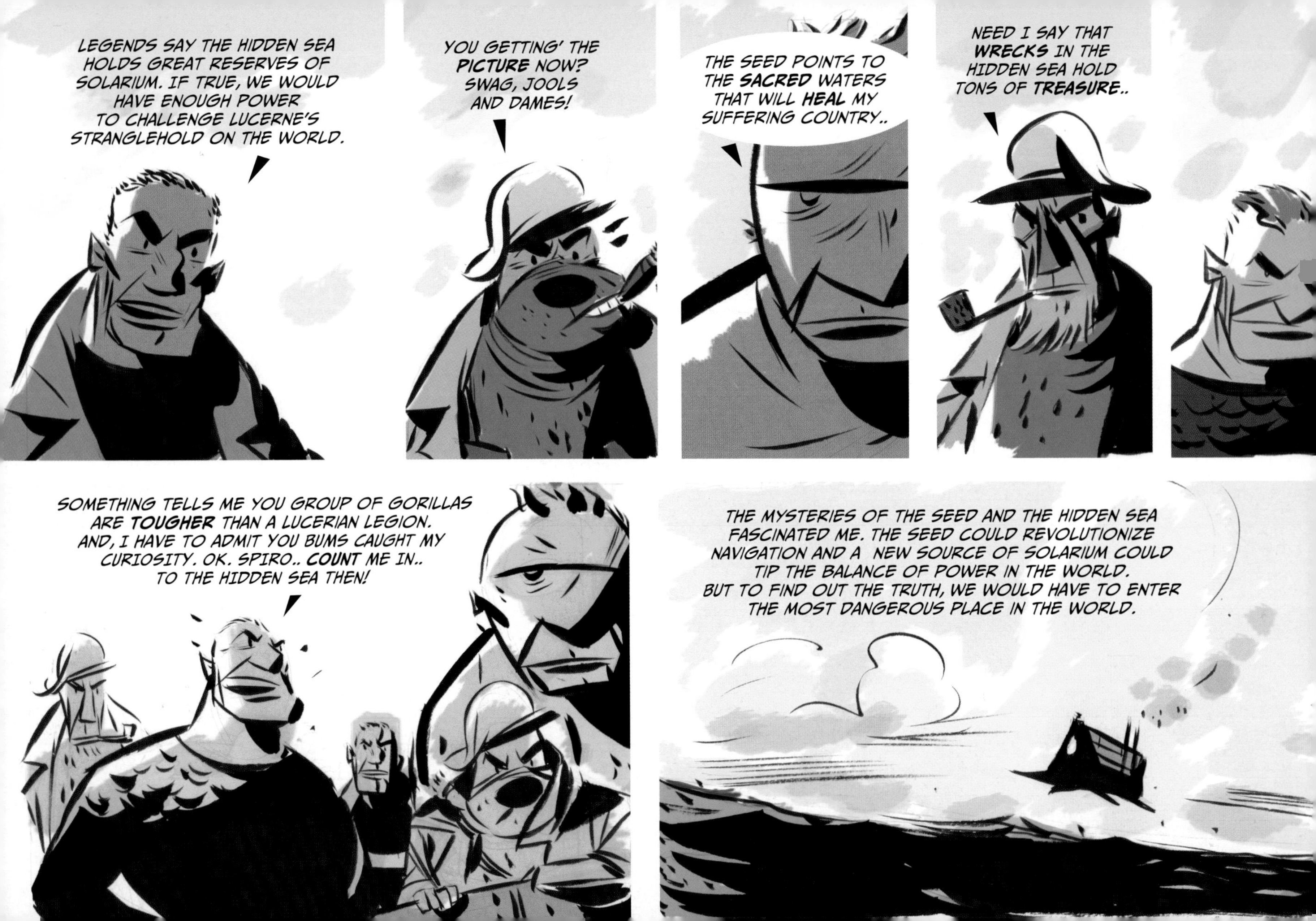
LEGENDS SAY THE HIDDEN SEA HOLDS GREAT RESERVES OF SOLARIUM. IF TRUE, WE WOULD HAVE ENOUGH POWER TO CHALLENGE LUCERNE'S STRANGLEHOLD ON THE WORLD.
YOU GETTING' THE **PICTURE** NOW? SWAG, JOOLS AND DAMES!
THE SEED POINTS TO THE **SACRED** WATERS THAT WILL **HEAL** MY SUFFERING COUNTRY..
NEED I SAY THAT **WRECKS** IN THE HIDDEN SEA HOLD TONS OF **TREASURE**..
SOMETHING TELLS ME YOU GROUP OF GORILLAS ARE **TOUGHER** THAN A LUCERIAN LEGION. AND, I HAVE TO ADMIT YOU BUMS CAUGHT MY CURIOSITY. OK. SPIRO.. **COUNT** ME IN.. TO THE HIDDEN SEA THEN!
THE MYSTERIES OF THE SEED AND THE HIDDEN SEA FASCINATED ME. THE SEED COULD REVOLUTIONIZE NAVIGATION AND A NEW SOURCE OF SOLARIUM COULD TIP THE BALANCE OF POWER IN THE WORLD. BUT TO FIND OUT THE TRUTH, WE WOULD HAVE TO ENTER THE MOST DANGEROUS PLACE IN THE WORLD.

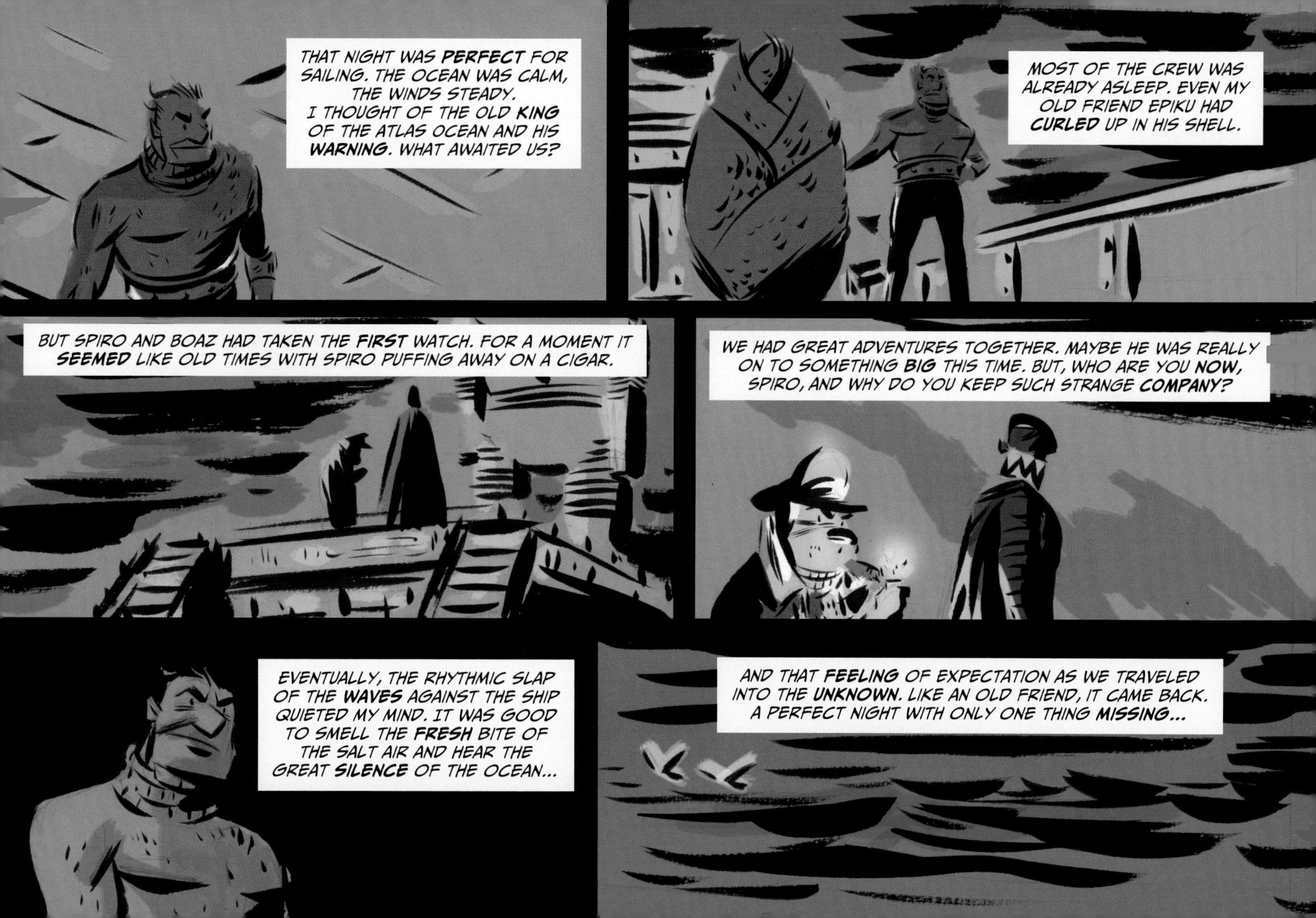
THAT NIGHT WAS PERFECT FOR SAILING. THE OCEAN WAS CALM, THE WINDS STEADY. I THOUGHT OF THE OLD KING OF THE ATLAS OCEAN AND HIS WARNING. WHAT AWAITED US?
MOST OF THE CREW WAS ALREADY ASLEEP. EVEN MY OLD FRIEND EPIKU HAD CURLED UP IN HIS SHELL.
BUT SPIRO AND BOAZ HAD TAKEN THE FIRST WATCH. FOR A MOMENT IT SEEMED LIKE OLD TIMES WITH SPIRO PUFFING AWAY ON A CIGAR.
WE HAD GREAT ADVENTURES TOGETHER. MAYBE HE WAS REALLY ON TO SOMETHING BIG THIS TIME. BUT, WHO ARE YOU NOW, SPIRO, AND WHY DO YOU KEEP SUCH STRANGE COMPANY?
EVENTUALLY, THE RHYTHMIC SLAP OF THE WAVES AGAINST THE SHIP QUIETED MY MIND. IT WAS GOOD TO SMELL THE FRESH BITE OF THE SALT AIR AND HEAR THE GREAT SILENCE OF THE OCEAN...
AND THAT FEELING OF EXPECTATION AS WE TRAVELED INTO THE UNKNOWN. LIKE AN OLD FRIEND, IT CAME BACK. A PERFECT NIGHT WITH ONLY ONE THING MISSING...

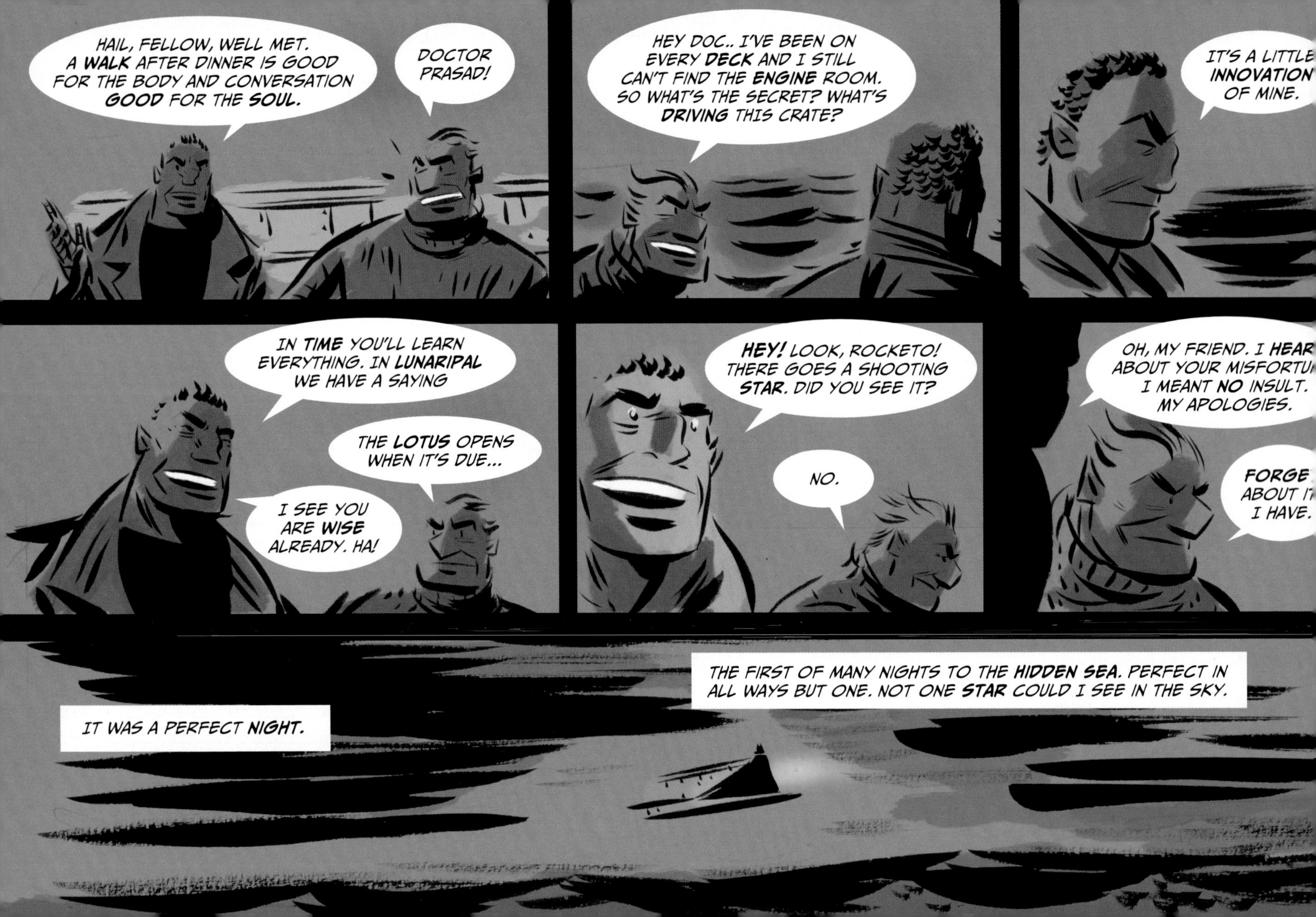
HAIL, FELLOW, WELL MET. A WALK AFTER DINNER IS GOOD FOR THE BODY AND CONVERSATION GOOD FOR THE SOUL.
DOCTOR PRASAD!
HEY DOC.. I'VE BEEN ON EVERY DECK AND I STILL CAN'T FIND THE ENGINE ROOM. SO WHAT'S THE SECRET? WHAT'S DRIVING THIS CRATE?
IT'S A LITTLE INNOVATION OF MINE.
IN TIME YOU'LL LEARN EVERYTHING. IN LUNARIPAL WE HAVE A SAYING
THE LOTUS OPENS WHEN IT'S DUE...
I SEE YOU ARE WISE ALREADY. HA!
HEY! LOOK, ROCKETO! THERE GOES A SHOOTING STAR. DID YOU SEE IT?
NO.
OH, MY FRIEND. I HEAR ABOUT YOUR MISFORTU I MEANT NO INSULT. MY APOLOGIES.
FORGE ABOUT I I HAVE.
THE FIRST OF MANY NIGHTS TO THE HIDDEN SEA. PERFECT IN ALL WAYS BUT ONE. NOT ONE STAR COULD I SEE IN THE SKY.
IT WAS A PERFECT NIGHT.

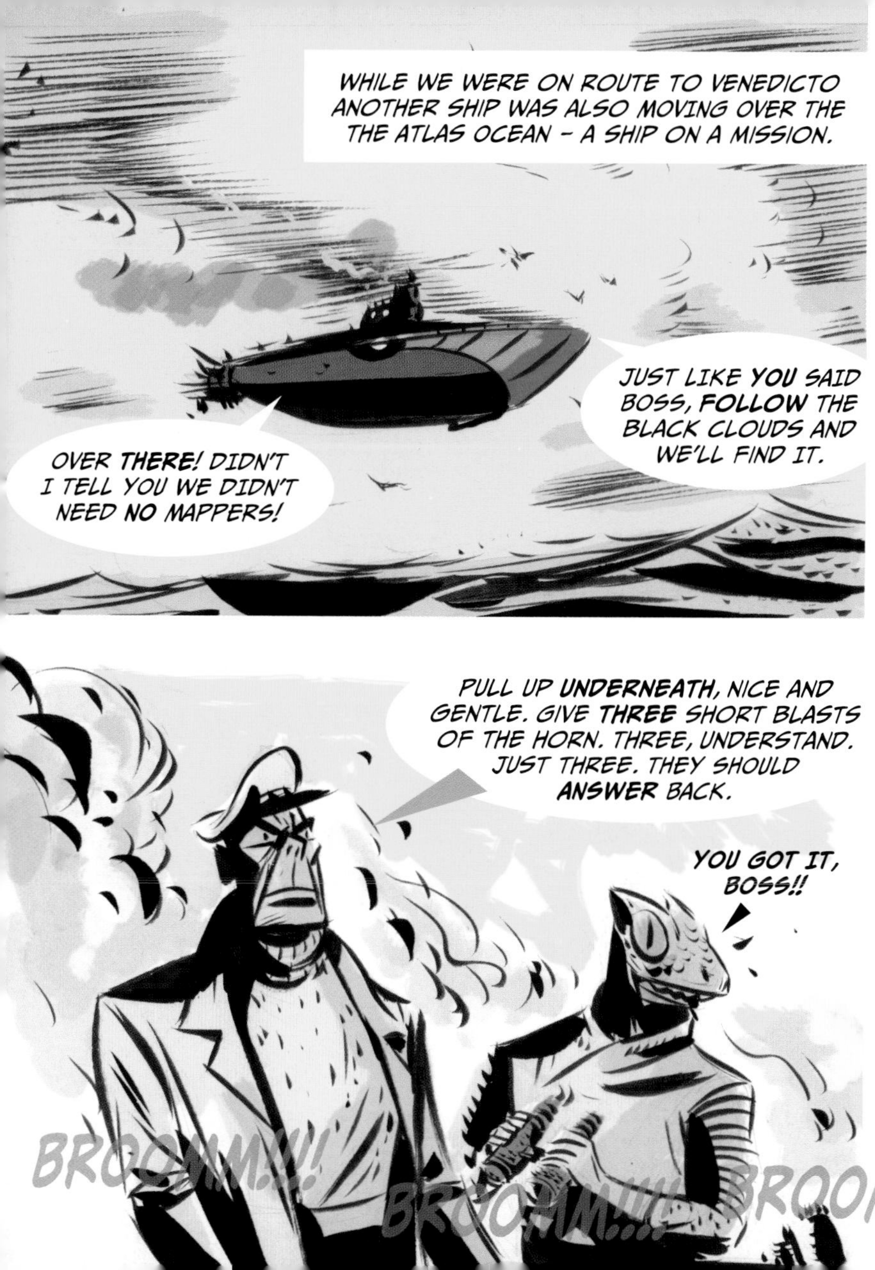
WHILE WE WERE ON ROUTE TO VENEDICTO ANOTHER SHIP WAS ALSO MOVING OVER THE THE ATLAS OCEAN – A SHIP ON A MISSION.
OVER THERE! DIDN'T I TELL YOU WE DIDN'T NEED NO MAPPERS!
JUST LIKE YOU SAID BOSS, FOLLOW THE BLACK CLOUDS AND WE'LL FIND IT.
PULL UP UNDERNEATH, NICE AND GENTLE. GIVE THREE SHORT BLASTS OF THE HORN. THREE, UNDERSTAND. JUST THREE. THEY SHOULD ANSWER BACK.
YOU GOT IT, BOSS!!
BROOMM!!!!
BROOMM!!!!
BROOMM!!!!

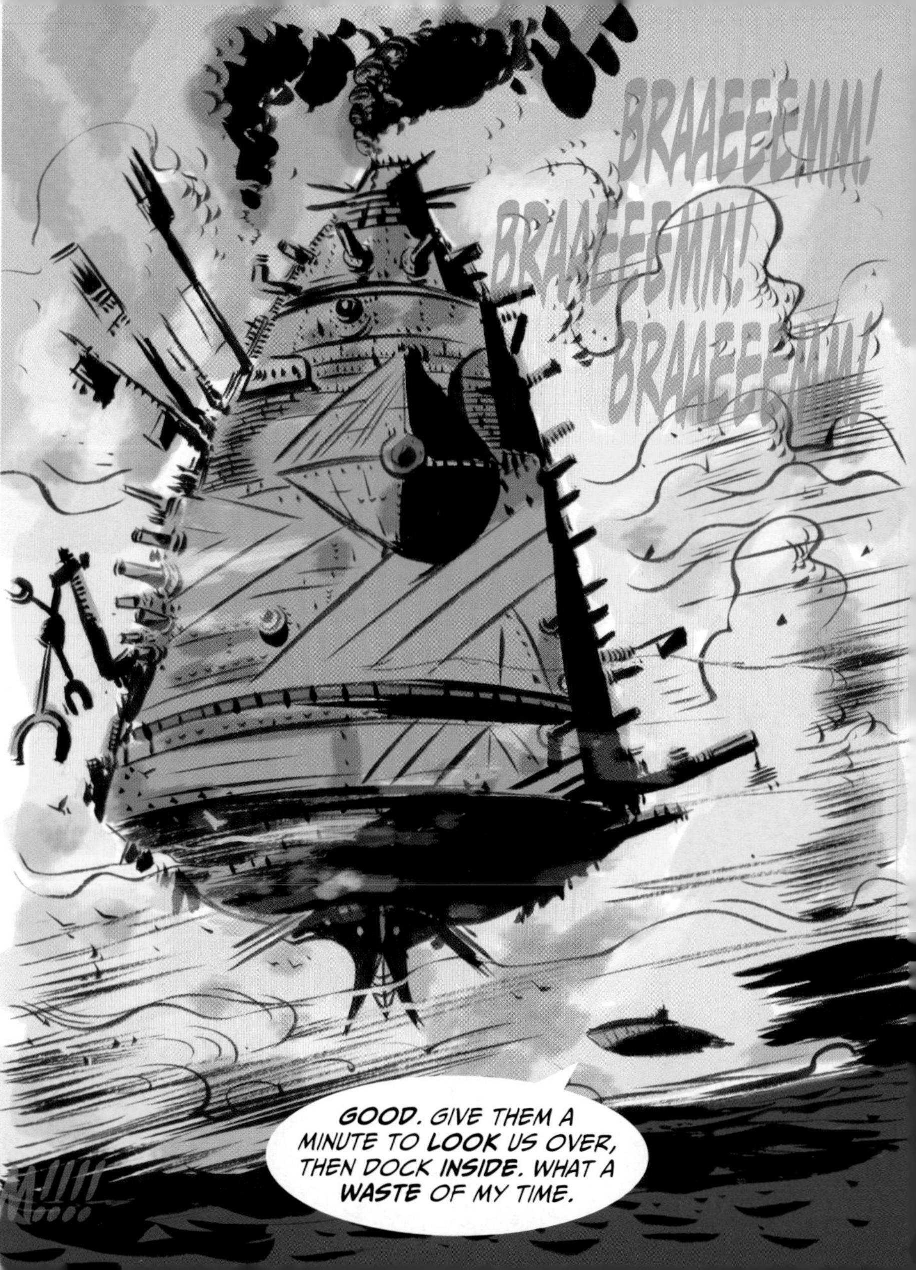
BRAAEEEMM!
BRAAEEEMM!
BRAAEEEMM!
GOOD. GIVE THEM A MINUTE TO LOOK US OVER, THEN DOCK INSIDE. WHAT A WASTE OF MY TIME.

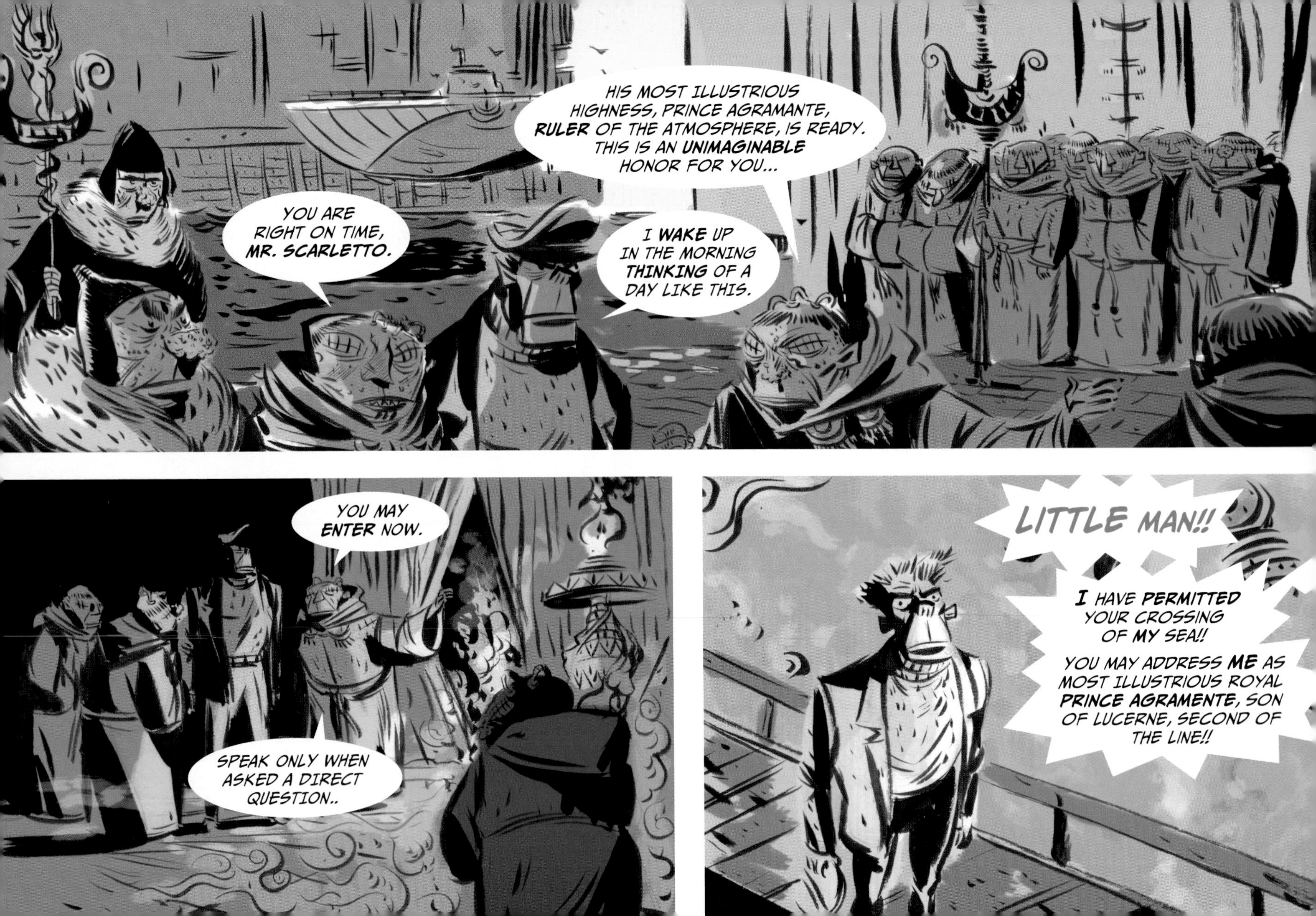
YOU ARE RIGHT ON TIME, MR. SCARLETTO.
HIS MOST ILLUSTRIOUS HIGHNESS, PRINCE AGRAMANTE, RULER OF THE ATMOSPHERE, IS READY. THIS IS AN UNIMAGINABLE HONOR FOR YOU...
I WAKE UP IN THE MORNING THINKING OF A DAY LIKE THIS.
YOU MAY ENTER NOW.
SPEAK ONLY WHEN ASKED A DIRECT QUESTION..
LITTLE MAN!!
I HAVE PERMITTED YOUR CROSSING OF MY SEA!!
YOU MAY ADDRESS ME AS MOST ILLUSTRIOUS ROYAL PRINCE AGRAMENTE, SON OF LUCERNE, SECOND OF THE LINE!!

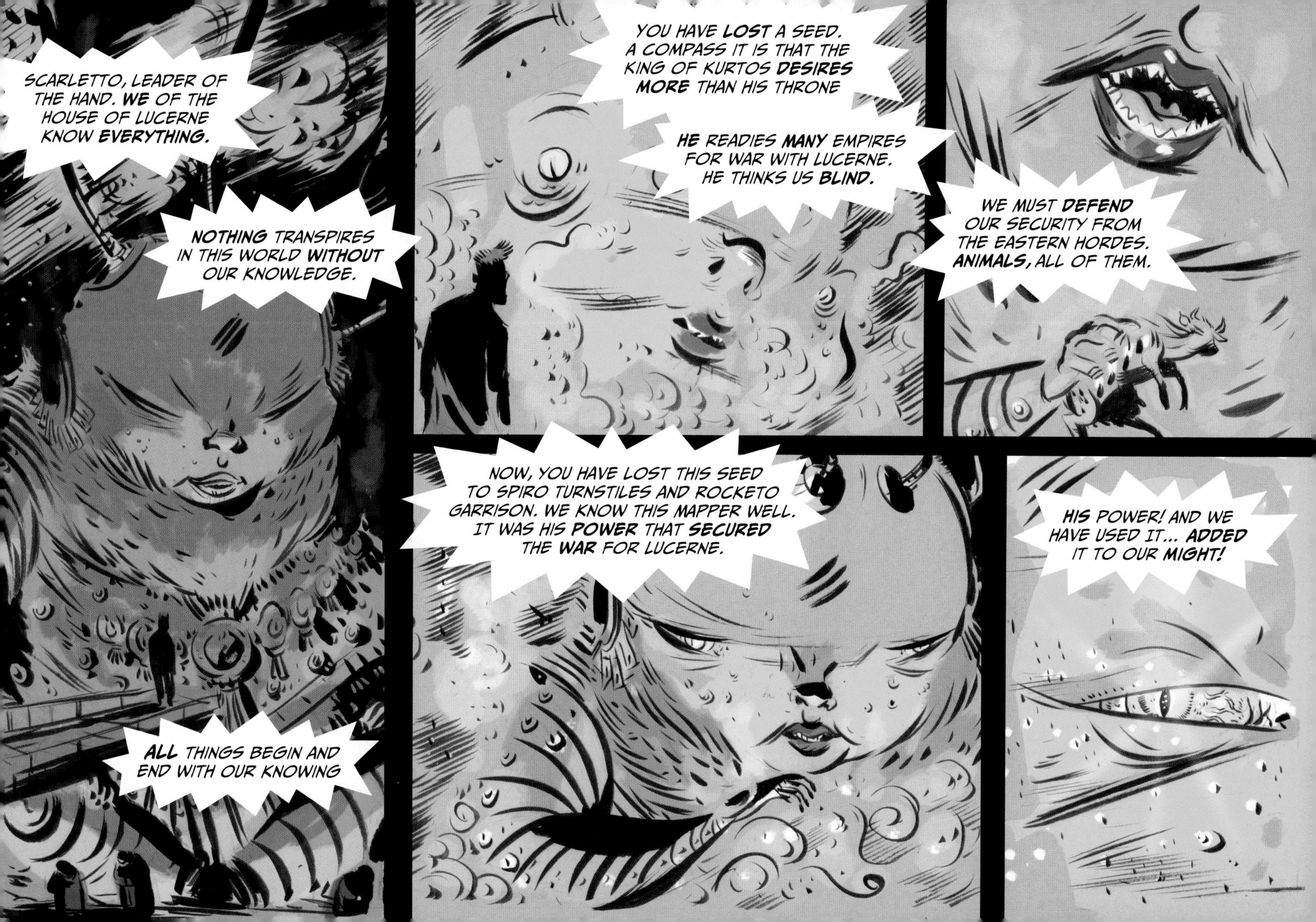
SCARLETTO, LEADER OF THE HAND. WE OF THE HOUSE OF LUCERNE KNOW EVERYTHING.
NOTHING TRANSPIRES IN THIS WORLD WITHOUT OUR KNOWLEDGE.
ALL THINGS BEGIN AND END WITH OUR KNOWING
YOU HAVE LOST A SEED. A COMPASS IT IS THAT THE KING OF KURTOS DESIRES MORE THAN HIS THRONE
HE READIES MANY EMPIRES FOR WAR WITH LUCERNE. HE THINKS US BLIND.
WE MUST DEFEND OUR SECURITY FROM THE EASTERN HORDES. ANIMALS, ALL OF THEM.
NOW, YOU HAVE LOST THIS SEED TO SPIRO TURNSTILES AND ROCKETO GARRISON. WE KNOW THIS MAPPER WELL. IT WAS HIS POWER THAT SECURED THE WAR FOR LUCERNE.
HIS POWER! AND WE HAVE USED IT... ADDED IT TO OUR MIGHT!

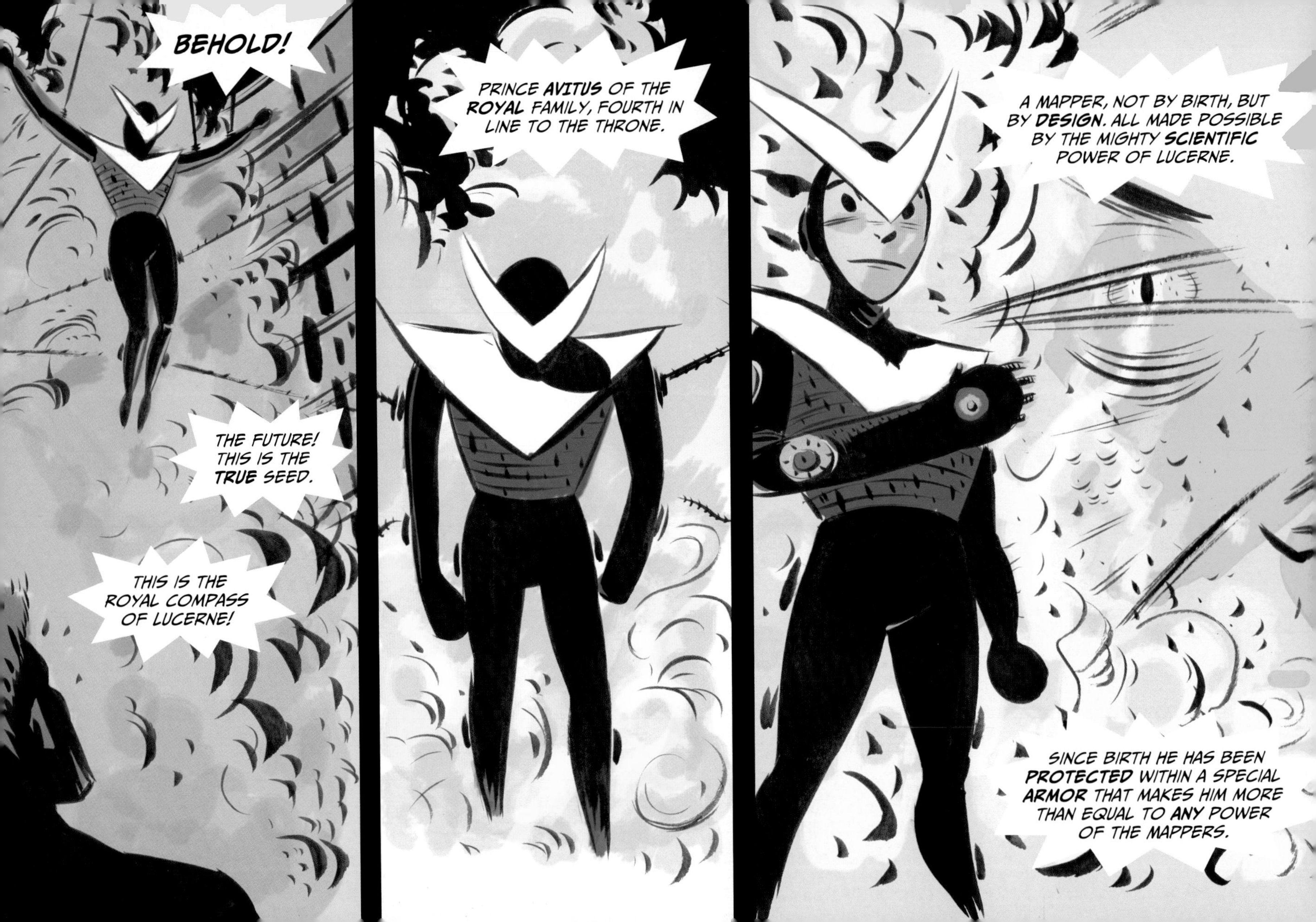
BEHOLD!
THE FUTURE! THIS IS THE TRUE SEED.
THIS IS THE ROYAL COMPASS OF LUCERNE!
PRINCE AVITUS OF THE ROYAL FAMILY, FOURTH IN LINE TO THE THRONE.
A MAPPER, NOT BY BIRTH, BUT BY DESIGN. ALL MADE POSSIBLE BY THE MIGHTY SCIENTIFIC POWER OF LUCERNE.
SINCE BIRTH HE HAS BEEN PROTECTED WITHIN A SPECIAL ARMOR THAT MAKES HIM MORE THAN EQUAL TO ANY POWER OF THE MAPPERS.

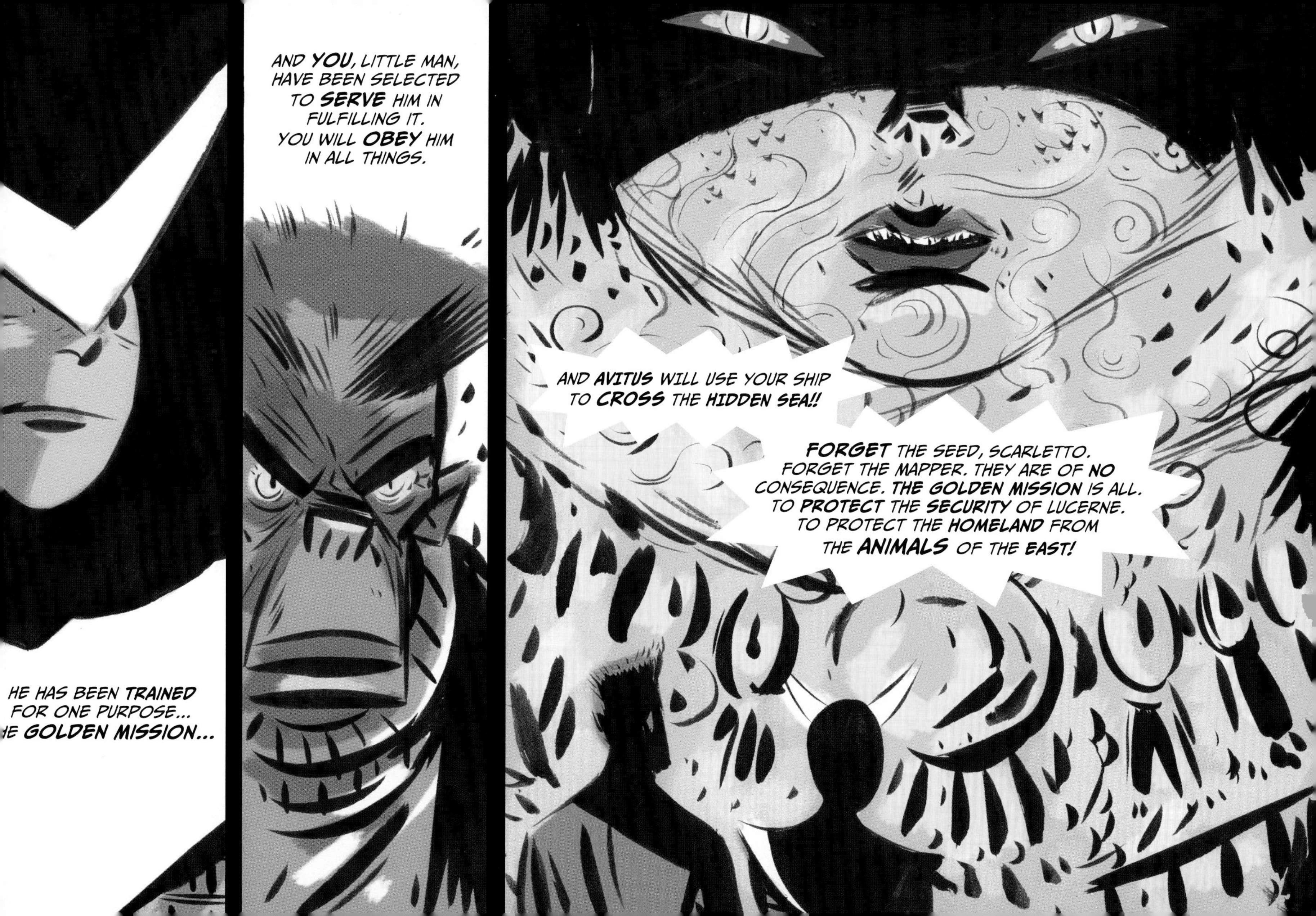
HE HAS BEEN TRAINED FOR ONE PURPOSE... HE GOLDEN MISSION...
AND YOU, LITTLE MAN, HAVE BEEN SELECTED TO SERVE HIM IN FULFILLING IT. YOU WILL OBEY HIM IN ALL THINGS.
AND AVITUS WILL USE YOUR SHIP TO CROSS THE HIDDEN SEA!!
FORGET THE SEED, SCARLETTO. FORGET THE MAPPER. THEY ARE OF NO CONSEQUENCE. THE GOLDEN MISSION IS ALL. TO PROTECT THE SECURITY OF LUCERNE. TO PROTECT THE HOMELAND FROM THE ANIMALS OF THE EAST!

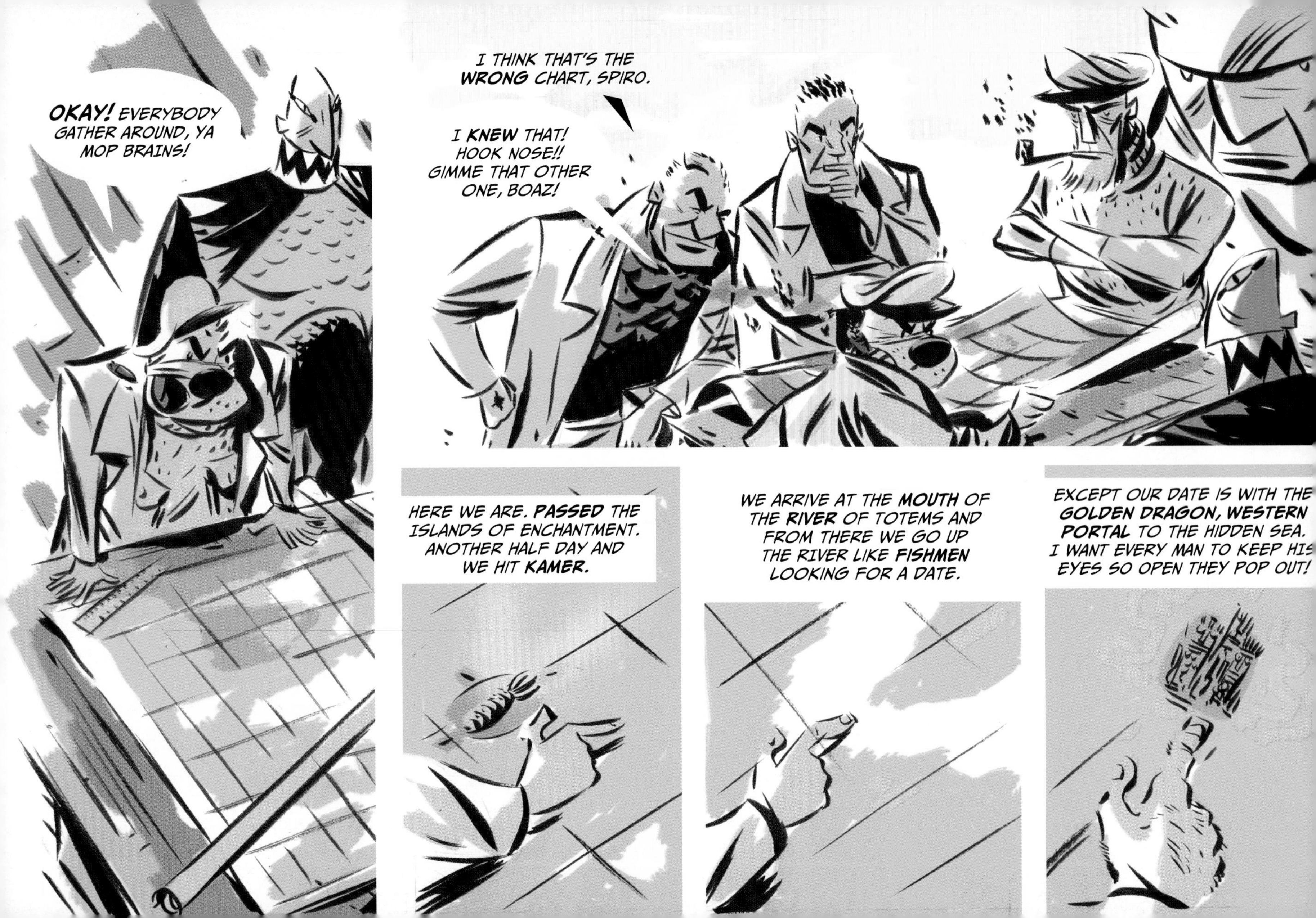
OKAY! EVERYBODY GATHER AROUND, YA MOP BRAINS!
I THINK THAT'S THE WRONG CHART, SPIRO.
I KNEW THAT! HOOK NOSE!! GIMME THAT OTHER ONE, BOAZ!
HERE WE ARE. PASSED THE ISLANDS OF ENCHANTMENT. ANOTHER HALF DAY AND WE HIT KAMER.
WE ARRIVE AT THE MOUTH OF THE RIVER OF TOTEMS AND FROM THERE WE GO UP THE RIVER LIKE FISHMEN LOOKING FOR A DATE.
EXCEPT OUR DATE IS WITH THE GOLDEN DRAGON, WESTERN PORTAL TO THE HIDDEN SEA. I WANT EVERY MAN TO KEEP HIS EYES SO OPEN THEY POP OUT!

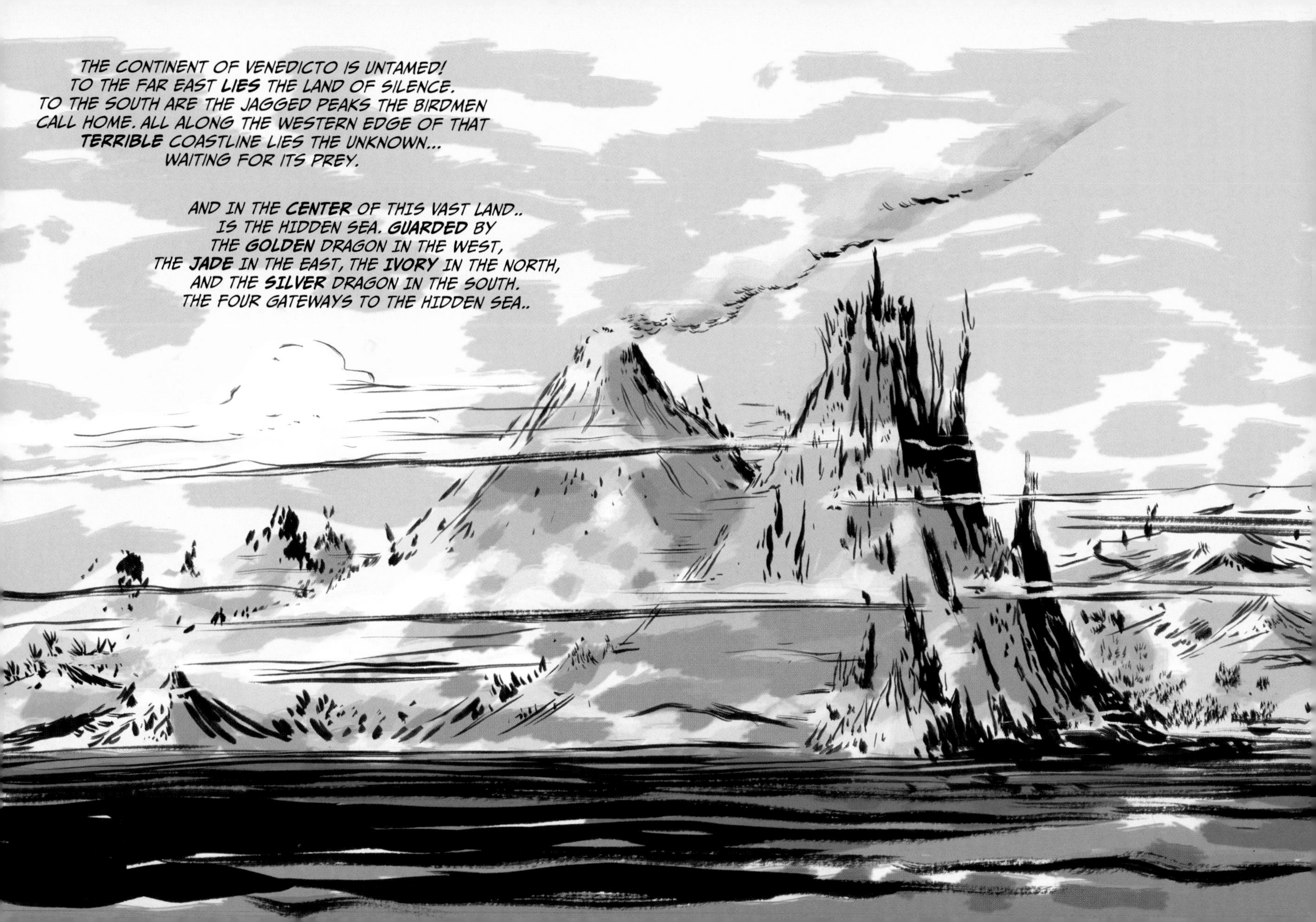
THE CONTINENT OF VENEDICTO IS UNTAMED! TO THE FAR EAST LIES THE LAND OF SILENCE. TO THE SOUTH ARE THE JAGGED PEAKS THE BIRDMEN CALL HOME. ALL ALONG THE WESTERN EDGE OF THAT TERRIBLE COASTLINE LIES THE UNKNOWN... WAITING FOR ITS PREY.
AND IN THE CENTER OF THIS VAST LAND.. IS THE HIDDEN SEA. GUARDED BY THE GOLDEN DRAGON IN THE WEST, THE JADE IN THE EAST, THE IVORY IN THE NORTH, AND THE SILVER DRAGON IN THE SOUTH. THE FOUR GATEWAYS TO THE HIDDEN SEA..

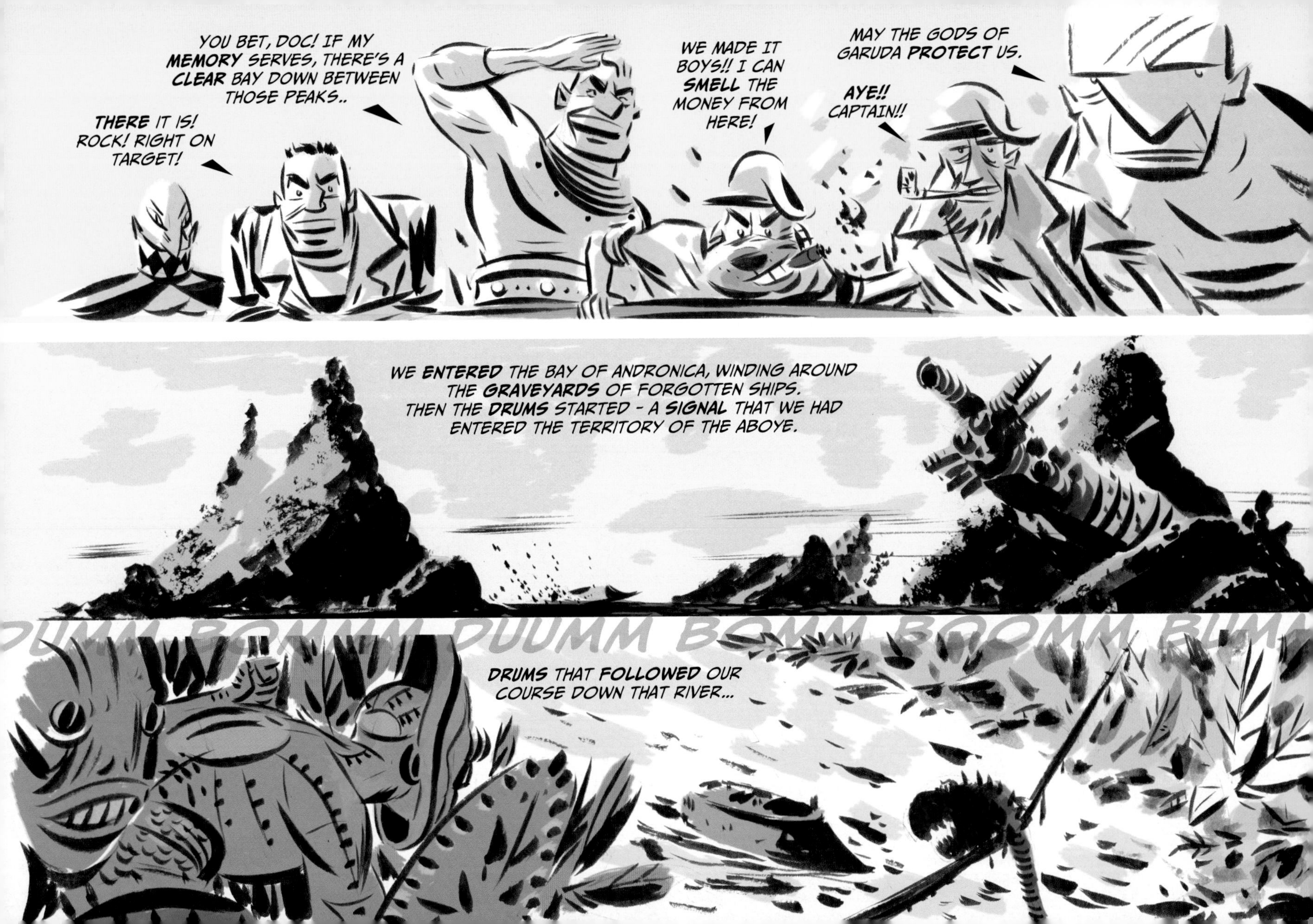
THERE IT IS! ROCK! RIGHT ON TARGET!
YOU BET, DOC! IF MY MEMORY SERVES, THERE'S A CLEAR BAY DOWN BETWEEN THOSE PEAKS..
WE MADE IT BOYS!! I CAN SMELL THE MONEY FROM HERE!
AYE!! CAPTAIN!!
MAY THE GODS OF GARUDA PROTECT US.
WE ENTERED THE BAY OF ANDRONICA, WINDING AROUND THE GRAVEYARDS OF FORGOTTEN SHIPS. THEN THE DRUMS STARTED - A SIGNAL THAT WE HAD ENTERED THE TERRITORY OF THE ABOYE.
DUUMM BOMMM BOOMM
DRUMS THAT FOLLOWED OUR COURSE DOWN THAT RIVER...

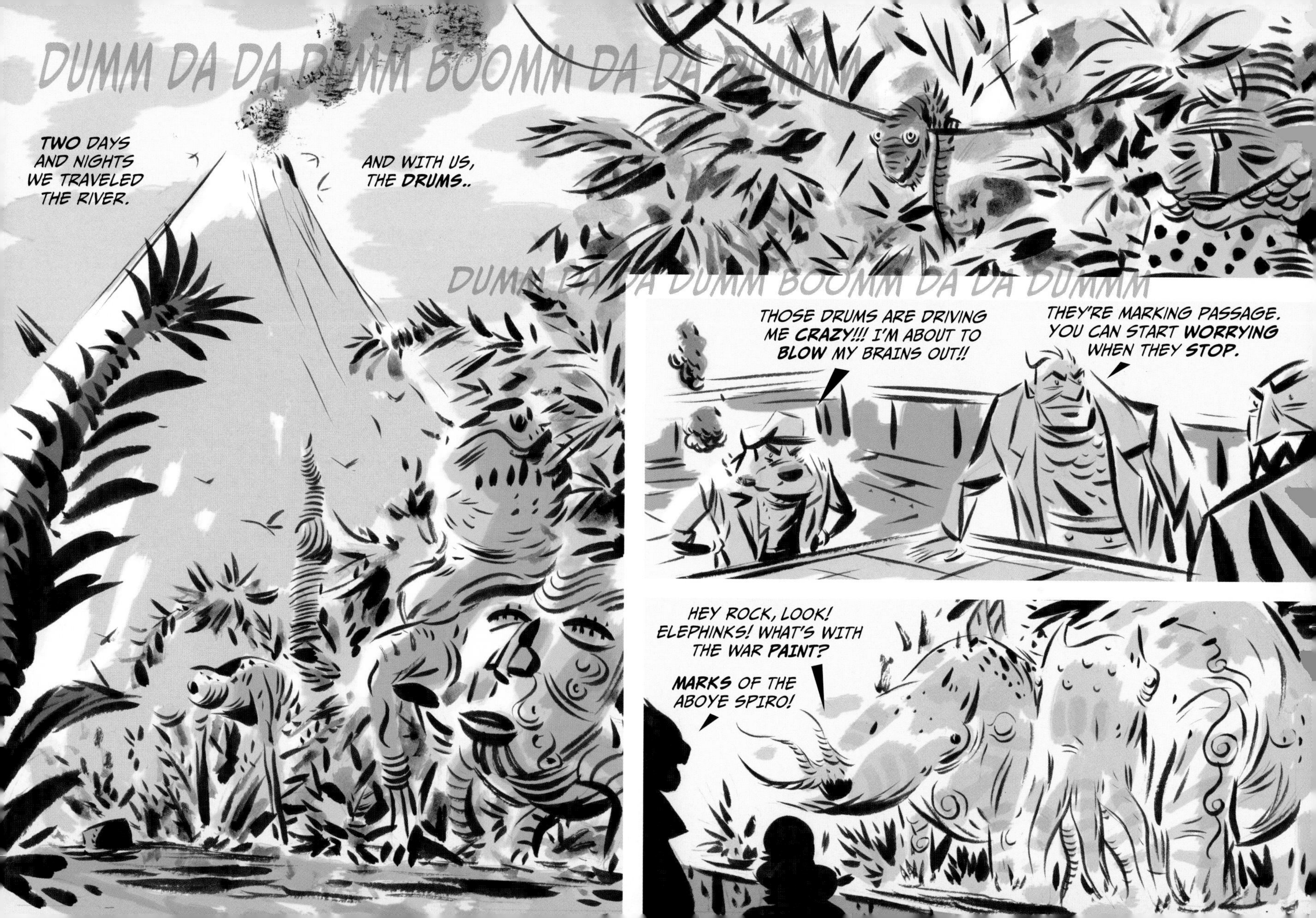
DUMM DA DA DUMM BOOMM DA DA DUMMM
TWO DAYS AND NIGHTS WE TRAVELED THE RIVER.
AND WITH US, THE DRUMS..
DUMM DA DA DUMM BOOMM DA DA DUMMM
THOSE DRUMS ARE DRIVING ME CRAZY!!! I'M ABOUT TO BLOW MY BRAINS OUT!!
THEY'RE MARKING PASSAGE. YOU CAN START WORRYING WHEN THEY STOP.
HEY ROCK, LOOK! ELEPHINKS! WHAT'S WITH THE WAR PAINT?
MARKS OF THE ABOYE SPIRO!

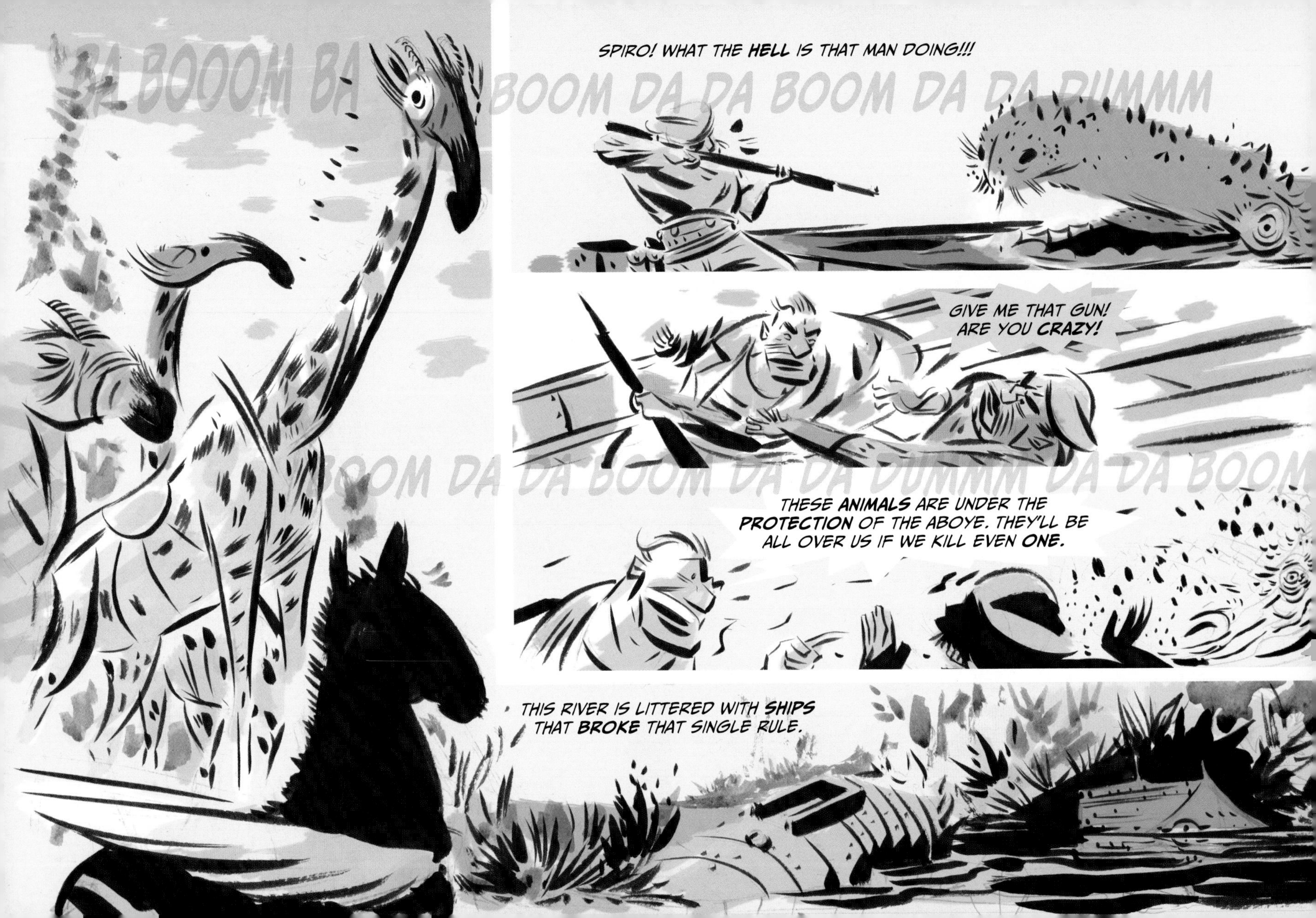
BA BOOOM BA BOOM DA DA BOOM DA DA DUMMM
SPIRO! WHAT THE HELL IS THAT MAN DOING!!!
GIVE ME THAT GUN! ARE YOU CRAZY!
BOOM DA DA BOOM DA DA DUMMM DA DA BOOM
THESE ANIMALS ARE UNDER THE PROTECTION OF THE ABOYE. THEY'LL BE ALL OVER US IF WE KILL EVEN ONE.
THIS RIVER IS LITTERED WITH SHIPS THAT BROKE THAT SINGLE RULE.

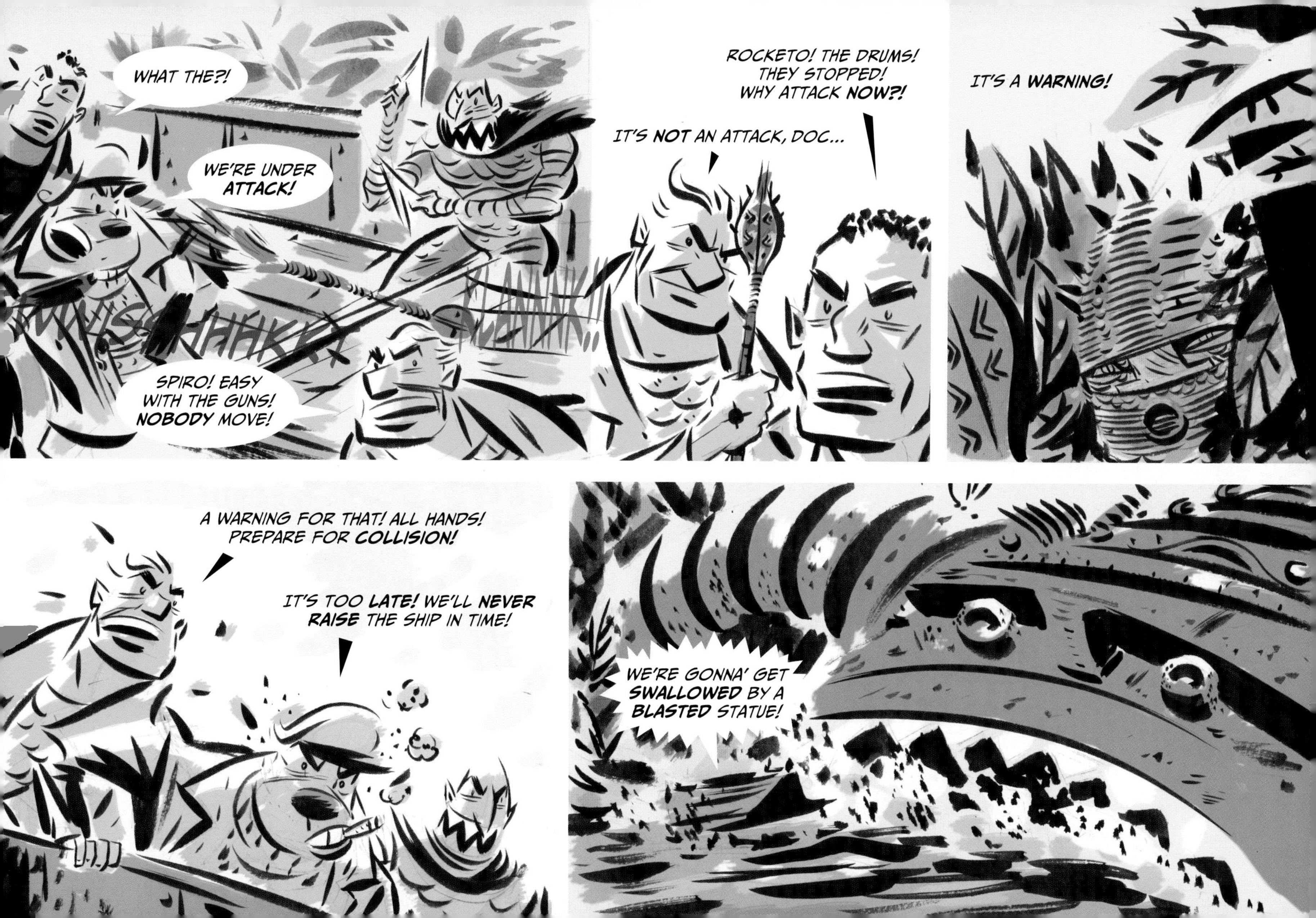
WHAT THE?!
WE'RE UNDER ATTACK!
SPIRO! EASY WITH THE GUNS! NOBODY MOVE!
ROCKETO! THE DRUMS! THEY STOPPED! WHY ATTACK NOW?!
IT'S NOT AN ATTACK, DOC...
IT'S A WARNING!
A WARNING FOR THAT! ALL HANDS! PREPARE FOR COLLISION!
IT'S TOO LATE! WE'LL NEVER RAISE THE SHIP IN TIME!
WE'RE GONNA' GET SWALLOWED BY A BLASTED STATUE!

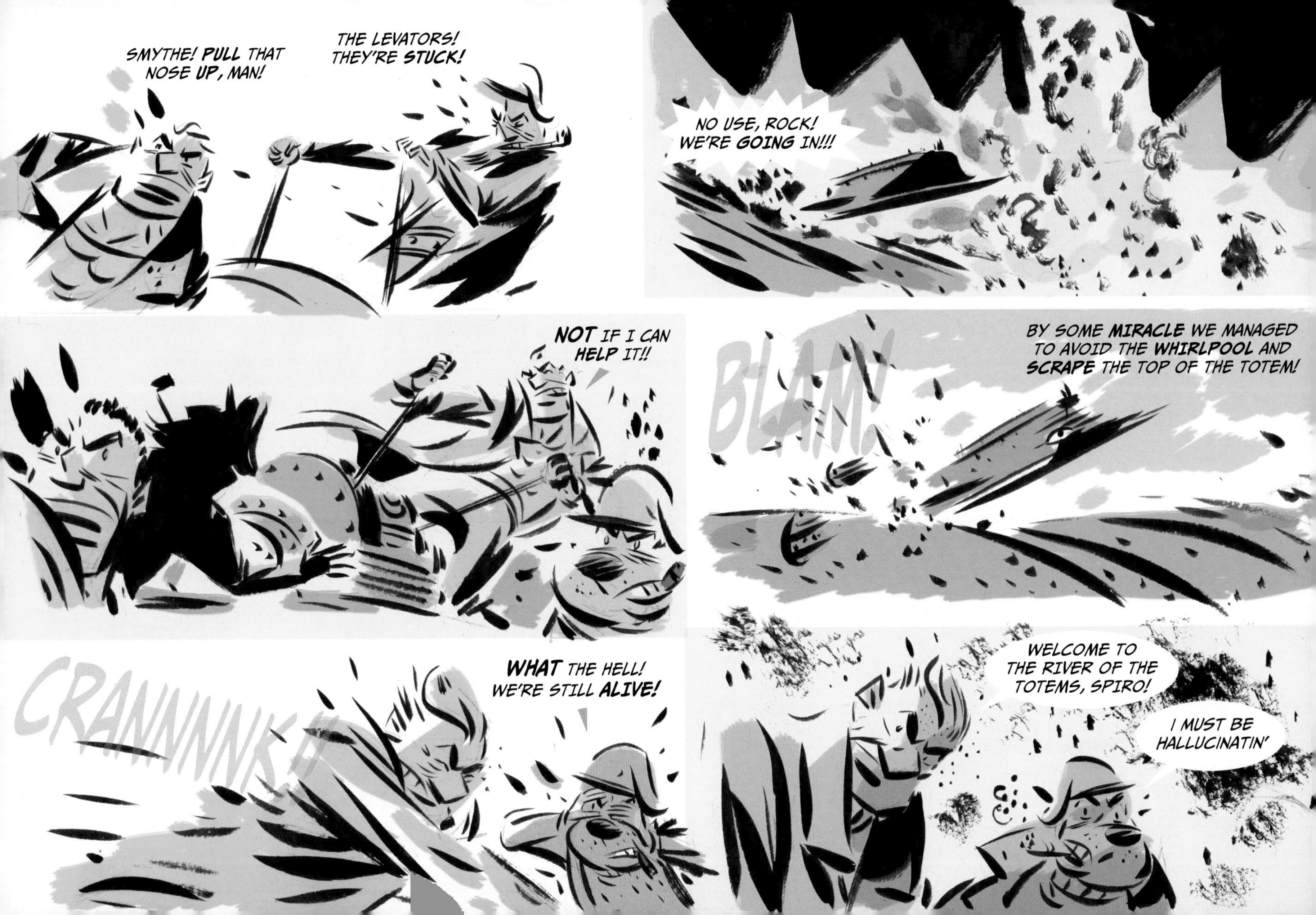
SMYTHE! PULL THAT NOSE UP, MAN!
THE LEVATORS! THEY'RE STUCK!
NO USE, ROCK! WE'RE GOING IN!!!
NOT IF I CAN HELP IT!!
BLAM!
BY SOME MIRACLE WE MANAGED TO AVOID THE WHIRLPOOL AND SCRAPE THE TOP OF THE TOTEM!
CRANNNNK!!
WHAT THE HELL! WE'RE STILL ALIVE!
WELCOME TO THE RIVER OF THE TOTEMS, SPIRO!
I MUST BE HALLUCINATIN'

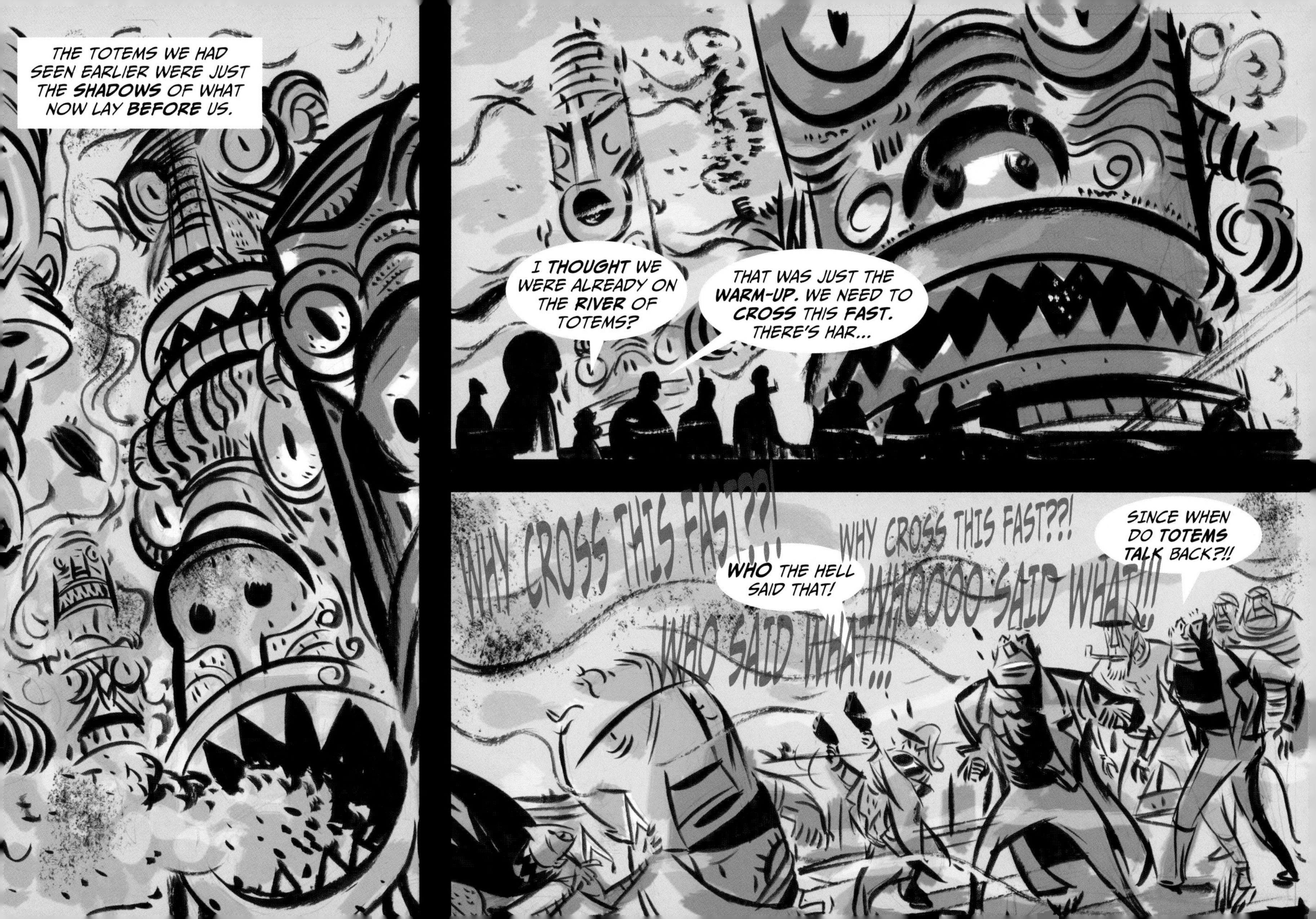
THE TOTEMS WE HAD SEEN EARLIER WERE JUST THE **SHADOWS** OF WHAT NOW LAY **BEFORE** US.
I **THOUGHT** WE WERE ALREADY ON THE **RIVER** OF TOTEMS?
THAT WAS JUST THE **WARM-UP.** WE NEED TO **CROSS** THIS **FAST.** THERE'S HAR...
WHY CROSS THIS FAST??!
**WHO** THE HELL SAID THAT!
WHO SAID WHAT!!!
WHY CROSS THIS FAST??!
WHOOOO SAID WHAT!!!
SINCE WHEN DO **TOTEMS TALK** BACK?!!

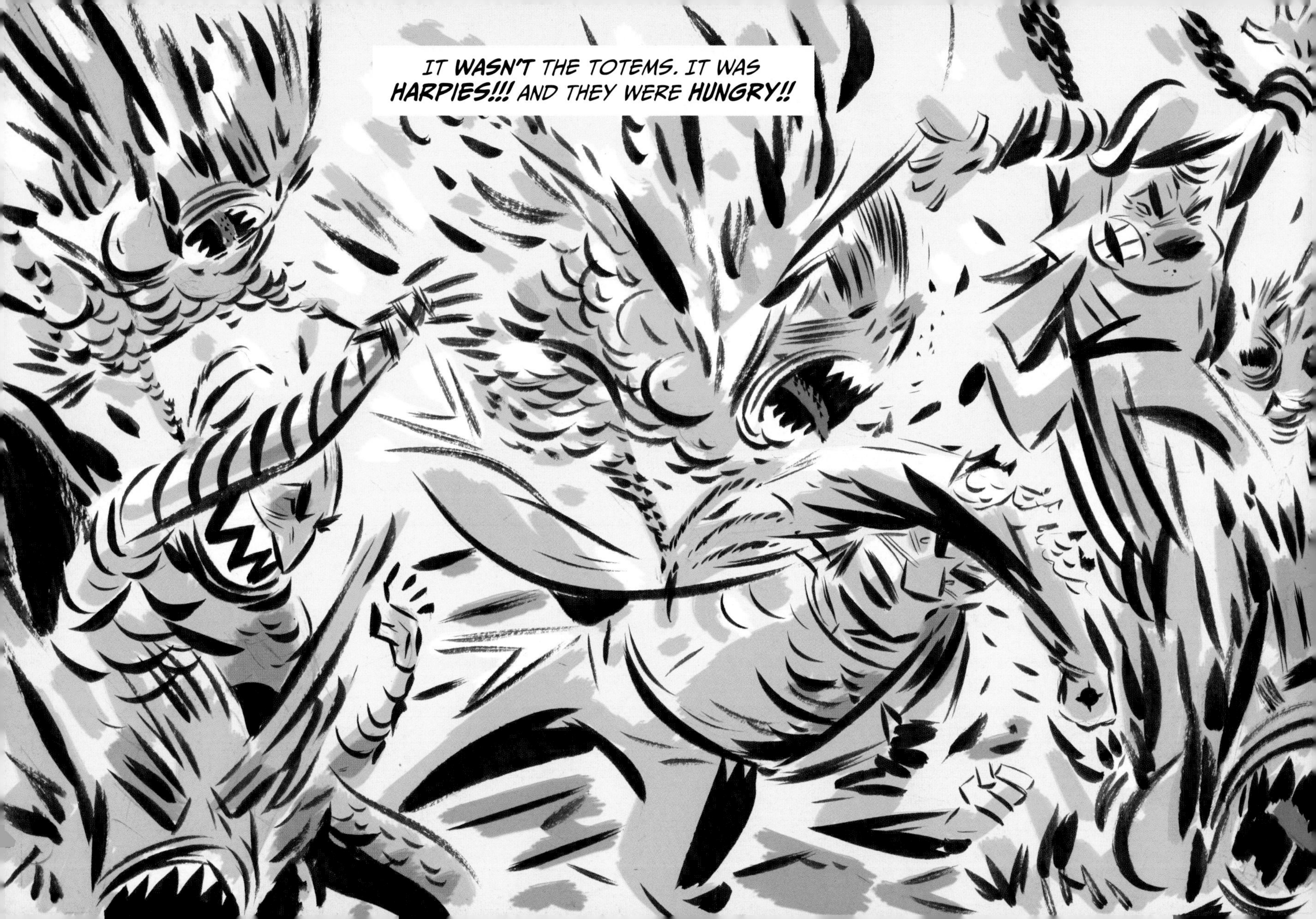
IT WASN'T THE TOTEMS. IT WAS HARPIES!!! AND THEY WERE HUNGRY!!

**ROCKETO**

THE RIVER OF TOTEMS AT THE EDGE OF THE HIDDEN SEA. THE YEAR, 1917 NW.

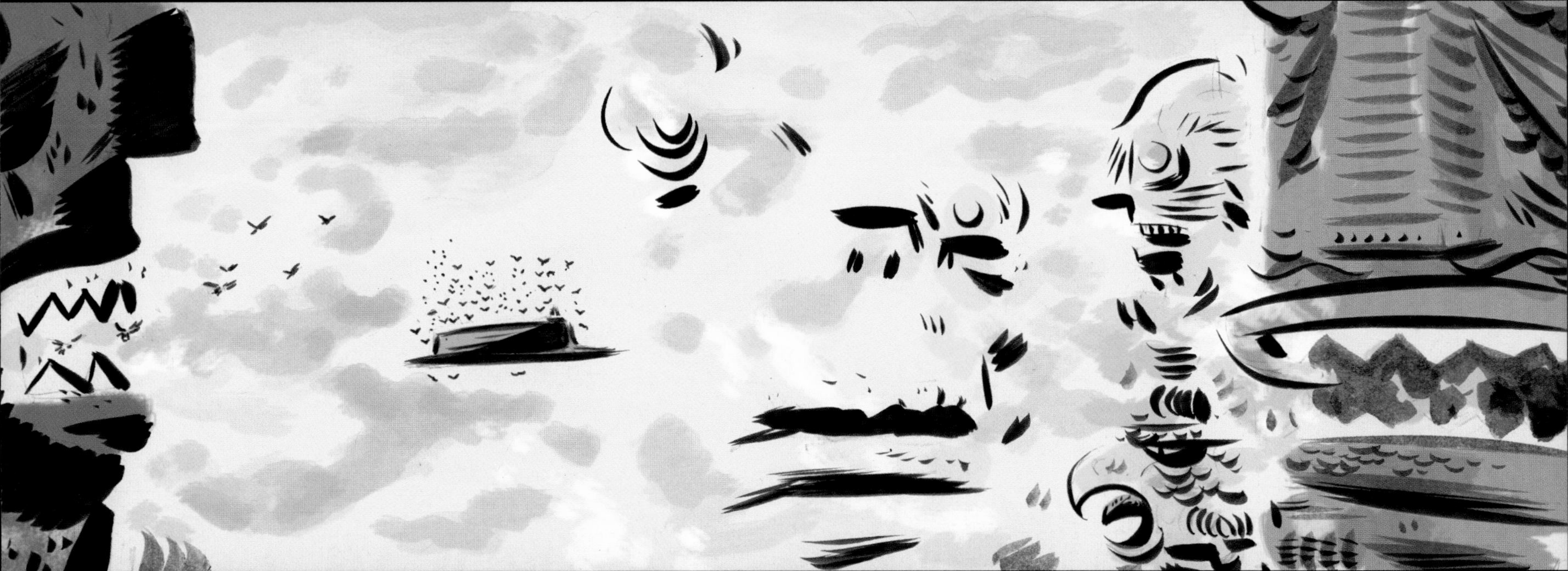

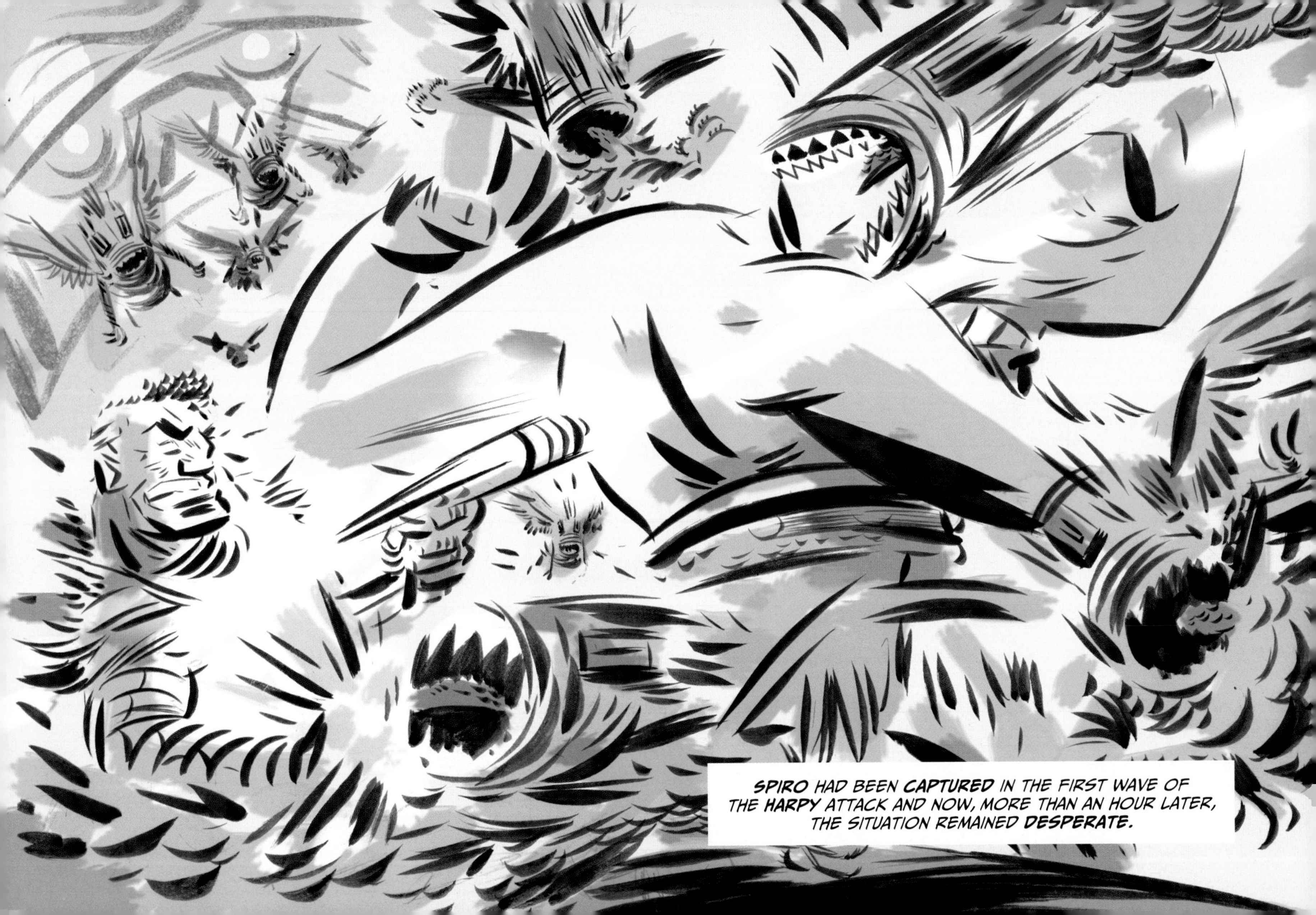
SPIRO HAD BEEN CAPTURED IN THE FIRST WAVE OF THE HARPY ATTACK AND NOW, MORE THAN AN HOUR LATER, THE SITUATION REMAINED DESPERATE.

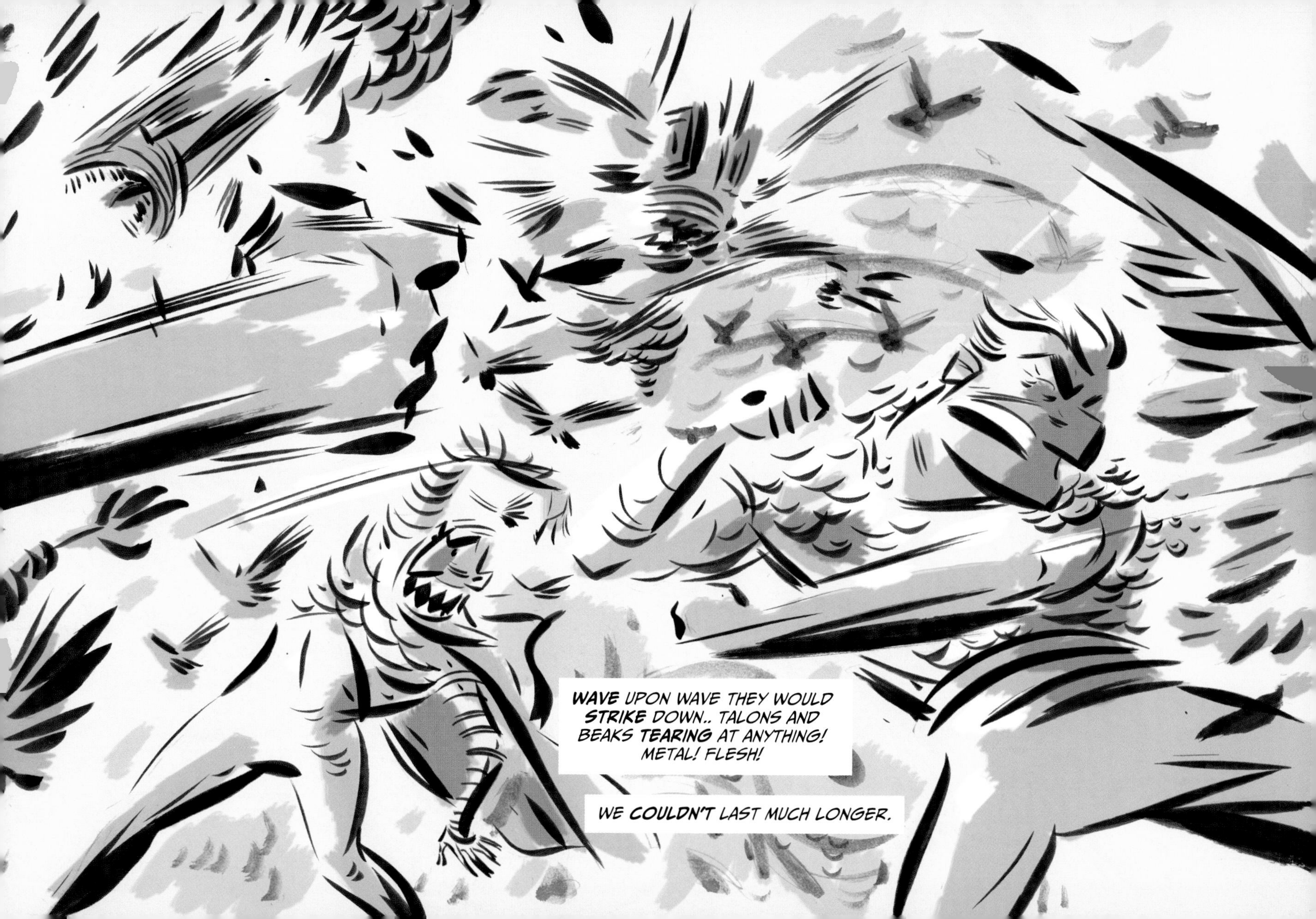
WAVE UPON WAVE THEY WOULD STRIKE DOWN.. TALONS AND BEAKS TEARING AT ANYTHING! METAL! FLESH!
WE COULDN'T LAST MUCH LONGER.

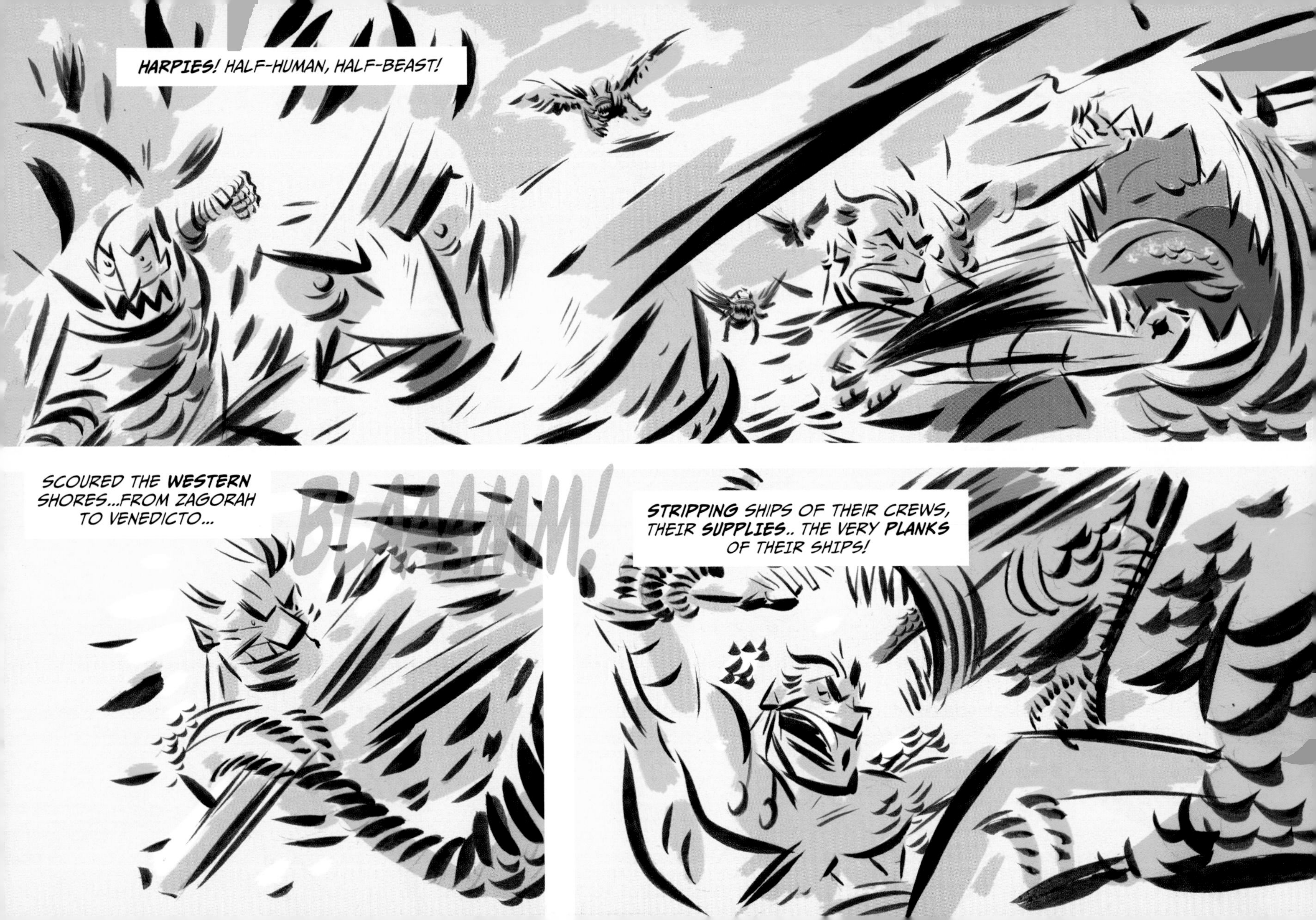
HARPIES! HALF-HUMAN, HALF-BEAST!
SCOURED THE WESTERN SHORES...FROM ZAGORAH TO VENEDICTO...
BLAAAMM!
STRIPPING SHIPS OF THEIR CREWS, THEIR SUPPLIES.. THE VERY PLANKS OF THEIR SHIPS!

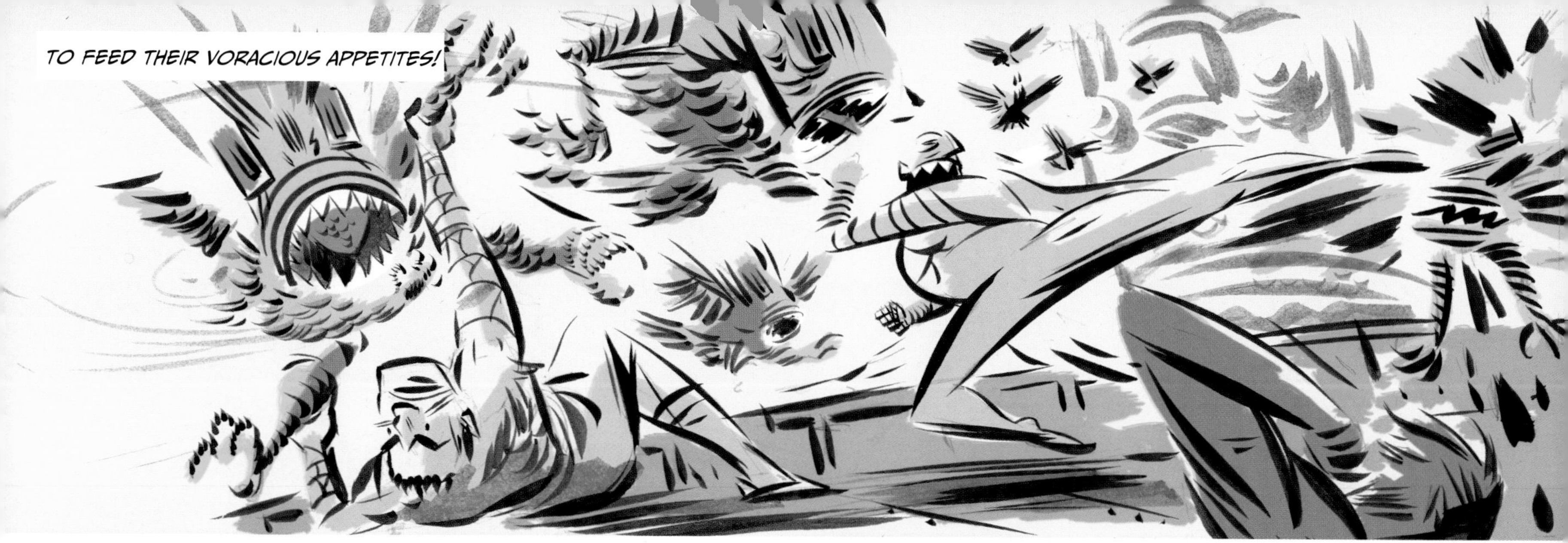
TO FEED THEIR VORACIOUS APPETITES!

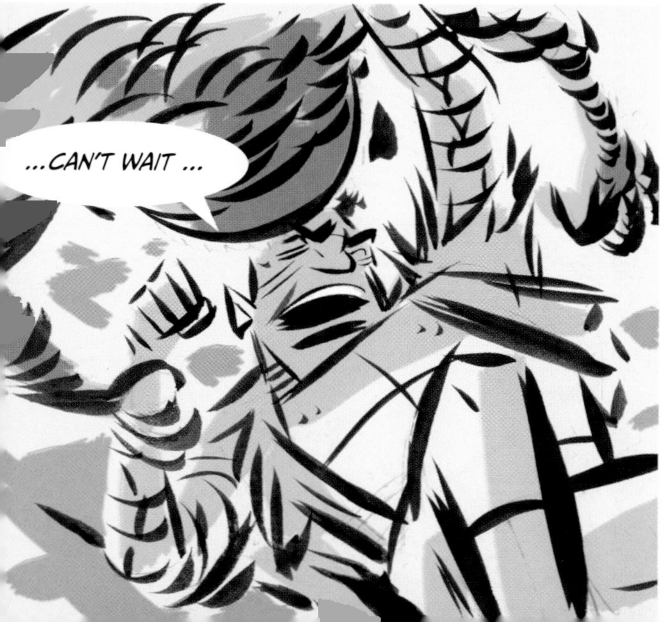
...CAN'T WAIT ...

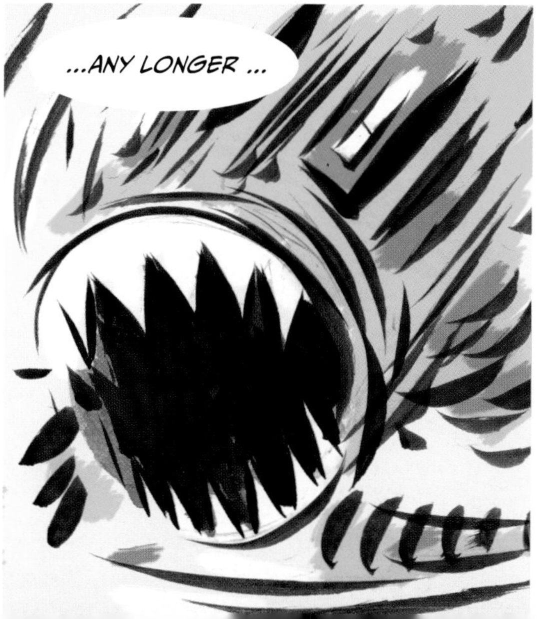
...ANY LONGER ...

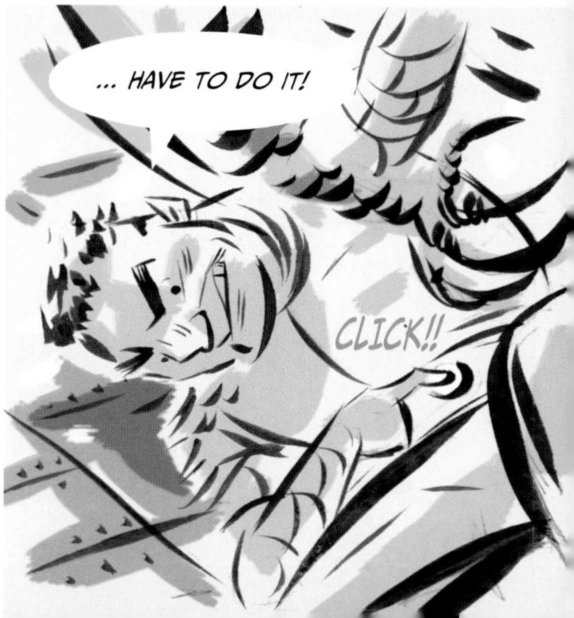
... HAVE TO DO IT!
CLICK!!

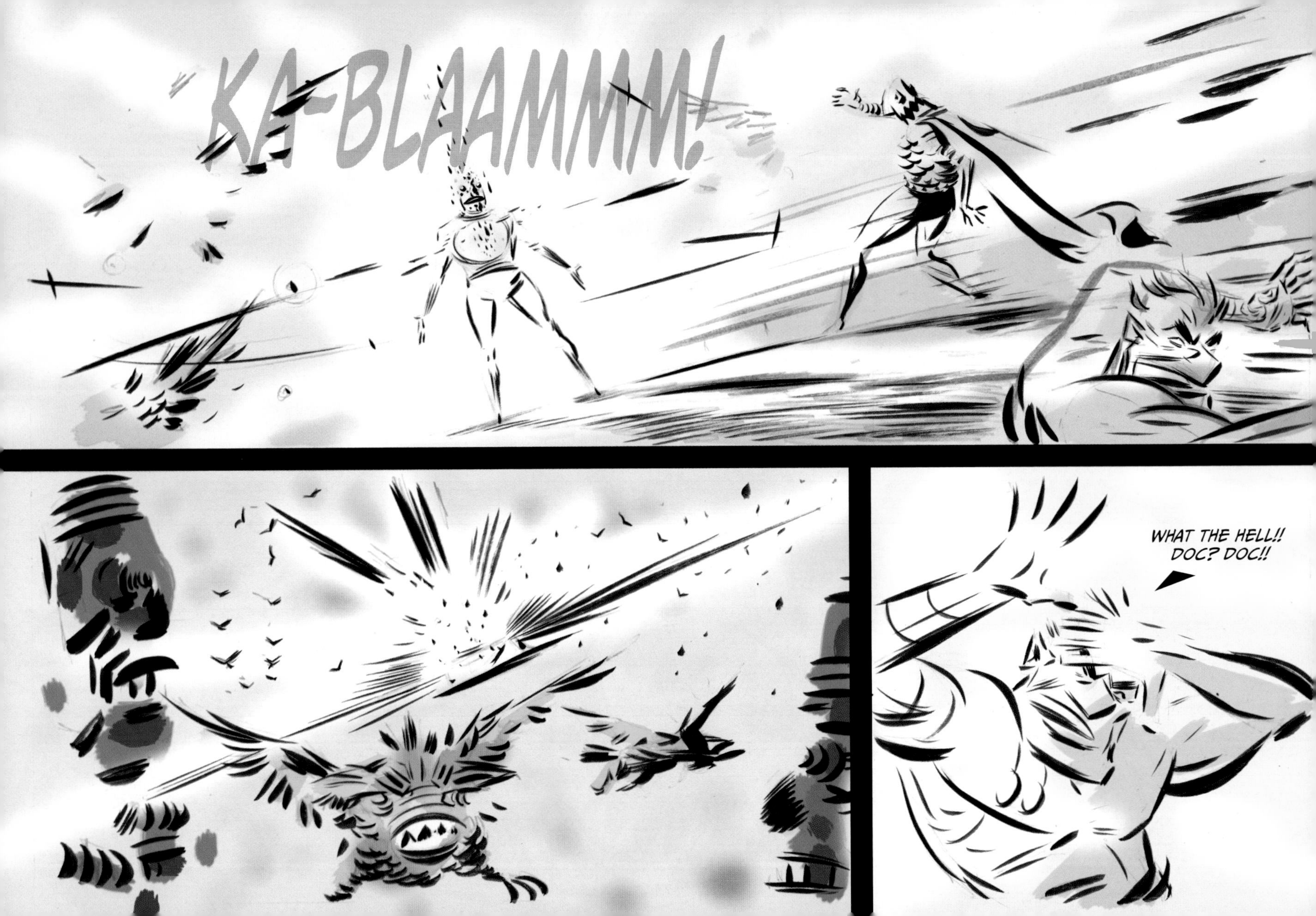
KA-BLAAMMM!
WHAT THE HELL!! DOC? DOC!!

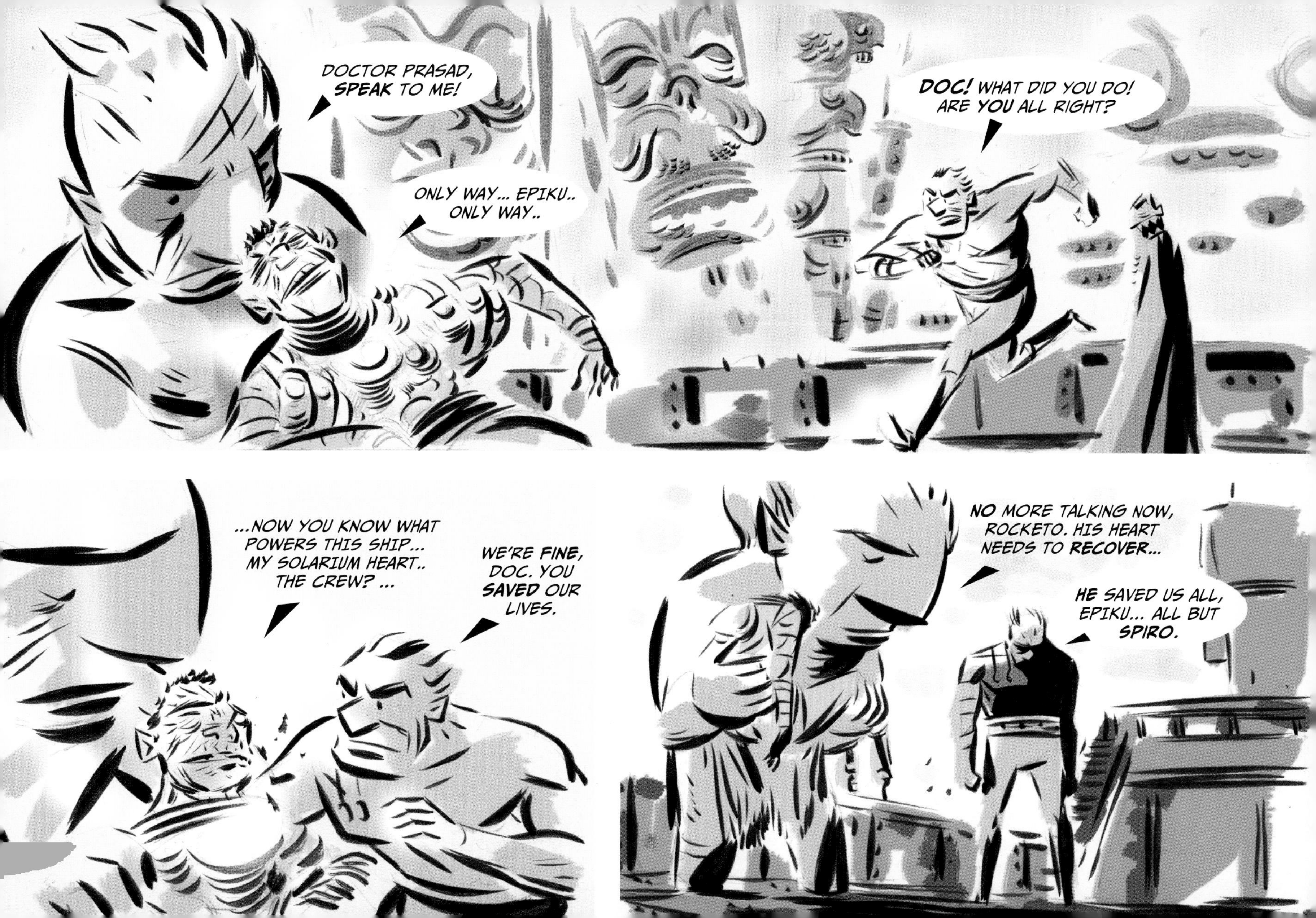
DOCTOR PRASAD, SPEAK TO ME!
ONLY WAY... EPIKU.. ONLY WAY..
DOC! WHAT DID YOU DO! ARE YOU ALL RIGHT?
...NOW YOU KNOW WHAT POWERS THIS SHIP... MY SOLARIUM HEART.. THE CREW? ...
WE'RE FINE, DOC. YOU SAVED OUR LIVES.
NO MORE TALKING NOW, ROCKETO. HIS HEART NEEDS TO RECOVER...
HE SAVED US ALL, EPIKU... ALL BUT SPIRO.

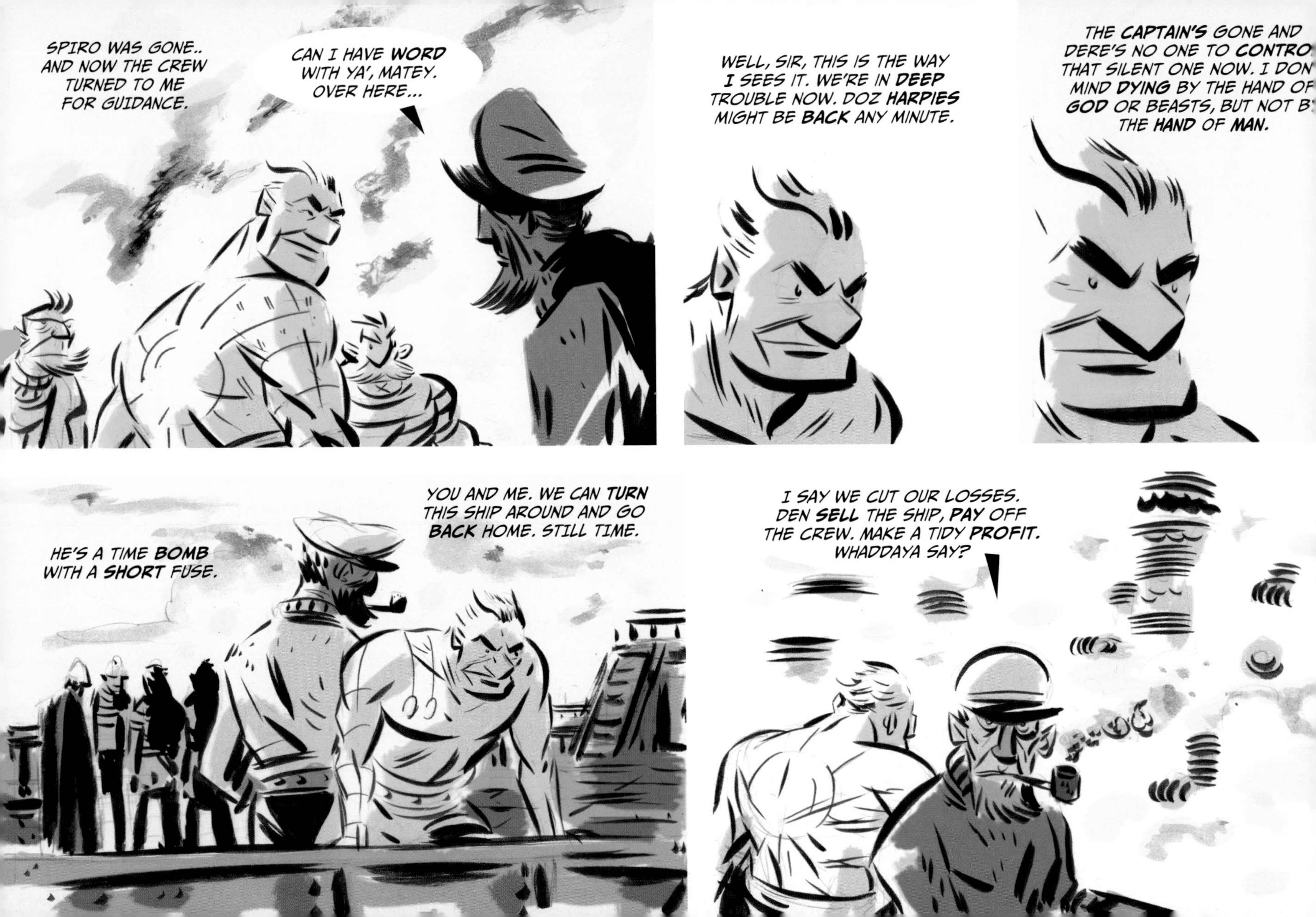
SPIRO WAS GONE.. AND NOW THE CREW TURNED TO ME FOR GUIDANCE.
CAN I HAVE WORD WITH YA', MATEY. OVER HERE...
WELL, SIR, THIS IS THE WAY I SEES IT. WE'RE IN DEEP TROUBLE NOW. DOZ HARPIES MIGHT BE BACK ANY MINUTE.
THE CAPTAIN'S GONE AND DERE'S NO ONE TO CONTRO THAT SILENT ONE NOW. I DON MIND DYING BY THE HAND OF GOD OR BEASTS, BUT NOT B THE HAND OF MAN.
HE'S A TIME BOMB WITH A SHORT FUSE.
YOU AND ME. WE CAN TURN THIS SHIP AROUND AND GO BACK HOME. STILL TIME.
I SAY WE CUT OUR LOSSES. DEN SELL THE SHIP, PAY OFF THE CREW. MAKE A TIDY PROFIT. WHADDAYA SAY?

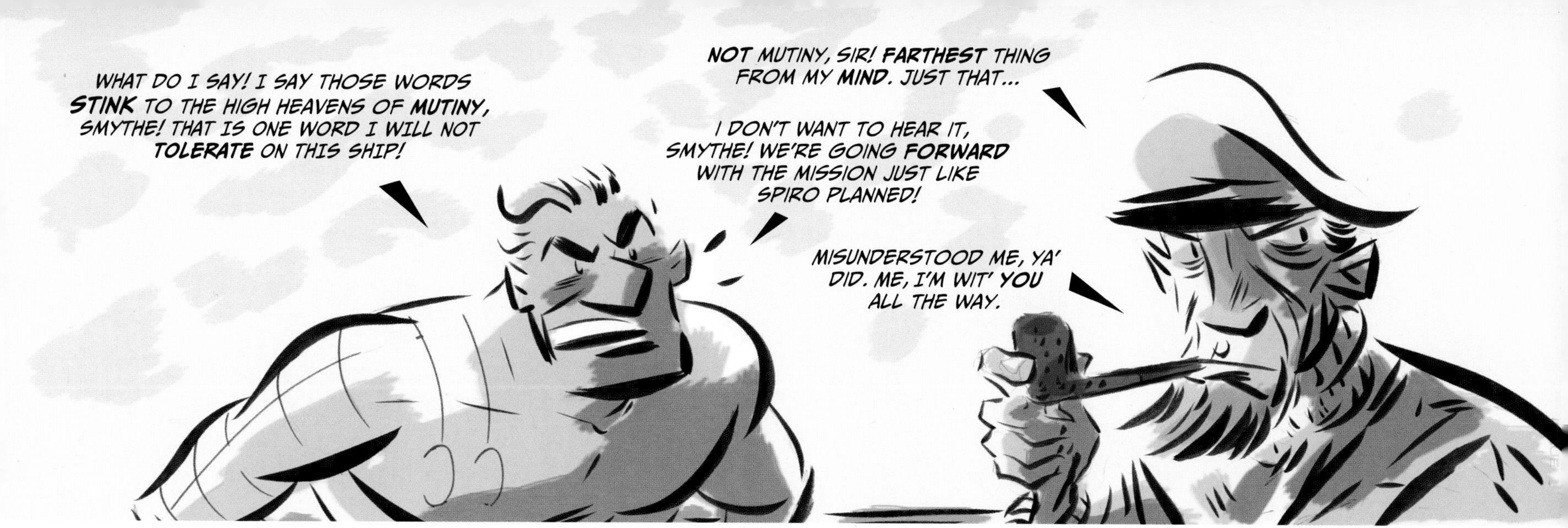
WHAT DO I SAY! I SAY THOSE WORDS **STINK** TO THE HIGH HEAVENS OF **MUTINY**, SMYTHE! THAT IS ONE WORD I WILL NOT **TOLERATE** ON THIS SHIP!
**NOT** MUTINY, SIR! **FARTHEST** THING FROM MY **MIND**. JUST THAT...
I DON'T WANT TO HEAR IT, SMYTHE! WE'RE GOING **FORWARD** WITH THE MISSION JUST LIKE SPIRO PLANNED!
MISUNDERSTOOD ME, YA' DID. ME, I'M WIT' **YOU** ALL THE WAY.

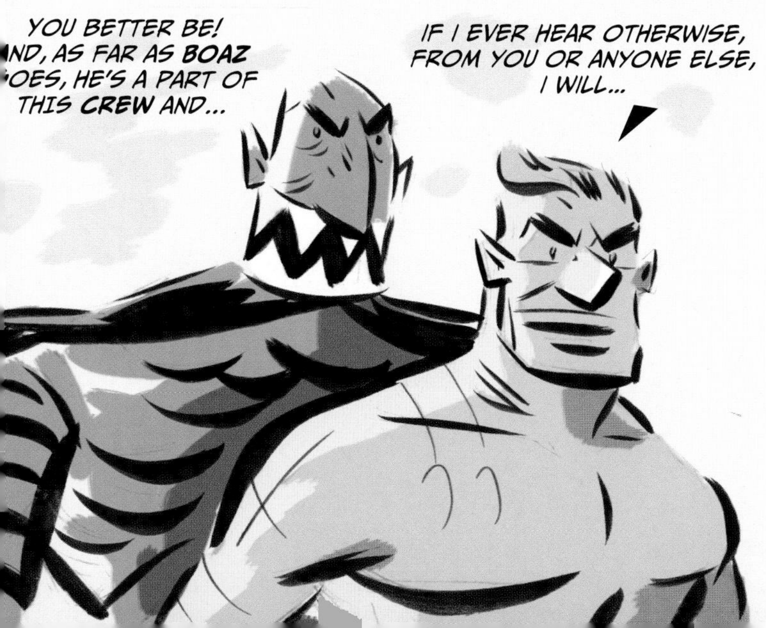
YOU BETTER BE! ND, AS FAR AS **BOAZ** OES, HE'S A PART OF THIS **CREW** AND...
IF I EVER HEAR OTHERWISE, FROM YOU OR ANYONE ELSE, I WILL...

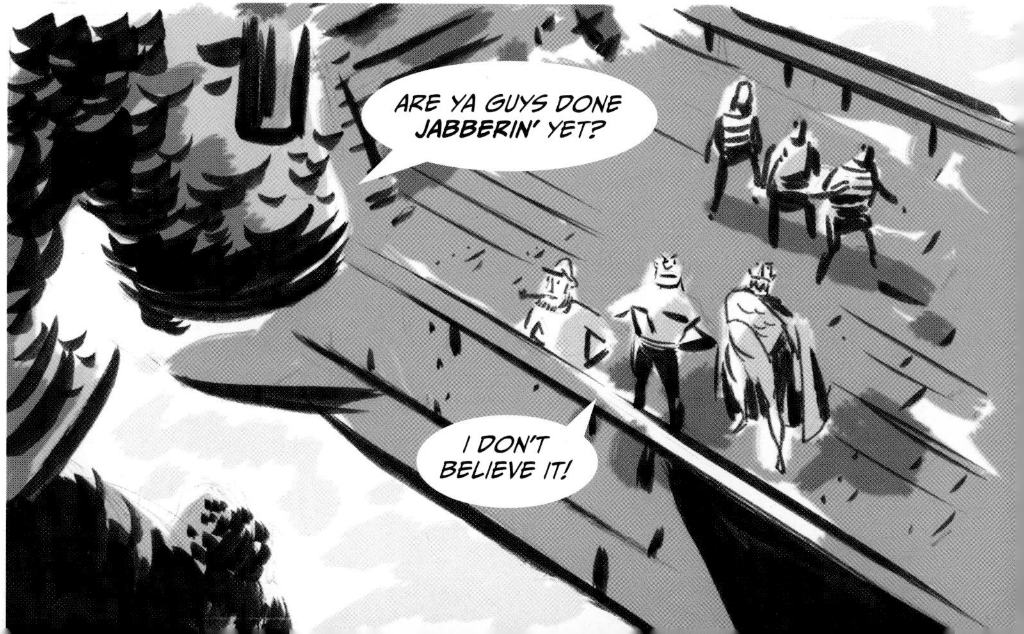
ARE YA GUYS DONE **JABBERIN'** YET?
I DON'T BELIEVE IT!

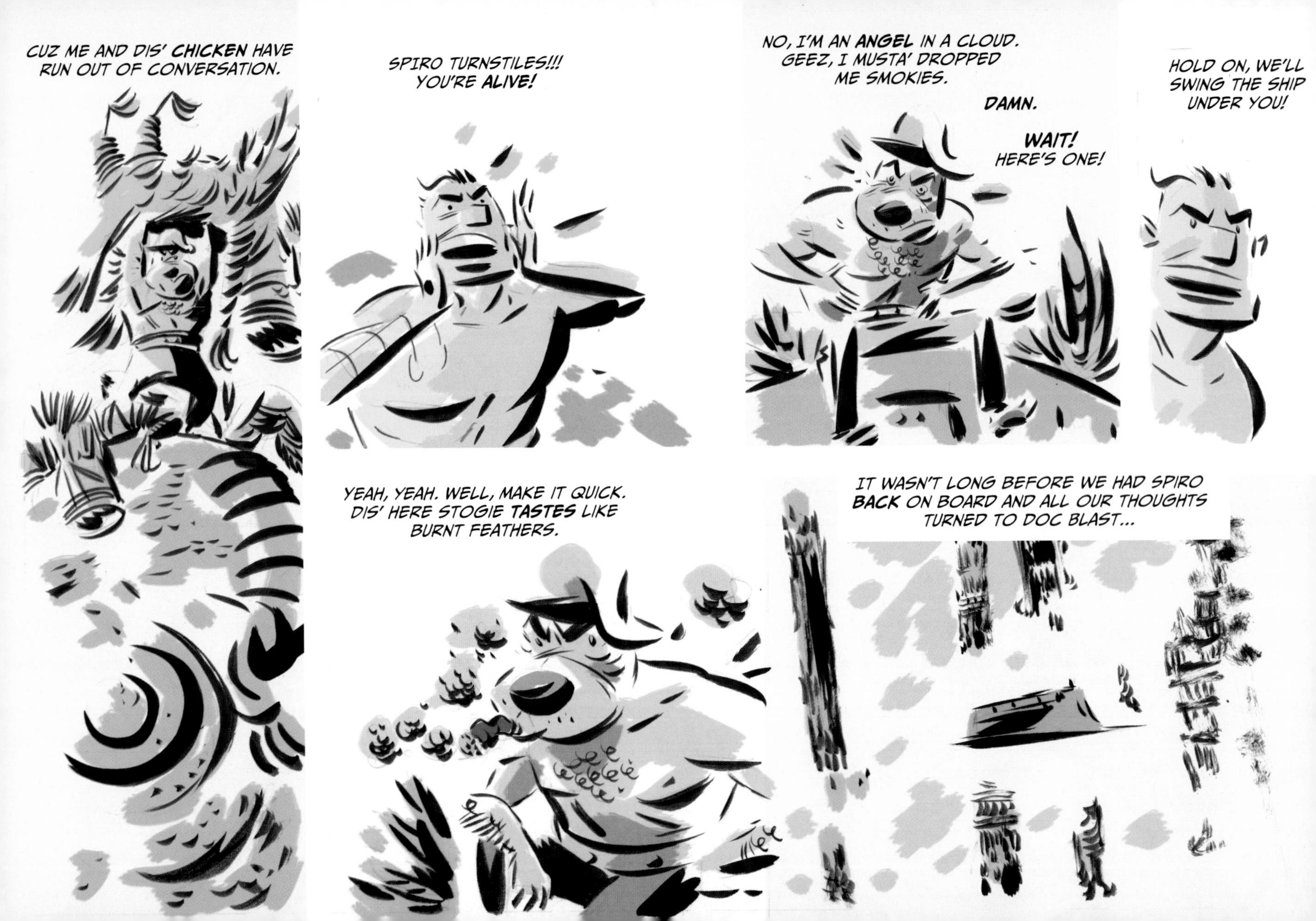
CUZ ME AND DIS' **CHICKEN** HAVE RUN OUT OF CONVERSATION.
SPIRO TURNSTILES!!! YOU'RE **ALIVE!**
NO, I'M AN **ANGEL** IN A CLOUD. GEEZ, I MUSTA' DROPPED ME SMOKIES.
**DAMN.**
**WAIT!** HERE'S ONE!
HOLD ON, WE'LL SWING THE SHIP UNDER YOU!
YEAH, YEAH. WELL, MAKE IT QUICK. DIS' HERE STOGIE **TASTES** LIKE BURNT FEATHERS.
IT WASN'T LONG BEFORE WE HAD SPIRO **BACK** ON BOARD AND ALL OUR THOUGHTS TURNED TO DOC BLAST...

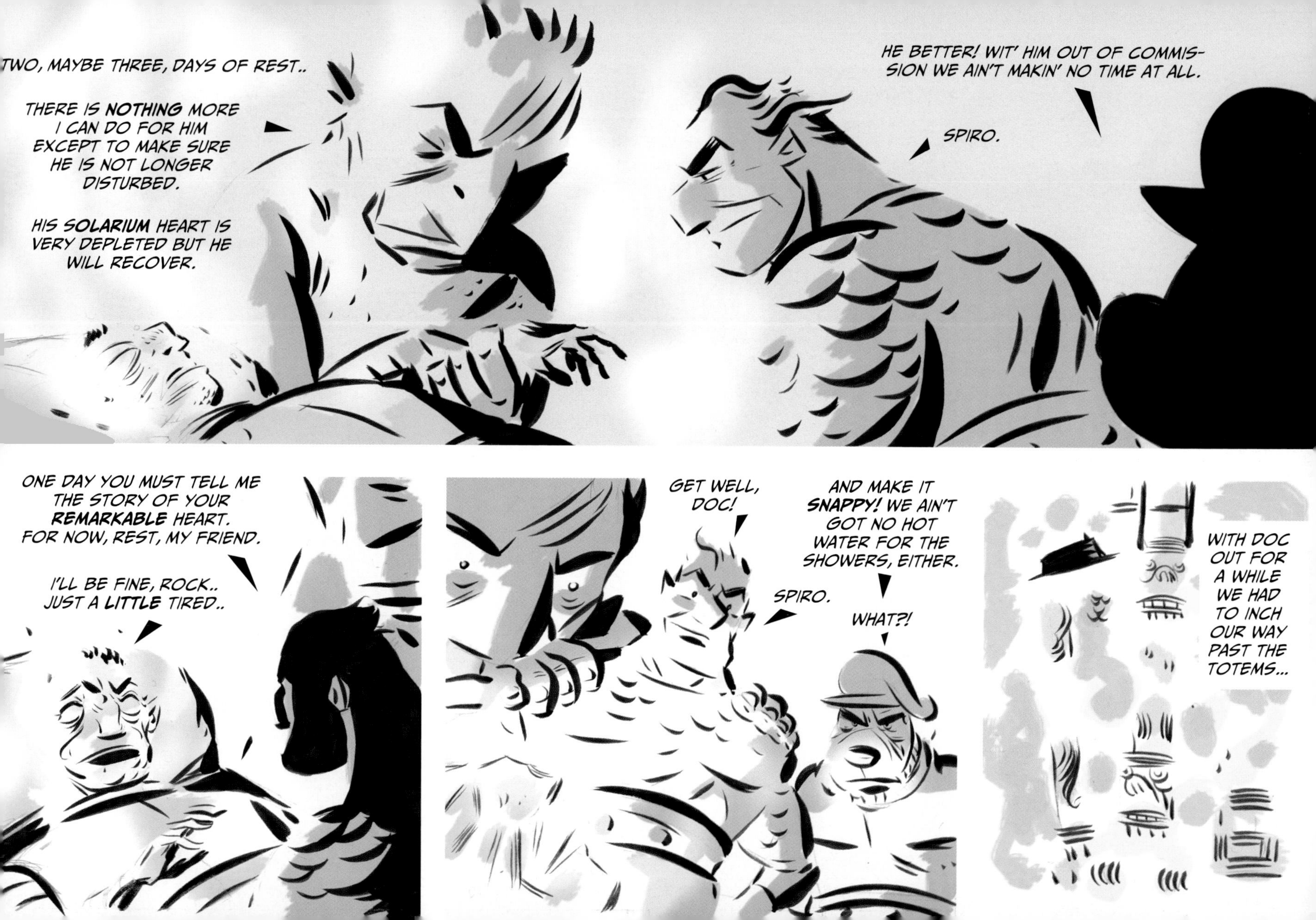
TWO, MAYBE THREE, DAYS OF REST..
THERE IS NOTHING MORE I CAN DO FOR HIM EXCEPT TO MAKE SURE HE IS NOT LONGER DISTURBED.
HIS SOLARIUM HEART IS VERY DEPLETED BUT HE WILL RECOVER.
SPIRO.
HE BETTER! WIT' HIM OUT OF COMMISSION WE AIN'T MAKIN' NO TIME AT ALL.
ONE DAY YOU MUST TELL ME THE STORY OF YOUR REMARKABLE HEART. FOR NOW, REST, MY FRIEND.
I'LL BE FINE, ROCK.. JUST A LITTLE TIRED..
GET WELL, DOC!
AND MAKE IT SNAPPY! WE AIN'T GOT NO HOT WATER FOR THE SHOWERS, EITHER.
SPIRO.
WHAT?!
WITH DOC OUT FOR A WHILE WE HAD TO INCH OUR WAY PAST THE TOTEMS...

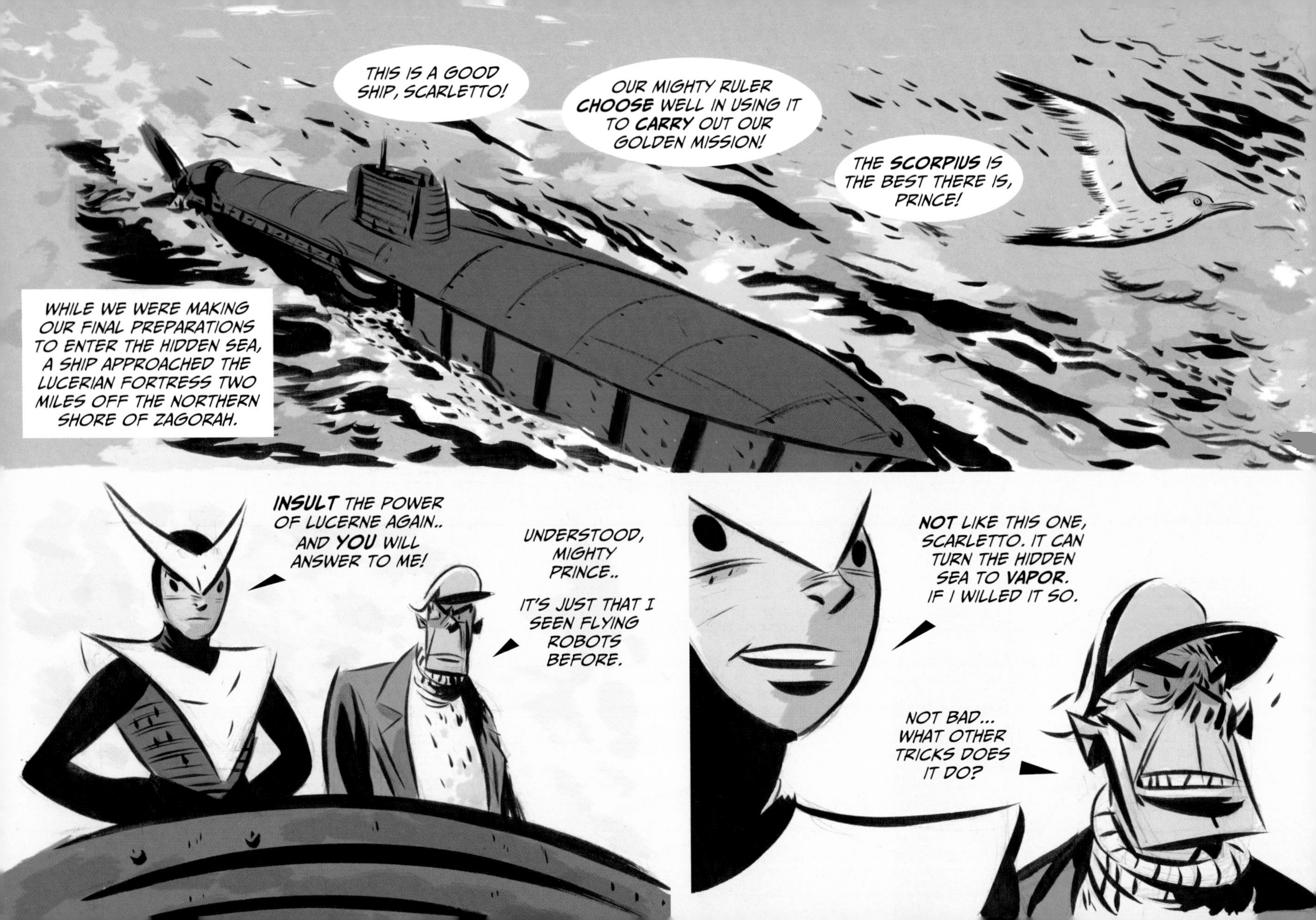

THIS IS A GOOD SHIP, SCARLETTO!
OUR MIGHTY RULER **CHOOSE** WELL IN USING IT TO **CARRY** OUT OUR GOLDEN MISSION!
THE **SCORPIUS** IS THE BEST THERE IS, PRINCE!
WHILE WE WERE MAKING OUR FINAL PREPARATIONS TO ENTER THE HIDDEN SEA, A SHIP APPROACHED THE LUCERIAN FORTRESS TWO MILES OFF THE NORTHERN SHORE OF ZAGORAH.
**INSULT** THE POWER OF LUCERNE AGAIN.. AND **YOU** WILL ANSWER TO ME!
UNDERSTOOD, MIGHTY PRINCE..
IT'S JUST THAT I SEEN FLYING ROBOTS BEFORE.
**NOT** LIKE THIS ONE, SCARLETTO. IT CAN TURN THE HIDDEN SEA TO **VAPOR.** IF I WILLED IT SO.
NOT BAD... WHAT OTHER TRICKS DOES IT DO?

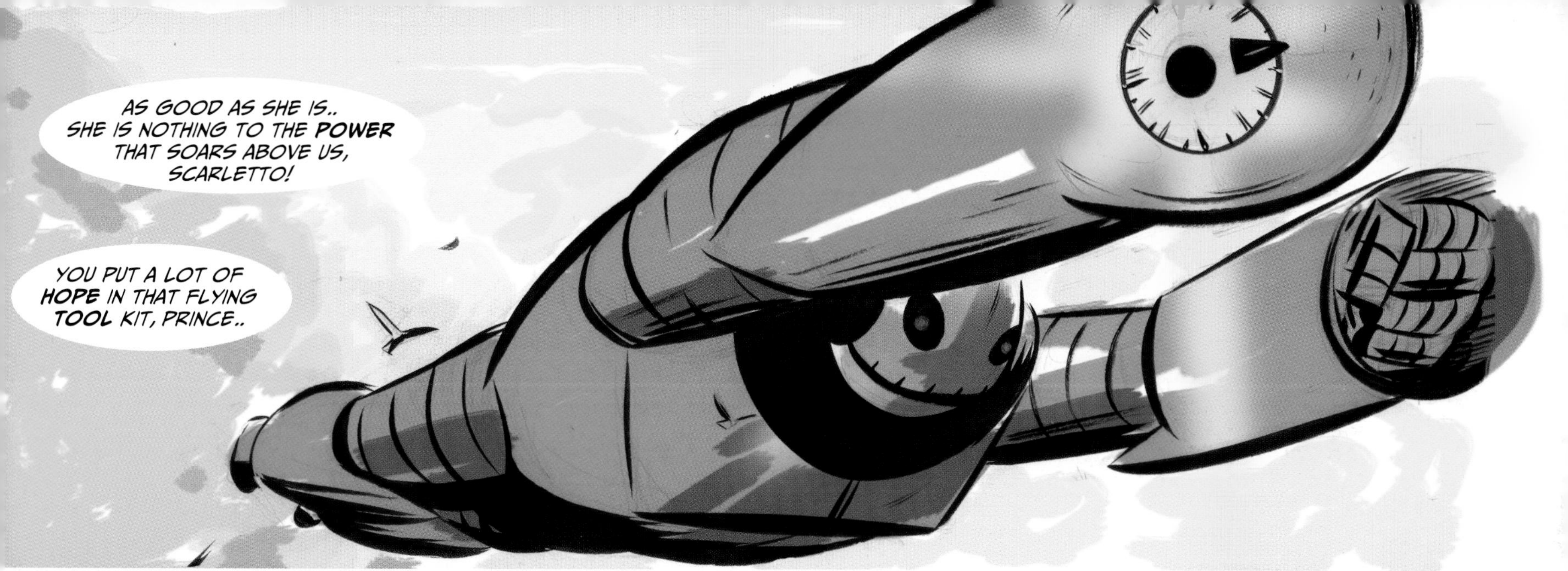
AS GOOD AS SHE IS.. SHE IS NOTHING TO THE **POWER** THAT SOARS ABOVE US, SCARLETTO!
YOU PUT A LOT OF **HOPE** IN THAT FLYING **TOOL** KIT, PRINCE..

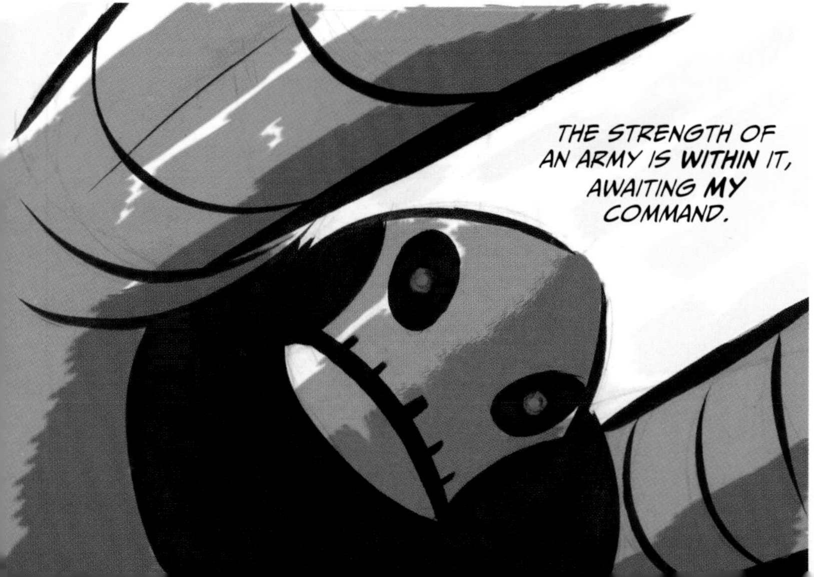
THE STRENGTH OF AN ARMY IS **WITHIN** IT, AWAITING **MY** COMMAND.

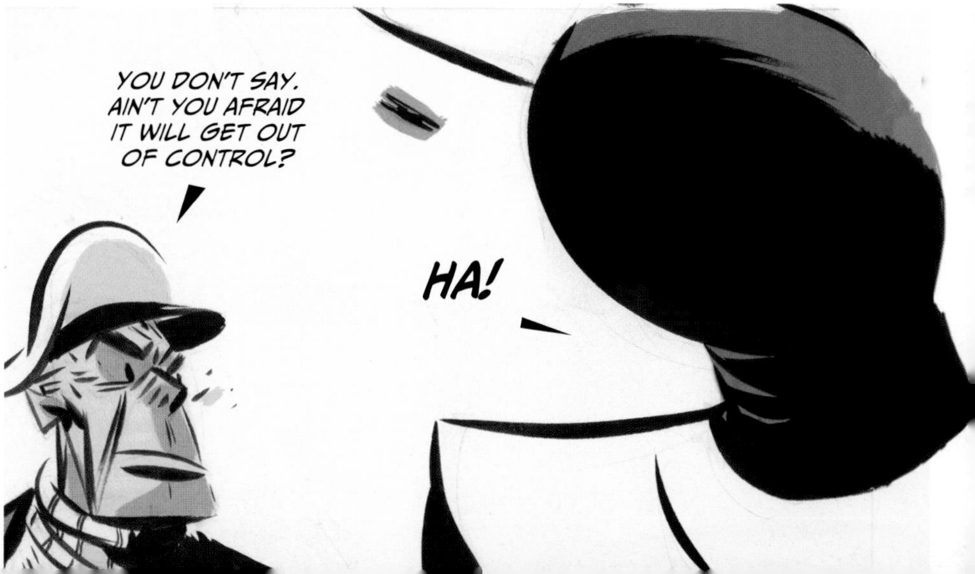
YOU DON'T SAY. AIN'T YOU AFRAID IT WILL GET OUT OF CONTROL?
HA!

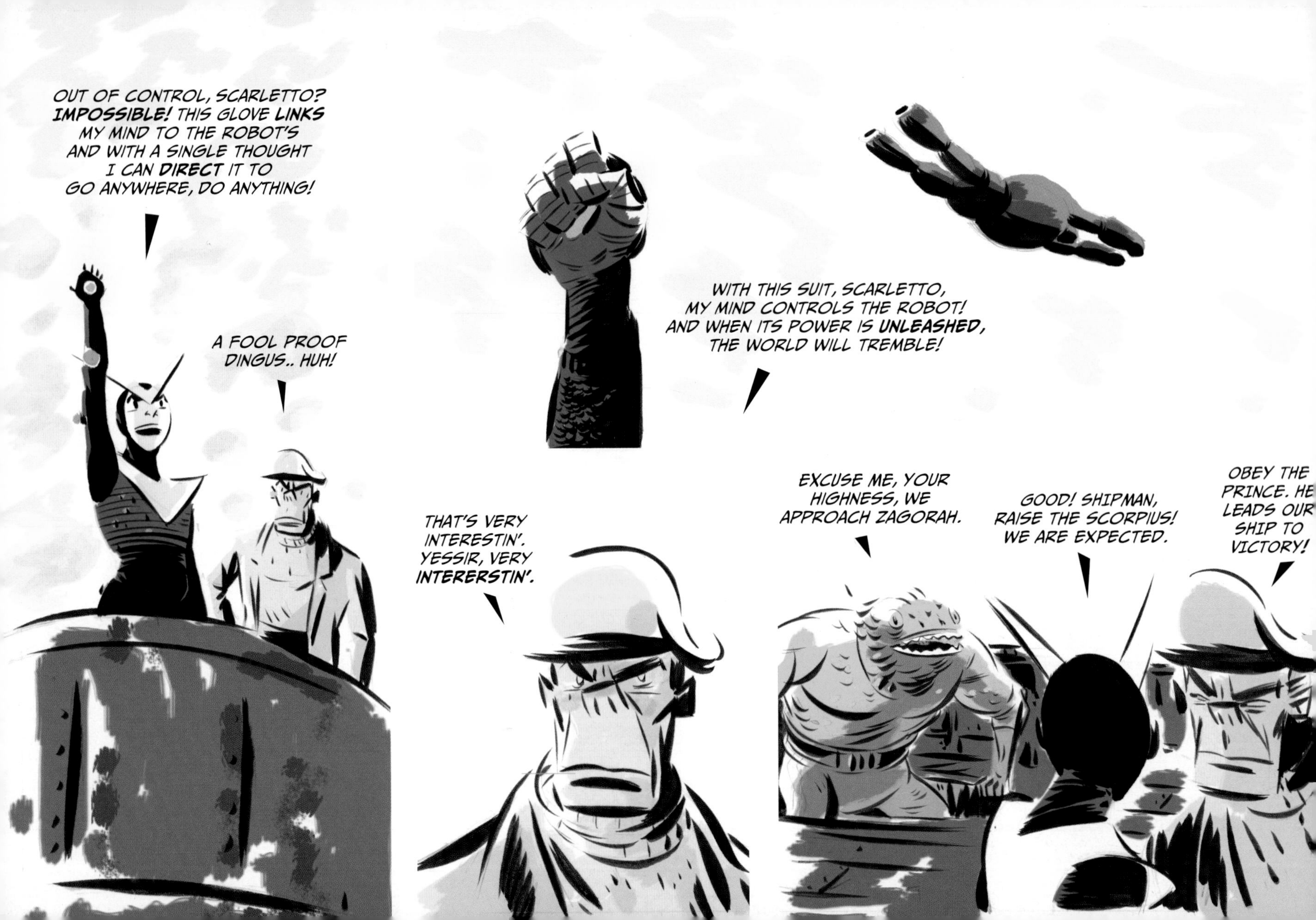
OUT OF CONTROL, SCARLETTO? IMPOSSIBLE! THIS GLOVE LINKS MY MIND TO THE ROBOT'S AND WITH A SINGLE THOUGHT I CAN DIRECT IT TO GO ANYWHERE, DO ANYTHING!
A FOOL PROOF DINGUS.. HUH!
WITH THIS SUIT, SCARLETTO, MY MIND CONTROLS THE ROBOT! AND WHEN ITS POWER IS UNLEASHED, THE WORLD WILL TREMBLE!
THAT'S VERY INTERESTIN'. YESSIR, VERY INTERERSTIN'.
EXCUSE ME, YOUR HIGHNESS, WE APPROACH ZAGORAH.
GOOD! SHIPMAN, RAISE THE SCORPIUS! WE ARE EXPECTED.
OBEY THE PRINCE. HE LEADS OUR SHIP TO VICTORY!

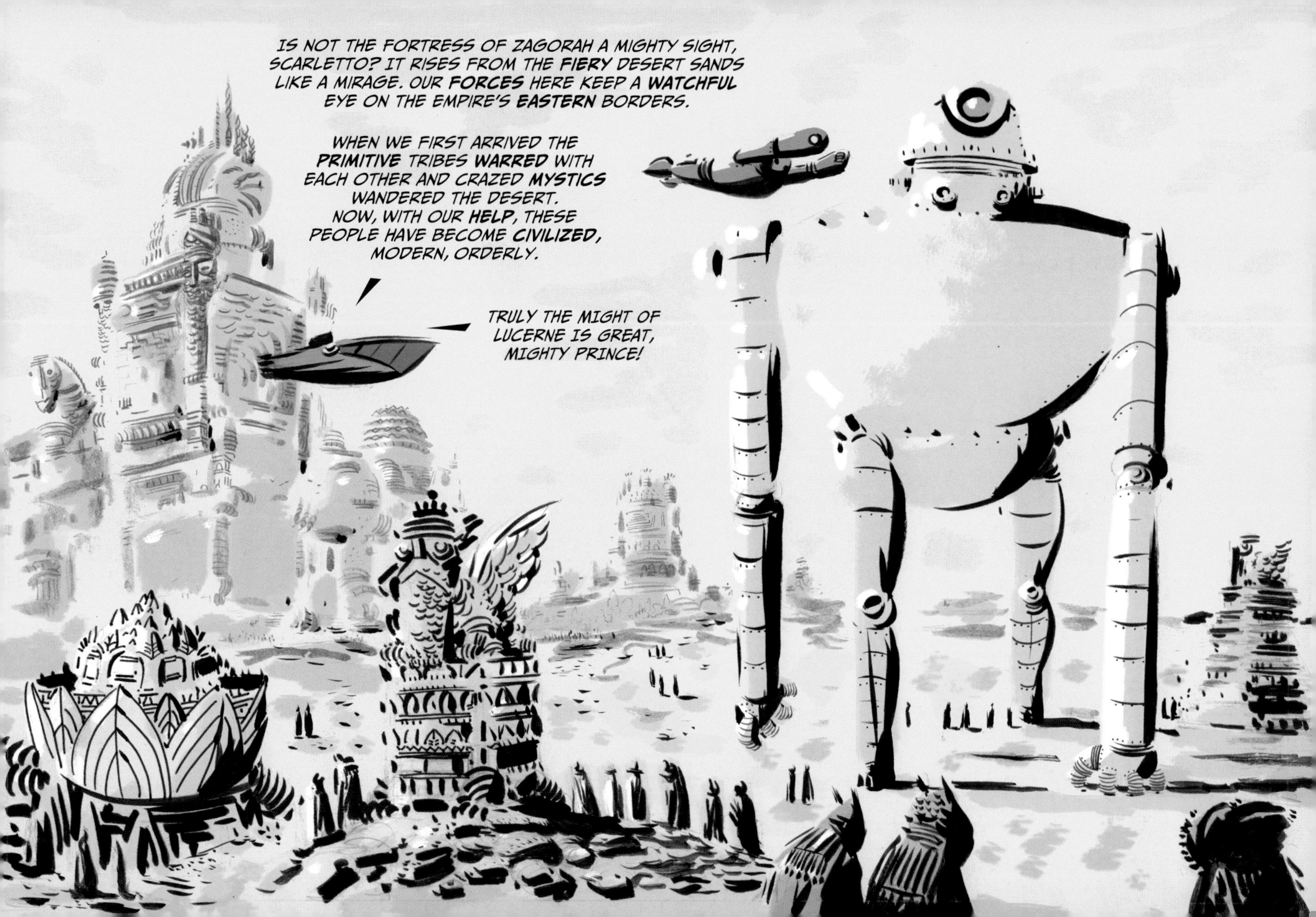
IS NOT THE FORTRESS OF ZAGORAH A MIGHTY SIGHT, SCARLETTO? IT RISES FROM THE **FIERY** DESERT SANDS LIKE A MIRAGE. OUR **FORCES** HERE KEEP A **WATCHFUL** EYE ON THE EMPIRE'S **EASTERN** BORDERS.
WHEN WE FIRST ARRIVED THE **PRIMITIVE** TRIBES **WARRED** WITH EACH OTHER AND CRAZED **MYSTICS** WANDERED THE DESERT. NOW, WITH OUR **HELP**, THESE PEOPLE HAVE BECOME **CIVILIZED**, MODERN, ORDERLY.
TRULY THE MIGHT OF LUCERNE IS GREAT, MIGHTY PRINCE!

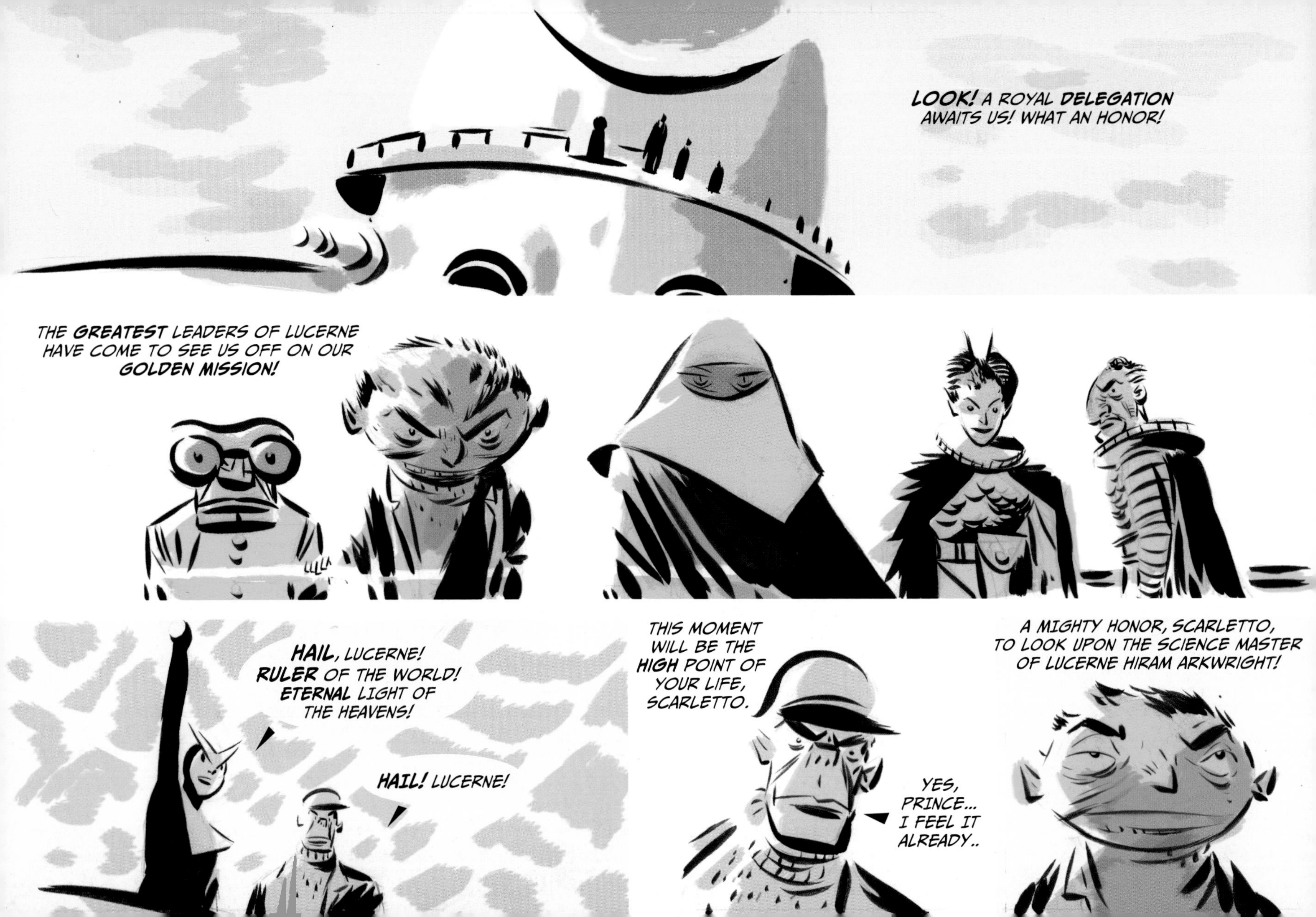

LOOK! A ROYAL DELEGATION AWAITS US! WHAT AN HONOR!
THE GREATEST LEADERS OF LUCERNE HAVE COME TO SEE US OFF ON OUR GOLDEN MISSION!
HAIL, LUCERNE! RULER OF THE WORLD! ETERNAL LIGHT OF THE HEAVENS!
HAIL! LUCERNE!
THIS MOMENT WILL BE THE HIGH POINT OF YOUR LIFE, SCARLETTO.
YES, PRINCE... I FEEL IT ALREADY..
A MIGHTY HONOR, SCARLETTO, TO LOOK UPON THE SCIENCE MASTER OF LUCERNE HIRAM ARKWRIGHT!

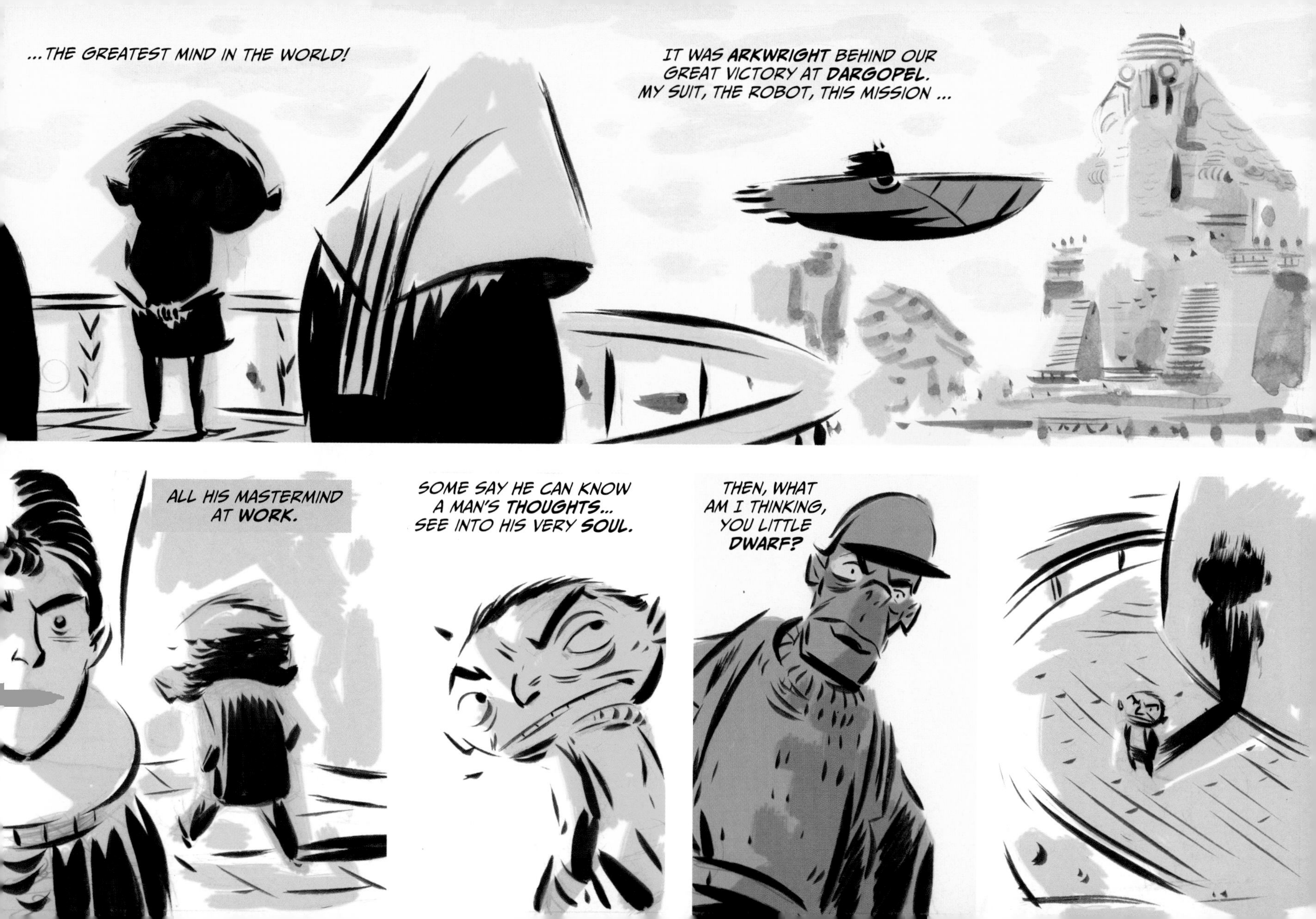
...THE GREATEST MIND IN THE WORLD!
IT WAS ARKWRIGHT BEHIND OUR GREAT VICTORY AT DARGOPEL. MY SUIT, THE ROBOT, THIS MISSION ...
ALL HIS MASTERMIND AT WORK.
SOME SAY HE CAN KNOW A MAN'S THOUGHTS... SEE INTO HIS VERY SOUL.
THEN, WHAT AM I THINKING, YOU LITTLE DWARF?

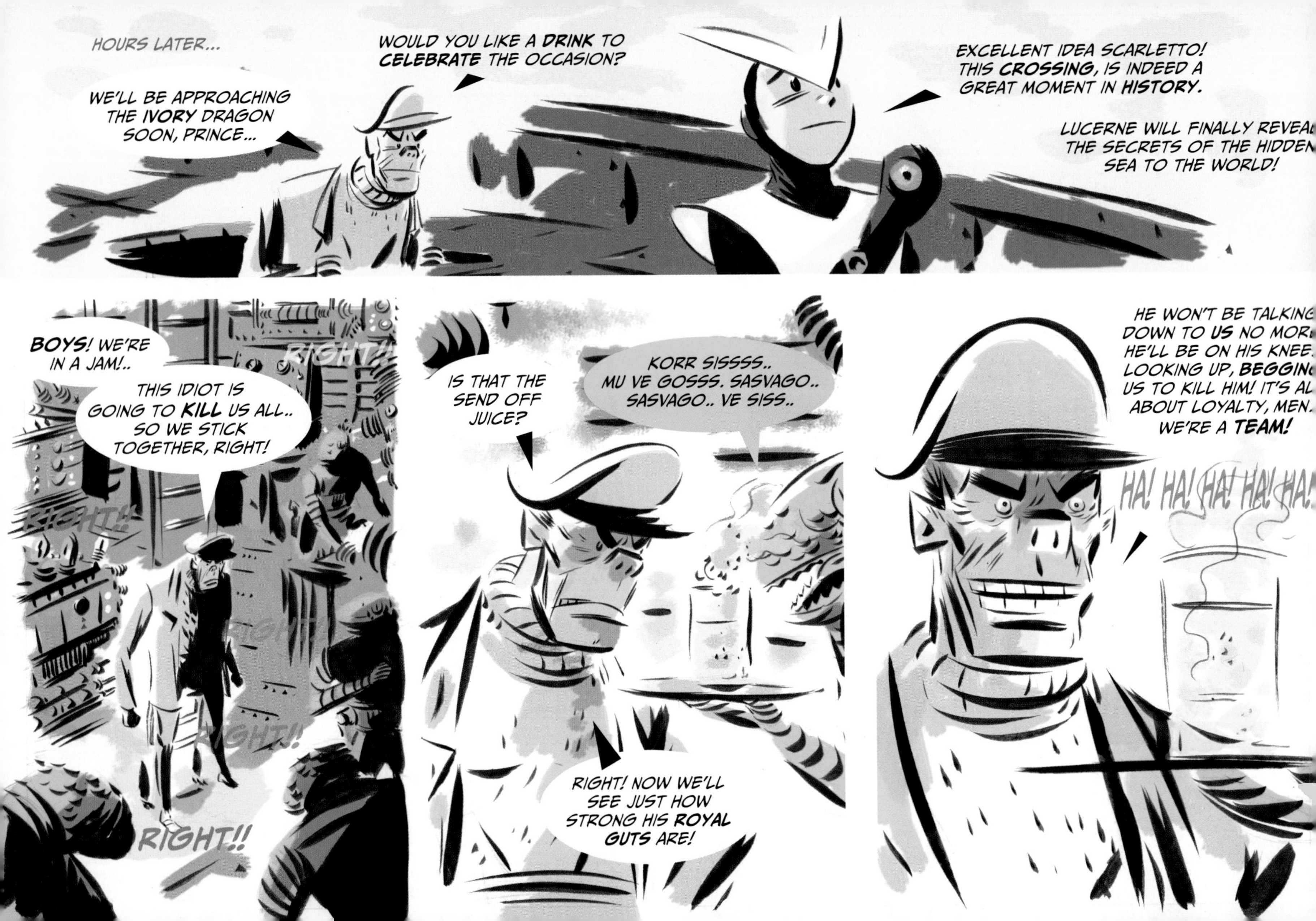
HOURS LATER...
WE'LL BE APPROACHING THE IVORY DRAGON SOON, PRINCE...
WOULD YOU LIKE A DRINK TO CELEBRATE THE OCCASION?
EXCELLENT IDEA SCARLETTO! THIS CROSSING, IS INDEED A GREAT MOMENT IN HISTORY.
LUCERNE WILL FINALLY REVEA THE SECRETS OF THE HIDDEN SEA TO THE WORLD!
BOYS! WE'RE IN A JAM!..
THIS IDIOT IS GOING TO KILL US ALL.. SO WE STICK TOGETHER, RIGHT!
RIGHT!!
RIGHT!!
RIGHT!!
RIGHT!!
RIGHT!!
IS THAT THE SEND OFF JUICE?
KORR SISSSS.. MU VE GOSSS. SASVAGO.. SASVAGO.. VE SISS..
RIGHT! NOW WE'LL SEE JUST HOW STRONG HIS ROYAL GUTS ARE!
HE WON'T BE TALKING DOWN TO US NO MOR HE'LL BE ON HIS KNEE LOOKING UP, BEGGIN US TO KILL HIM! IT'S AL ABOUT LOYALTY, MEN. WE'RE A TEAM!
HA! HA! HA! HA! HA!

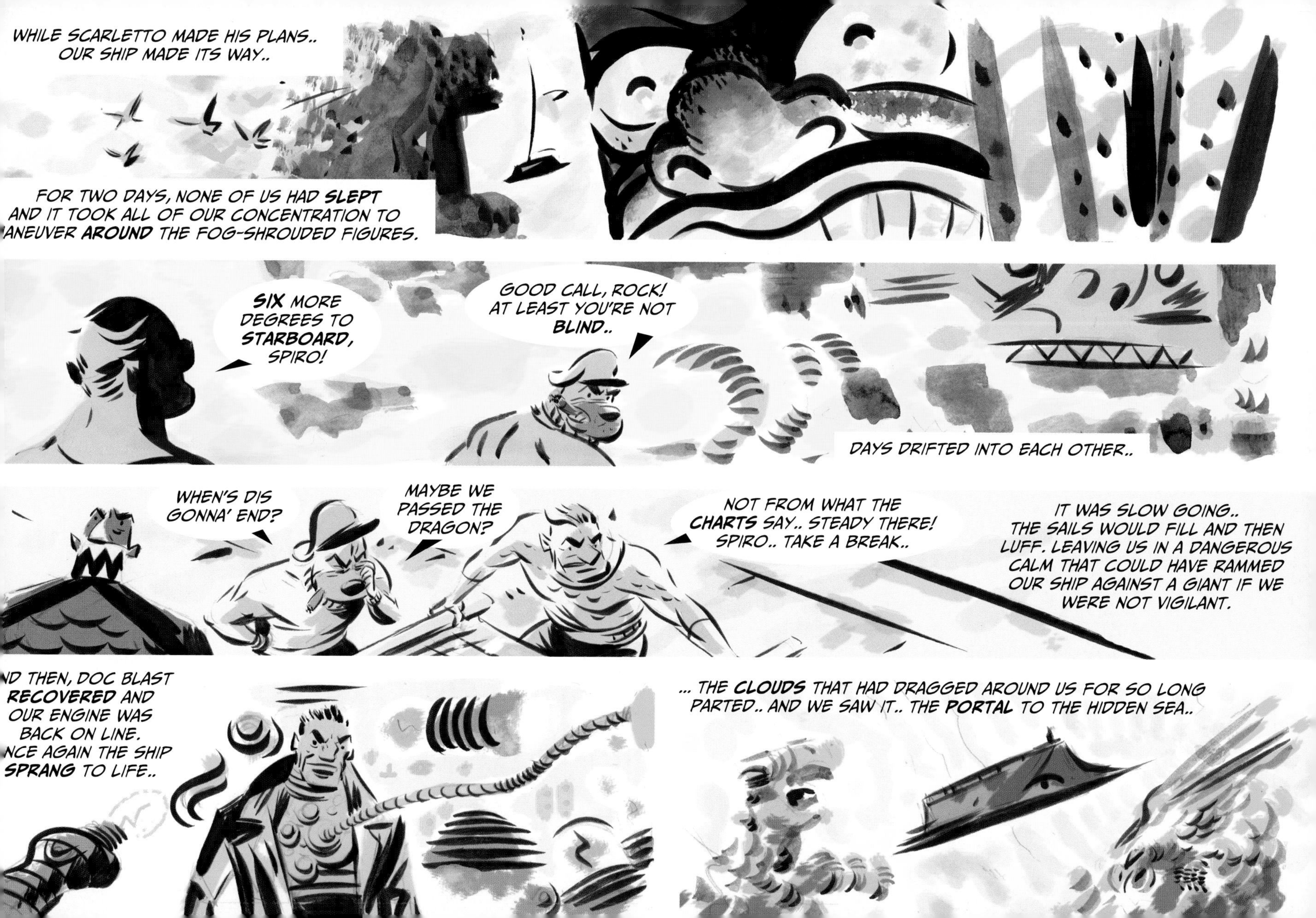
WHILE SCARLETTO MADE HIS PLANS.. OUR SHIP MADE ITS WAY..
FOR TWO DAYS, NONE OF US HAD SLEPT AND IT TOOK ALL OF OUR CONCENTRATION TO ANEUVER AROUND THE FOG-SHROUDED FIGURES.
SIX MORE DEGREES TO STARBOARD, SPIRO!
GOOD CALL, ROCK! AT LEAST YOU'RE NOT BLIND..
DAYS DRIFTED INTO EACH OTHER..
WHEN'S DIS GONNA' END?
MAYBE WE PASSED THE DRAGON?
NOT FROM WHAT THE CHARTS SAY.. STEADY THERE! SPIRO.. TAKE A BREAK..
IT WAS SLOW GOING.. THE SAILS WOULD FILL AND THEN LUFF. LEAVING US IN A DANGEROUS CALM THAT COULD HAVE RAMMED OUR SHIP AGAINST A GIANT IF WE WERE NOT VIGILANT.
ND THEN, DOC BLAST RECOVERED AND OUR ENGINE WAS BACK ON LINE. NCE AGAIN THE SHIP SPRANG TO LIFE..
... THE CLOUDS THAT HAD DRAGGED AROUND US FOR SO LONG PARTED.. AND WE SAW IT.. THE PORTAL TO THE HIDDEN SEA..

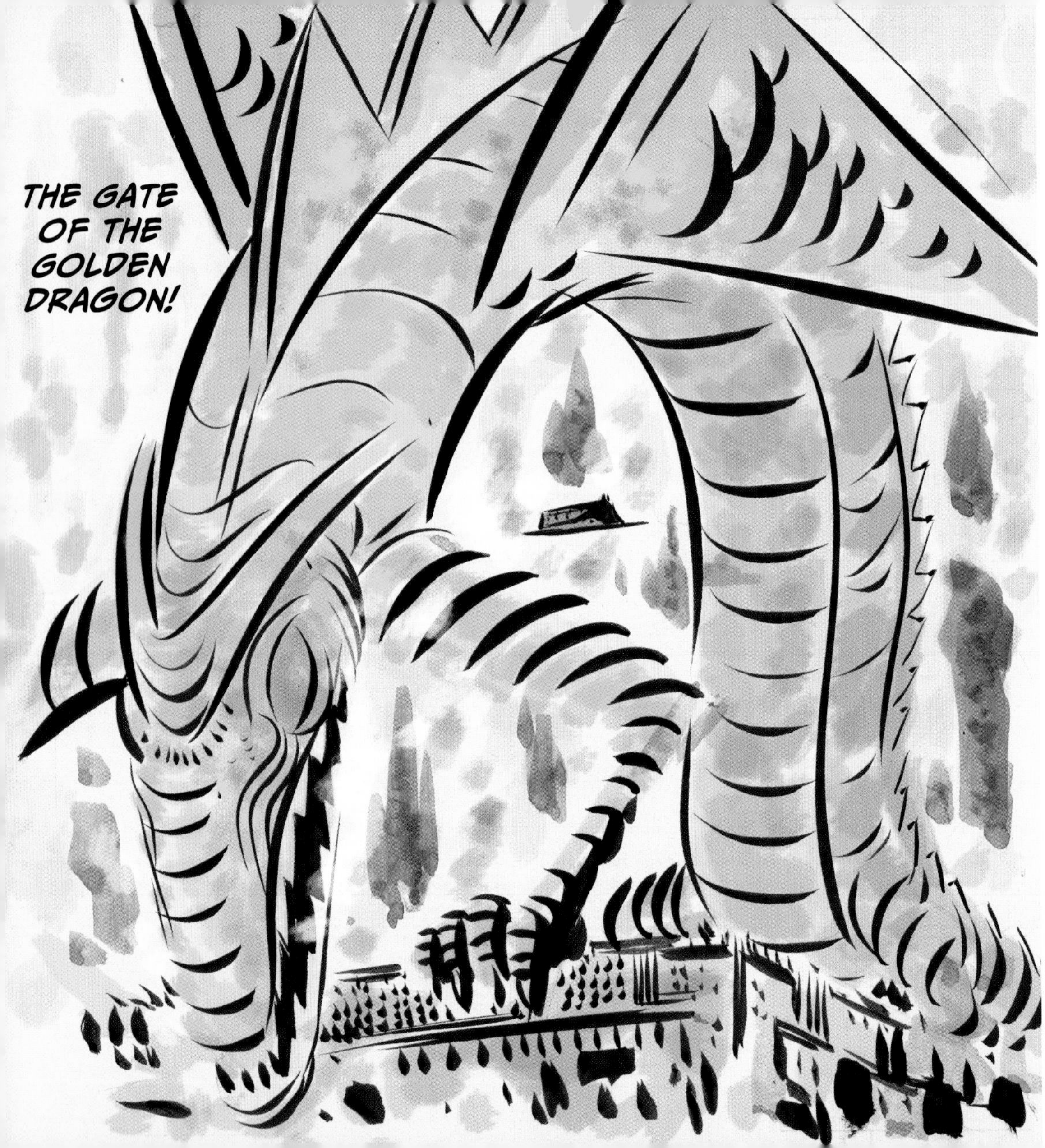
THE GATE OF THE GOLDEN DRAGON!

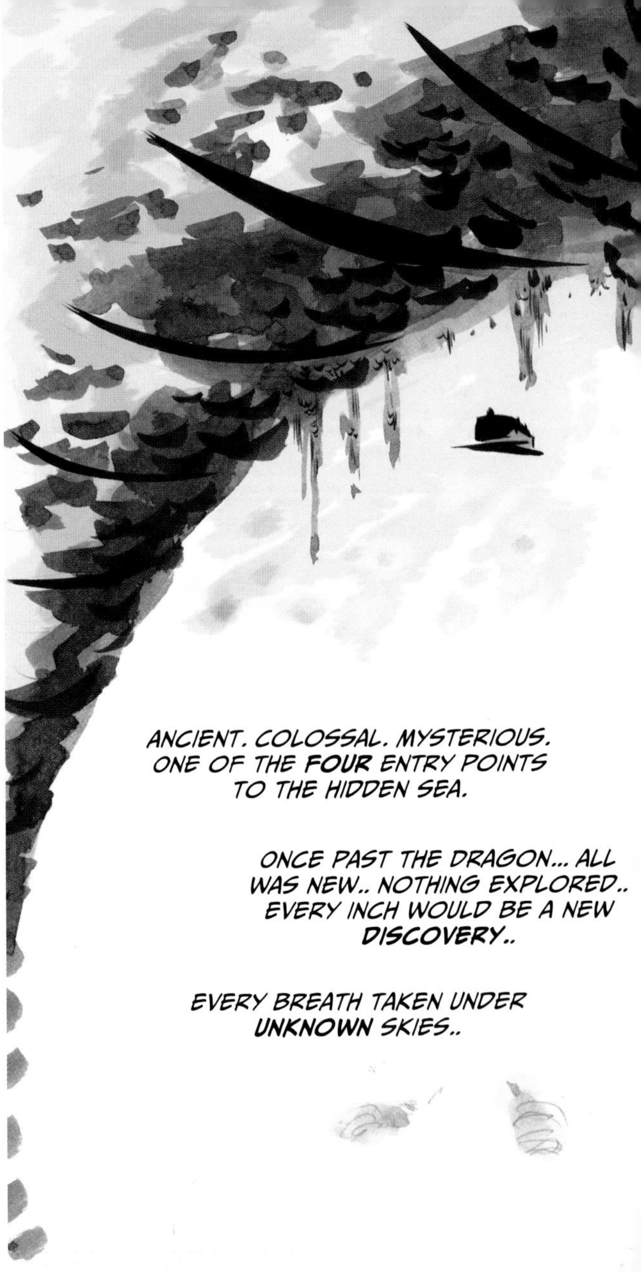
ANCIENT. COLOSSAL. MYSTERIOUS. ONE OF THE FOUR ENTRY POINTS TO THE HIDDEN SEA.
ONCE PAST THE DRAGON... ALL WAS NEW.. NOTHING EXPLORED.. EVERY INCH WOULD BE A NEW DISCOVERY..
EVERY BREATH TAKEN UNDER UNKNOWN SKIES..

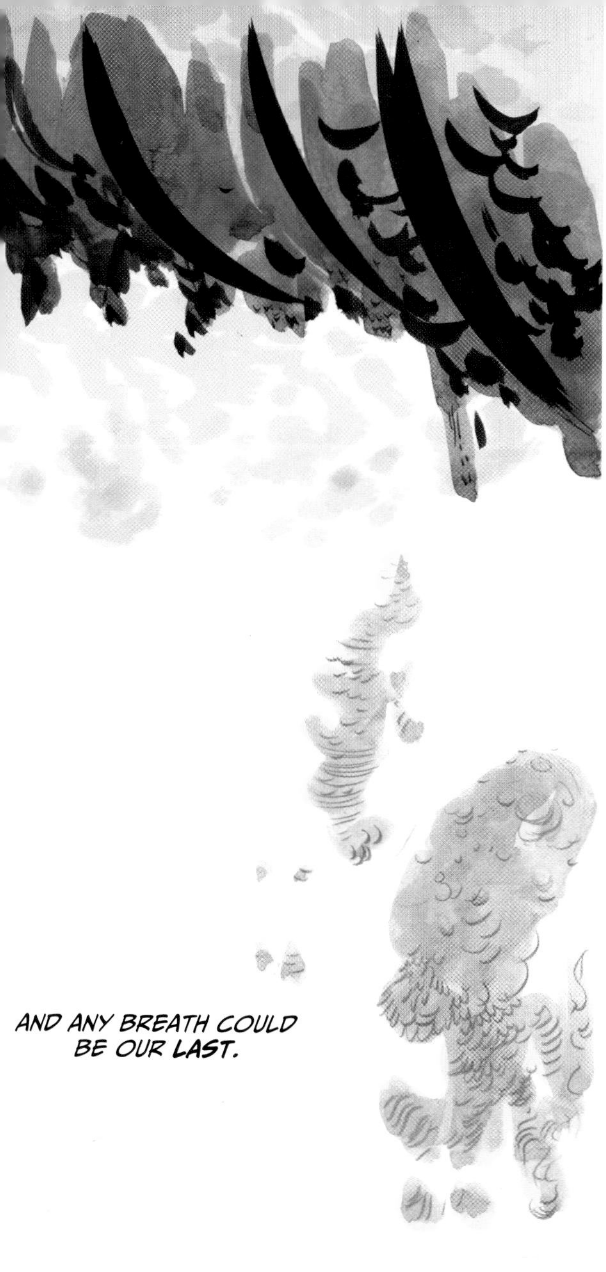
AND ANY BREATH COULD BE OUR LAST.

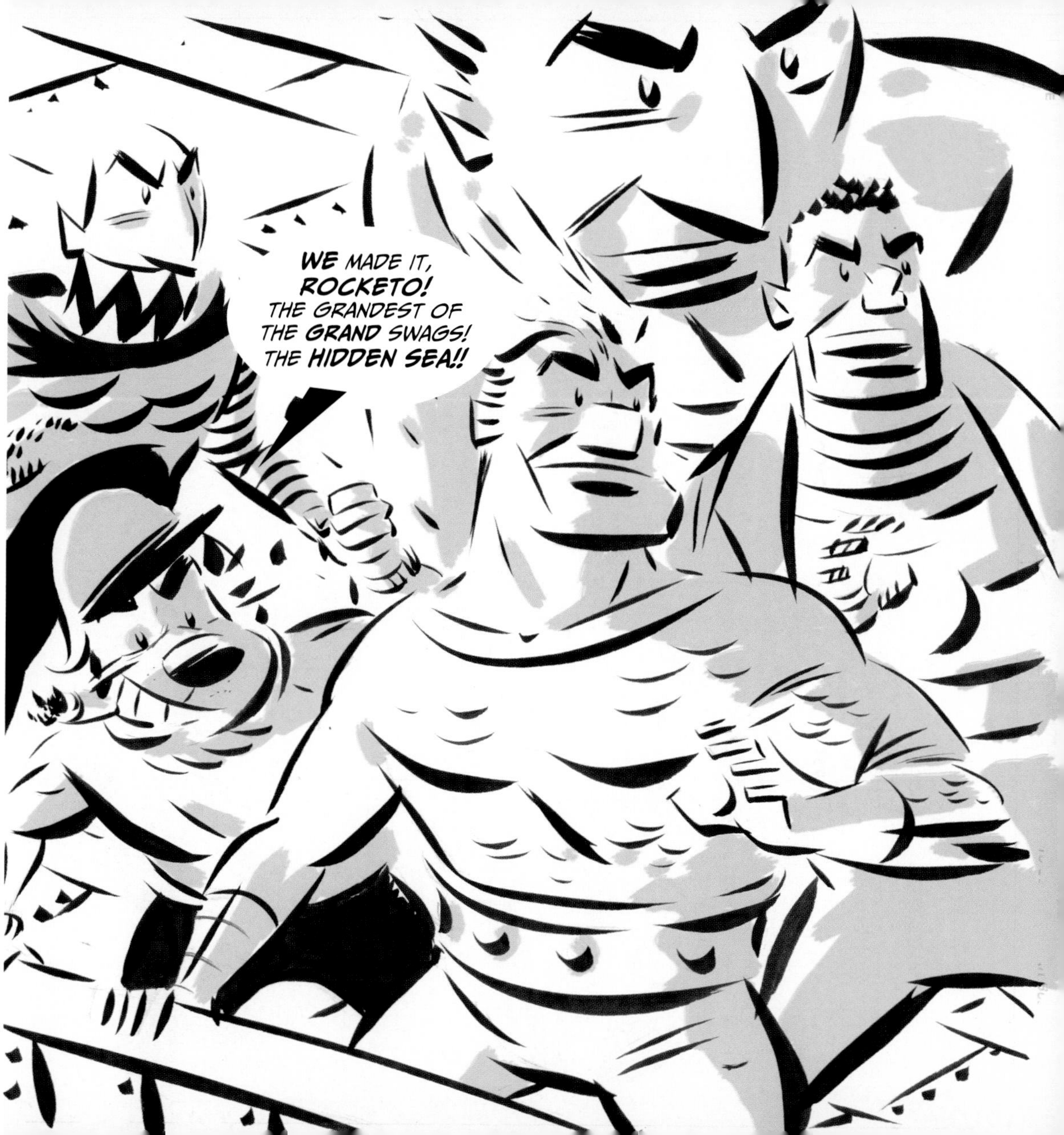
WE MADE IT, ROCKETO! THE GRANDEST OF THE GRAND SWAGS! THE HIDDEN SEA!!

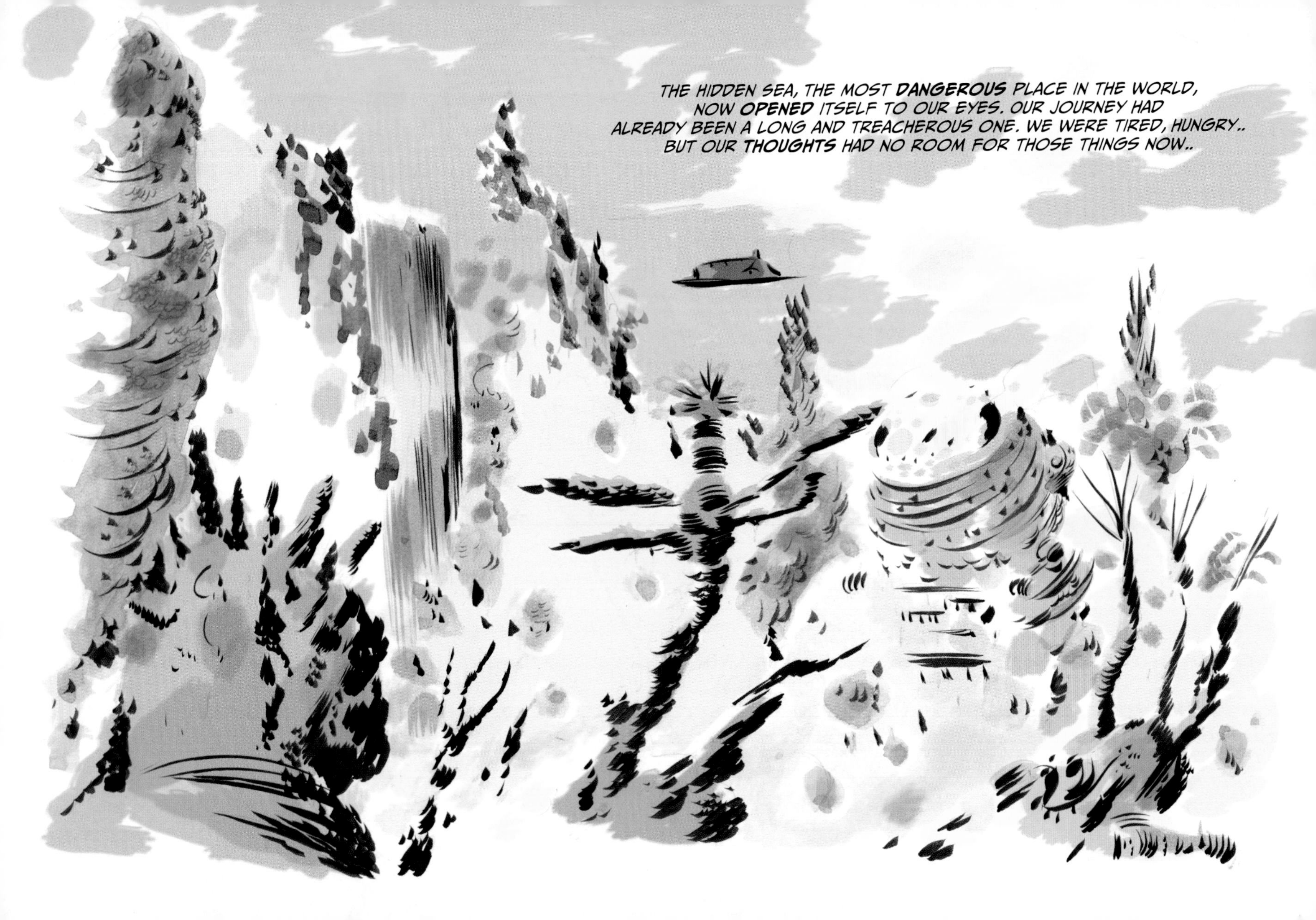
THE HIDDEN SEA, THE MOST **DANGEROUS** PLACE IN THE WORLD, NOW **OPENED** ITSELF TO OUR EYES. OUR JOURNEY HAD ALREADY BEEN A LONG AND TREACHEROUS ONE. WE WERE TIRED, HUNGRY.. BUT OUR **THOUGHTS** HAD NO ROOM FOR THOSE THINGS NOW..

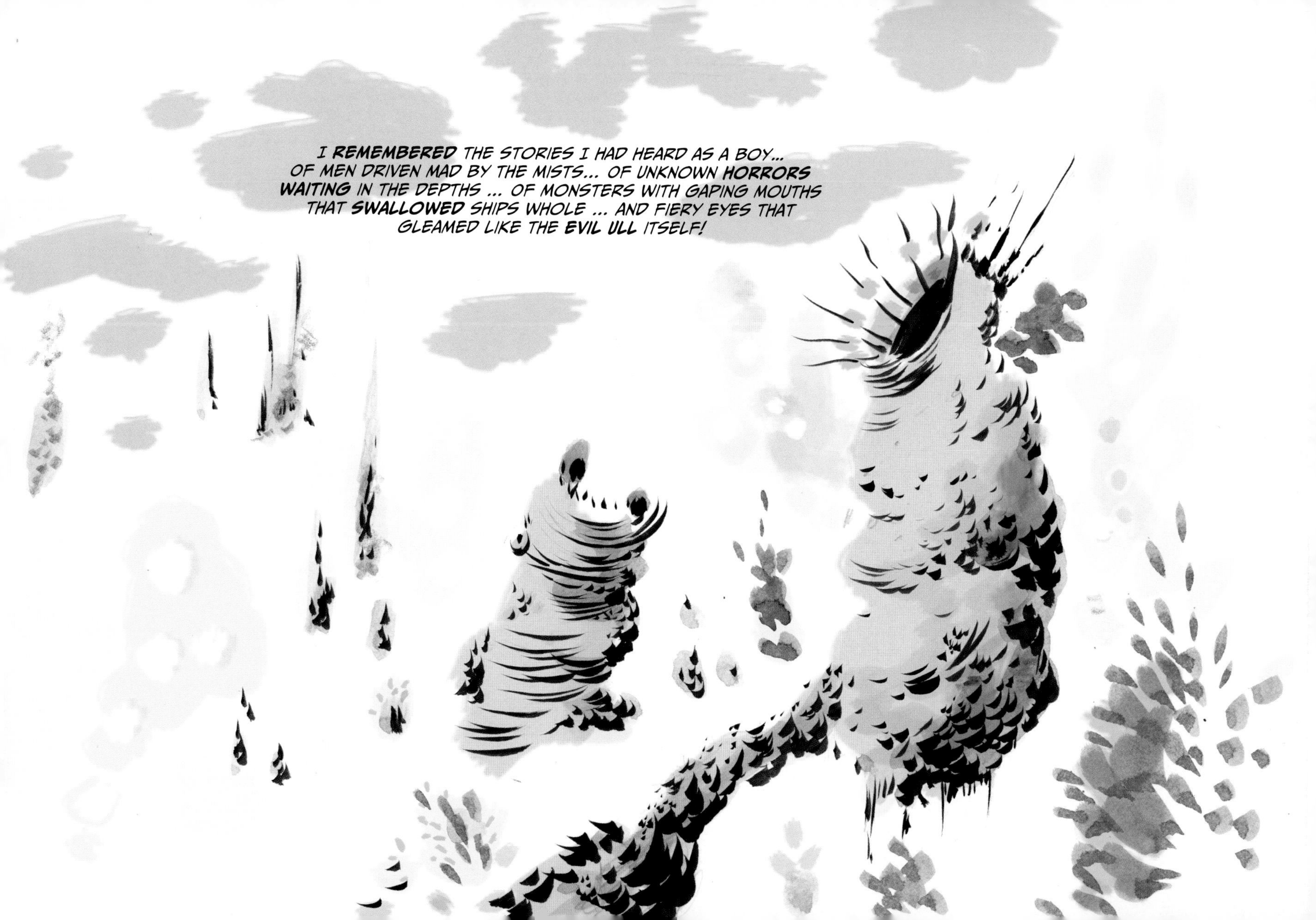
I REMEMBERED THE STORIES I HAD HEARD AS A BOY... OF MEN DRIVEN MAD BY THE MISTS... OF UNKNOWN HORRORS WAITING IN THE DEPTHS ... OF MONSTERS WITH GAPING MOUTHS THAT SWALLOWED SHIPS WHOLE ... AND FIERY EYES THAT GLEAMED LIKE THE EVIL ULL ITSELF!

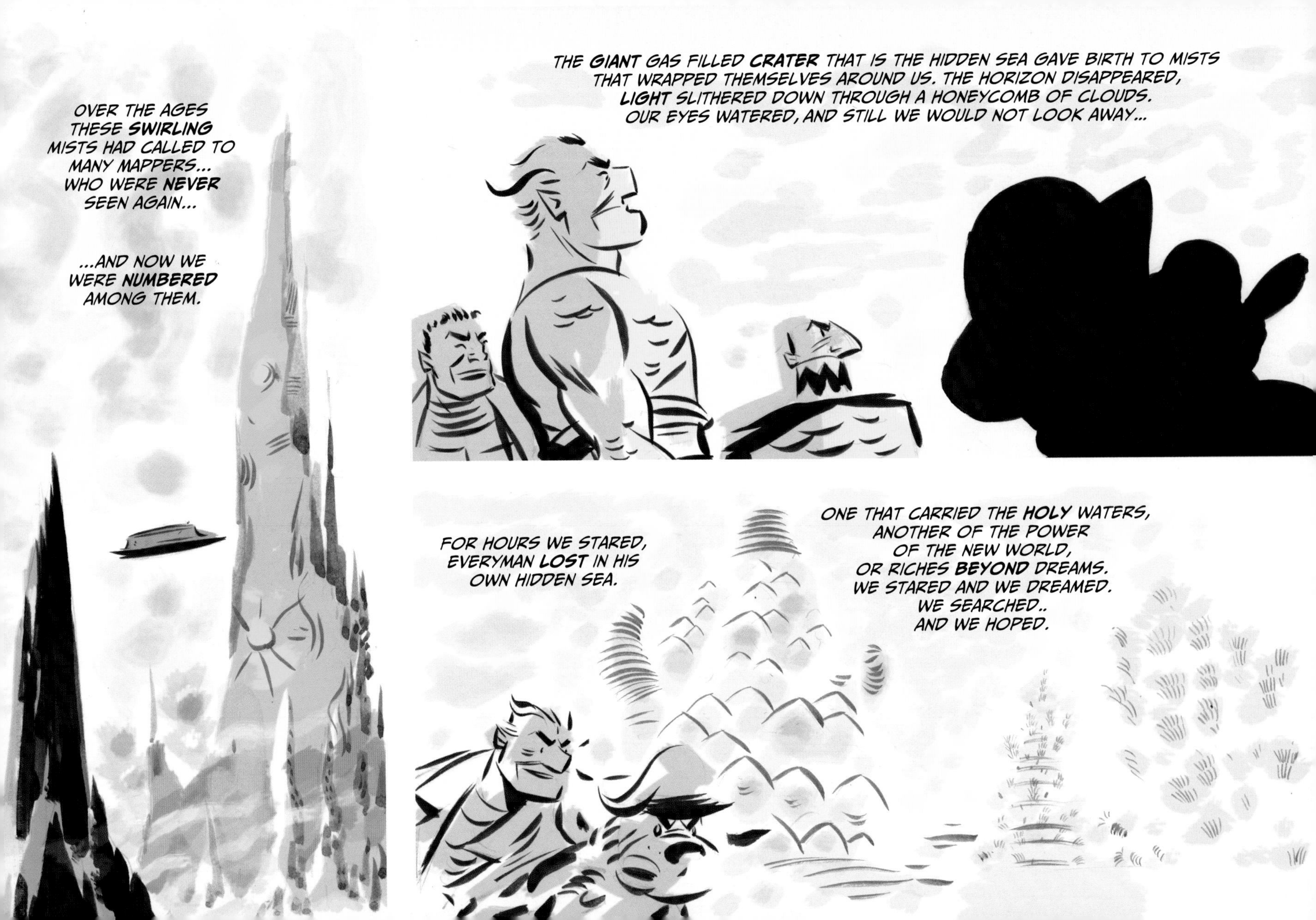
OVER THE AGES THESE SWIRLING MISTS HAD CALLED TO MANY MAPPERS... WHO WERE NEVER SEEN AGAIN...
...AND NOW WE WERE NUMBERED AMONG THEM.
THE GIANT GAS FILLED CRATER THAT IS THE HIDDEN SEA GAVE BIRTH TO MISTS THAT WRAPPED THEMSELVES AROUND US. THE HORIZON DISAPPEARED, LIGHT SLITHERED DOWN THROUGH A HONEYCOMB OF CLOUDS. OUR EYES WATERED, AND STILL WE WOULD NOT LOOK AWAY...
FOR HOURS WE STARED, EVERYMAN LOST IN HIS OWN HIDDEN SEA.
ONE THAT CARRIED THE HOLY WATERS, ANOTHER OF THE POWER OF THE NEW WORLD, OR RICHES BEYOND DREAMS. WE STARED AND WE DREAMED. WE SEARCHED.. AND WE HOPED.

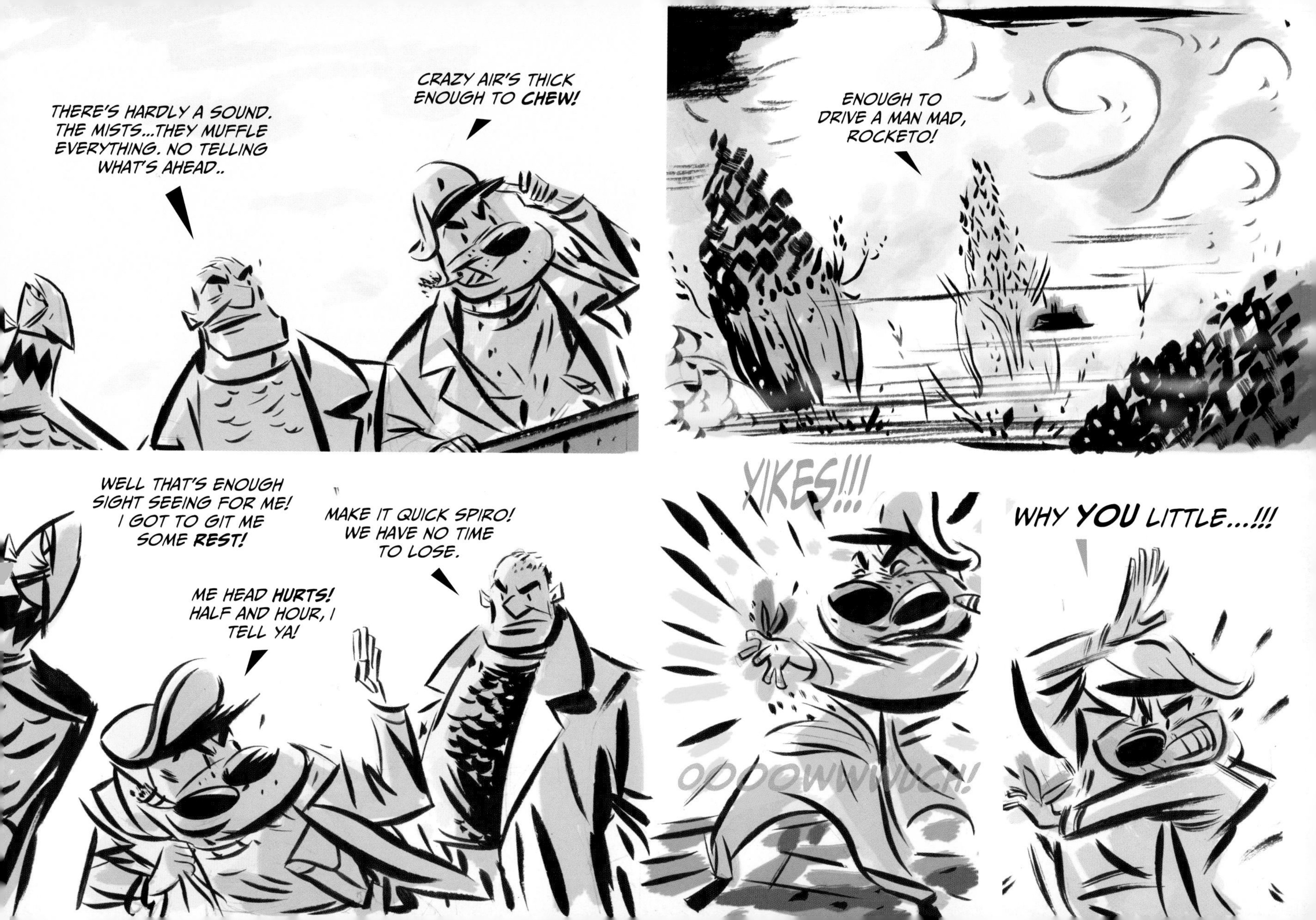
THERE'S HARDLY A SOUND. THE MISTS...THEY MUFFLE EVERYTHING. NO TELLING WHAT'S AHEAD..
CRAZY AIR'S THICK ENOUGH TO CHEW!
ENOUGH TO DRIVE A MAN MAD, ROCKETO!
WELL THAT'S ENOUGH SIGHT SEEING FOR ME! I GOT TO GIT ME SOME REST!
ME HEAD HURTS! HALF AND HOUR, I TELL YA!
MAKE IT QUICK SPIRO! WE HAVE NO TIME TO LOSE.
YIKES!!!
OOOOWWWUCH!
WHY YOU LITTLE...!!!

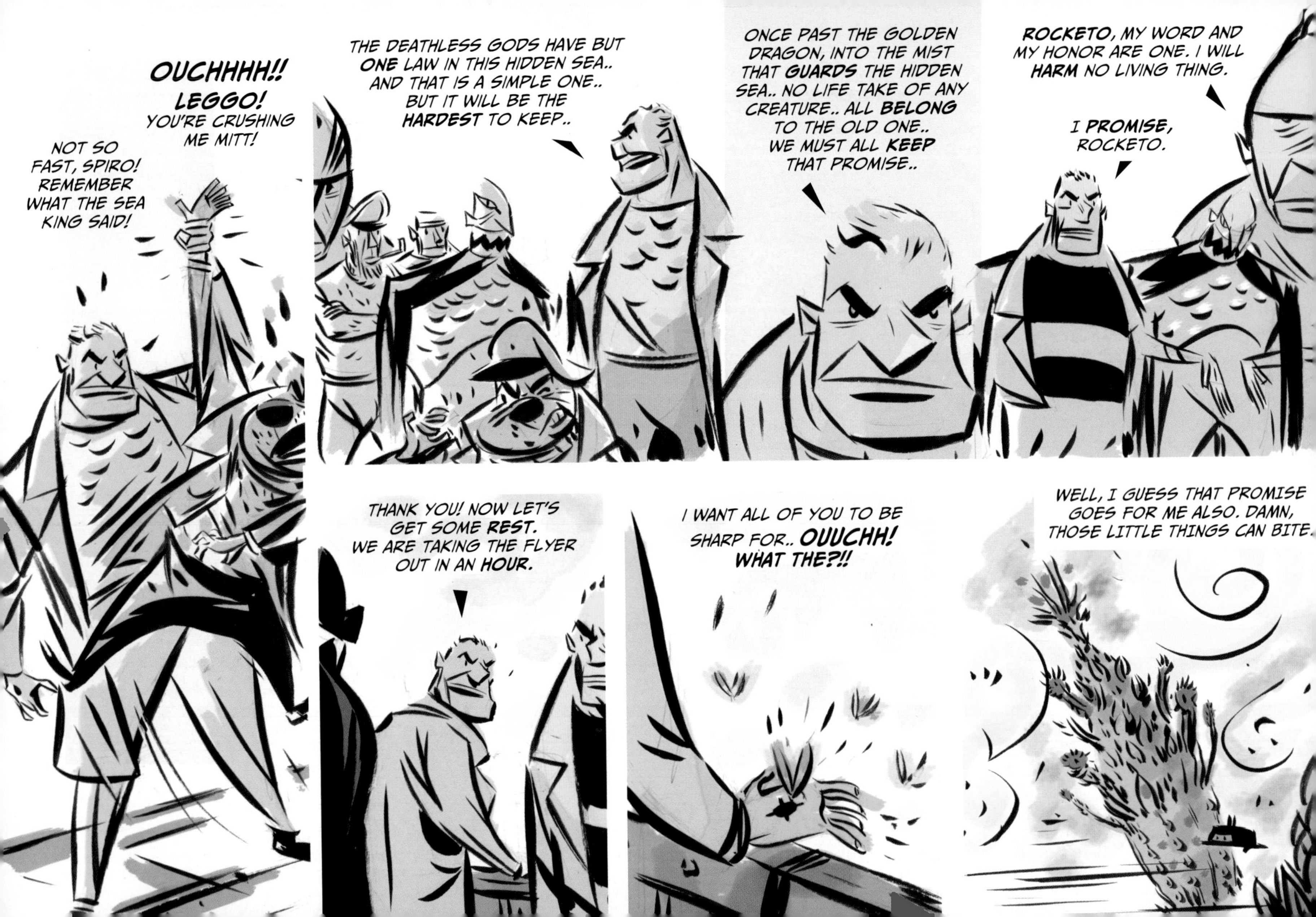
NOT SO FAST, SPIRO! REMEMBER WHAT THE SEA KING SAID!
OUCHHHH!! LEGGO! YOU'RE CRUSHING ME MITT!
THE DEATHLESS GODS HAVE BUT ONE LAW IN THIS HIDDEN SEA.. AND THAT IS A SIMPLE ONE.. BUT IT WILL BE THE HARDEST TO KEEP..
ONCE PAST THE GOLDEN DRAGON, INTO THE MIST THAT GUARDS THE HIDDEN SEA.. NO LIFE TAKE OF ANY CREATURE.. ALL BELONG TO THE OLD ONE.. WE MUST ALL KEEP THAT PROMISE..
ROCKETO, MY WORD AND MY HONOR ARE ONE. I WILL HARM NO LIVING THING.
I PROMISE, ROCKETO.
THANK YOU! NOW LET'S GET SOME REST. WE ARE TAKING THE FLYER OUT IN AN HOUR.
I WANT ALL OF YOU TO BE SHARP FOR.. OUUCHH! WHAT THE?!!
WELL, I GUESS THAT PROMISE GOES FOR ME ALSO. DAMN, THOSE LITTLE THINGS CAN BITE.

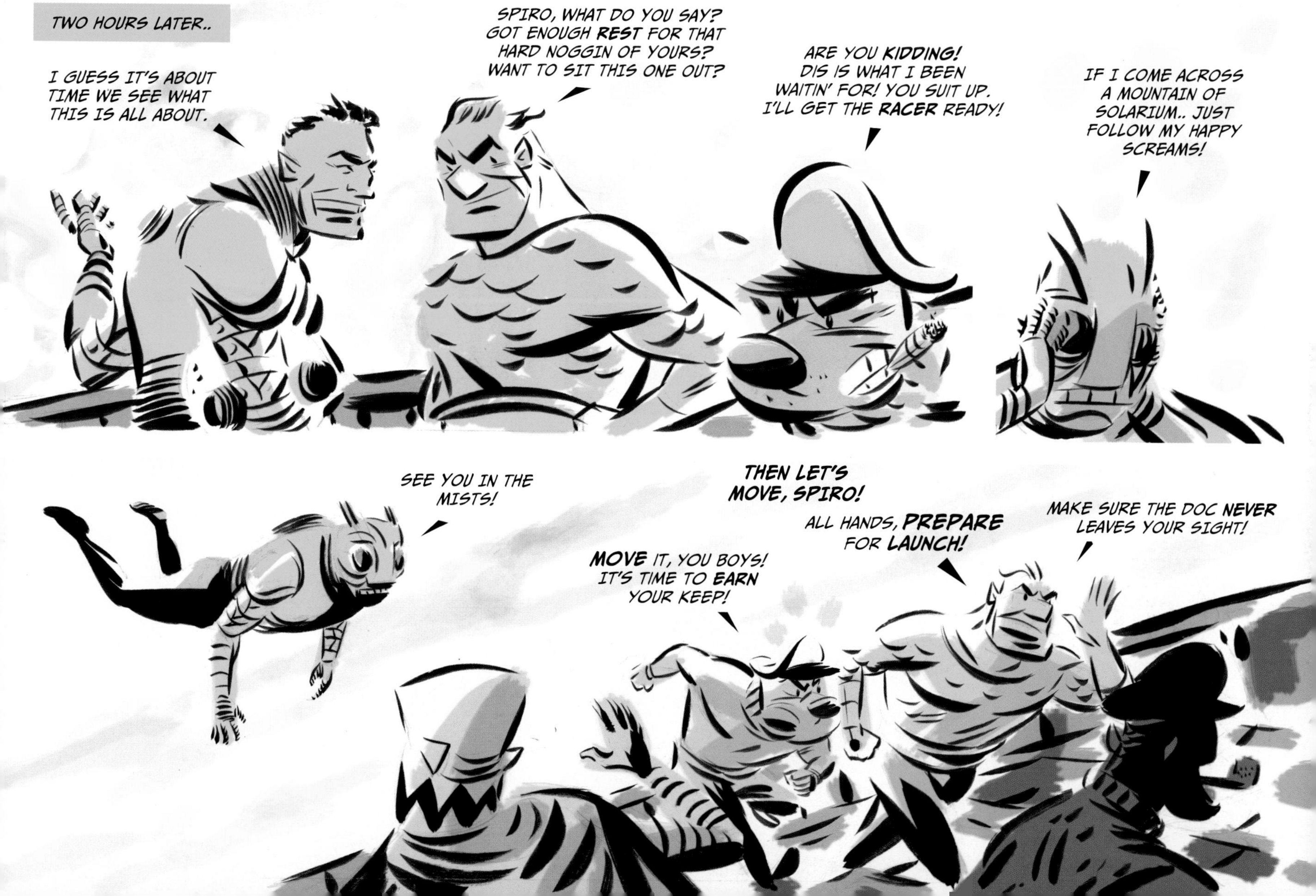

TWO HOURS LATER..
I GUESS IT'S ABOUT TIME WE SEE WHAT THIS IS ALL ABOUT.
SPIRO, WHAT DO YOU SAY? GOT ENOUGH **REST** FOR THAT HARD NOGGIN OF YOURS? WANT TO SIT THIS ONE OUT?
ARE YOU **KIDDING!** DIS IS WHAT I BEEN WAITIN' FOR! YOU SUIT UP. I'LL GET THE **RACER** READY!
IF I COME ACROSS A MOUNTAIN OF SOLARIUM.. JUST FOLLOW MY HAPPY SCREAMS!
SEE YOU IN THE MISTS!
**THEN LET'S MOVE, SPIRO!**
**MOVE** IT, YOU BOYS! IT'S TIME TO **EARN** YOUR KEEP!
ALL HANDS, **PREPARE** FOR **LAUNCH!**
MAKE SURE THE DOC **NEVER** LEAVES YOUR SIGHT!

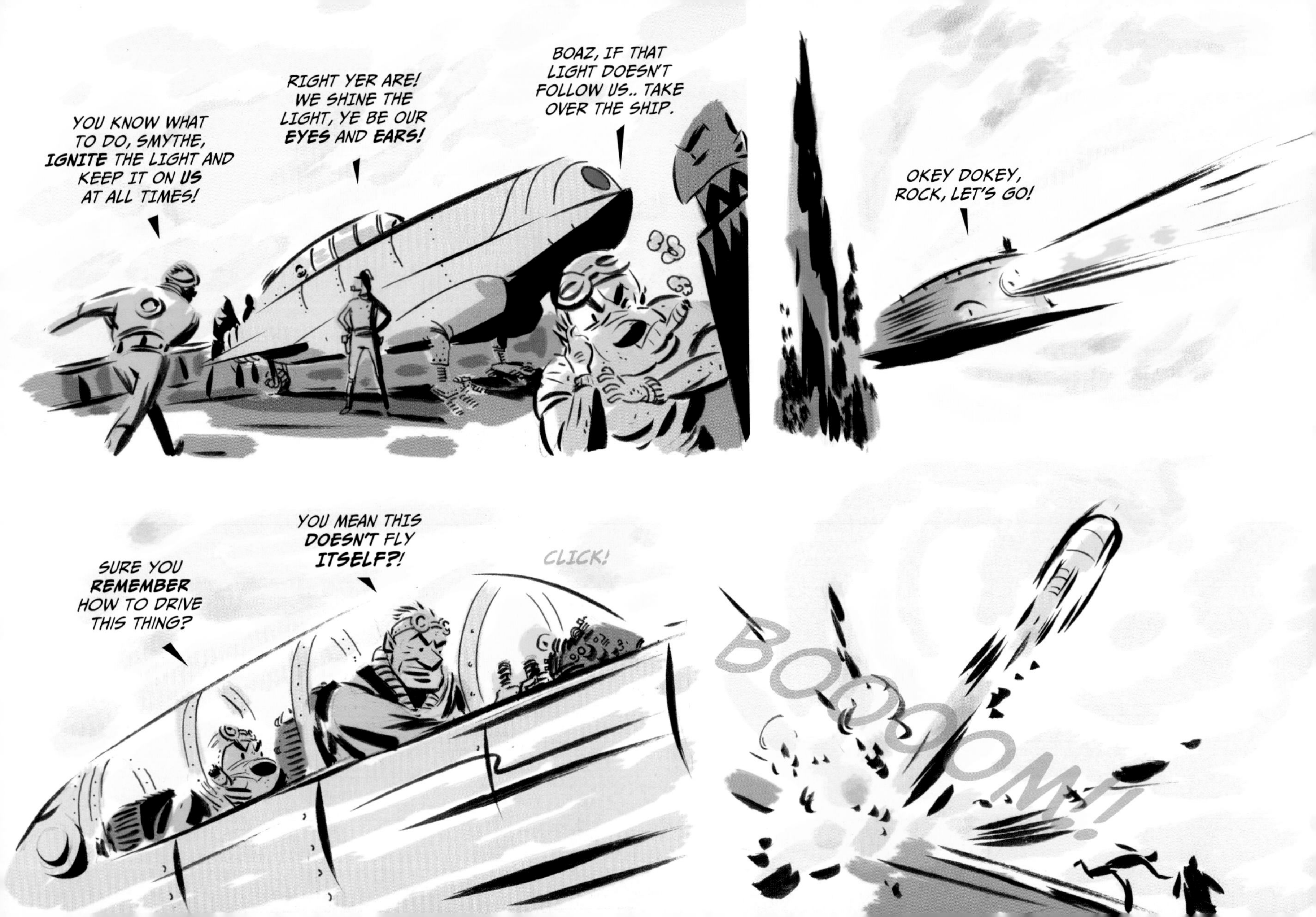
YOU KNOW WHAT TO DO, SMYTHE, IGNITE THE LIGHT AND KEEP IT ON US AT ALL TIMES!
RIGHT YER ARE! WE SHINE THE LIGHT, YE BE OUR EYES AND EARS!
BOAZ, IF THAT LIGHT DOESN'T FOLLOW US.. TAKE OVER THE SHIP.
OKEY DOKEY, ROCK, LET'S GO!
SURE YOU REMEMBER HOW TO DRIVE THIS THING?
YOU MEAN THIS DOESN'T FLY ITSELF?!
CLICK!
BOOOOOM!!

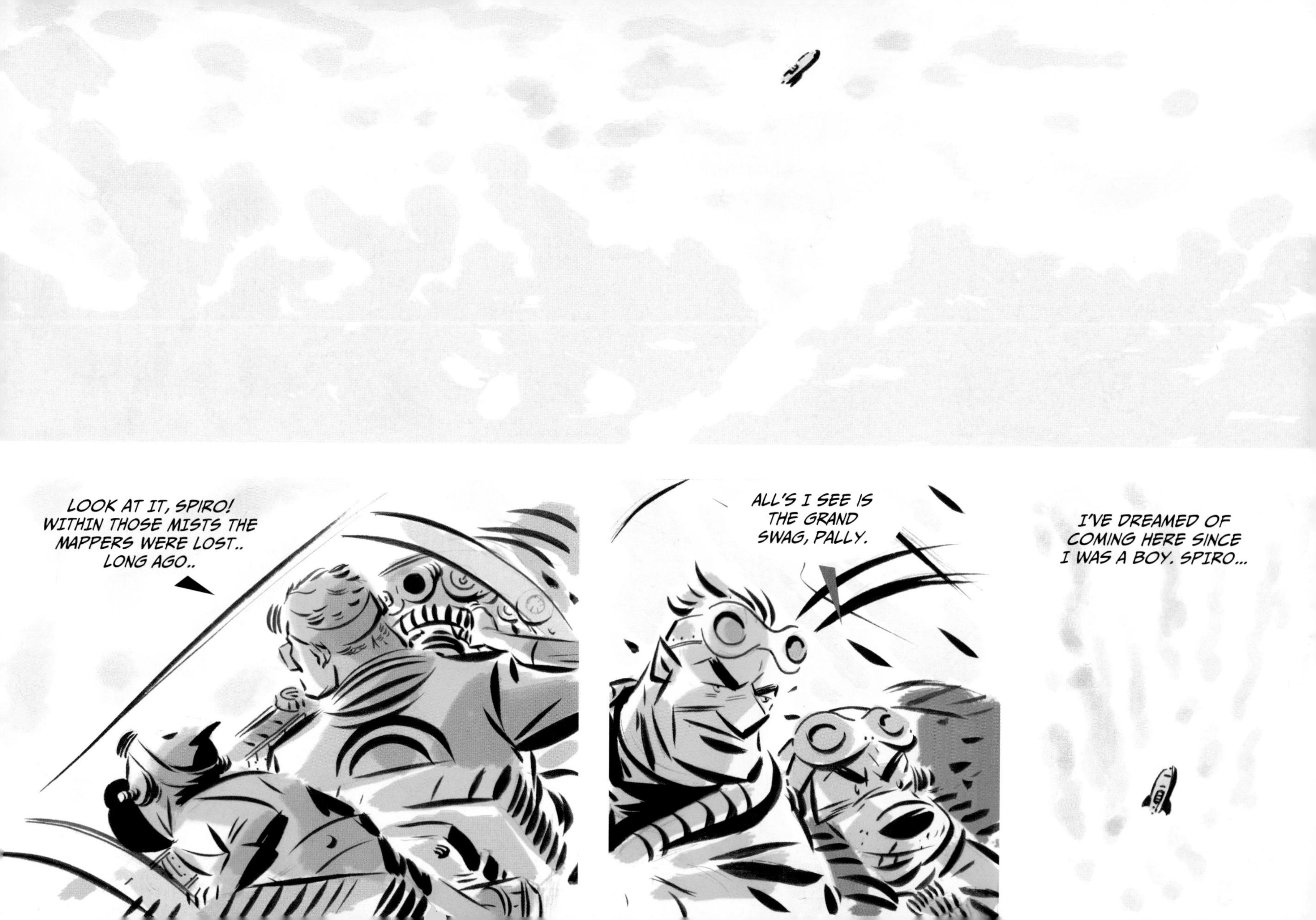
LOOK AT IT, SPIRO! WITHIN THOSE MISTS THE MAPPERS WERE LOST.. LONG AGO..
ALL'S I SEE IS THE GRAND SWAG, PALLY.
I'VE DREAMED OF COMING HERE SINCE I WAS A BOY. SPIRO...

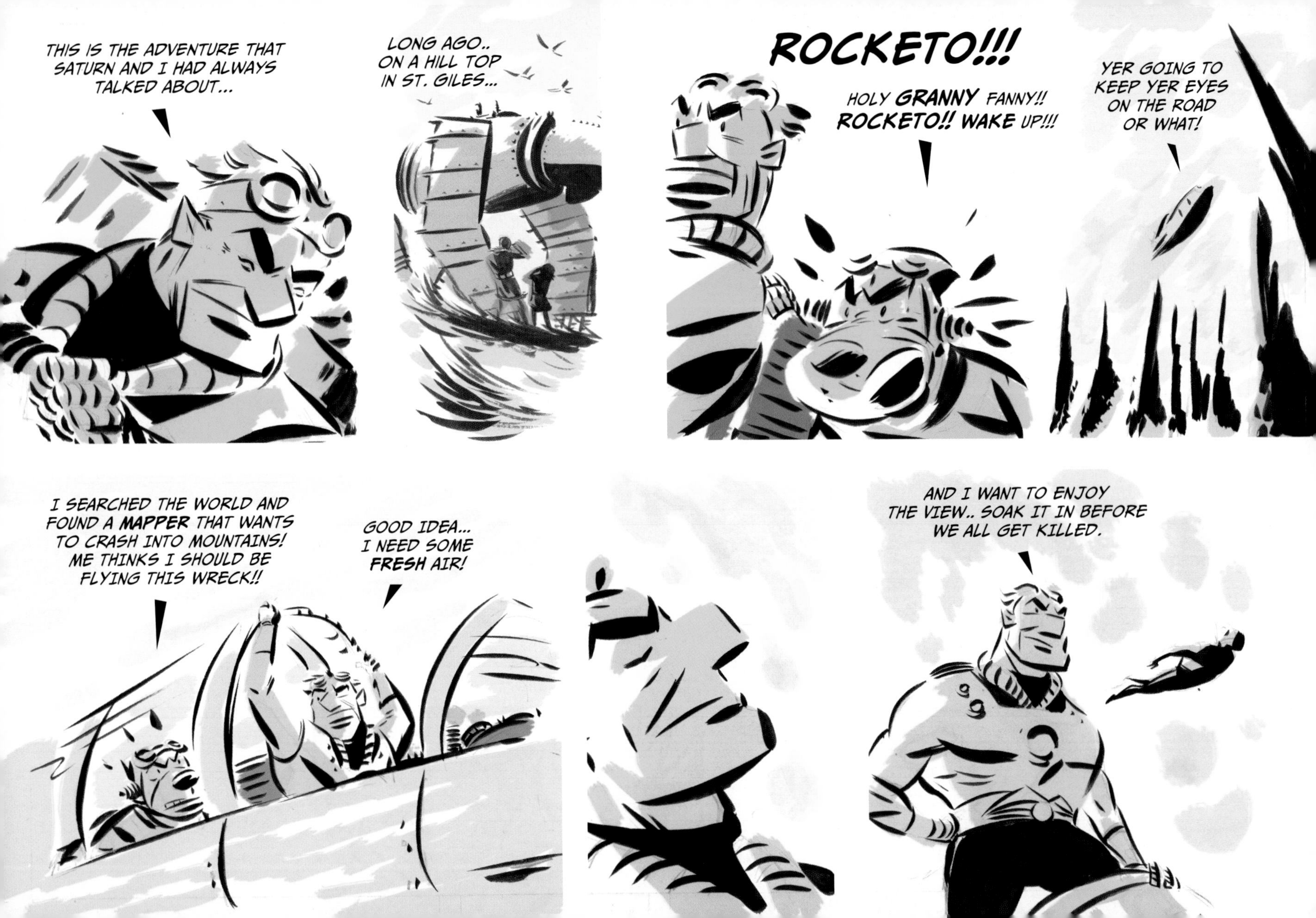
THIS IS THE ADVENTURE THAT SATURN AND I HAD ALWAYS TALKED ABOUT...
LONG AGO.. ON A HILL TOP IN ST. GILES...
ROCKETO!!!
HOLY GRANNY FANNY!! ROCKETO!! WAKE UP!!!
YER GOING TO KEEP YER EYES ON THE ROAD OR WHAT!
I SEARCHED THE WORLD AND FOUND A MAPPER THAT WANTS TO CRASH INTO MOUNTAINS! ME THINKS I SHOULD BE FLYING THIS WRECK!!
GOOD IDEA... I NEED SOME FRESH AIR!
AND I WANT TO ENJOY THE VIEW.. SOAK IT IN BEFORE WE ALL GET KILLED.

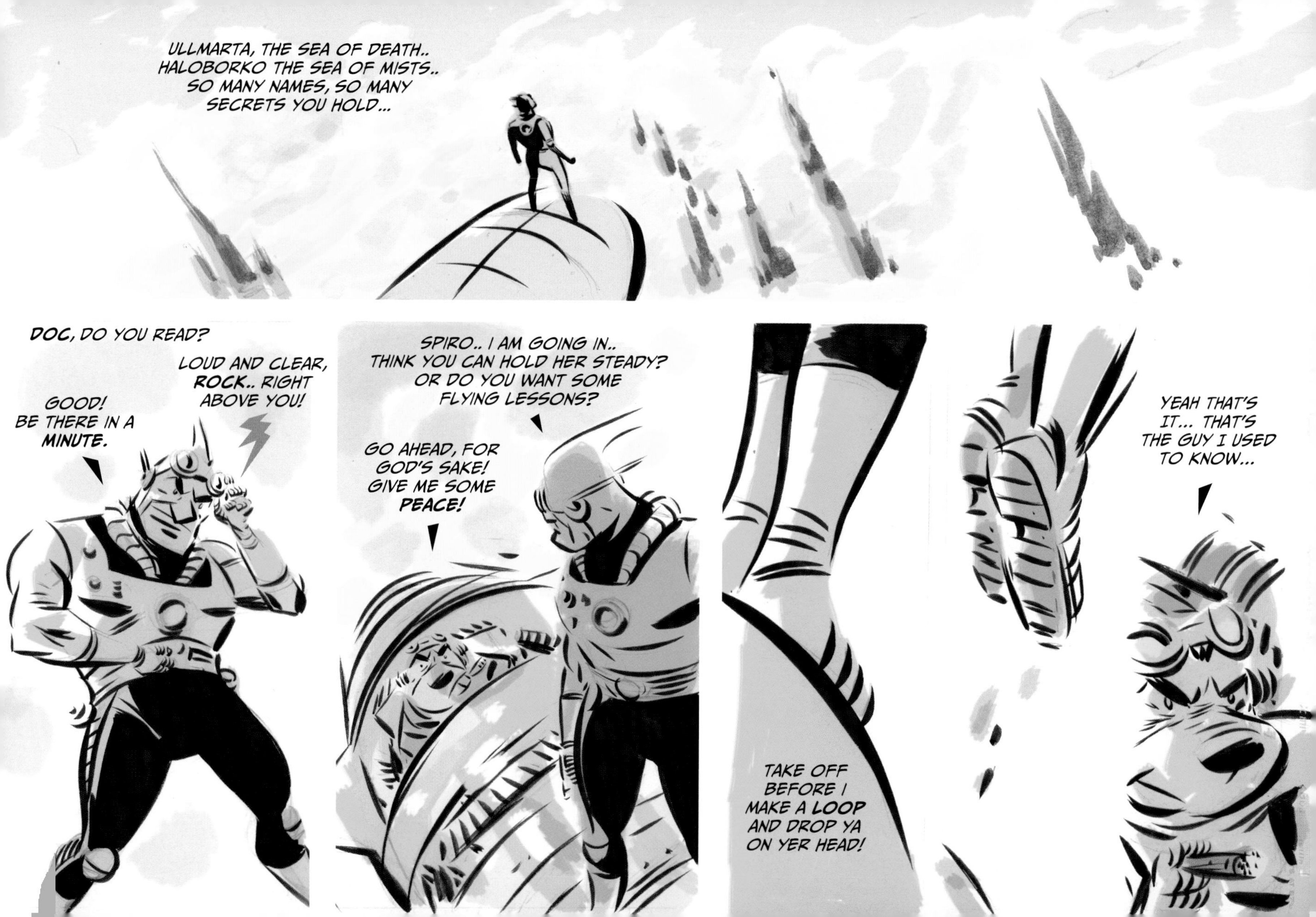
ULLMARTA, THE SEA OF DEATH.. HALOBORKO THE SEA OF MISTS.. SO MANY NAMES, SO MANY SECRETS YOU HOLD...
DOC, DO YOU READ?
LOUD AND CLEAR, ROCK.. RIGHT ABOVE YOU!
GOOD! BE THERE IN A MINUTE.
SPIRO.. I AM GOING IN.. THINK YOU CAN HOLD HER STEADY? OR DO YOU WANT SOME FLYING LESSONS?
GO AHEAD, FOR GOD'S SAKE! GIVE ME SOME PEACE!
TAKE OFF BEFORE I MAKE A LOOP AND DROP YA ON YER HEAD!
YEAH THAT'S IT... THAT'S THE GUY I USED TO KNOW...

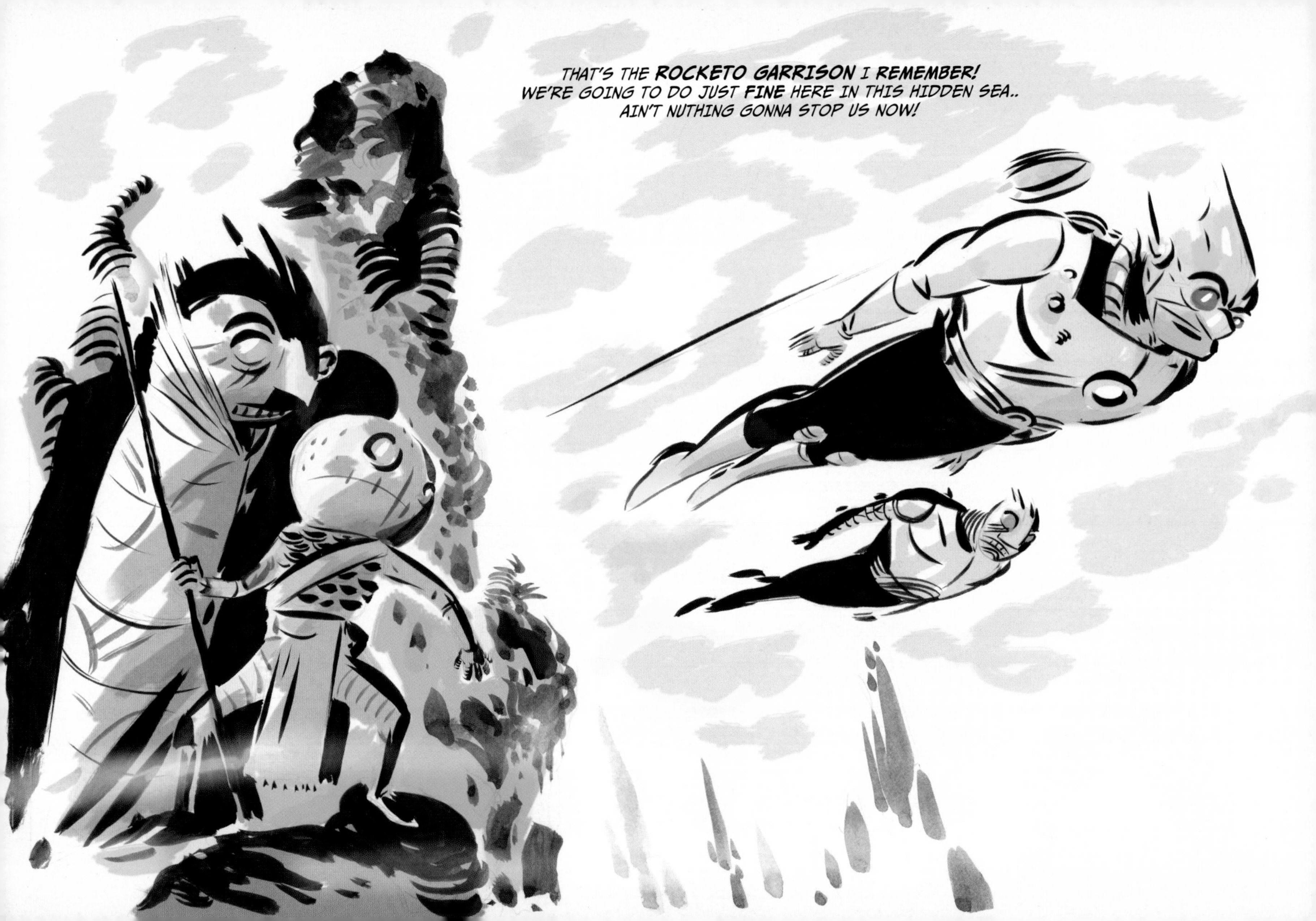
THAT'S THE ROCKETO GARRISON I REMEMBER!
WE'RE GOING TO DO JUST FINE HERE IN THIS HIDDEN SEA..
AIN'T NUTHING GONNA STOP US NOW!

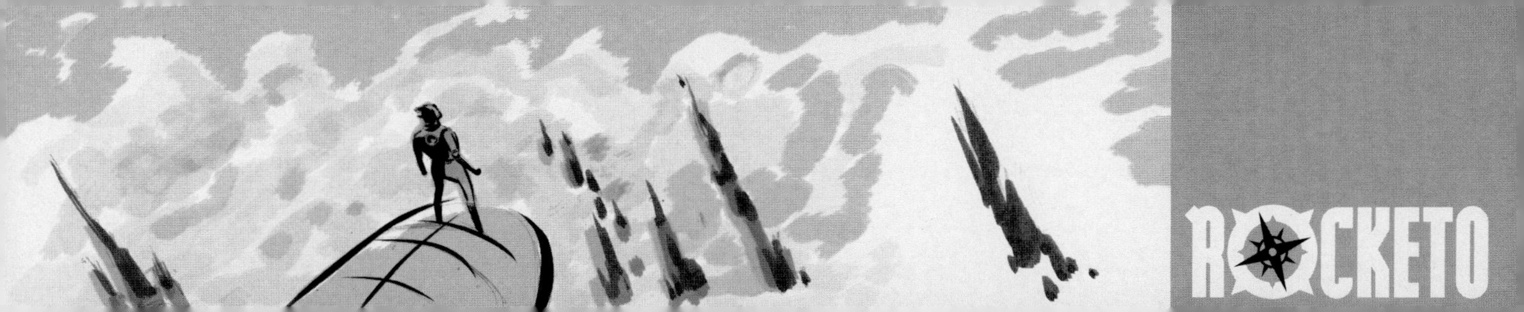

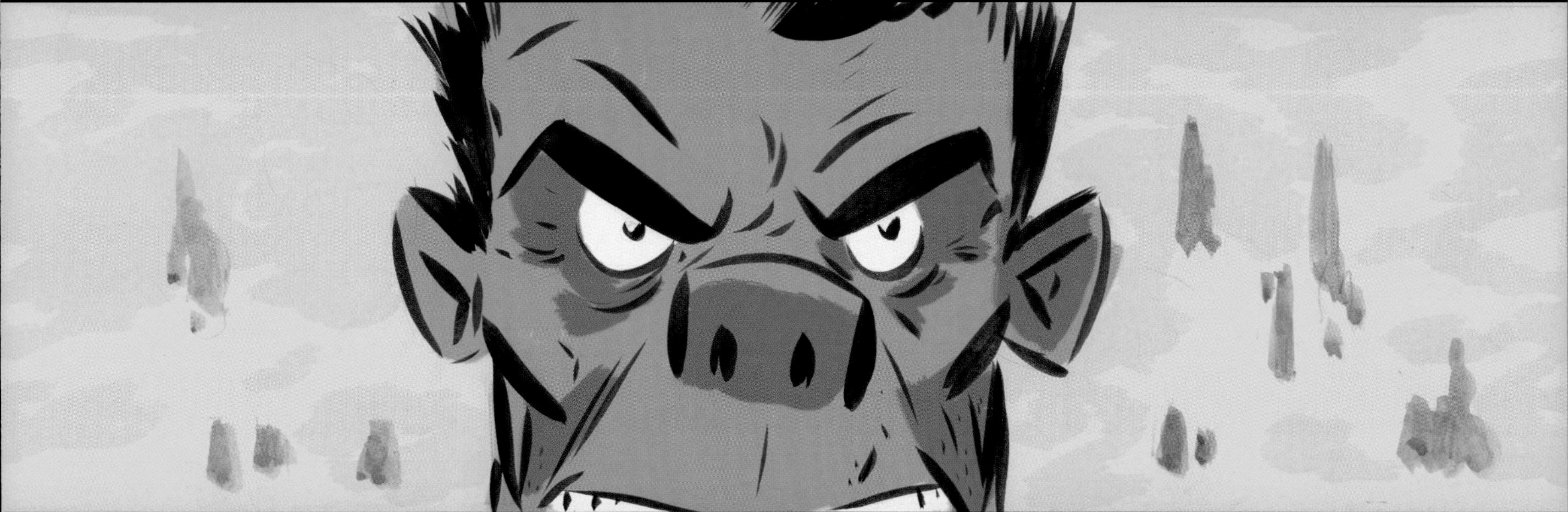

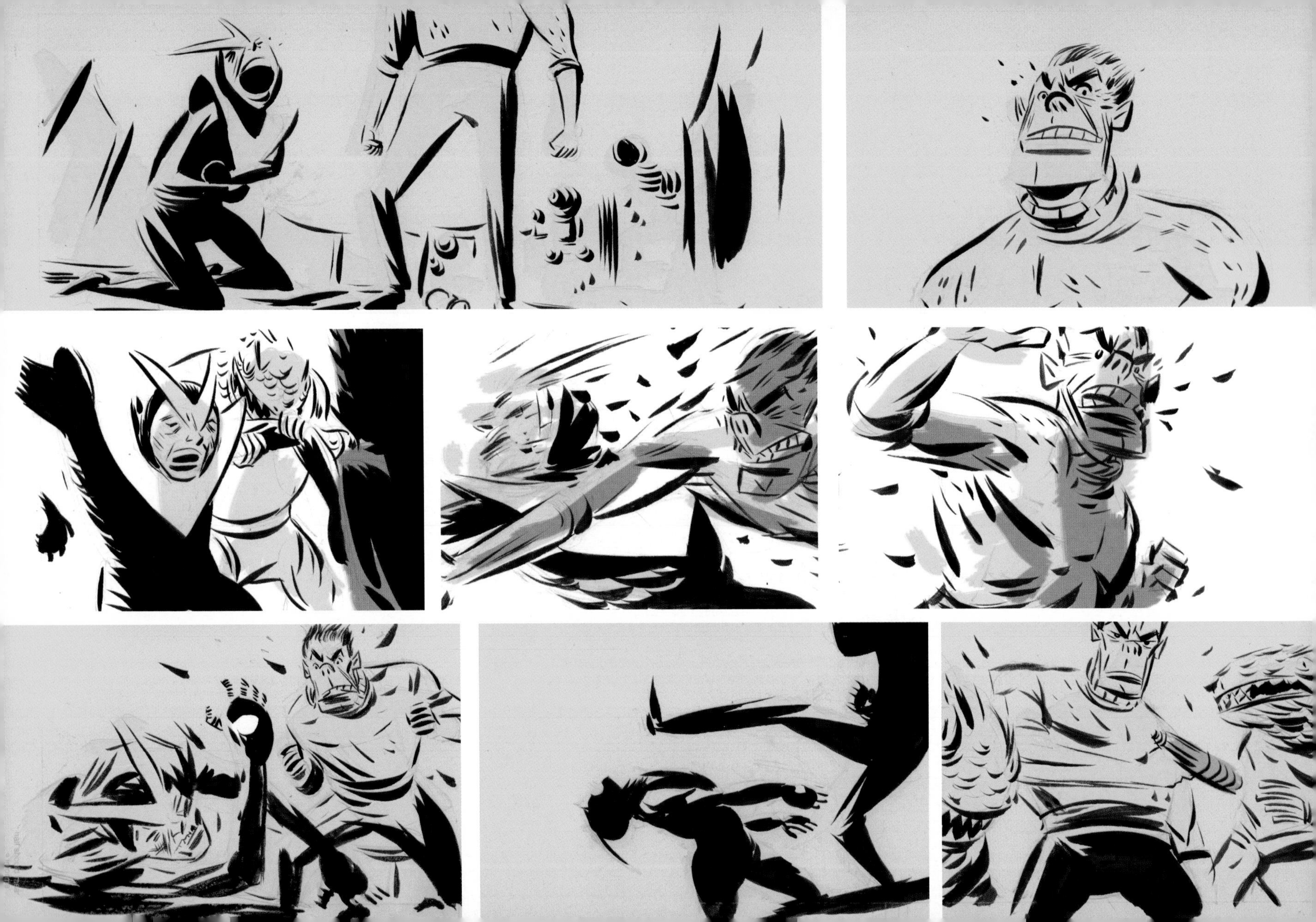

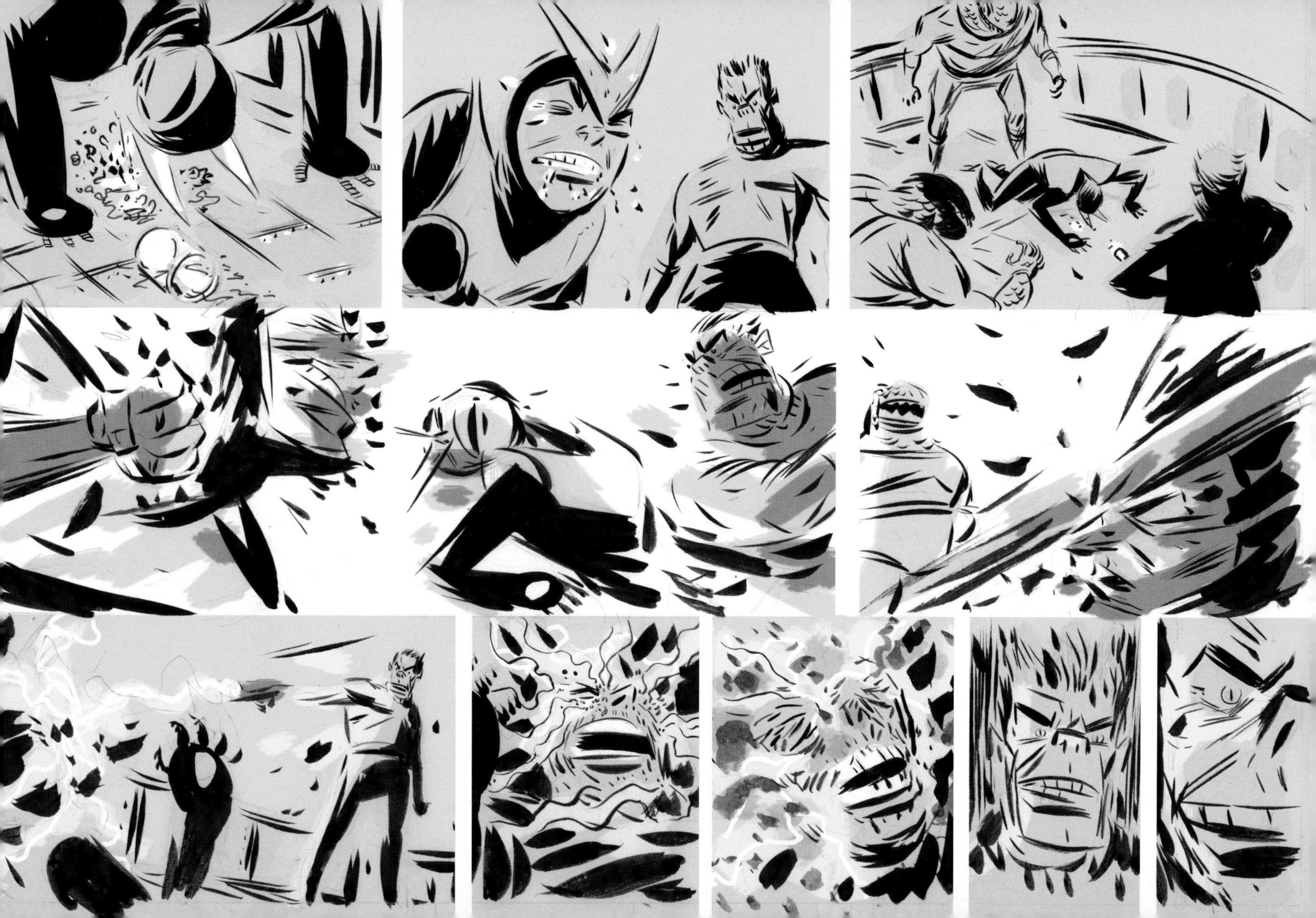

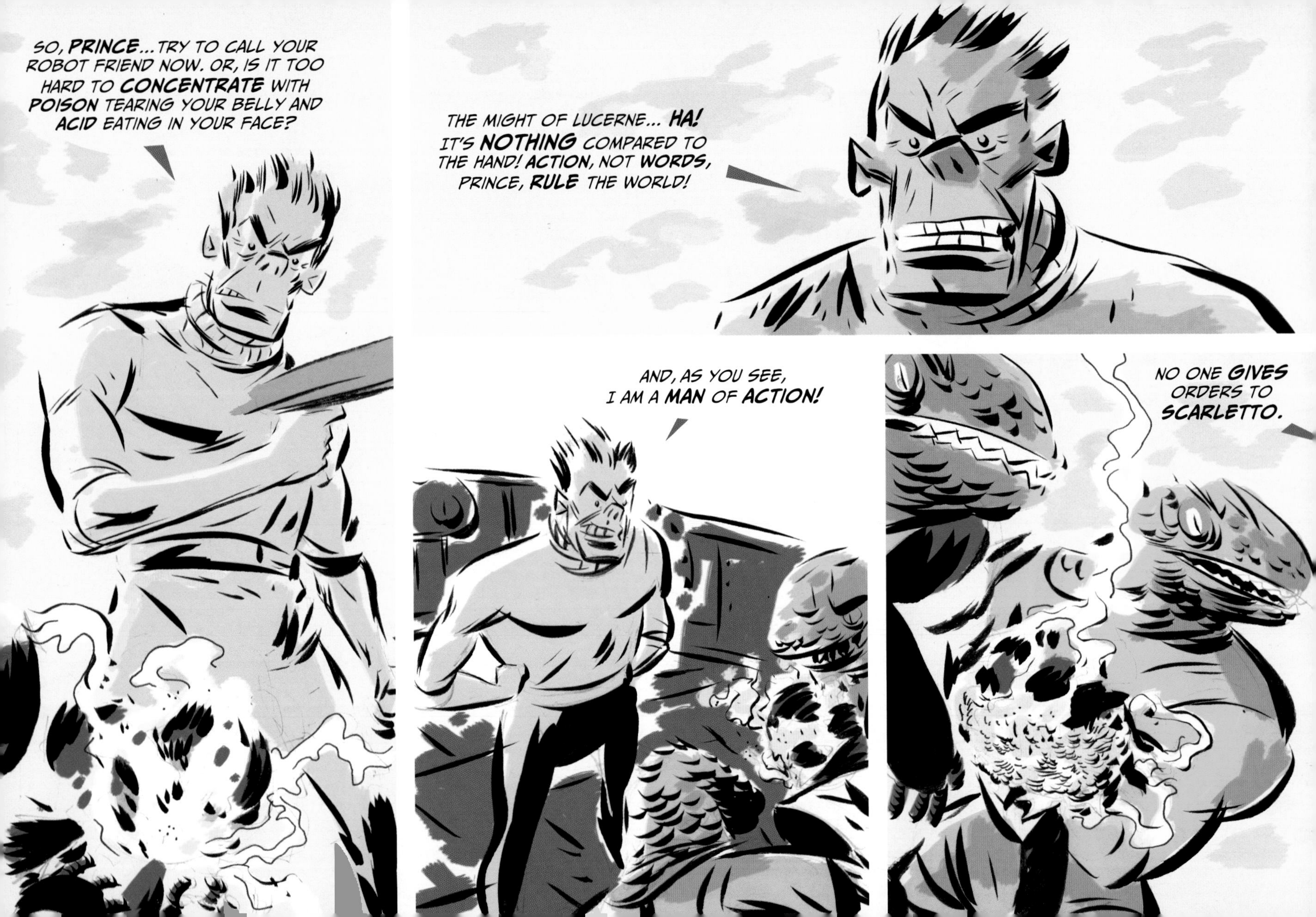
SO, PRINCE... TRY TO CALL YOUR ROBOT FRIEND NOW. OR, IS IT TOO HARD TO CONCENTRATE WITH POISON TEARING YOUR BELLY AND ACID EATING IN YOUR FACE?
THE MIGHT OF LUCERNE... HA! IT'S NOTHING COMPARED TO THE HAND! ACTION, NOT WORDS, PRINCE, RULE THE WORLD!
AND, AS YOU SEE, I AM A MAN OF ACTION!
NO ONE GIVES ORDERS TO SCARLETTO.

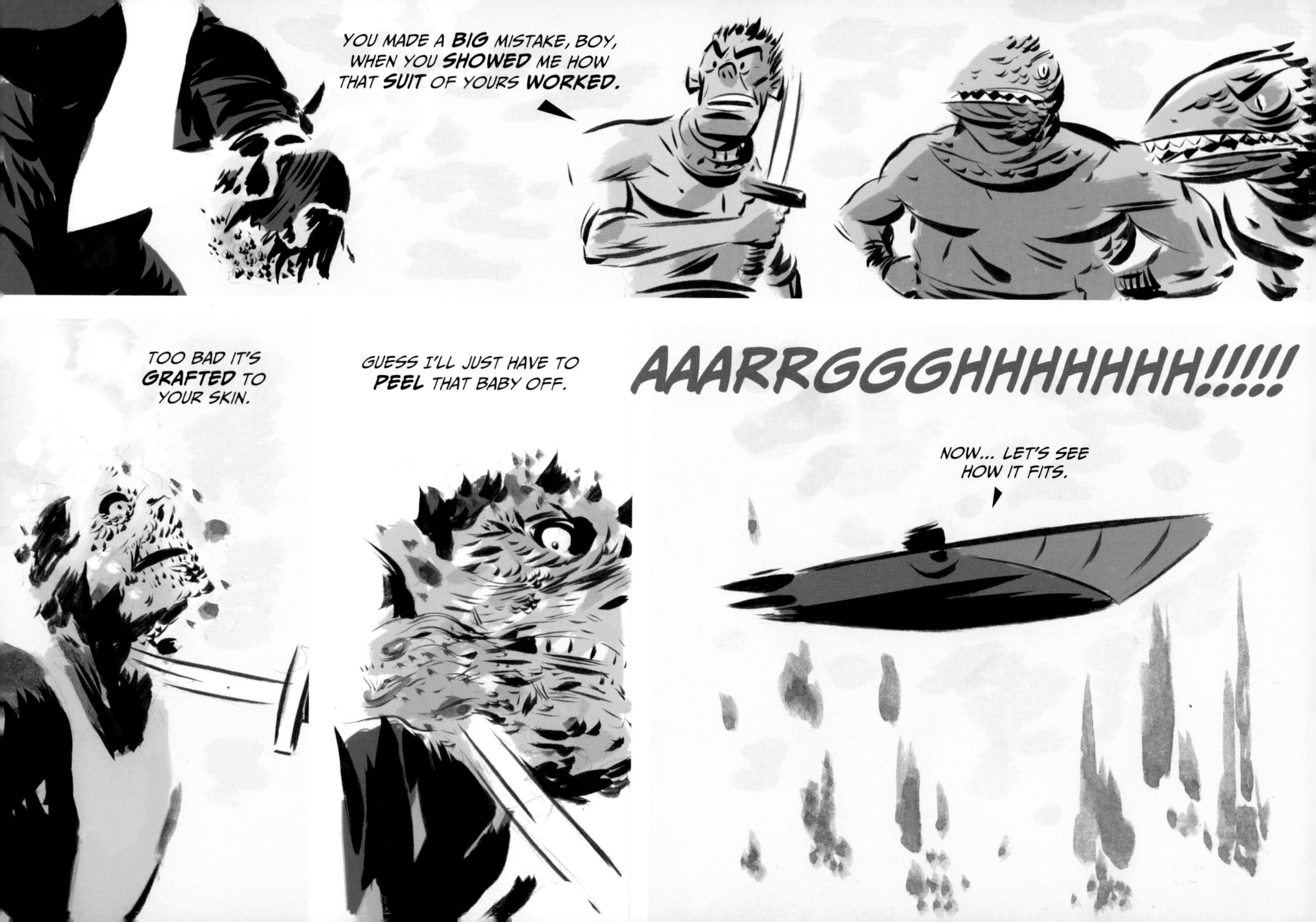
YOU MADE A BIG MISTAKE, BOY, WHEN YOU SHOWED ME HOW THAT SUIT OF YOURS WORKED.
TOO BAD IT'S GRAFTED TO YOUR SKIN.
GUESS I'LL JUST HAVE TO PEEL THAT BABY OFF.
AAARRGGGHHHHHHH!!!!!
NOW... LET'S SEE HOW IT FITS.

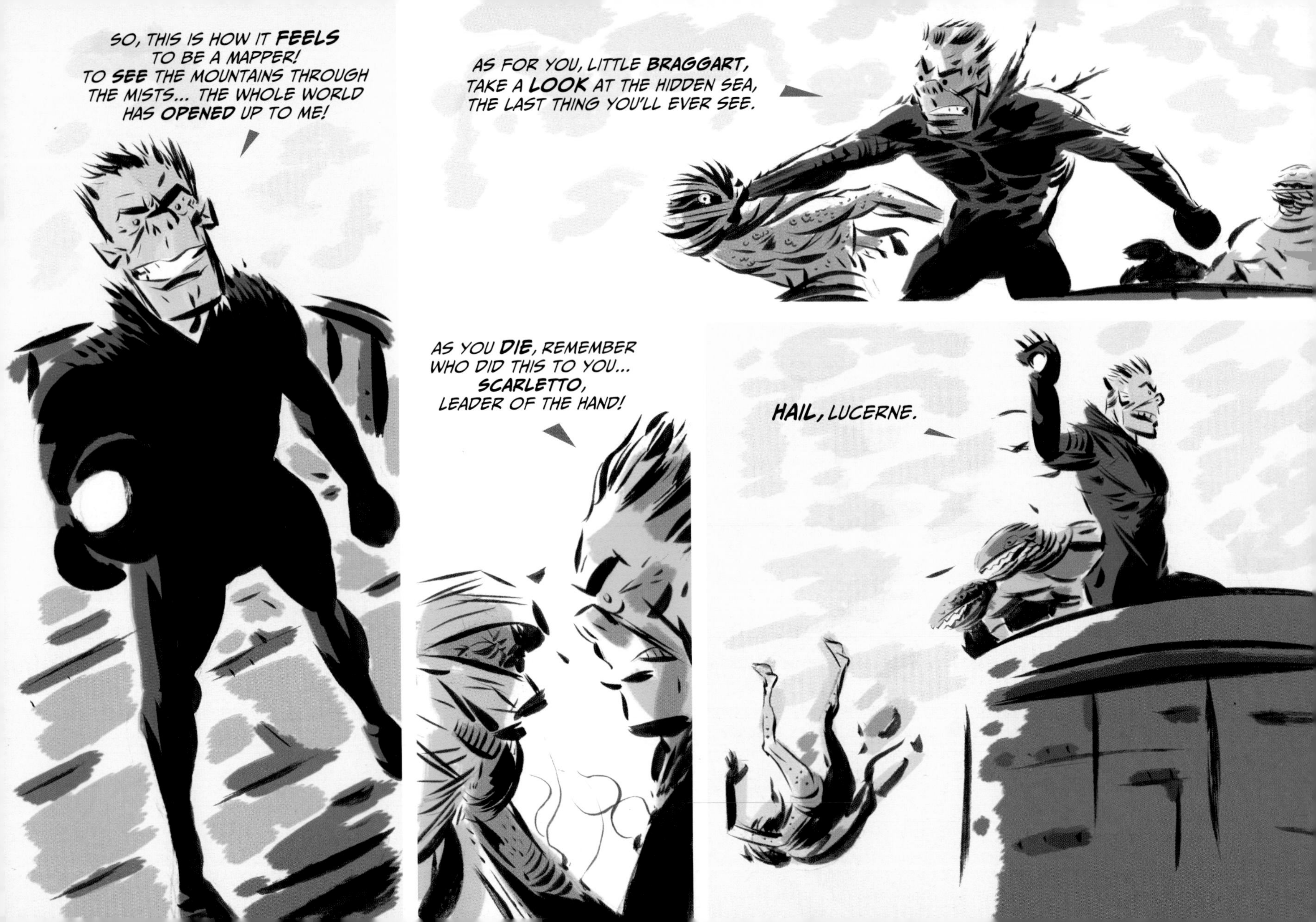
SO, THIS IS HOW IT FEELS TO BE A MAPPER! TO SEE THE MOUNTAINS THROUGH THE MISTS... THE WHOLE WORLD HAS OPENED UP TO ME!
AS FOR YOU, LITTLE BRAGGART, TAKE A LOOK AT THE HIDDEN SEA, THE LAST THING YOU'LL EVER SEE.
AS YOU DIE, REMEMBER WHO DID THIS TO YOU... SCARLETTO, LEADER OF THE HAND!
HAIL, LUCERNE.

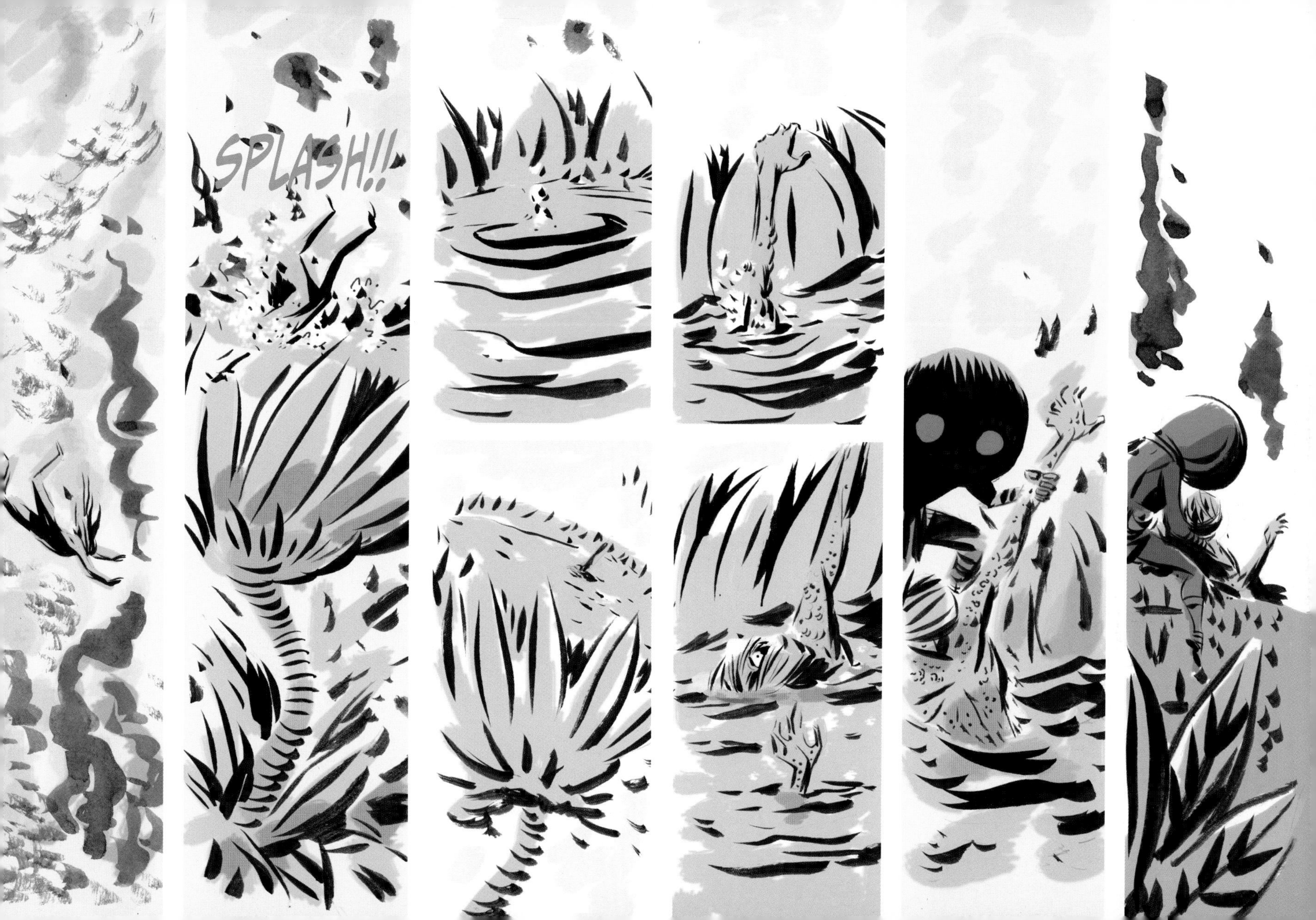
SPLASH!!

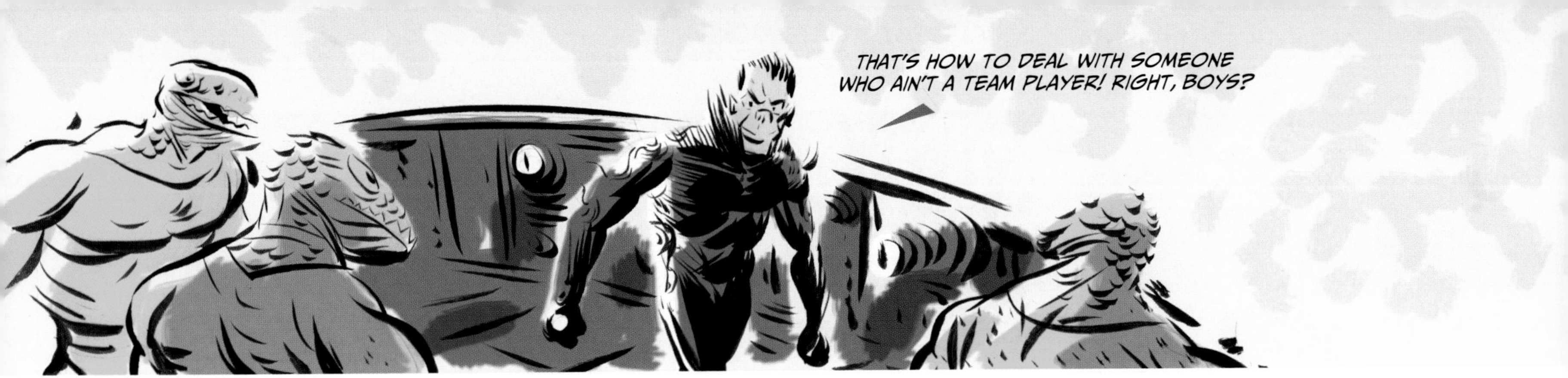
THAT'S HOW TO DEAL WITH SOMEONE WHO AIN'T A TEAM PLAYER! RIGHT, BOYS?

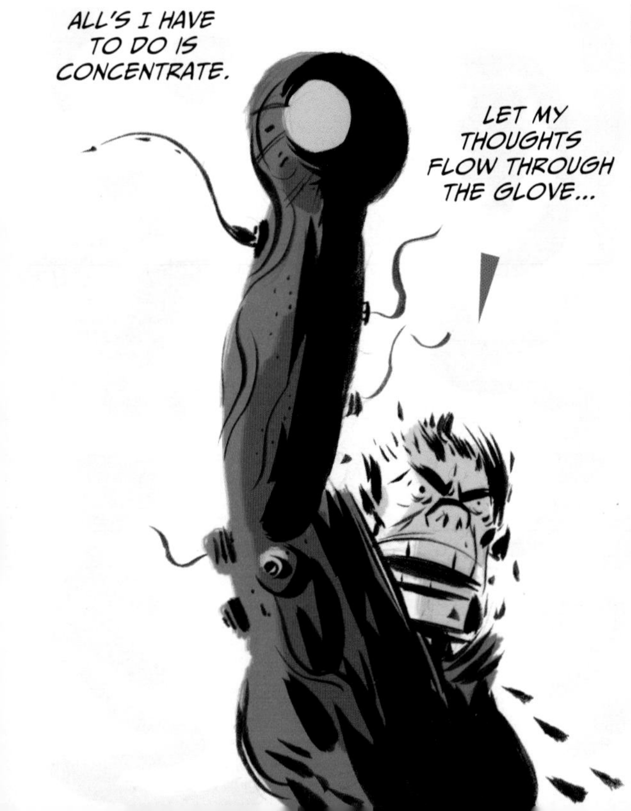
ALL'S I HAVE TO DO IS CONCENTRATE.
LET MY THOUGHTS FLOW THROUGH THE GLOVE...

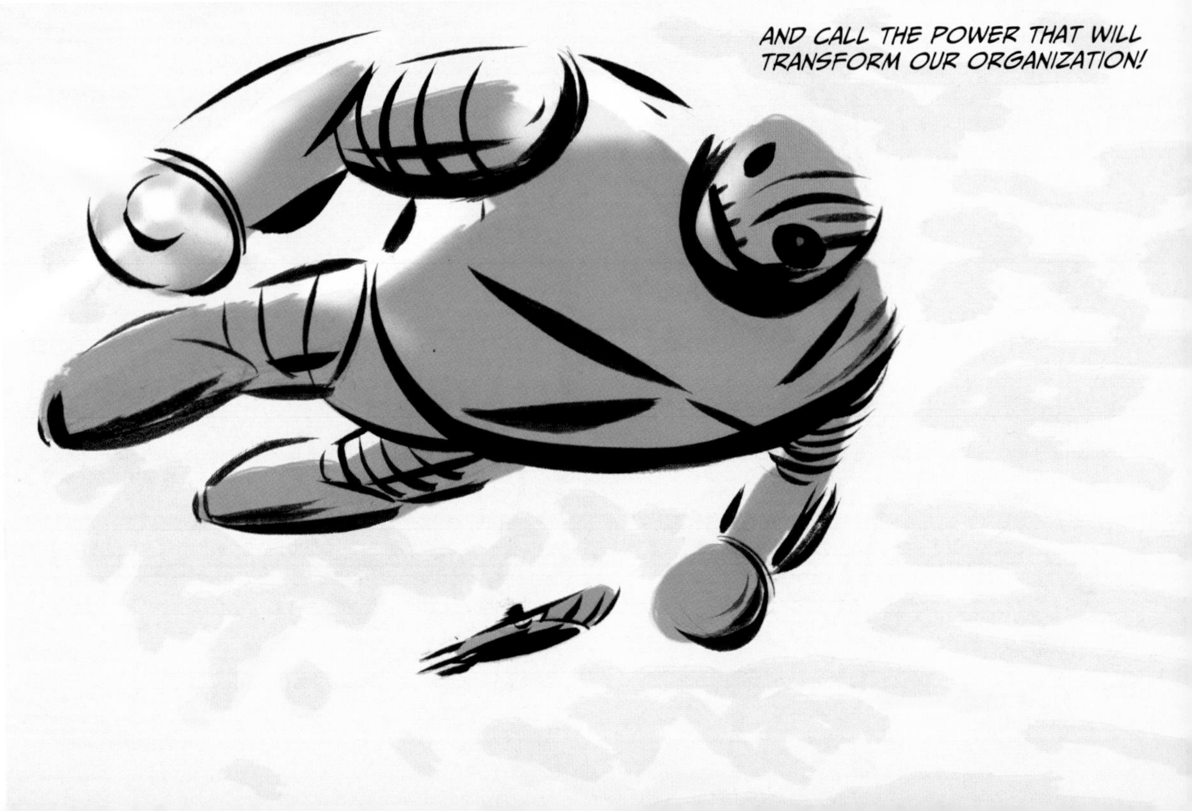
AND CALL THE POWER THAT WILL TRANSFORM OUR ORGANIZATION!

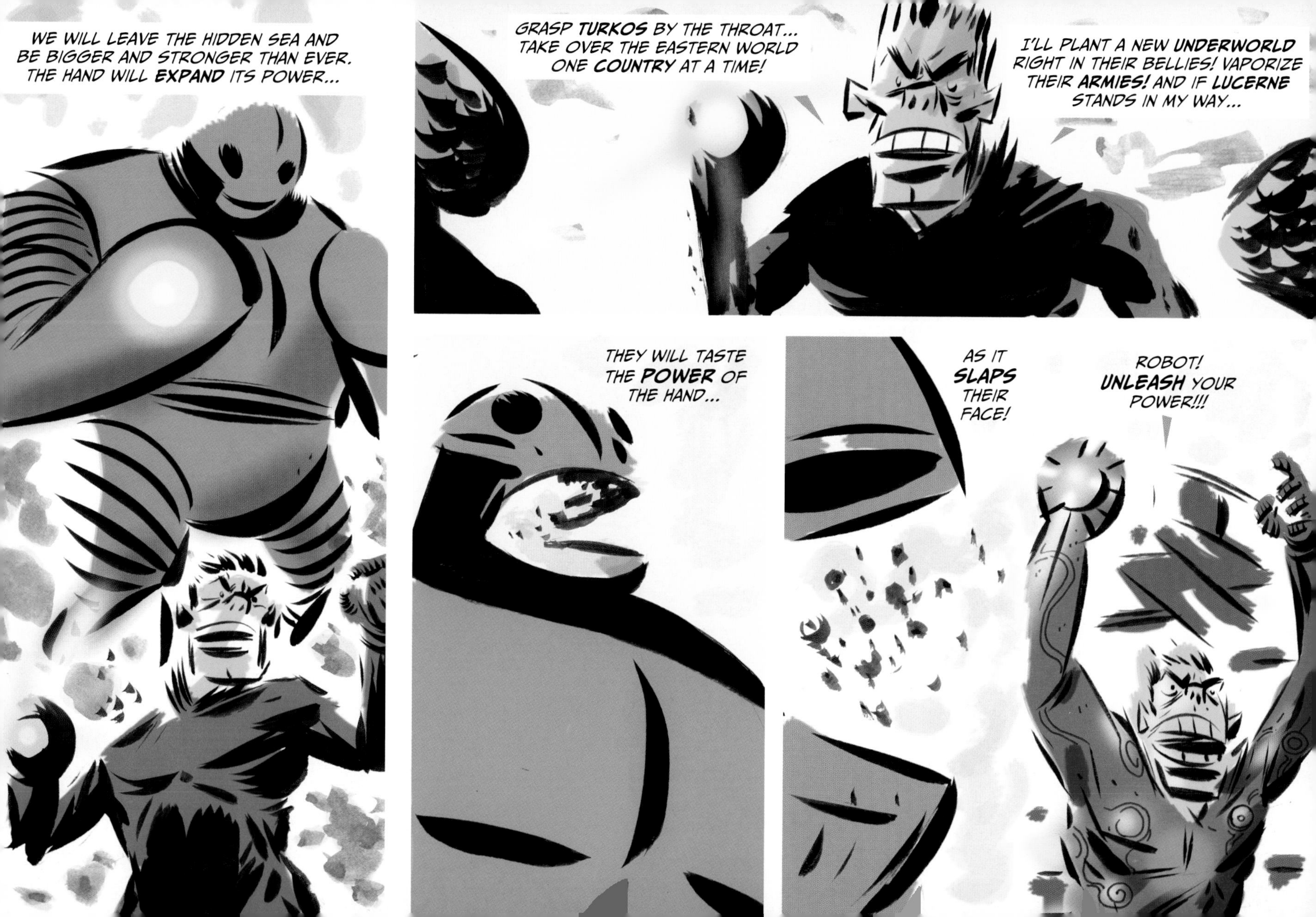
WE WILL LEAVE THE HIDDEN SEA AND BE BIGGER AND STRONGER THAN EVER. THE HAND WILL **EXPAND** ITS POWER...
GRASP **TURKOS** BY THE THROAT... TAKE OVER THE EASTERN WORLD ONE **COUNTRY** AT A TIME!
I'LL PLANT A NEW **UNDERWORLD** RIGHT IN THEIR BELLIES! VAPORIZE THEIR **ARMIES!** AND IF **LUCERNE** STANDS IN MY WAY...
THEY WILL TASTE THE **POWER** OF THE HAND...
AS IT **SLAPS** THEIR FACE!
ROBOT! **UNLEASH** YOUR POWER!!!

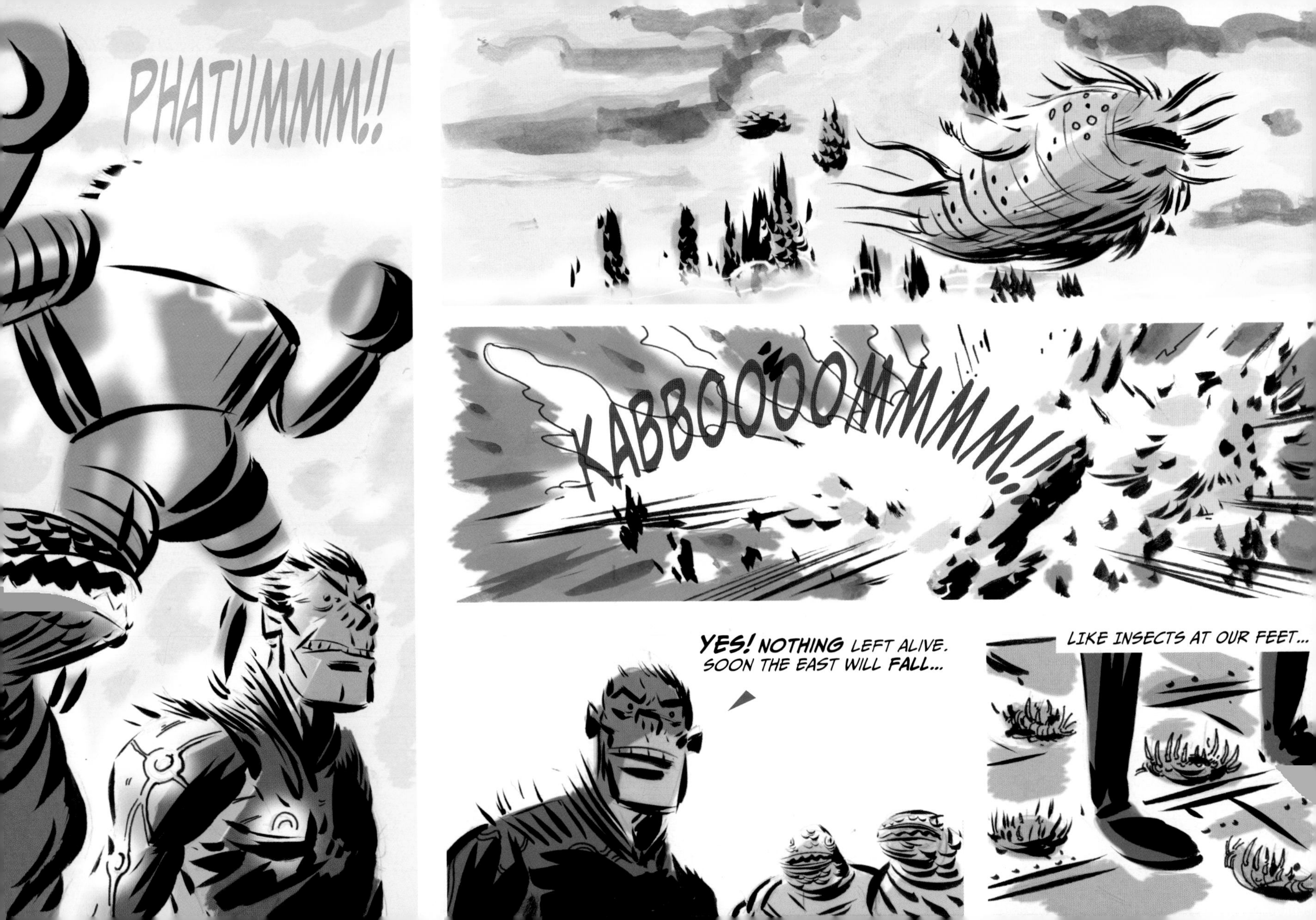
PHATUMMM!!
KABBOOOOMMMMM!!
YES! NOTHING LEFT ALIVE.
SOON THE EAST WILL FALL...
LIKE INSECTS AT OUR FEET...

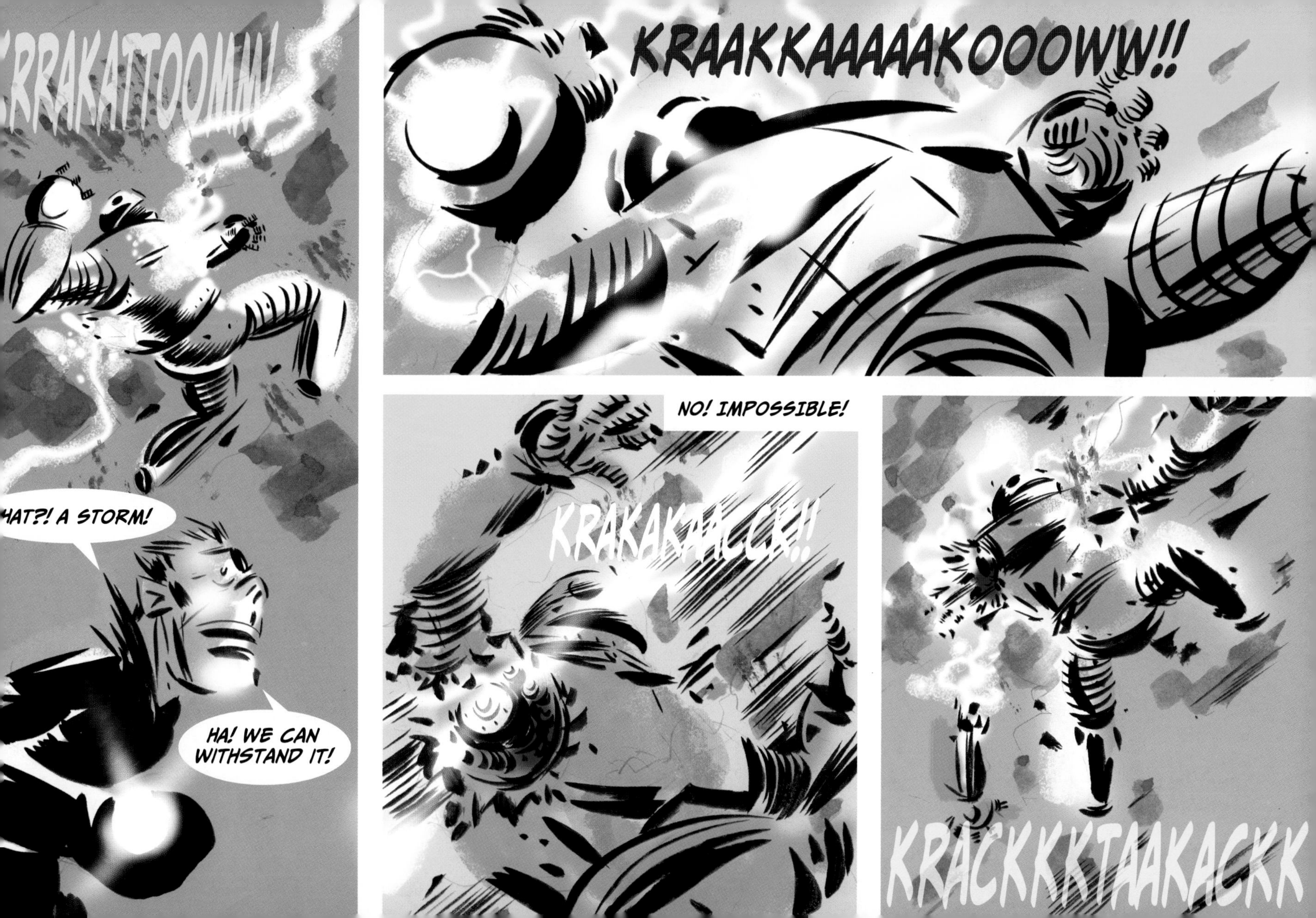

KRRAKATTOOMM!
HAT?! A STORM!
HA! WE CAN WITHSTAND IT!
KRAAKKAAAAAKOOOWW!!
NO! IMPOSSIBLE!
KRAKAKAACCK!!
KRACKKKTAAKACKK

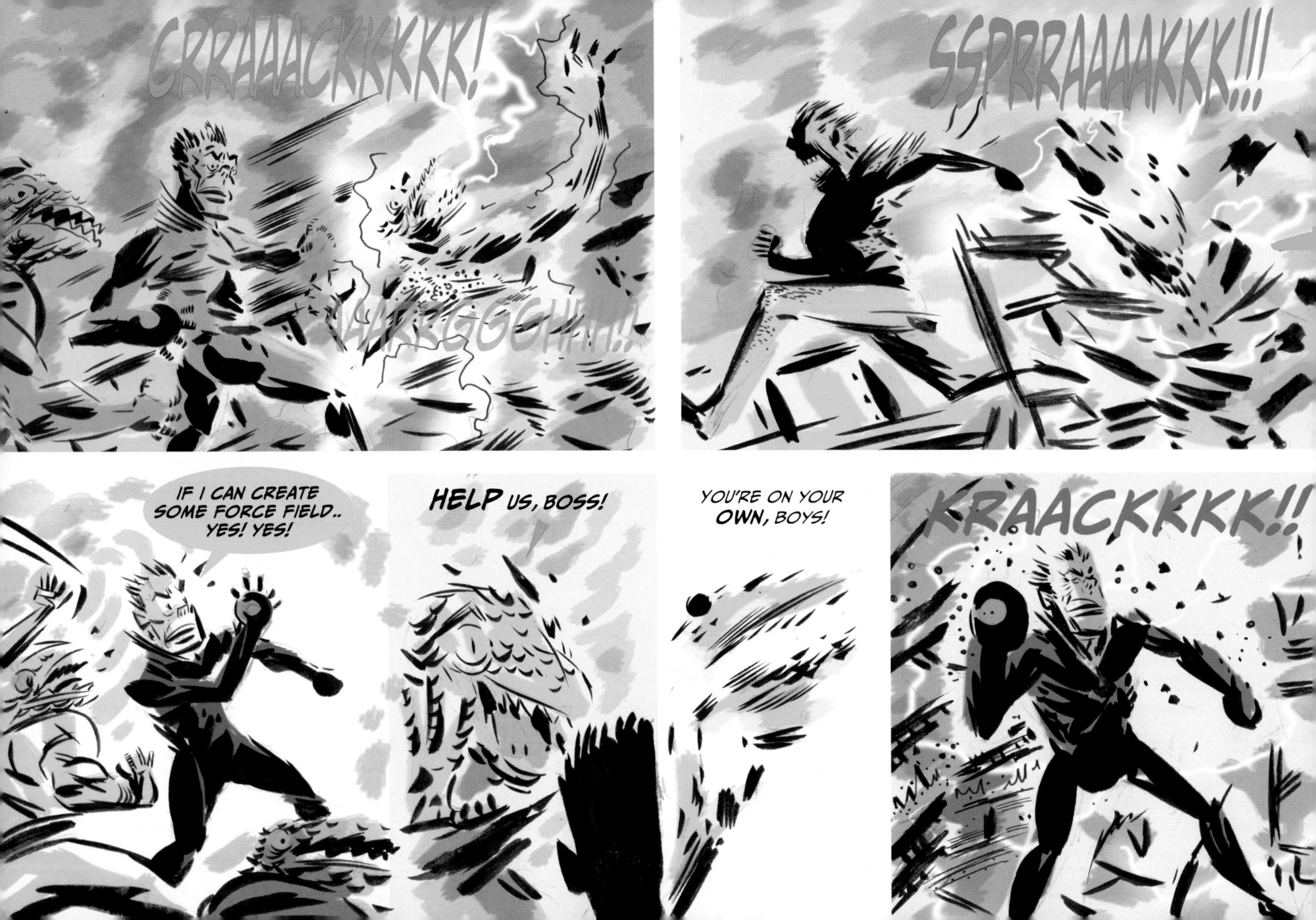
CRRAAACKKKKK!
AARRGGGHHH!!
SSPRRAAAAKKK!!!
IF I CAN CREATE SOME FORCE FIELD.. YES! YES!
HELP US, BOSS!
YOU'RE ON YOUR OWN, BOYS!
KRAACKKKK!!

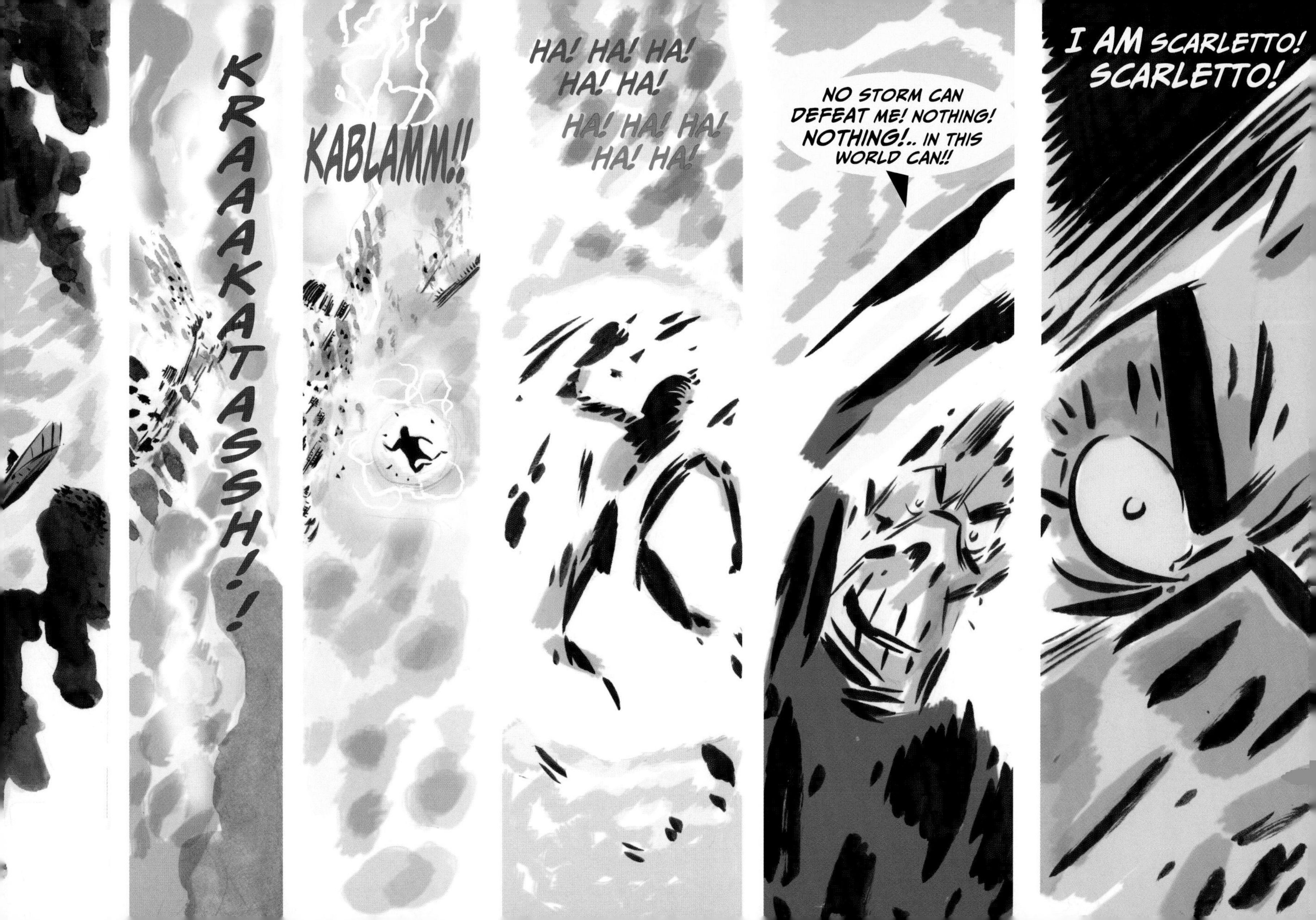
KRAAAAKATASSH!!
KABLAMM!!
HA! HA! HA! HA! HA!
HA! HA! HA! HA! HA!
NO STORM CAN DEFEAT ME! NOTHING! NOTHING!.. IN THIS WORLD CAN!!
I AM SCARLETTO! SCARLETTO!

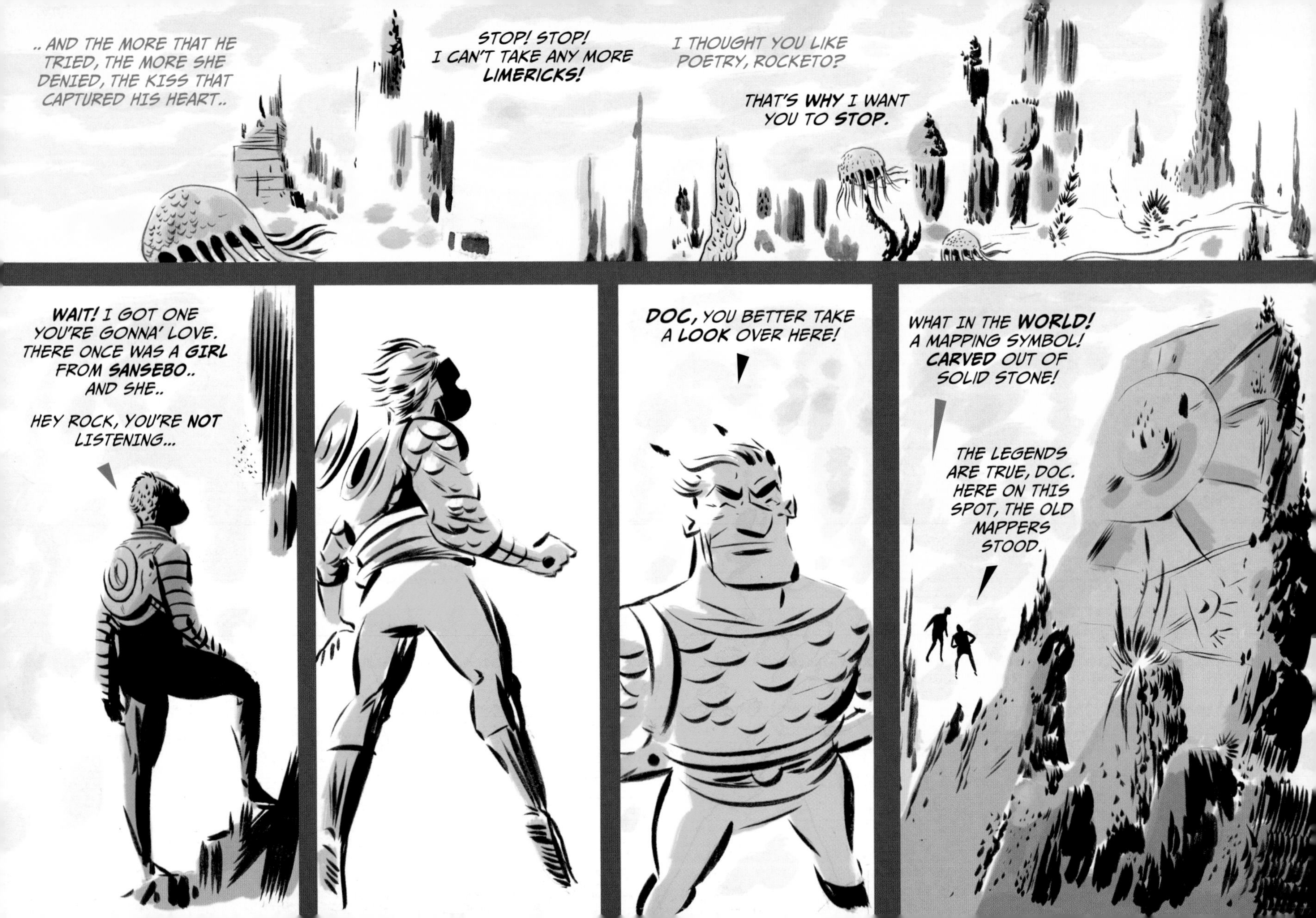

.. AND THE MORE THAT HE TRIED, THE MORE SHE DENIED, THE KISS THAT CAPTURED HIS HEART..
STOP! STOP! I CAN'T TAKE ANY MORE **LIMERICKS!**
I THOUGHT YOU LIKE POETRY, ROCKETO?
THAT'S **WHY** I WANT YOU TO **STOP.**
**WAIT!** I GOT ONE YOU'RE GONNA' LOVE. THERE ONCE WAS A **GIRL** FROM **SANSEBO..** AND SHE..
HEY ROCK, YOU'RE **NOT** LISTENING...
**DOC,** YOU BETTER TAKE A **LOOK** OVER HERE!
WHAT IN THE **WORLD!** A MAPPING SYMBOL! **CARVED** OUT OF SOLID STONE!
THE LEGENDS ARE TRUE, DOC. HERE ON THIS SPOT, THE OLD MAPPERS STOOD.

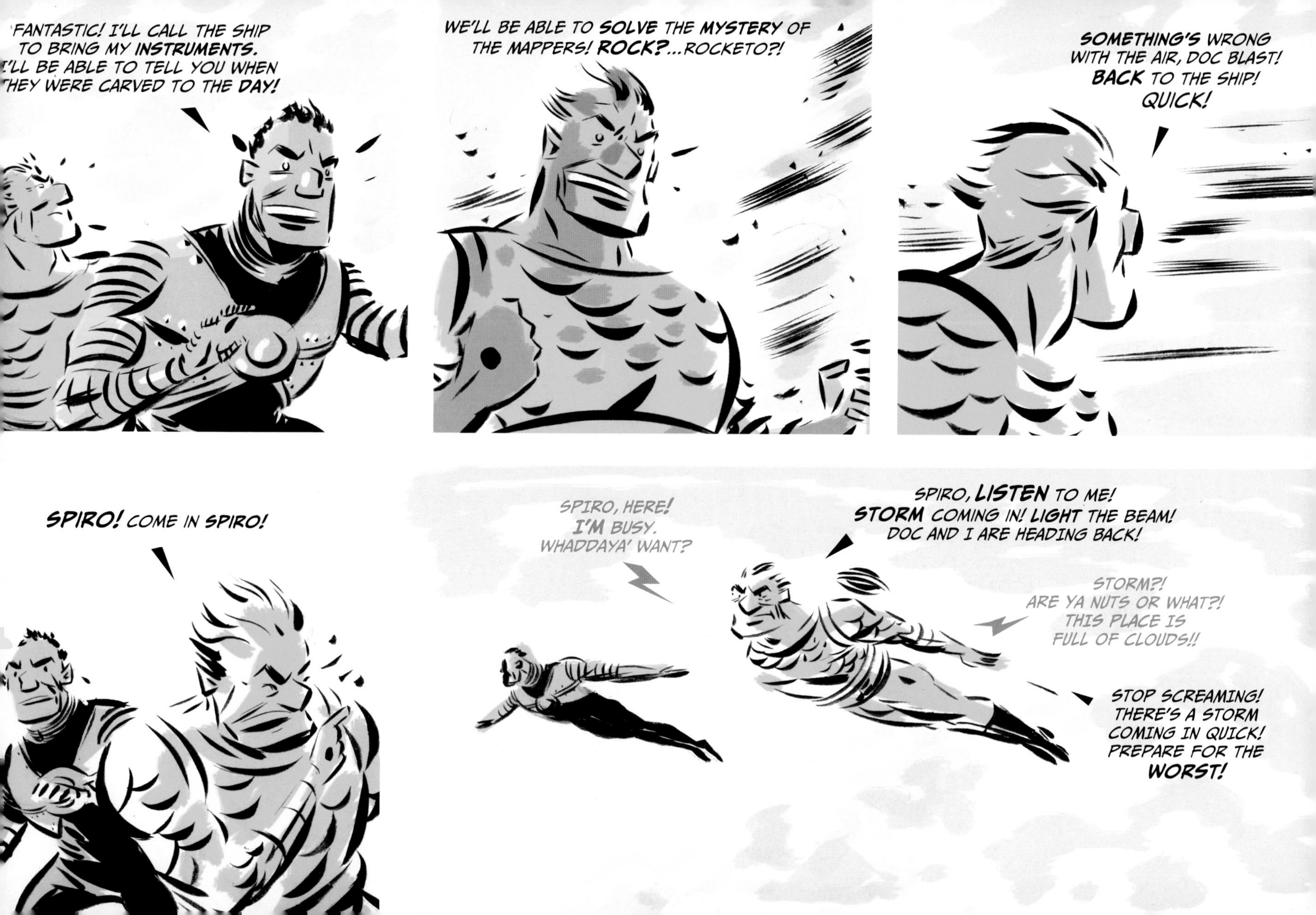
FANTASTIC! I'LL CALL THE SHIP TO BRING MY INSTRUMENTS. I'LL BE ABLE TO TELL YOU WHEN THEY WERE CARVED TO THE DAY!
WE'LL BE ABLE TO SOLVE THE MYSTERY OF THE MAPPERS! ROCK?...ROCKETO?!
SOMETHING'S WRONG WITH THE AIR, DOC BLAST! BACK TO THE SHIP! QUICK!
SPIRO! COME IN SPIRO!
SPIRO, HERE! I'M BUSY. WHADDAYA' WANT?
SPIRO, LISTEN TO ME! STORM COMING IN! LIGHT THE BEAM! DOC AND I ARE HEADING BACK!
STORM?! ARE YA NUTS OR WHAT?! THIS PLACE IS FULL OF CLOUDS!!
STOP SCREAMING! THERE'S A STORM COMING IN QUICK! PREPARE FOR THE WORST!

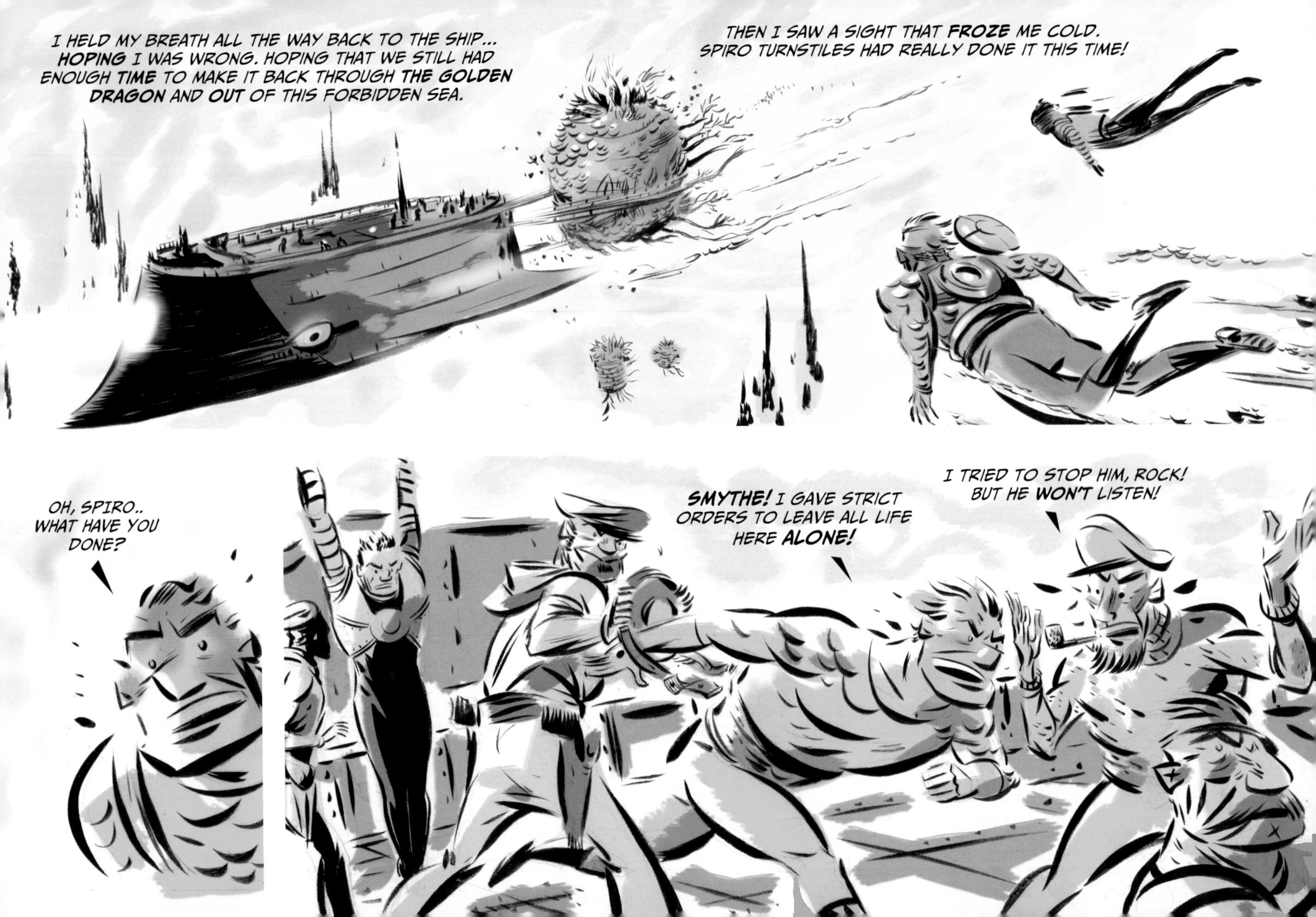
I HELD MY BREATH ALL THE WAY BACK TO THE SHIP... **HOPING** I WAS WRONG. HOPING THAT WE STILL HAD ENOUGH **TIME** TO MAKE IT BACK THROUGH **THE GOLDEN DRAGON** AND **OUT** OF THIS FORBIDDEN SEA.
THEN I SAW A SIGHT THAT **FROZE** ME COLD. SPIRO TURNSTILES HAD REALLY DONE IT THIS TIME!
OH, SPIRO.. WHAT HAVE YOU DONE?
**SMYTHE!** I GAVE STRICT ORDERS TO LEAVE ALL LIFE HERE **ALONE!**
I TRIED TO STOP HIM, ROCK! BUT HE **WON'T** LISTEN!

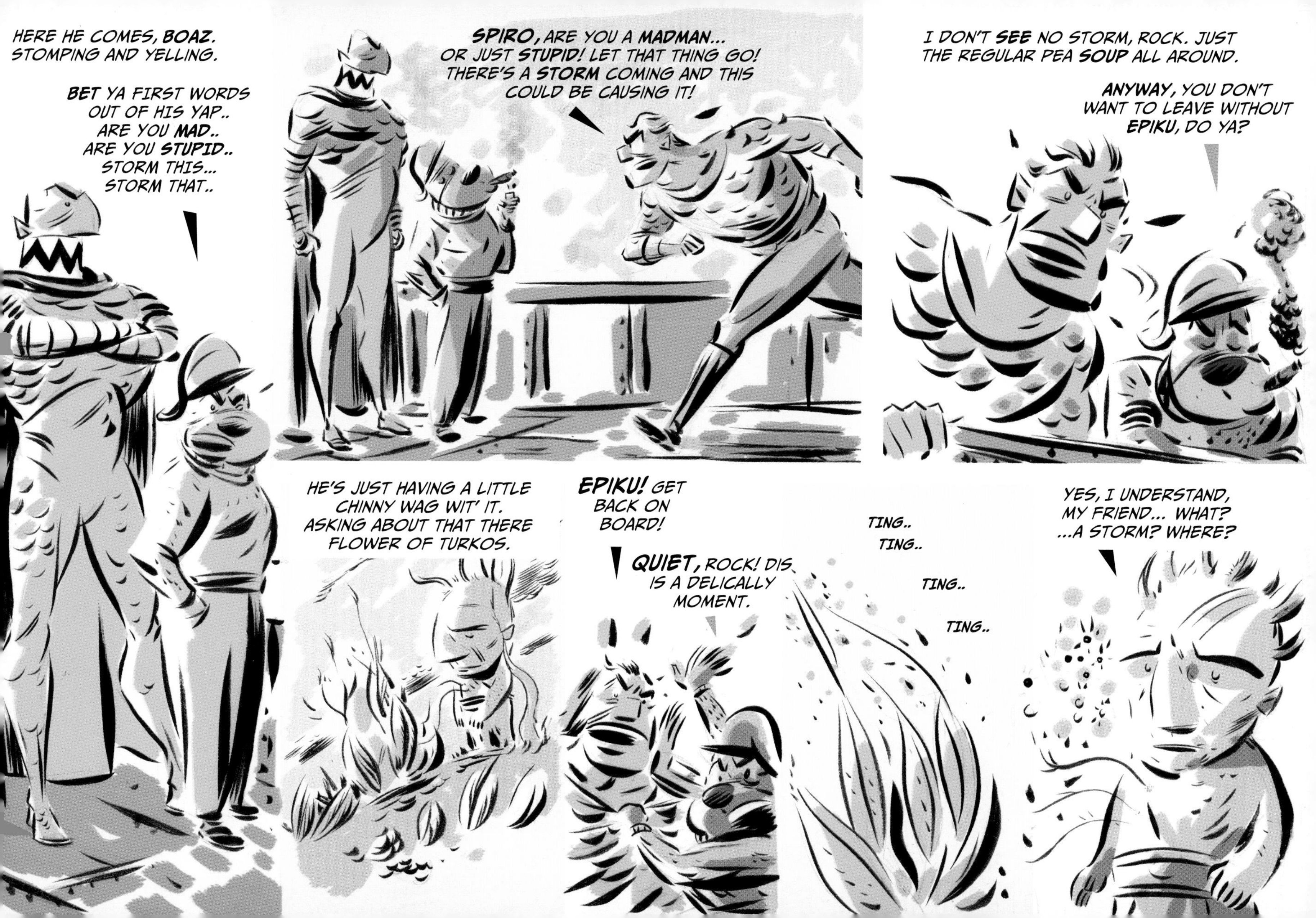
HERE HE COMES, BOAZ. STOMPING AND YELLING.
BET YA FIRST WORDS OUT OF HIS YAP.. ARE YOU MAD.. ARE YOU STUPID.. STORM THIS... STORM THAT..
SPIRO, ARE YOU A MADMAN... OR JUST STUPID! LET THAT THING GO! THERE'S A STORM COMING AND THIS COULD BE CAUSING IT!
I DON'T SEE NO STORM, ROCK. JUST THE REGULAR PEA SOUP ALL AROUND.
ANYWAY, YOU DON'T WANT TO LEAVE WITHOUT EPIKU, DO YA?
HE'S JUST HAVING A LITTLE CHINNY WAG WIT' IT. ASKING ABOUT THAT THERE FLOWER OF TURKOS.
EPIKU! GET BACK ON BOARD!
QUIET, ROCK! DIS IS A DELICALLY MOMENT.
TING..
TING..
TING..
TING..
YES, I UNDERSTAND, MY FRIEND... WHAT? ...A STORM? WHERE?

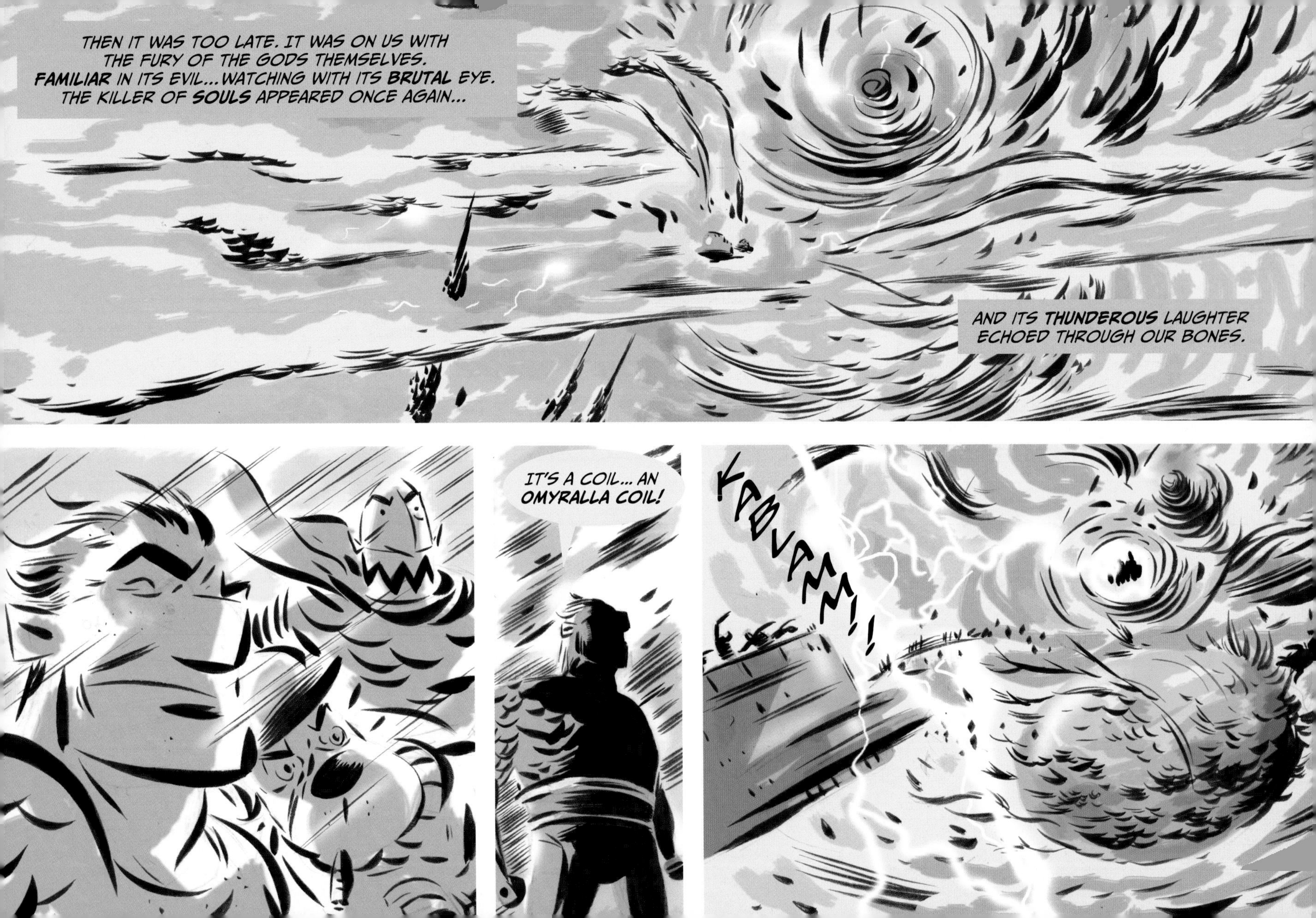
THEN IT WAS TOO LATE. IT WAS ON US WITH THE FURY OF THE GODS THEMSELVES. **FAMILIAR** IN ITS EVIL...WATCHING WITH ITS **BRUTAL** EYE. THE KILLER OF **SOULS** APPEARED ONCE AGAIN...
AND ITS **THUNDEROUS** LAUGHTER ECHOED THROUGH OUR BONES.
IT'S A COIL... AN **OMYRALLA COIL!**
KABVAMM!!!

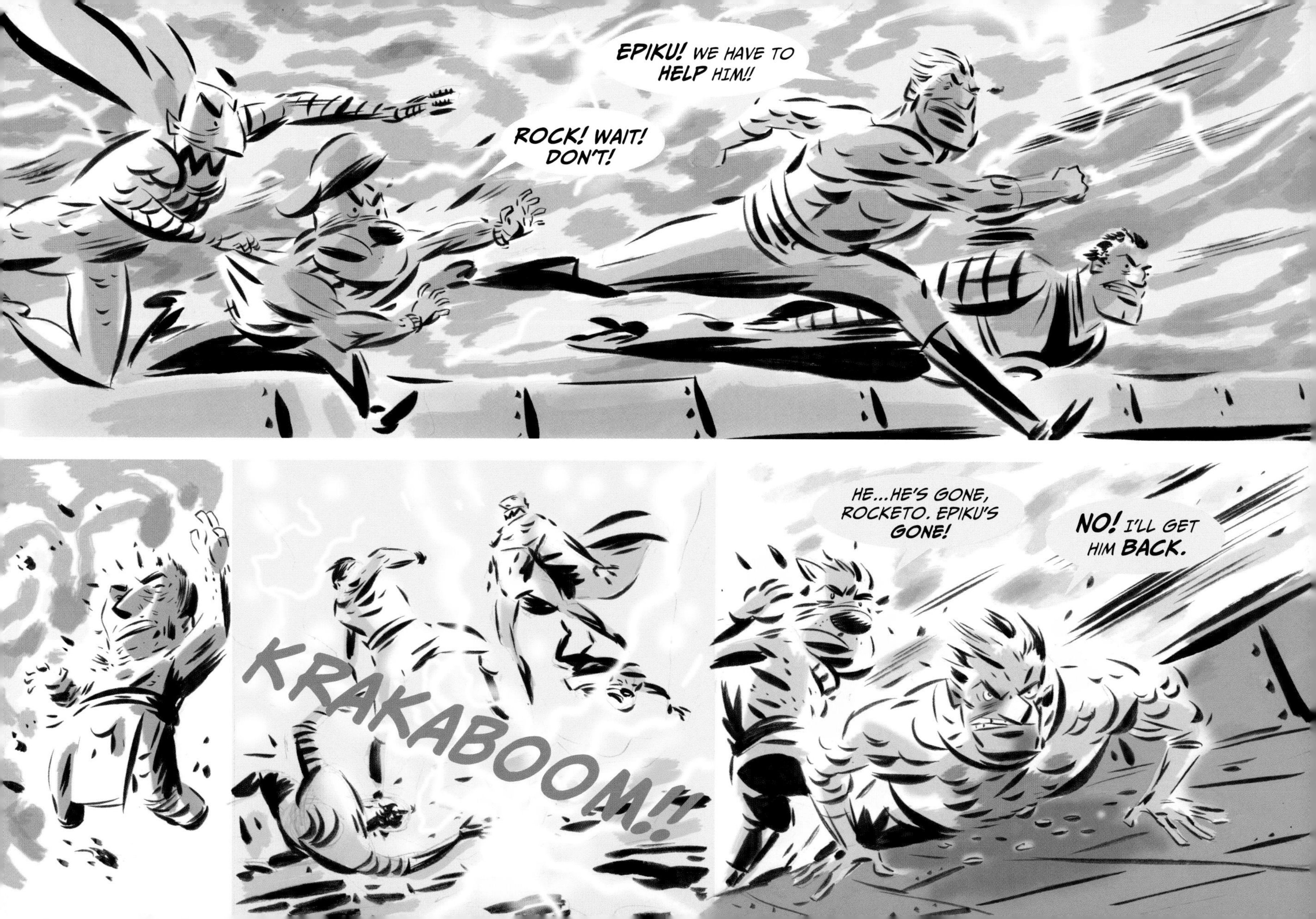
EPIKU! WE HAVE TO HELP HIM!!
ROCK! WAIT! DON'T!
KRAKABOOM!!
HE...HE'S GONE, ROCKETO. EPIKU'S GONE!
NO! I'LL GET HIM BACK.

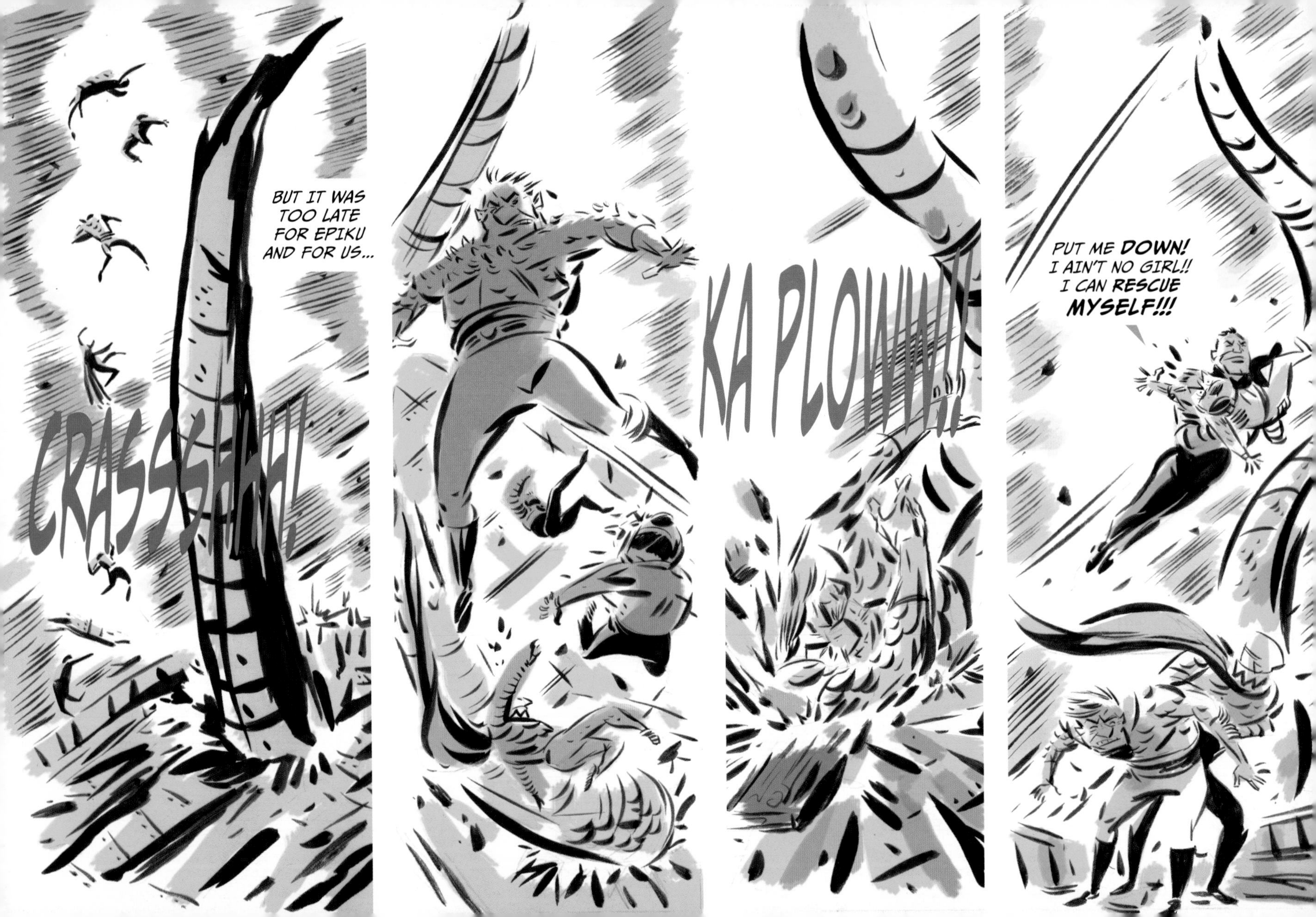
BUT IT WAS TOO LATE FOR EPIKU AND FOR US...
CRASSSHHH!
KA PLOWW!!!
PUT ME DOWN! I AIN'T NO GIRL!! I CAN RESCUE MYSELF!!!

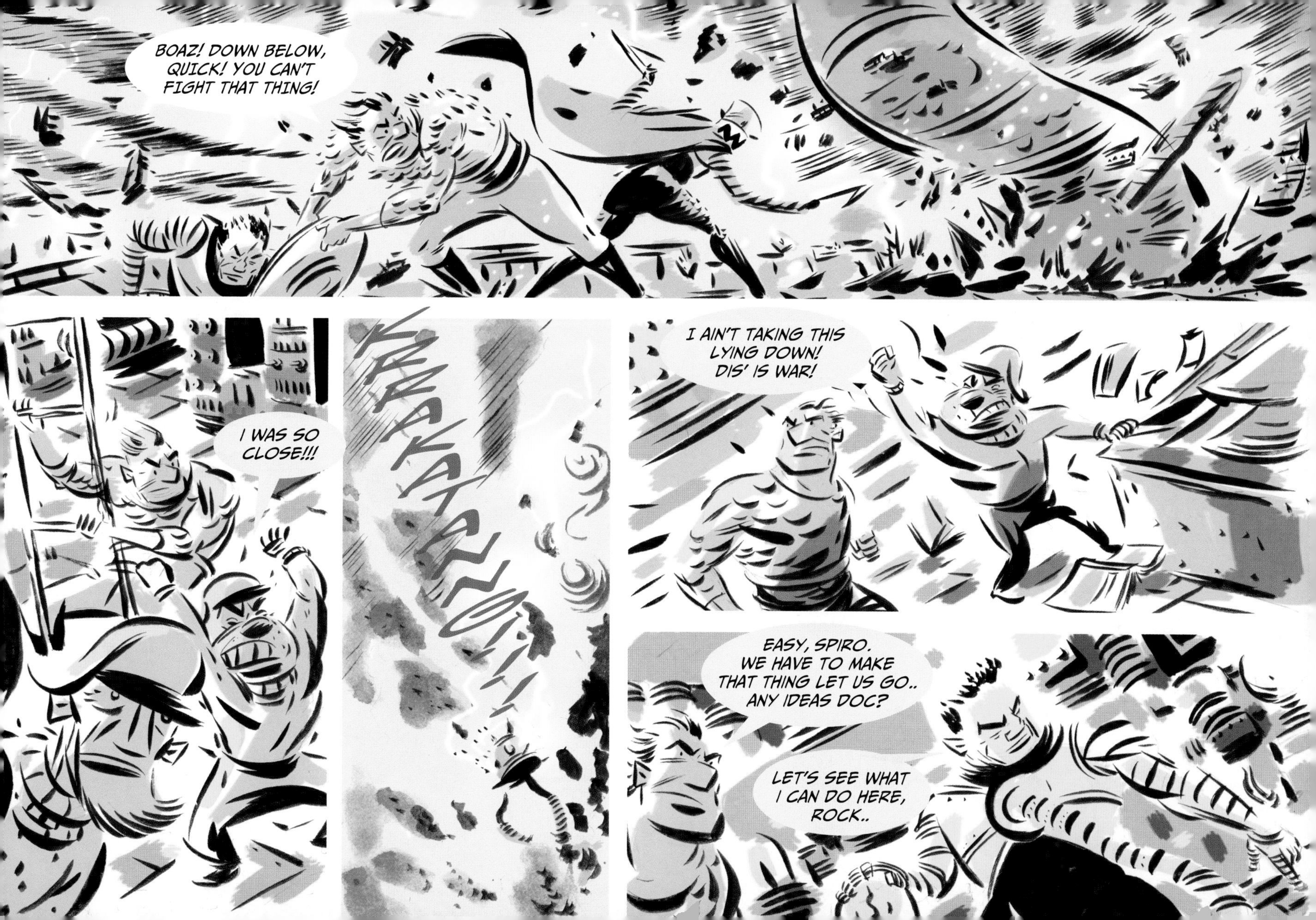
BOAZ! DOWN BELOW, QUICK! YOU CAN'T FIGHT THAT THING!
I WAS SO CLOSE!!!
KRAKAKAKOOOM!!!
I AIN'T TAKING THIS LYING DOWN! DIS' IS WAR!
EASY, SPIRO. WE HAVE TO MAKE THAT THING LET US GO.. ANY IDEAS DOC?
LET'S SEE WHAT I CAN DO HERE, ROCK..

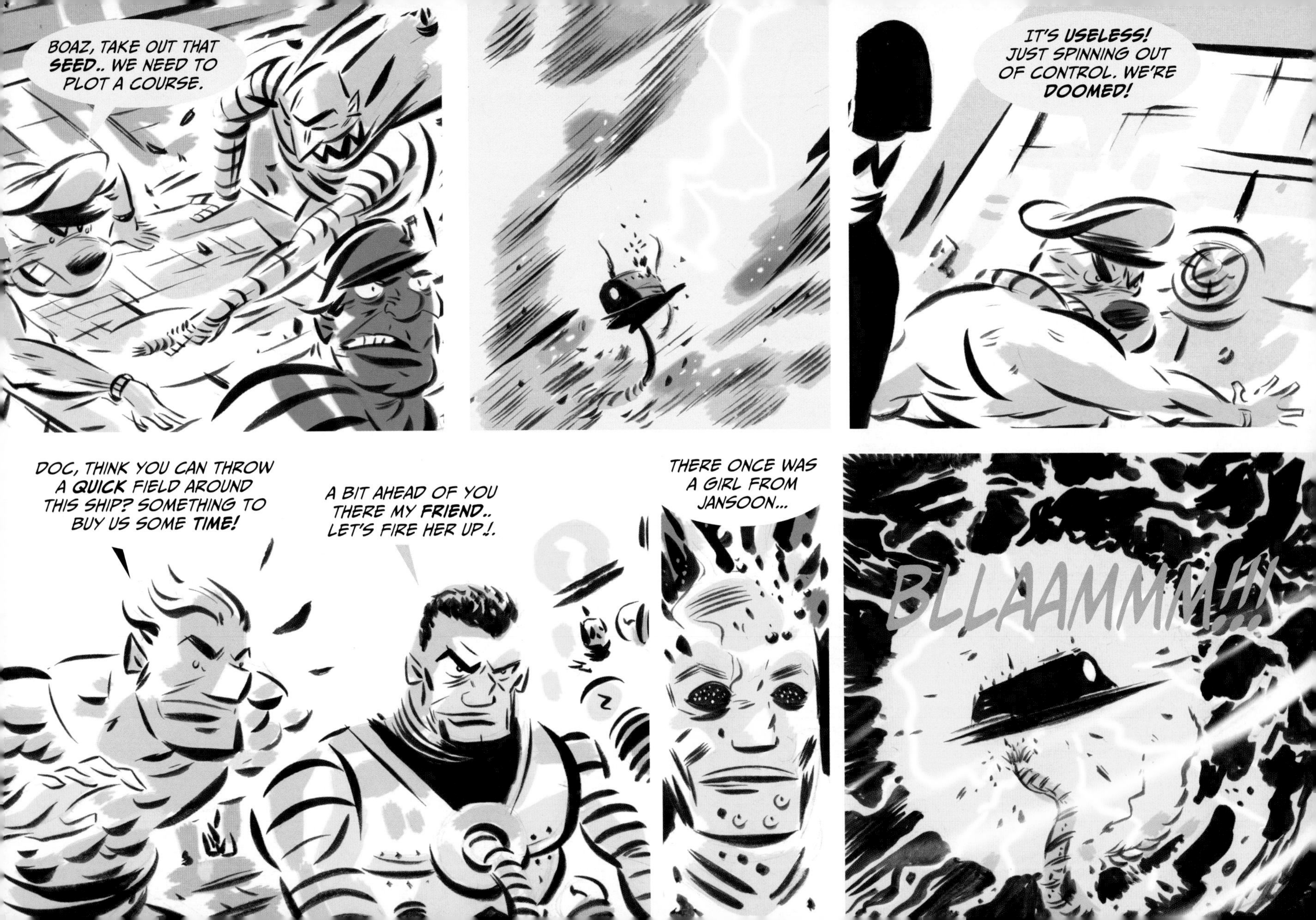
BOAZ, TAKE OUT THAT SEED.. WE NEED TO PLOT A COURSE.
IT'S USELESS! JUST SPINNING OUT OF CONTROL. WE'RE DOOMED!
DOC, THINK YOU CAN THROW A QUICK FIELD AROUND THIS SHIP? SOMETHING TO BUY US SOME TIME!
A BIT AHEAD OF YOU THERE MY FRIEND.. LET'S FIRE HER UP.!.
THERE ONCE WAS A GIRL FROM JANSOON...
BLLAAMMM!!!

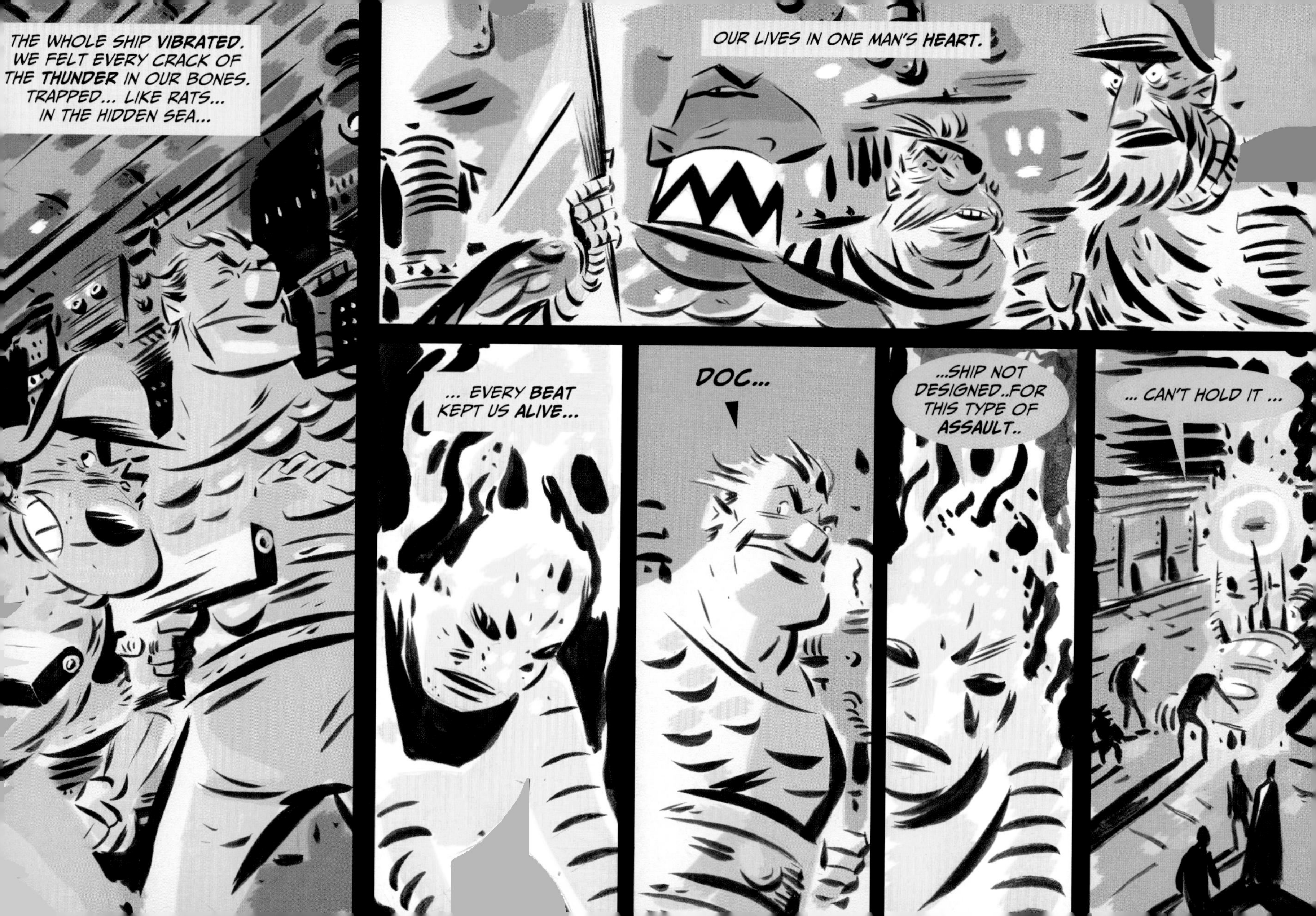
THE WHOLE SHIP VIBRATED. WE FELT EVERY CRACK OF THE THUNDER IN OUR BONES. TRAPPED... LIKE RATS... IN THE HIDDEN SEA...
OUR LIVES IN ONE MAN'S HEART.
... EVERY BEAT KEPT US ALIVE...
DOC...
...SHIP NOT DESIGNED..FOR THIS TYPE OF ASSAULT..
... CAN'T HOLD IT ...

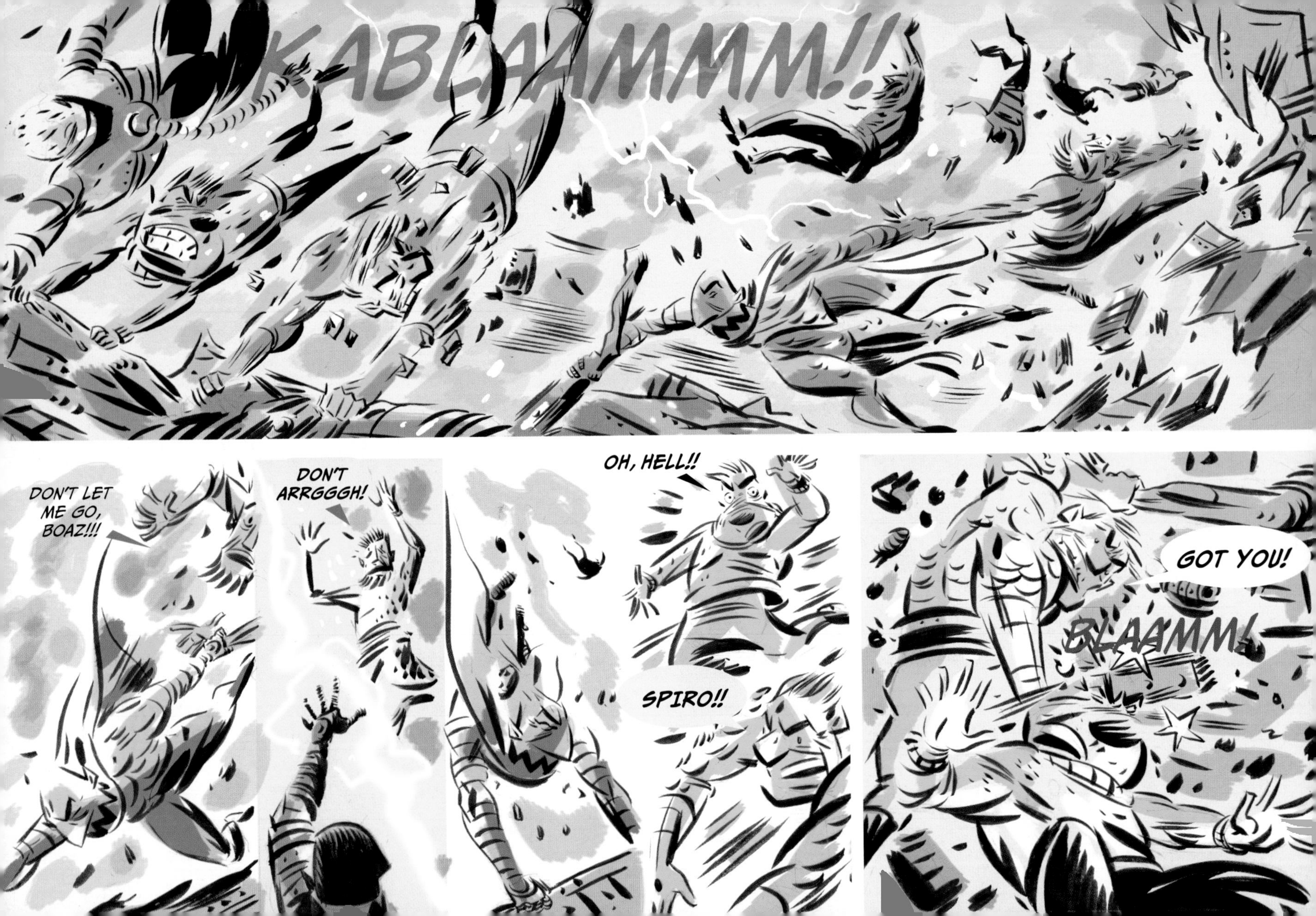
KABLAAMMM!!
DON'T LET ME GO, BOAZ!!!
DON'T ARRGGGH!
OH, HELL!!
SPIRO!!
GOT YOU!
BLAAMM!

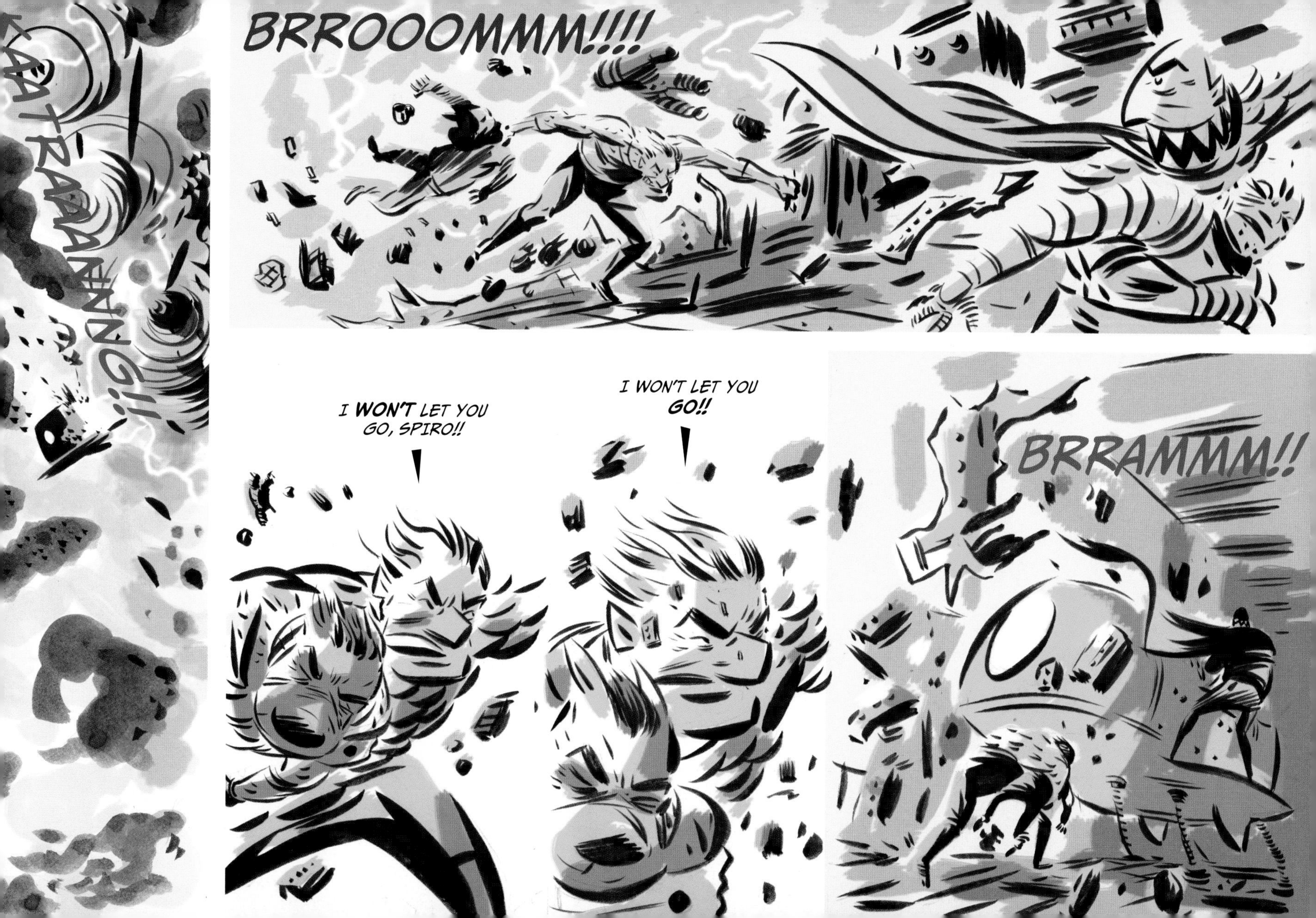
KAATRAAANNG!!
BRROOOMMM!!!!
I WON'T LET YOU GO, SPIRO!!
I WON'T LET YOU GO!!
BRRAMMM!!

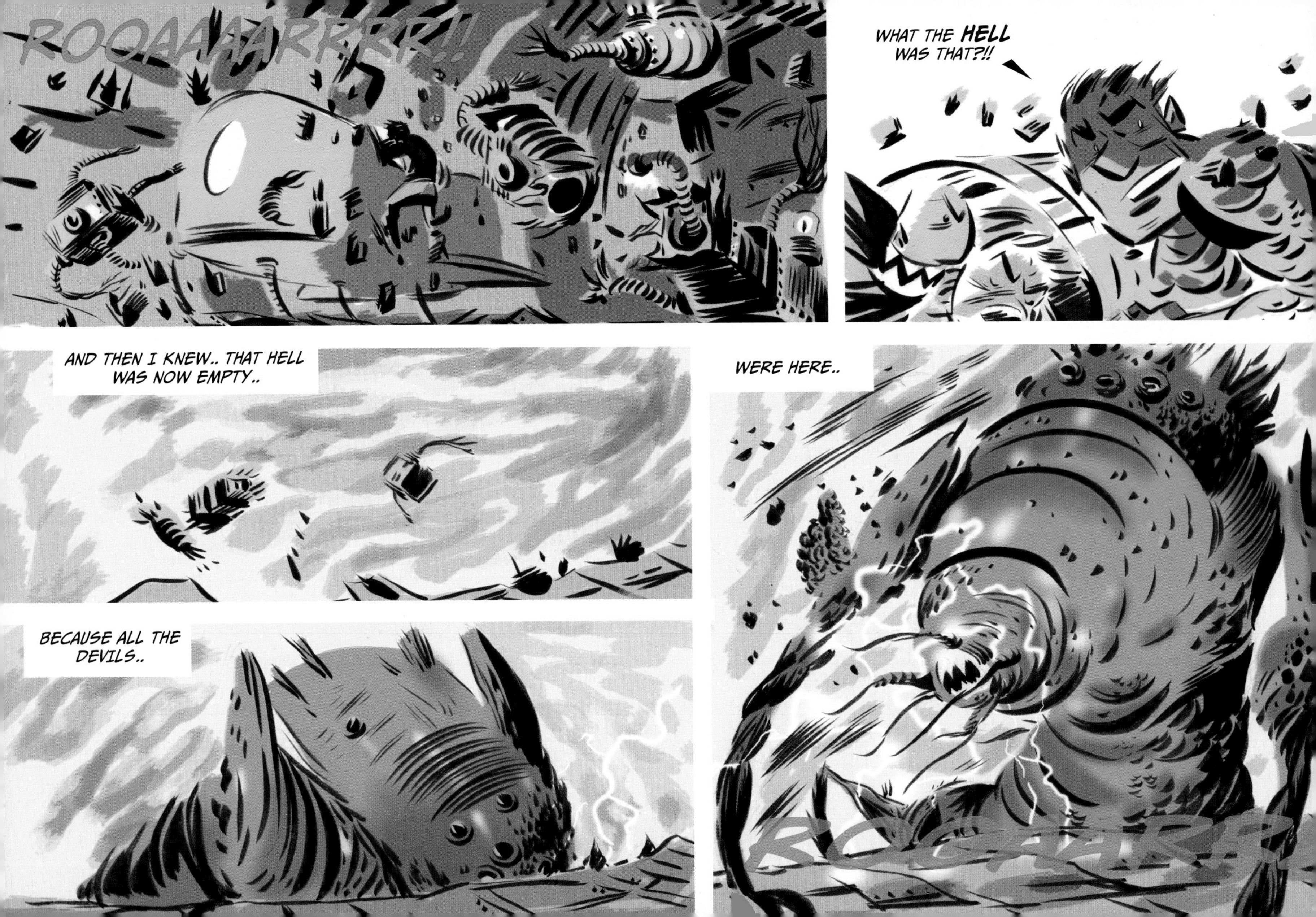
ROOAAAARRRRR!!
WHAT THE **HELL** WAS THAT?!!
AND THEN I KNEW.. THAT HELL WAS NOW EMPTY..
BECAUSE ALL THE DEVILS..
WERE HERE..
ROOARR

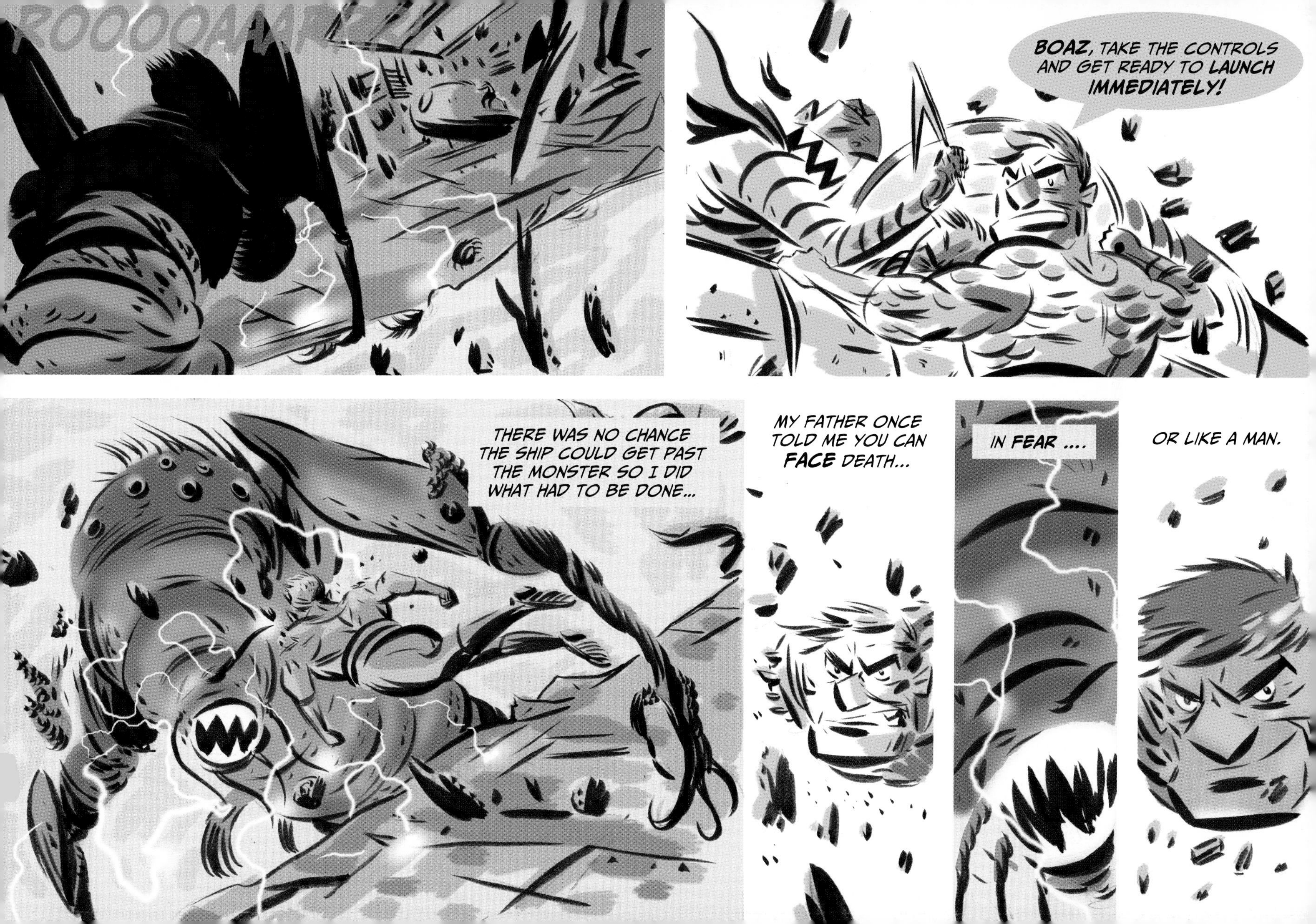
ROOOOAAARRR!
BOAZ, TAKE THE CONTROLS AND GET READY TO LAUNCH IMMEDIATELY!
THERE WAS NO CHANCE THE SHIP COULD GET PAST THE MONSTER SO I DID WHAT HAD TO BE DONE...
MY FATHER ONCE TOLD ME YOU CAN FACE DEATH...
IN FEAR ....
OR LIKE A MAN.

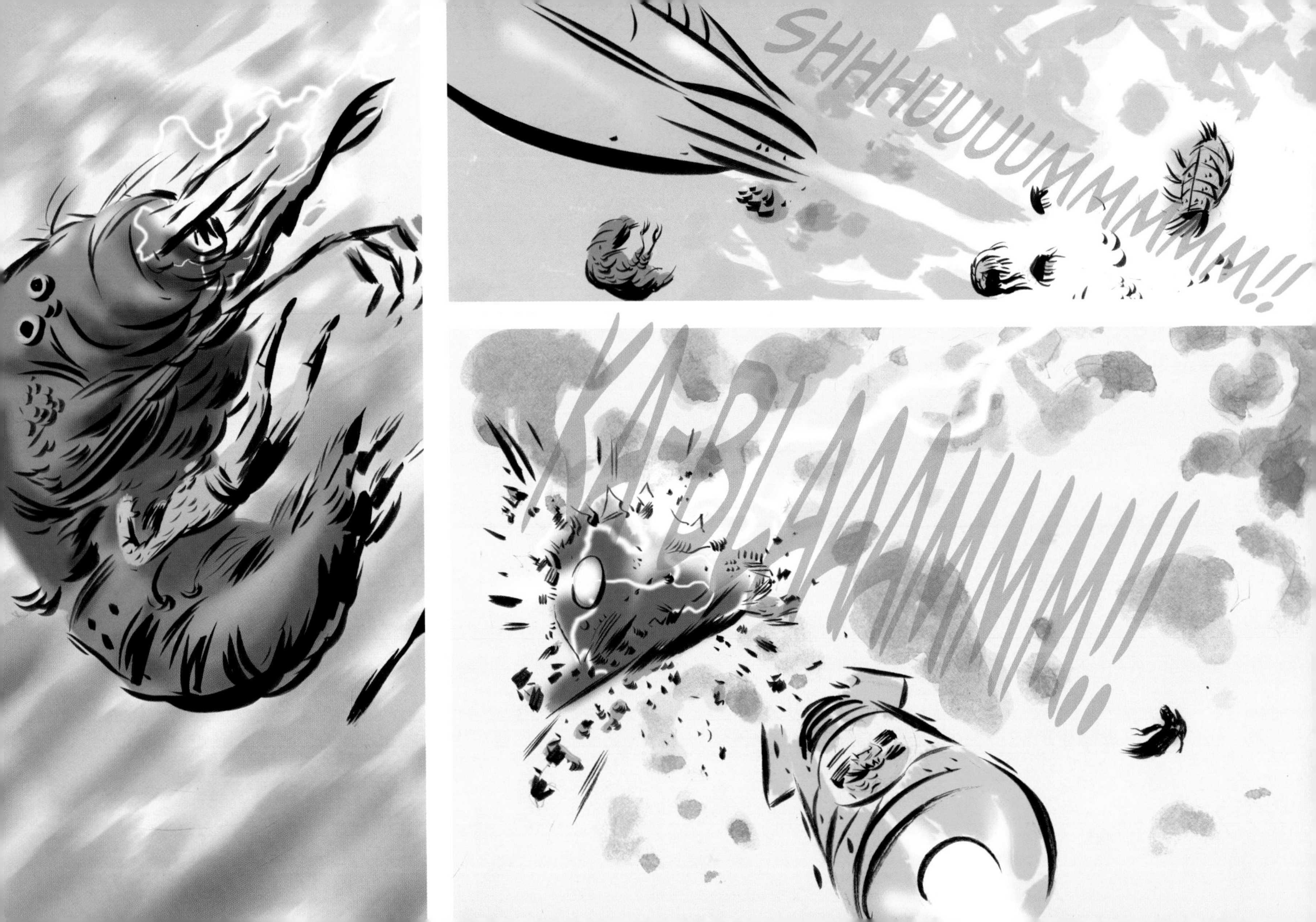
SHHHUUUUUMMMMMM!!
KA-BLAAAMMM!!

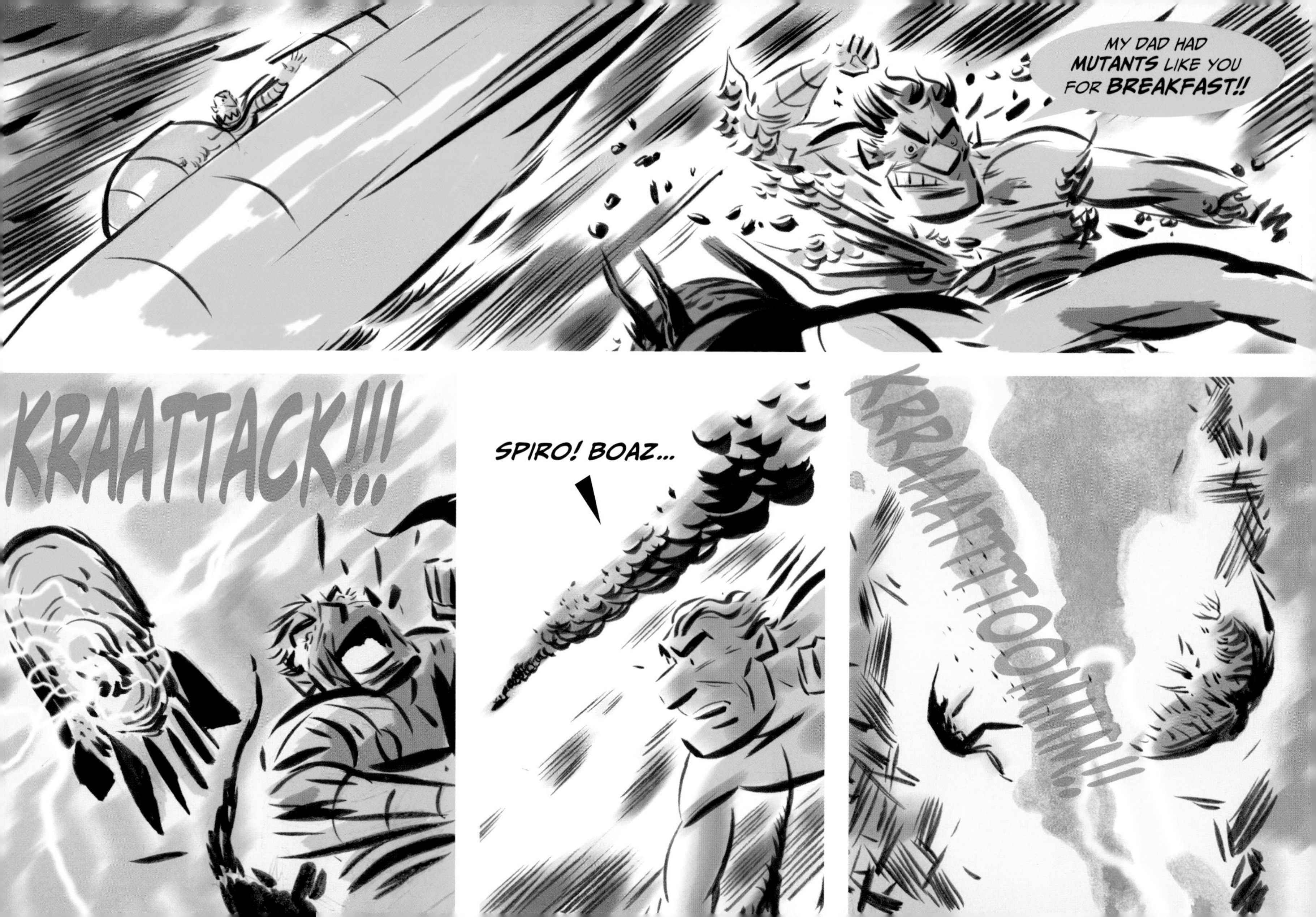

MY DAD HAD MUTANTS LIKE YOU FOR BREAKFAST!!
KRAATTACK!!!
SPIRO! BOAZ...
KRRAATTTOOMMM!!

THEN I WAS
FALLING..

INTO THE
SAME ABYSS..

MY PARENTS
HAD TRAVELED..

MANY YEARS
AGO..

FULL
CIRCLE..

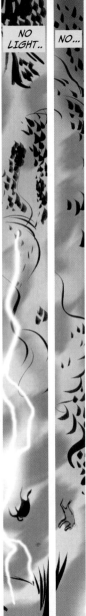

NO
LIGHT..

NO...

LIGHT.

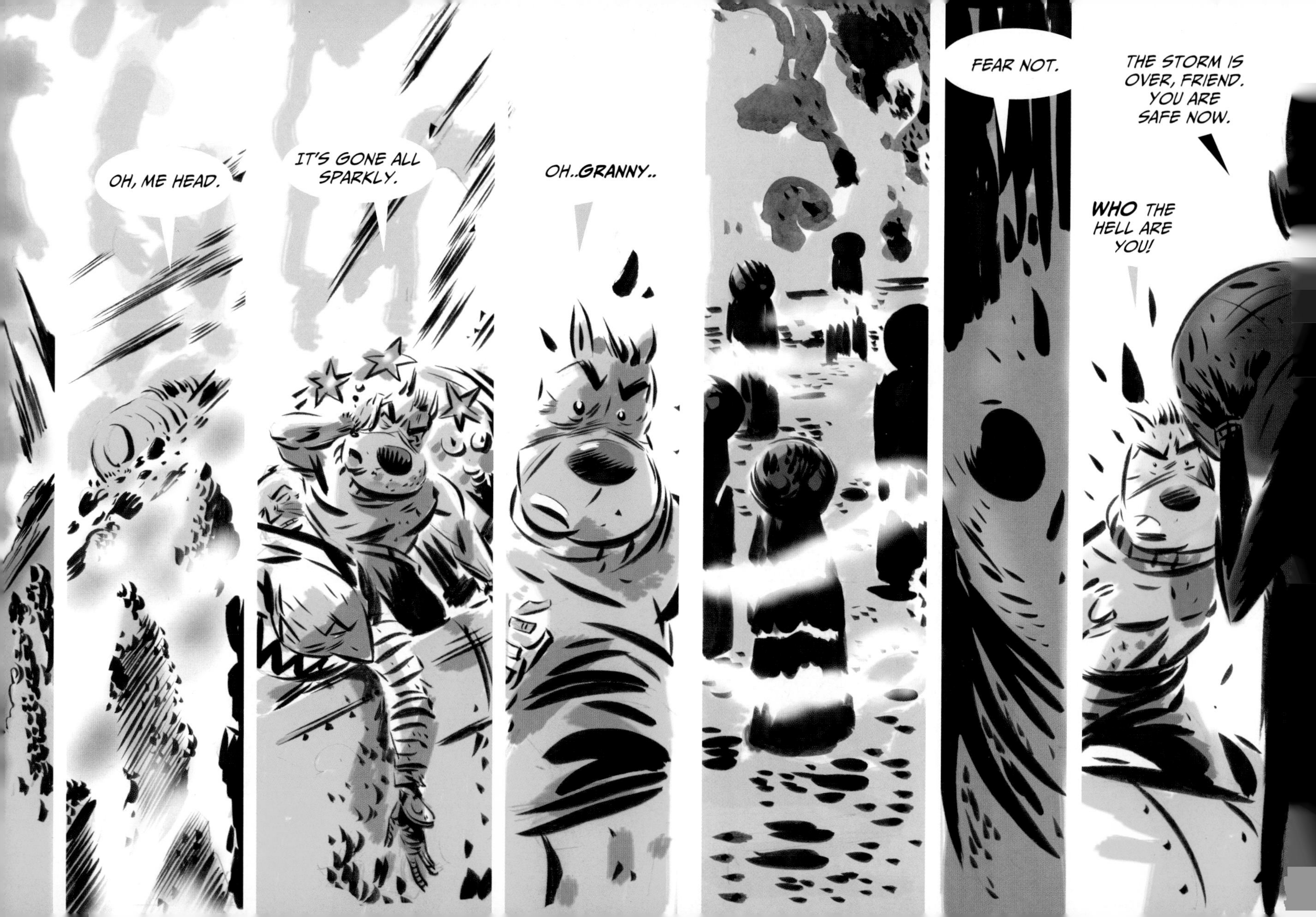
OH, ME HEAD.
IT'S GONE ALL SPARKLY.
OH..GRANNY..
FEAR NOT.
THE STORM IS OVER, FRIEND. YOU ARE SAFE NOW.
WHO THE HELL ARE YOU!

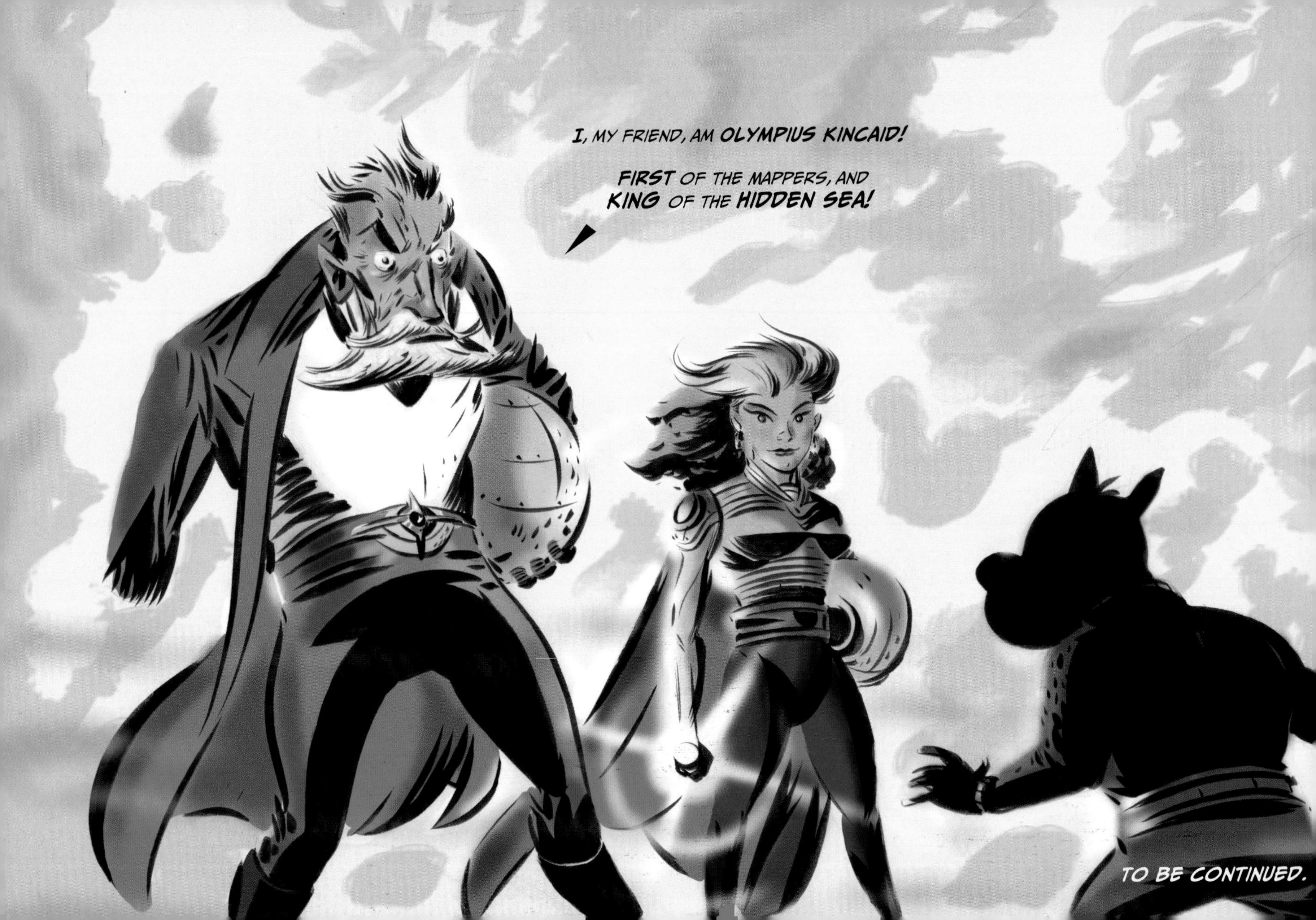
I, MY FRIEND, AM OLYMPIUS KINCAID!
FIRST OF THE MAPPERS, AND KING OF THE HIDDEN SEA!
TO BE CONTINUED.

ROCKETO

# MAP OF LUCERNE

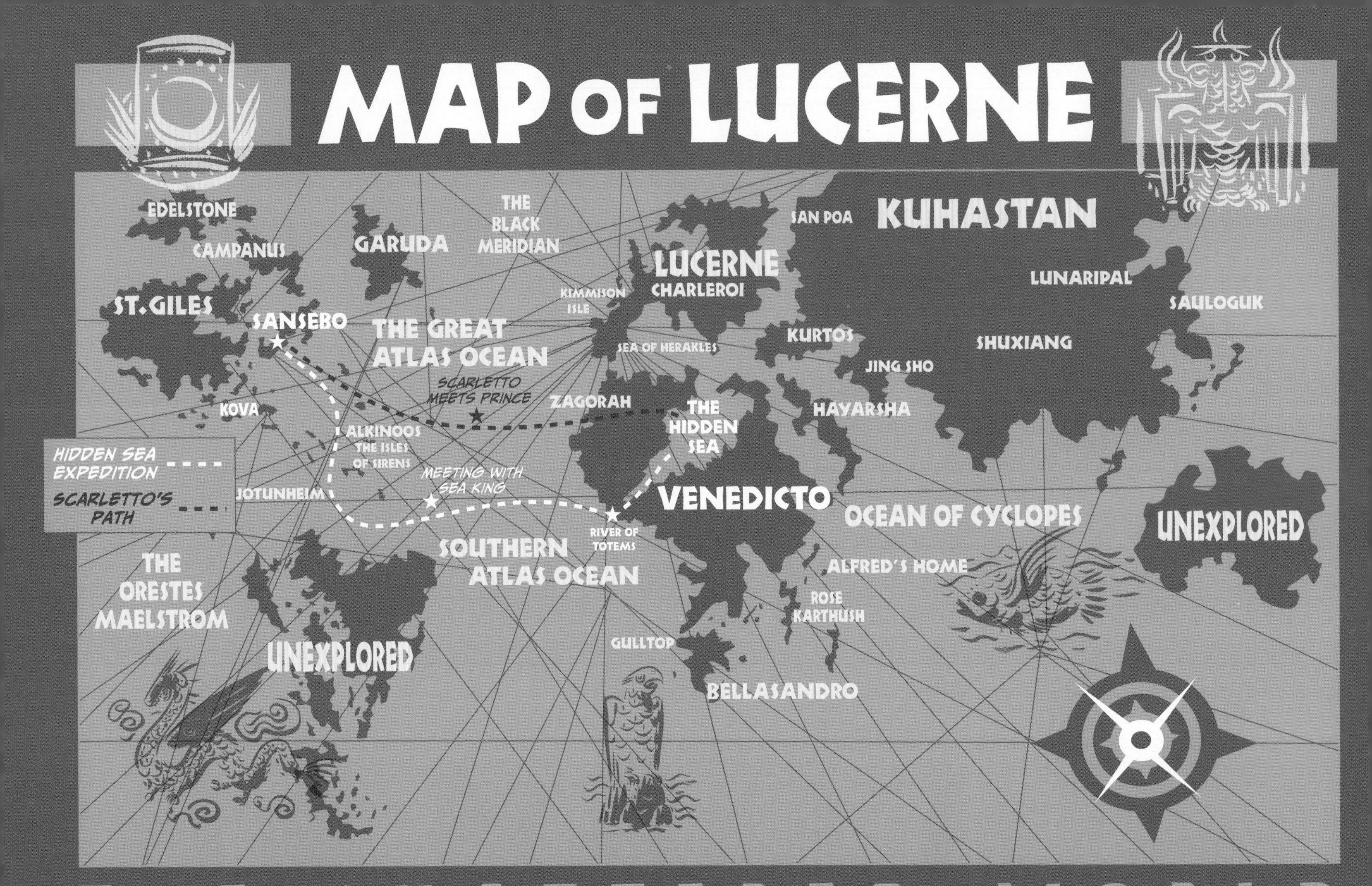

EDELSTONE
CAMPANUS
GARUDA
THE BLACK MERIDIAN
LUCERNE
CHARLEROI
SAN POA
KUHASTAN
LUNARIPAL
SAULOGUK
ST. GILES
SANSEBO
THE GREAT ATLAS OCEAN
KIMMISON ISLE
SEA OF HERAKLES
KURTOS
SHUXIANG
JING SHO
SCARLETTO MEETS PRINCE
ZAGORAH
THE HIDDEN SEA
HAYARSHA
KOVA
ALKINOOS
THE ISLES OF SIRENS
HIDDEN SEA EXPEDITION
SCARLETTO'S PATH
MEETING WITH SEA KING
JOTUNHEIM
VENEDICTO
OCEAN OF CYCLOPES
RIVER OF TOTEMS
UNEXPLORED
SOUTHERN ATLAS OCEAN
THE ORESTES MAELSTROM
ALFRED'S HOME
ROSE KARTHUSH
GULLTOP
UNEXPLORED
BELLASANDRO


THE SHATTERED WORLD

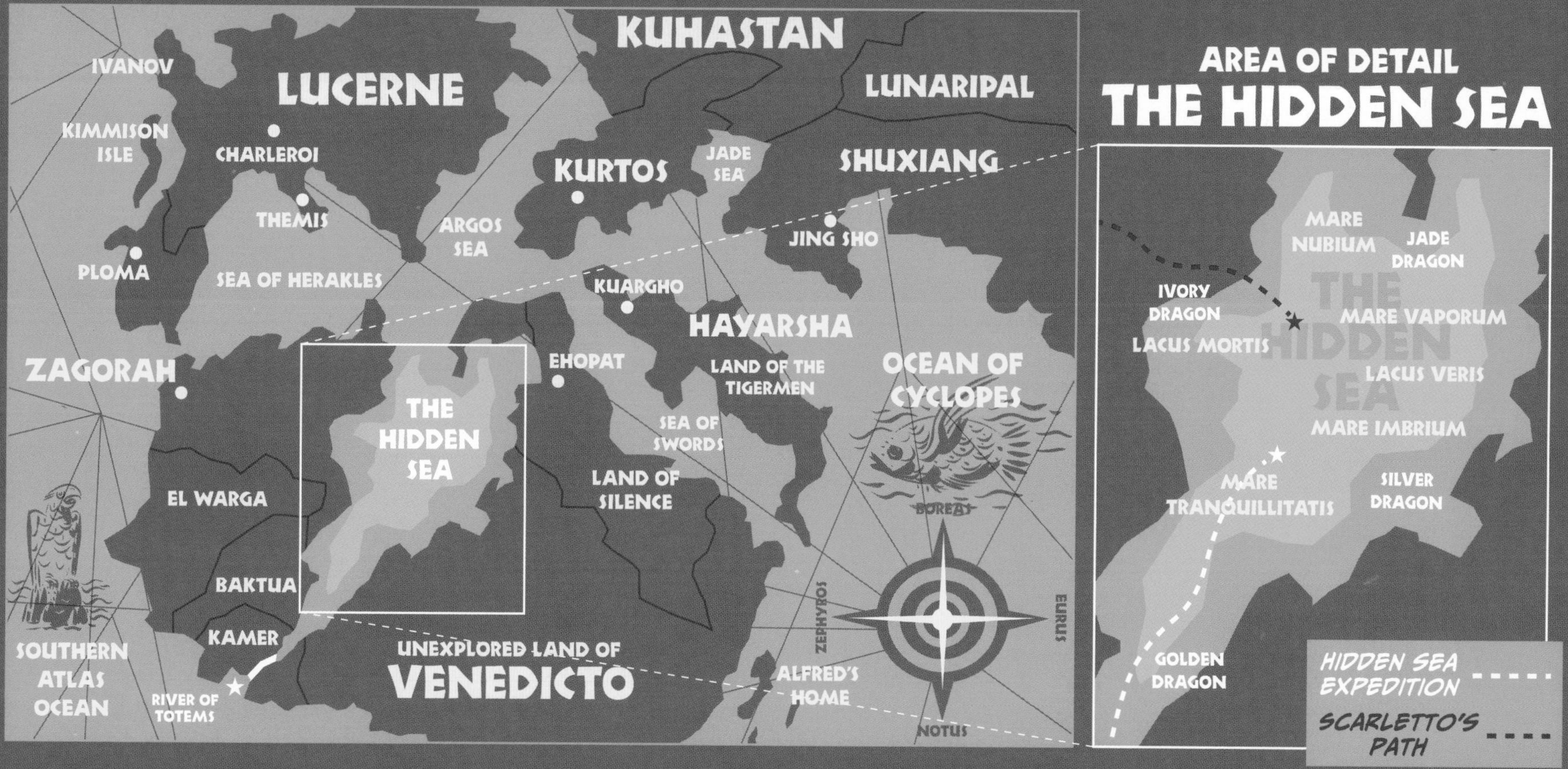
KUHASTAN
LUCERNE
LUNARIPAL
IVANOV
KIMMISON ISLE
CHARLEROI
KURTOS
JADE SEA
SHUXIANG
THEMIS
ARGOS SEA
JING SHO
PLOMA
SEA OF HERAKLES
KUARGHO
HAYARSHA
ZAGORAH
EHOPAT
LAND OF THE TIGERMEN
OCEAN OF CYCLOPES
THE HIDDEN SEA
SEA OF SWORDS
EL WARGA
LAND OF SILENCE
BOREAS
BAKTUA
ZEPHYROS
EURUS
KAMER
UNEXPLORED LAND OF
VENEDICTO
SOUTHERN ATLAS OCEAN
RIVER OF TOTEMS
ALFRED'S HOME
NOTUS
AREA OF DETAIL
THE HIDDEN SEA
MARE NUBIUM
JADE DRAGON
IVORY DRAGON
THE HIDDEN SEA
MARE VAPORUM
LACUS MORTIS
LACUS VERIS
MARE IMBRIUM
MARE TRANQUILLITATIS
SILVER DRAGON
GOLDEN DRAGON
HIDDEN SEA EXPEDITION
SCARLETTO'S PATH

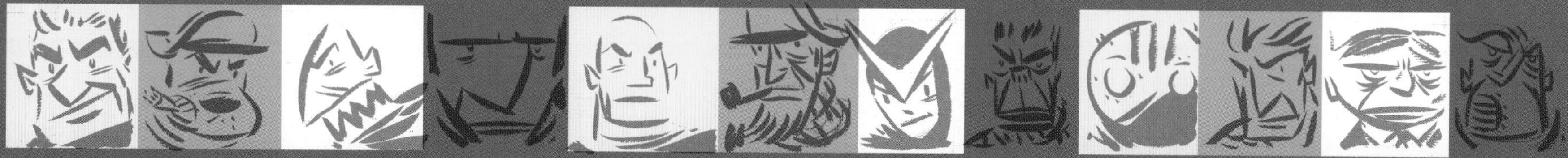

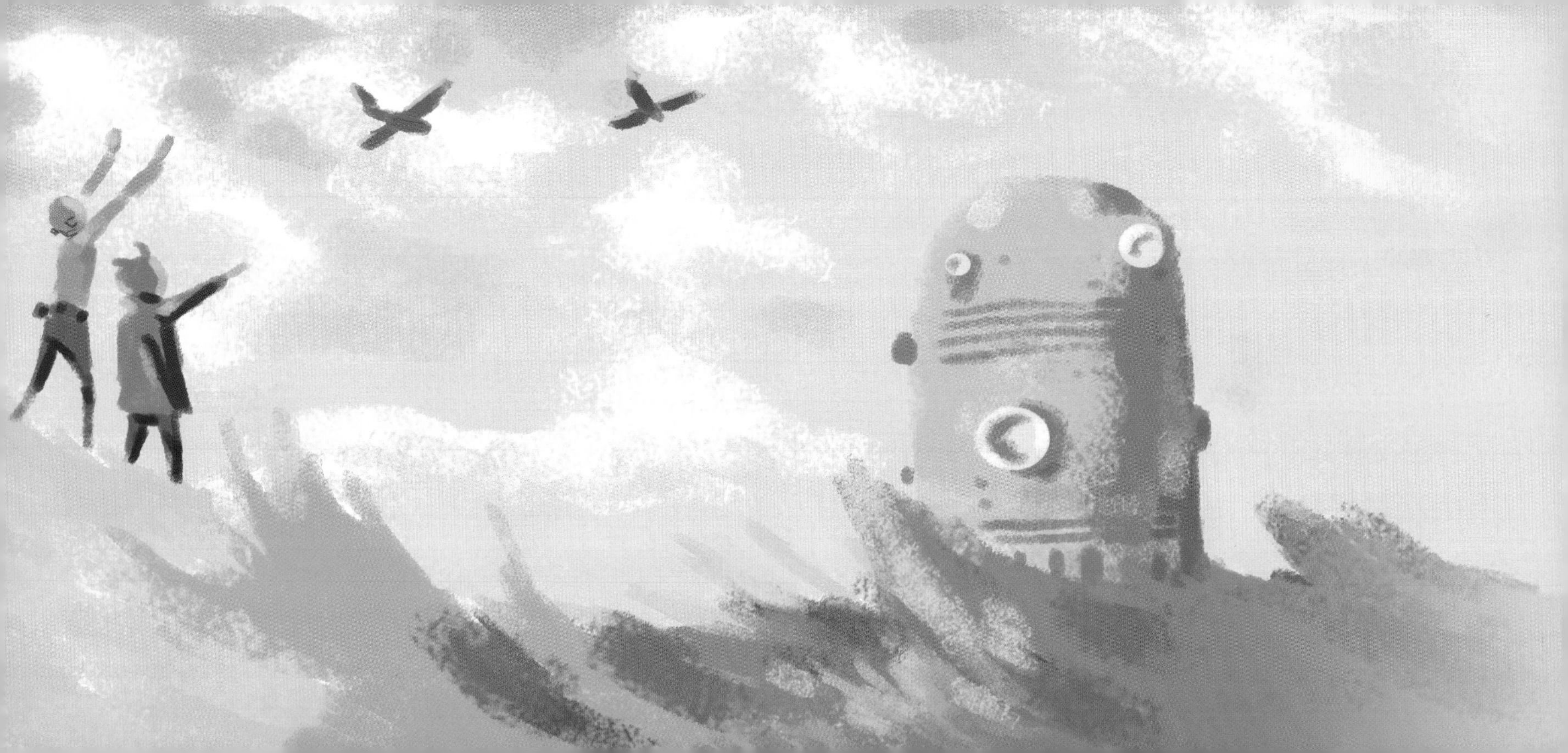

# THE ART OF ROCKETO™

NEW WORLD GEOGRAPHIC SOCIETY MUSEUM

SKETCHES

ILLUSTRATIONS

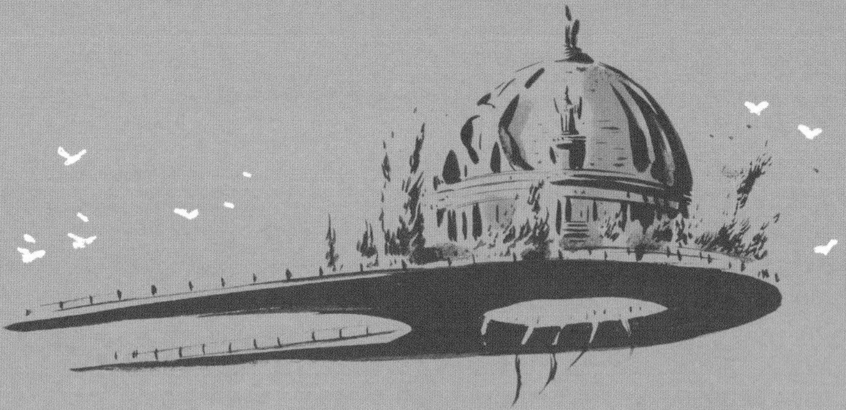

# New World Geographic Society Museum

## Porto Logas, St. Giles

### A Short History of the New World Geographic Society

The New World Geographic Society was founded in 1920 in Sansebo by noted Mapper, Rocketo Garrison, with the goals of promoting world-wide exploration, education and peace.

The New World Society quickly entered troubled waters and for many years was opposed by the powerful Mapping Guild. Viewing the Society as a rival organization, the Guild objected to the organization's political stance, training of female Mappers and promotion of an integrated world culture.

Matters came to a head in 1922 when a rash of murders occurred at San Pao, international headquarters of the Mapping Guild. (*1) The Society immediately came under suspicion and it was only through the efforts of Rocketo Garrison that the mystery was solved and the Society exonerated. (*2)

By 1926, the Society had over 300 members and exploration throughout the new world was extensive. It was during this period the history culture of Bellasandro was so fully documented by Petros Overfield and the initial explorations of the great land masses between the Southern Atlas Ocean and Orestes Maelstrom were begun.

Advances in the scientific fields and the shifting political alliances between Lucerne and the Eastern Block highlighted the next decade. With space travel now a possibility and not a dream, scientists and explorers flocked to join the New World Geographic Society. Again, conflict arose between the Society and the Mapping Guild over the limited resources available for space exploration. One of the greatest adventures yet recorded, narrated in Journey to the Shattered Moon, was led by Rocketo Garrison and his team of intrepid explorers. (*3)

When the Great Devastation came in 1942, the Society was among the leading forces in the defense of the world. (*4)

By the time that Rocketo Garrison mysteriously disappeared in 1945, he had set up the Porto Logas Foundation and arranged for the New World Geographic Society Museum to be located at the Porto Logas headquarters. The facility is now shared by the Society and Spiro Turnstiles, executor of Garrison's estate.

The Society hopes that you will enjoy the exhibits at the Museum and stop by our Gift Shop in the exit area.

To begin your tour, go to the Venedicto Room on the right.

*1: The Mapping Guild produced an alternative view of the events in The Murders of San Pao by Eurydice Smith, 1956, Pool Press.

*2: The Journey to the New World by Rocketo Garrison, New World Press, published 1928, offers a narrative of this period from the explorer's personal perspective.

*3: For another perspective, read My Life on the Moon by Penelope Wintergarten, Black Publishing, 1936.

*4: The Journey to Ultamo, Rocketo Garrison, New World Press, 1944, is the definitive text on this subject.

## The Museum

Welcome to the New World Geographic Society Museum located at the historic Porto Logas Observatory in St. Giles. The Museum is located on the lower level of the observatory.

The Museum is open to the general public every Thursday through Sunday from 10 a.m. to 7 p.m. Docent-led tours of the exhibits are scheduled on the hour. Private tours may be arranged by calling the administrative office during weekday business hours. There is a nominal charge for admittance with special rates for children, seniors and the handicapped.

The upper level of Porto Logas is the former residence of noted Mapper, Rocketo Garrison and there is absolutely no admittance without an appointment through museum management.

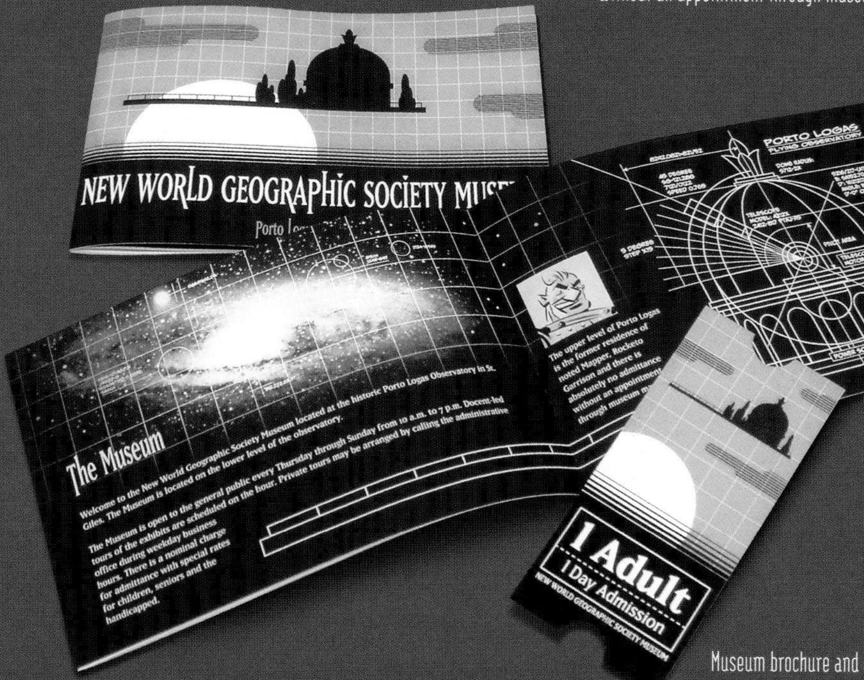
PORTO LOGAS
FLYING OBSERVATORY
The Museum
1 Adult
1 Day Admission
NEW WORLD GEOGRAPHIC SOCIETY MUSEUM

Museum brochure and admission ticket.

# Sketches

Some pages from my sketch books that I have kept throughout the development of this project. For me, the early part where it can go anywhere is always the time to play, think, explore.

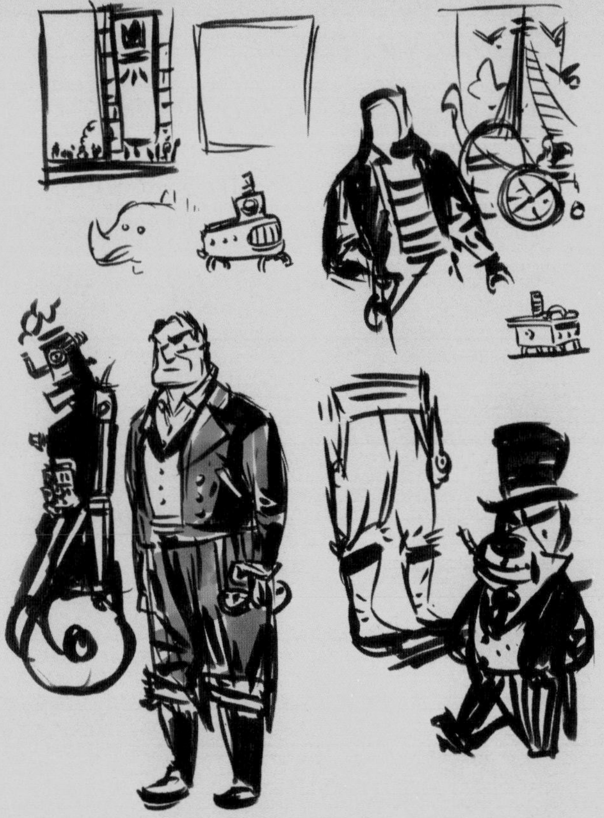

Some early work of Spiro and Rocketo. I really like the outfit Roc wears in this and now its finding the place for him to wear it. The initial idea behind these drawings was a more Jules Verne like version of St. Giles.

Rocketo after the Solarium war... Broken with no place to go... This is the sketch that started the story to move in that direction, and then I never used it in the actual book.

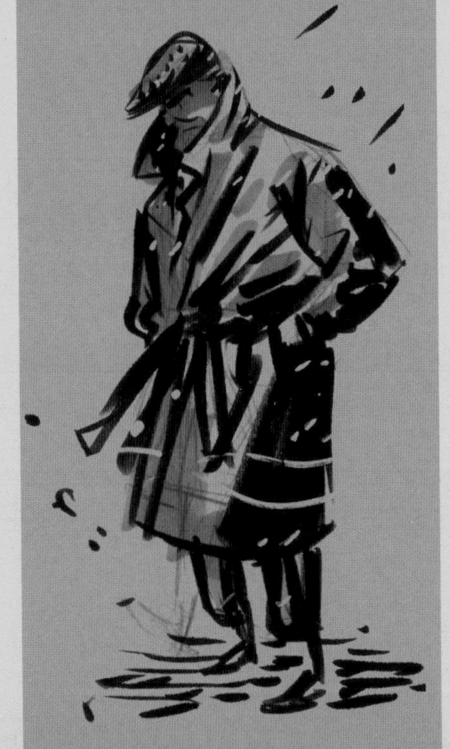

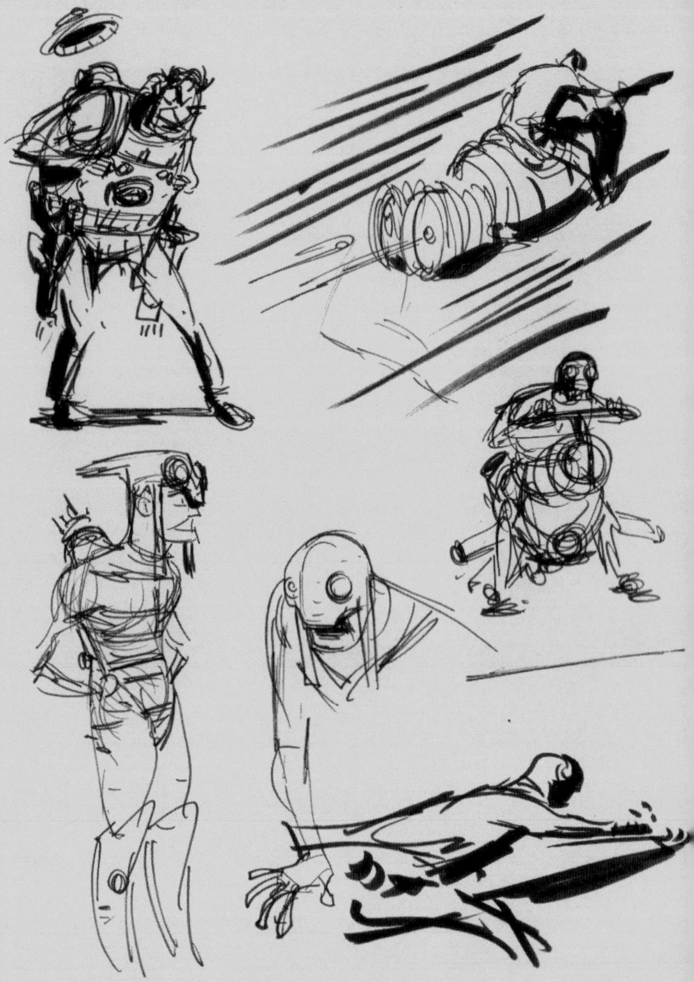

Some samples devices used for long range and short range flight. I settled on a spinning circular disc that somehow lifts the person through the air. Because in the New World technology is based more on genetics, the spinning disc would be a biological device instead of mechanical.

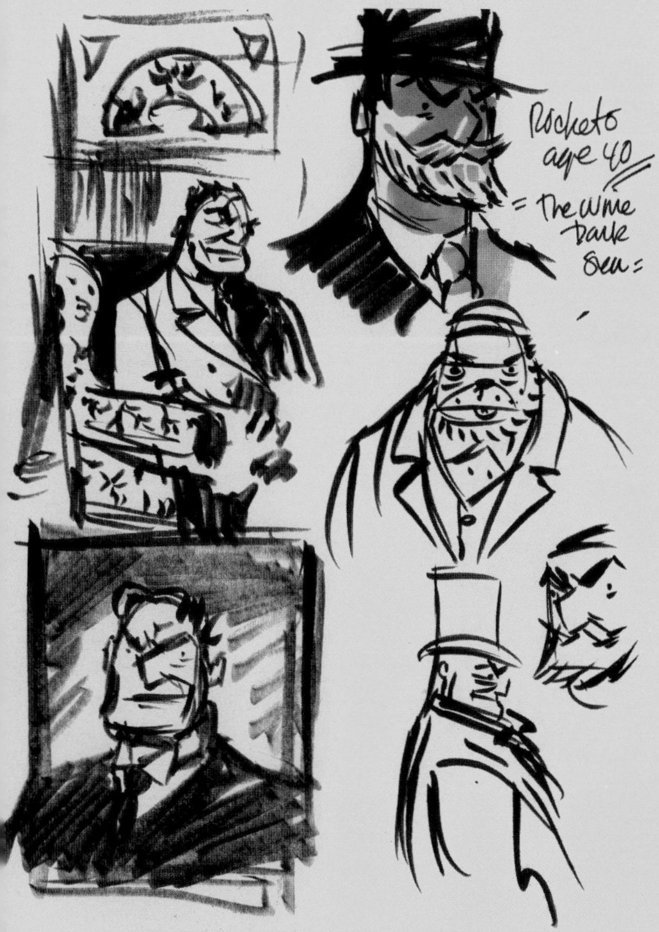
Rocketo age 40
= The Wine Dark Sea =

As the Journeys of Rocketo move forward in time naturally ages. In this sketches I am playing around with a beard for the earlier part of the story Journey to the Broken Moon.

Many drawings went into designing Rocketo, on of the earlier more interesting ideas was to have him scarred up after his torture by the Royalist. giving him a patchwork effect.

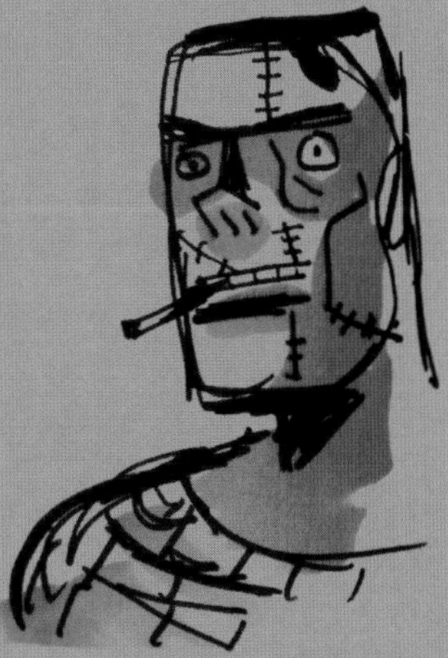

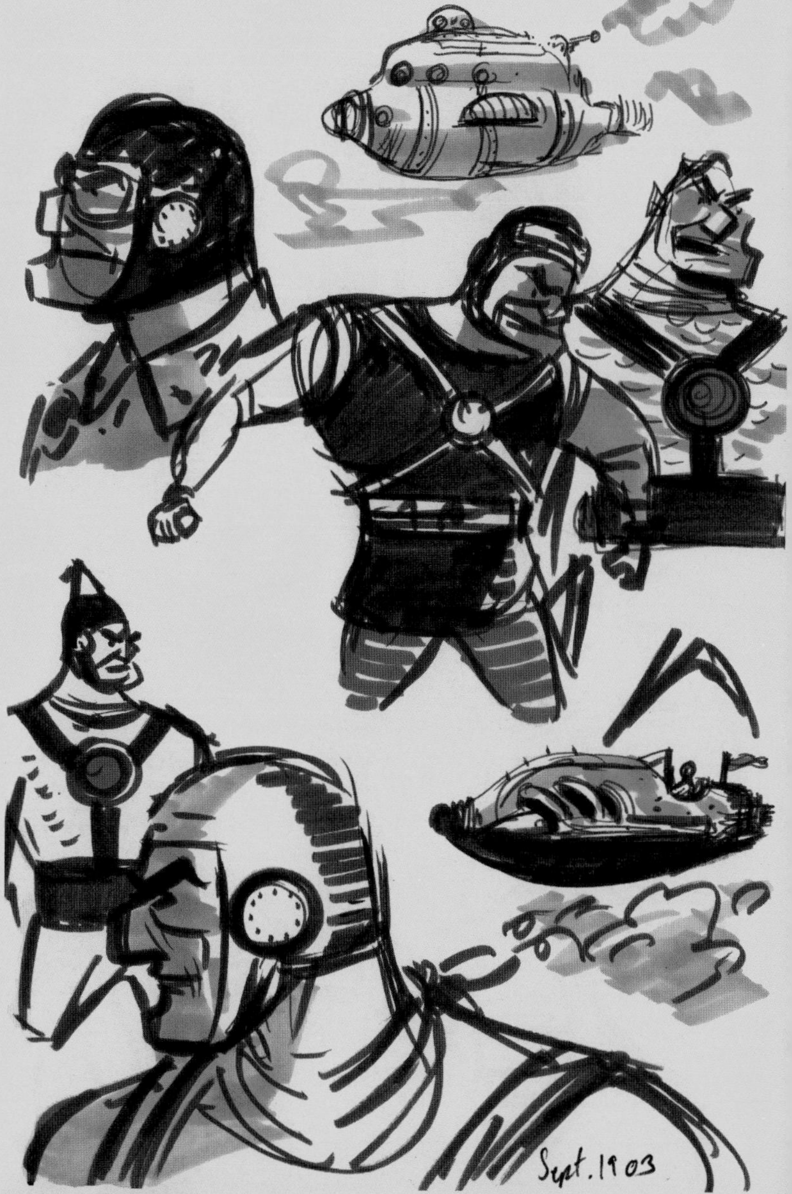
Sept. 1903

As Rocketo took form I wanted to see how graphic I could get with the profile shots. How much I could push that blasted nose. Also some experiments with different outfits he would don as the adventure requires.

PLAINS OF GARUDA / - The last
Battle was Fought -

meeting with
GARUDA / Nature
man...
one of ten
left in the
Planet...

come in ...

Poet.. Henning'-
Du lancet ....
From St. Giles ...

Sigfried knows
these fellows..
Rocketo doesn't

Tigerman?

Sigfried

BOAZ -

Jokon
and
ughtheanteln
Pal of
Rocketo.

Wizard
with machine

searching for
a piece of land to
claim for Garuda ...

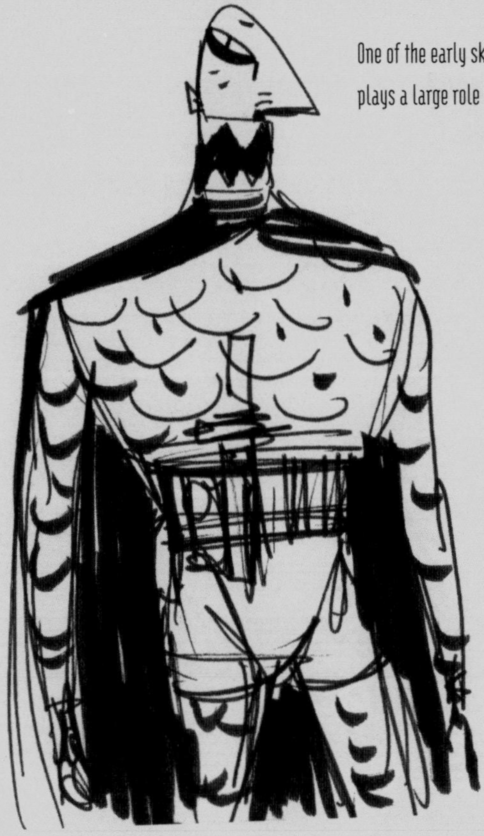

One of the early sketches of Boaz. Silent and mysterious Boaz
plays a large role in Rocketo Journey to the New World.

In this sketch we see Scarletto
very early in development. He
was much more realistic, and I
felt he need to become more
graphic and simple in his lines.

Some rough designs for Epiku, I wanted Epiku to look
like an Easter Island statue come to life, but still
play around with the idea that he was plant like.

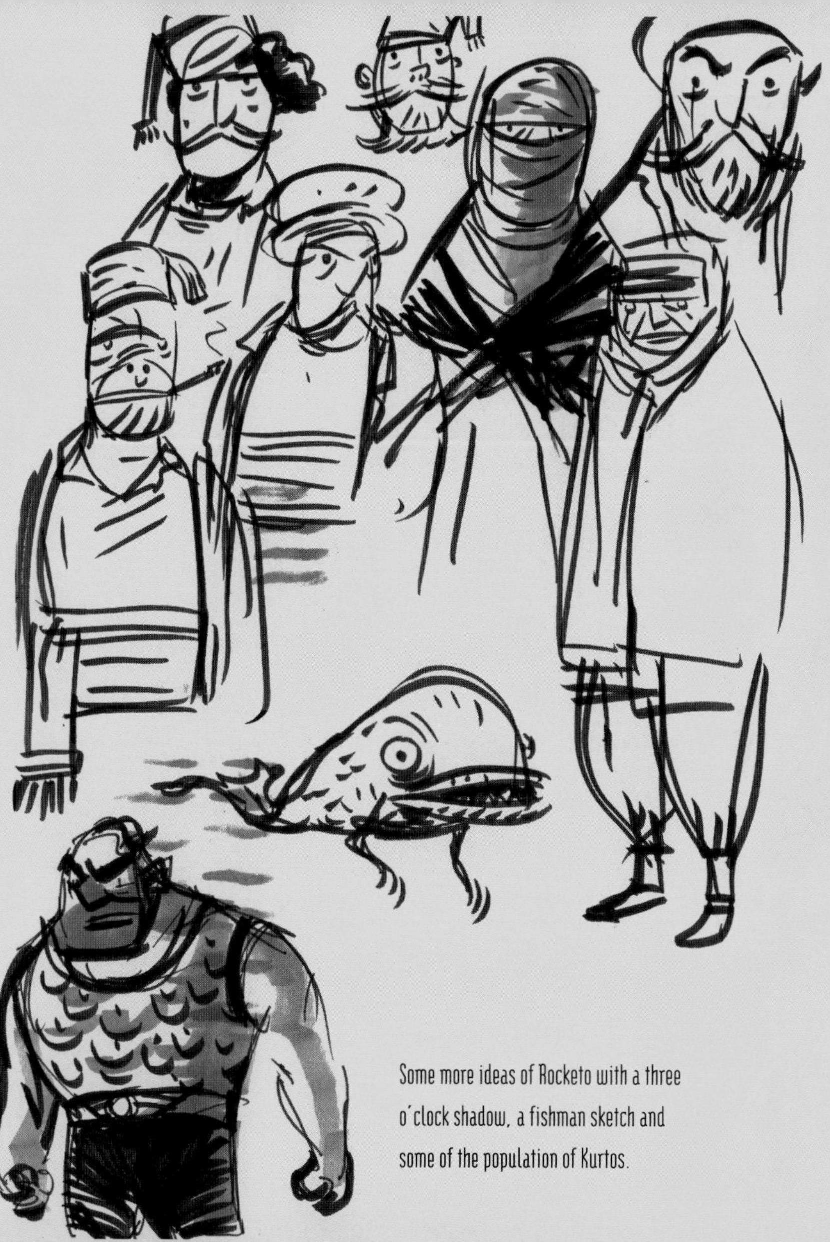

Some more ideas of Rocketo with a three o´clock shadow, a fishman sketch and some of the population of Kurtos.

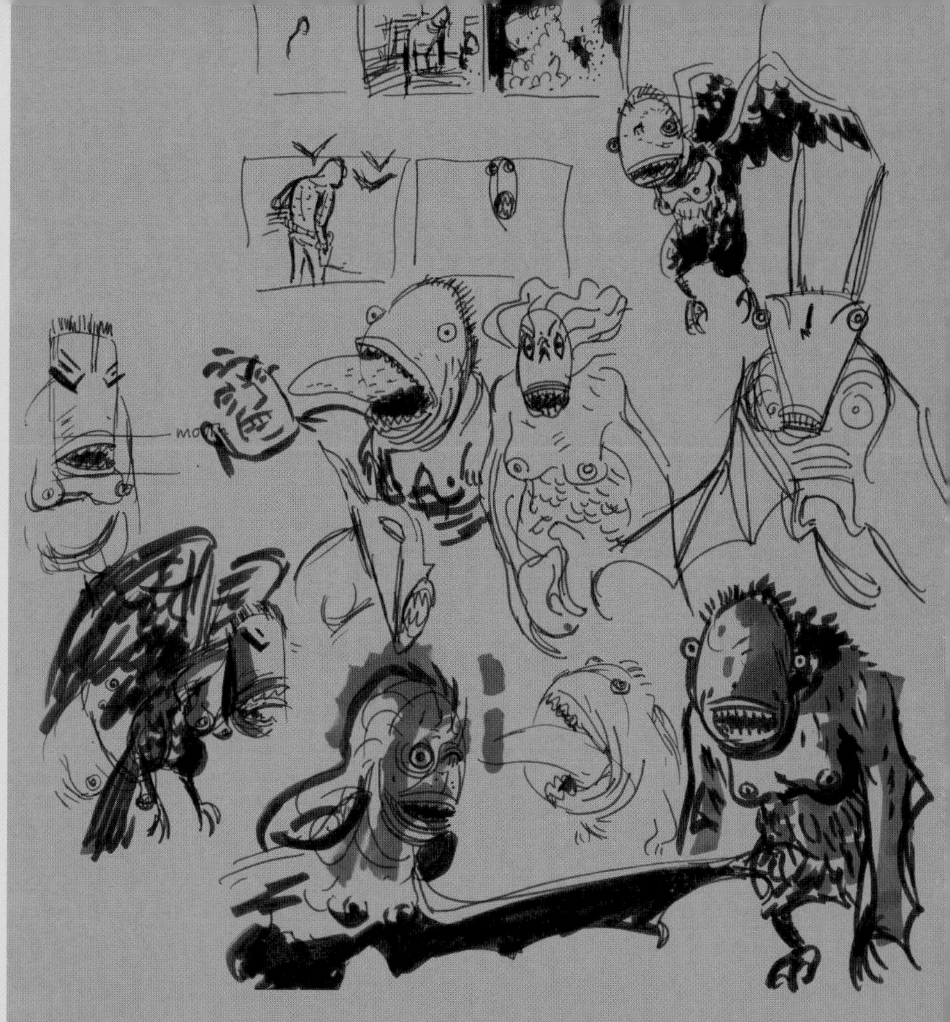

The Harpies of Venedicto were fun to play with and while only in this story for a short time will be back in the later books.

Here are some early studies of the Tigermen. I pretty much kept the same design for the books. It was one of the few characters that flowed easily. The notes stress the point that the Tigermen belong neither to the Commonwealth nor the Royalists.

FIREMOUNTS

Zonas steel can up to 10

Bandit tribes fig against one anot and also the Commo and Ro

KIN

NOMADIC MEN who live in the high hills .. of KAMBUL ..

The great Hiram Arkwright, the master mind of Lucerne, was another easy character to design. His roots go back more than ten years to when Rocketo was called Major Rocket, his first incarnation. I decided to bring back the original design, just making it a bit darker around the eyes.

That is Rocketo with the sword in his mouth in one of the early concepts of the Journey to the Hidden Sea. Rocketo came back from the war only to become an air pirate, a raider of ships. I was playing around with more of a Sinbad the Sailor feel that I later abandoned.

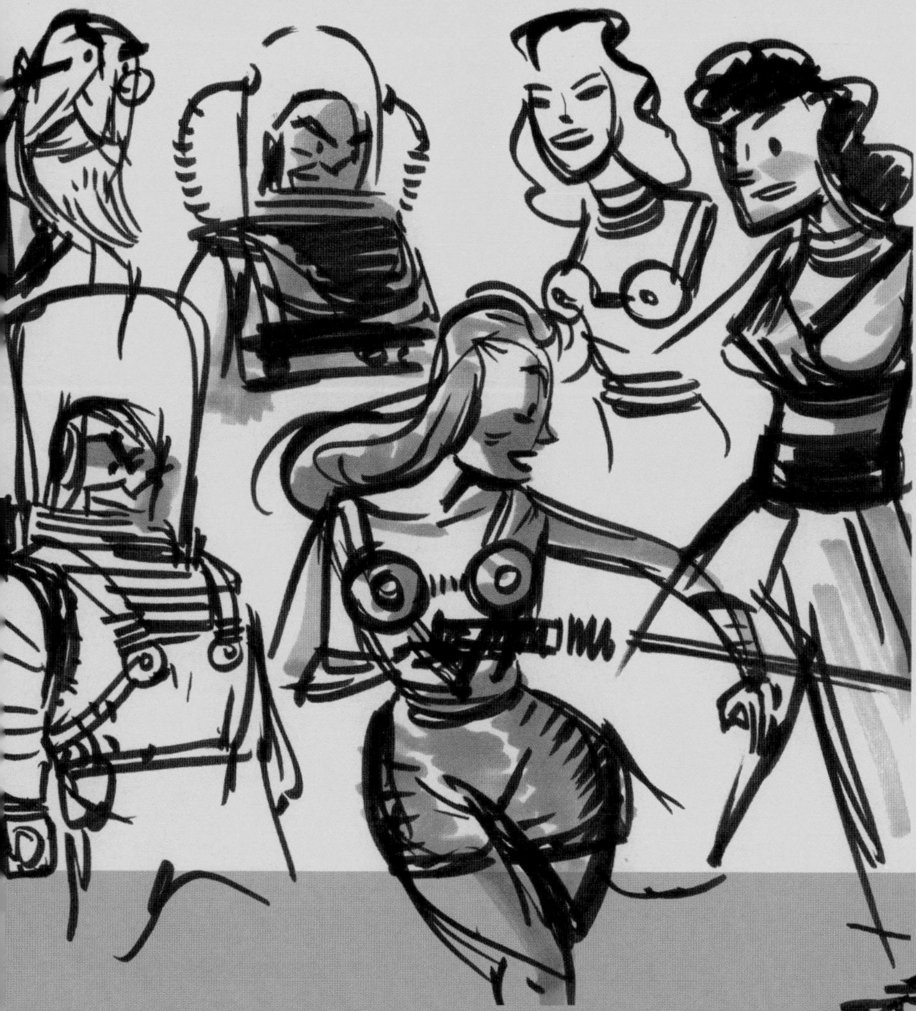

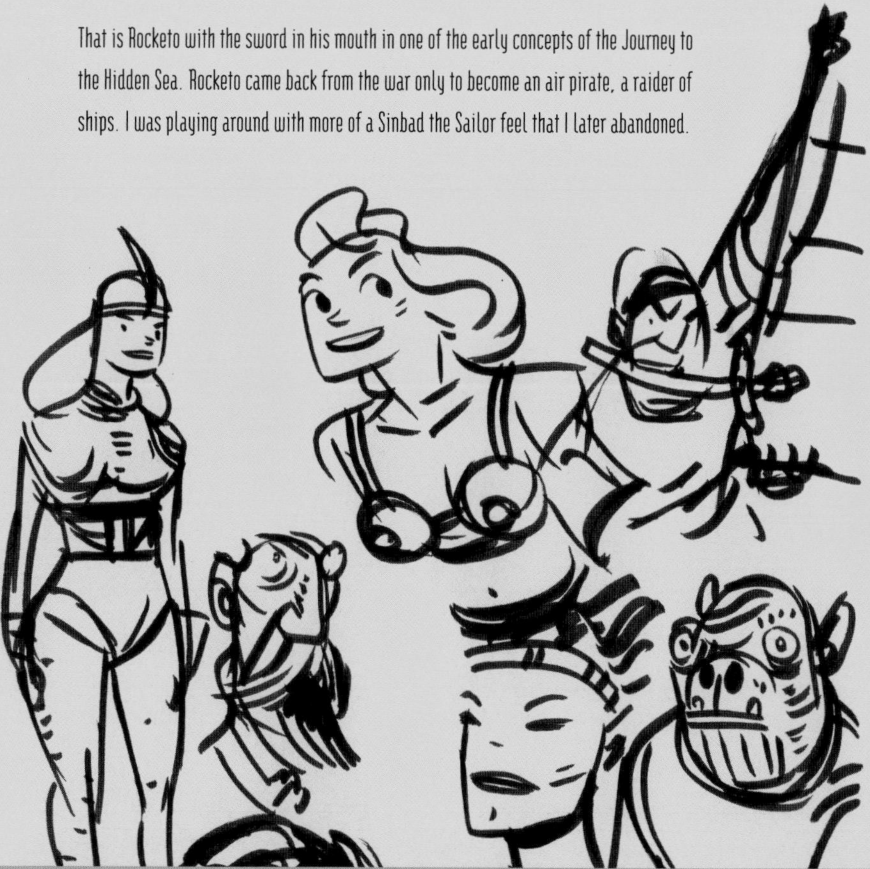

Here are some ideas for a girl character that Rocketo will meet in the later Journeys; some early concept work on the spacesuits; and some ships for the Journey to the Broken Moon.

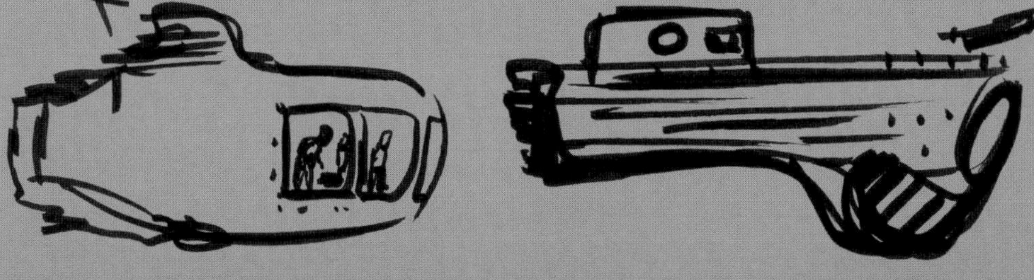

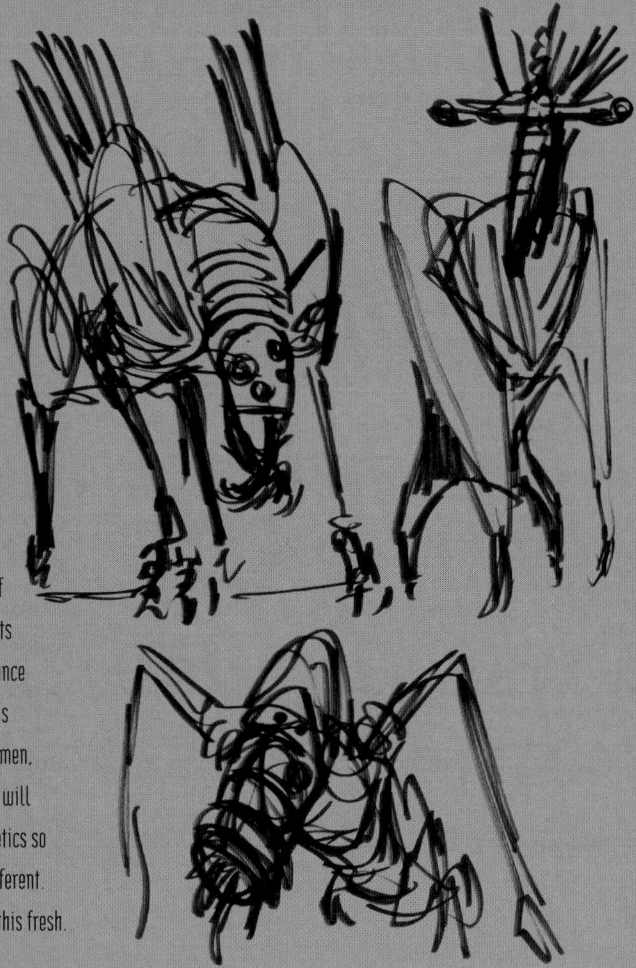

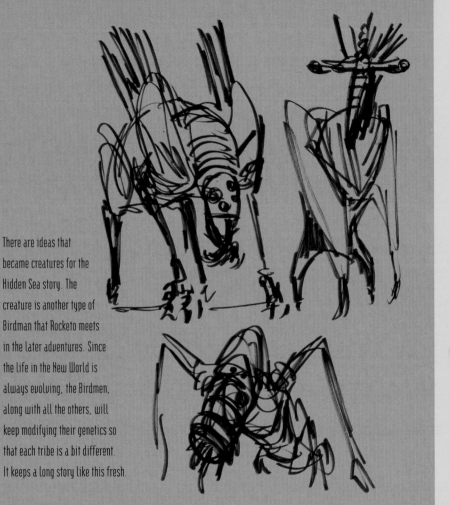

There are ideas that became creatures for the Hidden Sea story. The creature is another type of Birdman that Rocketo meets in the later adventures. Since the life in the New World is always evolving, the Birdmen, along with all the others, will keep modifying their genetics so that each tribe is a bit different. It keeps a long story like this fresh.

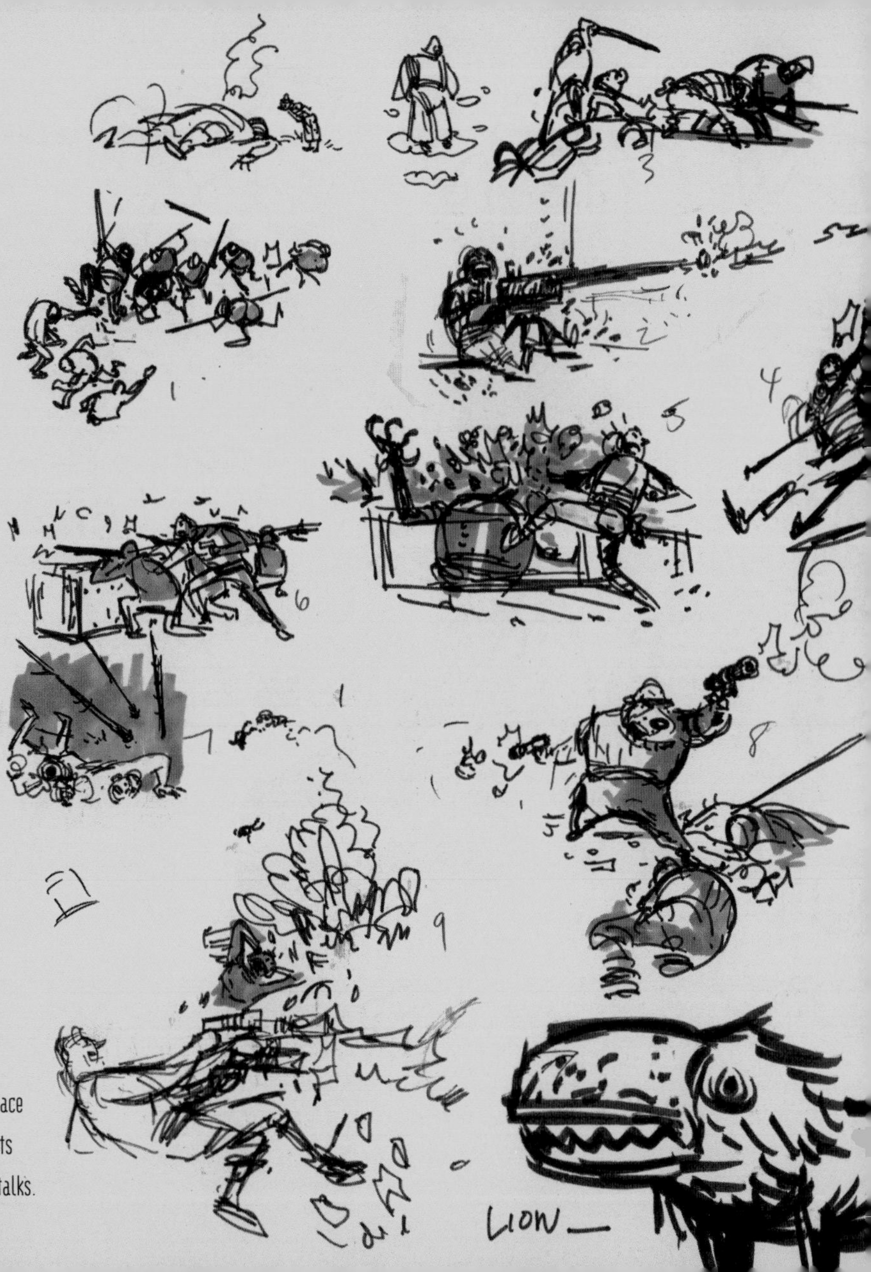
LION

These are some story ideas for a fight that was supposed to take place in the River of Totems. For timing, I cut out although it will make its way into another story. The Lion is one of my favorites and it also talks.

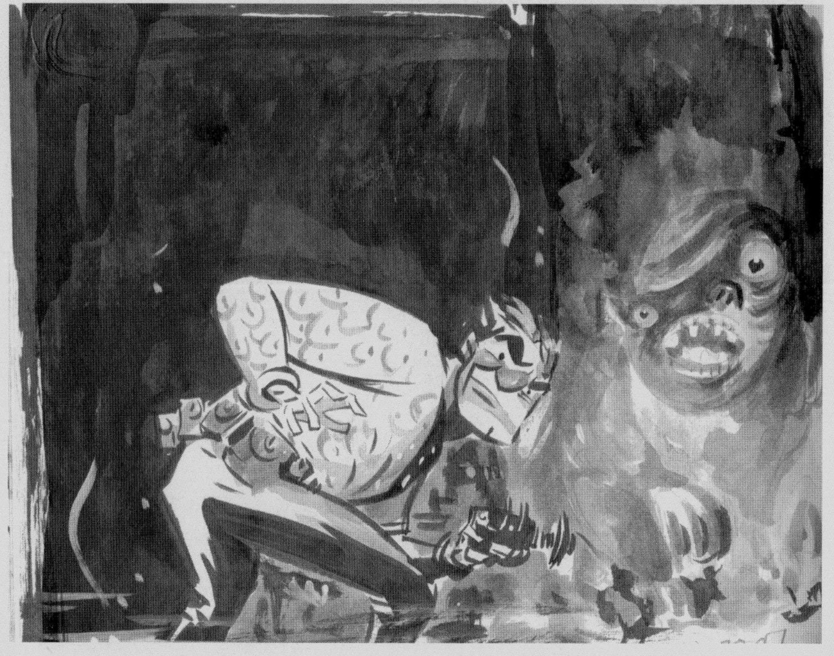

These were done early in the morning before work, playing around with wash. I love the look of ink and water when the tones mix and I have no idea what is going to happen next. They add a freshness that can never be repeated again. I would love to do a whole Rocketo book in pure dark washes.

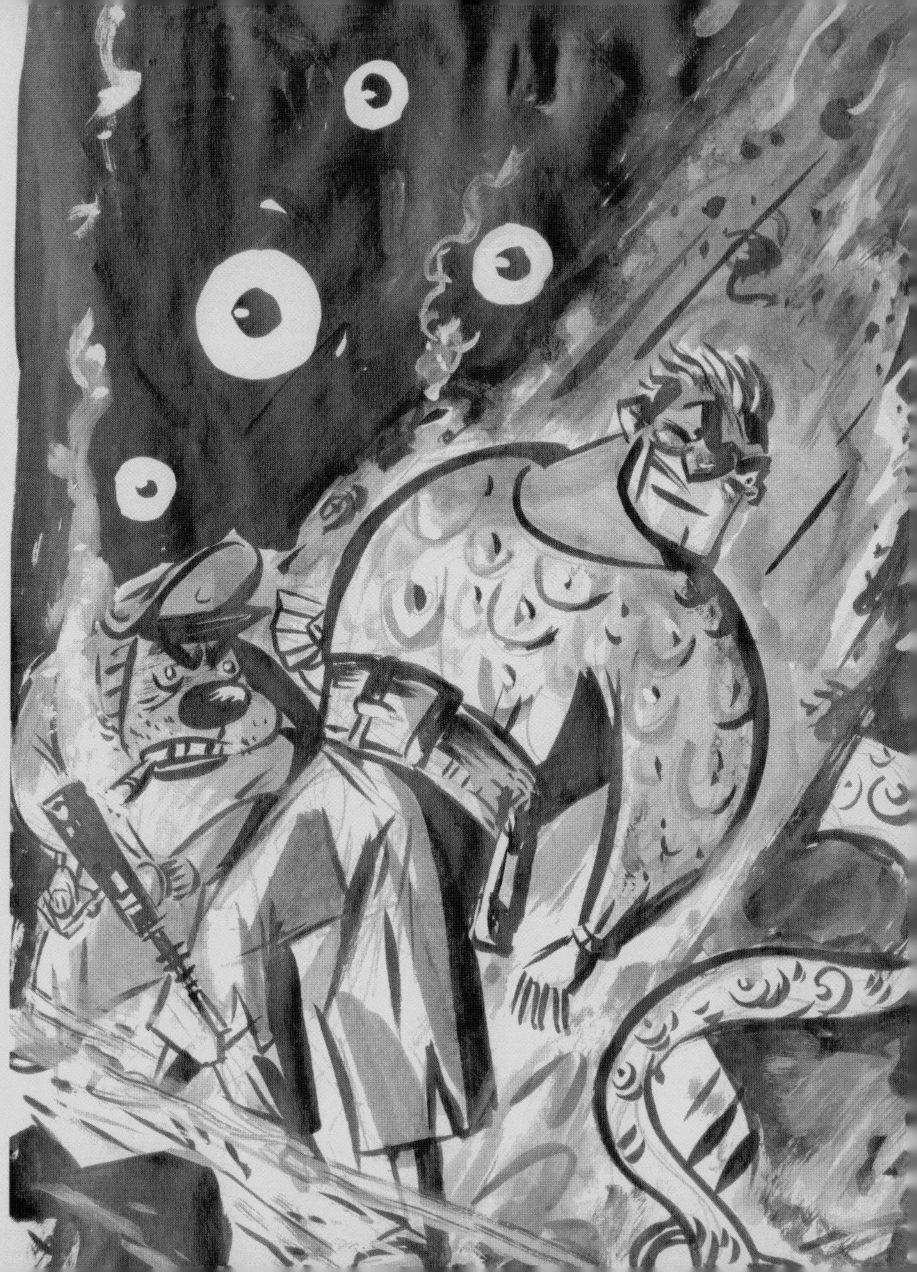

# ILLUSTRATIONS

Many of these paintings were done after the book was done, I wanted to revisit the early books and give them a new spin on color and style while trying to keep the spirit of the book.

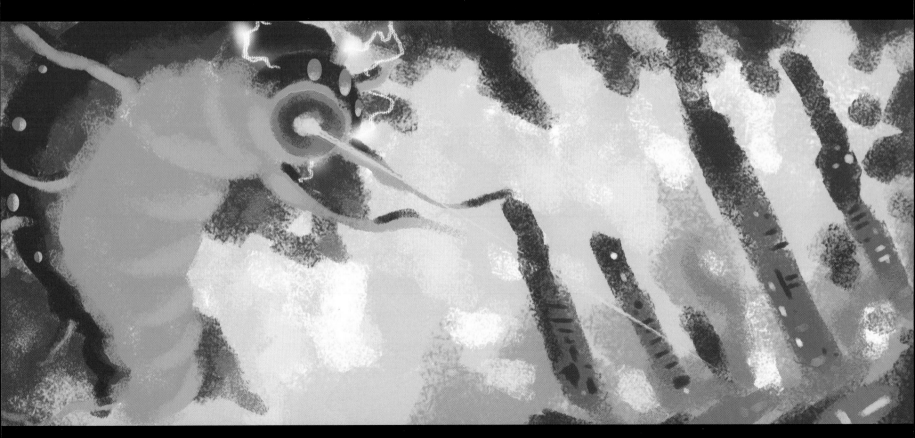

The great Ull attacks the Earth. Fire and devastation rain down on Mankind and sets the stage for the rebirth of the world.

The Mapping Guild was originally going to play a more important role in the early issues of Journey to the Hidden Sea. But I decided to leave it out and save it for the next book, **Journey to the New World**, where it is the central focus of the story.

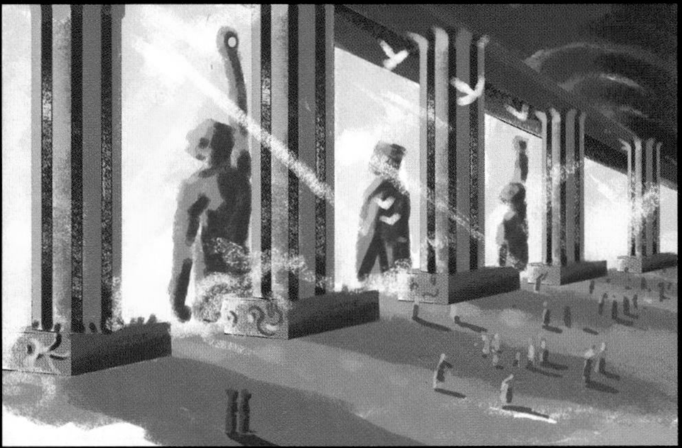

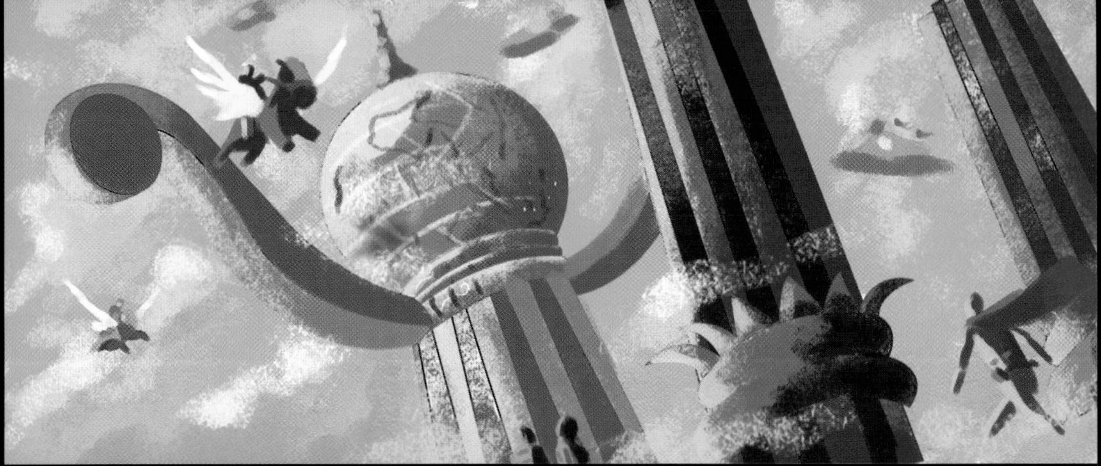

I'm still working out solutions for the visual look to the next series of books. Every gate in San Poa serves a different function in ritual and in design. The West Gate is the entry point the Mappers after a long Journey.

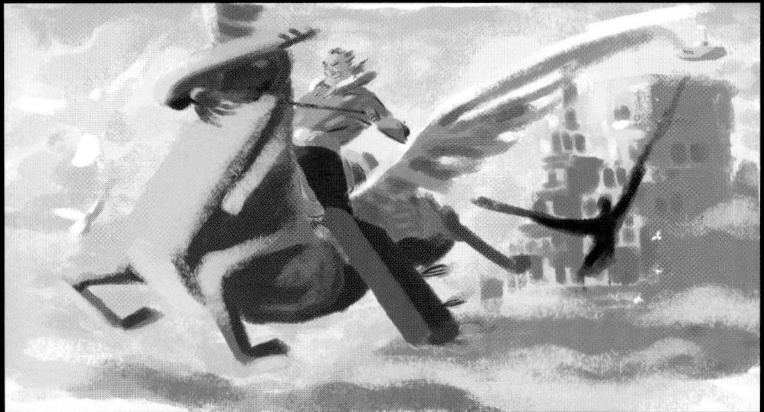

Originally Rocketo would go to San Poa and by asked to join the Mapping Guild. He would go through some training and from there begin his explorations.

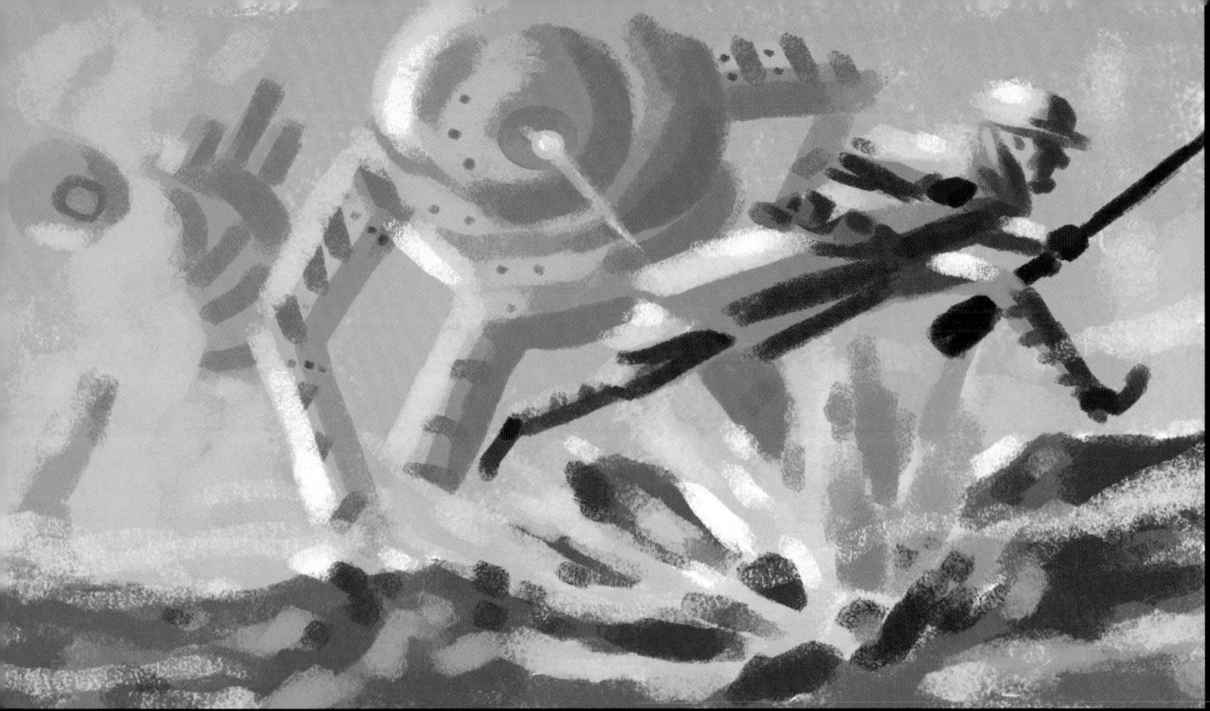

Rocketo joins the Solarium War. Because of time constraints I could not show the complete story behind Rocketo's role in the war. In this sketch he is fighting in the trenches.

Another sketch of Rocketo in the horrors of the war. Even though he joins the 7th Dragoons early on in the war, known for their flying horse attacks, Rocketo in my mind's eye would also spend many a day deep in a fox hole.

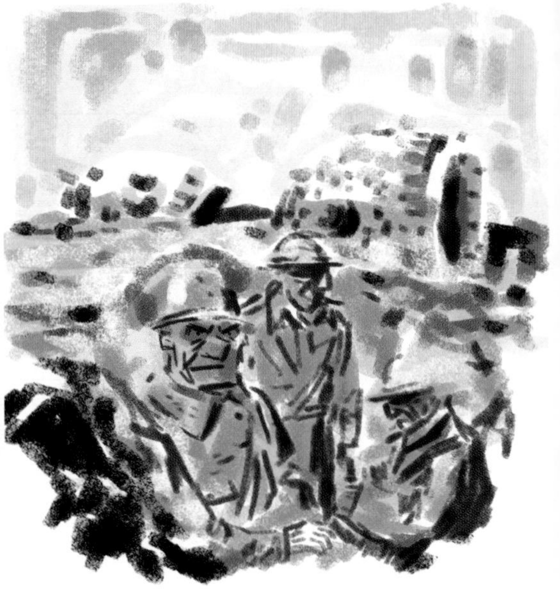

The conflict between the famous 7th Dragoons against the Royalist Mutants is one of my favorite battle scenes.
In this color study I wanted to bring it more into dimension and use it for a larger painting.

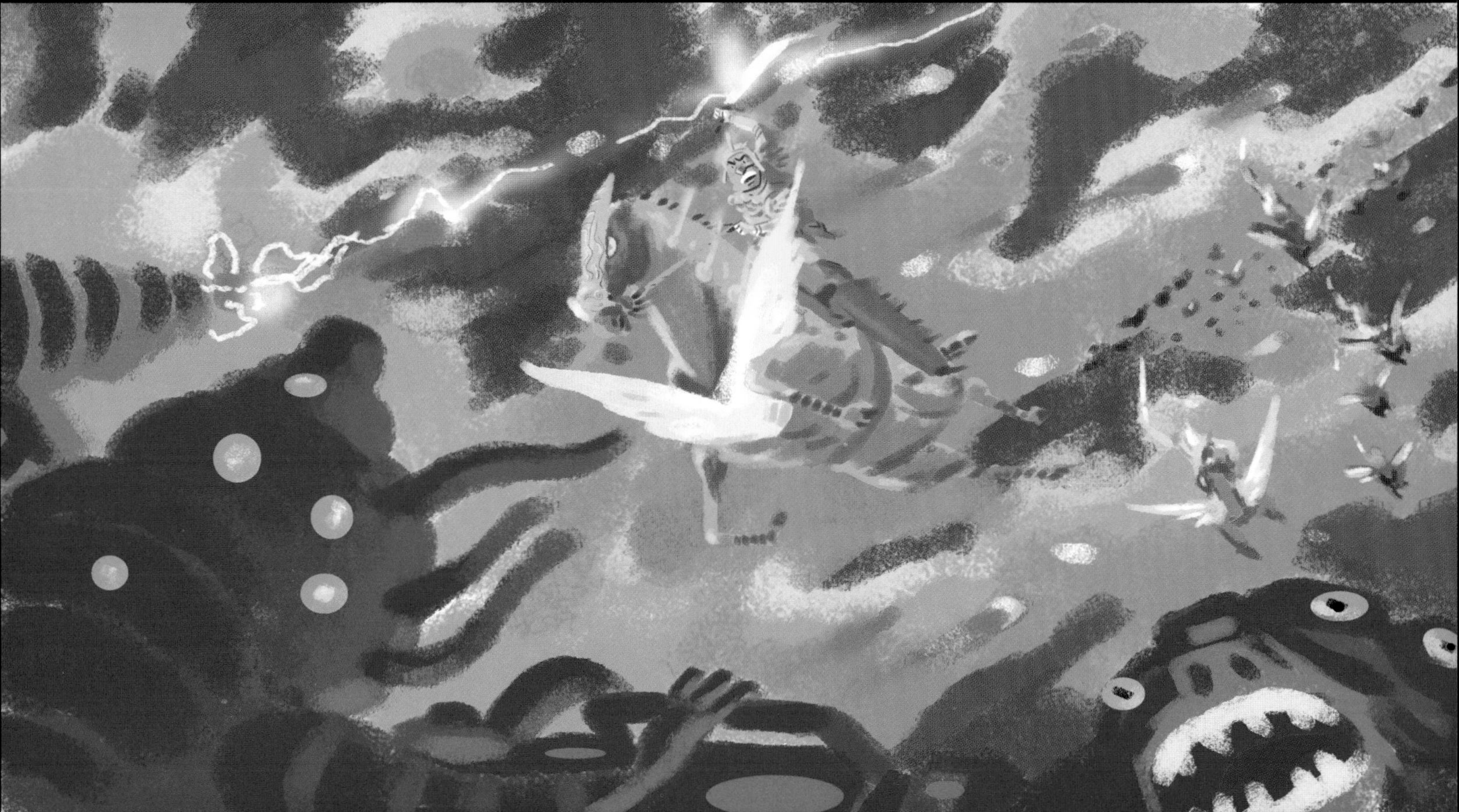

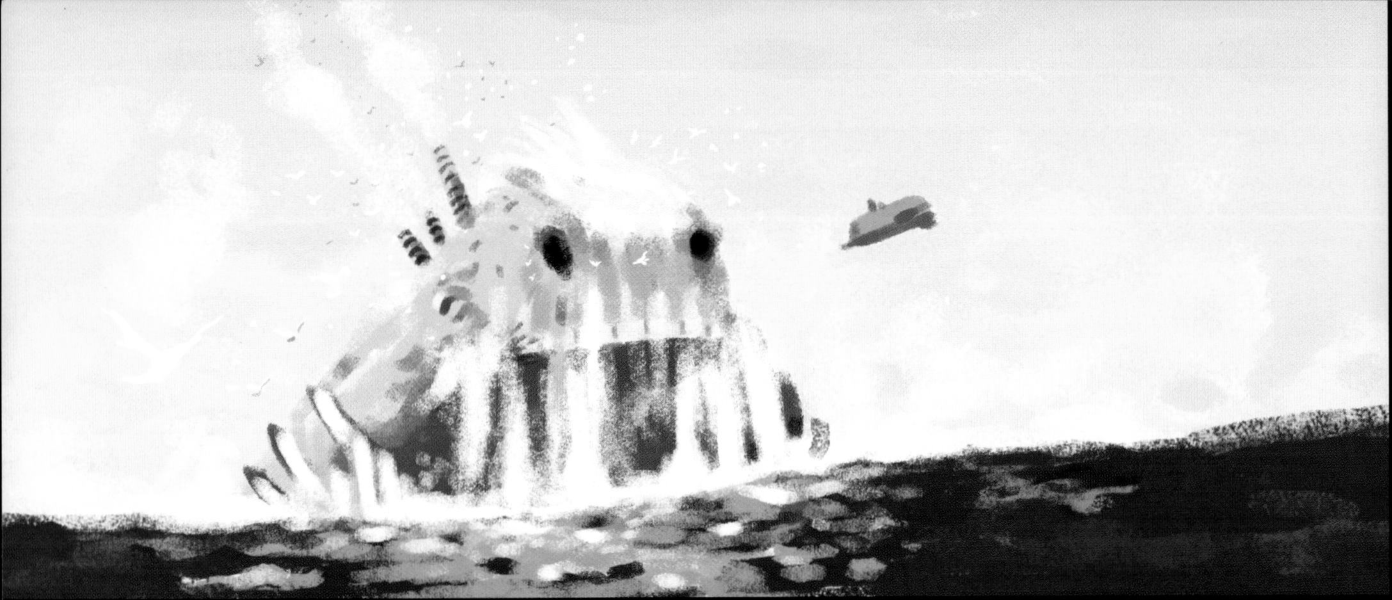

This is a study for the Sea King who will make some appearances in the later Journeys. The wise old man of the Sea is incredibly old and can remember all who cross his Ocean.

The flying carpet of the Silent Men, plays an important role in the **Journey to the Hidden Sea** as Rocketo and Scarletto come face to face in the Sea of Derelicts.

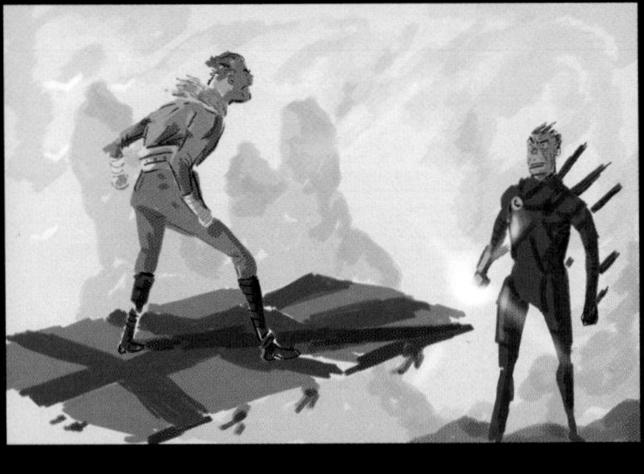

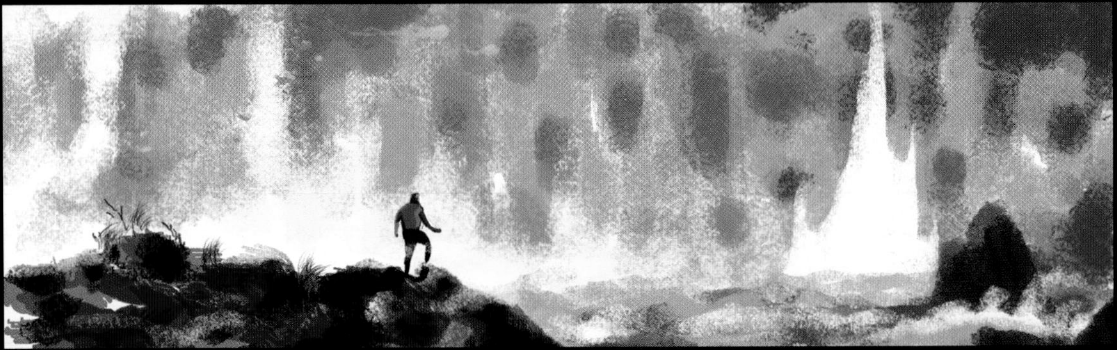

I was trying to figure out the colors and textures that I would play with to depict the Hidden Sea. A giant crater full of strange mists, it serves as the backdrop for more than half the book.

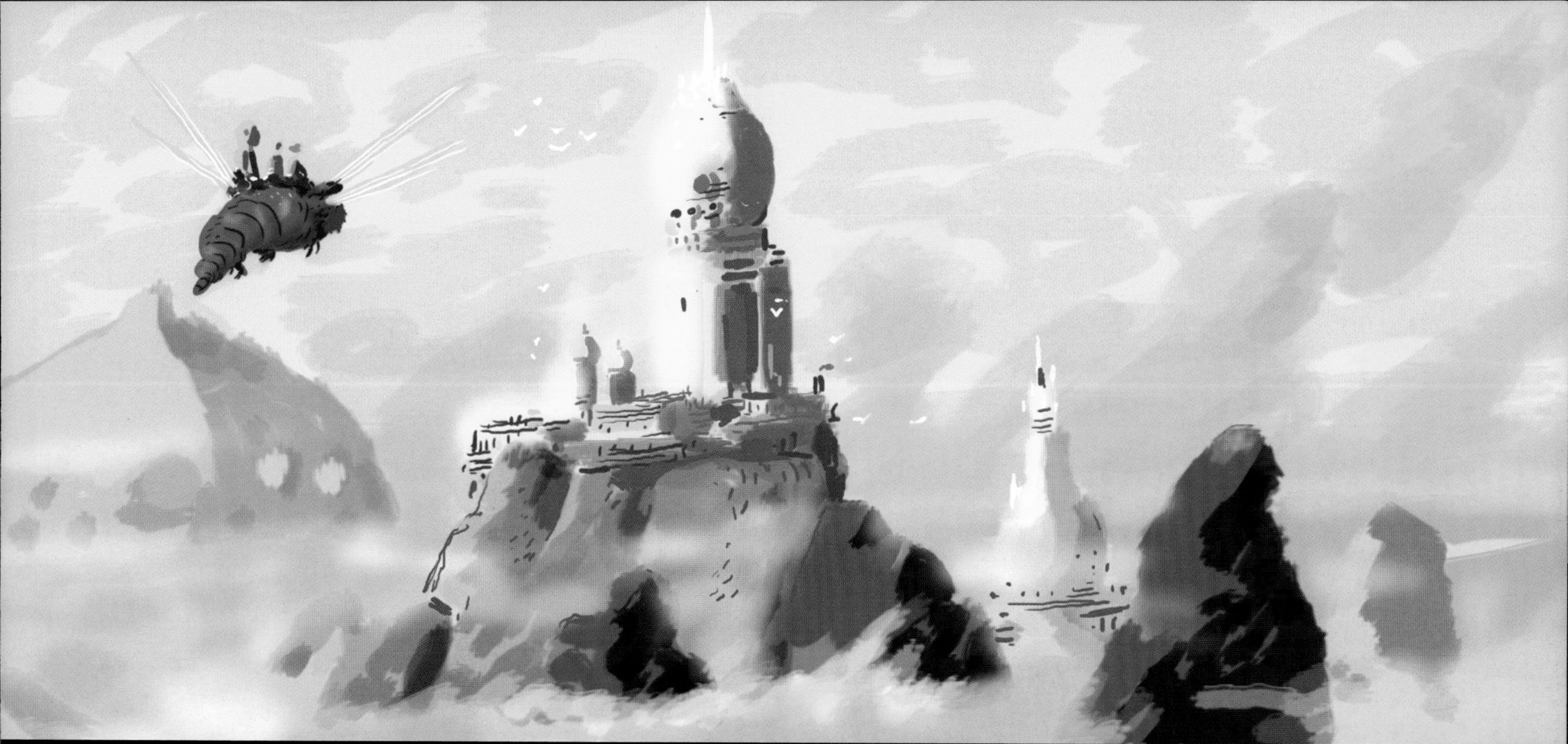

Some concepts for a city deep in the Hidden Sea. This city is one of the set pieces that Rocketo finds in the second half of the Journey to the Hidden Sea.

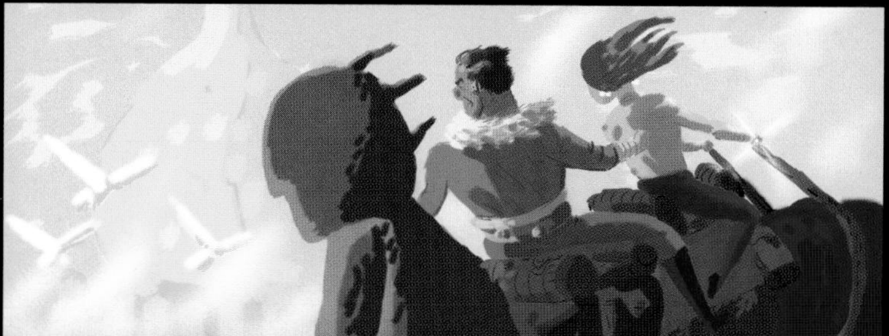

This study for a Birdman shows the colors and decorations along the belt and beak which serve as clan and status symbols. Here the Birdman flies in the mist of the Hidden Sea.

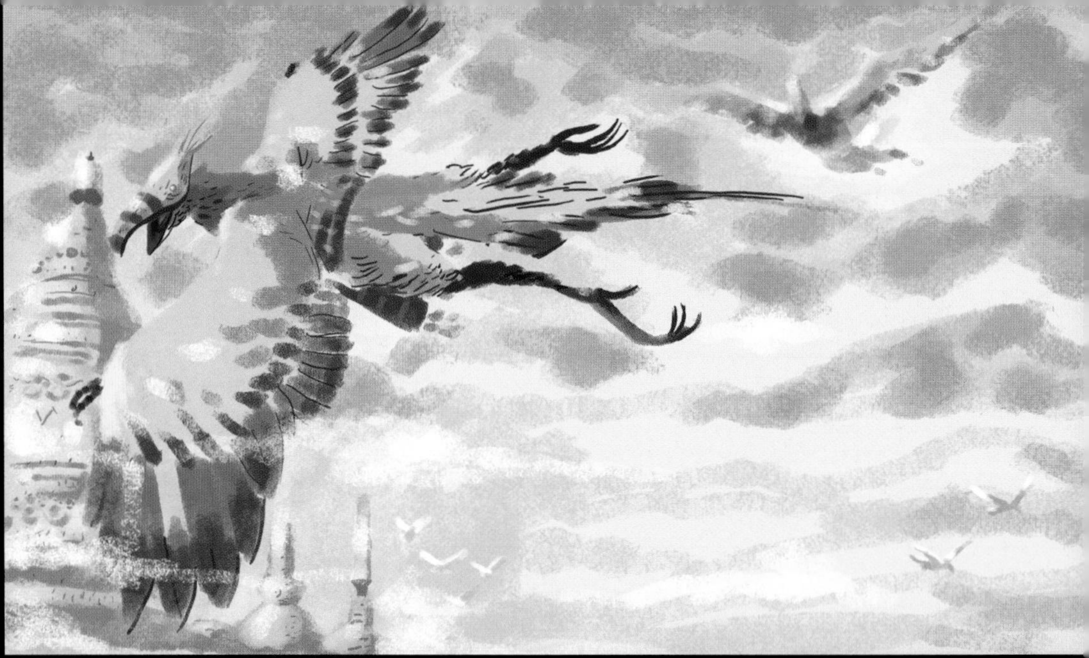

This is a shot of Rocketo in the later half of the **Journey to the Hidden Sea** where he meets the mysterious beings dwelling there.

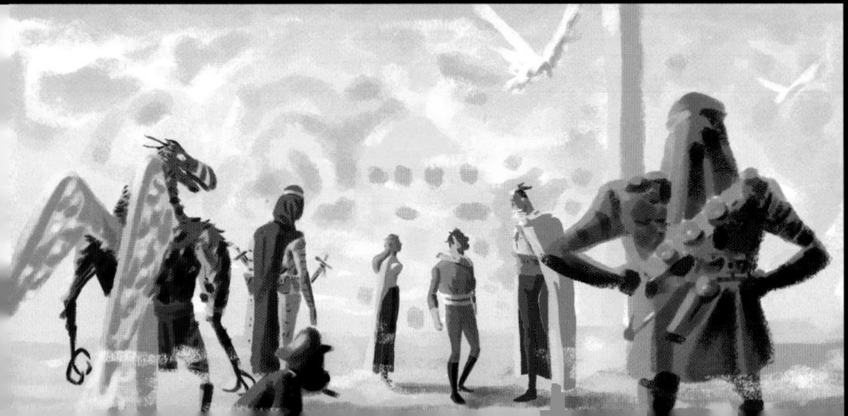

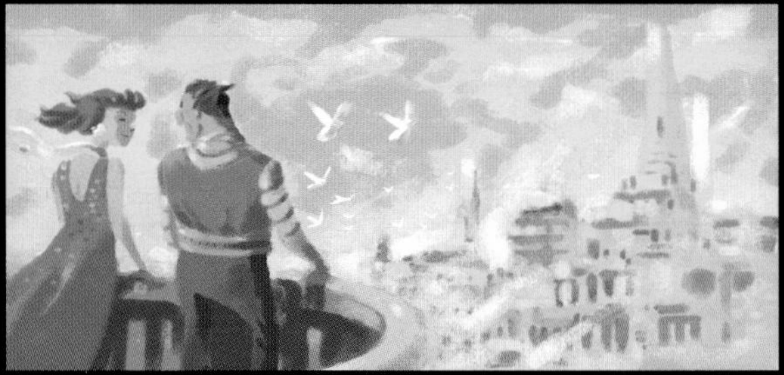

Rocketo looks upon a golden city he has always dreamed of.

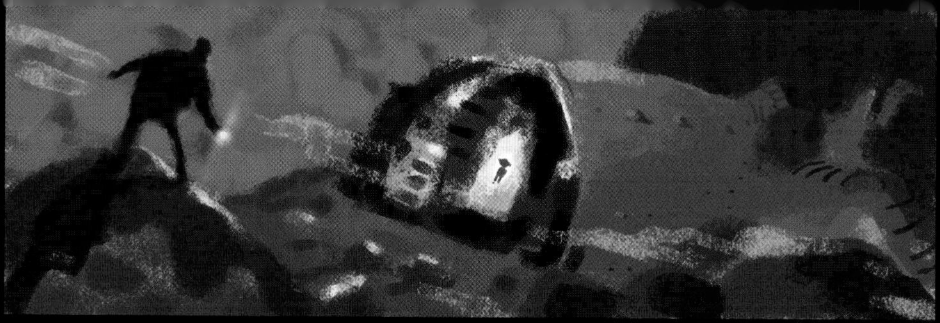

This is a color comp for a future event in **Journey to the Hidden Sea**.

One of the key elements in the next half of the **Journey to the Hidden Sea**.

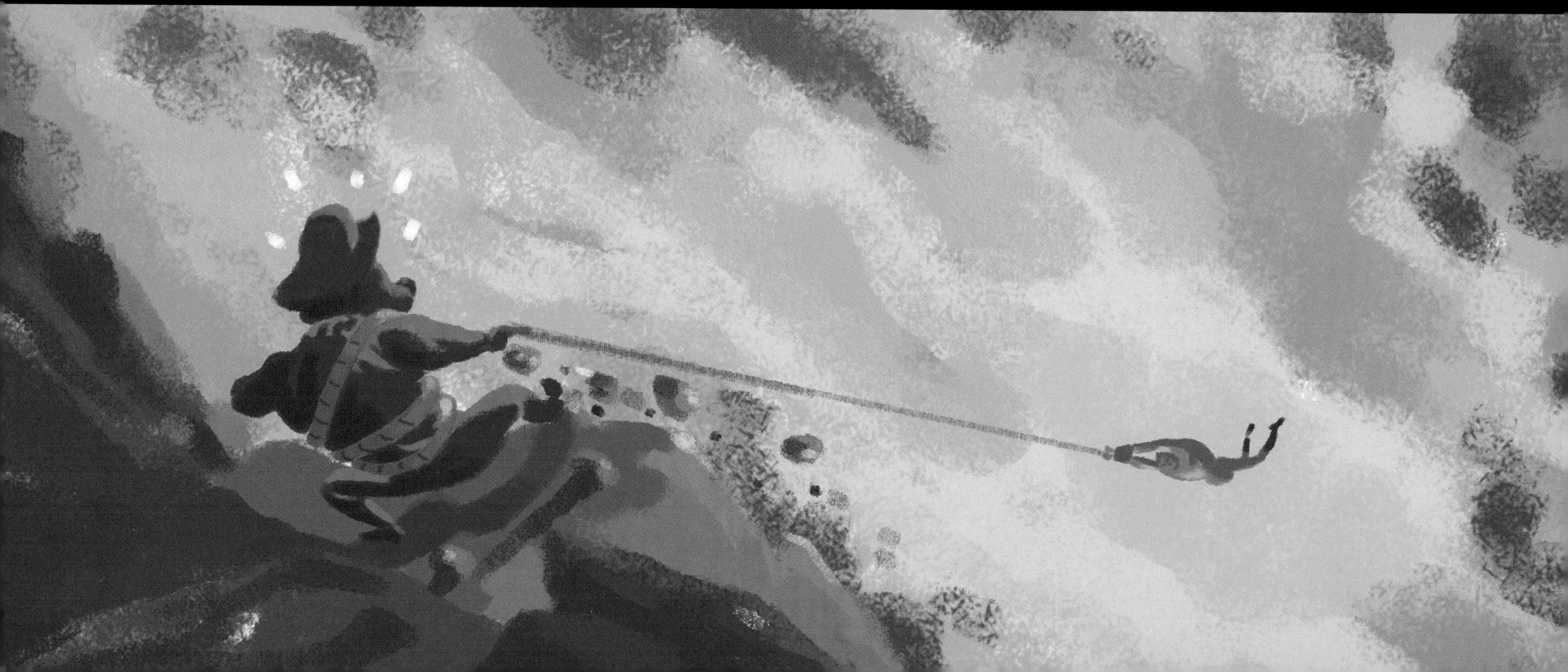

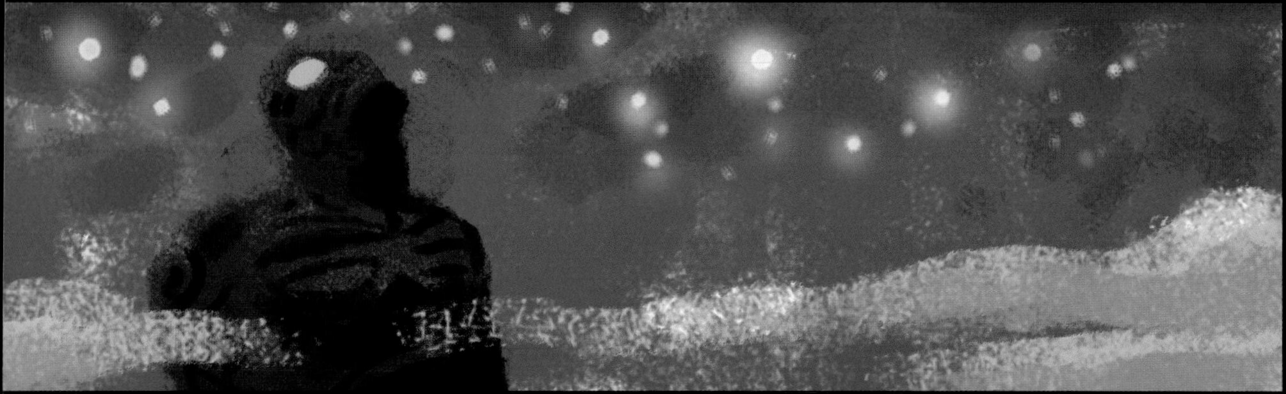

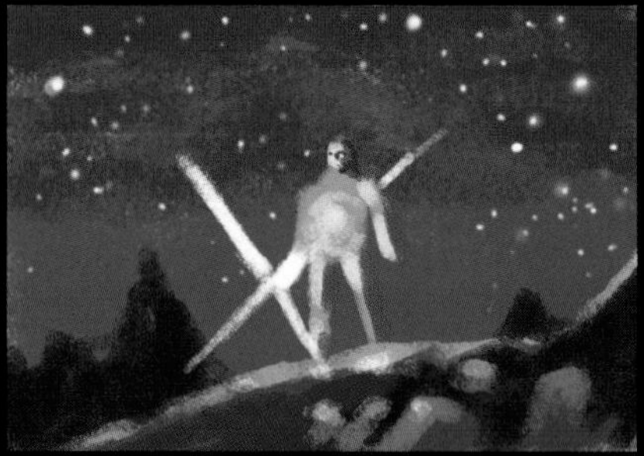

Color studies for **Journey to the Hidden Sea**.

Concept for a later point in the **Journey to the Hidden Sea**.

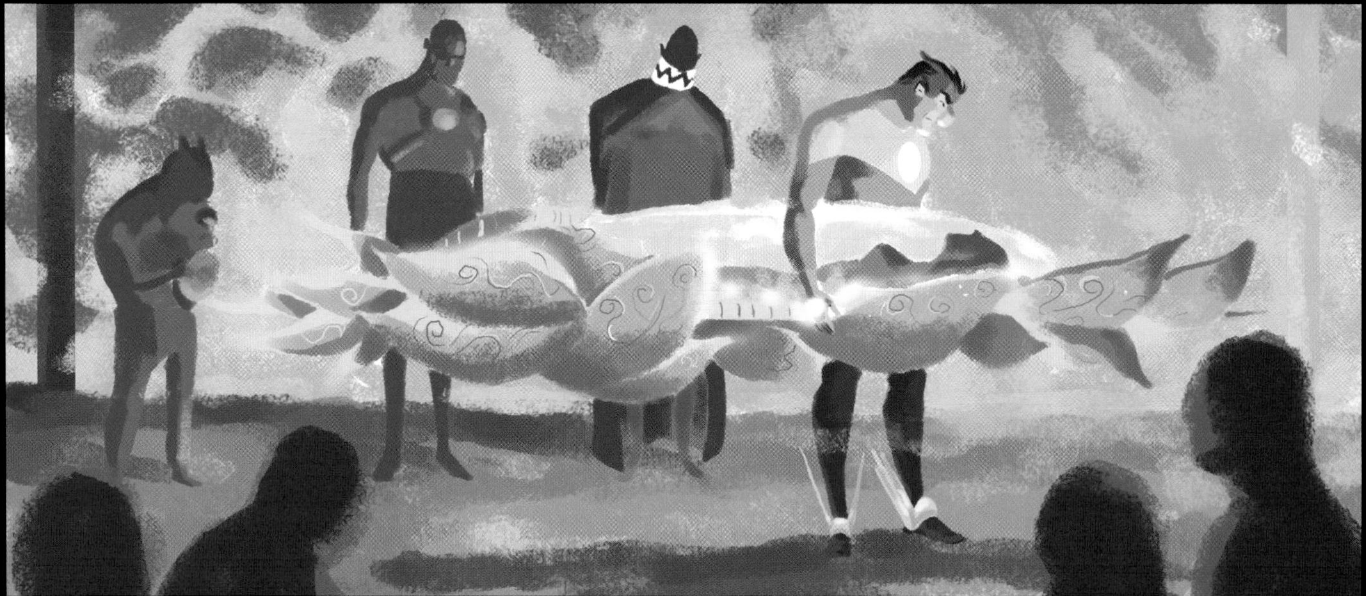

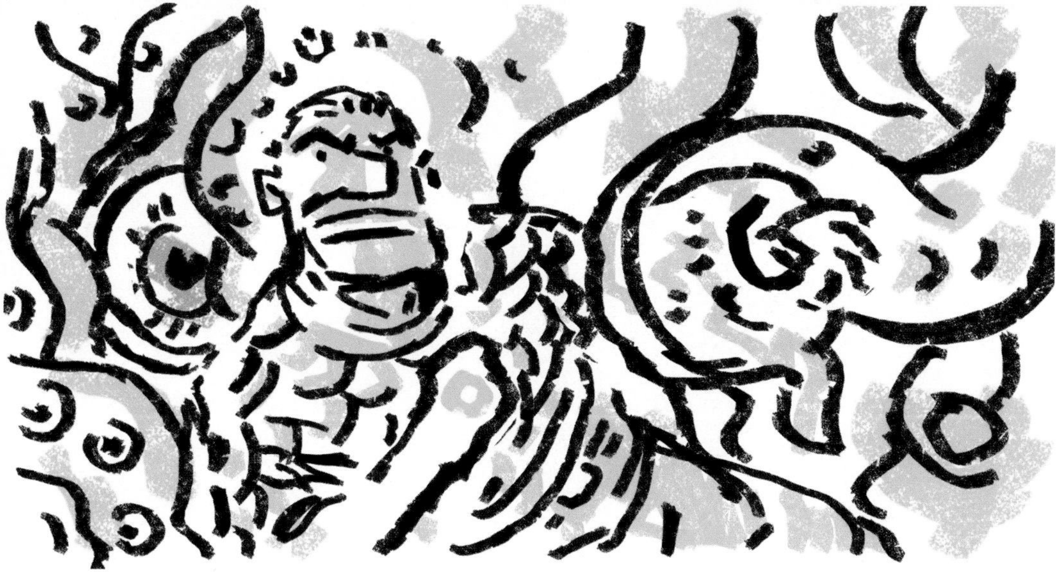

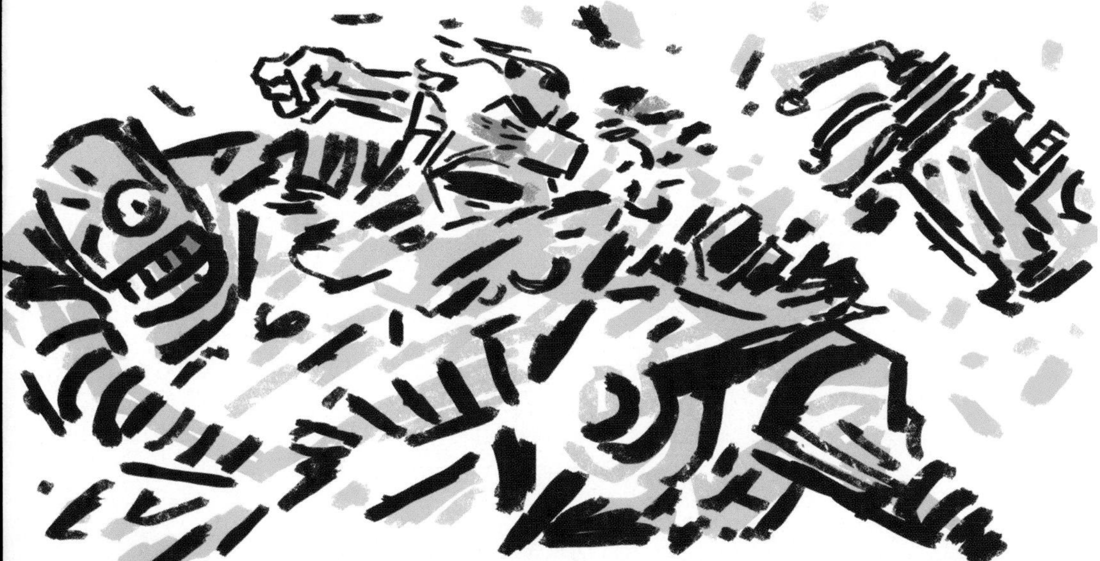

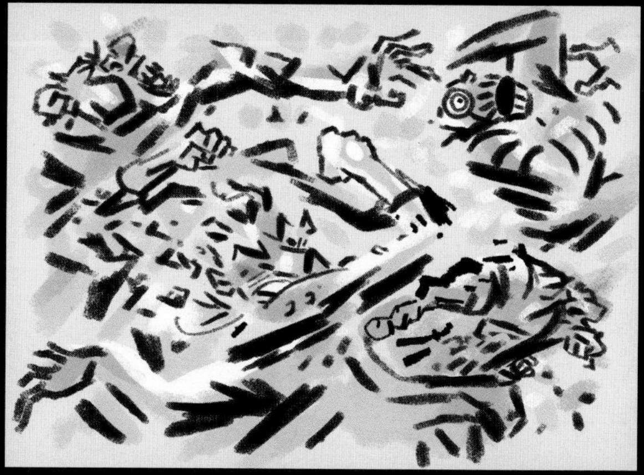

Some sketches showing variant action shots of Rocketo and experimenting with different textures and styles to capture movement.

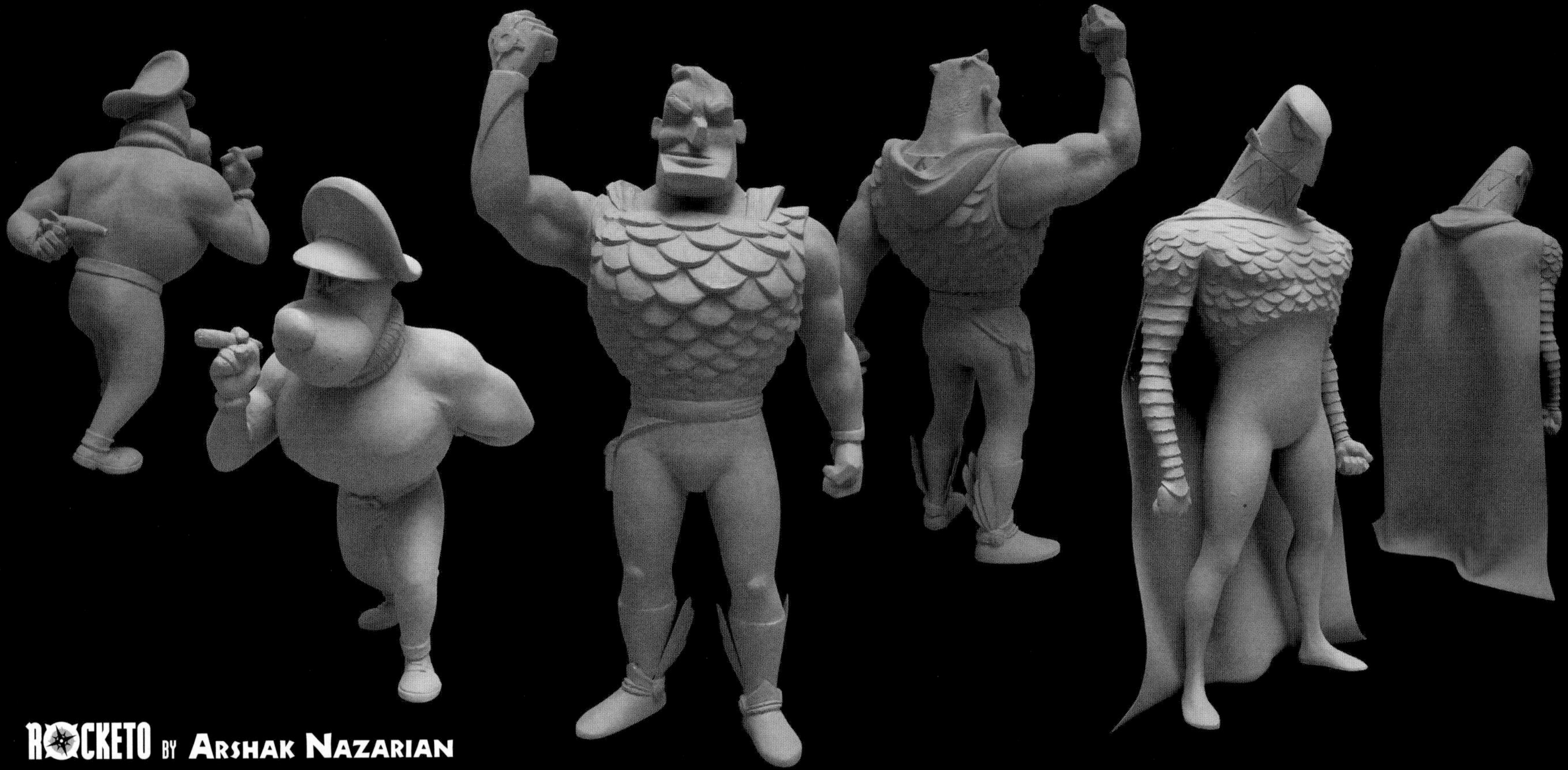

## ROCKETO BY ARSHAK NAZARIAN

I first met Arshak Nazarian when he walked into my office at Warner Bros. with a portfolio full of sculpts he had done in Armenia. Every piece was a work of art. Although there was not one cartoon character among the pieces his understanding was complete.

Arshak's understanding of sculpture, drawing and the fine arts brought truth to the characters. While holding on the foundations of solid form, Arshak evoked a highly stylized modern feel to all of them. Strong shapes seemed to leap out of some Art Deco period and combined with ones that defied gravity.

You can trust Arshak to take a sketch, a rough line drawn on paper and bring it with all its life into three dimensions. His tools are his hands, his fingers. With a pull of his thumb, Arshak shapes a bicep; another tug and a nose appears; a soft caress and the form is polished. He can shape feathers, chain mail or the illusion of a piece of paper out of clay. His eyes will know what shape to hide and which to show.

In the end your drawing will stand before you. The master.

# ROCKETO BY MATT CRUICKSHANK

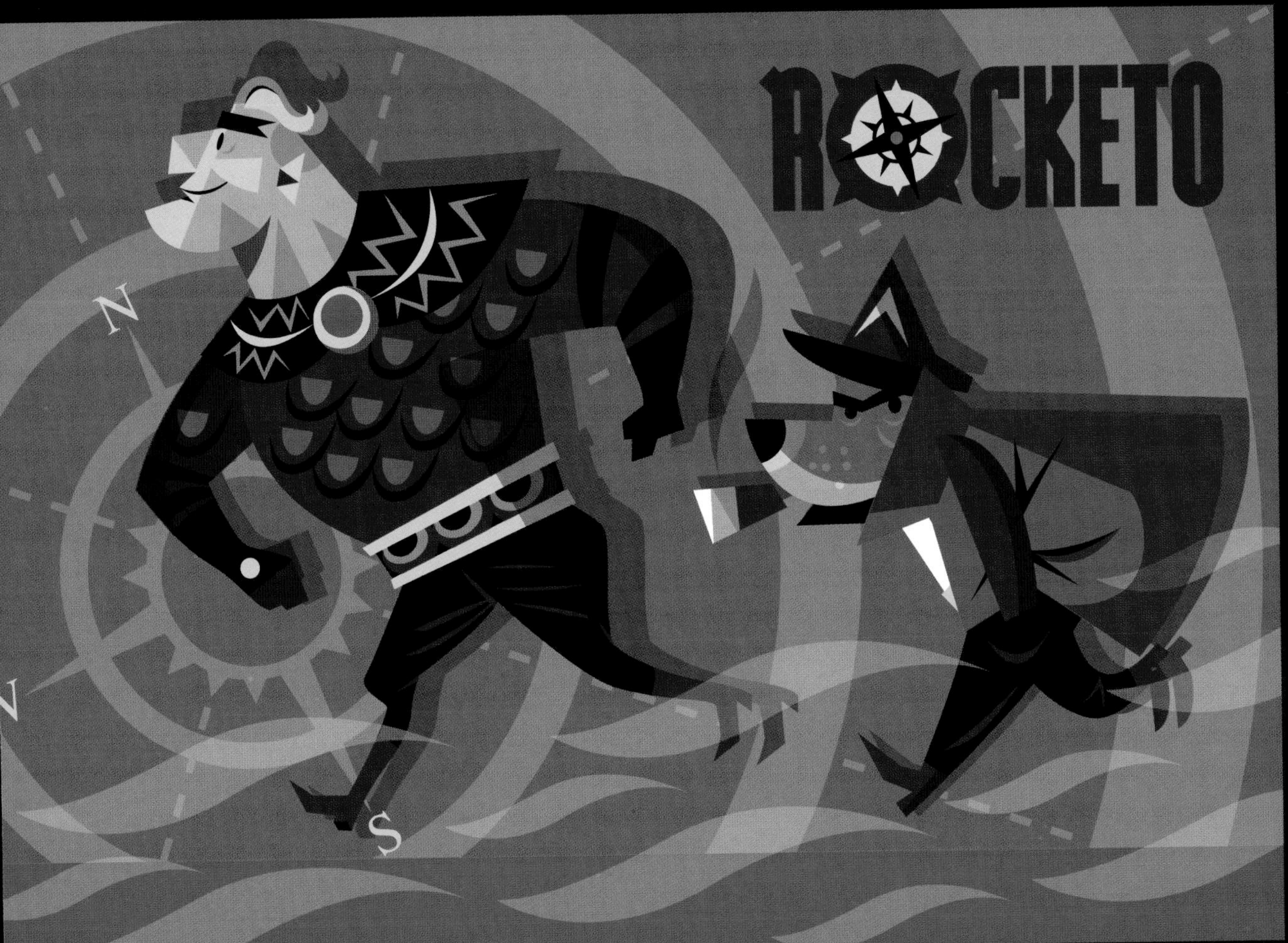
ROCKETO
N
S

Several years ago Matt Cruickshank visited Warner Bros. Consumer Products from the WB London Studios to pick up some tips on drawing the characters. Matt is a real artist and it didn't take him long to hone his skills.

Matt is what I would call a drawing mutant. He's one of those artists that can keep on drawing even while asleep. His sketch book is packed with gems – old Roman ruins, shattered old ships laying on pylons waiting for their time to sail again once more, old French cafes, puppies, cats, football players, lost dogs, more Roman ruins, caricatures, beast of fables. More… always more to draw.

One after another, his pen captures the world in bold strokes and crosshatches, splatters and graceful, never-ending, lines. With every addition to his sketch book his world grows and I learn more and more.

In those rare times he is not sketching, sculpting, or illustrating on the computer, Matt hurls himself and his snowboard at hair-raising speed down the slopes of European mountains. Now, if he would only combine the two.

I consider myself lucky to work with a talent like Masanori Hase. How rare to find a graphic artist that uses design to complement the characters rather than competing with them. With Masanori the design and the characters always work in total harmony.

Masanori not only designed the Rocketo logo but each month puts the pages in proper order, making adjustments here and there that makes my work look even better than I could imagined.

Mas did this piece of Rocketo in Adobe Illustrator, one of his favorite programs, bringing a new dimension to the character that I will learn from for a long time. His intuitive sense of design combined with his stylized and bold drawing skills give his work a graceful, modern and unique look that is original, daring and wonderful.

When not busy knocking out one fantastic design after another, Mas works on his own comic stories, which he writes and draws himself. To relax he hurls himself over twisting mountain lanes at whiplash speed on his wonderful Ducati motorcycle.

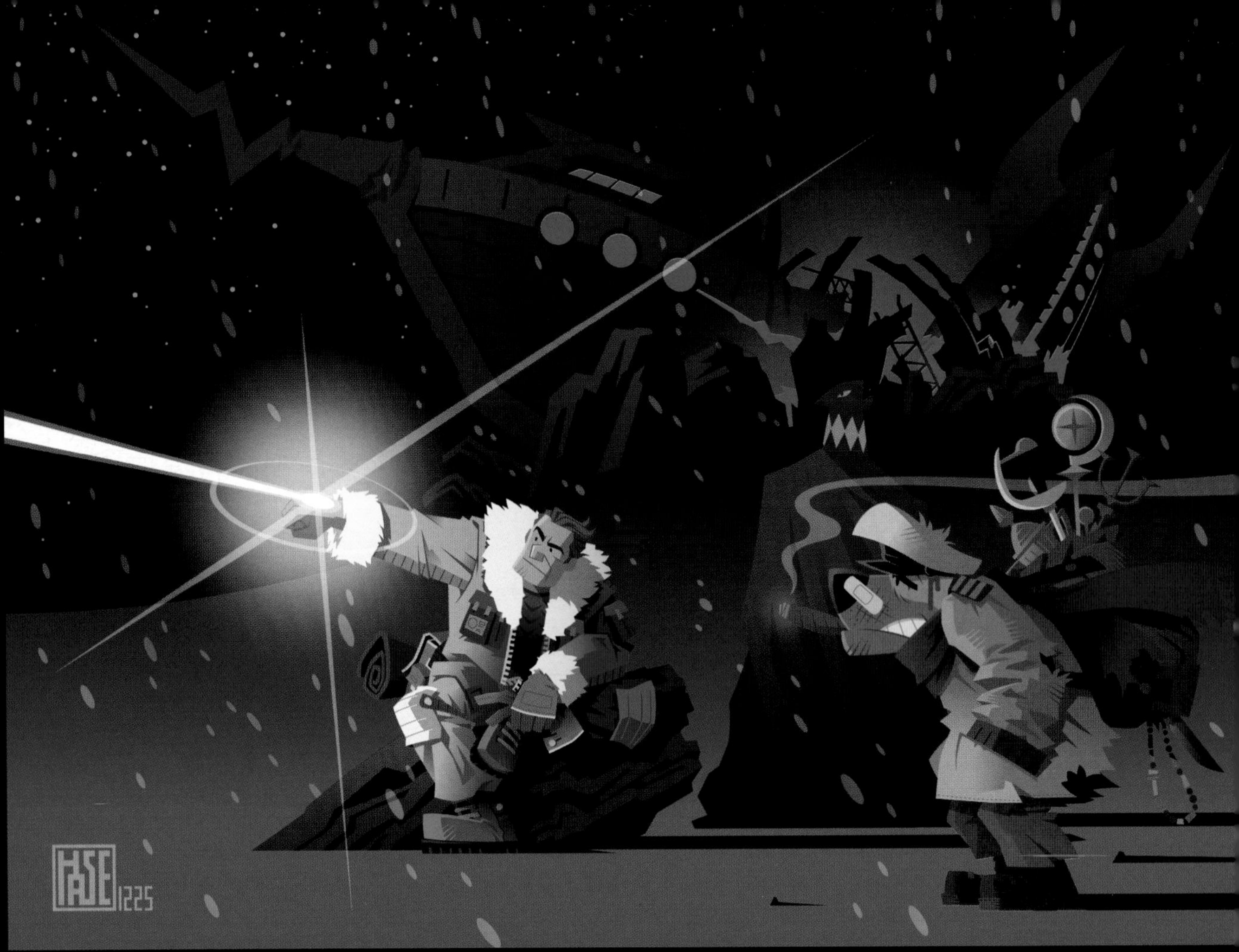
HASE 1225

ROCKETO BY MASANORI HASE

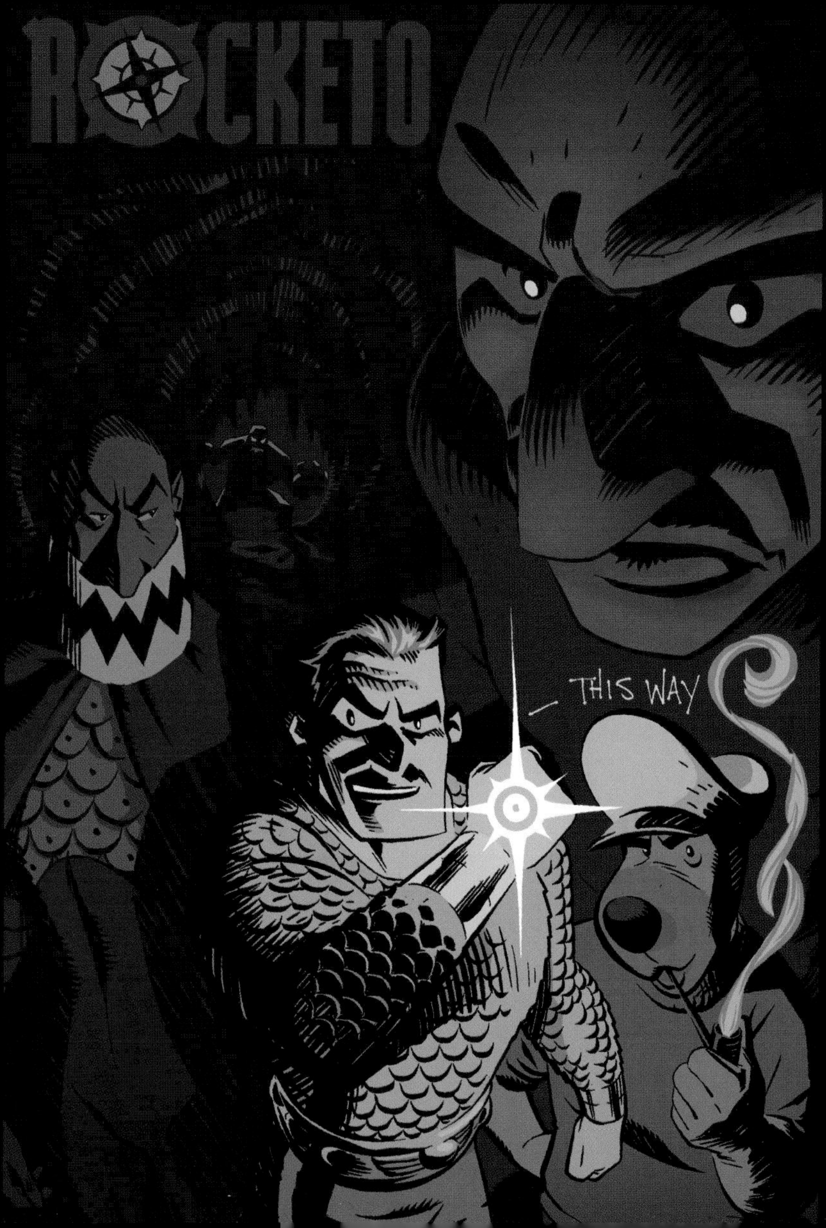
ROCKETO
THIS WAY

## ROCKETO BY DAVID WILLIAMS

David Williams is an elemental force with a pen. His art is full of an inner life that explodes off the page in strong solid shapes. With a sense for figure drawing that seems effortless, he pulls out lines, forms and silhouettes that read clear, strong and full of a dynamic energy that curls your hair. Pure energy.

David has worked in comics, animation, and almost everything else in between. He combines styles – from classic golden age and silver age comics to European and Japanese. You name it, it's in there. He gives his work a shot of pure adrenaline that makes his drawings soar, jump, fly and punch – all propelled by David's inner pulse.

David is currently working on his own graphic novel that will showcase his unique story telling style. When not drawing, he propels himself headlong into the world wide web... where he lurks somewhere in the shadows. He also has the amazing distinction of re-working Superman's costume more times than any artist I know.

There are many types of explorers in our world. Some cross jungles and vast oceans to discover new lands.
Then there are the ones who come to a new country and start life over again - learning a new language,
raising a family, surviving, growing, giving new hope where there was none.

This book is dedicated to my parents who charted the unknown and gave me the gift of the New World.

ZUM ZUM BOOKS offers special thanks to
LISETT TORRES, ALEX ROSS, DARWYN COOKE, ARSHAK NAZARIAN, DAVID WILLIAMS, FRANK BARRON,
KRISTINE HOPPE, BRIAN POOR, GLEN BRUSNWICK, JUNOT DIAZ, MAXWELL CONTON, MANNY TORRADO,
CHRIS MEADE, JONAH WEILAND, NANCY NOVAK, BETSY BAYTOS, DAVID MALAPOE.